LOCKE'S "ESSAY CONCERNING HUMAN UNDERSTANDING"

First published in 1689, John Locke's *Essay concerning Human Understanding* is widely recognized as among the greatest works in the history of Western philosophy. The *Essay* puts forward a systematic empiricist theory of mind, detailing how all ideas and knowledge arise from sense experience. Locke was trained in mechanical philosophy, and he crafted his account to be consistent with the best natural science of his day. The *Essay* was highly influential, and its rendering of empiricism would become the standard for subsequent theorists. The innovative ideas in this monumental work continue to speak to philosophers in the modern world.

This Companion volume includes fifteen new essays from leading scholars. Covering the major themes of Locke's work, they explain his views, while situating the ideas in the historical context of Locke's day and often clarifying their relationship to ongoing work in philosophy. Pitched to advanced undergraduates and graduate students, it is ideal for use in courses on early modern philosophy, British empiricism, and John Locke.

LEX NEWMAN is associate professor of philosophy at the University of Utah.

continued following the Index of Passages Cited

The Cambridge Companion to

LOCKE'S "ESSAY CONCERNING HUMAN UNDERSTANDING"

Edited by

Lex Newman
University of Utah

CAMBRIDGE
UNIVERSITY PRESS

CAMBRIDGE UNIVERSITY PRESS
Cambridge, New York, Melbourne, Madrid, Singapore, São Paulo

Cambridge University Press
32 Avenue of the Americas, New York, NY 10013-2473, USA

www.cambridge.org
Information on this title: www.cambridge.org/9780521834339

First published 2007

Printed in the United States of America

*A catalog record for this publication is available from the British
Library.*

Library of Congress Cataloging in Publication data

The Cambridge companion to Locke's essay concerning human
understanding / edited by Lex Newman.
p. cm. – (Cambridge companions to philosophy)
Includes bibliographical references and index.
ISBN 0-521-83433-3 (hardback) – ISBN 0-521-54225-1 (pbk.)
1. Locke, John, 1632–1704. Essay concerning human understanding.
2. Knowledge, Theory of. I. Newman, Lex, 1957–
II. Title. III. Series.
B1294.C36 2006
121–dc22   2006011712

ISBN 978-0-521-83433-9 hardback
ISBN 978-0-521-54225-8 paperback

Contents

List of Contributors

MARGARET ATHERTON is professor of philosophy at the University of Wisconsin, Milwaukee. She is the author of *Berkeley's Revolution in Vision* (1990) and the editor of *Women Philosophers in the Early Modern Period* (1994) and *The Empiricists* (1999). She is currently working on a second book about Berkeley's philosophy.

MARTHA BRANDT BOLTON is professor of philosophy at Rutgers University. She is the author of papers on a variety of figures and topics in seventeenth- and eighteenth-century philosophy, including Locke's theory of sensory perception and knowledge, his philosophy of language, and his views on substance and identity.

VERE CHAPPELL is professor of philosophy at the University of Massachusetts. In addition to editing *The Cambridge Companion to Locke* (1994) and a volume of writings by Hobbes and Bramhall on *Liberty and Necessity* (1999) for the Cambridge Texts in the History of Philosophy series, he is the author, with Willis Doney, of *Twenty-Five Years of Descartes Scholarship* (1987) and editor of the twelve-volume Essays on Early Modern Philosophers series (1992). He has also edited collections of recent articles on Descartes (1997) for Garland and on Locke (1998) for the Oxford Readings in Philosophy series.

LISA DOWNING is professor of philosophy at Ohio State University. Her publications include "The Status of Mechanism in Locke's *Essay*" (*Philosophical Review*, 1998) and "Berkeley's Natural Philosophy and Philosophy of Science" in *The Cambridge Companion to Berkeley* (2005). She is currently working on a book on empiricism and Newtonianism, among other projects.

MICHAEL JACOVIDES is assistant professor of philosophy at Purdue University. He is the author of several articles on Locke, including "Locke's Resemblance Theses" (*The Philosophical Review*, 1999).

NICHOLAS JOLLEY is chair and professor of philosophy at the University of California, Irvine. He is the author of *Leibniz and Locke: A Study of the New Essays on Human Understanding* (1984); *The Light of the Soul: Theories of Ideas in Leibniz, Malebranche, and Descartes* (1990); *Locke: His Philosophical Thought* (1999); and *Leibniz* (2005).

THOMAS M. LENNON is professor of philosophy at the University of Western Ontario. He is author of scores of books and articles on early modern philosophy, including *The Battle of the Gods and Giants* (1993).

MICHAEL LOSONSKY is professor of philosophy at Colorado State University. He is author of *Linguistic Turns in Modern Philosophy* (2005) and *Enlightenment and Action from Descartes to Kant: Passionate Thought* (2001) and editor of Wilhelm von Humboldt's *On Language* (1999). He is coauthor (with Heimir Geirsson) of *Beginning Metaphysics* (1998) and coeditor (with Geirsson) of *Readings in Language and Mind* (1996).

EDWIN MCCANN is professor of philosophy in the School of Philosophy at the University of Southern California. He has published a number of articles on early modern philosophy, emphasizing Locke.

LEX NEWMAN is associate professor of philosophy at the University of Utah. His numerous articles on Locke and Descartes have appeared in such journals as *Noûs*, the *Philosophical Review*, and *Philosophy and Phenomenological Research*.

DAVID OWEN is associate professor of philosophy at the University of Arizona. He has written several articles on Locke and Hume, and he is the author of *Hume's Reason* (1999).

SAMUEL C. RICKLESS is associate professor of philosophy at the University of California, San Diego. He is the author of articles on Locke's distinction between primary and secondary qualities and on Locke's theory of free action. He is at work on Locke's theory of knowledge and Berkeley's argument for idealism. He also writes on topics in ancient philosophy and is the author of *Plato's Forms in Transition: A Reading of the Parmenides* (2006). In respect of his project for this volume, he would like to thank Michael Hardimon,

Wayne Martin, Dana Nelkin, David Owen, Don Rutherford, and Eric Watkins for their constructive comments and suggestions. He is particularly indebted to Lex Newman, who helped him avoid a number of mistakes, and from whose advice he has greatly benefited.

G. A. J. ROGERS is professor of the history of philosophy emeritus at Keele University and the founder-editor of the *British Journal for the History of Philosophy*. He is the author of *Locke's Enlightenment* (1998) and the author of more than 100 articles on the history of seventeenth-century philosophy. He has recently edited Hobbes's *Leviathan* (with the late Karl Schuhmann) and is currently editing the drafts of Locke's *Essay* and related writings for the Clarendon Edition of Locke's Works (with Paul Schuurman).

CATHERINE WILSON is professor of philosophy at the Graduate Center, City University of New York. She works on seventeenth- and eighteenth-century philosophy and on moral theory. She is the author, most recently, of *Moral Animals: Ideals and Constraints in Moral Theory* (2004) and of other books and articles on the history and philosophy of science and the history of philosophy.

GIDEON YAFFE is associate professor of philosophy and law at the University of Southern California. He is the author of *Liberty Worth the Name: Locke on Free Agency* (2000) and *Manifest Activity: Thomas Reid's Theory of Action* (2004). His articles have appeared in such journals as the *Journal of the History of Philosophy*, the *History of Philosophy Quarterly*, and *Philosophical Topics*.

Note on Texts and Citations

Throughout the present volume, authors generally refer to *An Essay concerning Human Understanding* as simply the *Essay*. Quotations of the *Essay* are taken from the 1975 version, edited by Peter H. Nidditch. This edition is based on the original fourth edition of the *Essay*. The text has not been modernized, thus generally preserving Locke's original spelling, punctuation, italics, and case.

Works of Locke cited using abbreviations are the following:

C   *The Correspondence of John Locke*, ed. E. S. de Beer. 9 vols. (1976–).

CU   *Of the Conduct of the Understanding*, ed. Thomas Fowler (1901).

D   *Drafts for the* Essay concerning Human Understanding, *and Other Philosophical Writings*, ed. Peter H. Nidditch and G. A. J. Rogers. 3 vols. (1990–).

E   *An Essay concerning Human Understanding*, ed. Peter H. Nidditch (1975).

EL   *Essays on the Law of Nature*, ed. W. von Leyden (1954).

TE   *Some Thoughts concerning Education*, ed. John W. Yolton and Jean S. Yolton (1989).

W   *The Works of John Locke*, new ed., corrected. 10 vols. (1823; repr. 1964).

The majority of citations refer to the *Essay*. As per the abbreviation scheme above, these citations are marked with an E, and they specify the book, chapter, and article numbers, as well as page numbers: for example, E II.viii.15: 137 refers to Book II, Chapter viii, article 15, on page 137 of the Nidditch edition.

Citations to other works are given in parentheses, beginning with the uppercase abbreviation indicated, followed by a volume number (where relevant) and, finally a page number preceded by a full colon. For example, W IV: 36 refers to the *Works of John Locke*, volume IV, page 36.

Introduction

The *Essay* is first published in December of 1689 by a fifty-seven-year-old John Locke (1632–1704). (That same year Locke publishes the *Two Treatises of Government* and the *Letter Concerning Toleration*.) The philosophical themes of the *Essay* are the product of years of thought, as many as twenty in some cases. Locke continues working on the *Essay* in the decade following its initial publication. He produces three updates – a second edition in 1694, a third in 1695, and a fourth in 1700. He oversees a translation into French. And he writes three public responses to objections from Edward Stillingfleet, the bishop of Worcester, one of which is a book-length work in its own right. The result of Locke's efforts is an undisputed philosophical masterpiece. The systematic empiricism he develops would become the standard for subsequent theorists. The importance of some of the positions developed in the *Essay* continues to the present day.

The *Essay* is the product of more than simply the tireless efforts of a gifted philosophical mind. The seventeenth century is a period of significant intellectual development in Europe – developments to which the philosophical themes of the *Essay* are responsive. In the opening essay of the present volume (Chapter 1), "The Intellectual Setting and Aims of the *Essay*," G. A. J. Rogers details the historical factors influencing Locke.

Consistent with the title of the *Essay*, Locke refers to *"the Subject of this Treatise"* as being *"the* UNDERSTANDING*"* (E: 6). The Introduction states his *"Purpose"* as being "to enquire into the Original, Certainty, and Extent of humane Knowledge; together, with the Grounds and Degrees of Belief, Opinion, and Assent"

(E I.i.2: 43). The express concern with epistemology is reflected a few lines later in Locke's overview of his method:

First, I shall enquire into the *Original* of those *Ideas*, Notions, or whatever else you please to call them, which a Man observes, and is conscious to himself he has in his Mind; and the ways whereby the Understanding comes to be furnished with them.

Secondly, I shall endeavour to shew, what *Knowledge* the Understanding hath by those *Ideas*; and the Certainty, Evidence, and Extent of it.

Thirdly, I shall make some Enquiry into the Nature and Grounds of *Faith*, or *Opinion*: whereby I mean that Assent, which we give to any Proposition as true, of whose Truth yet we have no certain Knowledge: And here we shall have Occasion to examine the Reasons and Degrees of *Assent*. (E I.i.3: 44)

In the course of his inquiry, Locke explores topics that today are studied under such headings as action theory, epistemology, ethics, metaphysics, philosophy of language, philosophy of mind, philosophy of science, physics, and psychology, among others.

The *Essay* unfolds in accord with the threefold order just outlined, but with a rather different emphasis than is suggested by Locke's remarks. The topics Locke lists under *"First"* occupy the majority of attention and are distributed over the first three books of the *Essay*. The topics under *"Secondly"* and *"Thirdly"* are combined in the fourth and final book. The titles of the four books are as follows:

I.   Of Innate Notions
II. Of Ideas
III. Of Words
IV. Of Knowledge and Opinion

Books I and II are in some sense a two-part investigation into the origin of mental content. Book I gives a negative account, addressing the kinds of views Locke rejects. Book II gives Locke's positive account – a detailed empiricist account. "Let us then suppose the Mind to be, as we say, white Paper, void of all Characters, without any *Ideas*; How comes it to be furnished?" (E II.i.2: 104) The bulk of Locke's answer unfolds over the course of Book II, the longest book of the *Essay*. The present volume includes seven essays on topics connected with these first two books of the *Essay*.

The first such essay concerns Locke's rejection of *nativism*. Book I makes a series of attacks on nativism, arguing that our knowledge does not arise from *"innate Principles,"* or from notions "as it were stamped upon the Mind of Man" (E I.ii.1: 48). Unclear is whom Locke targets with these attacks, or how he understands their accounts. In "Locke's Polemic Against Nativism" (Chapter 2), Samuel C. Rickless attempts to clear up the confusion, along with clarifying both the structure of Locke's anti-innatist arguments and their success.

Locke holds that sense experience provides the building blocks of mental content – what he calls *simple* ideas. From these simple ideas the mind constructs *complex* ideas. At both levels of ideas, Locke makes further taxonomic divisions. The result is an elaborate taxonomy of ideas that helps define the organization of topics in Book II. In "The Taxonomy of Ideas in Locke's *Essay*" (Chapter 3), Martha Brandt Bolton clarifies this classification scheme, while addressing interpretative problems associated with the major divisions.

The theory has it that simple ideas of external sense are our window to the world. A corpuscularian understanding of body has implications for how the *qualities* of bodies help produce such ideas in the mind. What emerges is a famous distinction between two kinds of qualities. In "Locke's Distinctions Between Primary and Secondary Qualities" (Chapter 4), Michael Jacovides explains Locke's account while arguing that it is much richer than has been appreciated – Locke is in fact drawing several overlapping distinctions.

The longest chapter of the *Essay* concerns the idea of *power*. Ideas of power figure in numerous aspects of Locke's philosophy, including the centerpiece of the chapter – his treatment of human freedom. In "Power in Locke's *Essay*" (Chapter 5), Vere Chappell sorts out Locke's views on power – clarifying its widespread role in his philosophy, and defending a compatibilist interpretation of Locke's views on human freedom.

Appeals to *substance* have a distinguished philosophical history. The notion purports to get at what it is to be a *thing* in the most basic sense. Recent interpretations have tended to have Locke disavowing the traditional notion of substance. In "Locke on Substance" (Chapter 6), Edwin McCann carefully examines four influential such interpretations, concluding that an interpretation attributing to Locke a traditional conception of substance emerges as superior.

Related to our conceiving the world in terms of individual substances is that we have ideas of *identity over time* – ideas, for example, of a mature oak tree as being the same organism as some earlier tree that looked quite different, or of our own selves as being the same persons that performed actions years earlier. In "Locke on Ideas of Identity and Diversity" (Chapter 7), Gideon Yaffe explains Locke's account, focusing especially on his famous treatment of personal identity.

In significant respects, *ideas* take center stage throughout the *Essay*. Yet Locke scholarship is divided about how he understands the nature of ideas – whether he regards ideas as representational entities, and, if so, what this means. At stake is whether the mind directly perceives the world, or is instead trapped behind a veil of its own ideas. In "Locke on Ideas and Representation" (Chapter 8), Thomas M. Lennon clarifies the contours of the debate, while arguing that Locke does not regard ideas as imposing a barrier between mind and world.

Book III develops further the theory of ideas, notably in connection with general ideas and essences. In addition, Book III presents Locke's influential theory of language. The present volume includes two essays on Book III topics.

Experience leads us to *classify objects* into such kinds as trees, horses, gold, and so on. We tend to assume that the world naturally divides into such kinds – indeed, that the *essences* of the kinds are just as we conceive them. Locke rejects these assumptions. He distinguishes real and nominal essences, arguing that we classify external objects based on nominal essences. In "Locke on Essences and Classification" (Chapter 9), Margaret Atherton works through the texts and issues, developing an interpretation of Locke's account.

The traditional view of Locke's philosophy of *language* is that it presents a theory of linguistic meaning. Recent commentators have questioned this traditional account, arguing that it does not accurately portray Locke's understanding of the signification relation between words and ideas. In "Language, Meaning, and Mind in Locke's *Essay*" (Chapter 10), Michael Losonsky challenges these recent commentators and defends the traditional account.

Locke's theories of ideas and language having been expounded, Book IV turns to his theory of knowledge. Locke distinguishes two main sorts of propositional cognition: knowledge, wherein the mind has certainty; judgment, wherein it achieves only probability. Book IV presents separate accounts of knowledge and judgment, while treating a number of related issues. The present volume includes five essays on Book IV topics.

The opening lines of Book IV state that "Knowledge is only conversant" with ideas, because ideas are the only immediate objects the mind "does or can contemplate" (E IV.i.1: 525). Thus restricted to ideas, Locke defines *knowledge* as the perception of the agreement or disagreement of two ideas – a definition that has generated considerable scholarly debate. In "Locke on Knowledge" (Chapter 11), I defend an interpretation of Locke's account of knowledge that takes his controversial definition at face value.

In the course of developing the themes of Book IV, Locke makes claims bearing on his own *ontological commitments*. It has seemed to many readers that his claims are inconsistent – that they reveal tension in his views about the epistemic status of corpuscularianism, and further tension in his views about the nature of mind. In "Locke's Ontology" (Chapter 12), Lisa Downing examines the claimed tensions and argues that they can be resolved.

Locke maintains that inquiries into *morality* are those to which our natural faculties are "most suited," concluding that "*Morality is the proper Science, and Business of Mankind of general*" (E IV. xii.11: 646). Locke's claims about the nature of moral ideas and moral knowledge raise many questions. In "The Moral Epistemology of Locke's *Essay*" (Chapter 13), Catherine Wilson sorts through these various claims in an effort to clarify the account.

Locke generally reserves the language of *judgment* for contexts of probability, thus distinguishing it from knowledge. Since on his view strict knowledge is quite limited in scope, it emerges that judgment plays an extensive role in his broader philosophical system. In "Locke on Judgment" (Chapter 14), David Owen presents a general interpretation of Locke's theory of judgment, arguing, among other things, that the contributions of the intellect and the will in Locke's account make it importantly different from Descartes's well-known account.

Having explained knowledge and judgment, Locke discusses two further grounds of assent – divine revelation, and religious enthusiasm. That these further grounds of assent are bases of religious conviction raises questions about the balancing of faith and natural reason. In "Locke on Faith and Reason" (Chapter 15), Nicholas Jolley discusses Locke's overall philosophy of religion, his treatment of faith and reason, and his treatment of enthusiasm.

Locke's *Essay* covers far more topics of interest than are discussed here. That his *Essay* presents powerful and influential philosophical ideas in an uncommonly systematic fashion renders it a philosophical gold mine for both students and scholars. As the essays in the present volume collectively exhibit, Locke scholarship is alive and well. A host of interpretive issues continue to be debated, and much of the diversity of interpretive positions in the field is represented in these pages. That these interpretive debates do, in many cases, track ongoing philosophical debates attests to the ongoing relevance of Locke's philosophy. The philosophical world still has much to learn from the *Essay*.

1   The Intellectual Setting and Aims of the *Essay*

The *Essay Concerning Human Understanding*, though dated 1690, was published in late 1689, when its author was fifty-seven. It had been completed in Holland, where Locke had fled in 1683. It had a much longer gestation than this suggests, however. When it was published it was the product of a mature philosophical mind that had been reflecting on the issues that it considers for nearly twenty years. Locke tells us in the "Epistle to the Reader" something of its origin and history. He writes that five or six friends:

Meeting at my chamber, and discoursing on a subject very remote from this [i.e., human understanding], found themselves quickly at a stand, by the Difficulties that rose on every side. After we had a while puzzled our selves, without coming any nearer a Resolution of those Doubts which perplexed us, it came in to my Thoughts, that we took a wrong course; and that, before we set our selves upon Enquiries of that Nature, it was necessary to examine our own Abilities, and see, what Objects our Understandings were, or were not fitted to deal with. This I proposed to the Company, who all readily assented; and thereupon it was agreed, that this should be our first Enquiry. Some hasty and undigested Thoughts, on a Subject I had never before considered, which I set down against our next Meeting, gave the first entrance into this Discourse, which having been thus by Chance, was continued by Intreaty; written by incoherent parcels, and after long intervals of neglect, resum'd again, as my Humour or Occasions permitted; and at last, in a retirement, where an Attendance on my Health gave me leisure, it was brought into that order, thou now seest it. (E: 7)

We can now fill out this story in much detail, and some of that detail is directly relevant to understanding Locke's purposes in writing the book. To begin with, it is known that the subject matter of the discussion in which Locke and his friends were originally engaged was "morality and revealed religion."[1] The meeting itself took place in the winter, probably February, of 1671 and in Exeter House in the Strand, the London home of Lord Ashley, later first earl of Shaftesbury, situated where the Strand Palace Hotel now stands. Whether that first document that Locke prepared for the meeting is still in existence is not certain. What we have now are two early drafts of the *Essay*, both probably written in 1671 (though even this is not absolutely certain), known as Drafts A and B.[2] But in Locke's voluminous manuscripts there are many other references to material relevant to the background and production of the *Essay* through its five early editions. Further, in order to understand those drafts, and therefore the published book, we have to look to Locke's intellectual background as a philosopher, educated in the traditions of the more puritan strands of the Church of England, and as somebody who had entered deeply into studies in medicine, chemistry, and at least some other branches of natural philosophy before he began to write works of philosophy as now understood. And this was against a background in which Locke had taken his Oxford first degree and was thus familiar with the main tenets of Scholastic philosophy, and in the immediately following years had become familiar with and influenced by the new philosophy emanating from France, of which that of Descartes was by far the most important.

Locke had been a student and tutor at Christ Church, Oxford, the largest and most important college in the university, from the time that he graduated in 1656 until he moved to London to join Shaftesbury's household eleven years later in 1667, where he was to be based until 1675. Shaftesbury had by then become the leading Whig politician in the country, and much of his time was spent on government business. During those eight years Locke often worked as Shaftesbury's personal assistant in dealing with matters of politics and government. He was also responsible for finding Shaftesbury's son a wife and, in due course, for the education of the son produced from that marriage, the future third earl of Shaftesbury. He also, as secretary of presentations, became a civil servant and

[1] Locke's friend James Tyrrell, who was one of the five or six at that meeting, wrote as much in his copy of the *Essay*, now in the British Library.
[2] Published as John Locke: *Drafts for the* Essay Concerning Human Understanding, *and Other Philosophical Writings*.

was responsible for dealing with ecclesiastical matters that came under Shaftesbury's control as lord chancellor, the highest political appointment in the land. When possible, Locke was also engaged in medical practice with Thomas Sydenham, probably the greatest physician of the age. In 1668, he became a Fellow of the recently established Royal Society, attending its meetings when he was able and renewing contacts from his days with the Oxford Philosophical Society, of which the two most distinguished were Robert Boyle and Robert Hooke, but which also included many others, such as Christopher Wren, remembered as the architect of St Paul's Cathedral; the civil servant Samuel Pepys; Richard Lower, the physician; Sir Kenelm Digby; John Wilkins, who had been one of the moving forces behind the new science in Oxford and who later became Bishop of Chester; Nehemiah Grew, the botanist; and many other distinguished and not-so-distinguished men of science.

Perhaps enough has been said to indicate that Locke was far from being a standard academic philosopher in the modern sense. Indeed, as we shall see, the modern subject known as philosophy was in many respects to be created by his *Essay*. Although he had spent years teaching logic, rhetoric, and moral philosophy in Oxford, Locke's great intellectual passions in his earlier years were medicine and chemistry. It is of major significance for understanding his philosophy that in these disciplines he was actively engaged in research with the two outstanding figures in the respective fields, Thomas Sydenham and Robert Boyle.

The Royal Society was an institution that claimed to be putting into practice the plans for the increase in knowledge of the natural world that had been advocated by Francis Bacon at the beginning of the century. Supporters of the Baconian vision had been active in both Oxford and London during the period of the Commonwealth following the English Civil War and the execution of King Charles I in 1649, the year Locke had entered Christ Church. At the heart of Bacon's programme was the aspiration to increase people's knowledge of the natural world and to use that knowledge for practical benefit. Leading proponents of that movement in Oxford included Robert Boyle, an aristocrat of independent means, and John Wilkins, master of Wadham College and married to the sister of the man who was effectively the country's ruler, Oliver Cromwell. Locke attended the chemistry classes that Boyle introduced in

Oxford and began research on respiration and on human blood with Boyle. In 1660, at the Restoration of the monarchy, many of the Oxford group moved back to London, and it was this group, together with physicians and other men interested in natural philosophy, who were responsible for creating the new society. With royal patronage, it immediately achieved a status that would otherwise not have been available to it and soon provided a forum for the international exchange of information about a wide range of natural phenomena based on observation and experiment, in the way Bacon had advocated. Locke began to attend its weekly meetings in 1668, on his election to the Society, along with his medical work with Thomas Sydenham and his many commitments to Shaftesbury.

We shall look more closely at the connections between Locke and the Baconian movement associated with the Royal Society later. But let us now return to Locke and his studies in Oxford prior to his arrival in London. These fall into two very clear sections. As an undergraduate, Locke had to follow the reading prescribed for him by his tutor, but beginning in 1656 he could and did read much more widely and combined his reading with practical enquiries, especially in chemistry and medicine. The undergraduate course required him to advance further his mastery of Latin, mainly through rigorous and frequent exercises; logic, which was, of course, that of Aristotle's syllogistic; mathematics and astronomy, including Euclid and contemporary works of astronomy based on the heliocentric theory; and the classical texts of Greece and Rome.[3]

It is particularly interesting that in all such enquiries, there is little or no evidence that Locke would have encountered major works of what today would have been called the classics in philosophy. No doubt he would have been familiar with the major works of Aristotle, but perhaps not with those of Plato. Certainly he would not have encountered as a matter of course any of the major philosophers of the Middle Ages. Of Latin authors, only Cicero and Seneca would have been certainties. And by Locke's day none of the works of early modern philosophers such as Bacon, Descartes, Hobbes, and Gassendi would have been included as texts.

---

[3] For more on the courses at Oxford in Locke's day, see Feingold 1997: "The Humanities" and "The Mathematical Sciences and the New Philosophies." On Christ Church in particular, see Bill 1988.

This does not mean, however, that they would necessarily have been totally excluded from any teaching. In Christ Church, as in other Oxford and Cambridge colleges, each tutor had a fair amount of flexibility in what he encouraged his pupils to read. In 1667, for example, in Jesus College, Cambridge, John North as an undergraduate read Descartes's natural philosophy, presumably the *Principia Philosophia*, "three times," and he tells us that Descartes was studied quite widely, especially by "the brisk part of the university" (North 1959: 257–8).

When Locke began his studies, then, the intellectual forces gathering in the wider world, may be identified as, first, those associated with the advocacy and practice of the method of enquiry put forward by Francis Bacon in his *Great Instauration*, and more specifically in his *Advancement of Learning* (1605) and *Novum Organum* (1620), which lay at the base of the new enquiries supported by those who were to form the Royal Society. Second, there was the effect of the writings of Descartes, which almost from their inception had begun to make a significant impact on English thinking. This was not least because several of the leading philosophers in England had fled to France during the English Civil War and there had had direct contact with Descartes and other French thinkers such as Gassendi, Arnaud, and Mersenne. Of these, intellectually the most important was Thomas Hobbes, but Hobbes's immediate influence, though greater than often supposed, was somewhat diminished by the hostility with which he was generally regarded in his own country. Furthermore, his own personal rivalry with Descartes – each saw the other as a threat to his own standing as the leading philosopher of their generation – guaranteed that Hobbes was never to be a proponent of Cartesian philosophy. Others, such as Sir Kenelm Digby, Walter Charleton, and John Evelyn, all encouraged the study of Descartes. But the thinkers who probably did most to propel him in England were Henry More and others collectively, but perhaps not quite accurately, known as the Cambridge Platonists. This group of thinkers, perhaps surprisingly, were themselves to have something of an impact on Locke, a point to which we shall return.

The third great contemporary force acting on Locke's thinking was, of course, the traditional teachings and syllabus of the universities. These were still dominated by the works of Aristotle, for whom Locke was always to retain a high regard. It was his commentators and paraphrasers whom Locke came rapidly to hold in contempt. In England, Aristotle's teachings were given a significant Protestant twist in order to bring them in line with the theology of the Church of England, represented in Oxford by the teachings of two deans of Christ Church in Locke's time, the puritan John Owen, appointed by Oliver Cromwell, and John Fell, made dean at the restoration of the monarchy in 1660. Both of these men were well disposed toward Locke during his years at Christ Church, and Locke was careful not to court religious controversy until late in his life, which was in keeping with his generally cautious approach to all controversial issues.

Locke and his friends tell us that he did not much enjoy the undergraduate course at Oxford. He objected to the scholastic syllabus and the exercises in logic and Latin poetry. But his notebooks reveal that as soon as he graduated, if not before, he was turning to wider horizons. He told Damaris Masham that the first books "which gave him a relish of Philosophical Studys were those of Descartes,"[4] a claim that he confirmed himself in his *Letter to the Bishop of Worcester*, in which Locke writes, "I must always acknowledge to that justly-admired gentleman [Descartes] the great obligation of my first deliverance from the unintelligible way of talking of the philosophy in use in the schools." But he goes on to say that none of the mistakes to be found in the *Essay* can be attributed to Descartes, for its contents are "spun barely out of my own thoughts, reflecting as well as I could on my own mind, and the ideas I had there" (W IV: 48–9).

Precisely when Locke first read Descartes is not easily determined. The earliest notes that I have discovered are in Locke's Medical Commonplace Book, which is dated 25 February 1659 (1660 new style), and the latest publishing date for any book cited is 1660. The edition of Descartes that Locke used, according to his own reference, was the *Opera philosophica*, third edition, published in Amsterdam in 1656.[5] He enters short passages from the

---

[4] Lady Masham in a letter to Le Clerc (January 12, 1705, p. 7), a copy of which was given to me by Esmond de Beer, from a copy given him by Rosalie Colie taken from the original in the Remonstrants Library, Amsterdam.

[5] In Harrison and Laslett 1971 the date of Locke's copy is incorrectly given as 1658.

Meditationes, Principia philosophiae, Dioptrice, and *Meteora,* with most of the passages coming from the *Principia.*

It is plausible to put a construction on this last fact about Locke's interest in and debts to Descartes. What he found in Descartes's philosophy was a comprehensive and alternative account of the nature of the universe – alternative, that is, to that offered by the standard Aristotelian explanations. It was this wider vision that grabbed Locke's attention, not the particular epistemological concerns that occupy the early sections of the *Meditations.* There is no reason to see Locke at this early stage as being deeply engaged with any kind of epistemological enquiry, nor to see Descartes as holding any special interest for him in this direction. It is important to remember that when Locke was beginning his studies, the word 'philosophy' covered the whole of what we would today call natural science as well as epistemology, moral theory, and political philosophy. This wider understanding of the term is what Locke was suggesting when he claimed that Descartes had inspired his interest in 'philosophy'. Too often, on coming to learn of Locke's acknowledgment of his debt to Descartes, and influenced by a much narrower picture of philosophy (fostered in part by Locke's own work), commentators have come to assume that the issues that grabbed Locke's attention in the *Meditations* were the early concerns with scepticism. But there is no reason at all to believe this to be true. Indeed, there is no reason to believe that scepticism was an issue that greatly troubled Locke at all. What he found in the *Principia* was a powerful but conjectural account of the world, preceded by some methodological moves that he was later to find wanting in various ways but that did not, at this stage, engage him in any deep reflections. Those reflections were to come many years later. Nor is there any reason to suppose that Locke in any sense became a Cartesian as a result of those early readings. Certainly he was to be strongly influenced by Descartes in some particulars central to his philosophy. But he never showed any commitment to Descartes's method of enquiry and indeed had soon firmly rejected it, as we shall see. Nor is there any reason to believe that Locke followed Descartes in accepting an entirely mechanical account of causation in the physical world. Indeed, it would be very difficult to demonstrate that he held to any of the beliefs that were to become the dogmas of modern philosophy, whether speculative or natural, though no doubt some of the beliefs that are central to Locke's empirical epistemology were taking at least an informal place in his understanding of the world.

It is important for an appreciation of Locke's argument in the *Essay* to consider in more detail some of the many similarities as well as the differences between Locke and Descartes in their philosophical positions, differences that it is not always helpful to characterise as those between a Rationalist and an Empiricist philosopher. One relates to their objectives in writing a work of philosophy. Descartes tells us that what he was attempting to produce was a philosophy founded on the granite foundation of certainty. From impeccable premises the argument would proceed with ineluctable force to conclusions that could not be challenged. If Descartes in the end was not so confident that he had achieved his goal (as the closing sections of the *Principles of Philosophy* seem to suggest) or that it extended to the whole of the *Principia*, where the two later books may be read as invoking probabilist hypotheses, there can be little doubt about the original motivation.

The enemy was, then, the sceptic whose defeat was central to the project. Locke began with a quite different purpose. For the whole of his life he was quite sure that for large sections of human enquiry the outcomes could never be anything other than provisional. The state of 'mediocrity' – a word Locke often uses – in which we find ourselves was for him central to the human condition, and with it came a very clear view about the fallibility of the human intellect. Certainty was possible, but only in rather small quantities and in very particular areas of enquiry. To expect philosophy or any other enquiry to produce absolute certainty in large areas of human concern was whistling in the wind.

He was therefore interested in arguing from known self-evident principles to conclusions known equally to be certainly true in only three areas: mathematics, morals, and some few but important aspects of religion. Although Locke accepted the certainty of the existence of the self (Descartes's *cogito*), it was not for him, as it was for Descartes, taken as a foundational truth. Nor did he ever accept the very sharp dualism between mind and body that Descartes inferred from his first premise. Equally, Descartes's claim, in the way we have it in the *Meditations*, to have identified by introspection the essence of mind as thought and that of body as extension, he totally rejected. Locke accepted no such purely intellectual route to knowledge of the essence of substances. In short, Locke rejected completely the Cartesian route to knowledge of the essence of self and matter.

However, there were many areas where he was far from hostile to Descartes's method and innovations. How many of these he took over from his first readings we cannot with certainty say, but they were soon to appear in his philosophical writings and later to be incorporated into his mature work. By far the most important of these is that Locke adopted the Cartesian language of ideas to characterise our experience. That Descartes was the source for this aspect of Locke's thought is difficult to doubt. It was Descartes who first gave "ideas" a central place in his account of knowledge, whereas others who were strong influences on Locke did not. Thus Francis Bacon scarcely uses the term, and Boyle similarly eschews it. Hobbes, too, though not an overt influence, but perhaps more influential than Locke cared to admit, made no epistemically central use of the term.

Nor did it feature in the "language of the schools," the current discussions in the lecture theatres throughout the universities of Christendom that were equally despised by Bacon, Descartes, and Locke. The term was, however, to feature centrally in the writings of philosophers influenced by Descartes throughout the second half of the seventeenth century. Perhaps the most important of these for Locke was the *Logic or the Art of Thinking* (1662) by Antoine Arnaud and Pierre Nicole, but it is unlikely that this could have influenced Locke in these very early years, as he probably did not at this stage read French. His own copies of the *Logic* were the 1674 edition, which he acquired during his prolonged stay in France between 1675 and 1679.

Locke's rejection of syllogistic logic was clearly something that he shared with Descartes, but it would be rash to assume that it was Descartes who persuaded him of its redundancy. But he clearly came to agree with Descartes that intuition lies at the heart of knowledge. And perhaps even more importantly, he came to accept that clear and distinct ideas provide our best criterion of truth. Conversely, it was, again with Descartes, the indeterminate nature of many ideas that lead to confusion and mistakes in our reasoning.

There is no reason to doubt that Locke took many of these Cartesian thoughts away with him from his first reading of

Descartes's philosophy. No doubt he also took with him a respect for the power of mechanical explanation to account for change in the physical world. Descartes gave mechanical interaction the central place in his explanation of physical phenomena, from light to gravity and the circulation of the planets. But while for Descartes such interaction was the necessary consequence of his definition of matter, Locke was flexible enough to change his mind about "impulse," for example, in light of what he took to be the empirical evidence supplied by Newton's *Principia*. Thus in the first three editions of the *Essay* he had written that bodies operate *"by impulse,* and nothing else" (E II.viii.11: 135); this was changed in the fourth edition to *"Bodies* produce *Ideas* in us ... manifestly *by impulse,* the only way in which we can conceive Bodies operate in." Locke's change of wording is explained later in his *Second Reply to the Bishop of Worcester,* where he writes:

You ask, "how can my way of liberty agree with the idea that bodies can operate only by motion and impulse?" Answ. By the omnipotency of God, who can make all things agree, that involve not a contradiction. It is true, I say, "that bodies operate by impulse and nothing else". And so I thought when I writ it, and can yet conceive no other way of their operation. But I am since convinced by the judicious Mr. Newton's incomparable book, that it is too bold a presumption to limit God's power, in this point, by my narrow conceptions. The gravitation of matter towards matter, by ways inconceivable to me, is not only a demonstration that God can, if he pleases, put into bodies powers and ways of operation above what can be derived from our idea of body, or can be explained by what we know of matter, but also an unquestionable and every where visible instance that he has done so. And therefore in the next edition of my book I shall take care to have that passage rectified. (W IV: 467–8)

There were other reasons that might have led Locke in his for-mative years to doubt that mechanism was the only causal factor in bodies. To appreciate those other possibilities, we need to remem-ber that Locke was also on the way to becoming a chemist, as we shall see, and that chemistry in the early seventeenth century was not mechanical. One way into Locke's thoughts on such matters is to return to that early notebook.

This early notebook, as its attributed name implies, and like several other of his contemporary manuscripts, contains many notes that reflect Locke's reading in medical matters. It includes, for example, many notes from his medical friend and teacher Richard Lower, who had, like Locke, been educated at Westminster and Christ Church and who was destined to become, according to Anthony Wood, "the most noted physician in Westminster and London" (Wood 1813: IV: 98). Certainly his research in physiology gives him a high place in its history. Another senior member of Christ Church was Thomas Willis, whose work in medicine generally and on the brain in particular was of a ground-breaking order. Locke made many notes from his lectures and publications. Medicine, as practised in the later seventeenth century, was closely related to chemistry, specifically to iatrochemistry. The medieval domination of Galenic medicine was challenged in the early seventeenth century by the theories of Paracelsus, whose practical remedies based on a completely new theory of disease were playing a growing role in medical practice. Added to this was the new impetus to research in medicine created by Harvey's discovery of the circulation of the blood. The new role that Harvey gave to the heart – that of a pump – and the destruction thereby of the whole tradition of medicine as taught and practised in the medical schools of Europe invited a large number of research projects to make sense of this new physiology and to understand its implications for disease. Although the heart as a pump brought mechanism into biology in a large way, there remained a multitude of questions for which mechanical answers seemed less obvious. One of these was the place of respiration in the life cycle. Why do we breath? Why do we need to take air into our lungs so regularly? What happens to it when it encounters the blood vessels? These were difficult questions and ones for which there were no obvious answers. A whole research programme beckoned. It was one in which Locke was to become much engrossed and to play a significant role.

For Locke, and for Oxford science in particular, perhaps the single most important event at this time was the arrival in Oxford of Robert Boyle in 1656. He was to remain there until 1668, when he moved back to London, the year following Locke's own move to the capital. Boyle's role in Oxford for those years was of the greatest importance both for science and medicine and for Locke personally. In 1659, Boyle brought to Oxford a German chemist named Peter Sthael. This was just at the point when Locke's interest in medicine and chemistry was emerging strongly in his reading and, perhaps most importantly, in his observations and experiments. Locke joined Sthael's class in Boyle's house in the High Street, where, according to Anthony Wood (no friend of Locke), he was "prateing and troublesome." How accurate Wood's comment was we shall probably never know. But we might speculate that Locke was likely to ask questions and to challenge those claims of Sthael that Locke believed were not supported by the evidence offered. When we know that Sthael was a Paracelsian, with a commitment to accounts of chemical change that were highly theoretical, it would be no surprise to find that Locke sought justifications for claims for which he could see no reason. This may be challenged on the grounds that it presupposes that the Locke of 1659 held the same views about unsupported claims that find powerful justification in the *Essay*. But it is likely that by this time Locke was firmly committed to the position that belief should be carefully proportioned to the evidence. It is not too speculative to wonder if he sometimes found that the claims of Sthael exceeded the evidence offered.

Locke's relationship to Boyle involved much more than attendance at Sthael's chemistry classes. From his graduating B.A. in 1656 to his departure for London in 1667, a very high proportion of Locke's time was spent in one way or another on medicine and medical and iatrochemical research. Much of this was in the company of Lower, but from about 1660 onward Locke was heavily engaged not only with Lower but also with Robert Boyle. His notebooks show him engaged in fundamental research about the interaction between air, still imperfectly understood but no longer regarded as the simple element of Aristotelian and Galenic theory, and human blood in respiration. The great question was the nature of the physiological changes that occur in the lungs when we breathe, and this became the centre of their research. Locke's notebooks reveal him to have been a careful investigator at the frontier of contemporary medical science, engaged in careful experiment and observation to test hypotheses about the nature of the changes in the blood that are brought about by the act of breathing. His research reached a level of sophistication that led him close to very important discoveries, but he never quite made the breakthrough that would have given him a central place in the history of physiology.[6] The results of the work of Boyle and Locke were not to be published for another twenty years. They appeared in 1684 as *Memoirs for the Natural History of Humane Blood, Especially the Spirit of that Liquor by the Honourable Robert Boyle*. It was dedicated to the "very Ingenious and Learned Doctor J[ohn] L[ocke]." In the letter of dedication, Boyle described their work together, claiming that whilst observations of blood had often been made before, proper controlled experimentation on blood had never before been carried out. The work was, therefore, innovative and important.

Locke owned more of Boyle's books than he did those of any other author (though few authors had written nearly as many). His final library contained about sixty separate Boyle titles, some of them, theological works (but, curiously, not the *Natural History of Humane Blood*). There can be no doubt that Boyle's influence on Locke's thinking was considerable. But we must also remember that before they came into contact Locke had absorbed the spirit of experimental enquiry from other leading players in the new medical research, including his mentor, Richard Lower, and his colleague David Thomas.

This spirit was essentially the same as that whose great spokesman was Francis Bacon, the intellectual forerunner of the Royal Society and the man whom all of the followers, not least Boyle himself, constantly invoked as the inspiration for the new method being used for the understanding of nature to which they as a group subscribed. Central to this was the belief that careful observation and experiment were much more important than theory to a correct account of the natural world. Of course, there was a place for hypotheses, but any such hypotheses must be rigorously tested against the world. When the Royal Society was formed in 1662, it took as its motto '*Nullius in Verba*' – nothing in words. In so doing it committed itself to the notion that knowledge of the natural world was to be obtained not by verbal exchanges but by careful empirical enquiry. The title of Boyle's work immediately links it to the Baconian programme. Natural histories were understood to be records of careful observation and experiment uncontaminated by conjectured explanations of the supposed phenomena

---

[6] On Locke's place in medicine at this time, see Frank 1980, especially Chapter 7.

or hypotheses about their causes. Thomas Sprat, the first historian of the Royal Society, set out their objectives like this:

[T]heir purpose is, in short, to make faithful *Records*, of all the works of *Nature*, or *Art*, which can come within their reach: that so the present Age, and posterity, may be able to put a mark on the errors, which have been strengthened by long prescription: to restore the Truths, that have lain neglected: to push on those, which are already known, to more various uses: and to make the way passable, to what remains unrevel'd. This is the encompass of their Design. And to accomplish this, they have indeaver'd to separate the knowledge of *Nature*, from the colours of *Rhetorick*, the devices of Fancy, or the delightful deceit of *Fables*. (Sprat 1959: 61–2)

The goal was the production of knowledge that could be put to useful work in improving the lot of humankind. What better example of this was there than medical research of the kind that Locke conducted with Boyle?

But Boyle influenced Locke in other ways, too. The most famous way was with regard to the nature and properties of matter. It is often said, for example, and with reason, that Locke's famous account of the distinction between the primary qualities of bodies, such as size, location, and solidity, and the secondary qualities of colour, sound, taste, and smell was taken over from Boyle's account of matter. In his *Origine of Formes and Qualities* (1666), Boyle gave an account of the properties of bodies that was, at least superficially, very similar to that which appears in Chapter viii of Book II of Locke's *Essay*. Furthermore, Boyle was committed to a "corpuscular" account of matter and its properties and to a mechanical account of change in the physical world. Indeed, what Boyle stood for in the background to Locke's intellectual development was the corpuscular or "mechanical" philosophy (Boyle uses the two terms as virtual synonyms)[7] worked out in its most thorough way. But Boyle's mechanical philosophy was not the materialism of Hobbes, for the former was quite sure that it ranged over only part of God's creation.

Further, and this is of great importance in understanding his relationship to Locke, any account of the properties of matter that the corpuscular philosophy was able to offer could be understood

---

[7] On this, see Anstey 2000: 2 and passim.

only as a tentative explanation of the phenomena, constantly open to revision in light of further experimental or observational evidence. This, combined with his eclecticism, resulted in a lack of systematic explanation in his natural philosophy, even though the overwhelming theme is the power and persuasiveness of the corpuscular hypothesis. This in its turn depended on a thorough account of the qualities of bodies, and it is on these that much of his experimental research focussed. What Boyle was to do was to offer a new kind of explanation of the properties or qualities of bodies. In this he was not original. Like many other seventeenth-century philosophers, including Galileo, Descartes, Gassendi, and Walter Charleton, he followed the ancient Greek atomists, Democritus and Epicurus, in offering an atomistic account of matter and its properties that distinguished sharply between what, under the influence of Locke, came to be called the primary and secondary qualities of bodies. In fact, Boyle seems to have invented the term 'primary' in this context, but it was Locke who seems to have been the first to use the term 'secondary'. The distinction is drawn clearly by Boyle in *Forms and Qualities*. After distinguishing between "the two grand and most catholic principles of bodies, matter and motion" (Boyle 1979: 20), he continued by saying that matter must be divided into parts, each of which must have the attributes of size and shape, attributes that must apply to the minutest fragments of matters as much as to anything larger. So matter must always have size, shape, and either motion or rest. These, Boyle said, may be called the "*moods* or *primary affections* of bodies to distinguish them from those less simple qualities (as colours, tastes, and odours) that belong to bodies on their account" (1979: 21). It was thus that Boyle drew the famous primary/secondary quality distinction, which has challenged epistemologists, especially in its Lockean form, since Locke's day. But it is important to remember that in its original form it was offered by Boyle as part of a hypothesis (never more) about the nature of matter. And it is important to remember, when considering Locke's account of the distinction, that he treats the issue as an excursion into the physical sciences from his main enterprise in the *Essay*. After the discussion of primary and secondary qualities, he writes: "I have in what just goes before, been engaged in Physical Enquires a little farther than, perhaps, I intended." And as an excuse and explanation, he adds: "it being necessary to make the Nature of Sensation a little understood, and to make the *difference between the Qualities in Bodies, and the* Ideas *produced by them in the Mind,* to be distinctly conceived, without which it were impossible to discourse intelligibly of them; I hope, I shall be pardoned this little Excursion into Natural Philosophy" (E II.viii.22: 140).

There can be little doubt of Locke's debts to Boyle on this distinction, but it is also important to notice that Locke is quite clearly aware of the line between natural philosophy and the nature of his own, quite different, enquiry, and we shall return to this later. Let us just note one further aspect of Locke's debt to Boyle. It is a recurring issue amongst Locke commentators what place exactly the mechanical hypothesis and its linked corpuscular theory play in Locke's epistemology. But it is important to realize that Locke is usually careful to distinguish between the corpuscular theory, which he treats as an hypothesis, albeit the hypothesis most likely to be true, and his commitment to many other propositions that are not in the same sense regarded by him as conjectural. To argue, as many have, that Locke's epistemology presupposes the truth of mechanism is entirely to misconstrue the relationship between his philosophy as we have it in the *Essay* and his wider beliefs about the natural world, which he sees as conjectures open to revision in the light of further evidence. As he put it in *Some Thoughts Concerning Education*, with regard to natural philosophy: "though the world be full of Systems...yet I cannot say, I know any one which can be taught a Young Man as a Science, wherein he may be sure to find Truth and Certainty....Only this may be said, that the Modern *Corpuscularians* talk, in most Things, more intelligibly than the *Peripateticks*, who possessed the Schools immediately before them" (TE: 247–8).

A characteristic of Boyle's whole approach to natural philosophy is neatly captured by the title of a book about him, *The Diffident Naturalist* (Sargent 1995). Boyle was always careful to claim no more than he believed could be well supported by the empirical evidence. He was strongly conscious of the danger of claiming more certainty for his views than the evidence justified. Thus he refrained from following Descartes in supposing there to be vortices that carried round the planets and other heavenly bodies. Nor would he certainly decide whether the air pump that he used with Hooke to carry out many of his experiments generated a true vacuum or something less. Whether Locke learnt his own diffidence from Boyle or not, he certainly shared with him a reluctance to claim firm conclusions for positions that he was nevertheless inclined to believe were true. And such, as we have seen, was his position with regard to the corpuscular hypothesis itself.

In 1663, Locke was elected Senior Censor at Christ Church, a position that he held for twelve months and that required him to give a set of lectures. These have come down to us as Locke's *Essays on the Law of Nature*. They are important not only for an understanding of Locke's moral and political philosophy, but also for understanding his epistemology, for they contain in outline some of the main claims to be made later in both *Drafts* and in the published *Essay*.

Undoubtedly the most important of these is his early commitment to the empirical principle in epistemology. Indeed, we can go further and say that it was whilst writing the lectures that Locke came to accept it. Indeed, it is in many ways right to concur with the judgment of W. von Leyden that "it seems we are justified in regarding the [lectures] as being in some sense the earliest draft of the *Essay*" (EL Intro: 62). For in them we find argument and commitment to many of the claims of the final work and even passages that are carried over almost verbatim into the two early *Drafts* and from there into the published *Essay*. The *Drafts* have a considerably wider scope than the *Essays*, where he is concerned with the specific subject of the law of nature – contending, for example, that it is not known innately. But the epistemological implications are identical, even down to Locke's claims about the scope of knowledge being confined to the range of simple ideas that we have experienced. The two great faculties of knowledge, Locke claims, are reason and sense experience, but they have to work in tandem to produce knowledge:

...sensation furnishing reason with the ideas of particular sense-objects and supplying the subject-matter of discourse, reason on the other hand guiding the faculty of sense, and arranging together the images of things derived from sense-perception, thence forming others and composing new ones...but if you take away one of the two, the other is certainly of no avail, for without reason, though actuated by our senses we scarcely rise to the standard of nature found in brute beasts. . . . without the help . . . of the senses, reason can achieve nothing more than a labourer working in darkness behind shuttered windows. . . . The foundations . . . on which rests the whole of that knowledge that reason builds up are the objects of sense-experience. . . . (EL: 148–49)

For Locke, this includes our knowledge of a lawmaker, that is God, and our knowledge of that law. God is known to exist because we know through experience that the physical world exists and exhibits an order that could not occur by chance, and therefore there must exist a superior and much wiser power who has a just and inevitable power over us. It is equally obvious, Locke says, that God requires us to behave in certain ways that we can discover by considering our natures and the world in which we are situated.

It was already armed with these beliefs that Locke entered the meeting with his friends in London in 1671 that led to the early drafts of the *Essay*. He was already a committed empiricist, deeply knowledgeable about contemporary medical research, familiar with the writings of the leading intellectual figures of the century (of whom Descartes and Boyle were probably the most important), a Fellow of the Royal Society, and, as advisor to Shaftesbury, well acquainted with the political scene in England. Nevertheless, in that year he drafts the early versions of what was to become the *Essay Concerning Human Understanding*. The word *become* is used advisedly, because there is a great difference between the nature of the two drafts that bears comment. Draft A is written in a large folio notebook in which Locke also made many other entries. It is written for Locke's own personal use, though conceivably he could have read from it to a group of friends. Nor does the draft contain any indication that it is in any sense that of something which might at that stage be thought of as a book. It is also very heavily corrected. It is the working copy of something that might be the basis for something more substantial, but only at a very early stage. It was Locke's own first thoughts, or so it would appear. But running to about thirty thousand words, set out in forty-five numbered sections, it appears to be much longer than would be appropriate for its supposed intended purpose, an introductory paper on its subject to be read to friends. This raises the question whether it might itself be an expanded version of that first paper, one that

Locke had prepared for his own private use. Draft B, on the other hand, at 65,000 words and 162 numbered paragraphs, is about twice the length of Draft A, and much more like a finished work – more, in fact, like a draft book, and Locke uses the prefatory word 'Essay' for the first time in its title. From about this time Locke appears to have carried with him a folio notebook, 'De Intellectu', in which he began to draft a version of the *Essay*, obviously with the object of a book in mind. Unfortunately, that notebook appears not to have survived.

The final version of the *Essay* is, at about 290,000 words, almost five times the length of Draft B. Despite this it covers much of the same territory, but without nearly so much detail in its argument, presenting a thoroughly empiricist account of knowledge and its limits. Some of the topics that have since Locke's day received the most attention from commentators are, however, entirely or almost entirely missing from Draft B. Thus there is no considered treatment of the primary/secondary quality distinction, or of personal identity, or of the association of ideas. Indeed, these last two are covered only in chapters added to later editions of the *Essay*. Nor does Draft B give the attention to the whole subject of knowledge that we find in the final version as Book IV. As Book IV is that to which the prior three books are directed as an argument, it suggests that in 1671 Locke was, perhaps, not as clear as he was to become about the full implications of his empiricist premises for the nature and scope of knowledge that emerge in the published work. However, we can be fairly confident that the reason that Locke never produced a text for publication in the 1670s is not that he faced overwhelming intellectual difficulties with the topic but that, as he tells us, he had other commitments that took him away from sustained philosophical reflection. Soon Ashley was made an earl and was thereby destined for positions of power that required Locke to be active on his behalf. Philosophy had to be put aside.

When Shaftesbury was made lord chancellor in November 1672, Locke became first secretary of presentations and then, when Shaftesbury fell from power, secretary to the Council of Trade and Plantations. Later he went to France, perhaps as an agent for Shaftesbury; he was to stay there for four years, much of his time spent in Montpelier at the medical school there. But by early 1679 he was back in England, probably recalled by Shaftesbury, who had once again obtained high office and was in need of his services. From then until Shaftesbury's death in Holland in 1683, Locke was much engaged with work for him.

Earlier, whilst in France, Locke kept an annual journal that he continued to the end of his life. In it he entered a variety of information, but the journals show that he was still very much thinking about matters epistemological, for there are many entries on topics that were later to find a place in the *Essay*. And the entries also show that Locke still had an intention of presenting his ideas in the form of a book. These notes cover many of the central themes of that work, including, for example, knowledge, extension, species, and time. Some of them reinforce passages in the *Drafts*, and others show that Locke is extending his enquiries – he quotes from the Cambridge Platonists, Ralph Cudworth, and John Smith, for example – as well as showing that he has returned to thinking about central and contentious issues in the philosophy of Descartes.

Locke's interest in the Cambridge Platonists was undoubtedly stimulated by a new friendship he made in 1681. This was with Damaris Cudworth, daughter of the Cambridge Platonist, Ralph Cudworth, and herself to become a philosopher of real ability. Not surprisingly, she was much more sympathetic to the Cambridge school than was Locke, and she was quite prepared to engage him in philosophical exchange as an equal and later to publish her own philosophy. They were evidently strongly attracted to one another, but Locke's departure for Holland in 1683 broke their personal contact, and whilst he was away she married Sir Francis Masham and moved to his home at Oates in Essex. At their invitation, Locke was to spend his last years there as their paying guest. It is no surprise that Masham was herself much more influenced by Henry More, John Smith, and her own father than was Locke, but there can be no doubt that Locke's contact with her made him more aware of their philosophical positions and more sympathetic to them than he might otherwise have been. But it is also true that Locke could not but be aware of them because they were collectively the most interesting philosophers in England in the middle decades of the century.[8]

---

[8] On Locke's relationship to the Cambridge group, see Rogers forthcoming.

There is another strand to Locke's thought that ought also to be kept in mind when considering its aims and nature. It is his concern with political theory. Although the interaction between his political philosophy and his epistemology has often been regarded as minimal, at best, there can be little doubt that Locke did not himself see it that way. From the early *Essays on the Law of Nature* through to the last edition of the *Essay*, Locke was committed to the possibility of our being able to discover the law of nature, the moral law that should govern our lives, by intellectual enquiry. Morality for him was a collection of truths that could be reached by reflection on the human condition and the obligations to which social life gives rise. But he was also keenly aware from his examination of epistemological questions that reaching the truth about moral and religious issues is often very difficult and problematic. He therefore saw the issue of toleration of differing views on these contentious matters to be of great social and political importance. Indeed, the *Essay* might be seen as advocating what I have elsewhere called an epistemology of toleration. It would be claiming too much to hold that Locke was intent on producing an epistemology that would carry this implication. But that it did can be seen as giving his whole philosophy a strength that goes some way to explaining its continued influence.

All his life Locke enjoyed serious conversation with friends, and in France he was to make many new friends who shared his passion for intellectual exchange. Many of these new friends were French Protestants, and several were physicians associated with the famous medical school at Montpelier. Locke's flight to Holland in 1683 was almost certainly in part politically motivated. In 1685, with the revocation of the Edict of Nantes and the consequent excessive persecution of Protestants in France, some of Locke's French friends also fled to Holland, and Locke was to once more enjoy discussion with them. But, more importantly, the stay in Holland gave Locke the leisure that he had sought for some time, to return seriously to finishing his 'De Intellectu'. His departure to Holland had not gone unnoticed by the powers that be in England, and he was later accused of supporting those in Holland who were planning rebellion. The result, in November 1684, was expulsion from Christ Church at the express order of the king. The following year, after the death of Charles and the succession of his brother, the Catholic James II, he was suspected of helping to fund the duke of Monmouth's abortive rebellion.[9] When Locke was expelled from Christ Church, he wrote to his old pupil, the politically powerful earl of Pembroke, protesting his innocence of any involvement in plotting. He wrote:

My time was spent most alone, at home by the fires side, where I confesse I writ a great deale, I think I may say, more then ever I did in soe much time in my life, but noe libells, unlesse perhaps it may be a libell against all mankinde to give some account of the weaknesse and shortnesse of humane understanding, for upon that my old theme de Intellectu humano (on which your Lordship knows I have been a good while a hammering) has my head been beating, and my pen scribleing all the time I have been here except what I have spent in travelling about to see the country. (C 2: 665)

The long letter from which this passage is taken contains some dubiously true claims as to Locke's activities and contacts, but about his major engagement there can be little doubt. For much of the time he must have been writing the *Essay*. For nothing else would explain the production of a major work of nearly 300,000 words. By December 1686, Locke was able to send to his friend Edward Clarke "the [four]th and last book of my scattered thoughts concerning the *Understanding*" (C 3: 88). Locke went on to claim that until this point he had not read through the whole of the work, and that he was now painfully aware of its repetitions and other flaws. He recalls the meeting many years before at which Clarke was one of the friends, when his enterprise had been launched, and he continues with a description of his method:

For being resolved to examine *Humane Understanding*, and the way of our knowledge, not by others' opinions, but what I could from my own obser-vations collect myself, I have purposely avoided the reading of all books that treated any way of the subject, that I might have nothing to bias me any way, but might leave my thought free to entertain only what the matter itself suggested to my meditations. So that, if they at any time jump with others, 'twas not out of contradiction, or a mind to be singular. My aim has been only truth so far as my shortsightedness could reach it. (C 3: 89)

---

[9] This was almost certainly another 'Lock', a tobacconist from London. Cf. Cranston 1957: 251.

We know already of Locke's debts to Descartes and also something of his debt to Boyle, but as a general comment on Locke's method what he says appears to me to be true. It has often been suggested, not least by R. I. Aaron (1971: 31–5), that Locke appears to draw much of his account from Gassendi. But there is no evidence that Locke ever made a close study of Gassendi (cf. Milton 2000: 87–109), and it appears to me that insofar as they reach similar conclusions, it is as Locke says: if he jumps with others, it was not that he followed them but because they began from similar premises and agreed in the force of the argument.

Whilst Locke was in Holland, Newton's great work *Philosophiae Naturalis Principia Mathematica* was published in 1687. It has often been supposed that Newton's work had a great influence on the contents of Locke's *Essay*, as in so many ways they share a philosophy and as Newton is described in such glowing terms in Locke's "Epistle to the Reader" (of which more later). But we now know that Locke had substantially completed the *Essay* before reading Newton's work, which he did in 1687; he is probably the author of the review of it that appeared in the *Bibliothèque universelle* in March 1688.[10]

When Locke returned to England in February 1689, after the Revolution of 1688 had brought William and Mary to the English throne, it was as a recognised supporter of its outcome and on the same ship as the new queen. He immediately began to prepare the final text of several of his works for publication. The first to appear was his great work of political philosophy, the anonymous *Two Treatises of Government*, dated 1690 but licensed in October 1689. The *Essay* was available for sale in December. Its "Epistle Dedicatory" is dated May 24, 1689.[11] Between the previous February and their publication, Locke must have been extremely busy preparing the final versions of both. Although the text of the *Essay* was substantially ready perhaps two years prior to publication, it is virtually certain that Locke made some last-minute changes, including altering the order of presentation of his argument through

---

[10] On the relationship between the two books, see Rogers 1978. On the review, see Axtell 1965.

[11] This date was omitted in the first three editions but added by Locke to the fourth edition. It is in fact the date on which Locke signed his contract with his publisher, Churchill, upon delivery of the final manuscript.

modifications to the chapter order. He also wrote the already-mentioned famous "Epistle to the Reader." This serves both as an Introduction to the book and as a statement of Locke's objectives in publishing it. But there is also a further Introduction to the whole work, the first chapter of Book I, and we must look at both of these to gain a firmer hold on Locke's objectives.

In the "Epistle" Locke tells us that his subject is the understanding, which, as the greatest faculty of the "soul," we may use to pursue knowledge. Then, after apologising for various faults in his style and especially for the repetitious nature of some of the content, he tells us that he is interested only in obtaining truth and usefulness, "though in one of the meanest ways." That is to say, Locke makes no claim to be revealing grand truths about the world – no doubt men more clever than himself have long ago discovered all that he can offer. He continues by saying that he is well aware that he lives in a great age for discovery:

The Commonwealth of Learning, is not at this time without Master-Builders, whose mighty Designs, in advancing the Sciences, will leave lasting Monuments to the Admiration of Posterity; But every one must not hope to be a *Boyle* or a *Sydenham*; and in an Age that produces such Masters, as the Great *Huygenius*, and the incomparable Mr. *Newton*, with some others of that Strain; 'tis Ambition enough to be employed as an Under-Labourer in clearing the Ground a little, and removing some of the Rubbish that lies in the way to Knowledge. (E: 9–10)

This passage tells us much about Locke and his objectives and in many ways sets the agenda for philosophy, especially in the English-speaking world, for the next three hundred years. For what Locke is doing here is saying that his task is quite different from that of the natural scientist. The way in which the ground is to be cleared is essentially therapeutic. He tells us immediately after the passage just quoted that the "rubbish" that has been introduced comprises the "Vague and insignificant Forms of Speech and Abuse of Language" peddled as "Mysteries of Science." It is breaking into this "Sanctuary of Vanity" that will, he supposes, render some service to "Human Understanding." In other words, the task of the philosopher is to remove nonsense. Locke could not, of course, use the word 'philosopher' here, because the subject matter of philosophy in 1690 included all those enquiries in which his quartet had distinguished themselves. It is of some interest that Locke himself was good friends with all four and collaborated in important medical research with two of them, and in theology and perhaps some alchemy with Newton. It is much more doubtful that Locke saw himself as setting an agenda for philosophy with the *Essay*. But he was no doubt aware that there was nothing definitive about his achievement. He invited critical comment, which he says he would welcome. He need not have worried. He was to receive a great deal, some of it much more astute than others. His great critics were to be Bishop Stillingfleet and George Berkeley, but there were a host of others ready to wade in with their two penny worth well through the eighteenth century and beyond. His great heirs were Hume and Kant and virtually the whole of empirical philosophy in the nineteenth and twentieth centuries.

But there is another dimension to Locke's work that needs to be stressed and that was no doubt very much part of his objective in producing the *Essay*. The great French humanist Voltaire characterised the *Essay* as a "natural history of the human soul" (cf. Flower 1950: 177). There is a clear sense in which Voltaire is right about much of the *Essay*. The second book is in many respects a natural history of ideas, explaining the origin of complex ideas from their constituent simple ones, all themselves having their source in experience. Locke himself classified his procedure as following the "Historical plain Method" (E I.i.2: 44). So in some obvious sense the *Essay* was written as a natural history of the understanding, just as Locke and Boyle had collaborated to produce a natural history of blood, and as Sydenham was working toward a natural history of disease.

There might be thought to be something of a tension between these two objects of enquiry: the therapeutic and the Baconian. But that tension is hierarchical. The Baconian history requires clarity – clear and distinct ideas – in our concepts if the second is to be achieved. Locke set out his programme in his second "Introduction," Chapter I of the first book. His objective is to identify the bounds between opinion, on the one hand, and knowledge – genuine knowledge – on the other, and to provide the criteria for assigning the likelihood to truth of our beliefs or conjectures. To do so, he tells us he will enquire into the sources of our ideas. Second, he intends to show what knowledge we have through those ideas, including their certainty, evidence, and extent. Third, he will examine the grounds of belief, faith, and opinion and the appropriate degrees of assent. He combines these objectives with a firm belief that genuine human knowledge, contrasted with conjecture and speculation, and compared to the whole extent of creation, is very limited. If we agree with him on nothing else, we must surely agree with him about that!

2 Locke's Polemic against Nativism

In the seventeenth century, there was a lively debate in the intellectual circles with which Locke was familiar, revolving around the question whether the human mind is furnished with innate ideas. Although a few scholars declared that there is no good reason to believe, and good reason not to believe, in the existence of innate ideas, the vast majority took for granted that God, in his infinite goodness and wisdom, has inscribed in human minds innate principles that constitute the foundation of knowledge, both in practical and in theoretical matters. It was in opposition to the latter group, which included Descartes, leading Anglican divines, and the Cambridge Platonists, that Locke directed his attack upon innate ideas in the first book of the *Essay*.[1]

In the minds of those who weighed in on one side or the other, the importance of the controversy related to epistemological, moral, and religious doctrines. At the epistemological level, innatists (or, as I will also call them, nativists) held that all knowledge of the natural and supernatural world available to humans is based on fundamental "speculative" axioms, theoretical principles that neither require nor are capable of proof. These principles, such as the causal principle (that nothing comes from nothing) or the principle of noncontradiction (that nothing can both be and not be at the

---

[1] Aristotelian scholastics (including the logicians Burgersdicius and Sanderson, with whose works Locke was familiar – see W IV: 449) agreed with the purveyors of innate ideas that some principles (which they called "maxims" or "axioms") are foundational. But in accordance with the famous scholastic dictum *nihil est in intellectu quod prius fuerit in sensu* (nothing is in the understanding that was not earlier in the senses), they denied that these maxims are innate.

33

same time), were taken to be both universal and necessary, and hence impossible to derive from experience. To the mind of an innatist, if these principles are not based on experience and are not (as chimerical ideas were thought to be) constructed out of simpler elements by acts of volition, then they are neither acquired nor constructed, and hence must be built into the mind *ab initio*. At the moral and religious level, nativists held that knowledge of our duties is founded on innate "practical" axioms, the absence of which seemed to make room for moral disagreement or relativism profound enough to destabilize entire societies.

So the stakes could not have been higher when Locke first penned his anti-nativist polemic. It was held on all sides that any advance in the speculative or practical realm depends on the resolution of the controversy over innatism. It is therefore something of a pity that more philosophical effort has not been expended on gaining a clear understanding of the debate and of Locke's contribution to it.

The purpose of this essay is to shed light on Locke's polemic and the intellectual circumstances that prompted it. The basic interpretive questions to be addressed are these. First, who were Locke's opponents? What sorts of nativist doctrines did they hold? What reasons did they give in defense of nativism? Second, what are Locke's anti-nativist arguments in the *Essay*? Third, how successful are Locke's arguments, on their own and in the context of the *Essay* as a whole? Do they succeed in undermining nativism itself, the arguments therefor, or neither? Do some or all forms of nativism escape Locke's criticisms, or does Locke emerge victorious in the end?

It has long been held that Book I of the *Essay* is, to put it mildly, not one of Locke's best philosophical efforts. Some think that Locke's opponent in Book I is nothing but a straw man, others that his arguments are singularly ineffective. In the end, as I will argue, Locke successfully undermined naïve versions of nativism and shifted the philosophical burden onto the shoulders of those who defended a more sophisticated version thereof. Armed with a better appreciation of the historical context of the *Essay* and a clear reconstruction of Locke's anti-nativist arguments, we will see that Book I repays close attention and that Locke deserves significant philosophical rehabilitation on the relevant issues.

Of Locke's immediate predecessors, those who defended some version of nativism may be divided into three groups: (i) Descartes, (ii) prominent members of the Anglican Church, notably Edward Stillingfleet, Bishop of Worcester, and (iii) a number of Cambridge Platonists, including Henry More and Ralph Cudworth.

Descartes

Descartes, with whose views Locke was intimately familiar, holds that all ideas are adventitious, constructed, or innate (Descartes 1984: II:26 and III:183).[2] Among adventitious ideas, – that is, ideas occasioned by (brain) images received from the senses – Descartes counts the ideas of primary and secondary qualities, as well as "the idea we commonly have of the sun." Among constructed ideas, Descartes counts chimerical ideas, such as ideas of sirens and hippogriffs, as well as scientific constructs, such as "the idea which the astronomers construct of the sun by the reasoning." By contrast, Descartes holds that his understanding of "what a thing is, what truth is, and what thought is, seems to derive simply from [his] own nature," and also counts as innate "the idea of God, mind, body, triangle, and in general all those which represent true, immutable, and eternal essences."

Descartes's claim that some ideas (most notably, those that represent true and immutable essences) are innate was explicitly challenged by Thomas Hobbes (in the Third Objections) and by Pierre Gassendi (in the Fifth Objections). "When M. Descartes says that the ideas of God and of our souls are innate in us," objects Hobbes, "I should like to know if the souls of people who are in a deep, dreamless sleep are thinking. If they are not, they do not have any ideas at the time. It follows that no idea is innate; for what is innate is always present" (Descartes 1984: II:132). So Hobbes thinks there can be no innate ideas, because (i) innate ideas are always present, that is, conscious, and yet (ii) there are times when the mind is not conscious of any idea (e.g., during deep, dreamless

---

[2] Every one of the works of Locke's contemporaries and predecessors mentioned in this essay appears in the library that was part of Locke's estate upon his death; see Harrison and Laslett 1971.

sleep). As it happens, (ii) is something Descartes denies, in holding that the mind is a substance whose whole essence is to think (Descartes 1984: II:18). In response, Gassendi echoes Hobbes's criticism: "I want to stop here and ask whether, in saying that thought cannot be separated from you, you mean that you continue to think indefinitely, so long as you exist. . . . [This] will hardly convince those who do not see how you are able to think during deep sleep or indeed in the womb" (Descartes 1984: II:184).[3]

In response to Hobbes's "dreamless sleep" objection, Descartes writes (Descartes 1984: II:132): "Lastly, when we say that an idea is innate in us, we do not mean that it is always there before us. This would mean that no idea was innate. We simply mean that we have within ourselves the faculty of summoning up the idea." Expanding on this point, Descartes tells Regius that ideas are innate in "the same sense as that in which we say that generosity is 'innate' in certain families, or that certain diseases such as gout or stones are innate in others: it is not so much that the babies of such families suffer from these diseases in their mother's womb, but simply that they are born with a certain 'faculty' or tendency to contract them" (Descartes 1984: I:304). Descartes therefore holds that an idea that is neither constructed by an act of will nor prompted by the receipt of sense impressions is something of which the mind need not be conscious.[4]

---

[3] It is worth noting that Locke criticizes Cartesian nativism on just these grounds (E II.i.9–19: 108–16). Locke remarks that "it is an Opinion, that the Soul always thinks ... and that actual thinking is as inseparable from the Soul, as actual Extension is from the Body" (E II.i.9: 108). (In the French translation of the *Essay*, Coste makes clear that the philosophers holding this "opinion" are "Les Cartesiens.") In response, Locke claims that " 'tis doubted whether I thought all last night, or no" (E II.i.10: 109), and thus "every drowsy Nod shakes their Doctrine, who teach, That the Soul is always thinking" (E II.i.13: 111).

[4] In response to Gassendi's "deep sleep" objection, Descartes claims that the fact that we do not remember having any thoughts when we were infants or in a deep sleep does not show that we were not thinking at those times. For, as Descartes argues, it is necessary for the formation of (corporeal) memories that physical traces be "imprinted on the brain," and hence, since the brains of infants and those in a deep sleep are "unsuited to receive these traces," it is possible that such individuals have conscious thoughts without being able to remember at any later time that they had these thoughts (Descartes 1984: II:246–7). Locke himself criticizes this gambit of Descartes's in II.i.14–16. His main objections are two: first, that Descartes's hypothesis would have the absurd consequence that "[Socrates's] Soul when he sleeps, and Socrates the Man consisting of Body and Soul when he is waking, are

Descartes's brand of nativism is rather sophisticated. Unlike a more naïve innatist who holds that maxims are actually, and not merely potentially, in the mind, Descartes does not require that the ideas of which these maxims are composed be more than potentially there. Call the naïve innatism just described "occurrent nativism," and the sophisticated innatism of Descartes "dispositional nativism."[5] One of the questions I will be raising here is whether dispositional nativism is better able than occurrent nativism to withstand Locke's anti-innatist attacks.

Anglican Churchmen

In *Leviathan* (1651), Hobbes had argued that there are no incorporeal substances and hence, since God is a substance, that God is a body (Hobbes 1994: 540). Hobbes's materialism was widely thought to entail atheism, since it would seem impossible for bodies to be perfect, yet God was held to be perfect by definition. Numerous members of the Anglican Church felt it necessary to respond to what they perceived to be Hobbes's atheistic materialism. Perhaps the most intellectually gifted and prominent of these divines was Edward Stillingfleet, bishop of Worcester.

Stillingfleet gained fame with the publication of *Origines Sacrae* (1662), a book with which Locke was familiar. There Stillingfleet attempts to confute atheism by providing three main reasons for belief in God's existence, the first of which is that *"God hath stamped an universal character of himself upon the minds of men"* (Stillingfleet 1662: 383).[6] Stillingfleet then provides two reasons for accepting this result, the first being "because the whole *world* hath *consented* in it." The argument here is that *"no sufficient account can be given of so universal a consent, unless it be supposed to be the voice of nature,"* for *"a common and universal effect* must *flow*

---

two Persons" (E II.i.11: 110; E II.i.15: 112 – Locke expands his discussion of the point in E II.xxvii); and second, that "if [the Mind] has no memory of its own Thoughts" then its power of thought is "idlely and uselessly employ'd," a result that contradicts the assumption that "nature never makes excellent things, for mean or no uses" (E II.i.15: 113).

[5] Here I adopt terminology introduced in Kim 2003.

[6] Note that Locke uses the word "character" to describe the innatism he goes on to attack (see E I.ii.1: 48).

from some *common* and *universal cause"* (Stillingfleet 1662: 384).
Thus, if we find that human beings all agree that God exists, this
must be the result of "a natural *propensity* to *Religion* implanted in
them, and founded in the general *belief* of the *existence* of a *Deity"*
(Stillingfleet 1662: 389).

So one of Stillingfleet's main arguments for God's existence
relies on the claim that the idea of God is innate, a claim he defends
on grounds of universal consent. In his own defense, Stillingfleet
notes that he is not the first to have taken such a position. He refers
in particular to the Epicurean and Stoic arguments for God's existence in Cicero's *De Natura Deorum*. There, Velleius the Epicurean
claims that it is "a necessary *Prolepsis* or *Anticipation* of *humane
nature* ... that *nature* its self had *stamped* an *Idea* of *God* upon the
minds of men." As Stillingfleet puts it, Velleius then argues that
"since the *belief* of a *Deity*, neither *rise* from *custom* nor was
enacted by *Law*, yet is unanimously *assented* to by all *mankind*; it
necessarily *follows* that there must be a *Deity*, because the *Idea* of
it is so *natural* to us" (Stillingfleet 1662: 365–6). And Lucilius the
Stoic claims that "if there were no God, the belief [in a deity] would
not endure with such stability, it would not be strengthened by
lapse of time, nor could it have become fixed as the ages and gen-
erations of men advanced" (Stillingfleet 1662: 384 – Latin translation by Francis Brooks).[7]

In saying that innate ideas are akin to Epicurean or Stoic "pro-
lepses," Stillingfleet allies himself with dispositional, rather than
with occurrent, nativism. A prolepsis may (without excessive dis-
tortion) be identified with an innate disposition to form an idea.
And, as Stillingfleet sees it, it is only in this "proleptic" way that
the idea of God counts as innate. As he puts it: it is "not that there
is any such *connate Idea* in the *Soul*, in the sense which *connate
Idea's* are commonly understood; but ... there is a *faculty* in the

---

[7] Stillingfleet's argument for innatism on grounds of universal consent was also
anticipated by Lord Herbert of Cherbury. In *De Veritate* (1624), Herbert claims that
"universal consent [is] the final test of truth ... [and] the beginning and end of
theology and philosophy" (Herbert 1937: 117–18). Those propositions to which all
humans (apart from the mad and the weak-minded) assent, Herbert calls "common
notions." These common notions are not "conveyed by objects themselves," and
hence Nature must have "inscribed them within us" (Herbert 1937: 126).

Soul, whereby upon the free use of *reason*, it can *form* within its self a setled *notion* of such a *Being*" (Stillingfleet 1662: 369).[8]

Cambridge Platonists

In *Leviathan*, Hobbes had written that, in the state of nature, "the notions of right and wrong, justice and injustice, have...no place," and that "[w]here there is no common power, there is no law; where no law, no injustice" (Hobbes 1994: 78). To members of the Anglican Church, the idea that humans are not bound by a moral law promulgated by God was anathema. Anglican divines, such as Benjamin Whichcote, the father of Cambridge Platonism, pointed in particular to a well-known passage from Romans 2:15 in which the moral law is described as being "written on the hearts" of Gentiles. Whichcote and his brethren interpreted this passage to mean that there is a sense in which moral principles are "connatural": they are, in Whichcote's words, "truths of first inscription" that are "known to be true as soon as ever they are proposed." Thus when a human being flouts moral rules, he "confounds his own principles...and must necessarily be self-condemned" (see Whichcote 1901: 4–5).

Whichcote was more of a preacher than he was a philosopher. It was left to his philosophical descendants, particularly Henry More (and also Ralph Cudworth – see note 10), to clarify the sense in which practical and speculative principles are innate, and to provide philosophical (as opposed to merely scriptural) arguments for nativism.

In his *Antidote Against Atheisme* (1653), More argues, in opposition to the Aristotelian claim that *"the Soul of man* [is] *Abrasa Tabula, a Table book in which nothing is writ,"* that the Soul has *"some Innate Notions and Ideas in her self"* (More 1653: 13). More's conception of innateness is dispositional rather than occurrent:

[In saying that the mind has innate ideas] I doe not mean that there is a certaine number of *Ideas* flaring and shining to the *Animadversive faculty*,

---

[8] Like Stillingfleet, Herbert understands common notions to be latent, rather than occurrent. As he puts it: "It is the law or destiny of Common Notions...to be inactive unless objects stimulate them" (Herbert 1937: 120). Lord Herbert is the only one of Locke's nativist opponents to be mentioned by name in Book I of the *Essay*. For more on the nature of Locke's criticisms of Herbert, see note 18.

like so many *Torches* or *Starres* in the *Firmament* to our outward Sight, or
that there are any *figures* that take their distinct places, & are legibly writ
there like the *Red letters or Astronomical Characters* in an *Almanack*; but
I understand thereby an active sagacity in the Soul, or quick recollection as
it were, whereby some small businesse being hinted unto her, she runs out
presently into a more clear and larger conception. (More 1653: 13)

More compares the formation of innate ideas in the Soul to the
recollection of an entire song upon being presented with two or
three words of its beginning. It is in this way that "the *Mind* of *man*
being jogg'd and awakened by the impulses of outward objects, is
stirred up into a more full and cleare conception of what was but
imperfectly hinted to her from externall occasions" (More 1653: 14).

In arguing for nativism, More concentrates on speculative, rather
than practical, principles. More provides three reasons to accept
dispositional nativism. First, when geometrical figures are initially
presented to the senses, the mind can "straightway pronounce" that
all perfect versions of these figures have certain properties. For
example, when it has been proved in the case of a particular sensible
triangle that its three angles are equal to two right ones, the mind
immediately knows that this is true of all (perfect) triangles (More
1653: 14–15). Second, there are "*Relative Notions* or *Ideas*" that are
not "the impresses of any materiall object from without," and
hence "are the naturall furniture of the humane understanding."
Suppose, for example, that objects A and B are alike in color, but
that B is then whitened. A is now unlike B, even though A has not
been "touch'd or medled with." It follows that the idea of being
unlike is "not any *Physicall affection* that strikes the corporeall
Organs of the Body," but rather "the Souls own active manner of
conceiving those things which are discovered by the outward
Senses" (More 1653: 15–16).[9] Third, there are "severall complex
Notions…which are true to the soul at the very first proposal,"
truths to which the soul "will certainly and fully assent," which
"must therefore be concluded not fortuitous or arbitrary, but

---

[9] Though More does not accept Plato's doctrine of recollection, according to which
the souls of humans exist before they are born, notice the way in which More's
argument from geometrical figures resembles the point made in favor of the
doctrine in Socrates's examination of the slave boy in the *Meno*, as well as the way
in which More's argument from relative notions resembles Socrates's argument for
the doctrine at *Phaedo* 74ff.

Natural to the Soul." Among such complex notions, More lists: *"The whole is bigger then the part"*; *"If you take Equall from Equall, the Remainders are Equall"*; *"Every number is either Even or Odde"*; and *"The three angles in a Triangle are equal to two right ones"* (More 1653: 17–18).[10]

In arguing against innatism, Locke therefore faced a vast array of rationalist metaphysicians and Anglican divines. Apart from Hobbes and Gassendi, Locke had few anti-innatist friends. Still, the friends he had were not inconsequential. Before turning to Locke's

---

[10] In *A Treatise Concerning Eternal and Immutable Morality*, which was not published until 1731, but with the contents of which Locke was almost certainly familiar, Cudworth provides a kind of master argument for holding a version of dispositional nativism. According to this argument, there are many ideas that are not imprinted in the soul by means of the senses; and since what does not come from without must be excited from within, it follows that these ideas "must needs spring from the active power and innate fecundity of the mind itself" (Cudworth 1996: 83). As Cudworth sees it, the mistake of the anti-nativist is to infer from the fact that these ideas are first excited in the mind when the senses are stimulated that the ideas are "stamped upon the soul from the objects without." Rather, these ideas are merely awakened or occasioned, but not conveyed or transmitted, by the senses. Ideas that could not possibly be conveyed by the senses include (i) "ideas of cogitative beings, and the several modes of them" (Cudworth 1996: 101), such as the ideas of volition, cogitation, and sense, as well as the ideas of wisdom, prudence, knowledge, truth, virtue, honesty, justice, and their opposites (Cudworth 1996: 83); (ii) "all the logical and relative notions that are" (Cudworth 1996: 86), such as the relative ideas of cause and effect, means and end, similitude and dissimilitude, equality and inequality, symmetry and asymmetry, whole and part (Cudworth 1996: 84), and the logical ideas of essence, existence, thing, substance, something, and nothing (Cudworth 1996: 104); (iii) ideas of perfect geometrical objects (Cudworth 1996: 107–11); (iv) general ideas, such as "the idea of a triangle in general," which are not ideas of any particular thing (Cudworth 1996: 111); and those ideas of sense that do not resemble anything in the objects that occasion them, such as ideas of secondary qualities (Cudworth 1996: 112).

Like More, Cudworth does not think of intelligible ideas as "flaring and shining to the Anidmadversive faculty." Rather, "native and domestic" ideas are "inward anticipations" or "preconceptions" that are only "awakened by ... passive impressions" (Cudworth 1996: 98). In much the way that More compares the formation of innate ideas to the recollection of a song based on the hearing of a few notes, Cudworth compares the excitation of innate ideas to the recollection of a man's face based on the perception of a few "lines drawn with ink upon a piece of paper" (Cudworth 1996: 106). As Cudworth sees it, there is no explaining one's recognition of the man's face given the paucity of information derived from the senses without supposing that one's idea of the face is latently "pre-existent," waiting to be awakened by suitable stimulation. It is in this sense, and in this sense only, that Cudworth treats intelligible ideas as innate.

own objections to nativism, let us look briefly at the sorts of objections put forward by Samuel Parker.

In *A Free and Impartial Censure of the Platonick Philosophie* (1666), Parker, an Oxford don who was elevated to the bishopric of Oxford in 1686, gives short shrift to the argument from universal assent. Taking as his paradigm the "Maxime, That the whole is greater than its parts," Parker claims that the fact that "all men assent to it at the first proposal" is not to be explained by supposing it innate, but rather by the fact that "they are presented with innumerable instances thereof, every visible thing in the world being a whole compounded of parts sensibly smaller than it self." Furthermore, Parker argues that there would be no reason for Providence (or for God) to imprint such "maxims" on the soul from the beginning of its existence, since they are self-evident. As Parker pithily puts the point: "A man that has animadversive Faculties, has as little need to be minded of such obvious and apparent Certainties, as a man that has Eyes in his head, has to be taught that there is a Sun in the Heavens." And finally, Parker argues that even if there were such "congenite Anticipations," it does not follow from a principle's being "congenite" that it is true. After all, Parker writes, "'tis not impossible but the seeds of Error might have been the natural Results of my Faculties, as Weeds are the first and natural Issues of the best Soyles" (Parker 1985: 56).

Here then was the state of the debate when Locke first thought of entering it on the anti-innatist side. Locke faced a number of philosophers who favored dispositional nativism, some on grounds of universal assent (Lord Herbert), some on grounds of universal assent "upon the free use of reason" (Stillingfleet), and some on grounds of universal assent "at the very first proposal" (Whichcote and More). In addition, Locke faced dispositional nativists who argued that there are ideas (notably, relative, logical, and geometrical ideas) that "must needs spring from the active power ... of the mind itself" because they could not be conveyed to the mind through the senses (More, and also Cudworth). Occurrent nativism had already come under attack by philosophers who thought it inconsistent with the fact that fetuses and those in a dreamless sleep do not think (Hobbes and Gassendi). But it had also been pointed out that dispositional nativism is immune from this sort of criticism, since the latent ideas posited by dispositional nativists need not be conscious (Descartes).

And finally, some anti-innatists had argued (a) that nativism is not the only plausible explanation for the widespread acceptance of certain principles, (b) that the self-evidence of many of the principles commonly thought innate makes it unnecessary for God to imprint them on human minds, and (c) that a principle's being innate does not entail that it is epistemically trustworthy (Parker).

2. LOCKE'S ANTI-NATIVIST ARGUMENTS

In arguing against nativism, Locke adopts a two-pronged strategy. First, Locke attempts to undermine reasons that have been given in support of nativism. Second, Locke provides reasons for thinking that nativism is false. Most of these arguments appear in Book I of the *Essay*. As we'll see, the arguments belonging to the first prong are addressed, in systematic fashion, to the nativist arguments provided by Locke's immediate predecessors. It follows that the charge that Locke commits the straw man fallacy is without merit. As we'll also see, arguments belonging to one prong of the strategy are interwoven with arguments belonging to the other. Since Locke does not always make this interweaving explicit, some commentators, mistakenly thinking that a consideration that is part of one prong is part of the other, have charged Locke with the fallacy of affirming the consequent. These interpretive errors have contributed to the inadvisable lowering of Book I in the esteem of Locke scholars, and of historians generally. Once the dialectical structure of Locke's anti-nativist reasoning becomes clear and the interpretive errors are cleared away, we can see Book I for what it is: a reasonable attempt to demolish occurrent nativism and to shift the burden of proof onto the shoulders of dispositional nativists.

Before analyzing and evaluating the arguments themselves, it is important to clarify exactly what Locke takes himself to be arguing against. As Locke puts it, his nativist opponent holds that "there are in the Understanding certain *innate Principles*; some primary Notions, Κοιναι εννοιαι [common notions], Characters, as it were stamped upon the Mind of Man, which the Soul receives in its very first Being; and brings into the World with it" (E I.ii.1: 48). So Locke's target holds that there are innate principles. This much is clear. But what is less obvious is that this is not the only position Locke's target accepts.

First, Locke writes that his opponents hold that innate principles are "the foundations of all our other knowledge" (E I.ii.21: 59), that God (or Nature) has imprinted these principles on human minds "in indelible Characters, to be the Foundation and Guide of all their acquired Knowledge, and future Reasoning" (E I.ii.25: 62).[11] Packed into these quotations are the following theses: first, that God (or Nature) is the author of innate principles; second, that innate speculative principles serve an epistemically foundational role with respect to acquired speculative propositions and that innate practical principles serve as a guide to human action; and third, that the point or purpose of God's having imprinted them on human minds is that humans might thereby come to know what can be known and recognize what needs to be done in order to achieve happiness.

As will become clear later (particularly in our discussion of the Argument from Universal Consent upon the Use of Reason – see I.ii.8), Locke assumes in addition that his innatist opponents deny that all ideas are innate. In particular, as Locke sees it, self-respecting nativists should accept that at least some propositions, including most notably the theorems – as opposed to the axioms – of arithmetic and geometry, are not innate. Here it must be admitted that Locke is on shaky ground. It is true that *occurrent nativists*, committed as they are to the principle that a proposition's being innate requires that it be actually perceived and to the obvious fact that mathematical theorems are not actually perceived at birth, are ipso facto committed to the view that mathematical theorems are not innate. But the same is clearly untrue of nativists belonging to the dispositionalist persuasion. All of Locke's dispositionalist opponents (including, most notably, Descartes) took for granted (and not unreasonably) that the innateness of mathematical axioms entails the innateness of mathematical theorems. After all, if the use of reason is sufficient of itself to extract mathematical theorems from mathematical axioms, then it would appear that the mind is disposed to perceive and know mathematical theorems without assistance from the senses, and hence that such dispositional knowledge must be innate.

---

[11] Locke also takes his opponents to declare "That God has imprinted on the Minds of Men, the foundations of Knowledge, and the Rules of Living" (E I.iii.14: 76).

Second, Locke takes himself to "agree with these Defenders of innate Principles, That if they are *innate*, they must needs *have universal assent*" (E I.ii.24: 61). As Locke sees it, the reason for accepting the thesis that all innate principles are universally assented to derives from another, namely, that "every innate Principle must needs be [self-evident]" (E I.iii.4: 68). For example, as Locke argues, the principle of noncontradiction "carries its own Light and Evidence with it, and needs no other Proof: He that understands the Terms, assents to it for its own sake" (E I.iii.4: 68). The idea that innate principles are self-evident, and hence the objects of universal assent, arguably follows from (or, at least, harmonizes with) the claim that innate principles are meant to serve as the foundation of all our acquired knowledge. For it is reasonable to hold, as Locke's opponents did, that what makes a principle indubitable and foundational is the fact that understanding it is sufficient for recognizing its truth.

The First Prong: Arguments for Nativism Undermined

As Locke sees it, the master nativist argument, already familiar from our discussion of the views of the Epicureans, the Stoics, and Lord Herbert, is the Argument from Universal Consent: "There is nothing more commonly taken for granted, than that there are certain Principles both *Speculative* and *Practical* (for they speak of both) universally agreed upon by all Mankind: which therefore they argue, must needs be the constant Impressions, which the Souls of Men receive in their first Beings, and which they bring into the World with them" (E I.ii.2: 49). The argument, in a nutshell, is this:

Argument from Universal Consent (AUC)

(1) There are speculative and practical principles to which every human assents.

(2) If every human assents to P, then P is innate.

So, (3) There are innate speculative and practical principles.

Locke criticizes both premises of AUC. As against (1), Locke repeatedly points to evidence indicating that there is no one speculative or practical principle to which all humans assent. For example, Locke thinks it obvious that infants and the weak-minded do not assent to, let alone understand, the principle of non-contradiction (E I.ii.5: 49). And though it is commonly thought that everyone assents to the principle that one should do what is just, Locke thinks that simple observation of human behavior is sufficient to establish that when outlaws embrace this principle, they do so only as a rule of convenience, ready to be broken at a moment's notice (E I.iii.2: 66).

Nowadays, the lack of universal assent to these principles may seem obvious. But in Locke's time, divines never tired of referring to the latest far-flung area of the globe whose inhabitants were reported by European travelers to believe in the existence of a deity and to recognize the wrongness of such actions as murder and theft. What irked Locke was that the proponents of AUC needed to show more than just that there are principles to which *many* humans assent: they also needed to show that there are principles to which *no* humans *fail to* assent. Whence the importance of what might otherwise appear to be an unnecessary reminder of the existence of humans who are insufficiently mature, intelligent, or educated to assent to the principles commonly thought innate.

As Locke sees it, the main reason to believe (2) takes the form of an inference to the best explanation: given that some principle P is universally assented to, the best explanation for the existence of such universal assent is that P is innate. What Locke denies here is the assumption that the innateness of a principle is what best explains the fact that it is the object of universal assent. As Locke puts it: "This Argument, drawn from *Universal Consent,* has this misfortune in it, That if it were true in matter of Fact, that there were certain Truths, wherein all Mankind agreed, it would not prove them innate, if there can be any other way shewn, how Men may come to that Universal Agreement, in the things they do consent in; which I presume may be done" (E I.ii.3: 49). Locke later argues that universal consent to practical propositions can be explained as resulting from inculcation (E I.iii.22–26: 81–4) and that universal consent to speculative propositions can be explained as the concomitant of intuitive knowledge (see E IV.ii.1: 530–1). So, in the first place, the "unwary, and, as yet, unprejudiced Understanding" of children is ready to accept any practical doctrine taught by their caregivers, at a time "before Memory began to keep a Register of...when any new thing appeared to them." When these children become adults, they do not remember that the practical rules to which they now give ready assent were instilled in them by others, and so "make no scruple to *conclude, That those Propositions, of whose knowledge they can find in themselves no original, were certainly the impress of God and Nature* upon their Minds" (E I.iii.22–23: 81–2). And, in the second place, a person's ready assent to a speculative maxim may be explained by the fact that she intuits – that is, immediately perceives without relying on any further intervening ideas – that the ideas out of which the maxim is constructed agree (or disagree). As Locke sees it, the self-evidence of this intuitive knowledge engages the will inasmuch as the knowledge "is irresistible, and like the bright Sun-shine, forces it self immediately to be perceived, as soon as ever the Mind turns its view that way; and leaves no room for Hesitation, Doubt, or Examination, but the Mind is presently filled with the clear Light of it" (E IV.ii.1: 531).

Locke claims that, in order to avoid the deficiencies of AUC, "'tis usually answered, that all Men know and *assent* to [speculative maxims], *when they come to the use of Reason*, and this is enough to prove them innate" (E I.ii.6: 51). Which brings us to the following revision of AUC:

Argument from Universal Consent upon the Use of Reason (AUC-UR)

(4) There are speculative and practical principles to which every human assents *when he comes to the use of reason*.

(5) If every human assents to P *when he comes to the use of reason*, then P is innate.

So, (6) There are innate speculative and practical principles.

The point of turning AUC into AUC-UR, as Stillingfleet does (see Stillingfleet 1662: 369), is to replace (1) with (4), which, being weaker, has a better chance of being true.

Locke's reaction to AUC-UR begins with the claim that the phrase *"when he comes to the use of reason"* could mean one of two things:

(a) when the use of reason makes them known to him, or

(b) at the very time when he is first endowed with reason.

Upon disambiguation, AUC-UR turns into two arguments, AUC-UR (a) and AUC-UR(b):

AUC-UR(a)

(4a) There are speculative and practical principles to which every human assents when the use of reason makes them known to him.

(5a) If every human assents to P when the use of reason makes it known to him, then P is innate.

So, (6) There are innate speculative and practical principles.

AUC-UR(b)

(4b) There are speculative and practical principles to which every human assents at the very time when he is first endowed with reason.

(5b) If every human assents to P at the very time when he is first endowed with reason, then P is innate.

So, (6) There are innate speculative and practical principles.

Let us now consider Locke's reaction to each of these arguments, beginning with the first. Locke claims that mathematical theorems, no less than mathematical maxims, are such that every human assents to them when the use of reason first makes them known to him. It then follows from (5a) that "there will be no difference between the Maxims of the Mathematicians, and the Theorems they deduce from them: All must be equally allow'd innate" (E I. ii.8: 51). Recall now that Locke assumes (unfairly, as it turns out, in respect of dispositionalist nativists) that all of his nativist opponents are committed to the thesis that mathematical theorems are not innate. It follows that one who proposes AUC-UR(a) as his reason to accept nativism is caught in a bind, for he must either abandon one of the premises of this argument or abandon his commitment to the proposition that mathematical theorems are not innate. As we've seen, this problem should trouble the occurrent, but not the dispositionalist, nativist.[12]

---

[12] Locke also supposes that one who wishes to rely on (4a) over (1) presupposes that the propositions to which every human assents *when* the use of reason makes them known to him are *not* universally assented to *before* the use of reason makes them known. Such an opponent must therefore hold that "the Use of Reason is necessary to discover" these propositions (E I.ii.9: 51). As against this, Locke argues that such propositions cannot be innate. If they were, then reason would be needed to discover propositions that are already in the understanding,

In his response to AUC-UR(b), Locke makes two points. The first is that the evidence, such as it is, suggests that (4b) is simply false. For all maxims that are commonly thought innate "are not in the Mind so early as the use of Reason: and therefore the coming to the use of Reason is falsly assigned, as the time of their Discovery." For instance, the principle of noncontradiction is such that "Children . . . and a great part of illiterate People, and Savages, pass many Years, even of their rational Age, without ever thinking on this, and the like general Propositions" (E I.ii.12: 53). So if there are indeed any principles to which every human assents when he is first endowed with reason, they are not the ones commonly thought innate. The reason for this, Locke thinks, is that these principles are general, and, as he will argue in Book II, general ideas are created by the mental operation of abstraction, a faculty that (though innate) is not ready to be used until *after* children come to the use of the reason (E I.ii.14: 54; E II.xi.9: 159; E II.xii.1: 163).

Locke's second point is that (5b) is false as well. Suppose, to begin, that one is considering whether a given (mental) proposition is true. Such a proposition, Locke holds, consists of two ideas (E IV.v.5: 575), knowledge of which consists in the perception of the agreement or disagreement of those ideas (E IV.i.2: 525). Now sometimes, as we've seen, the fact that two ideas agree or disagree is something the mind immediately perceives, without the assistance of intermediate ideas (E IV.ii.1: 530-1). But it can also happen that the agreement or disagreement of the two ideas that make up a proposition is not immediately perceivable (E IV.ii.2: 531-2). In such cases, reason is the faculty whose function it is to discover and order the intermediate ideas that enable us to demonstrate truths that are not self-evident (E IV.xvii.2: 668-9). Now, as Locke assumes, nativists must surely admit that at least some of the ideas (both extreme and intermediate) on which

---

and hence, since one is conscious of whatever is in one's mind, already known. Yet if reason is *needed* to discover these propositions, then they cannot possibly be known before reason is used to discover them. Hence, before the use of reason, these propositions would be both known and not known at the same time. Contradiction. Notice that this argument relies on the assumption that one is conscious of whatever is in one's mind, an assumption that occurrent nativists accept, but that dispositional nativists reject.

reason operates are adventitious. The "province" of reason, as one might say, includes acquired ideas, as much as it is also held to include innate ideas. But, Locke objects, "by what kind of Logick will it appear, that any Notion is Originally by Nature imprinted on the Mind in its first Constitution, because it comes first to be observed, and assented to, when a Faculty of the Mind, which has quite a distinct Province, begins to exert it self?" (E I.ii.14: 54). Put simply: if the province of reason includes acquired ideas, why suppose that ideas discovered when reason first begins to exert itself must be innate?

Locke now claims that, in order to avoid the deficiencies of AUC-UR, "Men have endeavoured to secure an universal Assent to those they call Maxims, by saying, they are generally assented to, as soon as proposed, and the Terms they are propos'd in, understood: Seeing all Men, even Children, as soon as they hear and understand the Terms, assent to these Propositions, they think it is sufficient to prove them innate" (E I.ii.17: 56). Which brings us to a second attempt at revising AUC, one that might reasonably be laid at the door of Whichcote and More:

Argument from Universal Consent upon First Proposal (AUC-FP)

(7) There are speculative and practical principles to which every human assents as soon as they are proposed and the terms in which they are proposed in understood.

(8) If every human assents to P as soon as P is proposed and P's constituent terms understood, then P is innate.

So, (9) There are innate speculative and practical principles.

Locke replies by denying (8). To begin with, Locke notes that any true (particular) proposition of the form "A is not B" (e.g., "Yellow is not red"), where the idea expressed by "A" disagrees with the idea expressed by "B," will, according to (8), turn out to be innate. For such a proposition is universally assented to as soon as it is proposed and its constituent terms are understood. The problem is that there will be "a Million of . . . such Propositions, as many at least, as we have distinct *Ideas*" (E I.ii.18: 57). This again contradicts what Locke (perhaps mistakenly) sees as the nativist presupposition that innate principles are limited to a small number of general maxims.

A further problem arises when this result is combined with the assumption that (mental) propositions are composed of ideas (E IV.v.5: 575) and the further (reasonable) assumption that a whole cannot be innate unless its parts are innate. As Locke remarks, these assumptions entail (T) that "no Proposition can be innate, unless the *Ideas*, about which it is, be innate" (E I.ii.18: 58). Now it is plain that the proposition that yellow is not red is assented to as soon as it is proposed and its constituent terms are understood. Hence, by (8), this proposition is innate. Yet the ideas of yellow and red are acquired through sense perception, and so are not innate. It immediately follows from (T) that the proposition that red is not yellow is not innate. Contradiction.[13]

As should now be clear, none of Locke's criticisms of these three versions of the Argument from Universal Consent commits the straw man fallacy. The first targets Lord Herbert and those nativists who relied on Epicurean and Stoic arguments; the second targets Stillingfleet (and fellow travelers); and the third targets the Cambridge Platonists, particularly Whichcote and More. Thus, it cannot reasonably be argued that Locke was simply scoring rhetorical points at the expense of possible, but nonactual, adversaries.

---

[13] Locke also attacks a presupposition of (7), namely, that many of the propositions that are assented to *as soon as* they are proposed and the terms in which they are proposed in are understood are *not* assented to *before* they are proposed or *before* the terms they are proposed in are understood. If the presupposition were true, then there would be innate propositions to which some do not assent and to which they never have assented. But given that these propositions are self-evident and that one is conscious of whatever is in one's mind, this is impossible: if the propositions are innate, they are in the mind; so we are conscious of them; and if they are also self-evident, then we cannot help but assent to them. Moreover, even if lack of assent were no proof that the relevant propositions are not innate, we would need to explain why it is that people fail to assent to these propositions before they are proposed (even if the ideas out of which the propositions are composed are familiar), but then assent to them after they are proposed. One possible explanation is that "proposing [propositions] print[s] them clearer in the Mind" (E I.ii.21: 59). But if this were true, then it would follow that teaching (via proposal) makes innate propositions better known than they were before. And this contradicts the nativist presupposition that innate propositions are supposed to serve as the foundation of all our other knowledge. Notice again that Locke's attack on (7) depends on an assumption that the occurrent nativist accepts, but that the dispositional nativist rejects: namely, that one is conscious of whatever is in one's mind.

The Second Prong: Arguments Against Nativism

Having criticized AUC and the arguments it inspired, Locke turns
to his own criticisms of nativism. The first of these criticisms
appears in the middle of his discussion of AUC. Having stated that
AUC is unconvincing because there are reasons to think that universal assent is not sufficient for innateness (i.e., that (2) is false),
Locke seemingly attempts to turn AUC (including (2)) against the
nativist, claiming that "this Argument of Universal Consent,
which is made use of, to prove innate Principles, seems to me a
Demonstration that there are none such: Because there are none to
which all Mankind give an Universal Assent" (E I.ii.4: 49). It
therefore appears as if Locke is putting forward the following piece
of anti-nativist reasoning:

(10) There are no principles to which every human assents.

(11) If every human assents to P, then P is innate. (=(2))

So, (12) There are no innate principles.

The problem with this argument is that it commits something akin
to the fallacy of affirming the consequent: if P is not innate, then P
is not universally assented to; P is not universally assented to;
therefore, P is not innate.

But an interpretation that would foist such an unfortunate
argument on Locke would be exceedingly ungenerous. In the very
next paragraph, Locke makes it clear that he simply assumes
that "universal Assent . . . must needs be the necessary concomitant
of all innate Truths" (E I.ii.5: 49), and he later points out that in this
he is in agreement with his nativist opponents (E I.ii.24: 61). The
relevant assumption here is not that universal assent is *sufficient*
for innateness, but rather that universal assent is *necessary*
for innateness. So the innatist presupposition that Locke proposes
to turn against innatism isn't (11), but its converse. Whence
arises the first, and most important, of Locke's anti-nativist
arguments:

Argument from Lack of Universal Consent (ALUC)

(10) There are no principles to which every human assents.

(11c) If P is innate, then every human assents to P.

So, (12) There are no innate principles.

In making the case for (10), Locke's strategy is to argue, first, that the principle of noncontradiction (PNC) and the principle of equality (PE) are not universally assented to, and hence, since there are no speculative principles that have a better chance of gaining universal assent than these two self-evident maxims, there are no speculative principles to which all humans assent.[14] Second, Locke claims that it is even more obvious that no practical principle is the object of universal assent: as he puts it, "it is much more visible concerning practical Principles, that they come short of an universal Reception" (E I.iii.1: 65).

The text of the *Essay* at first suggests the following reconstruction of Locke's argument for (11c). Innate principles, by definition, are in each human mind. Now if a principle is in human mind M, then it must be perceived by M; "imprinting, if it signify anything, being nothing else, but the making certain Truths to be perceived" (E I.ii.5: 49). Moreover, all innate principles are self-evident: for if there were "natural Characters ingraven on the Mind..., they must needs be visible by themselves, and by their own light be certain and known to every Body" (E I.iii.1: 66). But if a principle is both perceived and self-evident, then it is "irresistible" (E IV.ii.1: 531), and hence compels assent. It follows that innate principles must be universally assented to.

However, Locke came to recognize that a principle P can be in mind M at time T without actually being perceived by M at T. This is emphasized in a section that was added to the second edition of the *Essay*. There Locke claims that "whatever Idea is in the mind, is either an actual perception, or else having been an actual perception, is so in the mind, that by the memory it can be made an actual perception again" (E I.iv.20: 96–8). It follows from this, not (A) that if P is in M at T, then M actually perceives P at T, but rather (B) that if P is in M at T, then *either* M actually perceives P at T *or* M perceived P at some time before T.

---

[14] The argument for the claim that PNC is not the object of universal assent relies on the premise that some humans do not so much as perceive or understand PNC. As Locke puts it: "'tis evident, that all *Children* and *Ideots*, have not the least Apprehension or Thought of [PNC]" (E I.ii.5: 49). This premise is then coupled with the assumption that assent to P at time T requires perception of P at T, so that "want of [apprehension] is enough to destroy...Assent" (E I.ii.5: 49).

If (A) is replaced by (B), then Locke must replace his argument for (11c) with the following argument for (11d):

(11d) If P is innate, then every human has at some time or other assented to P.

Innate principles, by definition, are in each human mind. Now if P is in M at T, then either P is perceived by M at T or P was perceived by M at some time before T. But all innate principles are self-evident and so assent-compelling when perceived. Thus, if P is innate, then either M assents to P at T or M assented to P at some time before T. QED.

But if (11c) is replaced by (11d), then (10) must be replaced by (10d) to preserve the validity of Locke's argument from lack of universal consent:

Argument from Lack of Universal Consent* (ALUC*)

(10d) There are no principles to which every human has at some time or other assented.

(11d) If P is innate, then every human has at some time or other assented to P.

So, (12) There are no innate principles.[15]

Before moving on, Locke considers an objection to (11d). It might be thought that for a principle to be innate is for the mind to possess the capacity to perceive and assent to it (E I.ii.5: 50). If this were

[15] There are clear textual indications that, even as early as the first edition, Locke intended to rely on (B), rather than (A), in arguing for (11d), rather than for (11c). As Locke puts it: "No Proposition can be said to be in the Mind, which it *never yet* knew, which it was *never yet* conscious of" (emphasis added – E I.ii.5: 50); or again, "to be in the Mind, and, *never* to be perceived, is all one, as to say, any thing is, and is not, in the Mind or Understanding" (emphasis added – E I.ii.5: 50–1). However, there are also clear textual indications that Locke refused to abandon (A), even as he was pushing it aside in favor of (B) in ALUC*. For (A) operates not merely in ALUC, but also in some of the arguments Locke uses to undermine AUC-UR(a) and AUC-FP (see notes 12 and 13). Given the evidence, the most reasonable hypothesis seems to be that Locke did not really think it important to distinguish between (A) and (B) until the second edition (which is when he chose to emphasize the distinction in E I.iv.20), at which time he simply forgot that (A) was implicated in some of the arguments he was relying on to undermine various versions of the nativist Argument from Universal Consent. Had he realized that (A) was so implicated, he would have either removed the texts in which (A) is relied on or altered them in such a way as to replace (A) with (B) without compromising soundness.

true, then (11d) would be false, for it could happen that, though M is always capable of perceiving and assenting to P, there is no time at which M actually assents to P. Locke's reply to this objection is this. If what it is for a principle to be innate is for every human mind to be capable of assenting to it, then, since every truth is such that every human mind is capable of assenting to it, it follows that every truth is innate. This result then contradicts the nativist presupposition that some truths are not innate.[16]

In addition to ALUC*, Locke provides three independent reasons for thinking that *practical* principles in particular are not innate. The first is based on an already-familiar assumption, namely, that all innate principles are self-evident:

Argument from Lack of Self-Evidence (ALSE)

(13) All innate principles are self-evident.

(14) No practical principles are self-evident.

So, (15) No practical principles are innate.

Locke does not think that this kind of argument will work to show that speculative maxims are not innate. This is because he thinks that speculative maxims, such as PNC and PE, are self-evident. But practical principles are a different kettle of fish, for, as Locke sees it, *"there cannot any one moral Rule be propos'd, whereof a Man may not justly demand a Reason"* (E I.iii.4: 68). Since it would not be appropriate or "just" to demand a reason for a self-evident principle, moral rules cannot be self-evident.[17] To bolster his case that every practical principle "need[s] proof to ascertain its Truth," Locke cites as his primary example the Golden Rule, *"That one should do as he would be done unto,"* which is commonly thought innate, but for which it would not be absurd to request justification (E I.iii.4: 68).

[16] Locke offers a "farther argument" against the innateness of speculative maxims. Innate principles, he writes, *"should appear fairest and clearest"* and "must needs exert themselves with most Force and Vigour" in those "least corrupted by Custom, or borrowed Opinions." But those who are least corrupted in this way are *"Children, Ideots, Savages,* and *illiterate* People." Yet it is to these individuals that speculative maxims are "least known." Consequently, no speculative maxims are innate (E I.ii.27: 63).

[17] Locke also argues, in defense of (14), that, though no self-evident proposition can be the object of widespread disagreement, there is a "great variety of Opinions, concerning Moral Rules, which are to be found amongst Men" (E I.iii.6: 68–9). It follows directly that no practical propositions are self-evident.

The second reason for thinking that practical principles are not innate concerns the peace of mind with which moral rules are routinely transgressed:

Argument from Confident Transgression (ACT)

(16) Human beings would not transgress innate practical principles with confidence and serenity.

(17) Every practical principle is such that there are human beings who transgress it with confidence and serenity.

So, (18) No practical principles are innate.

In defense of (17), Locke adduces evidence to suggest that many human beings have committed the worst kinds of atrocities (murder, rape, infanticide, cannibalism, etc.) "without scruple" (E I.iii.9: 71). In defense of (16), Locke argues that it is plain that innate moral rules would be laws and that every law has a lawgiver who rewards those who follow the law and punishes those who do not (E I.iii.12: 74; E I. iv.8: 87). Hence, since we are conscious of anything that is innate, we would all know, if moral rules were innate, that we will be punished for transgressing them (presumably by God in the afterlife, since it is clear that many do not suffer in this life for their moral transgressions). But the knowledge that one will be punished for transgressing a rule is sufficient to produce fear, and hence a lack of confidence and serenity when one actually transgresses.

Third, Locke argues that, though it should be easy to tell the difference between innate and adventitious propositions, "no body, that [he knows], has ventured yet to give a Catalogue of them" (E I.iii.14: 76):

Argument from Lack of a Catalogue (ALC)

(19) If there are any innate principles, then they are easily distinguished from non-innate propositions (i.e., propositions that are either deduced from innate principles or learned).

(20) If innate principles are easily distinguished from propositions that are not innate, then it should be easy for any human being to "know what, and how many, [innate principles] there were" (I.iii.14).

(21) It is not easy for human beings to know what, and how many, innate practical principles there are.

So, (22) No practical principles are innate.

Locke's guiding thought here is that a principle's innateness ought to be transparent to any mind on which it is imprinted: P's being innate is sufficient for my being conscious of the fact that P is innate.[18]

Locke completes his anti-nativist attack with a general argument that is intended to show that none of the constituents of any principle commonly thought innate is innate, and hence that no principle commonly thought innate is innate:

Argument from Lack of Innate Ideas (ALII)

(23) Principles are mental propositions that consist of the joining or separating of ideas.

(24) If a complex whole is innate, then its parts must also be innate.

(25) None of the ideas that compose the principles commonly thought innate is innate.

So, (26) None of the principles commonly thought innate is innate.

Taking (23) and (24) on board, Locke spends most of I.iv defending (25). Locke focuses on seven ideas in particular: the idea of impossibility (which is relevant to PNC), the idea of identity (which is relevant to PE), the idea of a whole and the idea of a part (which are relevant to the speculative maxim that the whole is bigger than a part – see E I.iii.1: 66), the idea of worship and the idea of God (which are relevant to Lord Herbert's practical maxim that God ought to be worshipped – E I.iii.15: 77), and the idea of substance (substratum).[19]

Here, in brief, are his reasons for thinking that these ideas are not innate:

Impossibility and Worship (E I.iv.3: 85–6; E I.iv.7: 87): Children lack these ideas. But an idea cannot be innate unless it is present to all

---

[18] In the way of an objection to (21), it was brought to Locke's attention that Lord Herbert had proposed a complete list of innate practical principles, as well as a list of six marks by means of which to distinguish them from non-innate practical propositions, in his *De Veritate*. Locke argues that none of the propositions that Lord Herbert considers innate satisfies all six marks of innateness (E I.iii.15–9). It follows that either (i) none of the practical propositions that Herbert thinks innate is innate or (ii) the list of marks Herbert proposes as his means of distinguishing between innate and non-innate propositions is inadequate.

[19] Locke does not mention any maxim that is commonly thought innate and that contains the idea of substance. But we can speculate. All of Locke's nativist opponents would have thought it an innate maxim that all accidents must inhere in a substance.

human minds. So the ideas of impossibility and worship are not innate. Moreover, only very few adults have a clear and distinct idea of worship. But an idea cannot be innate unless it is clear (see note 16). So the idea of worship is not innate.

Identity (E I.iv.4: 86): Suppose that X is a human composed of soul S and body B at time T1, while Y is a human composed of soul S and body B* at time T2 (where T1 is not identical to T2 and B* is not identical to B). It is difficult to say whether X is the same human as Y, and hence the idea of identity is not clear. But an idea cannot be innate unless it is clear (see above). So the idea of identity is not innate.

Whole and Part (E I.iv.6: 87): The idea of a whole and the idea of a part are relative to the ideas of extension and number. But if X is an idea that is relative to the idea of Y, and person P possesses X, then P also possesses Y. Hence, if X is an idea that is relative to the idea of Y, and X is innate, then Y is innate. It follows that if the idea of a whole and the idea of a part are innate, then the idea of extension and the idea of number must be innate as well. But the idea of extension and the idea of number are acquired by means of the senses, and hence are not innate. So the idea of a whole and the idea of a part are not innate.

God (E I.iv.8: 87–8; E I.iv.14–15: 92–3): Ancient philosophers report the existence of numerous godless men, and current anthropological evidence testifies to the existence of whole nations among whose members there is to be found no idea of God. Moreover, even among "civilized" nations, there are many whose idea of God is not clear. Finally, there are contrary and inadequate conceptions of God in the minds of different human beings. But an idea cannot be innate unless it is present to all minds, clear, adequate, and uniform (see above). So the idea of God is not innate.

Substance (E I.iv.18: 95): The idea of substance signifies only "an uncertain supposition of we know not what . . . , something whereof we have no particular distinct positive *Idea*," and hence is one of the most obscure and confused of ideas (E I.iv.18: 95). But an idea cannot be innate unless it is clear (see above). So the idea of substance is not innate.[20]

---

[20] From the result that the idea of God is not innate, Locke constructs a further argument against the claim that there are innate practical propositions. As he argues (see E I.iii.12: 74), one cannot have the concept of moral obligation without

3. LOCKE'S ANTI-NATIVIST ARGUMENTS EVALUATED

The First Prong: Arguments for Nativism Undermined

Locke's criticisms of AUC, AUC-UR, and AUC-FP are sufficient to establish that these arguments are unsound. Commentators have mostly complained, not that Locke's criticisms are off the mark, but that they are directed at the kind of argument for nativism that none of his contemporaries accepted. As we've seen, this is an uncharitable way to read the *Essay*. For there is plenty of evidence to suggest that Locke's criticisms were directed at the views of specific, albeit unnamed, writers with whose works Locke was familiar.

The Second Prong: Arguments against Nativism

ARGUMENT FROM LACK OF UNIVERSAL CONSENT. According to ALUC*, there are no principles to which all humans have at some time or other assented (10d). But if P is innate, then all humans have at some time or other assented to P (11d). Therefore, there are no innate principles.

Locke's reason for accepting (11d) is that whatever is in the mind must be either occurrently perceived or stored in memory. But why should we accept this? If memory is some sort of storehouse or repository of ideas, why couldn't there be another mental faculty whose function it is to store ideas and then, like memory, bring them to consciousness, but, unlike memory, without a consciousness of their having been in the mind before? If there were such a faculty, then ideas could be in the mind without being occurrently perceived or stored in memory.

In a later section on memory, Locke points out that the storehouse model of memory is misleading, for it is only in

---

having the concept of a law, and one cannot have the concept of a law without having the concept of a lawgiver (i.e., God). So, if the idea of God is not innate, then the idea of obligation is not innate. But every practical proposition is of the form, "One ought (not) to do X," and hence the idea of obligation is a component of every practical proposition. Given that no proposition can be innate unless its component ideas are also innate, it follows that no practical propositions are innate.

a figurative sense that an idea that is in one's memory is in one's mind:

> But our *Ideas* being nothing, but actual Perceptions in the Mind, which cease to be any thing, when there is no perception of them, this *laying up* of our *Ideas* in the Repository of the Memory, signifies no more but this, that the Mind has a Power, in many cases, to revive Perceptions, which it has once had, with this additional Perception annexed to them, that it has had them before. And in this Sense it is, that our *Ideas* are said to be in our Memories, when indeed, they are actually no where, but only there is an ability in the Mind, when it will, to revive them again; and as it were paint them anew on it self. (E II.x.2: 150)

Locke claims that the storehouse metaphor is just that: a metaphor. Importantly, we shouldn't think of memory as (or as anything like) a place where ideas are kept when they are not actually perceived: ideas that are not actually perceived are, as he says, "no where." Memory is nothing but a power to revive ideas with the perception of having perceived them before. Of course, the notion of "reviving" is metaphorical too, and also potentially misleading. For one natural way of thinking of "reviving" is as bringing something from a dormant state to a state of wakefulness. This suggests the possibility of an idea's being in the mind, but only in a dormant (i.e., unconscious) state. Locke is careful to warn his readers not to interpret "reviving" in this way. Ideas are "revived" only in the sense of being, as it were, repainted (yet another metaphor). If one thinks (as Locke does) of the mind as a canvas or slate, an idea that is "lodg'd in the memory" is an idea that used to be on the canvas but no longer appears on the canvas. Its being revived, then, is no more than its reappearing on the canvas.

There is clearly some tension in the metaphorical picture Locke paints here. If a forgotten idea (i.e., an idea that was once perceived but is no longer perceived) is "no where" (in metaphorical terms, does not appear on the canvas of the mind), then it stretches the metaphor of containment to the point of absurdity to say that forgotten ideas are *in* the mind. And what should we say of ideas that were once perceived but are never perceived again? According to Locke, the mind has the power to revive these ideas, to repaint them anew on the canvas of the mind. But what if the mind never exercises this power? Should we say, as Locke does, that forgotten ideas that are never "repainted" are still *in* the mind? And if we say this, then why can't we say, in defense of dispositional nativism, that ideas that are never brought to consciousness but that we have the ability to "paint" on the canvas of our minds without any accompanying perception of having had these ideas before are also *in* the mind? The problem here is that Locke's own account of the metaphysics of memory gives solace to the dispositional nativist.[21]

But the debate does not end here. As Locke argues, even if it were possible for innate principles to be in the mind without being present to the mind, it would be pointless for God to stamp merely latent principles in our minds. For as long as they are latent (possibly an entire lifetime), these principles do not help those who possess them attain knowledge of their circumstances or of their duties. As Locke puts the point: "If Men can be ignorant or doubtful of what is innate, innate Principles are insisted on, and urged to no purpose; Truth and Certainty (the things pretended) are not at all secured by them: But Men are in the same uncertain, floating estate with, as without them" (E I.iii.13: 75). But surely even nativists would agree that the point of God's having endowed us with innate principles is that they may serve to guide our actions and thoughts. Thus, assuming that God never acts in a pointless way, it follows either that all innate principles are occurrent (in which case dispositional nativism must give way to occurrent nativism, with its all-too-numerous theoretical drawbacks) or that God did not engrave them on our minds (in which case Parker's remark that they may, for all we know, be untrustworthy – "as Weeds are the first and natural Issues of the best Soyles" – is singularly a propos). The burden placed on the nativist is significant and underappreciated.[22]

---

[21] This problem also affects Locke's "farther argument" against the innateness of speculative principles, a piece of reasoning that relies on the claim that innate principles "should appear fairest and clearest" and "must exert themselves with most Force and Vigour" in uncorrupted minds (see note 16). In reply, the dispositional nativist might well argue that, if a principle can be in the mind without being brought to consciousness (a possibility for which Locke's account of memory makes room), then there is no reason to think that innate principles should "exert themselves," whether in corrupted or uncorrupted minds.

[22] I imagine a similar outcome to the debate over the soundness of the Argument from Confident Transgression. According to ACT, although human beings would

ARGUMENT FROM LACK OF SELF-EVIDENCE.   According to ALSE, whereas all innate principles are self-evident, no practical principles are self-evident, and hence no practical principles are innate. It would be difficult for any of Locke's immediate nativist predecessors to deny the assumption that innate principles are self-evident, since they held that innate principles are to serve as the foundations of the rest of our knowledge. But the most glaring problem with this argument lies with the assumption that no practical principles are self-evident, for this is an assumption that Locke himself rejects!

Here is where Locke stumbles. If no practical principles are self-evident, then morals cannot be a demonstrative science. The reason for this is that, for Locke, every principle of a demonstrative science is either a self-evident axiom or derived from self-evident axioms by self-evidently valid steps. Thus, if morals is a demonstrative science, there must be at least some self-evident moral axioms, that is, self-evident practical principles. The problem here is that Locke holds that a demonstrative science of morals is possible (see E III. xi.16: 516; E IV.iii.18: 549; E IV.xii.8: 643). Thus, Locke must hold that there are self-evident practical principles from which all other practical principles are validly derived.[23]

---

not transgress innate practical principles with confidence and serenity (16), every practical principle is such that there are human beings who transgress it confidently and serenely (17). It follows that no practical principles are innate. In defense of (16), Locke assumes that we are conscious of anything that is innate (see above). Although the occurrent nativist accepts this assumption, the dispositional nativist rejects it on the grounds that at least some innate principles are latent, and hence not present to the mind. It is the latency of these principles that explains why so many transgress them so confidently. It is at this stage that I imagine Locke falling back on his claim that it would be pointless for God to stamp merely latent principles in our minds.

[23] Consider, for example, Locke's derivation of the practical principle that where there is no property, there is no injustice (E IV.iii.18: 549). Locke affirms, first, (a) that to have property is to have a right to something, and second, (b) that injustice is the invasion or violation of a right to something. It follows from these two propositions that injustice is the invasion or violation of property, and hence that where there is no property there is no injustice. But what is the epistemic status of the two principles, (a) and (b)? It seems that they are self-evident, since Locke tells us that the idea of property is the idea of a right to something, and that the idea of injustice is the idea of the invasion or violation of a right. And aren't these self-evident principles themselves practical?

Of course, Locke could abandon the claim that a demonstrative science of morals is possible. If he did so, however, he would also need to give up his conception of God's goodness. As Locke sees it, it would be unkind in the extreme for God to create humans without giving them the wherewithal to determine what they need to do and to avoid doing in order to act rightly and merit eternal happiness in the afterlife. If morals were a demonstrative science, then humans could discover their duties (and so the way to eternal bliss) by exercising their (native) reason and their (native) ability to perceive the agreement and disagreement of ideas. But if morals is not a demonstrative science, then nothing guarantees that humans who exercise their native faculties properly will discover the way to happiness. Surely God wouldn't create human beings knowing that they would suffer through no fault of their own.

ARGUMENT FROM LACK OF A CATALOGUE. According to ALC, it should be easy to distinguish innate from non-innate propositions, in which case it should be easy to know what, and how many, innate principles there are. But, in fact, it turns out to be rather difficult to say what, and how many, innate practical principles there are. Consequently, no practical principles are innate.

Here, Locke assumes that a proposition's innateness ought to be transparent to any mind on which it is imprinted: P's being innate is sufficient for one's being conscious of the fact that P is innate. But why should this be? In the first place, the dispositional nativist will say that, since the fact that a proposition is innate isn't even sufficient for its being conscious, surely it can't also be that a proposition's innateness is sufficient for one's being conscious of its very innateness! But the occurrent nativist can object as well. For even if a proposition's being innate *is* sufficient for its being conscious, consciousness of a proposition need not entail consciousness of its origin. The entailment would hold if the origin of a proposition were somehow part of its content (so that mere awareness of the proposition would allow us to say where it came from). But, of course, a proposition's origin is rather conspicuously *not* part of its content. So why think that consciousness of an innate proposition automatically translates into consciousness of its origin? On balance, then, this argument is less than persuasive.

ARGUMENT FROM LACK OF INNATE IDEAS.   According to ALII, if the
ideas that compose principles are not innate, then the principles
themselves cannot be innate. But none of the ideas that compose
the principles commonly thought innate is innate. Hence, none of
the principles commonly thought innate is innate.

This argument, as Locke recognizes, is only as good as Locke's
case for thinking that none of the ideas commonly thought innate is
innate. Locke claims that the ideas of impossibility, worship, and
God are not present to all humans, and that the ideas of impossibility, worship, God, identity, and substance are unclear. Since
innate ideas must be clear and present to all humans, it follows that
these ideas are not innate.

As we've seen, the dispositional nativist denies that innate ideas
must be present to the mind. However, it is more difficult for the
dispositional nativist to deny that innate ideas must be clear. Were
God to create an obscure principle, what possible reason could He
have for stamping it on the minds of humans? If an innate principle's function is to guide a person's thoughts and actions, doesn't its
being composed of obscure ideas get in the way of its performing
this function well? And why would God endow us with principles
that perform their function poorly, if at all?

It would seem that it would best serve the dispositional nativist
to insist that the ideas Locke finds unclear are really clear. Locke
doesn't provide much in the way of argument for the claim that the
ideas of impossibility, worship, and God are not clear. But he does
argue that the idea of identity is not clear because there are situations in which it is difficult to say whether X is the same human as
Y, and he argues that the idea of substance is unclear because it
signifies only an "uncertain supposition of we know not what."

In reply, the nativist might point out that the argument that the
idea of identity is obscure is one that Locke himself rejects. Locke
claims that, where X is a human composed of soul S and body B at
time T1, and Y is a human composed of soul S and body B* at time
T2 (where B is not the same body as B*), it is difficult to say whether
X is the same human as Y. But this contradicts Locke's claim, in the
chapter "Of Identity and Diversity," that it is actually quite clear
that sameness of soul is not sufficient for sameness of human being.
Locke considers the question whether Heliogabalus, by supposition
a human being composed of a soul S and a human-shaped body B, is

the same man as a hog composed of the same soul S and a hog-shaped body B*. Locke's answer to this question is emphatically in the negative: "Yet I think no body, could he be sure that the Soul of Heliogabalus were in one of his Hogs, would yet say that Hog were a Man or Heliogabalus" (E II.xxvii.6: 332). Locke's point here generalizes: "[It is] a very strange use of the Word Man, applied to an Idea, out of which Body and Shape is excluded" (E II.xxvii.6: 332). Thus, in general, if X's body is of characteristically human shape whereas Y's body is not, then it follows immediately that X and Y are clearly not the same man.[24]

As for the idea of substance, the nativist might object that uncertainty as to the nature of what an idea represents does not entail that the idea itself must be obscure. As Frege might put it, the sense of a term might be clear, even as one is uncertain as to the nature of the term's referent. For example, the sense of "The Morning Star" might be clear, even to one who knows little or nothing about Venus itself.[25]

4. CONCLUSION

How in the end should we evaluate Locke's anti-nativist polemic? As I have argued, Locke's criticisms of the various versions of the nativist Argument from Universal Consent hit the mark, thereby shaking one of the reasons most commonly given in favor of nativism by Locke's opponents. By contrast, Locke's direct criticisms of nativism itself are a mixed bag. On the one hand, some arguments (e.g., the Argument from Lack of Universal Consent) rank as powerful indictments of occurrent nativism. On the other, some of the arguments (e.g., the Argument from Lack of Self-Evidence) are

---

[24] Since E II.xxvii was added to the second edition of the *Essay*, it is possible that Locke simply forgot to change (or even delete) his first edition argument in E I.iv.4 for the claim that the idea of identity is obscure.

[25] Concerning the ideas of whole and part, Locke's argument is that they are relative to the ideas of extension and number, which are themselves acquired through the senses. But, Locke claims, if X is an idea that is relative to the idea of Y, and X is innate, then Y is innate. Since the ideas of extension and number are not innate, it follows that the ideas of a whole and of a part are not innate. The real sticking point here is Locke's insistence that the ideas of extension and number are adventitious. This is something that Descartes, for one, denied. Adjudicating this dispute is beyond the scope of this essay.

inconsistent with other positions Locke holds, while others are less than persuasive (e.g., the Argument from Lack of a Catalogue). Moreover, none of the arguments can reasonably be read as a knockdown argument against dispositional nativism. Nevertheless, Locke's additional concern about the seeming pointlessness of God's providing humans with latent principles (especially considering the fact that God might have made these principles occurrent instead) successfully shifts the burden of proof onto the shoulders of dispositional nativists.

It might be thought that, after attending to arguments for and against nativism in Book I, Locke's attention shifts to other matters in Books II–IV of the *Essay*. This is not entirely accurate. In particular, it is possible to read much of the *Essay* as an extended answer to the nativist challenge propounded by Descartes and the Cambridge Platonists. More, for one, had argued that ideas of relations could not be "Impresses of any material Object from without [the mind]," and hence must be part of the "natural furniture of the humane Understanding." (And Descartes and Cudworth had argued, on similar grounds, that ideas of cogitative beings and their modes, and general ideas, must be innate – see note 10.) More had also argued that principles on which the mind can "straightaway pronounce," including such mathematical theorems as that the angles of a triangle are equal to two right ones, cannot be adventitious. In Book II, when Locke moves on to give his own empiricist account of how the human mind comes by ideas of relation (E II. xxv–xxviii), ideas of cogitative beings (E II.xxiii.15), ideas of cogitative modes (E II.xix–xx), and general ideas (E II.xii), we should read him as addressing, forcefully and directly, the nativist argument that these ideas cannot be either adventitious or constructed. And in Book IV, when Locke provides an empiricist account of demonstrative knowledge (E IV.ii), we should read him as countering the Morean argument that mathematical theorems must be innate. Overall, the polemic against nativism articulated in Book I does not merely introduce, but also frames, the main epistemological doctrines defended in the rest of the *Essay*. It is in this sense that a proper understanding of Locke's polemic serves to deepen one's understanding of the book as a whole.

3   The Taxonomy of Ideas in Locke's *Essay*

According to Locke's theory, ideas are the building materials of human understanding. They compose and combine in several ways. There are two main types of ideas, simple and complex, and there are several types of complex ideas differentiated by modes of construction. Moreover, although ideas direct the mind to objects of thought, ideas do not attain truth or falsity. Propositions, not ideas, are strictly true or false, according to the *Essay*; but propositions are composed of ideas and connective mental acts. The *Essay* is ultimately concerned with propositions, because they are what we know, believe, or judge to be true. The treatise aims to explicate the "Original, Certainty, and Extent of humane Knowledge; together with the Grounds and Degrees of Belief, Opinion, and Assent" (E I.i.2: 43). These topics are reached in Book IV after a thorough inquiry into the origin of the various types of ideas in Book II and an examination of names in Book III. The antecedent material on ideas is theoretical ground for the subsequent linguistic and epistemic theories. Names are typed and characterized in accord with the sorts of ideas that determine their signification. Propositions, too, are divided into types that have distinctive epistemic properties in virtue of the sorts of ideas that enter into their composition. The main purpose of this essay is to bring out the systematic theoretical uses to which Locke puts the taxonomic scheme, as well as to trace some strains they put on the classification.

A distinction between "simple apprehensions," which are not yet truth evaluable, and "complex apprehensions," which are, has deep roots in Aristotelian-Scholastic logic. A compositional view of propositions is part of this tradition. Late Scholastic logic texts commonly taught that mental, spoken, and written propositions are composite; basic mental propositions are composed of subject and predicate terms, the copula and mental acts that determine quality, quantity, modality, and so forth.[1] This was attractive, because it assigns propositions the structure required for evaluating syllogisms. Although Locke is impatient with syllogistic, he subscribes to a rudimentary compositional theory of mental and verbal propositions. Mental propositions (to stick with them) are formed out of ideas joined, in the affirmative case, or separated, in the negative, by one of several mental acts, and their truth conditions are determined by these constituents (E IV.v: 574–9; E IV.i.3: 525).

As for ideas, the thesis that ideas can be combined to form further ideas (as opposed to propositions) is abroad in early modern thought before Locke. Descartes recognizes our ability to make ideas by putting other ideas together, such as the idea of a golden mountain; he maintains that such ideas, unlike their simple components, typically fail to represent anything with a nature or essence.[2] According to the logic of Arnauld and Nicole, there are three main types of ideas: ideas of substances, modes, and modified things. This last sort consists of an idea of the first sort joined to an idea of the second sort, such as the idea of round body; again, the indeterminate idea of substance joined with the idea of a determinate mode (e.g., prudence) constitutes the idea of all things with that mode, all prudent men.[3] Gassendi invokes composition and other constructive techniques specifically for the purpose of expositing his empiricist view of the origin of ideas, or images; according to this account, all our ideas either come through the senses, as ideas of sun and man, or are formed from such ideas by operations of unification, enlargement, diminution, transference, adaptation,

---

[1] See Ashworth 1981; Ashworth 1974: 49–52. Compositional theories of the proposition are urged in Arnauld and Nicole 1996; Gassendi 1981; and Hobbes 1981. Descartes puts less importance on the distinction between ideas and bearers of truth; see, e.g., "Second Set of Replies" (Descartes 1984: II: 114) and letters to Mersenne (Descartes 1984: III: 186, 187); cp. *Meditation* III (Descartes 1984: II: 30).

[2] "First Set of Replies" (Descartes 1984: II: 83–4); *Principles of Philosophy* I: 47–8 (Descartes 1984: I: 208–9).

[3] Arnauld and Nicole 1996: 30–2, 40–4, 44–8. This classification of ideas is paired with a semantic theory on which names that express ideas of modified things – e.g., "round," "prudent" – directly (and distinctly) signify the things and indirectly (and confusedly) signify the mode.

analogy, and comparison.[4] Broadly speaking, Locke's theory about the structural differences among types of ideas and the composition of propositions implements strategies of a sort deployed by his predecessors to deal with diverse issues in the philosophy of human cognition. Nevertheless, Locke's account of the ways in which complex ideas are formed from simple ideas is the source of many of the most distinctive features of his account of human understanding.

Before continuing with the taxonomy of ideas, I want to bring out some general points. Ideas are fundamental in Locke's theory, because they account for the content of all conscious states – they account for what consciousness is *of*. There are two aspects of the content of consciousness, for Locke, and ideas address both. In the first place, ideas are present to awareness; when a person has in mind an idea, the person is aware of the idea (although perhaps not as such). So ideas constitute the "accessible content" of consciousness inasmuch as a person has awareness *of* ideas.[5] In addition, many (perhaps not all) ideas have intentional content, that is, they are "of" something.[6] Locke's theory is, roughly, that we think of actual and possible things by virtue of having ideas that represent those things. When one sees, remembers, or contemplates a cat, one has in mind an idea of a cat. The perceiver or thinker is aware of the idea and, for reasons we will consider more carefully, thereby sees or thinks of a cat. Inasmuch as ideas are present to awareness, they are designed to explain cognition internal to consciousness – the phenomenal character of sensory states and the appearances of things, ways of conceiving things and the evidential relations that underwrite knowledge, reasoning, and probable judgment, according to Locke. Inasmuch as a mind takes its ideas to represent things that exist, and inasmuch as they do, in fact, represent such things, ideas link internally accessible content with reality.

Often Locke's attention is focused on ideas as contents of immediate awareness. He maintains that ideas cease to exist when the mind ceases to be aware of them.[7] Nevertheless, a person "has"

---

[4] Gassendi 1981: 84–6.
[5] Locke sometimes says we "perceive" or "immediately perceive" ideas, e.g., E II. viii.8: 134.
[6] Sensory ideas of pleasure, pain, and the like are the likely exception.
[7] E II.x.2: 150.

ideas that are not, at the moment, in view, provided the person has been aware of them and is able to bring them back to awareness when needed. One is said to "have" an idea in either of two ways: occurrently or dispositionally.[8] On different occasions of thinking of the sun, as such, a person is aware of different tokens of the same idea-type, as we say; that is, two token ideas *of* exactly the same thing.

It is a matter of some theoretical importance, however, to specify what it is in virtue of which an idea represents a thing. We have said that there are two aspects of an idea: it is a content of awareness and it has intentionality – it is *of* something. Is an idea of a thing in virtue of the idea's presenting a content of awareness to which the things it represents conform or, alternatively, in virtue of the idea's being caused by, corresponding to, and being referred to things in the world that it represents? The former is a descriptive theory of representation, whereas the latter is a referential theory. For Locke, the answer varies with the sort of idea in question. In the case of general ideas, he takes the former, internalist approach apparently because it leaves no room for serious error about one's occurrent ideas, or what one is thinking of, classifying by, and so on.[9] Yet simple ideas of sensation represent in virtue of their causal connections, rather than in virtue of conformity or resemblance. For our purposes, it is enough to be aware that these two views are abroad in the *Essay*.

The taxonomy of ideas is on display in the analytical table of contents prepared by Locke.[10] It is reflected in the titles of many chapters and prominent in the topical outlines. Here is a sketch of the main divisions:[11]

---

[8] See E I.iv.20: 96–8; II.x.2: 150; IV.i.8: 527–8.

[9] See E II.xi.9: 159; on the certainty of ideas, see E II.xxix.5: 364; IV.ii.1: 531; cp. E II. xi.2: 156. On consequences for Locke's account of the signification of names of substance kinds, see Bolton 1998.

[10] E: 17–41.

[11] Fourth edition changes in II.xii.1 lead some scholars to think that in earlier editions, ideas of relations are a species of complex ideas, but that they are subsequently removed from that genus because they cannot be formed by composition. The significance of this change in II.xii.1 is debatable, because other pertinent passages remain unchanged from earlier editions. See, e.g., E II.xii.3: 164; II.xxix.1: 363; II.xi.4, 6: 157, 158. On this debate, see Gibson 1917; Aaron 1937; Carter 1963; Rabb 1974; Stewart 1979, 1980.

Simple ideas:
    Ideas of sensation
    Ideas of reflection
Complex ideas:
    Composite ideas of unitary things:[12]
        Ideas of modes:
            Ideas of simple modes
            Ideas of mixed modes
        Ideas of substances
    Ideas of relations

In addition, each of these classes is divided into ideas of particular things and ideas of kinds of things. Particular ideas are prior to general ones, for Locke, because experience delivers nothing but ideas of particulars. General ideas are made from these materials by a mental process, abstraction. The text is less than explicit about several aspects of this operation and the abstract ideas it yields. It "makes nothing new," yet begins with particular ideas and ends with a sortal one.[13] The particular/general idea distinction raises a number of issues not directly relevant to aspects of the taxonomy in focus in this essay.[14] Still, abstraction is a mental process performed on materials provided by experience. It will sometimes be necessary to take note of it, but little more is said about it here.

THE ORIGIN OF IDEAS

The taxonomy is used in Book II to elaborate the anti-innatist theory that all ideas are derived from experience. Experience is either sensory or reflective: "External Objects furnish the Mind with the Ideas of sensible qualities," and "the Mind furnishes the Understanding with Ideas of its own Operations." Referring to ideas acquired from these sources, Locke says: "These, when we have taken a full survey of them, and their several Modes, Combinations, and Relations, we shall find to contain all our whole stock of *Ideas*; and that we have nothing in our Minds, which did not come in, one of these two ways" (E II.i.5: 106). This theory is advocated

---

[12] Locke tends to speak of the operation, "combining" or "composition"; I use "composite" to mean the result of this operation. On the unitary character of ideas of modes and substances, as opposed to relations, see E II.xii.1, 6; II.xxv.1.

[13] E I.ii.15: 55; II.xi.9: 159; III.iii.6–9, 11: 410–12, 414; IV.vii.9: 596.

[14] The best available discussion is Ayers 1991: I: 259–63.

throughout Book II, and the taxonomy structures the argument. The book proceeds first to canvas the various sorts of ideas we receive in experience, then to review the various sorts of complex ideas we have, arguing that each can be formed from ideas received in experience. In effect, the argument employs the following criterion for distinguishing between simple and complex ideas: (a) simple ideas are those ideas a human mind can have only by encountering them in or abstracting them from experience; complex ideas are those a human mind can have without receiving them in or abstracting them from experience *because* it can form them from simple ideas.[15] The anti-innatist thesis is that this dichotomy strictly exhausts the class of human ideas.

The early chapters of Book II focus on the origin of simple ideas. To have the idea of blue, for example, one must be able to think of blue when appropriate. The theory is that a person acquires this ability by encountering external objects that cause her to have sensations of blue – presentations of phenomenal-blue. Although these early chapters may leave the impression that this ability is an immediate, nearly automatic effect of the sensation, Locke seems to think that some mental processing is required. At least a person needs to encounter phenomenal-blue often enough to retain the sensation in memory. This must somehow enable the person to recognize the sensation when it is presented again, to distinguish it from other sensations (D I: 1; E II.xi.8: 158; II.x.10: 154–5). Moreover, the account is plainly meant to cover both particular and general simple ideas, although no fuss is made over the distinction in these chapters. Abstraction, along with these other sorts of operations, is subsumed under the rubric "experience," which serves to gloss over them. This turns out to mask some complications, as we will see. Chapters ii through vii subdivide the class of simple ideas according to modes of reception. Some of these, such as ideas of colors, tastes, and so on, are received from external objects by one sense only; others, such as ideas of figure, motion, and extension, are conveyed by both sight and touch; ideas of affirming, perceiving, doubting, willing, and so on are acquired by

---

[15] This describes natural human faculties. The possibility of God's producing ideas directly in us is not, I think, ruled out by Locke's attack on innate ideas nor by his censure of enthusiasm.

reflection on the mind's own operations; some simple ideas are conveyed by both sense and reflection, namely, ideas of pain, pleasure, existence, unity, and power. The aim is to pick out, on empirical grounds, those ideas that are simple in the sense specified in the first clause of (a).

Thesis (a) focuses on the genesis of ideas, but the simple/complex distinction suggests a structural contrast as well. The plausibility of the empiricist claim depends largely on the contention that simple ideas are constituents, preferably the only constituent ideas, of the complex. The closer Locke comes to making out that complex ideas are composed of no ideas but those acquired in experience, the more support is gained for his empiricist theory. Whether he maintains that all complex ideas are strictly composed of simple ideas, rather than formed from simple ideas in some other way, deserves attention.

The syntactic structure of complex ideas is indicated, at least in part, by the mental operations that produce them. Combining, collecting, composing, and repeating are often cited, but comparing ideas is mentioned as well (e.g., E II.xi.4: 157; II.xii.1: 163; II.xxv.1: 319). This suggests that complex ideas of relations, in particular, comprise two or more simple ideas and a relation among them – the latter being a constituent of the complex, but not a compositional part. To be explicit, an idea A is composed of other ideas just in case A comprises other ideas each of which can exist apart from A.[16] By contrast, if an idea A is formed by comparing two ideas, then A consists of the two ideas compared and their comparison; the former two ideas can exist without A, but not the latter constituent of the idea.[17] This sort of complex idea has *non*compositional internal structure. To put it differently, combining ideas X and Y yields a novel composite idea comprising no ideas but X and Y; comparing X and Y yields a novel noncomposite idea comprising X, Y, and a novel constituent (their relation). This suggests that an empiricist has reason to be cautious about the operation of comparing because it yields ideas with an origin that is not entirely transparent.

[16] Cp. Gibson 1917: 46–7, where a composite idea is a mere aggregate without unifying structure; Locke's composite ideas have structure; see Losonsky 1989.

[17] This is not to deny that one might selectively attend to the relation between A and B, to the neglect of A and B; perhaps this is how we form abstract ideas, according to Locke (see Ayers 1991: I: 259–63).

As for complex ideas of substances and modes, they are strictly composed of simple ideas. Some passages may seem to express this view of complex ideas in general: "...all our complex *Ideas* whatsoever; which however compounded, and decompounded, may at last be resolved into simple *Ideas*,..." (E II.xxii.9: 292). Taken in a natural sense, this may indicate that the distinction between simple and complex ideas is strictly based on composition: (b) simple ideas have no compositional parts, whereas complex ideas are partwise composed of two or more other ideas (and ultimately of simple ones); this would allow that some simple ideas might have noncompositional internal structure. Yet Locke is attracted to the view that simple ideas, strictly so called, are radically simple – altogether without internal structure – and a corresponding notion of structure broader than strict composition. From this, we might draw a more restricted notion of simple idea and a more inclusive notion of complex idea: (c) a simple idea comprises no other ideas, whereas a complex idea comprises two or more other ideas and has either compositional or noncompositional structure. According to (c), we can say that simple ideas are strictly atomic and that some complex ideas are produced by comparing ideas.

Some scholars maintain that Locke adopts a wholly compositional theory of ideas.[18] M. A. Stewart argues that an atomic view of simple ideas and a compositional view of complex ideas is integral to Locke's scientific program. This is to treat ideas on analogy with Boyle's atomist mechanist physical theory. Locke does sometimes exploit this explanatory model. But ideas with the noncompositional structure required to represent things in relation drop out on this picture. Simple ideas are construed atomistically[19] (as on thesis (c)) and complex ideas as strictly compositional (as on thesis (b)). What makes this account of Locke's view of *complex* ideas plausible is that several ideas classed as simple in Book II, Chapters ii–vii are later acknowledged to comprise relations:

I confess *Power includes in it some kind of relation*, (a relation to Action or Change,) as indeed which of our *Ideas*, of what kind so-ever...does not? For our *Ideas* of Extension, Duration, and Number, do they not all contain a secret relation of Parts? Figure and Motion have something relative in them much more visibly: And sensible Qualities, as Colours and Smells, *etc.*

---

[18] Gibson 1917: 45–70; Stewart 1979, 1980.   [19] See especially Stewart 1979: 67.

what are they but the *Powers* of different Bodies, in relation to our Perception, *etc.* (E II.xxi.3: 234)

This gives some support to the view that all complex ideas have compositional structure, because it opens the prospect that complex ideas of relations might be strictly composed of simple ideas some of which are already ideas *of* relations. We will consider this later.

But the passage cuts against the atomic view of *simple* ideas in general. It shows no trace of the illusion that the idea of power is resolvable into nothing but ideas exclusive of relations. It gives no hint that, because the simple idea of power is the idea of a thing's relation to change, it is composed of the idea of change *inter alia*, and ultimately of nothing but (more) simple ideas. On the contrary, by allowing that relations are endemic to most, if not all, simple ideas, the passage implies that there is no ultimate composition base of nonrelational simple ideas. Here a functional notion of simple idea is invoked – not because the idea of power *ought* to be classed as complex, but still to enforce its right to be regarded as simple: "Our *Idea* therefore of *Power*…may well have a place amongst other simple *Ideas*,…being one of those, that make a principal Ingredient in our complex *Ideas* of Substances …" (E II. xxi.3: 234).[20] Locke may allude to a radical simplicity that the idea lacks, but he opts for a notion of simple idea tolerant of a certain internal structure (consistent with (b)). Even worse for the atomic view, Locke explicitly says elsewhere that some simple ideas have *compositional* structure. The simple idea of extension, for instance, is composed of other ideas of extension.[21]

The idea of power demands separate treatment, but a couple of points are in order here. It is, more exactly, the idea of a thing "able to make, or able to receive any change." It is acquired by both sense and reflection: we observe that qualities in outer objects and ideas in ourselves are regularly changed by other objects and by our volitions; from this, one infers that similar changes will be made by similar agents in future, "and so comes by that *Idea* which we call

---

[20] E II.xxiii.7–8: 299–300 invokes the functional notion of simple idea in connection with ideas of powers that are explicitly labeled complex; as such, they are evidently in the class of simple modes of the idea of power.

[21] E II.xv.9: 201–3; II.xvi.1: 205.

Power" (E II.xxi.1, 2: 233, 234).[22] In other words, experience leads us to expect that changes similar to those a thing is observed to make, or undergo, will take place in other similar things.[23] The point I want to make here is a general one: we observe things in relation in experience, according to Locke.[24] It is plain to him, for instance, that we observe things (actually) making changes – fire melting wax, giving pain, and so on.[25] Also, perhaps less controversial, we discover spatial and temporal relations by using our senses; we have, then, ideas of the distances between particular bodies, and the like. The point that our senses, in particular, do not just deliver ideas of isolated things, but rather ideas of things in causal, spatial, and temporal relations, would have had some importance for Locke. The opposite contention, that we have no merely sensory apprehension of relations, had been used to argue that all ideas of relations are innate.[26] Locke might have had a theoretical reason to admit simple ideas that represent things in relation.

Earlier chapters of Book II give the impression that Locke's notion of simple idea is the atomic one. This observation sets the tone: "For though the Sight and Touch often take in from the same Object, at the same time, different *Ideas;* as a Man sees at once Motion and Colour; the Hand feels Softness and Warmth in the same piece of Wax: Yet the simple *Ideas* thus united in the same Subject, are as perfectly distinct, as those that come in by different Senses" (E II.ii.1: 119). The passage goes on to say that each idea "being...in it self uncompounded, contains in it nothing but *one uniform Appearance,* or Conception in the Mind." In line with this in Book III, names of simple ideas, unlike names of complex ideas, are said to be incapable of definition. This may seem plausible for simple ideas proper to one sense modality, but it cannot be sustained for simple ideas in general. Although the atomic

---

[22] Should Locke have taken the fact that the idea is formed by an inference based on materials provided by experience to show that it is not simple, on thesis (a)? This might be argued. But I am inclined to say that recording the changes agents are observed to make and inferring abilities to make similar future changes are among the psychological processes at work in accumulating experience, as Locke sees it.

[23] E II.vii.8: 131.   [24] Cp. Gibson 1917: 67.

[25] See E II.xxvi.1: 324. I find it difficult to explain why Locke classes the idea of power, but not the ideas of cause and effect, as simple ideas.

[26] See More 1978: I: vi, 18; Cudworth 1996: 87, 90–2.

account of simple ideas evidently interests Locke, it is not, all things considered, his view.

Thesis (b) gets things wrong on two counts. In the case of simple ideas, it does not go far enough in tolerating internal structure. As we saw, some simple ideas are composed of other ideas, and some simple ideas have noncompositional structure. Is thesis (b) nevertheless correct about complex ideas? That depends largely on Locke's view of how complex ideas of relations are constituted. Does he envisage that their only relational constituents are *simple* ideas that include relations – ideas of power, motion, extension, and so on; that the complex is strictly composed of simple ideas, including some that represent relations? Locke pursues this program in some cases. He may justly suspect that ideas generated by acts of comparing two or more ideas are not fully traceable to experience. But the scheme is neither explicitly stated nor rigorously enforced. It seems unlikely, then, that it is essential to the division of ideas into simple and complex, or that Locke intends this fundamental dichotomy to be hostage to the success of a strictly compositional rendering of all complex ideas of relations. This argues for an inclusive notion of complex ideas as in (c). Taking all this into account, it seems best to say that *structure* is not what differentiates the classes of simple and complex ideas. Ideas that have compositional and noncompositional structure are found on both sides of the divide. Still, Locke's taxonomy of the structures of complex ideas is crucial to his case for empiricism. It gives specific content to (a) by identifying the patterns according to which complex ideas are formed from simple ideas if Lockean empiricism is true.

The role the fundamental division of ideas plays in expositing the empiricist theory can be summarized as follows. Simple and complex ideas might seem to be characterized in two logically independent ways: thesis (a) invokes origins – experience as opposed to operations performed on material supplied by experience; thesis (b) invokes internal structure. But thesis (a) is the pillar on which the distinction between simple and complex ideas rests. In connection with (b), two sorts of internal structure are abroad – compositional and noncompositional. Locke's initial exposition favors the assumption that simple ideas, as such, have structure of neither sort. This turns out to be an oversimple account, as the reader eventually learns. It makes Locke's case for empiricism seem more straightforward than it is; but it is not essential to the case he makes. Thesis (a) itself is more complicated than might at first appear. Ideas that originate in experience are not entirely innocent of mental processing, because experience involves memory, predictive inference, abstraction, and more (as we will see). To the extent that Locke provides no clear way to distinguish the sorts of mental processes that constitute experience and those operations that make further ideas from those delivered by sense and reflection, thesis (a) – and the empiricist argument that turns on it – is less than precise.

SIMPLE IDEAS OF SENSATION

Simple ideas of sensation are central in Locke's account of cognition of the external world. In the early chapters of Book II, they are treated as uniform, nondecomposable presentations to awareness. But more important for cognitive theory, they represent, and are taken to represent, qualities of things in the external world. It is central to this perceptual theory that all simple ideas of sensation, *qua* representative, are "real" and "adequate."

Locke does very often speak of simple sensory ideas as if they *were* qualities, not representative of qualities; for instance, simple *ideas* of softness and warmth are said to be "united in the same subject," a piece of wax – as much as to say, ideas depend on the wax roughly as accidents, on a substance. But more than once, when the dependence relation between ideas and bodies is the topic, Locke self-consciously corrects his own habit of speech (E II.viii.8: 134; II.xxxi.2: 375–6). He appears to ascribe some importance to the habit; but still, he argues that simple physical considerations show that ideas are not qualities in things, but rather mental effects "in us" caused by qualities, or modifications of the internal constitutions of bodies.[27]

These episodes are indicative of Locke's account of sensory cognition.[28] The key point is that humans are naturally disposed to ascribe sensory ideas to external objects, to ascribe them to one or more subjects on the model of accidents.[29] The fact taken from

---

[27] E II.viii.9–14: 134–7.   [28] See Bolton 2003, 2004.
[29] E II.viii.16–18: 137–9; II.xxxii.14: 388–9; II.xxx.2: 372.

rudimentary physics, that ideas and corporeal qualities are related by causality, leaves the natural disposition to refer ideas to external subjects, as if inhering in them, largely intact. And it brings into play the representative connection between ideas, on the one hand, and qualities and the subjects to which they belong, on the other. Sensory ideas thus serve us as generally reliable marks by which to distinguish different objects around us and their various qualities. To perform this role, simple ideas need not be images or resemblances of the qualities they represent, because their marking function is underwritten by causal connections alone.[30]

For this reason, all simple ideas of sensation are real. In general, an idea is "real," in Locke's technical sense, if (1) we suppose the idea represents something that exists in the world and (2) this supposition is correct.[31] We do suppose that simple ideas of sensation either are or represent the various qualities of things around us – we use them as distinguishing marks; the supposition is true because of the regular causal correspondence between those ideas and the qualities, or causal powers, of bodies around us. All simple ideas of sensation are thus real. (See E II.xxx.2: 372; IV.iv.4: 564.) For similar reasons, all such ideas are "adequate." That is, they are real and they "perfectly," as opposed to only "partially," represent the things we suppose them to represent. This is because simple ideas represent causal powers and, being regular effects of those powers, answer them completely.[32] The reality and adequacy of simple sensory ideas is assured precisely because they are passively received from external sources in accord with causal laws.[33]

These points in Locke's theory of sensory representation force a qualification of the view of paradigmatic simple ideas that pervades the early chapters of Book II. The idea of blue, for example, turns out to be more than a phenomenal presentation, "uniform in appearance" and ineffable. Even in II.ii.1, sensory awareness is said to be articulated by several distinct qualities *of one subject* – warmth and softness in the wax. As Locke puts it elsewhere, we "tacitly refer" the simple ideas we receive from the senses to external objects.[34] The point that sensory ideas are attended by acts

---

[30] E II.xxx.2: 372; IV.iv.4: 564.   [31] See E II.xxx.1: 372.   [32] E II.xxxi.2: 375–6.

[33] On the passive reception of simple ideas in general, see E II.xxx.3: 373; II.xxxi.2, 12: 375–6, 383; II.xii.1: 163; II.i.25: 118.

[34] E II.xxx.1–2: 372; II.xxiii.1: 295.

referring them to the world is reiterated in Book III: names of simple ideas *"intimate . . . some real Existence*, from which was derived their original pattern" (E III.iv.2: 421).[35] Perhaps the supposition that simple sensory ideas either are or represent qualities of external objects is best understood as an attitude toward the phenomenal content the idea presents to awareness.[36] It is not intrinsic to the phenomenal presentation, but it is surely essential to the idea of blue. It could not represent as it does or perform its marking function without the attendant reference. This is in tension with the thesis that names of simple ideas are indefinable, which naturally accompanies the atomic notion of simplicity. Because the idea of blue involves a phenomenal presentation and an "intimation" common to other simple sensory ideas, the name of the idea can be expressed by two names, neither of which is synonymous with the name defined. Strictly speaking, this undermines the thesis about language, and exposes Locke's tendency to neglect the intentional content of sensory ideas. Still, something can be saved even though the names of simple ideas can be defined, because at least the respects in which simple ideas of secondary qualities differ from each other cannot be defined.

With the doctrines about simple ideas in Book II, Chapters xxx and xxxi in place, Locke is poised to unfold his theory of sensitive knowledge in Book IV. Assent to what the mind supposes about its sensory ideas – that they indicate the presence of different external objects that unite different qualities – is, by and large, assent to the truth, because of the arrangements that guarantee the reality and adequacy of those ideas. Moreover, the claim that simple ideas of sensation are real accords with the simple/complex idea distinction – simple sensory ideas are direct effects of the physiological sensory system, undisturbed by mental operations.

It is remarkable, then, that these tenets of the theory of sensory representation are compromised in the chapter "Of Perception." It states that in grown people, ideas passively received from the senses are *"often . . . alter'd by the Judgement*, without our taking notice

---

[35] This is true also of names of ideas of substances, but not of names of other sorts; see E III.v.12: 435–6.

[36] Or we might treat it as a way of conceiving the content, which appears to be the approach to memory: the mind "renews its acquaintance with (ideas lodged in memory), as with *Ideas* it had known before" (E II.x.7: 153).

of it" (E II.ix.8: 145). This is all to the good, the passage suggests, because initially we may not take the ideas we receive by sight to represent the qualities they do. The example concerns the idea one receives when looking at an alabaster globe. It is, Locke says, the idea "of a flat Circle variously shadow'd." (The point seems to be that one's accessible content of awareness is the same as when one looks at the flat surface of a skillful painting of a globe.) But in the course of experience, one discovers the causes of such visual ideas and learns to collect the causally operative figure from patterns of light and shadow. Then "Judgment presently, by an habitual custom, alters the Appearances into their Causes" and, using the idea to mark its cause, "frames to it self the perception of a convex Figure, and an uniform Colour."

This gets the right result – an idea that marks, corresponds to, and represents the cause of the passively received idea. Accordingly, we correctly distinguish convex surfaces from flat ones by sight. Notice, however, that this success depends on the mind's intervening in the causal link between simple sensory ideas and qualities. This distorts the division between simple and complex ideas and, moreover, undermines the reality and adequacy of simple sensory ideas as such. The visual idea that successfully marks a globe is derived from other *ideas* – but nonetheless evidently ranks as a simple idea.[37] Locke's effort to build a theory of sensory cognition on the type simple idea is in jeopardy. This may suggest that his notion of simple idea won't bear the weight he puts on it in this connection, but let us look more closely.

It is likely Locke has a central problem of seventeenth-century optical theory in mind in II.ix.8.[38] William Molyneux's question poses an instance of a general issue about visual perception of figure, position, motion, and the like. To be brief, the problem is that the data the mind receives through the retinal image was thought to

[37] E II.v would seem to class all sensory ideas of figure (versus simple modes) as simple; in E II.viii.1 and elsewhere, ideas of primary qualities are ranked among simple ideas; in E II.ii.1, instances of visual ideas of motion and color. And sensory ideas altered by judgment fit none of the types of complex ideas in the taxonomy.

[38] Because the example is not only a case of visual perception of figure and distance, but also an example of *trompe d'oeille*, this may be a rare moment when Locke focuses on perceptual error; cf. E II.xi.3. But the fact that judgment affects mainly visual ideas, as opposed to other sense modalities, suggests this is not the problem in view.

underdetermine the distances and other spatial properties of objects in the line of sight.[39] The corporeal image does not vary as the distance of the object varies; nor does the image always vary in accord with the varying sizes, shapes, and motions of viewed objects. The two authors agree that a man born blind, but newly made to see, could not initially distinguish a globe from a cube on the basis of the visual impressions those objects would produce in him. The visual novice has "not yet attained the Experience" that would enable him to associate the figures, which he knows by touch, with their visual appearances (E II.ix.8: 146). Of course, a sighted person normally acquires visual ideas of figure, position, and so on; but only by forming the habit of altering the ideas that appear in the mind directly from external causes. For our purposes, the point is that although Locke ranks both visual and tactual ideas of extension, figure, motion, and so on as *simple*, he nevertheless maintains that the visual ideas are derived from other ideas.

This answer to Molyneux's question is undoubtedly tailored to empiricism about ideas; that's the main point. The specific intentional objects assigned to visual ideas are drawn from tactual ideas, and thus are within the scope of the Lockean theory of the origin of ideas. But the fact remains that in II.ix.8–10, judgment is said to mediate the connection between bodily qualities and the ideas that represent them – threatening the reality and adequacy of those ideas, and blurring the dichotomy of simple and complex ideas based on their origins.

How much damage does this do? I am inclined to think that the role given to judgment in II.ix.8–10 is a complication that effects where the line between simple and complex ideas is drawn, but does not detract from Locke's theory of the origin of ideas. It would do no harm if *visual* ideas of extension, figure, distance, and motion were classed as complex. Locke can be excused for not doing so. To frame claims about simple ideas around it would complicate almost everything said about simple ideas of sensation. It would introduce an additional type of complex ideas; and it would serve no useful purpose. It is true that the operation of judgment complicates the account of sensory representation, as well, but it does not affect its overall shape or plausibility, or so I would urge.[40] To be sure,

---

[39] See Bolton 1994; Lievers 1992.   [40] Cp. Schumacher 2003.

sensory ideas altered by a mental operation are not certified to be real and adequate. But this might lead us to conclude that the picture painted in II.xxx.2 and elsewhere is an idealization. Locke invokes it to explain the representative function of simple ideas, but he realizes that it is too simple. Certain physical and physiological facts require that passively received sensory input be adjusted if a mind is to achieve cognition of external things.[41] Yet, we might think, this does not embarrass the theory of representation, but only elaborates it. One further point: judgment is fallible; it cannot match the strict guarantee of reality and adequacy enjoyed by ideas passively received from external sources. Still, it produces results that approximate that ideal. Judgment tends, over time, to align with the optimal model, precisely because its operations are guided by experience, or so Locke might plausibly contend. But still, the insertion of judgment between passively received sensory input and the ideas delivered to sensory awareness raises a problem for Locke's claim that we have sensitive knowledge. He maintains that judgment, the faculty that affirms propositions on the evidence of what has been observed in the past, yields probable opinion, at best.[42] In view of this, the part given to judgment here would seem to be at odds with the doctrine presented in Book IV, that we know that particular things exist when we receive ideas owing to their causal powers – particular things that unite the qualities typical of, for instance, water or a man.

SIMPLE IDEAS OF PRIMARY QUALITIES

Ideas of primary qualities, unlike ideas of secondary qualities, are said to resemble the bodily modifications that cause them.[43] Specifically, ideas of primary qualities are said to be images of their causes. Yet II.xxx.2 leaves no doubt that the representative character of all simple ideas, images or not, rests on their causal connections; causality, not resemblance, underwrites the certainty of sensitive knowledge

---

[41] As earlier, other operations on simple ideas (e.g., abstraction) go unremarked in the discussion of reality.

[42] E IV.xiv; IV.xv.4–5: 655–7. In E II.ix.9–10, however, Locke stresses the habitual nature of the alteration made on sensory input, rather than the evidence provided by past experience.

[43] E II.viii.15, 18: 137, 138.

regarding the existence of particular things and their respective sensible qualities.[44] This allows scope for the question whether ideas of primary qualities are essentially images of bodily modifications – that is, in and of themselves – or whether they are instead images by virtue of the contingent fact that they are interpreted in terms of corporeal modifications in the course of experience.[45]

Construed as images, ideas of primary qualities would seem to have structural complexity. An image, like an icon, is a representation divisible into parts, each of which represents a part of what is represented by the image as a whole. When confronted with this, Locke manifests, once again, that he has no deep commitment to the atomic notion of simple idea. He accepts that ideas of space and duration "consist of Parts"; there are no indivisible ideas from which ideas of larger extensions and durations are composed. If Locke suggests that ideas of "the least portions of [duration or extension], whereof we have clear and distinct *Ideas*" are most fit to be considered the components of other ideas of duration and space, it is not because such an idea is atomic, but rather because it is clear and distinct.[46] A less welcome consequence of the theory that ideas of primary qualities are images of bodily modifications is that, as such, these (simple) ideas would seem to be capable of explication.

In the chapter "Of Solidity," oddly enough, the atomic view of simple ideas holds sway – here in connection with the idea of a primary quality. The chapter ends by declaring that the idea of solidity is an ineffable tactual sensation. We cannot say "wherein solidity consists," just as we cannot verbally convey ideas of color to a blind person (E II.iv.6: 127). Nevertheless, the chapter has a good deal to say about what solidity is, that is, what the idea is *of*: "That which...hinders the approach of two Bodies, when they are moving one towards another, ..." (E II.iv.1: 123). Solidity is defined in terms of a certain bodily interaction; perhaps this is not a definition in the strictest sense, because Locke tends to think solidity is the force that results in the mutual resistance of bodies. Yet if we are unable to define solidity, it is because of ignorance in natural

---

[44] See E IV.xi.

[45] The latter account of visual ideas is strongly indicated by Locke's answer to Molyneux's question.

[46] E II.xv.9: 202. The idea of space is treated both imagistically and discursively in this passage, but turns out to be composite either way.

philosophy, not because the idea is intrinsically inexpressible. As in other early chapters of Book II, the content a simple sensory idea presents to awareness is emphasized to the neglect of its intentional content. This raises no alarms until Locke offers to describe what such an idea is *of*, that is, to specify its intentional content. The oddity in II.iv is the appearance of there being two ideas *of* solidity – one a sensory presentation, the other expressed by a causal defini- tion; one is received via the senses, the other has a more obscure origin. Or, we might say, there is one idea, which presents an ineffable tactual content that nonetheless receives verbal articula- tion. I doubt that this appearance indicates an irresolvable incon- sistency. The immediate tension is relieved if we suppose that the idea of solidity is initially just an incommunicable sensory pre- sentation and, after due experience, the presentation is interpreted as a representation (image?) of other bodies' resisting the motion of one's own body. But this suggestion needs more careful considera- tion. For our purposes, it is enough to say that this chapter, espe- cially, shows that Locke's theory of how simple ideas are acquired – complete with intentional content – is more complicated than often assumed.

SIMPLE IDEAS OF REFLECTION

Book II, Chapter i names sensation and reflection as the sources of simple ideas. This suggests that we have experience of our own mental operations on a par with our sensory experience of things in the world. But, in fact, Locke does not treat them just alike. Whereas the perception of external things and their qualities is mediated by ideas, for Locke, ideas do not mediate perception of one's ongoing mental acts, or so I suggest. Like Descartes, Locke subscribes to the thesis that one is conscious of all one's acts of perceiving, thinking, and so forth. "It being impossible for anyone to perceive, without perceiving, that he does perceive."[47] The (meta)perception that necessarily attends all other acts of percep- tion and thought is not, so far, reflection.[48] Reflection is "that

---

[47] E II.xxvii.9: 335; see also E II.i.19.
[48] But reflection seems to come in degrees; for close consideration of relevant texts, see Kulstad 1984. The view urged here is in substantial agreement with Gibson 1917: 55–7.

notice which the Mind takes of its own Operations, and the manner of them" (E II.i.4: 105; II.vi.1: 127). And reflection is the source of ideas: "Whoever reflects on what passes in his own Mind, cannot miss it: And if he does not reflect, all the Words in the World, cannot make him have any notion of it" (E II.ix.1: 143; also E II.i.7–8: 107–8; II.i.24–5: 117–18). Taken together, these points strongly suggest that reflection occurs when one attends to a mental operation of which one would have some scattered awareness anyway. If so, it is natural to think, the content of immediate awareness reflection delivers is the act attended to – or, more exactly, an aspect of the act. Ideas are invoked only to explain the ability to recall an act previously reflected upon and to provide for general ideas of kinds of mental acts. Indeed, the whole theory of ideas is linked to the assumption that cognition of our own mental states is immediate in a way that cognition of external things is not. As Locke puts it: "... since the Things, the Mind contemplates, are none of them, besides it self, present to the Understanding, 'tis necessary that something else, as a Sign or Representation of the thing it considers, should be present to it: And these are *Ideas*" (E IV.xxi.4: 720–1).[49] Unraveling the reasoning behind this remark is difficult, to be sure. Still, it supports the view suggested here.

This may explain why simple ideas of reflection drop out of consideration in II.xxx–xxxi, chapters devoted to the reality, adequacy, and truth of ideas in respect of what they are supposed to represent. Simple ideas of reflection have no representative function in experience comparable to that sensory ideas have. In other respects, however, the two sorts of simple ideas play the same roles – they are components of complex ideas of substances, and some of them ground families of ideas of modes.

COMPLEX IDEAS

Although several simple ideas enter the mind at once, and a number of them are observed in the same thing, the senses do not deliver ready-made complex ideas. This follows from what we have already said about complex ideas: "... as the Mind is wholly Passive in the

---

[49] Likewise Arnauld and Nicole (1996: 25): "... we can have no knowledge of what is outside us, except by means of the ideas in us ..."

reception of all its simple *Ideas*, so it exerts several acts of its own, whereby out of its simple *Ideas*, as the Materials and Foundations of the rest, the other are framed" (E II.xii.1: 163). In effect, this passage acknowledges that the constituents of a complex idea are united by something more than mere co-presence (or succession) in awareness.[50] Mental operations are required both to select simple ideas and to provide a structure by virtue of which they constitute one idea.

More than one purpose is served by the main tripartite classification of complex ideas. As we have said, it is the framework of Locke's theory of the origin of ideas; each of the three types is defined, in part, by the operation that generates it, or by the structural pattern that unifies it. The typology is put to a different sort of use in Book IV, where it underwrites our capacities for knowledge and probable opinion. In what follows, we will look at the former issue and then briefly at the latter.

IDEAS OF MODES, SUBSTANCES, AND RELATIONS – STRUCTURE AND ORIGIN

Ideas of modes are distinguished from other complex ideas because they "contain not in them the supposition of subsisting by themselves, but are considered as Dependences on, or Affections of Substances" – for example, ideas of triangle, gratitude, murder (E II. xii.4: 165; also E II.xxii.1: 288). This sets up an important contrast with ideas of substances, which are "taken to represent distinct particular things subsisting by themselves" – for example, lead, sheep, man (E II.xii.6: 165; also E II.xxiii.1, 3: 295–7). In part, the difference turns on where the objects of ideas stand in, roughly, the familiar asymmetric dependence relation of accidents on substances. But it is at least as important that the two types of ideas carry different existential assumptions (see, e.g., E II.xxx.4–5: 373–4). Ideas of substances are supposed to represent one or more things that exist and, moreover, subsist by themselves. Opposed on both counts, ideas of modes represent entities that are not presumed to exist (nor presumed not to exist) and that (if they exist) depend on the existence of substance.

---

[50] See, e.g., E III.v.4: 429.

In fact, the pair of criteria that distinguish between ideas of substances and modes would seem to be capable of coming apart. Leibniz observes that diseases are like modes in their dependent metaphysical status but also "imitate substances" in respect of the difficulty we have understanding them[51] – the difficulty, namely, that we know a disease only from its observable manifestations. This is an epistemic trait closely tied to one of Locke's criteria, that ideas of substances are, and ideas of modes are not, meant to represent things that exist. Leibniz means to suggest that there are many natural phenomena, other than those that might qualify to be substances, that have this sort of epistemic status – natural events, processes, reactions, relations, and so on.[52] But oddly enough, ideas of such things have no place in Locke's taxonomy. Something more will be said about this later. But it remains rather puzzling, especially in view of Locke's interest in medicine.

IDEAS OF SUBSTANCES

The special function of ideas of substances is to represent certain things in the world that we know only by virtue of their effects on our senses or by reflection. As we saw, simple ideas of sensation are supposed to represent qualities of things in the world; by the same token, several simple ideas found "constantly together" are supposed to represent several qualities belonging to one thing.[53] Substance-ideas are intended to represent these things complete with their qualities. The point is central to Locke's anti-Cartesian theory of knowledge: whatever we know about substance is discovered in experience. Experience shows that there are substances in which certain causal powers are united, but leaves us ignorant of the internal source from which they arise.

The demand to represent a structure that we can identify via its effects but cannot otherwise knowledgeably describe is met, according to Locke, by the way complex ideas of substance are composed. Our idea of substance in general is made by uniting a number of ideas of sensible qualities found constantly together in

[51] Leibniz 1996: 426.
[52] Ayers 1991: II: 91–109 explores some of the metaphysical issues.
[53] II.xxiii.1: 295.

the same thing and the idea of a substratum in which those qualities "subsist" and from which they "result," but that otherwise
remains unknown.[54] Locke is committed to saying that we form the
idea of substratum – such as it is – from ideas acquired in experience; he undertook to explain this when Stillingfleet challenged
it.[55] Still, the schematic supposition that unifies the several components of the idea – many qualities *inhere in and result from* a
common substratum – would seem to be innate, yet arguably consistent with Locke's empiricism about ideas. As for ideas of particular sorts of substances – man, horse, gold, and so on – they are
composed of simple ideas of qualities supposed to *flow from, and
coexist in*, an unknown real essence or inner constitution.[56]

IDEAS OF SIMPLE AND MIXED MODES

Ideas of modes represent a variety of entities that, assuming they
exist, are substance-dependent: sorts of possible qualities, mental
operations, pleasures and pains, passions, actions, motions, powers.
Ideas of this type have a proprietary compositional structure: a base
simple idea is combined with other ideas that modify it. In Locke's
usage, "idea of mode" does not mean the idea of a modification of
substance (as it does for Arnauld and Nicole).[57] Instead, it refers to
ideas that represent modifications of a basic idea; there are, for
instance, modes of the idea of number, modes of the idea of motion,
modes of the idea of action. The template is conveyed in a marginal
addition to Draft B: "The Complex Ideas of Modes which are of
some one Simple Idea considered as chief & other simple Ideas
considered as modifying it whether they be the cause or the degree
or object or end or other circumstances, v.g. figure of extension,
Consideration of Thinkeing, runing or beating. of motion &c."[58]

This suggests that Locke takes up a challenge posed by Cartesian
doctrine. Descartes maintains that we have ideas of thought and
extension, two enduring substantial attributes that are intrinsically
indeterminate but capable of temporary determinate modifications.

---

[54] II.xxiii.1–2: 295–6.   [55] E I.iv.18: 95; W IV: 19–21.
[56] II.xxiii.3: 296 (and elsewhere); on inner constitution and substratum, see E II.
xxxi.13: 383.
[57] Locke notes that his use of the term is unusual (E II.xii.4: 165).
[58] D I: 162, note 4.

Moreover, the ability to think of particular modes of a substance presupposes an (innate) idea of its substantial attribute. For example, the idea of extension is conceptually prior to, and implicit in, ideas of the particular figures that bodies do or can have.[59] Of course, no indeterminate extension is discovered in experience. Locke's theory of ideas of modes is meant to provide an alternative explanation of the human ability to form indefinitely many ideas of variations of a single "attribute" (for lack of a better word) – extension and thought; and Locke also applies the model to motion, action, pleasure and pain, power, and more.

Paradigmatic ideas of simple modes are, naturally, modes of the simple idea of space. Initially, one acquires a sensory idea of some distance or volume – it doesn't matter what – from observing the intervals between bodies. This idea is subject to modification by repetition or division; in effect, it serves as the idea of a unit distance or volume. Whether Locke has in mind partwise image construction or numerical addition of units is, perhaps, unclear. But the latter would seem to be in view here: our "Power of repeating, or doubling any *Idea* we have of any distance, and adding it to the former as often as we will, without being ever able to come to any stop...is that, which gives us the *Idea* of *Immensity*" (E II.xiii.4: 168; also E II.xv.9: 201–3). The strategy exploits the fact that the potential limitability of space is intrinsic to any part of space: "Each different distance is a different Modification of Space, and *each* Idea *of any different distance, or Space, is a simple Mode of this* Idea" (E II.xiii.4: 167). Just as any finite space can be augmented or diminished, so the idea of any finite space represents, and exhibits, this potential. As a basis for modification (composition), then, the idea of a finite space serves just as well as the Cartesian idea of unbounded space. Still, one might object to this empiricist strategy, as Leibniz does, that nothing given to sensory awareness exhibits the endless potential for division intrinsic to the structure of space.[60]

Locke adopts a modal approach to simple ideas of secondary qualities, which may well come as a surprise. Simple modes of the

---

[59] *Principles* I, 63–5 (Descartes 1984: I: 213–15); see also the exchange with Arnauld, AT V, 214, 221; for the latter, Descartes 1984: III: 357. Also see Leibniz 1966: 444–5.
[60] Leibniz 1996: 158.

idea of white, for example, are "degrees of whiteness"; "shades" of a color are mentioned, too. The suggestion is that repeating an idea of white – superimposing it? – yields ideas of more intense white. Locke names ideas of "compound Tastes and Smells" as simple modes, apparently referring to the results of combining several tastes or aromas in imagination. This is, he says, like a musician who composes a tune or chord in the head before actually hearing it (see E II.xviii.3–6: 224–5). No doubt people can image compound sounds, tastes, smells, and colors, although artists, composers, and chefs might seem better at it than most. Accordingly, Locke points out that we do, or at least can, acquire (some) ideas of colors, and the like, by this technique, thereby circumventing the senses. But notice that modified ideas of colors, odors, and so on lack some important properties of Locke's simple ideas of sensation.[61] The latter are caused by, and tacitly referred to, things in the world; but modes of simple sensory ideas, being composed without concern for external causes, (so far) lack these external connections. They neither represent nor purport to represent existing qualities.

Ideas of mixed modes, in contrast to simple modes, are "compounded of simple *Ideas* of several kinds, put together to form one complex one" (E II.xii.5: 165). Here, too, the unity of ideas of this type is due to their comprising a base simple idea modified by other ideas. The simple ideas that *"have been most modified, and had most mixed Modes made out of them, with names given to them"* are "thinking, and Motion, (which are the two *Ideas* which comprehend in them all Action,) and Power, from whence these Actions are conceive to flow." The passage goes on to illustrate modes of action: "*Consideration* and *Assent*, which are Actions of the Mind; *Running* and *Speaking*, which are Actions of the Body; *Revenge* and *Murther*, which are Actions of both together..." (E II.xxii.10: 293). But Locke does not take the same care to explain the composition of these ideas as in the case of ideas of simple modes. In the end, mixed modal ideas are not even restricted to modifications of a central idea. Locke puts in this category ideas that express "the several Fashions, customs, and Manners" of different "Nations" (E II.xxii.6: 290). It includes ideas "made use of in Divinity, Ethicks, Law, and Politicks" (E II.xxii.12: 294). The emphasis is on things

---

[61] Conditions for reality of simple ideas and ideas of modes differ.

that owe their existence to conventional arrangements, whether social, legal, moral, political, cultural; examples include ideas of obligation, reprieve, triumph, beauty. This leaves Locke, as far as I can see, without a general account of the unifying structure that forges two or more simple ideas into one idea of a mixed mode. Indeed, to explain their unity he relies heavily on the fact that such ideas are given names.[62]

IDEAS OF RELATIONS

In the taxonomy of complex ideas, the last item is ideas of relations. We have already said something about the challenge this type of ideas poses for Lockean empiricism. It is difficult to see just how he means to say that this type of complex ideas is constituted. This is in part because chapters devoted to ideas of relations often speak of relations, relative denominations, and acts of comparing, but seem to have little to say about *ideas* of relations; for example: "... Relation is a way of comparing, or considering two things together; and giving one or both of them some appellation from that Comparison, and sometimes giving even the Relation it self a Name" (E II.xxv.7: 322). To my mind, such passages by no means settle the question whether all relations are mind-dependent, for Locke. Rather than addressing the metaphysical issue, the discussion is intended to bring out how we think of relations – how they are presented in thought. Above all, Locke wants to stress that the idea of a relation represents two or more things and a relation among them, whereas complex ideas of substance and modes represent unitary things:

Thus a Triangle, though the parts thereof compared, one to another, be *relative*, yet the *Idea* of the whole, is a positive absolute *Idea*. The same may be said of a Family, a Tune, *etc.* for there can be no Relation, but betwixt two Things, considered as two Things. There must always be in relation two *Ideas*, or Things, either in themselves really separate, or considered as distinct, and then a ground or occasion for their comparison. (E II.xxv.6: 321)

This is not to deny that a relation between A and B can be counted one thing, but just to emphasize that its status as relation is lost

---

[62] See E II.xxii.4: 289–90; III.v.10: 434.

unless A and B are regarded as distinct. But what is the syntactic structure of the complex idea of a relation?

Such ideas are regularly said to be "made up of" and to "terminate in" simple ideas.[63] This contrasts with the terminology of combining, collecting, and repeating simple ideas standard in connection with complex ideas of substances and modes. This, in itself, is some evidence that complex ideas of relations are constituted differently than complex ideas of these other sorts. But the text provides no general account of how complex ideas of relations break down. This much is clear, however. The idea of a relation includes ideas of the foundations of the relation and the relation so founded: "A Man, if he compares two things together, can hardly be supposed not to know what it is, wherein he compares them: So that when he compares any Things together, he cannot but have a very clear Idea of that Relation" (E II.xxv.8: 322; also E II.xxviii.19: 361). Still, the complex idea of a relation could be constituted in either of two ways: (i) a strict composite of simple ideas, including at least one simple idea of a relation; this would assimilate ideas of relations to ideas of modes, which elaborate or modify a central simple idea – a pattern might be found in the simple ideas of power and motion, which involve relations and are cited as the bases of ideas of simple and complex modes; or (ii) a complex comprising two or more simple ideas[64] that specify foundations and the idea of the relation they found; the complex idea is, then, constituted by other ideas, but not strictly composed of them. Perhaps the best evidence that Locke thought of treating all complex ideas of relations according to (i) is the sample analysis of the ideas of father and friend in II. xxviii.18.[65] Each is resolved into ideas some of which are plainly ideas of relations, namely, ideas of generation, child (of), love, disposition. These are not yet simple ideas. But perhaps they might be treated as modes of simple relational ideas.

But although this approach would have had understandable attractions for Locke, the groundwork for it is not laid in the *Essay*. The list of ideas comprising relations that are ranked as simple is short – ideas of power, sensible qualities, space, duration, and

---

[63] See, e.g. E II.xxv.11: 323–4; II.xxvi.6: 327; II.xxviii.18: 360–1.

[64] For brevity, I have omitted "or complex ideas formed from simple ideas."

[65] See Stewart 1980, which acknowledges that the plan to make all complex ideas of relations compositional is not fully worked out.

motion are the principal ones. Many relations that Locke plainly does not overlook, ones that occupy his attention even in the early drafts, cannot plausibly be treated as modes of this base set of simple ideas. This is especially true of ideas of civil, legal, and moral relations – citizen, constable, patron, right, duty – and the relation that constitutes morality, for Locke, "conformity of our voluntary actions with a law".[66]

IDEAS OF SUBSTANCES AND MODES (AND RELATIONS) – REALITY AND CONTRIBUTION TO KNOWLEDGE

Locke's theory of knowledge rests, in part, on the fit that generally obtains between the representative functions we ascribe to different types of ideas, on the one hand, and the foundations in reality those types of ideas have, on the other (as he sees it). Ideas are said to be real just in case they fit reality in this way (E II.xxx.1: 372). Unless our ideas are real, by and large, we have no prospect of acquiring knowledge of the world, for we cannot think of anything outside our own minds without having an idea of it, according to Locke. It is thus a matter of some importance for him to show that, for the most part, our ideas are real (E IV.iv). The taxonomy is essential to the argument; more will be said about it shortly.

The classificatory scheme has another crucial role in Locke's account of human knowledge. As we saw, ideas of substances purport to represent actual things, as do simple ideas of sensation, whereas ideas of modes and relations are meant to specify sorts of things with no presumption that such things exist. Locke builds a great deal on this carefully worked out distinction. Propositions composed of ideas that purport to represent actual things have an epistemic profile very different from that of propositions formed from ideas that carry no existential commitment. They demand opposite methods of inquiry, which yield different sorts and degrees of epistemic warrant and hold contrasting promise of advancement. Indeed, some philosophers regard this deep epistemic dichotomy as the *Essay*'s most important achievement. Yet its thorough grounding in Locke's typology of ideas is not often noted. In fact, it is little more than an extension of the central doctrine of Book II.

[66] E II.xxviii.3–4, 15: 350–1, 359.

The classificatory scheme is embedded in the catalogue of types of propositions, which shapes the account of the basis, scope, and limits of human knowledge (E IV.i.3: 525). To be sure, propositions are classified on the basis of types of "agreement or disagreement" among ideas that make propositions true; the terminology here is not that of the taxonomy. Nevertheless, Locke's assessment of the prospects for knowledge of "relations," as opposed to knowledge of "co-existence" and "real existence," can be traced directly to the fact (as he has it) that the former deal almost exclusively with ideas of modes and relations, and the latter with simple ideas and ideas of substances (IV.ii, iii, xi). After a quick look at the reality of ideas, we will turn briefly to the epistemic profile of substances, as opposed to modes, and finally to the use of the category of modal ideas in mathematical and moral epistemology.

The result that (nearly) all ideas are real, in Locke's technical sense, falls out of his account of the genesis of ideas – a neat result of his particular version of empiricism. For each type of ideas is acquired in a way that determines what that type is intended to represent, while it also assures that many, if not all, ideas of that type succeed in this. We saw this earlier, in the case of simple ideas. In virtue of their causal origins, simple ideas of sensation cannot fail to represent the different qualities of actual things, as we naturally take them to do. The case is different for ideas of substances, because their function is to represent *substances* – actual things that comprise a source of unity among qualities:

Our *complex* Ideas *of Substances*, being made all of them in reference to Things existing without us, and intended to be Representations of Substances, as they really are, are no farther *real*, than as they are such Combinations of simple *Ideas*, as are really united, and co-exist in Things without us. (E II.xxx.5: 374)

The idea of a mermaid belongs in the class of ideas of substances, but it is defective ("fantastical" is Locke's term). Lapses of this sort can, however, be avoided by diligent observation.

Ideas of modes and relations carry less demanding conditions for reality.[67] In accord with the dual criteria that differentiate ideas of

---

[67] In E II.xxx–xxxii, Locke seems to use "ideas of modes," "ideas of mixed modes," and "ideas of mixed modes and relations" indifferently to refer to all complex

modes, as opposed to substances (E II.xii.4–6: 165), the former are "Combinations of *Ideas*, which the Mind, by its free choice, puts together, without considering any connexion they have in Nature" (E IV.iv.5: 564). Behind this is a metaphysical picture on which substances are the only structures that effect a natural unity; events, processes, and relations are not plainly marked out in nature. Locke speaks as if changes mix and flow without having, or appearing to have, sharp natural contours. It is, then, up to us to form ideas of actions, motions, and so on to suit ourselves. This is not to deny that a person might form a modal idea – for instance, the idea of fencing or speaking – by observing things (E II.xxii.9: 291–2). Locke's thought seems to be that observers either establish for themselves the distinction between actions that constitute fencing, and those that don't, or they pick it up from preexisting social conventions. Such ideas are intended to define kinds – to delineate kinds – that can be applied in the world, if appropriate, and to enable us to consider actions (etc.) that are so far unrealized. For this reason, "there is nothing more required to those kind of *Ideas*, to make them *real*, but that they be so framed, that there be a possibility of existing conformable to them" (E II.xxx.3–4: 373; also IV.iv.5: 564).

To return briefly to a point mentioned earlier, the crux of this account of the reality of modal and relational ideas is that they have no external patterns. The existence of what we might call "natural processes," and the importance of framing ideas that are intended to represent them, is completely ignored. Above all, we might think that ideas of things related by cause and effect and ideas that modify the simple idea of power are intended to copy nature and are deficient if they fail to do so. But Locke's fitting the type in the direction of conventionally established kinds is preparation for his account of knowledge in the (nonphysical) sciences.

Further knowledge-theoretic implications of the typology of ideas are developed with the aid of Locke's notion of a real essence. He maintains that every kind for which we have a name has a real essence, that is, a foundation on which depend the several qualities that coexist in, or properties that necessarily belong to, all instances of the kind (E III.iii.15–18: 417–19). The real essence of a substantial

---

ideas other than ideas of substances; similarly, E IV.iv.5–11. In the next several paragraphs here, I follow this usage.

kind is the real internal constitution from which the species-typical qualities flow. Because the (real) idea of a substance, such as gold, represents actual things although we detect only a few of their qualities, the real essence of gold is hidden from us.[68] Thus "because we knowing not what real Constitution it is of Substances, whereon our simple *Ideas* depend, and which really is the cause of that strict union of some of them one with another, and the exclusion of others; there are very few of them, that we can be sure are, or are not inconsistent in Nature, any farther than Experience and sensible Observation reaches" (E IV.iv.12: 568; also IV.iii.9–16, 25–9: 544–8, 555–60). We are effectively blocked from having more than inductive empirical evidence with regard to the qualities that coexist in all samples of gold. The situation is very different for modal kinds.

Ideas of modes and relations represent kinds of things with real essences that are identical to those very ideas, because the ideas define those kinds, to begin with.[69] That is, by constructing a modal idea, or by modifying a base idea with another idea, humans do the work of constituting a kind as a subject of properties. This empiricist account of the genesis of modal ideas is a premise; from it, Locke concludes, the properties that belong necessarily to a mode, such as a triangle, are consequences of nothing but the idea of that mode – an idea that is, or can be, present to immediate awareness.

The epistemic consequences of the mode/substance distinction are now plain: "*We must* therefore ... *adapt our methods of Enquiry to the nature of the* Ideas *we examine*, and the Truth we search after" (E IV.xii.7: 643). Empirical methods are the best we have for inquiring about the existence, qualities, and powers of substances. It is fruitless to aspire to a "perfect *Science* of natural Bodies" – an explanatory order among many known general physical truths (E IV.iii.29: 560; also 26: 556; IV.xii.9–13: 644–8). Inductive evidence supports only probable judgment, which falls short of the certainty demanded of knowledge, in Locke's view.[70] By

---

[68] E III.iii.17–18: 417–18; E III.vi.3, 6: 439–40, 442; much of this chapter is devoted to urging that the boundaries of kinds for which we have names are determined by their nominal essences (the accessible content of our general ideas) rather than by real essences in the world.

[69] E III.iii.18: 418–19; E III.v.14: 436–7.

[70] E IV.xiv: 652–3; IV.xv: 654–7; the topic is discussed more fully in Owen 1993.

contrast, we need not resort to experience in order to prove general propositions with regard to a mode. Since a mode's properties are consequences of nothing but its idea, we need only attend to that idea and its relations to other modal ideas – relations that can, in principle, be exhibited to awareness, either immediately or by means of intermediary ideas. Locke concludes: "Because the Advances that are made in this part of Knowledge, depending on our Sagacity, in finding intermediate *Ideas*, that may shew the Relations and Habitudes of *Ideas*, whose Co-existence is not considered, 'tis a hard Matter to tell, when we are at an end of such Discoveries..." (E IV.iii.18: 548–9).

To Locke's mind, the success of mathematics as a science is explained by the fact that it deals with ideas of simple modes, which purport to represent things that are merely possible: "The Mathematician considers the Truth and Properties belonging to a Rectangle, or Circle, only as they are in *Idea* in his own Mind.... Is it true of the *Idea* of a *Triangle*, that its three Angles are equal to two right ones? It is true also of a *Triangle*, where-ever it really exists." Real things are considered only hypothetically: if a triangle exists, then the theorem is true of it.[71] On the strength of this analysis of mathematical knowledge, Locke envisages similar results for other ideas of the same type: "...if other *Ideas*, that are the real...Essences of their Species, were pursued in the way familiar to Mathematicians, they would carry our Thoughts farther, and with greater evidence and clearness, than possibly we are apt to imagine" (E IV.xii.7: 643). In particular, Locke argues that a demonstrative science of morality is possible.[72]

Many philosophers in Locke's time maintained that both mathematics and morality are, or could be, demonstrative sciences.[73] Locke has an original way to justify assimilating the two fields, namely, by appeal to the typology of ideas. Because the success of mathematics is attributed to the fact that it deals with ideas of modes, and the consequences this entrains, a similar result is anticipated for other ideas of modes. But despite its theoretical

[71] E IV.iv.6: 565.
[72] E IV.xii.8: 643–4; IV.iii.18–20: 548–52. The sciences of divinity, politics, and law are mentioned (E II.xxii.12: 294).
[73] The view can be traced to Erhard Weigel, and it was held by Pufendorf, Cudworth, and Leibniz, to name a few.

ground, the case is not strong. There are any number of ideas of Lockean modes that are plainly not subjects of nontrivial general necessary truths – ideas of beauty, a dance, modes of pleasure and pain, and many more. Yet these ideas share all the characteristics of mathematical ideas that, supposedly, explain why there is a science of mathematics. At this juncture, the taxonomic type cannot bear the weight that Locke's epistemology rests on it. But in other respects, the taxonomy holds up well under its epistemic uses.

CONCLUSION

Attention to the taxonomy helps one to understand some of the subtlety and power of Locke's overall theory of human cognition. In its role as scaffolding for the genetic story in Book II, it reveals the temper of his version of empiricism. Simple sensory ideas are presentations to immediate awareness; at least some of them are ineffable. But in the course of a person's experience, or cognitive development, such presentations are embedded in mental operations that bestow on them various representative contents and functions. As cognitive development – and chapters of the book – move on, the atomistic notion of sense impressions lingers only as an ingredient in more complicated mental constructions that constitute even simple ideas. It was mentioned earlier, but bears repeating, that the mental acts that refer sensory ideas to qualities of external objects, and the associated supposition that several such ideas inhere in a common subject, implicate intellectual resources in addition to passively received sensations. Indeed, at least some types of complex ideas have unifying structures – modification, coexistence in a subject – that are brought to (not found in) bare contents of immediate sensory awareness. Many, if not all, of these bases of unification are abstract schemata untouched by Locke's attack on innate propositional knowledge and ideas, or so I would argue. The assumption that humans have natural abilities to deploy such schemata allows the *Essay* to achieve a fairly sophisticated treatment of external reference, existential commitment, and the compositionality of ideas – all of which elude philosophers with more far-reaching versions of empiricism.

At the same time, the taxonomy constrains what Locke can say about ideas. Rather than sweep inconvenient facts about vision under the rug, he acknowledges that visual ideas are altered by mental operations; while they end up functioning as simple sensory ideas should, they do not fully accord with his general theory of simple ideas. But the type modal ideas, designed to avoid innately known extranatural standards, is allowed to yield an implausible assimilation of mathematical ideas and ideas of sorts of colors, thoughts, motions, and actions, which takes all of these ideas to specify sorts humans define at will. Locke's treatment of ideas of substances, however, credibly posits patterns in the natural realm, to which we have cognitive access only through experience. Each of these two types of ideas is neatly tailored to its particular function. Perhaps this helps to explain why the taxonomy fails to provide for any number of ideas we evidently possess – including ideas central to medicine, economics, applied mathematics, and so on. We may presume that Locke does not mean to deny that we have such ideas, but only to deny them a place in his basic theory of human cognition.

The typological developed in Book II is, after all, deployed throughout Book IV. The etiologies of different idea-types provide theoretical basis for Locke's contention that ideas are capable of informing us about reality. The earlier material is less conspicuous in the explications of sensitive knowledge, a priori knowledge, and empirical inquiry, but it is the ground on which the epistemology stands. The classificatory scheme thereby imparts considerable unity to the main components of the *Essay*'s treatment of human understanding. If readers fail to appreciate the powerfully systematic character of this theory, it is because they mistake the significance of the taxonomy of ideas.[74]

[74] I want to thank the organizers of and participants in the British Society for History of Philosophy conference on Locke in Oxford, 2004, for the chance to present and discuss some material that found its way into this essay. I also thank Lex Newman for helpful comments.

4   Locke's Distinctions between Primary and Secondary Qualities

Is there a distinction between primary and secondary qualities? The question may rest on a confusion. It is not obvious that it would be raised if the questioner knew what he meant by 'primary' and 'secondary' qualities.

There is at least this distinction. We may distinguish between the basic explanatory features of things and the derivative features they explain. In the disciplines that gave rise to chemistry, there's a long tradition of calling the fundamental explanatory qualities or principles 'firsts' (Baeumker 1909; Maier 1968: 17–18; Anstey 2000: 20–30). Aristotle's "first qualities" are hot, cold, dry, and wet; Paracelsus's *tria prima* ('three firsts') are salt, sulphur, and mercury. Boyle was willing to follow Aristotelian usage in calling hot, cold, dry, and wet 'first qualities'; he called what he considered to be the more fundamental attributes of size, shape, motion, and rest *"Primary Modes* of the parts of Matter, since from these simple Attributes or Primordiall Affections all the Qualities are deriv'd" (Boyle [1670] 1999: 6.267).

If Locke were only interested in advocating mechanistic physics, his discussion of primary and secondary qualities would be of marginal interest. Long before the publication of *An Essay concerning Human Understanding*, Boyle offers a defense of the thesis that "allmost all sorts of Qualities...*may* be produced Mechanically – I mean by such Corporeall Agents as do not appear, either to Work otherwise than by vertue of the Motion, Size, Figure, and Contrivance of their own Parts" (Boyle [1666] 1999: 5.302) – that is

---

[1] I thank Lex Newman, Matthew Stuart, Jonathan Walmsley, Martha Bolton, and Walter Ott for very helpful comments.

clearer and more developed than Locke's defense. The account in the *Essay* remains worth careful study because Locke fits the corpuscularianism with an epistemology, a philosophy of mind, a semantics, and a metaphysics.

His use of the expression 'I call' in E II.viii.9 suggests that Locke officially defines primary qualities as "such as are utterly inseparable from the Body." This definition doesn't seem entirely apt for his purposes. Richard Aaron (1971: 126; cf. Jackson 1929: 63–6; Mackie 1976: 20–1) observes that when Locke "first introduces primary qualities in II.viii.9 he seems to be thinking of them not as *determinates*, if I may use W. E. Johnson's terminology, but as *determinables*, not as particular shapes, for instance, but as shape in general." Determinate figures such as Locke's examples "Circle or Square" (E II.viii.18: 138) don't count as primary by his official definition unless we tacitly assume that qualities also count as primary if they are determinations of inseparable determinable qualities. Moreover, motion seems to be an intelligible, explanatory, yet separable quality by his lights. Locke can only get it to count as inseparable by putting it under the gerrymandered determinable quality *motion or rest* (R. Wilson 2002: 223).[2] If that gerrymandered quality is legitimate, then so are *transparent or colored* and *tasty or insipid*. Even so, the definition and the example that he uses to motivate it help to justify his theses that primary qualities are amenable to rational inference and that they are not powers to produce ideas in us.

Locke's use of the expression 'I call' in E II.viii.10 suggests that he officially defines secondary qualities as "Powers to produce various Sensations in us." The wider philosophical community calls this the Lockean account of secondary qualities, and I myself agree that we should accept this definition as definitive. There are, however, at least two weighty reasons for hesitating.

The first is that it seems indistinguishable from what seems to be his official definition of quality: "the Power to produce any *Idea* in our mind, I call *Quality* of the Subject wherein that power is" (E II. viii.8: 134). Locke offers, by way of illustration, "a Snow-ball having the power to produce in us the *Ideas* of *White, Cold*, and *Round*, the Powers to produce those *Ideas* in us, as they are in the Snow-Ball, I

---

[2] Anstey (2000: 46) observes that Boyle "wavers" on the inseparability of motion ([1666] 1999: 5.307).

call *Qualities*" (ibid.). Assuming that not all qualities are secondary qualities, commentators have some explaining to do. The problem splits those scholars who take his definition of qualities as powers to produce ideas in us seriously (Curley 1972: §3; Bolton 1976a: 306–7; Campbell 1980: 568–70; Alexander 1985: 165) from those who treat it as a mere slip (Jackson 1929: 71; Maier 1968: 65; Cummins 1975: 408–10; Mackie 1976: 11–12; Stuart 2003: 70). I am more sympathetic to the second group, but, in the spirit of compromise, I'll later describe two Lockean senses of power. In one of these senses, secondary qualities are powers; in the other, primary qualities are.

Here's a second reason for doubting that Locke genuinely intends to define secondary qualities as powers to produce sensations in us. Locke gives various examples of secondary qualities, including three in the passage where he seems to define them: "Colours, Sounds, Tasts, *etc.*" (E II.viii.10). And, while these examples are never offered as if they are exhaustive, one might doubt that there is any principled difference to be drawn between the power to produce the idea of red and the power to produce the idea of oblong. Why should our ideas of color pick out mere powers to produce ideas in us, while our ideas of shape pick out intrinsic, mind-independent qualities?

To answer this question is to unpack the argument of *Essay* II. viii. From an argument for a physical hypothesis, Locke draws conclusions about how our ideas represent. From that physical hypothesis and his theory of representation, he draws metaphysical conclusions about primary and secondary qualities. Because Locke believes that primary qualities are explanatory and that secondary qualities are not, he concludes that our ideas of primary qualities resemble and that our ideas of secondary qualities do not. Because our ideas of primary qualities resemble and our ideas of secondary qualities do not, he concludes that our ideas of primary qualities represent intrinsic, mind-independent, real qualities and that our ideas of secondary qualities represent powers to produce ideas in us.

Locke draws more than one distinction here; he wants to convince his reader that they overlap. If we oversimplify and try to boil his theses down to one essential distinction, his discussion loses part of its depth. The distinctions are:

1   Primary qualities are explanatory; secondary qualities are not deeply explanatory.

2   Ideas of primary qualities resemble something in bodies; ideas of secondary qualities do not.

3   Primary qualities are not dispositions; secondary qualities are dispositions to produce ideas in us.

4   The genera of primary qualities are inseparable from bodies; the genera of secondary qualities are separable.

5   Primary qualities belong to bodies as they are in themselves; secondary qualities do not.

6   Primary qualities, with the possible exception of some sorts of velocity, are real beings; secondary qualities are not.

Let me explain these six contrasts in some more detail.

FIRST DISTINCTION, PART I: PRIMARY QUALITIES ARE EXPLANATORY

Defending corpuscularianism is not the primary business of Locke's *Essay*, but it still contains arguments that a body "performs its Operations" through "the Mechanical affections" (E IV.iii.25: 556) of its microphysical parts. In particular, Locke argues that "Powers to produce various Sensations in us" work "by their *primary Qualities, i.e.* by the Bulk, Figure, Texture, and Motion of their insensible parts" (E II.viii.10: 135; cf. §§23, 26).

In §§11–14 of Book II, Chapter viii, Locke defends a corpuscularian theory of perception as follows. Bodies affect our sense organs through impulse, since alternative forms of corporeal interaction are inconceivable. When we perceive bodies at a distance, they affect our senses. Thus, there must be intermediate bodies between us and the perceived bodies. These intermediate bodies are imperceptible and so, presumably, too small to be perceived (McCann 1994: 62). To those who object that his explanation is vitiated by its postulation of an inconceivable, divinely instituted connection between motions in our sense organs and ideas of color and smell in our minds, Locke replies that it is "no more impossible, to conceive, that God should annex such *Ideas* to such Motions, with which they have no similitude; than that he should annex the *Idea* of Pain to the motion of a piece of Steel dividing our Flesh, with which that *Idea* hath no resemblance" (E II.viii.13: 136–7). Locke borrows this violent analogy from Descartes (Descartes 1984: I: 284; Maier 1968: 49–50, 66).

In E II.viii.21, after this initial defense of a corpuscularian the
of perception, Locke argues that it allows us "to give an Accou.
how the same Water, at the same time, may produce the *Idea*
Cold by one Hand, and of Heat by the other," when we've heate
one hand and cooled the other. On the hypothesis that "the Sen
sation of Heat and Cold, be nothing but the increase or diminution
of the motion of the minute Parts of our Bodies"[3] – that is, if sensations are determined by a change in the velocity of the particles in
our nerves – then the phenomenon "is easie to be understood" (cf.
W III: 328). The hypothesis is hinted at by Bacon ([1620] 2000: 126,
131), asserted by Descartes (1984: III: 66; [1637] 2001: 266), and
developed at length by Boyle ([1673] 1999: VII: 345–6, 350–4;
Woolhouse 1983: 150–2). When one hand is heated and the other
cooled, plunging both hands into the same water will speed up the
particles in one hand and slow down the particles in the other.
Edwin Curley (1972: 458) and J. L. Mackie (1976: 22–3) construe this
straightforwardly as an argument to the best explanation for a piece
of corpuscularianism.

In illustrating inference by analogy, Locke offers another defense
of a corpuscularian account of heat, this one concerned with heat
insofar as it is a mind-independent phenomenon. He writes,
"observing that the bare rubbing of two Bodies violently one upon
another, produces heat, and very often fire it self, we have reason to
think, that what we call Heat and Fire, consists in a violent agita-
tion of the imperceptible minute parts of the burning matter" (E IV.
xvi.12: 665–6). The analogy is between heat and fire that are
obviously caused by motion and heat and fire with an unknown
cause. Tendentiously, Locke moves from the premise that rubbing
macroscopic bodies *produces* heat and fire in some cases to the
conclusion that heat and fire *consist* in the violent motion of
imperceptible parts.

Often, Locke's analogies illustrate and justify his belief that
microphysical primary qualities explain the biological and chemical
capacities of bodies. Death is like the stopping of a clock through
the filing of a gear; sleep is like the stopping of a clock through
placing a piece of paper on the balance; dissolving a metal with an

---

[3] At the end of this sentence, Locke gives what I think is his considered view: the
sensations of heat and cold "depend" on increases and decreases of motion.

acid is like opening a lock with a key (E IV.iii.25: 556); the internal structure of a human being is like the internal structure of the clock at Strasbourg (E III.vi.3: 440; Woolhouse 1983: 99–103; cf. Laudan 1966). Generally speaking, Locke thinks that mechanical explanations work for artifacts. He insinuates that similar explanations would work in the natural world, if we could perceive the real essences of natural objects.

As we have seen, according to Locke, secondary qualities depend on primary qualities. Let me defer the question of whether he thinks that secondary qualities are explanatory at all until I have more pieces of his metaphysics on the table.

SECOND DISTINCTION, PART I: IDEAS OF PRIMARY QUALITIES RESEMBLE SOMETHING IN BODIES

Locke feels the need to explain his digression into "Physical Enquiries" in a book devoted to the study of human understanding (E II.viii.22: 140). He makes this detour in part to establish something about the relation between our ideas and the external world, a central topic of Book II of the *Essay* (Maier 1968: 64; Bolton 1983: 359). After advancing his account of perception, he writes,

From whence I think it is easie to draw this Observation, That the *Ideas of primary Qualities* of Bodies, *are Resemblances* of them, and their Patterns do really exist in the Bodies themselves; but the *Ideas, produced* in us *by* these *Secondary Qualities, have no resemblance* of them at all. (E II.viii.15: 137)

St. Thomas, a target here, had written, "colors are on a wall, the resemblances [*similitudines*] of which are in the sight" (ST 1a 76 A1; Cohen 1982); Descartes, an ally here, classified his previous beliefs that there is something in bodies "exactly resembling" our ideas of heat, colors, and tastes among his "ill-considered judgements" (Descartes [1641] 1984: II: 56–7; M. Wilson 1994)

Today, some commentators think it is so obvious that ideas cannot resemble bodies that they insist on reinterpreting philosophers who write that some ideas do. Jonathan Bennett (1982) states this position with special vigor. For Locke, they have argued, an idea resembles a quality in the corresponding thing just in case the scholastic theory of perception applies to that idea (Woolhouse 1983: 159–61; Heyd 1994; McCann 1994: 63–4), or if the quality helps to explain the production of the idea (Bennett 1971: 106; Curley 1972: §5; Cummins 1975: 402–5), or if the thing has the quality that the idea represents it as having (Woozley 1964: 32–5), or if just one fine structure corresponds to the simple idea (Campbell 1980: 582). In my opinion (Jacovides 1999: §2.1), these readings either stretch the meaning of 'resemblance' too far or don't completely fit Locke's text (but cf. Hill 2004).

I think, following Thomas Reid ([1764] 1877: 1.131), Hilary Putnam (1981: 57–8), Michael Ayers (1991: I: 63–5), and Kenneth Winkler (1992: 154–6), that the best reading of Locke's theses takes them literally. However few philosophers today think that ideas can resemble bodies, in the seventeenth century the doctrine was commonplace. More specifically, it was a common doctrine that sense production causes a corporeal image somewhere in the head (Descartes [1637] 2001: 87–105; Willis [1661–64] 1980: 139). Though Locke is agnostic about the relation between matter and ideas (E I.i.2: 43–4; Acworth 1971: 10), this background shows that we can't just dismiss a literal reading as uncharitable. Moreover, other texts support a literal reading (E II.viii.18: 138; E II.ix.8: 145; E II.xvi.1: 205; E IV.iv.6: 565).

Whatever Locke means by 'resemblance', the relation is one of the two ways that he believes that ideas can represent external objects. The other way is by brute causal connection. According to Locke, since the mind can't make simple ideas on its own, they "must necessarily be the product of Things operating on the Mind in a natural way, and producing therein those Perceptions which by the Wisdom and Will of our Maker they are ordained and adapted to" (E IV.iv.4: 563–4). In Ayers's apt phrase (1991: I: 62), some of our simple ideas are mere 'blank effects' of their causes. Though they do represent the outside world by signaling various features of it, the connection isn't intelligible: they "can, by us, be no way deduced from bodily Causes, nor any correspondence or connexion be found between them and those primary Qualities which (Experience shews us) produce them in us" (E IV.iii.28: 559; cf. E IV.iii.13: 545; McCann 1994: 69–72). Thus, they don't give any insight into the nature of the causes.

According to Locke, resemblance allows us to represent external objects in a way that preserves the truth of theorems: "Is it true of the *idea* of a *Triangle*, that its three Angles are equal to two right ones? It is true also of a *Triangle*, wherever it really exists" (E IV. iv.6: 565). Not only does resemblance give him a second mechanism for mental representation, it also gives the possibility of something more than the mere awareness of the presence of some external quality; resembling ideas give the possibility of an intelligible grasp of the workings of external objects (Downing 1998: 388–9 note 15).

Once we realize that Locke believes that only resembling ideas can underwrite an accurate, explanatory physical theory, we can understand his inference from his corpuscularian theory of causation to his resemblance theses in §15. Consider first the reasoning behind the positive resemblance thesis. Assume that Locke's argument for a corpuscularian theory of perception succeeds and yields a right and intelligible account of the external world. If we can have right and intelligible theories only on the condition that our ideas of the explanatory qualities of that theory resemble those qualities, then it follows that our ideas of the explanatory qualities of corpuscularianism (that is, our ideas of primary qualities) resemble those qualities (Alexander 1985: 195–6).

SECOND DISTINCTION, PART II: IDEAS OF SECONDARY QUALITIES DON'T RESEMBLE ANYTHING IN BODIES

Because Locke believes that ideas are the immediate object of the understanding (E II.viii.8: 134) and because he worries whether and how our ideas represent external objects, he believes that there ought to be a presumption against thinking that our ideas resemble external things. He defends this presumption in the three sections immediately following his statement of his resemblance theses. In what follows, I'll take Locke's talk of 'ideas being in things' to be another way of saying that the idea resembles something in the object. This reading fits the texts and his marginal summary of the passages including §§16–18. It also has Locke defending a position that is substantial, controversial, and (by his lights) true.

In all three sections, he compares ideas of secondary qualities to pain (Atherton 1992: 118; McCann 1994: 65–6). He borrows Descartes's thought experiment of walking closer and closer to a fire (Descartes [1641] 1984: II: 57; Maier 1968: 49, 66) to show that the idea of warmth is as likely to resemble external objects as the idea of pain.[4] According to Locke, this similarity establishes a presumption that ideas of warmth and ideas of pain stand in the same relation to the outside world. Someone considering such a fire, "ought to bethink himself, what Reason he has to say, That his *Idea* of *Warmth*, which was produced in him by the Fire, is actually *in the Fire*; and his *Idea* of *Pain*, which the same Fire produced in him the same way, is *not* in the *Fire*" (E II.viii.16: 137). There's no such reason, Locke believes, and without some such, we ought to say that neither our idea of warmth nor our idea of pain resembles something in the fire.

He next compares the ideas of whiteness and cold that snow produces with the pain it can also produce (E II.viii.16: 137), and the ideas of whiteness and sweetness with the pain and sickness that a laxative produces (E II.viii.18: 138), both times challenging his opponent to give "some Reason to explain" (ibid.) the difference between the two cases that justifies thinking that ideas of secondary qualities, but not ideas of pain, resemble something in bodies (Rickless 1997: 311–12).

So Locke has a presumption against believing that ideas resemble something in bodies. He thinks that ideas of primary qualities overcome that presumption, since they are elements of the most intelligible theory that explains the workings of bodies, and he thinks that the only way that a theory could intelligibly explain the workings of bodies is if our ideas resemble the explanatory qualities in that theory. No similar argument is available to overcome the presumption that ideas of secondary qualities do not resemble anything in bodies, so Locke concludes that they don't.

Consider in this light Locke's diagnosis of why people mistakenly think that the causes of our ideas of secondary qualities resemble those ideas. When we see the sun burn a fair face or whiten a lump of wax, "we cannot imagine, that to be the Reception or Resemblance of any thing in the Sun, because we find not those different Colours in the Sun it self" (E II.viii.25: 142; cf. Palmer 1974: 44–5). By contrast, "our Senses, not being able to discover any unlikeness between the *Idea* produced in us, and the Quality of the Object producing it, we are apt to imagine that our *Ideas* are resemblances of something in the Objects" (ibid.). We can't

---

[4] Locke offers a teleological explanation of the phenomenon at E II.vii.4.

compare our ideas of things and the things themselves, since the ideas get in the way (Palmer 1974: 46). Locke's diagnosis, like his main argument, requires a veil of ideas to generate the presumption that our ideas don't resemble external objects.

Another argument for the conclusion that ideas of secondary qualities don't resemble anything in bodies is worth mentioning. When Locke presents the example of water seeming hot and cold in his Second Reply to Stillingfleet, there's no mention of corpuscularianism, just an argument that it's impossible for ideas of hot and cold to be "the likenesses and the very resemblances of something in the same water, since the same water could not be capable of having at the same time such real contrarieties" (W IV: 399). If, as Aristotle said (GC 329b19), hot and cold are contraries, then they can't both be in the water (Heyd 1994: 27). If we further assume that both hands have been stressed equally by unusual temperatures, there's no reason to think that the idea produced by one and only one hand resembles something in the water (Bolton 1983: 365–6; Rickless 1997: 317–18). Still, this point can't be directly generalized to cases where our sense organs aren't distressed (Aaron 1971: 120), and Locke doesn't explicitly make that generalization either at E II. viii.21 or in the Stillingfleet correspondence.

THIRD DISTINCTION, PART I: SECONDARY QUALITIES ARE DISPOSITIONS TO PRODUCE IDEAS IN US

Locke defines 'secondary qualities' as "Such *Qualities*, which in truth are nothing in the Objects themselves, but Powers to produce various Sensations in us by their *primary Qualities*" (E II.viii.10: 135). He defines 'quality' as "the Power to produce any *Idea* in our mind" (E II.viii.8: 134). Which of these definitions should we take more seriously? What was Locke thinking when he offered these strangely overlapping definitions? Why does he believe that secondary qualities are nothing but powers to produce ideas in us?

With respect to the first question, there are at least three reasons to take the definition of secondary qualities more seriously. First, only it is supported by other texts. If the definitions in §§8 and 10 were both deleted, we would have no idea that Locke ever considered primary qualities to be powers, but we would have plenty of texts where he declares secondary qualities to be powers (e.g., E II.

xxiii.8: 300; E II.xxxi.2: 375–6), including passages in Book II, Chapter viii where he is contrasting secondary qualities with primary ones (e.g., §§15, 22–3, 26; Stuart 2003: 70). Second, Locke denies that primary qualities are powers by writing, "the simple *Ideas* whereof we make our complex ones of Substances, are all of them (bating only the figure and Bulk of some sorts) Powers" (E II. xxxi.8: 381; Stuart 2003: 70 – 'bating' means 'with the exception of').[5] Third, as I'll show, we can easily reconstruct a sound argument against the thesis that primary qualities are powers to produce ideas in us from materials that Locke provides us. Sound arguments for interesting conclusions are so rare in philosophy that I would hate to think that he stumbled across one without realizing it.

Even though Locke's definition of quality as a power to produce ideas doesn't cohere with the rest of the *Essay*, I think that something can be said about why he offered it. He uses the word 'power' in two different ways (Leibniz 1981: 216, Jacovides 2003: 332–3).[6] His usual sense of 'power' is deflationary. On this account, powers are merely capacities to do things and not explanatory entities. We might call these bare powers (cf. E II.viii.25) or dispositions. To say that a bare power such as "the *digestive* Faculty" answers the question "what it was that digested the Meat in our Stomachs . . . is, in short to say, That the ability to digest, digested" (E II.xxi.20: 243–4). A different, explanatory notion of power shows up at E II. xxii.11. Locke there asserts, "*Power* being the Source from whence all Action proceeds, the Substances wherein these Powers are, when they exert this Power into Act, are called *Causes*." We might call these robust powers.

When Locke characterizes qualities as powers to produce ideas in us, he is mixing bare powers and robust powers (Bolton 2001: 111). Primary qualities are powers in the sense that they are responsible for producing the relevant ideas. A body produces sensations "*by* Reason of *its* insensible *primary Qualities*" (E II.viii.23: 140).

---

[5] According to Alexander (1985: 166), Locke's point here is only that some sorts of substances don't include shapes in their abstract ideas. The passage makes clear that he thinks that shapes are in our ideas of some sorts and not in others, but what Locke asserts is that all of the ideas in our abstract ideas of substantial sorts are powers except for our ideas of figure and bulk (Stuart 2003: 94–5 note 24).

[6] Three, if you count the normative sense of 'power' in E II.xxviii.3 and in *The Second Treatise of Government*, §3.

Secondary qualities are powers in the sense that having a secondary quality entirely consists in being able to produce a certain idea in perceivers. Such powers don't give a serious explanation of the corresponding actuality.

Locke's occasional suggestions that he uses the word 'quality' loosely need to be understood in light of its traditional status in the table of categories. He tells us that features that enter the mind through more than one sense, such as "Extension, Number, Motion, Pleasure, and Pain," aren't classed as qualities "in its ordinary acception" (E III.iv.16: 428). His point is they were traditionally classed as quantities, actions, and passions. Rickless (1997: 302) argues that the problem with the excluded features is that they aren't powers, but that wasn't the ordinary usage of 'quality'. According to Locke, powers to affect bodies have as much right to be called qualities as secondary qualities (E II.viii.10: 135). His point is that a scrupulous metaphysician might class them as relatives (cf. Jackson 1929: 61–2).

Locke's clearest exposition of the hybrid nature of his conception of qualities comes in a memorandum at the end of Draft A of the *Essay*. He first stipulates that when he speaks of ideas existing out in the world, he means what is "the cause of that perception. & is supposed to be resembled by it." Of such a cause, he tells us, "this also I call quality. whereby I meane anything existing without us which affecting any of our senses produces any simple Idea in us" (Draft A 95: D I: 82–3). These qualities are supposed to be resemblances, and they affect our senses, so we may think of this passage as an early description of primary qualities.

Locke goes on to define 'quality' in its application to what we may recognize as secondary and tertiary qualities:[7] "because the powers or capacitys of things which too are all conversant about simple Ideas, are considerd in the nature of the thing & make up a part of that complex Idea we have of them therefor I call those also qualities" (Draft A 95: D I: 83). Powers or capacities are counted as qualities because people think that they are parts of the natures of

---

[7] 'Tertiary quality' is what commentators call Locke's "third sort" of quality (E II. viii.10: 135), which he describes as "The *Power* that is in any body, *by* Reason of the particular Constitution of *its primary Qualities, to* make such a *change* in the *Bulk, Figure, Texture, and Motion of another Body,* as to make it operate on our Senses, differently from what it did before" (E II.viii.23: 140).

things and because the corresponding ideas are constituents of our complex ideas. By saying that he "also" calls powers 'qualities', Locke implicitly contrasts powers with the first sort of qualities.

He then somewhat artificially distinguishes between primary and secondary qualities on the one hand, and what his commentators will call tertiary qualities:

> destinguish qualities into actuall & potential v:g: all the actuall qualitys in salt are those which any way affect our senses being duely applied to them & soe cause simple Ideas in us as its tast colour smell & tangible qualitys. the potentiall qualitys in it are all the alteration it can of its actual qualitys receive from any thing else, or all the alteration it can make in other things v:g solution in water, fusion in a strong fire corrosion of Iron &c. (ibid.)

Powers that would affect our senses if duly applied count as actual qualities here. Judging by his examples, potential qualities are either capacities to be affected or capacities to affect things other than the senses.

Martha Brandt Bolton describes Locke's contrast between "actual" and "potential qualities" and rightly concludes, "This is surely not the doctrine of primary and secondary qualities" (1976a: 308). Jonathan Walmsley quotes Locke's proto-description of primary qualities and writes, "Locke put all the attributes of bodies and the respective ideas they caused in us on an equal footing" (2004: 31). Indeed, the passages they quote don't draw the distinction between primary and secondary qualities, but nearby lines in the memorandum do draw a distinction between the causes of our ideas and mere powers or capacities.

In Draft A, the purportedly resembling causes of our ideas, what he came to call primary qualities, are not called powers.[8] This two-part

---

[8] In correspondence, Walmsley emphasizes that the resemblance is merely supposed and that in the corresponding passage in Draft B (178: D I: 164), the resemblance is "vulgarly supposed." Let me suggest that the difference between the draft treatments and the published treatment of resemblance is connected with a change in Locke's account of primary qualities. In the drafts, the first sort of quality comprises whatever causes our sensations; the resemblance comparison is between cause and effect; and the vulgar often mistakenly suppose a resemblance between an idea and its cause. In the published version of the *Essay*, the first sort of quality comprises the inseparable qualities of bodies and their determinations; the comparison is between those qualities and the ideas that best represent those

definition is revised into a glib patchwork definition, in both Draft C (quoted in Aaron 1971: 69–70) and in the published version, where we are left with the brief and misleading description of a quality as "the Power to produce any *Idea* in our mind" (E II.viii.8: 134).

If Draft A is the frame upon which the *Essay* was built (and it is), then secondary and tertiary qualities are bare powers. Why does Locke believe that our ideas of secondary qualities represent mere capacities? Recall that Locke believes that the redness, the squeakiness, and the sourness that you find in your ideas don't resemble anything out in the world. He would not, however, be at all happy to say that our judgments about color, sound, smell, and taste are all false. He wants our ideas of secondary qualities to provide us with knowledge (E IV.iv.4: 563–4), and he recognizes that ordinary judgments about these qualities allow us to distinguish objects for our uses (E II.xxxii.15: 389). These antiskeptical and pragmatic attitudes push him to interpret ordinary utterances about secondary qualities so that they come out right. According to Locke, we can do that by analyzing secondary qualities as powers: "if Sugar produce in us the *Ideas*, which we call Whiteness, and Sweetness, we are sure there is a power in Sugar to produce those *Ideas* in our Minds, or else they could not have been produced by it" (E II.xxxi.2: 375; Ayers 1991: I: 38–9).

Locke draws the consequence that there would be no "Imputation of *Falshood* to our simple *Ideas, if* by the different Structure of our Organs, it were so ordered, That *the same Object should produce in several Men's Minds different* Ideas at the same time" (E II. xxxii.15: 389). According to Locke, "all things that exist are only particulars" (E III.iii.6: 410). The relevant idea that determines whether an object is to be called 'red' is thus only a particular idea in the speaker's head, and this can't steer us wrong, no matter what's inside the heads of others (Ayers 1991: I: 207–9).

Because Locke thinks that primary qualities are inseparable from bodies, he believes that primary qualities aren't powers to produce ideas in us. I'll discuss his argument for that conclusion after I've discussed his inseparability theses.

---

qualities; and Locke himself believes that those ideas resemble those qualities. For Walmsley's different view of the matter, see Walmsley 2004: 28–31.

FOURTH DISTINCTION, PART I: THE GENERA OF PRIMARY
QUALITIES ARE INSEPARABLE FROM BODIES

Locke advances four propositions about the inseparability of primary qualities at the beginning of E II.viii.9. Primary qualities are (1) "such as are utterly inseparable from the Body, in what estate soever it be," (2) "such as in all the alterations and changes it suffers, all the force can be used upon it, it constantly keeps," (3) "such as Sense constantly finds in every particle of matter, which has bulk enough to be perceived," and (4) such as "the Mind finds inseparable from every particle of matter, though less than to make it self singly be perceived by our Senses."[9] Thesis three is clearly an a posteriori claim. Thesis one seems to summarize the theses that follow.

The epistemic status of theses two and four is controversial. Some argue that they are trifling, that is, mere enunciations of the qualities in the abstract idea of body (Bennett 1971: 90; Davidson and Hornstein 1984: 285; Atherton 1992: 115; Downing 1998: 401–3). In favor of this, we may observe that Locke's rejection of *de re* inseparability (E III.vi.4: 440) seems to contradict any other reading. On the other hand, this account doesn't fit with the brevity of Locke's descriptions of the constituents of the abstract idea of body (at E II.xiii.11: 171; E II.xxiii.22: 307; E III.vi.33: 460; E III.x.15: 498; and E IV.vii.13: 604), nor with his implication that the result of pounding a body with "all the force that can be used upon it" will still have primary qualities (E II.viii.9: 134). Moreover, it would be odd for Locke to put so much effort into justifying what would be, by his lights, a trifling thesis.

Arnold Davidson and Norbert Hornstein and Robert Wilson rightly emphasize Locke's use of transdiction, that is, his inference from perceptible cases to imperceptible cases. They (Davidson and Hornstein 1984: 285–9; Wilson 2002: 204–11), however, restrict the inference to mere inductive extrapolation: in perceptible cases, bodies have primary qualities, so they probably have them in imperceptible cases as well. McCann (1994: 61–2, 65) considers the inference to be substantive yet known independently of experience (in Lockean terms, a nontrifling proposition, known through intuition or demonstration).

---

[9] My enumeration follows R. Wilson 2002: 203.

Locke defends his inference as follows:

For division (which is all that a Mill, or pestel, or any other Body, does upon another, in reducing it to insensible parts) can never take away either Solidity, Extension, figure, or mobility from any Body, but only makes two, or more distinct separate masses of Matter, of that which was but one before. (E II.viii.9: 135)

The modal expression 'can never' suggests that McCann is right, since, as Kant once said, experience tells us what is, but not that it is necessarily. The inseparability Locke asks us to consider in E II. viii.9 is something like the connections between primary qualities that he describes in E II.xxiii.17, E III.x.15, and E IV.iii.14, and even more like the processes that he says that watchmakers and lock-smiths can make without trial in E IV.iii.25 (cf. Winkler 1992: 153–4).

THIRD DISTINCTION, PART II: PRIMARY QUALITIES ARE NOT DISPOSITIONS TO PRODUCE IDEAS IN US

Locke chooses the example of wheat with imperceptible particles in mind. Ground wheat is flour, of course, and since flour is a powder, it is difficult to see the features of its smallest constituents. If a perceiver's vision is weak enough or if the flour is very well ground, then each of the smallest particles in the flour is "less than to make it self singly be perceived by our Senses" (E II.viii.9: 135). Though we cannot perceive these particles with the naked eye, Locke believes that reason tells us that these small particles exist and that, no matter how small, they possess primary qualities (Maier 1968: 64). Here Locke follows Democritus (A37 Barnes 1987: 247), Descartes ([1644] 1984: I: 286–87), and Boyle ([1666] 1999: 5.307; Aaron 1971: 121–2).

Locke's concern to show that imperceptible particles possess primary qualities should be seen as part of a tacit argument for the thesis that primary qualities are not dispositions to produce ideas in us. If all imperceptible bodies possess primary qualities, then those primary qualities are not dispositions to produce ideas in us, since imperceptible bodies have no such dispositions (Cummins 1975: 409–10; Stuart 2003: 70). For his purposes, Locke tells us, he needs to distinguish the *primary*, and *real Qualities* of Bodies, which are always in them, (*viz.* Solidity, Extension, Figure, Number, and Motion or Rest; and are sometimes perceived by us, *viz.* when the Bodies they are in, are big enough singly to be discerned) from those *secondary* and *imputed Qualities*, which are but the Powers of several Combinations of those primary ones, when they operate, without being distinctly discerned. (E II.viii.22: 140)

The contrast that he wants us to heed is between qualities that are possessed by every material body, including imperceptible ones, and qualities that are not possessed by imperceptible bodies, since those qualities are dispositions to produce ideas in us.

This argument for the separability of powers to produce ideas in us is most convincing if we take the relevant powers to be mere dispositions, but the argument is strong on any plausible construal of 'powers to produce ideas in us'. There is no interesting sense in which a picometer (a trillionth of a meter) is a power to produce the corresponding idea in perceivers. Are we supposed to imagine that, for Locke, a picometer is the power to produce the idea of a meter in humans, when combined with a trillion other particles of the same size? I suppose it's true that picometer-wide corpuscles have that power, but so do smaller particles. I doubt that that or anything like it is his considered analysis of the primary quality.[10]

Bolton thinks of primary qualities as explanatory "causal powers" (1976b: 494). She tries to make Locke's definition of qualities as powers to produce ideas in us compatible with the inseparability of primary qualities from insensible particles by arguing, "The fact that a particle is insensible, however, does not show that it has *no* powers to produce ideas." She offers three reasons: first, "it would produce ideas if suitably magnified" (ibid.). Perhaps and perhaps not, but when Locke defends the inseparability of primary qualities from the fragments of the flour, he surely isn't making a point about the possible capacities of microscopes. We are supposed to divide the grain fragments in thought and conclude that the results possess primary qualities whether or not they have powers to produce ideas in us. If

---

[10] If the example seems anachronistic, Locke's millionth part of a gry (E IV.x.10: 623–4) is about eighty-three picometers. A gry is 1/3,000 the length of a pendulum with a period of one second. For a simple pendulum with a small amplitude, the length of the pendulum should be about twenty-five centimeters.

the flour argument shows anything, it shows that corpuscles possess primary qualities independently of whether they can be seen by any means at all. Next, Bolton argues, "Locke holds that it is by means of the primary qualities of insensible particles that our ideas of colours, odours, etc. *are* produced" (ibid). Fair enough. We should therefore restrict our focus to those corpuscles that are not involved in the production of sensation. "Finally," Bolton argues, "it is because of the primary qualities of insensible particles that a body has its 'tertiary' powers, or powers to cause changes in other bodies, thereby altering the ideas they produce" (ibid.). Generally speaking, however, individual corpuscles make no difference at the level of experience, and Locke believes that primary qualities are inseparable from individual corpuscles, not just inseparable from their aggregates.

Setting aside worries arising out of Locke's misbegotten definition of 'quality', we should be careful to avoid a fallacy. It does not always follow from the premise that a determinable quality F is G that the determinate qualities that fall under F are also G. After all, the determinable quality *extended* is inseparable from bodies, but the determinate quality *one foot tall* is not. Let me go slowly and explicitly, so that we may see that Locke's swift and tacit inference is valid.

Divide the primary qualities into three groups. Begin with those qualities that are determinate and inseparable: solidity and mobility. If imperceptible bodies without any dispositions to produce ideas in us possess these qualities, then these qualities are not dispositions to produce ideas in us. In a second group, include determinate primary qualities that can be possessed by both imperceptibly small bodies and ones that are visibly large. *Sphericity, single, convex everywhere*, and *traveling at ten meters per second* may be possessed by a corpuscle or by a baseball. If a corpuscle does not have any power to produce ideas in us, then none of its qualities is a power to produce ideas in us, no matter where these qualities are instantiated. The remainder are varieties of extension and bulk. Those bodies that are too small to be seen possess different determinate qualities in this group than bodies of perceptible size. However, it would be incredible if *being one meter long* were a bare power to produce ideas in us while *being ten microns long* were not. Lengths and volumes are too homogenous for that to be a serious possibility. Therefore, we may conclude that primary qualities are not essentially dispositions to produce ideas in us.

THIRD DISTINCTION, PART II: THE GENERA OF SECONDARY
QUALITIES ARE SEPARABLE FROM BODIES

In E II.viii.9, Locke argues that portions of matter continue to possess primary qualities, even after they have been pulverized to imperceptible pieces. The complementary thesis is that portions do not continue to possess secondary qualities after they have been pulverized into imperceptible pieces. Secondary qualities are dispositions to produce ideas in us, and imperceptible bodies are imperceptible because they lack such dispositions (Bolton 2001: 111).

Locke makes two other suggestions about the separability of secondary qualities that are worth examining. The first has to do with transparency and flows from Locke's adoption of a Boylean theory of colors. Insipid, silent, odorless, transparent bodies don't fall under any of the genera of secondary qualities (Rickless 1997: 303; Downing 1998: 402–3 note 46). According to Locke, 'insipid' and 'silence' signify the absence of ideas of taste and sound (E II. viii.5: 133; Woolhouse 1983: 150).

One might have thought that transparency was the least common of these privative attributes, but Locke suspects that, viewed with sufficiently strong lenses, everything is transparent. There are three reasons for thinking that he believes this. First, in discussing the role of analogy in natural philosophy, he offers as examples the production of colors by "the different refraction of pellucid Bodies" (he must have in mind prisms and the like) and the production of color by different arrangement of "watered Silk." (The latter phenomenon is actually produced by diffraction, though Locke couldn't have known that.) He concludes "that the Colour and shining of Bodies, is in them nothing but the different Arangement and Refraction of their minute and insensible parts" (E IV.xvi.12: 665–6), that is to say, in something like the way different arrangements of prisms produce colors.

Second, in discussing the possibility of microscopical eyes, Locke supposes that if we could see much better, the colors that we see would "disappear" and be replaced with "an admirable Texture of parts of a certain Size and Figure" (E II.xxiii.11: 301). His examples from the microscope intended to illustrate his thesis (sand, pounded glass, hair, and blood) are all cases in which an object that looks entirely colored under ordinary conditions turns out to be either entirely or mostly transparent when viewed under a microscope (Maier 1968: 66–7). Third, Boyle had observed, "multitudes of Bodies, there are, whose Fragments seem Opacous to the naked Eye, which yet, when I have included them in good *Microscopes*, appear'd Transparent" ([1664] 1999: 4.52; C. Wilson 1995: 230), and tentatively suggested that this might be true universally. Locke often borrowed physical doctrines wholesale from Boyle. Indeed, this is an interesting case of borrowing a near-contradiction, since the doctrine that all color is the result of refraction and that every body is transparent under sufficient magnification seems to be in some tension with corpuscularianism. The smallest corpuscles themselves can't be transparent, one might have thought, since transparent objects let light pass through them.[11]

One final way in which Locke believes that secondary qualities might be separated from bodies is by removing all perceivers from the world:

were there no fit Organs to receive the impressions Fire makes on the Sight and touch; nor a Mind joined to those Organs to receive the *Ideas* of Light and Heat, by those impressions from the Fire, or the Sun, there would yet be no more Light, or Heat in the World, than there would be pain if there were no sensible Creature to feel it, though the Sun should continue just as it is now, and Mount *Ætna* flame higher than it ever did. (E II.xxxi.2: 376)

Alexander (1985: 176) argues that in this context, 'light' and 'heat' refer to ideas. I'm not inclined to agree (nor is Rickless [1997: 303–4]), but, even if Alexander were right, the doctrine that powers to produce ideas in animals would vanish if all the animals vanished follows from Locke's metaphysical premises.

According to Locke, "*Powers* are Relations" (E II.xxi.19: 243; cf. E II.xxxi.8: 381; Boyle [1671] 1999: 6.521–2; Anstey 2000: 86–7). He also asserts that relations cease to obtain whenever one of the relata ceases to exist: "if either of those things be removed, or cease to be,

---

[11] Newton develops this tension in a fruitful way, building on the proposition that "the least parts of almost all natural Bodies are in some measure transparent: And the Opacity of those Bodies ariseth from the multitude of Reflexions caused in their internal Parts. That this is so has been observed by others and will easily be granted by them that have been conversant with Microscopes" (*Opticks*, Book 2, Pt. 3, Prop. 2, Thackray 1968).

the Relation ceases, and the Denomination consequent to it, though the other receive in it self no alteration at all" (E II.xxv.5: 321). I doubt that either of these premises is universally true: the capacity to grow is a power in Locke's dominant sense but not a relation, and I don't think that Bridget Fonda ceased to be Henry Fonda's granddaughter when Henry ceased to exist. Still, those assumptions, along with Locke's thesis that secondary qualities are powers to produce ideas in us, entail that secondary qualities are separable from bodies by eliminating us, which is what Galileo ([1623] 1957: 274) had concluded.[12]

FIFTH DISTINCTION, PART I: SECONDARY QUALITIES DO NOT
BELONG TO BODIES AS THEY ARE IN THEMSELVES

Lucretius argued from the variable colors of objects that they had no color in the dark (*De Rerum Natura* 2.799–809; Guerlac 1986: 10). Sextus Empiricus appealed to variable appearances as a mode of bringing about the suspension of judgment (*Outlines of Pyrrhonism* 1.91–9; Bolton 1983). Locke argues from the variable appearances of the colors in porphyry to the conclusion that those colors don't belong to porphyry as it is in itself. Actually, his main conclusion is, once again, that ideas of colors don't resemble anything in the stone, but, in my judgment, the subconclusion that colors don't represent intrinsic qualities of porphyry is more interesting.

   Locke asks us to

consider the red and white colours in *Porphyre*: Hinder light but from striking on it, and its Colours Vanish; it no longer produces any such *Ideas* in us: Upon the return of Light, it produces these appearances on us again. Can anyone think any real alterations are made in the *Porphyre*, by the presence or absence of Light; and that those *Ideas* of whiteness and redness, are really in *Porphyre* in the light, when 'tis plain *it has no colour in the dark*? It has, indeed, such a Configuration of Particles, both Night and Day, as are apt by the Rays of Light rebounding from some parts of that hard Stone, to produce in us the *Idea* of redness, and from others the *Idea* of whiteness: But whiteness or redness are not in it at any time, but such a texture, that hath the power to produce such a sensation in us. (E II.viii.19: 139)

[12] Boyle's view of the question is slippery ([1666] 1999: 5.309–22) and much discussed (Jackson 1929: 59–60; Curley 1972: §4; Alexander 1985: 70–84; Anstey 2000: Chapter 4).

I would reconstruct his premises as follows:

1   Porphyry is red and white in the light.

He asks us to consider the red and white colors in porphyry and says that they vanish when we obstruct the light.

2   Porphyry is not red and white in the dark.

Locke tells us that porphyry "has no colour in the dark." According to Samuel Rickless (1997: 315), Locke just assumes that bodies lack colors in the dark, and this assumption saps the argument's persuasive force. I think rather that the argument turns on peculiarities of porphyry, a slightly reddish rock with little crystals in it. Up close, the crystals look white, and observers can see the reddish color. At a moderate distance, even in good light, the stone looks merely grey.

The third premise is

3   Neither the presence nor the absence of light causes a real alteration in porphyry.

This is the obvious assertoric content of the rhetorical question "Can anyone think any real alterations are made in the Porphyre, by the presence or absence of light?"

Peter Geach (1994: 71–2) calls the following proposition the Cambridge criterion of change: "The thing called 'x' has changed if we have 'F(x) at time t' true and 'F(x) at time t^{1}' false, for some interpretation of 'F', 't', and 't^{1}'." Geach calls a thing's meeting the Cambridge criterion without really changing 'a mere Cambridge change', as when the number five ceases to be the number of someone's children. The premises just reviewed amount to saying that porphyry loses its red and white colors in a mere Cambridge change (cf. Heyd 1994: 22–3). Behind Locke's claim that porphyry doesn't really change when the light is blocked off must be something like the following dependency thesis: if a body undergoes a real change from being F to not being F, that change must depend on a change in constitution or on a change in fundamental explanatory qualities.[13] Hindering light from striking a rock doesn't do either of those things.

---

[13] To avoid circularity, the fundamental explanatory qualities may be given by other considerations, such as the ones that Locke offers. A change in those qualities is

There are two more principles that Locke tacitly relies upon to get from the premises to the conclusion. The first is a representational principle:

4   If an idea resembles a quality in a body, then the quality belongs to the thing as it is in itself.

Locke believes that only resembling ideas represent things as they are in themselves (Goldstick 1986; Downing 1998: 389–2). He writes,

the greatest part of the *Ideas*, that make our complex *Idea* of *Gold*, are Yellowness, great Weight, Ductility, Fusibility, and Solubility, in *Aqua Regia*, etc. all united together in an unknown *Substratum*; all which *Ideas*, are nothing else, but so many relations to other Substances; and are not really in the Gold, considered barely in it self. (E II.xxiii.37: 317)

Earlier, I argued that we should interpret Locke's writing of 'ideas not being in things' as meaning that the ideas don't resemble anything in the things. Given that interpretation, Locke here asserts that most of our ideas in the complex idea of gold represent relational features and don't resemble anything in the gold. This suggests (though it does not imply) that, on his view, if an idea represents a relational quality, then it doesn't resemble a feature in the body. The conditional statement would make the argument in E II.viii.19 work, and it fits with Locke's theory of representation.

The second principle he needs is a metaphysical principle:

5   If a body can lose a quality in a mere Cambridge change, then the quality doesn't belong to it as it is in itself.

I think that this principle is both ancient (*Theaetetus* 154b) and plausible. Locke concludes that no reasonable person can believe that "those *Ideas* of whiteness and redness are really in *Porphyre* in the light," and that "whiteness or redness are not in [porphyry] at any time." As I've argued, he uses 'whiteness' and 'redness' as

---

just a matter of meeting the Cambridge criterion for change with respect to them. I have added the clause about constitution to save Locke from a counterexample that Brian Weatherson has presented on his weblog ("Change," September 21, 2003, http://tar.weatherson.org/2003/09/21/change).

names for ideas here. He is, once again, arguing for a special case of his negative resemblance thesis (Bolton 1983: 355). So,

6   The ideas of red and white don't resemble qualities in porphyry.

Supplemented by his tacit principles, Locke's argument is valid. Setting aside worries about premise four and Locke's theory of representation, it seems to me that porphyry is red all the time (though its redness is sometimes hard to see) and that the crystals are never white (it's just a trick of the light), so premises one and two are false. There are, perhaps, better examples of mere Cambridge changes of color (Bennett 1968: 105–7; Guerlac 1986: 8, 10; Jacovides 2000: 150–5, 159).

FIFTH DISTINCTION, PART II: PRIMARY QUALITIES BELONG TO OBJECTS AS THEY ARE IN THEMSELVES

Locke tells us that the idea of a primary quality is "an *Idea* of the thing, as it is in it self, as is plain in artificial things" (E II.viii.23: 140). Why should artifacts (as opposed to animals, plants, or minerals) make it plain that primary qualities belong to things as they are in themselves? The salient feature about primary qualities in the artifacts that Locke has in mind, such as clocks and locks, is that they explain how the artifacts work. The implicit principle that Locke relies upon in his justification is that if a quality is explanatory in a relatively deep way, then it belongs to a thing as it is in itself.

With that principle in mind, consider E II.viii.20, which describes a phenomenon and adds a rhetorical question: "Pound an Almond, and the clear white *Colour* will be altered into a dirty one, and the sweet *Taste* into an oily one. What real Alteration can the beating of the Pestle make in any Body, but an Alteration of the *Texture* of it?" The answer must be 'only that', but it isn't obvious what the question means.

In light of his treatment of real alterations in the porphyry argument, I suggest that Locke thinks of real alterations as changes in a thing's intrinsic features. The reader who considers the example is supposed to consider the interaction as an interaction of intelligible features and come to the conclusion that the only intelligible and explanatory feature that will be changed in the almond is its texture (Alexander 1985: 127; Heyd 1994: 25–6; McCann 1994: 66). Since Locke believes that only deep explanatory features are intrinsic, he concludes that the almond's texture, as opposed to its color and taste, belongs to the almond as it is in itself.

FIRST DISTINCTION, PART II: SECONDARY QUALITIES ARE NOT DEEPLY EXPLANATORY

As I said in the last section, Locke's assertion that artifacts make it obvious that primary qualities belong to things as they are in themselves shows that he believes that deeply explanatory qualities belong to things as they are in themselves. That conditional doctrine helps prove what has thus far gone without saying. Since Locke believes that secondary qualities are relational, we may conclude that he believes that they aren't deeply explanatory.

The conditional principle, alongside Locke's thesis that all powers are relations, implies that no power is deeply explanatory. It isn't at all obvious that such qualities as *fragile*, *malleable*, and *conductive* are never explanatory. The denial that any power is explanatory does fit with his repeated claims that powers to affect bodies are akin to powers to produce ideas (E II.viii.10, 23); he goes so far as to call powers to affect bodies "Secondary Qualities, mediately perceivable" (E II.viii.26: 143). More broadly, it fits well with his model of explanation, in which ideas and *propria* flow from intrinsic essences, and relations all "terminate" (E II.xxv.9: 323) in the comparison of ideas (Woolhouse 1983: 92–4).

I should point out a wrinkle in this relatively neat story. In E II. viii.26, Locke not only asserts that secondary qualities (mediately and immediately perceived) depend on primary qualities, but also asserts that secondary qualities are those "whereby we take notice of Bodies, and distinguish them one from another." If we lean on this in a certain way, the passage suggests that secondary qualities explain facts about human awareness and classification. Perhaps the most precise thing to say is that Locke has a hierarchy of explanatory features. Primary qualities are more fundamental than secondary qualities, and relational qualities, in his view, cannot be explanatory at a certain depth.

SIXTH DISTINCTION, PART I: SECONDARY QUALITIES ARE
NOT REAL BEINGS

Ontological questions are not at the forefront of the chapter on primary and secondary qualities, but remarks scattered through the *Essay* do suggest that Locke denies that secondary qualities, like other powers, are real beings that ultimately constitute elements of the world. So far as we know, the oldest way to contrast secondary and primary qualities is with respect to their reality. Democritus wrote, "By convention colour, by convention sweet, by convention bitter: in reality atoms and void" (B125, Barnes 1987: 254). Locke tells us that one of the points of his excursion into natural philosophy is "to distinguish the *primary*, and *real Qualities* of Bodies...from those *secondary* and *imputed Qualities*, which are but the Powers of several Combinations of those primary ones" (E II. viii.22: 140). By real qualities, Locke certainly didn't mean what Ockham or Descartes meant (Menn 1995). That is, Locke doesn't believe that primary qualities can exist independently of their bodies. Rather, he explains, he calls them *"real Original*, or *primary quali-ties*, because they are in the things themselves, whether they are perceived or no: and upon their different Modifications it is, that the secondary Qualities depend" (E II.viii.23: 141; cf. E II.viii.14, 17, 18, 24, 25; cf. Rickless 1997: 305; Stuart 2003: 93n5). He calls them real (and original and primary) because they belong to things as they are in themselves, because they belong to imperceptible bodies, and because they are explanatory – considerations that we have already touched upon.

Other passages suggest a further, ontological significance to Locke's description of primary qualities as real.[14] First, at E II. xxxi.2, Locke complains that our terminology is misleading: "the Things producing in us these simple *Ideas*, are but few of them denominated by us, as if they were only the causes of them; but as if those *ideas* were real Beings in them" (cf. Boyle [1666] 1999: 5.310–15; Alexander 1985: 71–2; Anstey 2000: Chapter 4). Fire, for exam-ple, "is denominated ... Light, and Hot"; it would be more accurate to call it lightful and hotful, since our present terminology gives us

---

[14] John Carriero has written a manuscript in which he argues for an ontological interpretation of *Essay* E II.viii. I wasn't convinced when I first read it, but I've come around.

the false impression that light and hot are real beings in the fire. Along the same lines, Locke denies that faculties are "real beings" (E II.xxi.6: 237). When he says this, he doesn't mean to "deny there are *Faculties* both in the Body and Mind: they both of them have their *powers* of Operating, else neither the one nor the other could operate. For nothing can operate, that is not able to operate; and that is not able to operate, that has no *power* to operate" (E II.xxi.20: 243). Locke believes talk of powers and faculties is legitimate in philosophy "cloathed in the ordinary fashion and Language of the Country" and intended for a general audience; he believes that references to powers may be paraphrased away by talking about what a thing is able to do; and he believes that ordinary ways of speaking mislead us into thinking that powers are agents (E II.xxi.20: 243–4). Finally, recall that Locke believes that secondary qualities, like all powers, are relations. He doesn't think much of the ontological status of relations, describing them as "having no other *reality*, but what they have in the Minds of Men" (E II.xxx.4: 373).[15]

Rejecting the existence of secondary qualities as real beings does not commit one to believing that no object can be rightly described as colored, noisy, tasty, smelly, or warm. A reasonable philosopher may believe that barns are red without believing that any rednesses, either particular or universal, inhere in them (Quine 1980: 10). Galileo had written, "tastes, odors, colors, and so on are no more than mere names so far as the object in which we place them is concerned, and that they reside only in the consciousness" ([1623] 1957: 274). Locke's work may be taken as an elaboration on that theme. Concrete secondary-quality terms rightly apply to bodies, but the only existing entities denoted by our secondary-quality words are ideas.

According to Locke, secondary qualities are not real entities that exist in bodies, and, thus, philosophers need not investigate deeply the conditions under which they come into existence and go out of existence. On his view, the real and explanatory entities are primary qualities, the bodies in which they inhere, ideas, and the minds in which they inhere. The states of affairs in which these entities are arrayed are the basic facts that make our assertion about secondary qualities true or false. There is nothing to keep us from

---

[15] Here I am indebted to Walter Ott.

decreeing that an object is properly described as 'red' if it appears red to some observer (Bennett 1968: 115).

SIXTH DISTINCTION, PART II: PRIMARY QUALITIES, WITH THE POSSIBLE EXCEPTION OF SOME SORTS OF VELOCITY, ARE REAL BEINGS

Locke's chapter on primary and secondary qualities begins with six sections on whether positive ideas might have privative causes. His answer is yes. Part of his discussion assumes a kind of folk metaphysics that he calls "the common Opinion" (E II.viii.6: 134). Shadows (E II.viii.5: 133) and holes (E II.viii.6: 133–4) may cause ideas of black even if they are mere privations. Another part of his argument considers the hypothesis that our ideas are caused by a change in the velocity of the corpuscles in our animal spirits. If ideas are "produced in us, only by different degrees and modes of Motion in our animal Spirits, variously agitated by external Objects," then a privative cause would cause a positive idea, since "the abatement of any former motion, must as necessarily produce a new sensation, as the variation or increase of it" (E II.viii.4: 133). In the end, Locke tells us, the question of whether there are privative causes turns on *"Whether Rest be any more a privation than Motion"* (E II.viii.6: 134). This remark may seem to neglect the preceding suggestion that the abatement of motion might be a privative cause, but really it doesn't. Locke's thought is that, for reasons of Galilean relativity, it may turn out that velocity is always relative to a frame of reference, and if that were true, then neither rest nor deceleration would be intrinsically privative. (Ayers 1991: I: 223–36 argues that Locke moved away from relativism and toward the doctrine of absolute space.) Locke sets aside shadows and holes as candidate privative causes, because of his commitment to corpuscularianism. He believes that the only possible privative causes will be primary qualities, since he believes that

When we go beyond the bare *Ideas* in our Minds, and would enquire into their Causes, we cannot conceive any thing else, to be in any sensible Object, whereby it produces different *Ideas* in us, but the different Bulk, Figure, Number, Texture, and Motion of its insensible Parts. (E II. xxi.73: 287)

Moreover, the only primary qualities that Locke suspects might be privations are connected with motion – rest and the abatement of motion. He believes that the other primary qualities are real beings and that they are part of the furniture of the world in a way that secondary qualities could not be.

5   Power in Locke's *Essay*

Locke devotes a whole chapter – Chapter xxi of Book II, the longest in the *Essay* – to the idea of power. After a few remarks on power in general, this chapter contains an extensive account of two particular powers belonging to human beings, the power of willing and the power of acting freely. But power also appears at several other places in the *Essay*. The qualities of material substances, treated in E II.viii and elsewhere, are powers for Locke; the mental operations, described in E II.ix–xi, of which we have ideas of reflection, are exercises of powers of the mind, which Locke calls faculties; and ideas of powers also "make a great part of our complex ideas of substances" (E II.xxiii.7ff.).

In this chapter I propose, first, to consider Locke's conception of power in general; second, to sketch his views of qualities, faculties, and substances; third, to lay out his accounts of the will and of freedom; and finally to outline his views on motivation, which are connected to his treatment of the will and of freedom and which take up a large part of Chapter xxi. Since qualities and substances are being treated in other chapters in this volume, I shall deal very briefly with these two topics, and concentrate most of my attention on power in general and on the particular powers of will and freedom.

I. POWER IN GENERAL

Powers for Locke are modifications or affections – or, as philosophers nowadays would say, properties – of substances. By possessing a power, a substance is able to do or to suffer something, to perform an action or undergo a passion. The power is said to be the source or basis of the action or passion, and the action or passion is called the actualization or realization of the power. Actualizations of power are often directly observable, but powers themselves never are: their presence in the doing or suffering substance must be inferred; and if a substance does do or suffer something, then the inference to its having the corresponding power is immediate and certain (E II. xxi.4: 235).

Locke takes most of the foregoing doctrine and language for granted. Many of his seventeenth-century contemporaries and most of his medieval predecessors held the same opinions and used the same vocabulary.

Locke begins his discussion in the chapter *Of Power* by explaining how the mind acquires the idea of power. It does so, he says, by observing changes in things, both within itself and in the world outside: it observes the latter by means of the senses, the former by "reflecting on its own Operations." It then notices that these changes occur, always or at least more often than not, in the same ways; and it "concludes" that there is some constant item or factor, both in the things suffering the changes and in the things causing them, that accounts for these regularities. This i em or factor is the power such things have to change or to be changed in the ways they do or are.

The idea of power is thus linked for Locke with the ideas of change and causation. A power is necessarily a power of doing or suffering something, and the actualization of a power either produces or constitutes a change in a substance, either the same substance as the one that possesses the power or a different one. Furthermore, all changes have causes for Locke, and the cause of a change that occurs when a power is actualized is either that power itself, or the substance possessing that power: he speaks in both ways.

Because every power is a power to do or to suffer something, something different from the power itself, Locke says that the idea of power includes that of relation, "a relation to Action or Change": powers are, in other words, relational properties of their bearers. Yet Locke also says that the idea of power is a simple idea. This is surprising, since in an earlier passage he had characterized a simple idea as one that is "in it self uncompounded, [and] contains in it nothing but *one uniform Appearance*, or Conception in the mind, and is not distinguishable into different *Ideas*" (E II.ii.1: 119). By that standard, power is anything but a simple idea. But in II.xxi, Locke gives as his reason for considering power a simple idea, that "it make[s] a principal ingredient in our complex *Ideas* of Substances" (E II.xxi.3: 234); and at the end of the chapter, he includes power among "our *original Ideas*, from whence all the rest are derived, and of which they are made up" (E II.xxi.73: 286). Here he seems to be introducing a new conception of simplicity, different from the one he had before. (In a later passage, Locke acknowledges that the ideas of some powers that we find in substances "though not simple *Ideas*, yet ... for brevity's sake, may conveniently enough be reckoned amongst them" [E II.xxiii.7: 299]. This is still a different conception of simplicity, or rather, use of "simplicity.")

Locke distinguishes two species of power, active and passive. An active power is not merely a power of doing as opposed to undergoing something. That distinction itself is uncertain, given the plasticity of the verb "do": undergoing may itself count as doing, as may resting or staying. (A: "Don't just stand there, *do* something! B: "I *am* doing something. I'm *standing* here.") In any case, that's not the basis on which Locke draws the distinction. An active power, he says, is one whereby a substance is "able to make ... any change"; a passive power is one whereby a substance is "able to receive any change." Thus the notion of causing is explicitly built into the idea of an active power; with that of a passive power, causation is only implied.

But even this is not all there is to Locke's conception of active power. To exercise an active power is not merely to act, or to cause a change in something; it is also to initiate or create the change all by oneself, entirely on one's own. When a moving billiard ball causes another ball to move by striking it, the first ball is not exercising an active power, Locke says, because it has not put itself into motion "by its own Power." It has rather "receive[d] the impression whereby it is put into that *Action* purely from without," that is, "from some external Agent"; and this power "is not properly an *Active Power*, but a mere passive capacity in the subject" (E II. xxi.72: 285). And in general, whenever one body impels another, the one does not "produce" motion in the other, but only "transfers" or "communicates" its own motion, which it has "received" from something else. Indeed, Locke suggests that no body is ever able to produce motion in itself, and hence that no body is possessed of any active power at all. If we reserve the term "agent" for a substance that has (and exercises) active powers, then Locke's position is that no body is an agent, properly speaking.

Where then do we find active powers in the universe? Only, Locke thinks, in God and in finite spirits, including (in the latter category) our own minds, and so (by extension) ourselves. For we are able, "barely by a thought of the Mind," which is to say, "by willing it," to move our own bodies, and parts of our bodies, and so to produce or initiate motion in something. (Locke sometimes identifies this something as oneself, but he does not usually think of one's body as a thing distinct from oneself.) We are also able, just by willing, to produce or direct thought in ourselves, though we cannot do this on every occasion, any more than we can move our bodies in every way and under all circumstances. This power of willing, what most philosophers (including Locke) call "the will," is thus an active power, the clearest example we have thereof in our experience.

At this point in Chapter xxi, Locke embarks on his discussion of this active power of the will and of willing. Before we follow him on that journey, however, we should consider one further point in his account of power in general, and also deal briefly with qualities, faculties, and substances.

Locke seems to assume that every power is either active or passive, and thus that these are the only two kinds of power there are. But recent philosophers have identified various further kinds, and subkinds, of these two. They often use the word "disposition," as Locke does "power" (and as Aristotle did *dunamis* and Aquinas *potentia*), as a general term covering all of these kinds. But then they distinguish capacities and abilities from liabilities and susceptibilities, and these from inclinations and tendencies, and all of them from one another (see Ryle 1949: 116ff.) Only abilities and capacities would fall under Locke's active powers, though not all of them would; susceptibilities and liabilities would all be passive powers; and inclinations and tendencies would have instances under both headings.

2. QUALITIES

Qualities for Locke are primarily properties of material substances. Immaterial spirits and souls have modifications and affections, but these are not generally called qualities (one passage in which they are, however, is E II.xxiii.30: 313). Locke introduces qualities in Chapter viii of Book II, under the heading "*Some farther Considerations concerning our simple Ideas.*" Qualities are presented as correlates in the material world of the simple, sensory ideas we have in our minds: they are described from the outset as "Power[s] to produce [such] *Idea*[s] in our mind" (E II.viii.8: 134) and are said to be "in Bodies" or "Objects," which is to say, material objects (ibid. and E II.viii.9).

The best-known feature of Locke's account of qualities is the distinction he draws between primary and secondary qualities. Primary qualities (of bodies) include "Solidity, Extension, Figure, Motion, or Rest, and Number." (The primary qualities of spirits, which he mentions in E II.xxiii.30, are "Thinking, and a power of Action," what he elsewhere calls "Will.") Secondary qualities (of bodies) are "Colours, Sounds, Tasts, *etc.*" (No secondary qualities of spirits are listed in E II xxiii.30.) Secondary qualities, he says, are "nothing in the objects [which have them] themselves, but Powers to produce various Sensations in us," whereas primary qualities are

such as are utterly inseparable from [any] Body, in what estate soever it be; such as in all the alterations and changes it suffers ... it constantly keeps; and such as Sense constantly finds in every particle of Matter, which has bulk enough to be perceived, and the Mind finds inseparable from every particle of Matter, though less than to make itself singly be perceived by our Senses. (E II.viii.9: 134–35)

(Locke obviously is referring here not to determinate size, shape, etc., but to corresponding determinable qualities.) Since in this definition of primary qualities, Locke doesn't explicitly say that they also are powers, some scholars have supposed that he does not take them to be. But that is a mistake. Not only has Locke said, without qualification, that qualities in general are powers, but in later passages he makes it explicit that primary qualities too cause simple ideas in perceivers, for example, "These ... *original* or *primary Qualities* of Body ... produce simple *Ideas* in us," and so must be powers to do so. The difference between primary and secondary qualities, apart from the fact that a body may lack one or more species of the latter, is that secondary qualities are nothing but powers, whereas primary qualities are powers and something besides. What this extra something might be, Locke never explicitly says, though some scholars have tried to work out what he must have had in mind (see Campbell 1980).

In addition to primary and secondary qualities, Locke distinguishes a third category, though he doesn't call these tertiary qualities. These are the powers that some bodies have to change the qualities of other bodies: "the power in Fire to produce a new Colour, or consistency in Wax or Clay ... , is as much a quality in Fire, as the power it has to produce in me a new *Idea* or Sensation of warmth or burning" (E II.viii.10: 135).

Secondary qualities are linked by Locke to human minds: they produce sensations in the latter. He also connects them to the primary qualities of the bodies that possess them, or rather to the primary qualities of the insensible parts of such bodies. Secondary qualities "depend on" primary qualities, he says: the color, taste, and smell of objects are "Powers [in them] to produce various Sensations in us by their *Primary Qualities*, *i.e.* by the Bulk, Figure, Texture, and Motion of their insensible parts" (E II.viii.10: 135). Locke is here acknowledging a point that has been prominent in recent discussions of dispositional properties, that such properties in some way presuppose the existence of nondispositional ones, called "categorical" or "intrinsic" properties, belonging to the same subject. Properties of the former sort appear or manifest themselves only on occasion, when certain conditions involving objects or situations external to their bearers are satisfied. In the case of Locke's secondary qualities, the condition is that a human mind properly connected to properly functioning and properly situated sense organs is present. But the primary qualities of the insensible parts of the property bearer are always and unconditionally present within it.

3. FACULTIES

Locke is famous for having ridiculed the "faculty psychology" of earlier philosophers, which still was prevalent among his contemporaries. On this view, the mind was held to consist of, or to contain, a number of faculties, including ones for understanding and willing; and the presence of these faculties was thought to explain how it is that minds perform these activities. In truth, these faculties are nothing but powers in the minds that possess them and in themselves are perfectly innocent: Locke himself refers quite often to the powers of the mind as faculties. The problem is that other philosophers have treated these faculties as if they were not merely powers but "real Beings in the Soul," which themselves have powers and activities belonging to them. Thus the faculty of will was said to "direct the Understanding," and the faculty of understanding to "obey, or obey not the Will"; and in the same vein the will was said to be or not to be free, although freedom is itself a power, as much as the will is. But this way of talking, Locke says, is "absurd" and "unintelligible," and has "produced great confusion" (E II.xxi.18: 242).

4. SUBSTANCES

Locke says that "our *Idea* ... of *Power* [is one of those] simple *Ideas*" that "make a principal Ingredient in our complex *Ideas* of Substances" (E II.xxi.3: 234). A few lines before he had been more specific: it is *"active Powers"* that "make so great a part of our complex *Ideas* of natural Substances" (E II.xxi.2: 234). Two questions arise. First, if natural substances include bodies, as it seems past doubt they do, how can they have active powers? This appears to be another expression of the tension we noted earlier in Locke's thinking about power and bodies.

The second question is, how is the idea of power involved in our ideas of substances? In the chapter on substance, Chapter xxiii, Locke explains that, in the case of a material substance, we have "no other *Idea* of any [such] *Substance* ... but what [we have] barely of those sensible Qualities" that we have observed to exist in it, together "with a supposition of such a *Substratum*, as gives as it were a support to those Qualities" (E II.xxiii.6: 298); these qualities, of course, are "the Powers, [that] Substance [has] to produce several *Ideas* in us by our Senses" (E II.xxiii.9: 300). In this passage it appears that the qualities Locke has in mind are primary and secondary qualities, but elsewhere in the chapter (sections 7 and 9: 299 and 300), he makes it clear that he takes the ideas of their tertiary qualities to be included in our ideas of material substances as well. The situation is a bit more complicated in the case of spiritual substances, including our minds. Here the simple ideas we have are ideas of "those Operations of our own Minds, which we experiment daily in ourselves [sc. by reflection], as Thinking, Understanding, Willing, Knowing, and Power of beginning Motion, *etc.* co-existing in some [Substratum]" (E II.xxiii.15: 305). It is true that thinking and such are not powers but actions, but their presence in a subject entails the existence of the corresponding powers to perform them. If we observe thinking going on in our mind, then we immediately "collect a Power [in that mind], able to make that [Action]" take place (E II.xxi.4: 235). So our ideas of all substances consist entirely of ideas of powers or of activities that entail powers, together with the idea of a substratum. But the latter is a thin idea, with little content: "we have no idea of what [this substratum] is, but only a confused obscure one of what it does" (E II.xiii.19: 175).

5. THE HUMAN WILL

Before considering Locke's view of the will and of freedom, we must note that his thinking on these topics changed considerably during the years 1690–1704. These changes are reflected in the alterations he made in the text of the five different editions of the *Essay* that were published during this period. The first edition appeared in 1690, the second in 1694, the third in 1695, the fourth in 1700, and the fifth in 1705, shortly after his death. In my account here, I shall mostly expound the views expressed in the fourth edition, which is the one Peter Nidditch used as the copy-text for his now-standard edition of Locke's work (Locke 1975). But sometimes I refer to views presented in different editions, and when I do I shall so indicate by including a bold numeral in the citation, **1**, **2**, or **5** (the third edition was a virtual reprint of the second, with no substantive changes).

Locke introduces the will in Chapter xxi as an active power, the only one whose operation we have any experience of. The will is the power to perform acts of willing, or what Locke (and many other philosophers) call volitions. Volitions are actions, and since they are exercises of an active power, the things that perform them are agents. Volitions also have objects: every volition is a volition *to* something. In particular, a volition is a volition to *act*, or to *do something*; hence the object of a volition is also an action, a different one from the volition itself. But this action does not actually exist at the time the volition occurs: "object" here means "inter-nal" or "intentional object": it is something projected or to-be-accomplished and not something already existing or done.

Locke sets two further requirements for the object of a volition: it must be (a) an action that is to be performed "presently" (that is, soon after the volition takes place) and (b) an action that the agent believes to be in his power to perform (though he may be mistaken in this).

Very often, when an agent performs a volition to ϕ, he does ϕ, and he ϕ's because he has performed a volition to do so. In such a case, Locke says, the agent acts voluntarily; ϕ is a voluntary action on his part, and he has acted according to his will. (Locke also says that a voluntary action "conforms to" the agent's volition or will.) The relation between a voluntary action and the volition that precedes it is in some way causal: the volition is the cause or part of the cause of the action. Locke never gives an explicit account of this relation, although in one passage he allows that "the actual choice of the Mind [may be] the cause of actual thinking on this or that thing" (E II.xxi.19: 242–3) (see Lowe 1986 on this question).

Locke says that human agents engage in two (and only two) sorts of voluntary actions, thinking and moving. Thinking is an action of or in our minds, moving an action of or in our bodies. But not every thought or movement we engage in is a voluntary action. We are sometimes caused to move by some (already moving) object other than our own bodies, or to think by some (e.g., sensible) object outside our own minds. Such motions and thoughts are not voluntary on our part. Since we do not ourselves, by ourselves, initiate them, they are not even actions in the strict sense of being exercises of active powers. They are really only passions.

When an agent performs a voluntary action, the volition that brings or helps to bring the action about is "successful" or "satis-fied." But a volition may fail: an agent may will to ϕ and yet not ϕ, for any of several reasons (he is prevented from doing so, or he changes his mind, or he is distracted, or the action turns out not in fact to be in his power, etc.).

Still, volitions normally do not fail in this way. When an agent wills to walk, then normally he does walk, and normally his walking is voluntary. Because of this, Locke sometimes identifies the exercises of an agent's will with voluntary actions, and not with the volitions that prompt them: walking as opposed to willing to walk. He even defines the will on occasion as the power "we find in ourselves ... to begin or forbear, continue or end several actions of our minds, and motions of our Bodies, barely by the thought or preference of the mind ordering ... the doing or not doing such or such a particular action" (E II.xxi.5: 236). Notice that the power specified here is not merely the power to perform these actions of our minds and bodies, but the power to perform them by willing, and indeed "barely by" willing: if they were performed by some other means, they would not be voluntary, and would not even seem to be exercises of the will. Even so, this is loose talk on Locke's part. Strictly speaking, it is only the volition to walk that counts as the exercise of the will; the external action is "consequent to" the volition. It is true that in saying that the will is the power to perform such consequent actions *by* willing, Locke is indicating that these actions are not direct exercises of this power, but that willing somehow intervenes to play a causal or at least instrumental role. But even so, this way of speaking could be misleading.

Locke thinks that not only positive actions such as walking but also negative ones such as not walking may be voluntary. Instead of saying that agents sometimes "will not to walk," however, he tends to describe them as "willing to forbear walking." This expression could cause confusion, since willing is built into forbearing. An agent who forbears to walk is one whose not walking is voluntary, that is, one who wills not to walk, does not walk, and does not walk because he has willed not to do so. Such forbearances (that is, actions forborne) must be distinguished from mere nonactions, such as not walking without having willed not to do so, as when a man ambles about aimlessly, moving his legs automatically. (For illuminating discussions of negative actions and some cousins thereof, see Ryle 1973 and Stuart unpub.)

Locke supposes that willing is a specific sort of mental action, and that it has a distinctive appearance or phenomenal quality that distinguishes it from other mental actions. In the second edition of the *Essay*, he says that "whosoever desires to understand what [willing] is, will better find it by reflecting on his own mind, and observing what it does, when it *wills*, than by any variety of articulate sounds whatsoever" (E 2–5 II.xxi.30: 249). Nonetheless, in both the first and the second editions, Locke tries to describe "the act of *Volition*" by using words. In both editions, he employs verbal expressions that are supposed to have the same meaning as "willing," mainly "choosing" and "preferring." In the first edition, he says that "preference" is a better term than "choice" to "express the act of Volition," because "choice is of a more doubtful signification, bordering more on Desire, and so is referred to things remote; whereas Volition, or the Act of Willing, signifies nothing properly, but the actual producing of something that is voluntary" (E 1 II.xxi.33: 258–9). It is puzzling that Locke is willing to equate preferring with willing in this passage, where he explicitly identifies willing as an action. For to prefer something is not to perform any action, but rather to have a certain disposition or power, and so to be in a passive state: a man can prefer vanilla (to chocolate, say) without even thinking of ice cream, let alone be engaged in the process of deciding which to buy in the shop.

Matthew Stuart has provided a neat solution to this puzzle. There is, he has found, a sense of the verb "prefer," which is now obsolete but was current in the seventeenth century, according to which to prefer is "to forward, advance, promote (a result); to assist in bringing about" (Stuart unpub.: Chapter A, pp. 8f., citing the OED). In this sense, preferring might well be counted an action.

Neat though it is, however, this solution can be applied only to some occurrences of "prefer" in Locke's text. In an important passage in the first edition, after declaring again that willing "is nothing but the *preferring* the doing of any thing, to the not doing of it," Locke goes on to identify such preferring with "the *being pleased more with the one, than the other*" (E 1 II.xxi.28: 248). By no stretch can, or could, the passive form "be pleased with" be taken to signify an action of the mind, as opposed to a passion thereof.

In the second edition, besides continuing to use "preferring" and even "choosing" to render "willing," Locke makes use of expressions that are not so much synonyms of "willing" as metaphors for willing. Thus the mind, in willing, is "ordering, or as it were commanding the doing or not doing such or such particular action" (E 2–5 II.xxi.5: 236). Locke also says that, in willing, the mind "directs" particular actions. But then in a later passage, he comes back to his main point, warning his reader that none of these terms, "*Ordering, Directing, Chusing, Preferring*, etc. will ... distinctly enough express *Volition*" to him "unless he will reflect on what he himself does, when he *wills*" (E 2–5 II.xxi.15: 240). It hardly needs remarking that someone who doesn't already know what willing is, is unlikely to find it helpful to be told to reflect on what he does when he wills.

Despite his caveats, however, Locke himself sometimes tends to assimilate willing to other mental phenomena, both actions and passions. It is this tendency that accounts, I believe, for his mishandling of some of the examples he employs in his discussion of freedom, as I hope to show in the next section.

6. HUMAN FREEDOM

Locke defines freedom as the power a man has "to think, or not to think; to move, or not to move, according to the preference or direction of his own mind" (E II.xxi.8: 237). Some commentators have claimed that his view is the same as that of Hobbes, who indeed defines a free agent in his *Treatise of Liberty and Necessity* as one "that can do if he will and forbear if he will" (Hobbes 1999: 39). But Hobbes speaks misleadingly in this passage: it does not accurately express the position he actually held. He states it better in *Leviathan* xxi, where he defines a free man as "he that ... is not hindered to do what he has a will to," that is, who "finds no stop in doing what he has the will ... to do" (Hobbes 1999: 95). What Hobbes should have said in the *Treatise*, therefore, is that a man is free to do something if, having willed it, he can do it; and he is free to forbear doing something if, having willed not to do it, he is able not to do it. Locke's position, by contrast, is that a man is not free to do something he has willed to do unless he not only is able to do it but also is able not to do it; and he is not free to forbear doing something he has willed not to do unless, besides being able not to do it, he also is able to do it if he wills to do it. Locke makes this clear in the sentence that directly follows the one just quoted: "Where-ever any performance or forbearance are not equally in a Man's power; where-ever doing or not doing, will not equally follow upon the preference of his mind, there he is not *Free*" (E loc. cit.) – although, he immediately adds, "perhaps the Action may be voluntary." The action he refers to here is either that of thinking or that of not thinking (forbearing to think), either that of moving or that of not moving (forbearing to move). It suffices for any one of these actions to be voluntary that the agent wills to do it, does or is able to do it, and does or is able to do it just because he wills it.

On Locke's view, then, freedom is a two-way power belonging to an agent, both a power to ϕ and a power not to ϕ, whichever way the agent wills. Further, although being voluntary is not sufficient for an action to be free, it is a necessary part of it. Locke makes this point explicitly when he says that *"Liberty* cannot be, where there is no Thought, no Volition, no Will; but there may be Thought, there may be Will, there may be Volition, where there is no *Liberty"* (E II.xxi.8: 238). Here is further evidence of the difference between the views of Locke and Hobbes: Hobbes explicitly says that he takes "all voluntary acts to be free" (Hobbes 1999: 82).

(Some terminological points: (a) "Liberty" and "freedom" are synonyms for Locke. (b) The adjective "free" is almost always applied to agents, and not to actions, but agents are often said to be free with respect to particular actions. So there is no reason not to apply "free" to particular actions as well: a free action is just one with respect to which an agent is free. (c) The contrary of "free" is "necessary," and Locke does often speak of necessary actions, as well as of necessary agents. (d) The sense of "necessary" in which it means "not free" is quite different from that of logical or metaphysical necessity, on the one hand, and that of nomological necessity, on the other, in both of which senses Locke uses "necessary" in other chapters of the *Essay*. What this necessity amounts to, however, apart from precluding freedom, Locke does not say.)

Locke's claim, that being voluntary and being free, as he understands these notions, are different, seems incontestable. Nonetheless, he seeks to bolster it by describing some examples in which an agent is supposed to do something that is voluntary and yet is not free. These examples have been the target of much critical attention on the part of Locke scholars.

The most famous such example is that of the man in the locked room. Here is Locke's presentation of it:

[S]uppose a Man be carried, whilst fast asleep, into a Room, where is a Person he longs to see and speak with; and be there locked fast in, beyond his Power to get out: he awakes, and is glad to find himself in so desirable

Company, which he stays willingly in, *i.e.* preferrs his stay to going away. I ask, Is not this stay voluntary? I think, no Body will doubt it: and yet being locked fast in, he has not freedom to be gone. (E II.xxi.10: 238)

It is clear that Locke's conclusion from this example, that an action may be voluntary and yet not free, is not established unless the action in question, namely, the man's staying in the room, is both not free and voluntary. Locke assumes that it is both, but this assumption is open to question. The question is not whether the action is really not free by Locke's definition, for it obviously is not. The question is whether the action of staying is really voluntary. It is not a voluntary action by Locke's definition unless the agent has performed a volition to stay, and it is doubtful that he has: at least, none is mentioned. Locke says that the man stays willingly, but doing something willingly is different from, and does not entail, willing or having willed to do it. Locke also says that the man prefers staying to going away. But his preferring in this case is not any act of volition on his part, but only a passive disposition. This is one of those instances in which Locke's equation of willing with preferring brings him to grief.

But even if Locke's point, that there are voluntary actions that are not free, is not established by the locked room example as he presents it, the point is correct, and it can be confirmed by making a small change in the example. Suppose that the man, having been carried into the room while asleep, wakes up, looks around, and is tempted to leave, but then on thinking it over decides to stay and enjoy the company of the person he finds there. In that case the man performs, or could well be supposed to perform, an actual volition, and then to stay because of that volition. With this change in the example, the man's staying would be "truly voluntary," and it still would not be a free action.

Locke holds that a free action must be voluntary, and we noted earlier the passage in which he claims that only a being that is capable of thought has a will, which is the power to perform acts of willing and thence voluntary actions. ("We conceive not a Tennis-ball to think, and consequently not to have any [power of] Voli-tion.") This is true if only because willing is itself a species of thinking: volition is one kind of thought. But Locke's position goes considerably further than this. He holds that a being that is able to will must have a faculty of understanding, and so be capable of cognitive thought, and indeed rationality. In taking this position, Locke was aligning himself, perhaps unwittingly, with Thomas Aquinas, who insisted on this very point (Aquinas 1964ff.: Vol. 17, p. 13 [ST I–II.vi.2. *ad* 1]).

Questions about human freedom have been discussed by philosophers since ancient times. One reason for their popularity has been the widely perceived connection between freedom and morality. Thinkers of quite different persuasions have agreed that agents cannot be held morally responsible for their actions unless those actions are free (or the agents are free with respect to them). Some have gone further, claiming that no action has moral properties or moral significance, no action is morally good or bad, right or wrong, unless it is performed freely, or at least by a free agent. Locke takes no notice of this issue, and says nothing explicit about it. But there is an interesting passage that first appeared in Book IV of the fourth edition of the *Essay* that gives a clear indication of his stand on it. This occurs in the chapter on reason. Locke is discussing the structure of deductive reasoning, arguing that it need not be, and in real life most often is not, syllogistic. As an alternative to the syllogistic model, he proposes that reasoning be conceived as a series of propositions in each of which two ideas are connected, with each proposition forming a link in a chain wherein each link follows logically from its predecessor, and whereby the first idea contained in the first proposition is connected to the second idea contained in the last proposition in the chain. He then gives as an example a chain of propositions starting with (the premise) "Men shall be punished in another world" and ending with (the conclusion) "Men can determine themselves." We need not be concerned with all of the intervening steps, but the following are relevant. The proposition that "a man is justly punished for doing something" is supposed to entail that "he is guilty of that action"; that in turn entails that "he could have done otherwise," and from that in turn it follows that "he did what he did freely" (E 4–5 IV. xvii.4: 672–3). It is obvious from this that Locke accepts the traditional position on this issue: that a man is morally responsible only for actions with respect to which he is free.

One of the most prominent questions addressed in recent discussions of freedom is that of the relation of freedom to determinism – the doctrine that everything that happens, including human actions, is antecedently determined to happen, either by God or by natural causes or causal laws. The question is whether free agency is logically compatible with determinism. Some, the compatibilists, have answered yes; others, the incompatibilists, have answered no; and the latter have gone two ways: those who believe in freedom (and hence reject determinism) are libertarians; those who embrace determinism (and eschew freedom) are hard determinists. So in which of these camps should Locke be placed? Locke certainly believes in freedom, so he is not a hard determinist. But is he a compatibilist or a libertarian? Some scholars have defended the former option (Chappell 1998), others the latter (Schouls 1992); whereas Matthew Stuart has claimed that Locke took "no forthright stand on the issue of determinism" (Stuart unpub.: Chapter A, p. 32).

It is true that Locke made no explicit pronouncement either pro or contra determinism. But there is enough evidence to warrant the conclusion that, had he been given the choice, he would have accepted determinism, with respect to the action both of God and of natural causes.

Thus, in his proof of the existence of God in Book IV of the *Essay*, Locke asserts as a premise, known "by an intuitive Certainty, that bare *nothing can [not] produce any real Being*," or, as he shortly restates it, "what had a Beginning, must be produced by something else" (E IV.x.3: 620). Here he is speaking of natural causation, since the beings in question are those that have beginnings. More particularly, in his discussion of willing, Locke not only states but also argues that, to be exercised, the will must be "determined by something without it self" (E 1 II.xxi.28–9: 248). (I shall return to this argument.)

On the other hand, Locke wrote the following to his friend Molyneux:

I own freely to you the weakness of my understanding, that though it be unquestionable that there is omnipotence and omniscience in God our maker, and I cannot have a clearer perception of any thing than that I am free, yet I cannot make freedom in man consistent with omnipotence and omniscience in God, though I am as fully perswaded of both as of any truths I most firmly assent to. (C 4: 625–6, letter #1592)

This statement might seem to indicate that Locke is an incompatibilist after all, though he also believes both in freedom and in the determination of everything by God. But in fact, Locke does not say here that freedom and determination *are* incompatible, or that they *cannot* be reconciled, merely that he cannot understand *how* the two can both obtain. This is a familiar stance for Locke. At several points in the *Essay* he encounters situations in which his understanding falls short of his conviction. In this case, his conviction, clearly, is both that human beings are free and that everything in the universe is determined, both by the nature of God and by natural causes. He is committed, therefore, to compatibilism, despite his failure to embrace this position explicitly.

Since freedom according to Locke is primarily a property of agents, which are substances, it is simply absurd, he says, a mistake of language, to attribute freedom to the will, as many of his predecessors and contemporaries had done. Even to ask "whether the *Will has Freedom*, is to ask, whether one Power has another Power, one Ability another Ability; a Question at first sight too grossly absurd to make a Dispute, or need an Answer" (E II.xxi.16: 241). To ask "whether Man's *Will* be free [is as insignificant], as to ask, whether his Sleep be Swift, or his Vertue Square: *Liberty* being as little applicable to the *Will*, as swiftness of Motion is to Sleep, or squareness to Vertue" (E II.xxi.14: 240). Nonetheless, Locke concedes that those who ask this question may be intending to ask something different, something that is not only significant but also worth trying to answer.

This different question concerns willing rather than the will, the exercises of a power rather than the power itself. Locke contrasts willing with action that is "consequent" thereto, that is, with voluntary motion and thought. But willing itself is an action for Locke, so it is natural to ask whether willing counts among those actions that can be voluntary and, if so, whether willing is ever a free action. Locke divides this question into two: (1) Whether "*a Man in respect of willing any Action in his power once proposed to his Thoughts*" can be free (E 1–4 II.xxi.23: 245); and (2) "*Whether a Man be at liberty to will which of the two he pleases, Motion or Rest*" (E II.xxi.25: 247). To the first question Locke gives a straightforwardly negative answer; the second, he says, is an absurd question that "needs no answer," and yet he thinks it follows from the absurdity of the question that the answer to it too is negative. He offers an argument for each of these negative answers. The first argument, presented in §23 and summarized in §§24 and 25, is fully stated, but recent scholars have had different opinions on how to construe it. The second argument is only hinted at in a couple of highly compressed sentences, one (in editions 1–4) at the end of §23, and the other (in all editions) at the end of §25. Scholarly opinion is less sharply divided on the proper interpretation of this argument than it is on the first one, but even so, no complete consensus has been reached (see Chappell 1994a; Rickless 2000; Yaffe 2000: 27ff.; and Stuart unpub.: Chapter A, pp. 40ff.).

Rather than examine these interpretive controversies, I will simply and dogmatically summarize the view I have myself defended as to the shape and import of these two arguments, and proceed on that basis.

The first argument has the structure of a destructive dilemma, and its conclusion is that in the case of a prospective action that an agent is considering, the agent cannot avoid willing either to do it or not to do it. So with respect to that sort of action, willing something with respect to it is unavoidable. This conclusion might be called the Unavoidability Thesis. But this argument is unsound, because one of its premises (not one that Locke states explicitly, but one that is required for the argument to be valid) is false, a criticism that was also pointed out by Leibniz in the *New Essays* (Leibniz 1981: 181).

The other argument is a reductio ad absurdum of the proposition that there are free volitions. The conclusion is that an infinite series of free volitions must be performed before the free one in question can be accomplished. But this conclusion is reached on the basis of certain premises (in addition to the one that is supposed to be reduced to absurdity), some of which are not acceptable to Locke's libertarian opponents, who are presumably the argument's targets, and some of which are unacceptable to Locke himself. So this argument cannot be effective for the purpose for which Locke evidently intended to use it. (For details, see Chappell 1994a; for criticisms of and alternatives to Chappell's readings, see especially Rickless 2000. and Stuart unpub.).

On my reading, then, both of Locke's arguments in support of the view that agents are never free with respect to acts of volition are faulty: neither does support the conclusion Locke intended it to support. In any case, that he held this view seems clear, though some recent scholars dispute even that. Locke's position is that freedom extends only to actions that are consequent to volition, not to volitions themselves. In taking this position, Locke joined forces with Hobbes, and set himself against an array of libertarian philosophers, both before and during his time: the Jesuit Molina, Hobbes's adversary Bramhall, the Cambridge Platonist Cudworth, and the Arminians, whose number included Locke's friends Philip Van Limborch and Jean Le Clerc. These philosophers not only thought it possible for acts of willing to be free; they held that no action is free unless it is preceded and determined by a free volition.

7. MOTIVATION

From his discussion of freedom, Locke is led to consider motivation. His treatment of this topic, however, is really a continuation of his account of willing and of action rather than of freedom. The discussion of motivation carries through to the end of Chapter xxi, and it is both rich and tangled – tangled in large part because this is the material to which Locke made the most changes for the second and later editions. The majority of these changes consist of additions to, rather than alterations of, the existing text. Locke did drop a few first edition passages, but most he retained, sometimes rearranging them and adding new material around them. The result is hard to follow, and even harder to make sense of.

For Locke, the question of motivation is the question of what determines the will when an agent performs a volition and thence a voluntary action. We might wonder why the will needs determining in the first place. In the first edition, Locke offers an argument for holding that it does:

Volition or Willing ... is nothing but the preferring the doing of any thing, to the not doing of it; ... Well, but what is this Preferring? It is nothing but the being pleased more with the one, than the other. Is then a Man indifferent to be pleased, or not pleased more with one than another? Is it in his choice, whether he will, or will not be better pleased with one thing than another? And to this, I think, every one's Experience is ready to make answer, No. From whence it follows, ... That the Will, or Preference, is determined by something without it self.... (E 1 II.xxi.28–9: 248)

One problem with this argument is that it equates willing with being pleased, which, as we have seen, conflicts with Locke's dominant conception of willing as an action, as opposed to a mere passive state. Furthermore, Locke's position here, the conclusion of his argument, seems to conflict with his account of the will as an active power. For an active power, we saw earlier, is a power that can be exercised by its possessor all by himself, entirely on his own. That sounds like the very antithesis of being determined "by something without it self."

Be that as it may, Locke is evidently committed to the position that the human will must be so determined if it is to be exercised. In the passage just quoted, he seems to regard it as an empirical fact that the will does not determine itself. But he also has the two arguments we examined earlier, which lead to a similar conclusion. So it looks as if he can claim ample reason for holding this position. But even if these arguments are faulty, even if the empirical claim is false, and even if the position itself is at odds with Locke's conception of the will as an active power, we must try to understand his view and see what more he has to say about it.

Note first that in Locke's view it is inaccurate to speak of *the will* as being subject to determination. In a passage added to the second edition, he says that since the will is "nothing but a power in the Mind to direct the operative faculties of a Man to motion or rest,... the true and proper Answer... to the Question, what is it determines the Will?" is: the agent, that is, the man whose will it is. "For that which determines the general power of directing, to this or that particular direction, is nothing but the Agent it self Exercising the power it has" (E 2–5 II.xxi.29: 249). So the question should be altered to: what determines a man to will something? – as Locke himself puts it, "What moves [the Agent], in every particular instance, to determine [his] general power of directing, to this or that particular Motion or Rest?" (ibid.) So in the second edition as well, Locke is holding fast to the position that the thing being determined, whether agent or will, does not determine itself: what determines it is something "without it self."

It appears that determination is a kind of causation for Locke, and in the case of the will (or of agents with wills) there are two sides to it. On the one hand, to determine the will of an agent is to cause the will to be exercised, that is, to cause the agent to exercise his will, so that an act of volition is produced. On the other hand, to determine the will is to specify an action to be willed, that is, to cause the agent to perform a volition with a specific object or content. The distinction here corresponds to Aquinas's distinction between the exercise and the specification of the act of willing (Aquinas 1964ff.: Vol. 17, pp. 66–7 [ST I–II.ix.1. *ad* 3]; Vol. 17, pp. 86–7 [ST I–II.x.2. *corpus*]). Aquinas indicates that the former is brought about by efficient causation, whereas the latter is accomplished by formal causation. Locke does not make explicit use of this Thomistic (and Aristotelian) language, but invoking it can help us to understand his thinking. The main point to keep in mind is that, for Locke, what determines the will must serve both as an efficient cause, prompting or inducing the agent to activate his power of willing at a particular time, and as a formal cause, providing the agent with a specific action to direct his willing upon.

In the first edition, what determines the will of an agent, Locke says, is happiness, which is "that ... we call Good" (E 1 II.xxi.29: 248). Good, in turn, is identified with pleasure; and the contrary of happiness, which he calls misery or evil, is the same as pain, though he conceives these two broadly, "there being pleasure and pain of the Mind, as well as the Body" (ibid.). Locke makes it clear that it is the agent's own pleasure and pain that determines his will: Locke is an egoist as well as a hedonist.

Happiness or good, or in case there are several goods, the greatest good among the alternatives: this is Locke's initial answer to the question he poses. But he soon qualifies this initial answer, one reason being, apparently, that, for a nominalist like Locke, good itself is not the sort of thing that could cause any agent to do anything at a time: it could not serve as an efficient cause of an act of willing. Rather, Locke says, it is "the appearance of Good, greater Good" that determines the will (E 1 II.xxi.33: 256). By "the appearance of Good, ... " here he means "what appears to be good, or better [than the alternatives], to the agent at the time and in the circumstances in which he is willing." In other words, what determines the agent's will is what he perceives or believes to be good or best, or, as Locke prefers to say, the agent's judgment of good. Perceptions and judgments, and also in this context beliefs, are occurrent states of the agent's mind, thus datable events, and so are fit to serve as efficient causes of acts of his will. So what determines the will of an agent on any occasion, according to Locke in the *Essay*'s first edition, is the agent's judgment of what is best for him to do in the circumstances in which he finds himself, where "what is best" means "what will or is likely to produce or lead to the most pleasure for him, either in the next moment or at some time in the future."

The *Essay* was published at the end of 1689 (although it was dated 1690). Within a couple of years, Locke began making plans for a second edition. He solicited his acquaintances for suggestions for improving his work. One who obliged was William Molyneux, whom Locke had come to know through correspondence in 1692. Molyneux at first had nothing but praise for Locke's book, but upon being prodded he did venture a few critical comments, including some about the chapter on power. He found Locke's "Discourse about Mans Liberty and Necessity" to be "wonderfully fine spun," he said, but thought it required "some Farther Explication." But the only specific criticism he even hinted at was one about motivation: "you seem," he wrote to Locke, "to make all Sins to proceed from our Understandings, ... and not at all from the Depravity of our Wills." And yet, he added, "it seems harsh to say, that a Man shall be Damn'd, because he understands no better than he does" (C 4: 600–1: letter #1579). In essence, Molyneux was accusing Locke of overintellectualizing motivation, of making an agent's volitions depend too heavily on his judgments regarding the truth of certain propositions, even though these propositions concern the agent's own pleasure and pain. Molyneux was thus attributing to Locke the position of Socrates: to know the good is to do it, so that when wrong or evil occurs, it is because of some cognitive fault on the part of the agent: ignorance or error.

Whether Locke thought this accusation just, or took intellectualism to be a bad thing, is unclear. But he was moved by his friend's concern to undertake "a closer inspection into the working of Men's Minds, and a stricter examination of those motives and views, they are turn'd by," in consequence of which he "found reason somewhat to alter the thoughts [he] formerly had concerning that, which gives the last determination to the Will in all voluntary actions" (E 2–5 "Epistle to the Reader": 11). That which Locke now thinks is "the great motive that works on the Mind to put it upon Action, which for shortness sake we will call *determining of the will*, is always some *uneasiness*" (E 2–5 II.xxi.29: 249).

Uneasiness Locke takes to be a state of the mind, an occurrent feeling of discomfort or dissatisfaction that either is the same as, or at least always accompanies, desire. It is an affective rather than a cognitive state, though it has an (intentional) object: when a man is uneasy, there is always some thing or circumstance, actual or possible, that he is uneasy about. Indeed, Locke holds that the object of uneasiness is always some evil, or at any rate some absent good, and he still equates good and evil with pleasure and pain, as he had done before. Or rather, again as before, it is the pain or pleasure that the agent believes will ensue or be lost that causes his uneasiness or desire. But the new position differs from the earlier one in that the agent's judgments of good and bad affect not his will (at least directly), but rather his desire, which Locke now makes a point of distinguishing from will (as he had not done in the first edition). In the new view, the only thing that actually touches the will, so to speak, so as "to set us on work," is uneasiness: "'tis uneasiness alone [that] operates on the will"; nothing but uneasiness "immediately determines [it] to [any] voluntary action" (E 2–5 II.xxi.33–6: 252–4).

It might look, therefore, as if Locke has now made his position immune to the charge of intellectualism. What determines the will is not a judgment, or any cognitive state of the agent, but rather a feeling or emotion. And the new view allows for *akrasia* or weakness of will, as, notoriously, the Socratic view does not. That there are cases in which an agent fails to will the action that he knows is best for him, or wills to do what he knows is bad, is made evident, Locke says, by "every one's Experience." A poor man may be convinced of the advantages of plenty over poverty; yet he may be content with his state, and as long as he "finds no *uneasiness* in it, he moves not; his *will* never is determin'd to any action, that shall bring him out of it." And on the other side, "let a Drunkard see, that his Health decays, his Estate wastes; Discredit and Diseases ... attend ... him in the course he follows: yet the returns of *uneasiness* to miss his Companions; the habitual thirst after his Cups, at the usual time, drives him to the Tavern. ... 'Tis not for want of viewing the greater good: for he sees, and acknowledges it ... but when the *uneasiness* to miss his accustomed delight returns, the greater acknowledged good loses its hold, and the present *uneasiness* determines the *will* to the accustomed action" (E 2–5 II.

xxi.35–36: 253–4). It appears indeed that one of Locke's reasons for abandoning his earlier view of motivation is just that it precludes such cases. The same thought may have prompted Molyneux's objection too.

An important feature of Locke's new view of motivation is the doctrine of suspension. Here is the passage in which he introduces it.

> There being in us a great many *uneasinesses* always solliciting, and ready to determine the *will*, it is natural … that the greatest, and most pressing should determine the *will* to the next action; and so it does for the most part, but not always. For the Mind having in most cases … a power to *suspend* the execution and satisfaction of any of its desires, and so all, one after another, is at liberty to consider the objects of them; examine them on all sides, and weight them with others. … during this *suspension* of any desire, before the *will* be determined to action, and the action (which follows that determination) done, we have opportunity to examine, view, and judge, of the good or evil of what we are going to do; and when, upon due *Examination*, we have judg'd, we have done our duty, all that we can, or ought to do, in pursuit of our happiness. … (E 2–5 II.xxi.47: 263–4)

The significance of this power of suspension for Locke is that it enables an agent to have some control over when and what he wills, control which the new theory seems otherwise unable to provide for. For according to that theory, an agent cannot exercise his will except in response to some antecedent desire, and his willing is then dictated by both the timing and the content of the desire. But many if not most of our desires come to us unbidden; they are caused by conditions in our bodies, or by instinct, or habit, and are beyond our power either to initiate or to stop. It is paradoxical, to say the least, that, with such a causal history, an act of willing could give rise to an action that is free. And yet, on Locke's account of freedom, there is no free action that is not produced by such acts of willing. The doctrine of suspension provides the means by which an agent can prevent at least some of his desires from being effective. He may not be able to keep these desires from occurring, but he can keep them from determining his will and so keep himself from performing voluntary actions in accord with it.

Of course, suspension is a temporary state, and when it lifts or is lifted by the agent, there will again be a multitude of desires "solliciting, and ready to determine the will to the next action." So are we back where we started? Not necessarily, according to Locke. What happens during the suspension of our desires is that we "consider the objects of them; examine them on all sides, and weigh them with others." In other words, we deliberate; and when we have finished deliberating, we "judge, of the good or evil of what we are going to do." As a result of these judgments, our desires may change: some of those we had before may disappear; those that remain may gain or lose strength and so be reordered; some entirely new ones may arise. This could not happen if our cognitive states were not capable of influencing our desires, at least sometimes and to some degree. But Locke maintains quite explicitly that they do have this capacity. Thus "due, and repeated Contemplation [can bring some absent good] nearer to our Mind, give ... some relish to it, and raise ... in us some desire" (E 2–5 II.xxi.45: 262). Again, "by a due consideration of the true worth" of a great and weighty good, we are able to "form ... appetites in our minds suitable to it, and [make] our selves uneasie in the want of it. ... this is in every ones power. ... Nor let any one say, he cannot govern his Passions, nor hinder them from breaking out, and carrying him into action; for what he can do before a Prince, ... he can do alone, or in the presence of God, if he will" (E 2–5 II.xxi.53: 268). Locke does not maintain that we are able, merely by changing our opinions, to bring about changes in our wills, or in any case to do so directly. But we can bring about changes in our desires by this means, which then in turn determine our wills to various actions.

So cognitive states are effective in influencing our wills. Locke's new position thus reflects the intellectualism of his first edition view, but with this difference: though judgments of good or bad still have a place in the motivational process, their influence on the will is partial and indirect: it is not they, or they alone, that account for either the exercise or the specification of the will. In the new view, it is true that "Good and Evil, present and absent, ... work upon the mind. But that which immediately determines the *Will*, from time to time, to every voluntary Action, is *uneasiness* of *desire*, fixed on some absent good, either negative, as indolency to one in pain; or positive, as enjoyment of pleasure" (E 2–5 II.xxi.33: 252).

Still, there are a number of difficulties with Locke's new view, and especially with the doctrine of suspension, as several commentators have pointed out (see especially Chappell 1994b;

Magri 2000; and Stuart unpub.). Rather than discuss these difficulties, however, I will devote my remaining space to a further
question about the doctrine of suspension.

Locke claims that this doctrine has important implications for
our understanding of freedom. That there is a connection between
suspension and freedom is indicated in several passages.

We have a power to *suspend* the prosecution of this or that desire. ... This
seems to me the source of all liberty; in this seems to consist that, which is
(as I think improperly) call'd *Free will*. (E 2–5 II.xxi.47: 263)

This is the hinge on which turns the *liberty* of intellectual Beings in their
constant endeavours after, and a steady prosecution of true felicity, that
they can *suspend* this prosecution in particular cases, till they have
looked before them, and informed themselves, whether that particular
thing, which is then proposed, or desired, lie in the way to their main end,
and make a real part of that which is their greatest good. (E 2–5 II.xxi.52:
266–7)

The great inlet, and exercise of all the *liberty* Men have, are capable of, or
can be useful to them, and that whereon depends the turn of their
actions, ... lie[s] in this, that they can *suspend* their desires, and stop them
from determining their *wills* to any action, till they have duly and fairly
examin'd the good and evil of it. ... (ibid.)

Some scholars have thought that Locke is introducing a new
account of freedom in these passages, different from the one he put
forward in the first edition (see, e.g., Yaffe 2000). But if so, then
either the new account is intended to replace the original, or else it
is meant merely to supplement it in some way.

If there is a new account of freedom, it is clear that it is not
intended to replace the original definition. For that same definition
is stated several times in Locke's revised text, not merely in passages taken over and repeated from the first edition but in some
newly written. In the first edition, freedom is defined as the "power
in any Agent to do or forbear any Action, according to the determination or thought of the mind" (E II.xxi.8: 237) or again as "our
being able to act, or not to act, according as we shall chuse, or *will*"
(E II.xxi.27: 248). Both these passages are repeated, verbatim, in the
second edition. (See also E II.xxi.12: 239; II.xxi.21: 244; and II.xxi.23:
245.) In addition, Locke added passages to later editions in which

the same definition is repeated, for example: "Liberty 'tis plain consists in a Power to do, or not to do; to do, or forbear doing as we *will*" (E 5 II.xxi.56: 270).

So if Locke did mean to introduce a new account of freedom in the second edition, he must have meant it as a supplement to his original account. But in what way exactly? Matthew Stuart has proposed an answer to this question. In the original account, two requirements are set: for an agent m to be free with respect to an action ϕ, it is necessary (1) that m will to ϕ, and (2) that it be possible both for m to ϕ and for m not to ϕ, just by willing to do the one or the other. Stuart suggests that, in the second edition, Locke is specifying a third requirement for m's being free with respect to ϕ, namely, (3) that m have the capacity to suspend the desire that immediately precedes the volition to ϕ (Stuart unpub.: Chapter B, pp. 39–43). But Stuart does not claim that (3) is distinct from (1) and (2), such that an agent could satisfy them and not satisfy it. His position, rather, is that "the capacity to suspend desire [is] ... 'the hinge on which liberty turns' because it is a prerequisite for genuine agency." Locke's statements connecting suspension with freedom in the second edition do "not reflect a change in [or addition to] his view of what is required for an agent to be free with respect to a type of action; they ... serve [rather] to make more explicit his presumption about what is required for agency in the first place" (Stuart unpub.: Chapter B, pp. 40–1). Stuart's suggestion is both ingenious and entirely plausible, and in my view it resolves an interpretive problem that has puzzled several scholars in the past few years (see Yaffe 2000 and Chappell 2004).

6 Locke on Substance

The category of substance is a venerable philosophical concept. It was the first and most fundamental of Aristotle's logical categories, and even though it underwent a bewildering set of changes as it came down through the later Scholastic tradition, and was often the subject of heated disputes between various metaphysical camps, it remained a concept of central importance even into the seventeenth century. Descartes, for example, needs the notion of substance (although he understood it quite differently from Aristotle and the tradition) to formulate his famous claim that the mind is a substance that is really distinct from the body, which is also a substance; and he makes central use of it as well in his cosmological argument for God's existence (where the dependence relations of modes on substances, and of finite substances on an infinite substance, are taken to correspond to "degrees of reality," so that the ideas we have of these entities exhibit similar degrees of reality).

Corresponding to the foundational role the notion of substance plays in metaphysics, it enjoys epistemological priority as well. In the Aristotelian/Scholastic tradition, it is one of the first ideas of reason, and is a simple notion that is foundational to many of the more specific notions involved in the deductions of necessary truths that comprise *scientia*, the certain knowledge that we have of the world and the natural things within it. For Descartes, it is not so much the notion of substance as the notions of extended substance (which he equates with body) and thinking substance (which he equates with mind, or soul) that are clear and distinct, and which enable us to conceive minds and bodies as simple natures.

Against this august background, on Locke's account our idea of substance in general, or substratum, looks very much like a poor cousin. The most oft-repeated formulation he gives, one that has played into the hands of critics ever since Berkeley, is that substance in general, or substratum, is "something, [I] know not what." Here's the crucial passage from the *Essay*, quoted in full:

So that if any one will examine himself concerning his *Notion of pure Substance in general*, he will find he has no other *Idea* of it at all, but only a Supposition of he knows not what support of such Qualities, which are capable of producing simple *Ideas* in us; which Qualities are commonly called Accidents. If any one should be asked, what is the subject wherein Colour or Weight inheres, he would have nothing to say, but the solid extended parts: And if he were demanded, what is it that Solidity and Extension adhere in, he would not be in a much better case than the *Indian* before-mentioned [the reference is to E II.xiii.19]; who, saying that the World was supported by a great Elephant, was asked what the Elephant rested on; to which his answer was, a great Tortoise: But being again pressed to know what gave support to the broad-backed Tortoise, replied, something, he knew not what. And thus here, as in all other cases where we use Words without having clear and distinct *Ideas*, we talk like Children; who being questioned what such a thing is, which they know not, readily give this satisfactory answer, That it is *something*; Which in truth signifies no more, when so used, either by Children or Men, but that they know not what; and that the thing they pretend to know and talk of, is what they have no distinct *Idea* of at all, and so are perfectly ignorant of it, and in the dark. The *Idea* then we have, to which we give the general name Substance, being nothing, but the supposed, but unknown support of those Qualities we find existing, which we imagine cannot subsist, *sine re substante*, without something to support them, we call that support *Substantia*; which, according to the true import of the Word, is in plain English, *standing under*, or *upholding*. (E II.xxiii.2: 295f)

Although, as I've said, this is the most widely known of Locke's characterizations of the idea of substance in general, he does say more about it in the Stillingfleet correspondence. In the first of his letters to Stillingfleet, he specifies its content a little more fully, even if, as he admits, and indeed emphasizes, it doesn't come out looking any more clear and distinct. Correcting an evident misunderstanding on Stillingfleet's part, Locke writes:

... I never said, That the *general Idea of Substance comes in by* Sensation *and* Reflection: Or, that it is a simple Idea of Sensation or Reflection, tho' it be ultimately founded in them; for it is a complex Idea, made up of the general *Idea* of *something*, or *being*, with the Relation of a Support to Accidents. (1697: 35; W IV: 19)[1]

The idea of substance in general, then, is a complex idea consisting of the idea of something or being (which is among the most general or abstract ideas we can form, which in the case of this idea helps to make for obscurity), together with the idea of the relation of support (which itself is none too clear, at least in this context).[2]

[1] This quotation is from Locke's first letter to Stillingfleet (1697), which, I will sometimes refer to as the First Letter. All quotations from the letters to Stillingfleet are taken from the original, which varies somewhat from the reprint. (The citations included in the main text will include also the location of the quotation in the reprint.) Something should be said in defense of using these letters as evidence of Locke's views. Bennett, for example, rejects the correspondence as a source of evidence, asking, "is Locke likely to have been less clear and candid in his magnum opus than in his letters to a touchy and not very intelligent bishop?" (1971: 61) This question overlooks some important facts about the correspondence, however. It was not a private exchange; each of the so-called letters was a published book. Stillingfleet was an important figure of the time who enjoyed a solid reputation as an intellectual and a friend of the new science, and who had a high position in the Church of England (he was bishop of Worcester). The charge to which Locke was responding was a grave one, to wit, that he was at least a fellow traveller of the Socinian heresy. The correspondence was important enough to draw a two-part review in the *Nouvelles de la Republique des Lettres* for October and November 1699, and Leibniz was writing extensive comments on the correspondence during 1698–1700 (see Leibniz 1962: 16–37). Perhaps the most important fact is that, as I interpret Locke's doctrine of substance, there is no conflict between what Locke says in the *Essay* and what he says in the correspondence, so there is no need to question the reliability of statements Locke makes in the latter. Indeed, I think the same thing holds for all points of doctrine discussed in the correspondence. (For a similar evaluation of the Stillingfleet correspondence, see Ayers 1977a: 80, note 7.)

[2] Locke emphasizes the obscurity of the notion of a support to qualities, as it figures in the context of the idea of substance in general, by contrasting it with the use of the notion in more standard contexts:

> If your Lordship has any better and distincter Idea of Substance than mine is, which I have given an Account of, your Lordship is not at all concern'd in what I have there said. But those whose Idea of *Substance*, whether a *rational* or not rational Idea, is like mine, something he knows not what, must in that, with me, talk like Children, when they speak of something they know not what. For a Philosopher that says, That which supports Accidents is *something* he knows not what; and a Country-man that says, The Foundation of the great Church at *Harlem* is supported by *something* he knows not what; and a Child that stands in the dark upon his Mothers Muff, and says he stands upon *something* he knows not what, in this respect talk all Three alike. But if the Country-man knows, that the Foundation of the Church at *Harlem* is supported by a Rock, as the Houses about *Bristol* are; or by Gravel, as the Houses about *London* are; or by Wooden Piles, as the Houses in *Amsterdam* are; it is plain, that then having a

I. THE TRADITIONAL INTERPRETATION OF
LOCKE'S DOCTRINE OF SUBSTANCE

We've seen enough already to appreciate that Locke's doctrine of substance in general has at its core the idea of substance as substratum. Locke is at pains to stress that the idea of substance in general, as he explains it, is the same as the idea of substance he takes to be the inheritance of the long Scholastic tradition. He is no innovator, he assures Stillingfleet; to the latter's complaint that he has allowed only a very obscure idea of substance, Locke replies:

He that would shew me a more clear and distinct Idea of Substance, would do me a kindness I should thank him for. But this is the best I can hitherto find, either in my own Thoughts, or in the Books of Logicians; for their Account or Idea of it is, that it is *Ens* or *res per se subsistens & substans accidentibus*; which in effect is no more but that Substance is a *Being* or *Thing*; or in short, *Something* they know not what, or of which they have no clearer Idea, than that it is something which supports Accidents, or other simple Ideas or Modes, and is not supported it self as a Mode or an Accident. (1697: 10–11; W IV: 8)[3]

Locke goes on to mention Burgersdijk and Sanderson as two among "the whole Tribe of Logicians" who agree on this account of substance; and in a subsequent letter he explains that he mentioned them not to ridicule them but "for being of the same Opinion with me" (1699: 381; W IV: 449). Further on in the first letter, Locke responds to Stillingfleet's suggestion that "the best Authors" – to wit, Cicero and Quintilian – use the word "substance" in a different

---

clear and distinct Idea of the thing that supports the Church, he does not talk of this Matter as a Child; nor will he of the Support to Accidents, when he has a clearer and more distinct Idea of it, than that it is barely *something*. But as long as we think like Children, in Cases where our Ideas are no clearer nor distincter than theirs, I agree with your Lordship, *That I know not how it can be remedied*, but that we must talk like them. (1697: 15–17, W IV: 10)

See also the disparaging remarks Locke makes about *Inhaerentia* and *Substantia* in E II.xiii.20, to be quoted later.

[3] The accuracy of Locke's report about the views of logicians is confirmed by a sampling of contemporary logics: in Franco Burgersdijk (Burgersdicius), we have as Theorem I: "Substantia est ens per se subsistens, & substans accidentibus" (1637: I: ch. iv: 15); in Robert Sanderson, we have as the "definition" of substance: "Substantia est *ens per se subsistens*" (1640: I: ch. ix: 31). The same definition is given in Johannes Combach (1633: I: ch. 29: 311), a book on which Locke took notes. See J. R. Milton (1984) for further discussion of these sources.

sense, "a sense wherein it is not taken for the substratum of accidents," but instead is "the same with Essence," by saying:

However I think it a sufficient Justification of my self to your Lordship, that I use it in the same Sense your Lordship does. ... But if your Lordship and I (if without presumption I may join my self with you) have, in the use of the word *Substance* quitted the Example of the *best Authors*, I think the Authority of the Schools, which has a long time been allowed in Philosophical Terms, will bear us out in this Matter. (1697: 45–6; W IV: 23–4)

These passages leave no doubt that Locke meant his account of the idea of substance to capture the traditional logical notion of substance as a substratum to qualities.

What I am going to call "the traditional interpretation" takes straight, and at face value, Locke's portrayal of the idea of substance in general as simply the notion of substratum as it figured in the logical tradition. It's a traditional interpretation in two senses: first, it locates Locke's idea of substance within the tradition of Aristotelian logic, broadly construed; and second, it was the most widely accepted interpretation of Locke's doctrine of substance among Locke's contemporaries and critics,[4] and it was a standard view among commentators, down to about thirty years ago.

As traditionally interpreted, Locke's theory of substance includes the following central theses: (i) each individual object (individual substance) has a *substratum*; (ii) this substratum is conceived of, in the first instance, as the *support* to the qualities and powers of that individual substance; (iii) the substratum's being the support to qualities and powers is glossed in turn by the claims that (a) the qualities and powers of the individual *inhere in* the substratum, and cannot otherwise exist, whereas (b) the substratum *subsists* of itself (which means that it does not exist or inhere in anything else); (iv) the inherence relation is in some sense a *logical*, *noncausal* relation, in that it holds in exactly the same way for each of the powers and qualities, and it is not supposed that the substratum itself undergoes any change if and when the object undergoes a change with respect to any of its powers or qualities; (v) in line with this, the substratum is not supposed to have any nature or internal

---

[4] See McCann 2001. The interpretation of Locke's theory of substance offered there, the "no-theory" theory of substance, is the same as the one defended here.

differentiation of its own, and is thus *distinct from the real essence* of the object; finally, (vi) because the substratum is not directly available to sensory observation (or, in the case of the substratum to mental states, to internal reflection), the qualities and powers being the only things that are thus available, and because it has no intrinsic nature of its own, it is in principle *unknowable*.

In recent years, however, this interpretation of Locke's theory of substance has fallen out of favor. One important reason for this is reluctance on the part of recent commentators to ascribe to Locke a theory that seems to them to commit him to *bare particulars*, a commitment that the substratum theory is widely thought to carry. A bare particular is an entity that has no qualities, properties, or affections beyond bare subsistence (existing in such a way as to need nothing else – at least, no other finite entity – in order to exist) and perhaps, as on some views, a primitive identity.[5] No doubt to their credit (in point of charity, at least) commentators do not wish to saddle Locke with such a doctrine unless there is no way to avoid it.[6]

It's important to note not only that it is possible to be a substratum theorist without taking them to be bare particulars, but also that Locke says nothing that would invite reading substrata as bare particulars. It is, after all, one thing to say that we know of nothing besides subsistence or being, and being a support, that pertains to substratum, or that that's all that is contained in our conception of it; it's quite another thing to attribute to Locke the positive claim that there is nothing more to substance or substratum, so that as a matter of metaphysical fact we must deem them to be bare particulars.

[5] Many philosophers would agree with Anscombe's characterization of the notion of a bare particular as "incredibly idiotic," and even those who might find this characterization a bit harsh would be hard pressed to give a coherent formulation of the notion (see Anscombe and Geach 1961: 11). There is another understanding of the notion of a bare particular on which it is somewhat less implausible. According to this view, a bare particular is an entity having none of its properties essentially. But since Locke does not think that any individual substance has any of its properties essentially (see E III.vi.4), this would not differentiate substratum from the individual object itself.

[6] Interestingly, those commentators who were largely influential in bringing the traditional interpretation into the twentieth century were highly critical of the substratum theory. See, e.g., T. H. Green, the most influential British Hegelian of the late nineteenth century (1874–75), and James Gibson (1931: 190ff.).

Another factor, no doubt, behind the recent tendency to challenge the traditional interpretation has been the growing awareness of the extent to which Locke's philosophy is shaped by his commitment to the Gassendi–Boyle theory of mechanistic atomism, or corpuscularianism. There seems to be no role in corpuscularian theory for the notion of substratum to play; indeed, the notion may actually be incompatible with corpuscularianism, if the substratum is taken to be an actual component of a body, over and above (or rather, below or beneath) the aggregated solid parts of the body. The corpuscularian theory, after all, holds that the only real constituents of bodies are their solid parts.

Faced with these prima facie problems with the traditional interpretation, recent commentators have come up with a number of alternatives. There have been interesting, and competing, proposals from such leading figures as Peter Alexander, Michael Ayers, Jonathan Bennett, Martha Bolton, Maurice Mandelbaum, and John Yolton, among others. In spite of all the ingenuity, learning, and close attention to details of the text that mark the work of these mostly sympathetic interpreters, there are, it seems to me, serious problems with each of these interpretations. In what follows, I will consider four leading recent contenders, and will point out the shortcomings of each; we will see that in each case the traditional interpretation does better, so that it is the only interpretation that fits the whole range of Locke's pronouncements about substance. We will also see, not only that Locke's treatment of substance as substratum is not in conflict with corpuscularianism, but that it is an important part of his attempt to buttress corpuscularianism by ruling out on philosophical grounds its leading competitors, Aristotelianism and Cartesianism. What is more, when we appreciate the motivation behind the theory, we will see Locke's account of the idea of substance in general to be philosophically defensible, and even subtle. So I will urge a return to something very like the traditional interpretation. It may not always be true that the old ways are best, but in this case I think they are.

2. FIRST BENNETT

Jonathan Bennett has over the years offered not one but two rival interpretations to the traditional interpretation. The first of these is

presented in Bennett's very influential 1971 book (1971: 59–63).
Bennett was perhaps the first commentator to draw attention to the
prima facie conflict between the largely positive tone of some of the
main passages in the *Essay* concerning the idea of substance
(including the very important opening sections of the *Essay*'s
chapter on our ideas of substances (II.xxiii, especially sections 1–5),
and the quite negative tone found in the prominent and extended
discussion of the idea of substance in the *Essay*'s chapter on space
(II.xiii.17–20). The former set of passages emphasize the centrality
of the idea of substance in our thought about the world, and can be
taken (as Bennett took them) as attempts on Locke's part to argue
for the utility of the notion of substance and substratum – for
example, in explaining the nature of predication. The latter passages
are almost unrelievedly negative, claiming that the idea of substance is confused and obscure, and consequently of no use in
philosophy; indeed, as we'll see later, First Bennett seems to read
them as a denial of either the existence of substratum or the
meaningfulness of the notion of substratum, with perhaps the latter
denial as the ground of the former.[7] This apparent textual schizo-
phrenia should be regarded as a basic datum that any interpretation
of Locke's doctrine of substance must explain, or explain away, and
as much as anything else is responsible for the perplexities of
interpretation attending Locke's doctrine of substance. The major
difference between Bennett's two interpretations comes down to
whether the negative remarks are given precedence (First Bennett)
or the positive ones (Second Bennett).

Let us turn now to the details of Bennett's first interpretation.
Bennett describes "a certain line of thought about substance" that
he says Locke "entertained – I would not say adopted," although
halfway through the discussion this qualification threatens to
become lost amid the talk of "the Lockean analysis" and "the
Lockean theory of property-instantiation." As Bennett sets it out,
this line of thought takes off from the observation that the notion of
a "thing which" must be invoked in the analysis of any sentence
such as "The pen in my hand is valuable"; in this example, the

---

[7] The passages do not divide as neatly as this may suggest. There are echoes of the
negative remarks in E II.xiii.17–20 in some of the seemingly positive passages at the
opening of E II.xxiii; see particularly section 2.

subject term would be broken out as "thing which is in my hand and is a pen." The notion of a "thing which" cannot in turn be analyzed in terms of any "descriptive concepts" whatsoever, according to Bennett, because "the concept of a 'thing which'...is an ingredient in the concept of a 'thing which is F' for each value of F, and so it cannot be *identical* with the concept of a 'thing which is F' for any value of F" (1971: 59). Bennett identifies this concept of a "thing which" with that of a subject or bearer of properties, that is, a substratum.

So far, this line of thought has been exclusively about concepts; it says that every subject-concept has as a constituent the (unanalyzable, at least in terms of "descriptive concepts") concept of "a property-bearer, or of a possible subject of predication – let us call it the concept of a *substance*" (1971: 59–60). As Bennett presents it, however, the Lockean line of thought leaps to a metaphysical conclusion:

> So, if any existential or subject-predicate statement is true, then there are two sorts of item – substances, and properties or qualities. The former have the privilege of bearing or supporting the latter without being in the same way borne by anything. We imply the existence of "substances" in this sense every time we imply that some property is instantiated. (1971: 60)

Bennett goes on to criticize – rightly, it seems to me – the immediate move from a conceptual to an ontological claim. Indeed, in Bennett's view the mistake is compounded by the Lockean's insistence that substrata can have no other characteristics than that of being a property-bearer; as he puts it, "The Lockean analysis implies that nothing could count as experience of substratum-substance, but there is also a deeper objection, namely that Lockean substratum-substance *cannot have a 'nature' at all*" (1971: 62, emphasis in original). Bennett's Lockean, therefore, ends up committed to the existence of substrata as bare particulars. Thus, Bennett notes in closing, "The theory's crucial error is the move from 'There is a concept of a *thing which* ... , which enters into every subject-concept' to 'There is a kind of item about which nothing can be said except that such items bear properties'" (1971: 63). This is, of course, the recipe for bare particulars.

As I've noted already, Bennett does not interpret Locke himself as being finally committed to the correctness of this whole line of thought, or to its conclusion. Instead, he takes it as the target of Locke's negative comments about substance, concluding that "Locke's treatment of 'substance in general' is mainly skeptical in content and ironical in form" (1971: 61).[8]

Bennett is certainly right about the irony. At E II.xiii.19, Locke first regales us with the story of the Indian philosopher who supports the world by an elephant, and the elephant by a tortoise. If that philosopher had only thought of "the word *Substance*," Locke says, he could have used that to support the Earth, without troubling with the menagerie. For it's just as good an answer to the question of what supports the Earth:

...as we take it for a sufficient Answer, and good Doctrine, from our *European* philosophers, That *Substance*, without knowing what it is, is that which supports *Accidents*. So that of *Substance*, we have no *Idea* of what it is, but only a confused obscure one of what it does. (E II.xiii.19: 175)

Locke concludes the discussion with this:

But were the Latin words *Inhaerentia* and *Substantia*, put into the plain English ones that answer them, and were called *Sticking on*, and *Underpropping*, they would better discover to us the very great clearness there is in the Doctrine of *Substance* and *Accidents*, and shew of what use they are in deciding of Questions in Philosophy. (E II.xiii.20: 175)

In case any reader is deaf to the sarcasm, Locke spells out the message in his marginal summary for sections 19 and 20: "Substance and Accidents of little use in Philosophy."

Even if Bennett is right about Locke's ultimate aims, it will be worth our while to determine how much of the line of thought that Bennett initially describes is actually to be found in Locke, whether put forward as theory or set up as foil. Bennett quotes two passages from the *Essay* in connection with this line of thought. The one that seems to come closest is E II.xxiii.3: 297. It runs in part:

...we must take notice, that our complex *Ideas* of Substances, besides all these simple *Ideas* they are made up of, have always the confused *Idea* of *something* to which they belong, and in which they subsist: and therefore

---

[8] In a subsequent paper (1987), Bennett retracts the claim that in these passages Locke means to deny that there is such a thing as the substratum of an object. Although Bennett's current position is much closer to the one I defend, there are some important differences, which I'll note as we go along.

when we speak of any sort of Substance, we say it is a *thing* having such or such Qualities, as Body is a *thing* that is extended, figured, and capable of Motion; a Spirit a *thing* capable of thinking; and so Hardness, Friability, and Power to draw Iron, we say, are Qualities to be found in a Loadstone. These, and the like fashions of speaking intimate, that the Substance is supposed always *something* besides the Extension, Figure, Solidity, Motion, Thinking, or other observable *Ideas*, though we know not what it is.[9]

In this passage Locke is avowedly describing only what is "intimated" by our "fashions of speaking," and this is nothing more than that the substance is (supposed by us to be) something other than any one of the observable qualities of the thing, or the combination of them. The notion that Locke means to be describing an inference to an occult entity of some sort is belied by the last clause of the first sentence just quoted, when he says that hardness, friability, and so on are qualities to be found in a lodestone (as opposed to a substratum), and this common name he treats as on all fours with the "thing which" he had been speaking of in the preceding clause. So this passage does not provide evidence from Locke's text for the inference Bennett ascribes to the Lockean.

The other passage Bennett quotes is from E II.xxiii.2: 296, which I quoted in full at the beginning of this essay. Bennett quotes the last sentence:

The *Idea* then we have, to which we give the general name Substance, being nothing, but the supposed, but unknown support of those Qualities, we find existing, which we imagine cannot subsist, *sine re substante*, without something to support them, we call that Support *Substantia*; which, according to the true import of the Word, is in plain *English, standing under*, or *upholding*.

If this is supposed to be textual evidence of the Lockean inference to the bareness, or complete lack of a nature or of any qualities of its own, of a substratum, it similarly falls short. For it evidently concerns the poverty of our conception of substratum, which is, after all, only supposed because "we imagine" that the qualities cannot subsist without a support. There is no claim made here about the

---

[9] Part of this passage is quoted by Bennett (1971: 60) in connection with his exposition of the Lockean line of thought, although he begins his quotation earlier in the passage and, significantly, ends it earlier (before the bit about the lodestone).

nature, or lack thereof, of the substratum, but only about the shortcomings of our conception of substance in general.

This interpretation of the quoted passages is confirmed, I think, when we consider what is Locke's fullest statement of the process by which we come by the idea of substance in general. It is found in his first letter to Stillingfleet, where, after having characterized the idea of substance as "a complex Idea, made up of the general *Idea* of *Something*, or *being*, with the Relation of a Support to Accidents," Locke sketches how it is acquired:

All the Ideas of all the sensible Qualities of a Chery come into my Mind by Sensation; the Ideas of *Perceiving*, *Thinking*, *Reasoning*, *Knowing*, &c. come into my Mind by *Reflection*: The Ideas of these Qualities and Actions, or Powers, are perceived by the Mind to be inconsistent with Existence; or, as your Lordship well expresses it, *We find that we can have no true Conception of any Modes or Accidents, but we must conceive a Sub-stratum or Subject, wherein they are; i.e.* that they cannot exist or subsist of themselves. Hence the Mind perceives their necessary Connection with Inherence or being Supported, which being a relative Idea, superadded to the *red Colour* in a Chery, or to Thinking in a Man, the Mind frames the correlative idea of a *Support*. For I never denied, That the Mind could frame to it self Ideas of Relation, but have shewed the quite contrary in my Chapters about *Relation*. But because a Relation cannot be founded in nothing, or be the Relation of nothing, and the thing here related as a *Supporter* or *Support* is not represented to the Mind by any clear and dis-tinct Idea; therefore the obscure, indistinct, vague Idea of *thing* or *some-thing*, is all that is left to be the positive Idea, which has the relation of a *Support* or *Substratum* to Modes or Accidents; and that general, inde-termined Idea of *something*, is, by the abstraction of the Mind, derived also from the simple Ideas of Sensation and Reflection: And thus the Mind, from the positive, simple Ideas got by Sensation or Reflection, comes to the general, relative Idea of *Substance*; which without these positive, simple Ideas, it would never have. (1697: 39–40; W IV: 21–2)

Of course, the main burden of this passage is to show how the idea of substance in general is derived from sensation and reflection, as, according to Locke, all ideas must be; but it also shows that the idea of substance in general is not the result of a considered analysis of the subject-predicate sentence structure, but instead is the best we can do, in our ignorance, by way of marking our conviction that qualities cannot subsist in themselves or in one another. Locke says just this in a very important passage from near the beginning of the chapter, one to which both he and Stillingfleet made frequent reference in their correspondence:

Hence, when we talk or think of any particular sort of corporeal Substances, as *Horse, Stone, etc.* though the *Idea,* we have of either of them, be but the Complication, or Collection of those several simple *Ideas* of sensible Qualities, which we use to find united in the thing called *Horse* or *Stone,* yet because we cannot conceive, how they should subsist alone, nor one in another, we suppose them existing in, and supported by some common subject; *which Support we denote by the name Substance,* though it be certain, we have no clear, or distinct *Idea* of that *thing* we suppose a Support. (E II.xxiii.4: 297)

It was the language of "supposing" a substratum that drew Stillingfleet's ire; we'll return to this point later, but for now let us note Locke's suggestion that we settle on this supposition *faute de mieux.*

Our review of the relevant textual evidence has shown that it does not support the attribution to Locke, whether *in propria persona* or otherwise, of even the beginnings of the line of thought that Bennett ascribes to the Lockean. There is thus no question of his being committed to the doctrine of substrata as bare particulars, at least as reached by the route Bennett outlines.[10] Locke does not in those passages (or anywhere else) make use of the idea of substance in general to explain anything, nor does he attribute to the common folk, the nonphilosophers, all of us who find the idea of substance inescapable, the belief that it genuinely explains anything. They (we) certainly are not worried about providing a theory of predication or property instantiation, and Locke shows no sign of worrying about this either. He certainly does not claim to explain or analyze property instantiation or predication in terms of this idea (or any other) in these passages (or any other).[11] This is, of course, just what

---

[10] We will consider later, in connection with Bennett's 1987 interpretation, the Leibnizean criticism that Locke is stuck with bare particulars, whether or not he intends to be.

[11] This is not surprising, given his hostility to formal logic (i.e., the logic of the Schools). No doubt he would see the theory of predication as just another issue that is an artifact of the misplaced subtleties of Scholastic philosophy. See Wilson 1967: 347–66 for a valuable discussion of Locke's attitude toward formal logic; and see E IV.vii, viii, and xvii, passim. I take my claim that Locke is not interested in using the

one would expect after the brusque rejection of the usefulness of the doctrine of substance and accidents we found in E II.xiii.17–20.[12]

Now we need to consider the other part of Bennett's 1971 interpretation, which is encapsulated in the formula that Locke's treatment of substance in general is "mainly skeptical in content and ironical in form." Bennett evidently takes Locke to intend to reject the claim that there are any such things as substrata, on the ground that the affirmation (and hence, denial) of the existence of substrata does not even make sense given Locke's empiricist theory of meaning.[13] Bennett thinks that this is the better of Locke's two lines of thinking about substratum.

We can note, first, that given Locke's affirmation that we have an idea of substance in general, and the account he provides of how it is derived from simple ideas given in sensation and reflection, there would be no ground even on the most stringent empiricist theory of meaning for denying either the meaningfulness or the truth of the claim that there are substrata. There is, in addition, very strong textual evidence for Locke's commitment to the existence of substrata to be found in Locke's correspondence with Stillingfleet. In his 1697 book *A Discourse in Vindication of the Doctrine of the Trinity*, Stillingfleet had accused Locke of having "almost discarded *Substance* out of the reasonable part of the World" (Stillingfleet

---

idea of substance in general in developing a theory of predication, or in explaining anything, to be in conflict with that part of Bennett's interpretation that has not changed since the book. In his 1987 article, Bennett offers to explain the "two-faced" appearance of the passages on substance in general as the result of a conflict between Locke's semantic theory and his recognition that we "must" have the idea of substance. (See the first five sections of Bennett's paper.) As I read Bennett, he thinks that Locke thinks that we need the idea to explain property instantiation. Giving up this picture in favor of the one I have been urging, namely, that Locke thinks that we are stuck with the idea of substance as a way of marking our inability to conceive that qualities should exist by themselves or one in another, with the consequence that our idea of substance is irremediably obscure and so of no use in explaining anything, restores a single face to Locke's treatment of substance.

[12] In his 1987 article, Bennett correctly emphasizes that it is the common folk's idea of substance that is described in the *Essay*. He finds the passage at II.xiii.18 to be the only place where Locke "treats substratum not as an embarrassing bit of public property but rather as a gratuitous, dispensable, and wholly criticisable invention of certain philosophers" (1987: 209). But there Locke is not criticizing the idea of substance, particularly not as ordinary people hold it, but rather the attempt of philosophers to press such an obscure notion into philosophical service.

[13] This is also asserted in the 1987 paper.

1697b: 234).[14] Locke returned to this charge a number of times throughout the correspondence; at one of the first places where he takes it up, he says:

The other thing laid to my Charge, is, as if I took the *being* of *Substance* to be doubtful, or render'd it so by the imperfect and ill-grounded Idea I have given of it. To which I beg leave to say, That I ground not the *being* but the *Idea* of *Substance*, on our accustoming our selves to suppose some *Substratum*; for 'tis of the *Idea* alone I speak there [referring to E II.xxiii.1 and 4], and not of the *being of Substance*. And having every where affirmed and built upon it, That a *Man* is a Substance, I cannot be supposed to question or doubt of the *being of substance*, till I can question or doubt of my own being. (1697: 32; W IV: 18)

This might seem to be mere punning on the word "substance," that is, running together the claim "There are substances, that is, individual natural objects" with the more contentious claim "There is substance, that is, substratum." More than that is going on here, however; elsewhere in the first letter, Locke makes it clear that what licenses the inference in the passage above (Some man, to wit, John Locke, exists; ergo, some substance, i.e., a thing that has properties and qualities that cannot exist otherwise than in a substratum, exists; ergo, a substratum exists) is the general principle that sensible qualities (such as those had by a man, or defining the kind *man*, i.e., the qualities included in the nominal essence of man) cannot be conceived to exist except in a substance, or substratum. Thus

... as long as there is any such thing as Body or Spirit in the World, I have done nothing towards the *discarding substance out of the reasonable part of the World*. Nay, as long as there is any simple Idea or sensible Quality left, according to my way of Arguing, Substance cannot be discarded, because all simple Ideas, all sensible Qualities, carry with them a supposition of a *Substratum* to exist in, and of a Substance wherein they inhere. (1699: 9–10; W IV: 445–6)[15]

---

[14] This is in Chapter 10, entitled "The Objections against the Trinity in Point of Reason answer'd"; although it is "the Gentlemen of this new way of reasoning" (i.e., "the new way of certainty by Ideas") who are said to have almost discarded substance out of the reasonable part of the world, all the references that Stillingfleet gives are to the *Essay*. Note the adjective "reasonable"; Stillingfleet is plainly charging Locke with making substance unintelligible, i.e., not evident to reason as to either its nature or its existence.

[15] See also 1697: 57–8 and 65–6; W IV: 29 and 33. Note that this passage undermines Bennett's proposal that substratum functions as a genuine causal explainer of the unity of qualities in an individual object (see his 1987: 211–12).

This is all of a piece with the opening sections of the *Essay*'s chapter on substances, or at least Locke supposed it so. He copiously cites those sections (especially II.xxiii.1, 2, and 4) in the correspondence, in particular in connection with the passages just quoted, and in the fifth edition of the *Essay* both of the passages are added as footnotes to those very sections.[16]

Locke is even more explicit in his third letter to Stillingfleet. Here he responds to Stillingfleet's criticism that in saying, for example at E II.xxiii.1: 295, that we "accustom ourselves to suppose" a substratum underlying a thing's sensible qualities, Locke was demoting a "Consequence of Reason" or "Deduction of Reason" (Stillingfleet 1698: 12) to a mere usage of custom. "Your lordship goes on to insist mightily upon my supposing," Locke says in reply, and continues:

> Your Lordship...concludes, That there is Substance, *because it is a repugnancy to our Conceptions of Things...that Modes or Accidents should subsist by themselves;* and I conclude the same thing, because we cannot conceive how sensible Qualities should subsist by themselves. Now what the difference of *Certainty* is from a *Repugnancy to our Conceptions,* and from our not being able to conceive; I confess, my Lord, I am not acute enough to discern. And therefore it seems to me, that I have laid down the same *Certainty* of the Being of Substance, that your Lordship has done. (1699: 375–6; W IV: 445–6)

Locke finishes off this discussion by affirming that "there must be Substance in the World, and on the very same Grounds, that your Lordship takes it to be certain" (1699: 377; W IV: 446).[17]

---

[16] According to Nidditch, the excerpts from the correspondence included in the posthumous fifth edition (1706), which Locke identified in his will as the definitive edition, must at least have been approved by Locke's executor, Peter King. If there were any obvious departures from the *Essay*'s doctrines in these passages, King, as a sympathetic relative and a man well versed in Locke's philosophy, would no doubt have elected not to include them. See Nidditch's preface to the hardcover edition of the *Essay* (1975), pp. xxxii–iii; for the location of the footnote quotations of the two passages cited, see the fifth edition of the *Essay*, pp. 190 and 192, respectively.

[17] It is important to note that these formulations from the Stillingfleet correspondence go beyond anything that is said in the *Essay*; there he never says, flatly, that it is certain that there is substratum. He talks, instead, of "supposing" that there is substratum, because we're not able to "imagine" how simple ideas (qualities) can subsist by themselves (E II.xxiii.1: 295), or to "imagine" how they might subsist *sine re substante,* without something to support them (E II.xxiii.2: 296), or to

How are the seemingly skeptical passages from the chapter on space to be reconciled with these? Luckily, we don't have to guess. Locke tells Stillingfleet that the passages about the elephant and the tortoise

were not intended to ridicule the *Notion* of *Substance*, or those who *asserted it*, whatever that "it" signifies. But to shew, that though *Substance* did support Accidents, yet Philosophers, who had found such a support necessary, had no more a clear Idea of what, that support was, than the *Indian* had of that, which supported his Tortoise, tho' sure he was, it was something. (1699: 379; W IV: 448)

Locke had already warned us earlier in the first letter against inferring that substratum doesn't exist based on the obscurity of our idea of it:

So that I think the *being of Substance* is not shaken by what I have said: And if the Idea of it should be, yet (the *being* of things depending not on our *Ideas*) the *being of Substance* would not be at all shaken by my saying, We had but an obscure, imperfect *Idea* of it, and that Idea came from our accustoming our selves to suppose some *Substratum*; or indeed if I should say, We had no *Idea* of Substance at all. For a great many things may be and are granted to have a *being*, and be in nature of which we have no Ideas. (1697: 33; W IV: 18)

We can grant to Bennett that Locke's treatment of substance in the *Essay* is both ironical in tone and skeptical in content, so long as we

---

"conceive" how they should subsist alone, or one in another (E II.xxiii.4: 297). We should probably read Locke's insistence that he gives the same ground of certainty to the claim that there is substance in the world as does Stillingfleet as more an attempt to deflate the force of Stillingfleet's "certainty of Reason" and "repugnance to our first conceptions of things" than an attempt to promote our inability to imagine or conceive how qualities might subsist by themselves or in one another to the level of an inference yielding certainty. Note, however, the claim made in the First Letter derivation of the idea of substance in general from simple ideas given in sensation and reflection (quoted earlier), namely, that "the Ideas of these Qualities and Actions, or Powers, are perceived by the Mind to be inconsistent with Existence," so that "the Mind perceives their necessary Connection with Inherence or being Supported" (1697: 39–40; W IV: 21–2). Locke would be hard pressed, to put it mildly, to explain how it is that the mind perceives these things, and to the extent that his claim that we know for certain that substance exists depends on the correctness of the claims made in this passage, he'd do well to retreat from it. The point would still remain that we are completely at a loss when we try to conceive how qualities might exist without existing in some sort of support.

take the skepticism to concern only the clarity and distinctness of our idea of substance, and not whether there is something answering to this idea. On the latter question, Locke is no skeptic.

3. SECOND BENNETT

Now we can consider Bennett's second interpretation, offered in his 1987 paper "Substratum." Bennett rejects his old wrong answer – as he describes it (1987: 197) – in favor of one according to which Locke does not deny the existence of substratum. On the new answer to the question about the status of substratum in Locke, Bennett holds Locke to be torn between a felt need to recognize that there is some sort of conceptual demand to recognize that there is a support to qualities[18] and his commitment to an empiricist theory of meaning according to which the idea of substance can have no content.

Bennett's new emphasis on the positive side of Locke's remarks about substance, and his soft-pedaling of the negative or skeptical-seeming side, and in particular his continued appreciation that the role of substratum as support to qualities is the core of the idea of substance in general, are all quite in line with the interpretation I'm developing here. The part of the old interpretation that he hasn't jettisoned, and one that is still crucial to his interpretation, is the idea that Locke offers his account of substance in general as part of an explanation of predication, or of the property instantiation relation. We saw in the preceding section that Locke emphasizes over and over that the way in which the idea of substance in general is derived from simple ideas given in sensation and reflection leaves it a hopelessly and irremediably obscure and confused idea. Indeed, we've seen that the very passages that drove the First Bennett interpretation were designed to deliver the conclusion that "Substance and Accidents [are] of little use in Philosophy" (the marginal summary for E II.xiii.19 and 20). Locke would be confused, as Bennett suggests, if he tried to put such an obscure and confused idea to explanatory use, as part of an endeavor to explain the semantics of predication; but as I have argued, there is no reason to think he tried to do this.

---

[18] Bennett thinks this felt need to be finally wrongheaded: see the criticisms given in his section III (1987: 198–9).

This makes pressing the question why Locke advanced an account of substance at all. There is, as he himself insists, no innovation in his description of the content of the idea of substance; he never puts the idea to use in explaining anything, and indeed insists that it is so obscure as to be incapable of explanatory use; he has no interest in giving a theory of predication or property instantiation; and the idea has no role to play in the corpuscularian theory of nature that he accepted. Why doesn't he simply dispense with the idea of substance?

The mystery is dispelled when we consider that it is one of the major aims to the *Essay* to provide a catalogue – a natural history, as it were[19] – of all the ideas we have and an account of how they derive from sensation and reflection. As we have seen, one of Stillingfleet's main charges was that Locke couldn't provide for an idea of substance on the basis of sensation and reflection alone; this charge was pressed by other contemporary critics of Locke as well.[20] To have failed to account for an idea that, in the words of E I.iv.18: 95, "would be of general use for Mankind to have, as it is of general talk as if they had it," would thus have been a large lacuna in the project of accounting for all the ideas we have. Locke sincerely thinks that we have an idea of substance, such as it is, and he aims at giving an honest account of it, even if that account must leave us with an idea that is woefully obscure and confused.

Beyond the need for showing that the idea of substance does indeed derive from simple ideas given in sensation and reflection, Locke's account of the idea of substance in general can be put to other, and more subversive, uses in connection with Scholastic logic and metaphysics. We have already seen that the category of substance is the first and most important of the categories of Aristotelian/Porphyrian logic; it was a central assumption of the Scholastics that this logic limns the basic structure of reality, and thus provides a privileged framework for the formulation and accretion of knowledge. What becomes of this claim if that central notion is hopelessly confused and obscure, the result of an inability

[19] Thus at E I.i.2: 44 he says he will follow "the Historical, plain Method" in giving his account of the ideas we have and how we acquire them; see also E I.ii.1 and II.i.1.

[20] Prominent among them were Henry Lee and John Sergeant. For a very useful account of the contemporary criticism of the *Essay* on this point, see Yolton 1956: 126–48; also McCann 2001.

to imagine how qualities might exist by themselves rather than an insight vouchsafed by the light of reason? Not only will the Scholastic claim to possess a foundation for knowledge be undermined, but several important metaphysical doctrines will be threatened as well.

One of the leading Scholastic criticisms of atomism, for example, held that atomists could not account for the special unity possessed by an individual substance. For followers of Aristotle, it is the hallmark of an individual substance that it is a per se unity, as opposed to a mere aggregate of component parts. Atomists, according to this criticism, can see bodies only as accidental unities (as *entia per accidens*), and thus must treat individual substances as loosely and accidentally organized aggregates of material atoms. It is the substantial form that makes a parcel of matter into a unified object; it does this by organizing the constituent matter of the body in a certain way and providing for principles of growth, life, and continuity.

Locke in fact has a number of lines of reply to this criticism. One is to develop an account of identity for bodies that does not demand what Locke calls "Unity of Substance";[21] this he does in the *Essay*'s chapter on identity, providing an account on which a body may survive changes in its constituent matter (so that it is not strictly identical with the aggregated atoms, or "parcel of matter" that constitute it at any time), but without having a substantial form or other nonmechanistic principle of unity to keep it the same through change. Locke also has a battery of direct arguments against substantial forms, contained largely in E III.vi and focusing on the alleged connections between substantial forms, essences of species, and essences of individuals.[22]

Yet another line of defense is made available by Locke's treatment of the idea of substance in general. If we ask what basis there is for the claim that individual substances have a special unity, one going beyond mere unity by aggregation, the only plausible answer the Scholastic can give is that it comes from our knowledge of the

[21] E II.xxvii.7: 332. For a discussion of Locke's account of identity that pictures his theory in this way, see McCann 1987: 54–77.

[22] These are mainly to be found in the *Essay*'s chapter on the names of substances (III.vi), and have to do with the notion of species as natural kinds. For helpful discussions of these arguments see Ayers 1981 and Atherton 1984a.

nature of substance, which we have by virtue of our intellectual grasp of the category of substance. To call into question the competence of the idea of substance to give us nontrivial knowledge about the nature of substance, or anything else, thus helps to answer an important objection against mechanistic atomism.

Of course, it would take more discussion than I have space for here to determine how far Locke actually succeeds in undermining Scholastic attempts to draw rich metaphysical conclusions from the notion or category of substance. I hope enough has been said to indicate how Locke's account of the idea of substance could be seen to further his argument against Scholastic Aristotelianism and in favor of the Mechanical Philosophy. Locke's remarks on substance all have a single face, and that face is set firmly against Aristotelianism. As we'll see in the next section, he also uses his account of the role played by the idea of substance in general in our ideas of the two major kinds of (finite) substances, body and spirit, against that other archrival to corpuscularian mechanism, Cartesianism.[23]

4. ALEXANDER

There are two other recent interpretations besides Bennett's that stand as rivals to the interpretation offered here. In general, they see Locke as having more positive aspirations for the idea of substance than I have done; I will argue that they are not justified in this.

I will consider first Peter Alexander's recent, and ingenious, interpretation. Alexander sees Locke as denying that there is any wholly general notion of substance, one that could be common to body and spirit. Instead, there are two basic and fundamentally different kinds of substance-in-general, spirit and matter or body. In the case of matter this claim plays out as follows:

Matter is a solid stuff which is what, in material bodies, is qualified by specific shapes, sizes, and mobilities. My suggestion is that this is what Locke meant by substance-in-general for material things. It is not featureless

---

[23] Before leaving Second Bennett, I want to acknowledge that his 1987 paper makes an important contribution in pointing out some important formulations of Locke's that are very hard to interpret (1987, sections XIII–XV). I hope to discuss some of the issues raised by these formulations in future work.

because it is solid and solidity is its essential characteristic although it is not a quality; it does not exist independently of qualities since being solid entails having shape and size. (Alexander 1985: 224)[24]

Spirit is a different substance-in-general, whose essence, Alexander says, is "perceptivity," or power of perception and thinking (1985: 233–4). There is no more general notion of substance than either of these.

Let's consider first the claim that solidity is not a quality. The interpretation requires it, for if solidity were counted a quality, it would be as much in need of support as any other quality. There is plenty of evidence, however, that Locke takes solidity to be a quality of bodies. To mention just some central passages, we have Locke listing solidity as one of the *"original* or *Primary* Qualities of Body"* in the passage introducing the distinction between primary and secondary qualities (E II.viii.9: 135); later in the chapter, at II. viii.22: 140, it is called one of the *"primary*, and *real* Qualities of Bodies."* At E II.xxiii.30: 313, "solid coherent parts" is listed as one of the "Two primary Qualities, or Properties of Body" (and compare E II.xxiii.17). Throughout the Stillingfleet correspondence Locke speaks of solidity as a quality, and although Alexander argues (1985: 232) that Locke is simply deferring to Stillingfleet's formulations, there is no reason to think that Stillingfleet took these formulations from any source but the *Essay*. Locke's talk of solidity in the correspondence is all of a piece with that in the *Essay*.

Alexander's main reason for thinking that solidity is not a quality is that it cannot serve to differentiate bodies one from another: every body has solidity, and to exactly the same extent as every other body (speaking, that is, of absolute solidity or impenetrability, as opposed to relative solidity, or hardness). There are problems with this, however. In the first place, Locke never makes it a criterion of something's being a quality that it admit of variation or degree with respect to the things that have it, nor is there any independent reason to accept such a criterion. Second, if Alexander's idea is that something is a quality only if it qualifies some subjects and not others, so that it can serve as a point of

---

[24] The point that being solid entails having a determinate bulk and figure was made by Boyle, although he adds the required qualification that the body in question be finite. See Boyle 1667: 9 (reprinted in 1979: 20).

differentiation, then solidity would be a quality, for it would (and does, according to Locke and Boyle) distinguish bodies from immaterial spirits (angels, at least, and human minds if it isn't the case that God has made them by granting suitably framed systems of matter the power of thought).[25] Third, and most telling, mobility or motion-or-rest (the capacity to move or be moved, as distinguished from being actually in motion), another primary quality of bodies, is a quality that cannot vary in degree: either something has it or it doesn't, and anything that has it has it to exactly the same extent as any other thing that has it. Yet there is no question that it is a quality, a primary quality, of bodies. The same goes for the quality of extension, that is, having spatial dimension.

So much for the claim about solidity. Alexander's interpretation founders not just on this point, however. It has deeper problems. Specifically, it threatens to make hash of a central doctrine of Locke's, one that he defends at length in the Stillingfleet correspondence: the doctrine, namely, that it is possible, for all we know, that God gives thinking things the power of thought by superadding this power directly to merely material bodies. Alexander thinks that Locke is a dualist (1985: 225), pointing to those passages in the *Essay* and the correspondence where Locke says that it is "the more probable Opinion" that the thing that thinks within us is immaterial.[26] But Locke is not a dualist, at least not one of the Cartesian

---

[25] See E IV.iii.6.

[26] E II.xxvii.25: 345. See also 1697: 67 and 75; W IV: 33 and 37. In the First Letter, Locke cites his argument at E IV.x.16 as showing that it is "in the highest degree probable, that the thinking Substance in us is immaterial" (1697: 67; W IV: 33). But the argument there concerns the supposition that a system of matter could fortuitously or randomly, as it were, come to constitute an intelligent thinking thing. (The main consideration against: "For unthinking Particles of Matter, however put together, can have nothing added to them, but a new relation of Position, which 'tis impossible should give thought and knowledge to them.") Even if we overlook the fact that this argument begs the question against the materialist, it does not reach the point at issue. Stillingfleet saw this; quoting E IV. x.5, where Locke says that "it is repugnant to the Idea of senseless Matter, that it should put into itself Sense, Perception, and Knowledge," he comments: "But this doth not reach the present Case; which is not what Matter can do of it self, but what Matter prepared by an Omnipotent Hand can do. And what certainty can we have that he hath not done it?" (Stillingfleet 1697b: 242, quoted in Locke 1697: 74; W IV: 36) What Stillingfleet says here obviously goes for the E IV.x.16 passage as well, and for probability as well as certainty.

stripe; he famously (in the seventeenth century, notoriously) argues at E IV.iii.6 that we cannot demonstrate the truth of either dualism or materialism, and in this connection introduces the possibility of God's superadding the power of thought directly to systems of matter (i.e., certain sorts of bodies).

How would this possibility be understood, on Alexander's model? If one and the same individual object had both the quality of solidity and the power of thought (or perceptivity), it would have two distinct natures, and would belong to each of the two general kinds of substance. This in fact is the basis of an objection that Stillingfleet puts to Locke:

We do not set bounds to *God's Omnipotency*: For he may if he please, change a Body into an *Immaterial Substance*; but we say, that while he continues the Essential Properties of Things, it is as impossible for Matter to think, as for a Body by Transubstantiation to be present after the manner of a Spirit.... For if God doth not change the *Essential Properties of things*, their Nature remaining: then either it is impossible for a *Material Substance* to think, or it must be asserted, that a Power of thinking is within the *Essential Properties* of *Matter*; and so *thinking* will be such a Mode of *Matter*, as *Spinoza* hath made it.... (Stillingfleet 1697a: 78–9)

Locke's response, which Alexander seems to misunderstand (1985: 231–2),[27] is to point out that Stillingfleet cannot allow God the power to change a body into a thinking substance if he identifies the substance of a thing with its nature:

For if the same Substance remain not, *Body* is not *changed into an Immaterial Substance*. But the solid Substance and all belonging to it is Annihilated, and an Immaterial Substance Created, which is not change of one thing into another, but the destroying of one and making another *de novo*. (1699: 412; W IV: 470)

---

[27] There is nothing in Locke's reply taking Stillingfleet to task for counting solidity as a quality; and rather than "glossing" Stillingfleet's proposal that God may change a body into an immaterial substance, Locke is arguing that Stillingfleet cannot accommodate this possibility because he cannot recognize that one and the same substance could be first an extended solid substance and then (through God's intervention) a thinking one. Far from "denying the possibility" of God's removing the quality of solidity from a substance, leaving pure substance-in-general, which is then given the power of thinking, Locke's account of the change of a body into a spirit, and so his argument against Stillingfleet, requires that that be possible.

As the wider context of his argument makes plain, Locke is not arguing *in propria persona* that to take away the solidity of a body is to take away the individual substance itself, but is instead remarking that Stillingfleet's commitment to the identity of the substance of a body with its nature (an identification that Locke rejects, as Alexander himself notes [1985: 217–21]) leaves him unable to accord God as much power as he wishes, and claims, to do. Locke's point, then, is that on his view God has the power to change a body into an immaterial substance (or vice versa) by stripping the substance of its extension and solidity (or perceptivity) – that is, by removing what Stillingfleet had called its essential qualities and thus, according to Stillingfleet, destroying the substance – and adding the qualities appropriate to the other. Locke's God can do things – consistently describable things – that Stillingfleet's God cannot do. But Locke's God could not do these things (because they would no longer be coherently describable) if we interpret the notion of substance along Alexander's lines.

This difficulty is closely related to one that Alexander admits that he finds in an important passage from Locke's first letter to Stillingfleet.[28] Locke writes:

your Lordship will argue, That by what I have said of the possibility that God may, if he pleases, super-add to Matter a Faculty of Thinking, it can never be proved that there is a spiritual Substance in us, because upon that supposition it is possible it may be a material Substance that thinks in us. I grant it; but add, that the general Idea of Substance being the same every where, the Modification of *Thinking*, or the Power of *Thinking* joined to it, makes it a *Spirit*, without considering what other Modifications it has, as whether it has the Modification of *Solidity* or no. As on the other side *Substance*, that has the Modification of *Solidity*, is Matter, whether it has the Modification of *Thinking* or no. (1697: 66; W IV: 33)[29]

Alexander says that in this passage Locke is falling in with Stillingfleet's assumption that he is a doctrinaire materialist, and agreeing with Stillingfleet that this would involve one substance having both the modification of solidity and the modification of thinking. Locke's aim in this passage, according to Alexander, is to

---

[28] This passage is, Alexander admits, "the most difficult passage for my view" (1985: 228).

[29] Note that Locke calls both thinking and solidity "modifications" of substance.

show that even doctrinaire materialism does not have the consequences Stillingfleet supposes it to have.

This account of the passage won't hold up. In the first place, Stillingfleet never accuses Locke of being a materialist, nor does Locke take him to do so; they were both well aware that the point at issue between them is whether the immateriality of the soul can be rationally demonstrated. Second, Locke's own view that it is possible for God to superadd thought to material bodies is clearly interpreted by him to entail that a single substance can have the modifications of thought and solidity at the same time, and he explicitly avows this; there is no need to misinterpret him as a materialist in order (correctly) to attribute this view to him. Locke is simply arguing, *in propria persona*, that there is no special nature of the substance of a material thing that either necessarily ties it to solidity (so that solidity would be one of its essential properties) or prevents its having the power of thought, just as there is no special nature of the substance of a thinking thing tying it to thinking or preventing its also being solid. And Locke locates this sameness of the substance of each kind in the (wholly generic) content of the general idea of substance. When he says that the general idea of substance is the same everywhere, he means that one and the same idea is a component of the idea of body or matter (when the modification of solidity is added), and a component of the idea of spirit (when the modification of thinking is added).[30]

Admittedly, there is some talk in the *Essay*'s chapter on substances that seems to make better sense on Alexander's view than on mine. In E II.xxiii.5, 16, 23, and 30, Locke talks of "the substance of Body," "the substance of Matter," and "the substance of Spirit." Despite Locke's remarks in the Stillingfleet correspondence about the proper use of *"substantia"* in the Scholastic tradition, there is a fairly common use by some Scholastic writers of the locution "the substance of" where it does mean something like the nature or essence of the thing. (Note that in the first three editions of the *Essay*, Locke spoke of "the Nature, or Substance of Spirit [and] Body" at II.xxiii.5.) As Bennett notes (1987: 210), this phrase is anomalous in Locke; Bennett speculates that it is left over from an earlier stage of Locke's thought, where "substance" may have been

[30] My understanding of this passage is the same as Ayers's; see Ayers 1977a: 91.

used for other purposes. The fact that in the fourth and fifth editions of the *Essay* Locke altered the phrase in II.xxiii.5 but left "Substance of" argues against its being an unthinking holdover. We can make sense of Locke's use of this phrase by noting that the nominal topic of these passages, and indeed of a large stretch of the chapter, is the question whether mind is better known than body. He plays the middle against Descartes and Malebranche; where the former had held, famously, that mind is better known than body, the latter had held, in Locke's time equally famously, that body is better known than mind. Locke maintains that the two are equally well-known, or rather, ill-known. We know the observable, defining qualities of each (extension and solidity in the case of body, thinking and willing in the case of spirit), and beyond that, there is only the same obscure idea of substance underlying these qualities.[31]

Locke's further purpose in this discussion is that of undermining the notion that "the substance of body" (or "spirit") refers to an underlying nature that would causally explain the possession of extension and solidity, the defining characteristics of body (or of thought and volition, in the case of spirit). He offers a reductive account of these locutions, on which the general kinds of substance are defined simply by the observable qualities themselves (extension and solidity, thinking and willing), inhering in a substratum that, because our conception of this substratum is so obscure, cannot be taken to be the causal basis of the observable qualities, or

---

[31] Of course, the claim that mind is no better or worse known than body, and that each are equally badly known, depends on the fact not only that we know almost nothing of the nature of substance in general (given the obscurity of our idea of it), but also that we know very little about what the nature of thinking is, or how it is that thinking things perform this action, just as we have no conception of what holds together the parts of a body to make it a single extended thing. On the first part of our ignorance, see particularly E II.xxiii.15: 305: "For our *Idea* of Substance, is equally obscure, or none at all, in both [the Idea of Matter, and the Idea of Spirit]; it is but a supposed, I know not what, to support those *Ideas*, we call Accidents." For the other parts of our ignorance, see, for example, E II.xxiii.23: 308: "If any one says, he knows not what 'tis thinks in him; he means he knows not what the substance is of that thinking thing: No more, say I, knows he what the substance is of that solid thing. Farther, if he says he knows not how he thinks; I answer, Neither knows he how he is extended; how the solid parts of Body are united, or cohere together to make Extension."

to be any more or less tied to extension and solidity than it is to thinking and willing.[32]

We can understand in the same way the puzzling opening clause of E II.xxiii.6: 298. It runs: "Whatever therefore be the secret and abstract Nature of *Substance* in general..." Good nominalist that he was, Locke cannot be maintaining that there actually is such a thing as an abstract nature, whether of substance or of anything else.[33] Here we have two choices, equally good: we could see Locke as waving aside the issue whether substratum is to be seen as a causal (in the Aristotelian sense of formal cause) basis for the manifest defining qualities, or instead as simply something in which those qualities inhere (and from which they may be separated, leaving the same substance), and forging ahead to his point in this section that the ideas of the sorts of substances (man, horse, etc.: not the general kinds of substances) are simply collections of sensible ideas taken to exist in a subject,[34] where the emphasis is on the fact that the sensible ideas are all we really have access to; or, the alternative I prefer, since the talk of a 'secret and abstract nature' is so unusual for Locke, we could see here once again the sarcastic tone that Locke favors in discussing the metaphysical excesses of the Schoolmen.

Alexander's interpretation runs afoul of too many central Lockean doctrines to be acceptable. It has the right motivation, for it sets out to undermine the view of Locke's notion of substance as "an absolutely indeterminate and unknowable substratum in which all

---

[32] Note that on this reading of these passages they are of no help at all to what Bennett takes (1987: 208–10) to be Ayers's interpretation.

[33] Compare this from the first letter to Stillingfleet: "By *general Substance* here, I suppose, your Lordship means the general Idea of Substance:...and if your Lordship should mean otherwise, I must take the liberty to deny there is any such thing in *rerum Natura* as a *general Substance* that exists it self, or makes any thing" (1697: 52; W IV: 26). Of course, Locke does allow that there are general or abstract ideas, but these don't refer to real natures of things. See E III.iii.

[34] Here Locke speaks of this subject as a "Cause of their [the simple ideas, or more exactly the qualities they represent] Union," but this can be understood along the lines suggested earlier: the substratum can be taken to unify a collection of qualities if each of the qualities individually inheres in the substratum. This reading is helped by the further specification: "in such, though unknown, Cause of their Union, as makes the whole subsist of itself." Also, note the occurrence of the phrase "unknown common Subject, which inheres not in anything else" just a couple of lines further down (E II.xxiii.6: 298).

qualities, whether observable or not, and whether material or mental, must inhere" (1985: 221), where this is taken to involve ontological commitment to an entity distinct from the individual object itself. As we've seen, however, the traditional interpretation isn't committed to any such entity, and it can accommodate all of the relevant passages.

5. SUBSTANCE AND SUBSTANTIAL FORM

The other rival to the traditional interpretation is probably the currently most widely accepted interpretation of Locke's doctrine of substance.[35] On this interpretation, Locke identifies substance with real essence. The claim is not that he identifies the concept or notion of substratum with the concept or notion of real essence,[36] but rather that he holds that these concepts pick out the same thing, so that the real essence of the thing is what "supports" the thing's qualities.

The reasoning that leads to this interpretive claim runs roughly as follows: A significant difference between the sensible qualities or powers of a thing and its substance or substratum, according to Locke, is that the former are observable, while the latter is not. Similarly, Locke holds that the real essence of a body is not observable by us (at least not under present conditions), while, as before,

---

[35] Maurice Mandelbaum first put forward this interpretation (1964); it is also advanced by John Yolton (1970: Chapter 2) and Martha Brandt Bolton (1976b). Ayers (1977a) is widely taken to identify substance (substratum) with real essence, but this is a mistaken interpretation of his view. His arguments against the view that Locke is committed to substratum as an actual entity distinct from the real essence (and from the individual object) are, some of them, similar to arguments given by Mandelbaum and others, so this may have aided the misconstrual of Ayers's position. Since Ayers's article does contain forceful and influential presentations of some of these arguments, I will sometimes cite his article for them, even if he does not take them to yield the conclusions that many of his readers have drawn from them. But it is important to note that the view presented in Ayers 1977a is the same as that outlined more fully in his magisterial 1991 book, *Locke* (see Volume II, Part One, especially Chapters 3, 4, 8, and 9) and in a very helpful summary presentation in Ayers 1996; in none of these presentations does Ayers identify substance or substratum with real essence.

[36] Alexander's criticism of the interpretation seems to rely on this misapprehension; see Alexander 1985: 217–21. The passages Alexander cites from the Stillingfleet correspondence only go against the view that the concepts of substance and of real essence are the same.

the sensible qualities that "flow" from it are observable. This is not, according to the new interpretation, "a two-fold ignorance" of substance and of real essence (Pringle-Pattison's phrase)[37]; we are ignorant of the nature of that which underlies or lies behind the observable qualities, that from which they "result" or "flow," whether we call this thing "substratum" or "real essence." Thus Mandelbaum says that the idea of a substratum is "a surrogate for what in the object is material and exists independently of us...an indeterminate and general notion standing for something in the object which makes that object a self-subsisting thing...", because of its indeterminacy, the idea "stands in need of correction by inferences based on the observation of the powers of objects: it is the atomic constitutions of objects, not 'pure substance in general', which cause the ideas of them which we actually have, and which also cause the effects, whether perceived or unperceived, which objects have upon one another" (1964: 39). Ayers says something similar: "The concept of 'substance', 'substratum', or 'thing (having such and such properties)' is thus a concept by means of which we refer to what is unobserved and unknown – or known only through its effects and relatively to the level of observation. In other words, substance is a 'dummy' concept like power..." (1977a: 85; see also 77–80, 84–5, 90–6). Again,

What underlies "the powers and qualities that are observable by us" in anything is a substance constituted (or modified or determined) in certain ways. There are not two underlying levels, first the real essence, then, beneath it, the substance. (1977a: 94)

On this view, we can expect that the notion of substance will finally be displaced by that of real essence as science progresses.

This line of reasoning is both plausible and appealing, but there is no textual evidence that directly supports it. Locke nowhere explicitly identifies substance and real essence, not even in such propitious places as the long and involved discussion of real and nominal essences in E III.iii and III.vi, or in the lengthy controversy with Stillingfleet (who did identify substance and essence at the conceptual level). Locke puts the two notions to quite different work in different stretches of the Essay, even in those few passages

---

[37] Pringle-Pattison 1924: 233–4.

where they rub up against each other. There are some parallels in the way the respective notions are sometimes treated, but these are few and weak.[38]

We can't suppose that Locke would have thought that the identity of substance and essence went without saying, given the background to his argument. The long history of the Scholastic tradition gave rise to a number of conflicting views concerning the substratum: some held that it was the matter of which the thing is composed (with additional latitude for controversy over whether it was prime matter or so-called designated or signate matter), others that it was the composite of form and matter, still others that it was the form itself. The real essence of a thing, both as traditionally conceived (as substantial form) and as thought of by Locke,[39] is the causal basis of that thing's powers and qualities (or in the case of substantial form, the basis of the thing's essential properties and associated *propria*). The substratum, or subject of properties and qualities, is related to the qualities in a different way: it supports them; they inhere in it; and this relation is in a certain sense logical. Now of course there is no inconsistency in one and the same thing being related both causally and "logically" to the same properties and qualities.[40] Nonetheless, the notions of substratum and of real essence are highly theoretical ones with quite different theoretical roles to play, so that an identification of the two is not at all obvious. (Indeed, it is hard to see what the grounds would be for such an identification.) In any case, Locke would have known that to identify the substratum with the essence of a thing is to take a position on a long-standing and highly contentious issue.

Locke would have known this because of his Scholastic training and because of Boyle's discussion of a related issue in his major work, *The origine of Formes and Qualities*. One of the traditional difficulties for the view that form is the substratum to properties

---

[38] Both Alexander (1985: 217) and Bennett (1987: 202–3) make similar points.

[39] The corpuscularian notion of real essence was regarded by Locke as a replacement for the Scholastic notion of substantial form: both were supposed to satisfy the traditional definition of the *essentia* of a thing as "that which makes a thing to be what it is" (where this "making" is causal), and Locke presents the dispute between the corpuscularians and the proponents of substantial forms as a conflict of opinions about the nature of real essence. See E III.iii.15 and 17.

[40] Some of the critics of the identification of substance and real essence seem to have overlooked this point. See, e.g., Woolhouse 1969: 130–5 and Buchdahl 1969: 222–3.

was that it seemed to make the substantial form of a thing unqualifiedly a substance in its own right, that is, a thing able to subsist independently of anything else, and in particular, of matter. This threatened to make ordinary individual substances – men, horses, bronze spheres, and so on – into composites or accidental unities. Boyle brings it up as an example of the confusions attending the doctrine of substantial forms:

... so those things which the Peripateticks ascribe to their substantial Forms, are some of them such, as, I confess, I cannot reconcile my Reason to: for they tell us positively, that these Forms are Substances, and yet at the same time they teach that they depend upon Matter, both *in fieri* and *in esse*, as they speak, so that out of the Matter, that supports them, they cannot so much as exist, (whence they are usually call'd Material Forms,) which is to make them Substances in name, and but Accidents in truth: for not to ask how (among Physical things) one Substance can be said to depend upon another *in fieri*, that is not made of any part of it [Boyle has in the preceding pages been criticizing the Scholastic doctrine that forms are "educed out of the power of matter"], the very notion of a Substance is to be a self-subsisting Entity, or that which needs no other Created Being to support it, or to make it exist.

And a little further on in the same paragraph:

... for if a Form be a true Substance really distinct from Matter, it must, as I lately noted, be able to exist of it self, without any other Substance to support it; ... whereas they will have it, that in Corruption the Form is quite abolish'd, and utterly perishes, as not being capable of existing, separated from the Matter, whereunto it was united: so that here again what they call a Substance they make indeed an Accident....[41]

It is not clear how representative a picture this is of late Scholastic views about substantial forms;[42] it is possible, for example, that

---

[41] Boyle 1667: 155–6 (reprinted in 1979: 57); previous quotation, Boyle 1667: 154–5 (reprinted in 1979: 57).

[42] Boyle is careful to note that these views are not Aristotle's; he prefaces the discussion from which I have been quoting with the caveat that he is discussing only the "general opinion of our modern Aristotelians and the schools":

> I say, the *Modern* Aristotelians, because divers of the *Antient*, especially *Greek* Commentators of *Aristotle*, seem to have understood their Masters Doctrine of Forms much otherwise, and lesse incongruously, than his Latin followers, the Schoolmen and others, have since done. Nor do I expressly mention *Aristotle* himself among the Champions of substantial Forms, because though he seem in

Boyle is missing a qualification frequently attached to the claim that the differentia, and/or the substantial form underlying them, are in the category of substance: they are so, it was said, only "reductively," and thus are not to be considered substances in the primary or focal sense.[43] Whatever the accuracy of Boyle's presentation, there can be no question that Locke would have been well aware of the difficulties of identifying substance and real essence, if not from his Scholastic training, then from Boyle's discussion.

The most difficult passage for the identification of substratum with real essence comes from the correspondence with Stillingfleet. We have already seen Locke firmly rejecting Stillingfleet's identification of the nature or essence of a thing with its substance, even though he admits that "the best authors" make this identification; while this doesn't count against an ontological reduction of substance to real essence, still, given Locke's strategy of maximizing (at least the appearance of) agreement with Stillingfleet, he might have been expected to note the reduction if he had had it in view. Continuing his discussion of the relation between substance and essence, Locke says:

Here I must acknowledge to your Lordship, That my Notion of these Essences differs a little from your Lordship's; for I do not take them to *flow* from the Substance in any created Being, but to be in every thing that *internal Constitution*, or Frame, or Modification of the *Substance*, which God in his Wisdom and good Pleasure thinks fit to give to every particular

---

a place or two expressly enough to reckon Formes among *Substances*, yet elsewhere the examples he imploies to set forth the *Forms* of Natural things by, being taken from the *Figures* of artificial things, (as of a Statue, &c.) which are confessedly but *Accidents*, and making very little use, if any, of Substantial Forms to explain the *Phaenomena* of Nature, He seems to me upon the whole matter, either to have been irresolv'd, whether there were any such Substances, or no, or to speak ambiguously and obscurely enough of them, to make it questionable, what his opinions of them were. (1667: 144–5; 1979: 53)

Recent writers in the Scholastic tradition mentioned by Boyle in the *The Origine of Formes and Qualities* (1667) include, prominently, Giacomo Zabarella, J. C Scaliger, and Daniel Sennert (Sennertus), but Boyle does not cite particular works, nor does he mention these names expressly in connection with the making of forms into substances.

[43] Thanks to Calvin Normore for explaining to me the significance of this qualification.

Creature, when he gives it a Being: and such *Essences* I grant there are in all Things that exist. (1697: 187–8; W IV: 82)

I see no reason for reading "modification" in any other than the usual sense. Locke is saying that a body's matter being arranged in this or that particular way (i.e., its having constituent atoms each with its particular bulk, figure, motion, and relative situation) *is* its having a particular real essence or internal constitution; the atomic structure, or particular arrangement of the matter of a thing, is a modification (or mode) of the substance. Locke would certainly hold that it is possible for a thing to have its internal structure (slightly) rearranged while remaining the same substance. Holding to the traditional terminology, real essences would then be modifications of substances, not substances themselves.

This doesn't amount to a decisive refutation of the interpretation identifying substratum with real essence. That interpretation is an ingenious one, and it neatly avoids saddling Locke with a commitment to substrata as real, distinct entities. The problem with it is, as we have seen, that it has nothing going for it in the way of textual evidence. More than this, it seems to leave Locke in the uncomfortable position of issuing a promissory note about the advancement of our scientific understanding of nature, a promissory note that Locke himself says we probably won't be able to cash.[44]

The version of the traditional interpretation that I have defended here does not commit Locke to a mysterious entity that is distinct from the individual object and entirely undifferentiated in its own nature; it does not rest on any promissory notes about the future progress of science; and it fits with, and does not go beyond, the textual evidence. Moreover, it pictures Locke as having offered in his account of substance an effective wedge against a number of central Scholastic metaphysical doctrines, some of which were supposed to provide the basis for criticisms of mechanistic atomism.

6. CONCLUSION

The main points of the interpretation for which I have argued are these. Locke thinks we have an idea of substance in general whose

---

[44] See E IV.iii, IV.vi, IV.xii.

content is just as logical tradition has it to be: it is the idea of a support or substratum to qualities, that is, something in which qualities inhere but that does not in turn inhere in anything else. Against the tradition, however, Locke insists that the idea is confused and obscure, affording us no clues about the nature of this substance; the only knowledge we can base on this idea is the certain knowledge that substance exists. This does not, however, commit us to the existence of any entity over and above, or below or beneath, the body itself with all of its qualities and powers; nor are we bound to identify the substratum to qualities with the real essence of the body. All that we are in a position to say, given the obscurity of the idea of substance, is that *something* supports the qualities and powers of the body. And to say this is not to explain, or even begin to explain, anything.

Locke's treatment of the idea of substance is, like most everything else in the *Essay*, aimed at advancing the claims of the mechanical philosophy against the Aristotelianism of the Schools. It is, I hope to have shown, a treatment that is not shabby by any reasonable philosophical standards. What is more, it worked. Locke was on the winning sides in what Michael Ayers has called his two big battles, against Cartesian and Aristotelian dogmatic philosophy; and as Ayers remarks, "His capacity for winning, in metaphysics as in politics, should not be despised."[45] If my interpretation is right, Locke's treatment of the idea of substance is an important part of this winning strategy.[46]

[45] Ayers 1977b: 227. It is obvious how a denial that we have a clear and distinct idea of substance would cut against Cartesianism.

[46] This chapter started life as an invited paper read at the Pacific Division meetings, of the American Philosophical Association, March 1986. The commentator was Margaret Atherton; I thank her, Barry Stroud, and Jonathan Bennett for their very helpful remarks at that session. The paper was subsequently read, in different versions, to colloquia at Claremont Graduate School, the University of California at Irvine, and the University of California at Santa Cruz. In addition to thanking the members of the audiences at those occasions, I also want to thank Michael Ayers, Michael Friedman, Jeremy Hyman, Thomas Lennon, Janet Levin, Brian Loar, Calvin Normore, and Margaret Wilson for their valuable criticisms. I am grateful to referees for the *Philosophical Review* for their helpful comments. I am especially grateful to Lex Newman for his penetrating and helpful comments on recent drafts.

7   Locke on Ideas of Identity and Diversity

INTRODUCTION

Identity is a relation: it is the relation that each thing bears to itself. It is not the only relation that a thing can bear to itself. You can point at yourself, for instance. But identity is the only relation that each and every thing necessarily bears to itself and that no thing could bear to anything distinct from itself.[1] By contrast, some things don't point at all, much less point at themselves, and sometimes you point at things other than yourself. For any relation, there are criteria that objects must meet if one is to bear the relation to the other: you are pointing at yourself, for instance, only if your finger is directed toward your body. Locke's Scholastic and Cartesian predecessors used the term "principium individuationis," or the principle of individuation, to refer to the criterion that two things meet just in case they are, indeed, two things and not one. The flip side of the principle of individuation is what we might call the principle of identity, a criterion that two things meet just in case they are not two things at all but are, in fact, one. Imagine, for instance, that you are looking at a picture, taken some years ago, of a baby, and you are wondering if it is a picture of you. A specification of the principle of identity of persons would be a specification of a rule, or principle, that would be met by you and the baby in the picture just in case you *are* the baby in the picture. The principle of identity (and the corresponding principle of individuation) is a filter: it allows pairs (like the baby in the picture and you) to pass

---

[1] Strictly speaking, identity is the only relation that is both symmetric and transitive. A relation R is symmetric if and only if (aRb ↔ bRa). R is transitive if and only if ((aRb & bRc) → aRc).

through it if they are identical, and only if they are identical. The principle of identity would not necessarily tell you how to *find out* if you and the baby in the picture are the same person – perhaps you do that by looking on the back of the photo to see if your name is written on it – but would tell you, instead, what the fact is that you are discovering when you discover an identity; it would tell you what identity is.

Locke's most important discussion of identity in the *Essay* (E II. xxvii: 328–48, "Of Identity and Diversity") appears in Book II alongside chapters concerned with various other relations, such as the causal relation. (The concept of identity is discussed explicitly in a few other places in the *Essay* as well. See E I.iv.4–5, where Locke claims that the idea of identity cannot be innate, and E II. i.11–12, where he claims that the Cartesian claim that the mind is always thinking is contradicted by what we know of personal identity.) Like the other chapters of Book II, the ostensible purpose of "Of Identity and Diversity" is to offer an account of the mechanism through which we acquire particular ideas. However, also like other chapters of Book II, Locke leaves aside the question of the acquisition of the idea rather quickly and launches into a discussion of philosophical questions that arise about what the idea is of. What he offers are accounts of the principles of individuation, and corresponding principles of identity, of many things, including, although not limited to, persons. Locke's account of personal identity, and the method that he uses to defend it, influenced his immediate successors tremendously and remains to this day the starting point for much thinking about the nature of personal identity. It is one of the *Essay*'s enduring legacies.

Although we care about the identity of many things – it could be quite disconcerting to find that the toaster on the counter when you wake up is not the same one as the one that was there when you went to bed – the identity of persons has peculiar importance. It is impossible, in fact, to go through a day, or even an hour, without having a thought intertwined with thoughts about the identity of yourself or others. When you step onto a rollercoaster, you might feel a peculiar form of apprehension that you don't feel about, say, your next-door neighbor's stepping onto the rollercoaster. That feeling of apprehension is a feeling of doubt, however slight, that you will survive the ride. But the question "Will I survive?" always has the same answer as the question "Will a person get off the rollercoaster at the end who is identical to me?" To want to survive, or to worry that you might not, is to want a future person and your present self to be the same person. So, and this is of importance to Locke, to believe that there is an afterlife is to believe that after your body's last breath there will still be, somewhere in the world, a person identical to your present self. Similarly, if you sit on a jury, you are asked to pronounce as to whether or not the person in the courtroom and the person who committed some crime in the past are the same person. It wouldn't do to conclude that the defendant *has a lot in common* with the criminal. Nothing short of identity will serve for the justice of punishment. And, correlatively, if the defendant does not believe himself identical to the man who committed the crime, a variety of self-directed moral emotions are out of place: it would make no sense for him to feel guilt or remorse, for instance, if he didn't think himself the same person as the one who committed the crime.

Locke uses the term "concernment" to refer to that special emotionally entangled attitude that you have toward future and past persons whom you judge to be identical to yourself and that you don't normally have in the absence of a belief in identity. His primary aim in "Of Identity and Diversity" is to discover the basis, or the grounds, for concernment. What fact are we tracking in our emotions when we feel concernment? What is personal identity? However, answering this question requires, first, thinking about identity in general and how we acquire the idea and, second, thinking about what it is that makes for the identity of many ordinary objects that we encounter every day.

I. THE ACQUISITION OF THE IDEA, THE PRINCIPLE OF INDIVIDUATION, AND RELATIVE IDENTITY

It is by engaging in the mental operation that Locke calls "comparing" that we acquire our ideas of relations (cf. E II.xi.4). Comparing, like abstracting, composing, and enlarging, is a way of creating a new idea from ideas you already have. You have an idea of the cup and an idea of the coffee, for instance, and by comparing the two you come up with the idea of a relation between them, an idea that you express with the words "is in," when you say, "The coffee *is in* the cup." So we would expect Locke to say that the idea of identity is acquired by comparing any idea with itself. This, however, is not what he says. He begins the chapter on identity, instead, with the following remark:

ANOTHER occasion, the mind often takes of comparing, is the very Being of things, when considering any thing as existing at any determin'd time and place, we compare it with it self existing at another time, and thereon form the *Ideas* of *Identity* and *Diversity*. (E II.xxvii.1: 328)

In order to acquire the idea of identity (and the idea of diversity), we need to compare two *distinct* ideas of the same thing to each other, rather than comparing any one idea of a thing to itself; the two ideas represent the thing at different times. So, for Locke, a creature that had ideas only of things existing in the present – perhaps an entity that has ideas only of things that it is sensing – would lack an idea of the relation of identity. Such a creature wouldn't have the kinds of ideas needed to compare, and so wouldn't have the tools for creating the idea of identity.

In the first instance, then, the idea of identity is formed in order to formulate a question about the identity of objects encountered at different times. You wonder if the piñata that the children were pounding on an hour earlier, when you passed, is the same one they pound on now. You didn't wonder, when you walked by the first time, if the piñata on which they pounded was the same one on which they pounded; obviously it was, and so there was no question to ask, no need to formulate an idea of the relation of identity. But, Locke points out, if you think there's a determinate answer to the question – if you think it either is or is not the same piñata with which the children earlier labored – it is because you are tacitly assuming that what you looked at earlier was not, itself, two things but one. Your question – "Same piñata?" – wouldn't have a determinate answer if, for instance, there had been two piñatas hanging in exactly the same place when you passed earlier. Locke puts the point like this:

When ... we demand, whether any thing be the same or no, it refers always to something that existed such a time in such a place, which 'twas certain, at that instant, was the same with it self and no other: From whence it follows, that one thing cannot have two beginnings of Existence, nor two things one beginning, it being impossible for two things of the same kind, to be or exist in the same instant, in the very same place; or one and the same thing in different places. (E II.xxvii.1: 328)

Whenever we ask whether an object before us is the same, we always refer back in time to some object that we know to have existed at an earlier time. A thing is never rightly described as "the same" without specifying what formerly existing thing it is the same *as*. From this observation Locke concludes that any time we wonder about identity, we must be assuming the general principle that *no two things of the same kind can occupy the same place at the same time*. We are assuming that there could not have been two piñatas occupying the same exact place when we earlier passed. Call this the "Place-Time-Kind Principle."[2]

Why does the Place-Time-Kind Principle include *kind*? The answer is that sometimes different kinds of things can occupy the same place at the same time. Shortly after stating the Place-Time-Kind Principle, Locke tells us that the world is made up of only three basic, or fundamental, kinds of things: God, finite minds, and bodies (E II.xxvii.2). God, Locke believes, is at all times everywhere. But the fact that you are where you are now doesn't make you God. Similarly, at least according to Descartes and his followers, the mind is one thing, the body another, and yet it seems that if there is to be causal interaction between the two, and no action at a spatial or temporal distance, then there must be moments in which the mind and the body are at exactly the same place and time. As Locke puts the point elsewhere in the *Essay*, as part of an argument to the effect that immaterial spirits are capable of motion,

Every one finds in himself, that his Soul can think, will, and operate on his Body, in the place where that is; but cannot operate on a Body, or in a place, an hundred Miles distant from it. No Body can imagine, that his Soul can think, or move a Body at *Oxford*, whilst he is at *London*. (E II.xxiii.20: 307)

If a body and soul are both at Oxford when the one acts on the other – and not just at Oxford but at a particular, precise place in Oxford – then the body and the soul can be in the same place at the same time and yet be distinct.

---

[2] In the passage just quoted, Locke also points out that it follows from the Place-Time-Kind Principle that no two things can be of the same kind and yet have begun to exist at precisely the same time and place.

The Place-Time-Kind Principle, and the fact that anyone capable of asking identity questions is committed to it, has, Locke thinks, important philosophical implications:

From what has been said, 'tis easy to discover, what is so much enquired after, the *principium Individuationis*, and that 'tis plain is Existence it self, which determines a Being of any sort to a particular time and place incommunicable to two Beings of the same kind. (E II.xxvii.3: 330)

Locke's claim is that a specification of the conditions that must be met for a thing of a particular kind to exist at a particular time and place is, at once, a specification of the conditions that must be met for objects of the same kind, existing at different times, to be identical. If you know what it is for a thing to exist, then, because of the Place-Time-Kind Principle, you know what it is for a thing to *exclude others* of its kind from its location. But then you must know what makes that thing *distinct* from others of its kind and, correlatively, what makes it identical to some (future and past) of its kind. Or, to put the point in the context of our example, if you know what it is for a body to be a piñata, and thereby to make it impossible for any other piñata to occupy its location at a time, then you will know what criterion must be met by the piñata that you pass at the later time for it to be the same piñata that you passed at the earlier time. We might, then, put Locke's claim like this: the synchronic conditions for a thing's existence (the conditions that must be met for a thing to exist at a time) necessarily entail the diachronic conditions for a thing's identity (the conditions met by objects encountered at different times just in case they are identical). To know what it is that makes a thing the particular individual it is at a time is to know what makes it capable of excluding others of its kind from its location; and to know that is to know what makes it the same individual later.

Although this result informs the rest of Locke's discussion of identity, it is important to highlight that it is also Locke's way of lampooning his predecessors' approach to questions of identity. Locke is rejecting the possibility of a general and informative account of the principle of individuation, applicable across the board in answer to the full range of identity questions ("Same apple?" "Same tree?" "Same corpse?" "Same soul?" "Same person?" etc.). It is only at a very high level of abstraction that there is anything in common among the facts that determine the answers to these questions. All such answers depend on some kind of assumption about what it is for a thing of the requisite sort to exist at a time, but there is no reason to think that those assumptions, guiding our answers to identity questions about a wide variety of things, have anything else in common. It might be (and, it turns out, it *is*) a very different thing for, say, an oak tree to exist than it is for a mass of matter, or a soul, or a person to exist. And, thus, the principles of individuation for oaks, masses, souls, and persons might (and do) turn out to be entirely different from one another except in this limited sense: each is linked to the conditions that a thing of that sort must meet to exist at a particular time and to exclude others of the same sort from its location.

Before turning, in the next section, to Locke's particular accounts of the identity of various sorts of things, it is important to take a short detour into a debate among scholars about exactly what Locke is committed to by the link that he evidently sees between the identity of things at different times and the kinds to which they belong.

Some interpreters think that Locke commits himself to a two-part position known as the "Relative Identity Thesis."[3] According to the first part of the Relative Identity Thesis, every statement of the form "x is the same as y" or "x is identical to y" must, to be meaningful, contain a tacit reference to a particular kind of which x and y are both members. To put it another way, determining what, exactly, is being asserted by someone who says, "x is the same as y" requires an answer to the question "Same what?," where what is being asked for is a specification of a kind. When you are wondering if the thing hanging from the tree now is the same thing as the thing that hung there an hour ago, you are wondering if it is the same piñata.

According to the second part of the relative identity thesis, it is perfectly possible for two things to be the same F, but not the same G, where F and G are different kinds, even though both are Fs and at least one is a G. Say, for instance, that you tear out this page of this book. According to the Relative Identity Thesis, the book after this

---

[3] Geach 1967: 11; Odegard 1972: 38; Langtry 1975: 401; Mackie 1976: 151; Griffin 1977: 131; and Noonan 1978.

event is the same *book* as the book before; but it is not the same *bound set of pages*. By tearing out this page you have destroyed one bound set of pages and created another, but the book persists, one page shorter. Add to this the claim that at any given moment in time the book *just is* the bound set of pages and the Relative Identity Thesis seems to point to a metaphysical marvel: it is possible for two things to be one; or, put less provocatively, it is possible for two objects to be coincident at one time and not at another.

Does Locke accept either half of the Relative Identity Thesis? Take the first part first. Does Locke think that what a speaker who says, "This is the same as that," means can be understood only by supplementing what is explicitly said with a specification of a kind to which the speaker refers? No. In a passage normally discussed in connection with Locke's view of kinds and our talk of them, he writes,

'Tis necessary for me to be as I am; GOD and Nature has made me so: But there is nothing I have, is essential to me. An Accident, or Disease, may very much alter my Colour, or Shape; a Fever, or Fall, may take away my Reason, or Memory, or both; and an Apoplexy leave neither Sense, nor Understanding, no nor Life. Other Creatures of my shape, may be made with more, and better, or fewer, and worse Faculties than I have: and others may have Reason, and Sense, in a shape and body very different from mine. None of these are essential to the one, or the other, or to any Individual whatsoever, till the Mind refers it to some Sort or *Species* of things; and then presently, according to the abstract *Idea* of that sort, something is found *essential*. (E III.vi.4: 440)

Locke invites us to imagine how we would think of things if we resolutely refused to classify them into kinds – if, that is, we had no abstract ideas – and he claims that we would not consider any properties to be essential. But, to test whether or not we would find any properties to be essential, he imagines himself altered in various ways and wonders if the resulting creature would, without being placed into a kind, be thought identical to himself. In each instance the answer is "yes." Would he be the same if his color or shape were altered? Yes. Would he be the same if he lost his reason or his memory? Yes. This shows that he does not accept the first part of the Relative Identity Thesis, for under it these questions are not even meaningful, much less rightly answered in the affirmative, given the hypothetical situation that Locke is asking us to imagine.

If there were no kinds to which he belongs, as Locke is imagining, and if "the same" were only meaningful when a kind is specified, then there would be no asking whether or not he would be the same given various changes.

What of the second part of the Relative Identity Thesis, the claim that x and y could be the same F but not the same G, where F and G are distinct kinds? The best (perhaps the only) evidence that Locke accepts this claim comes from his statements of various examples. For instance,

An Oak, growing from a Plant to a great Tree, and then lopp'd, is still the same Oak: And a Colt grown up to a Horse, sometimes fat, sometimes lean, is all the while the same Horse: though, in both these Cases, there may be a manifest change of the parts: So that truly they are not either of them the same Masses of Matter, though they be truly one of them the same Oak, and the other the same Horse. (E II.xxvii.3: 330)

If Locke is saying here that the colt is a mass of matter, and that the adult horse is a different mass of matter, and yet the colt is the adult horse, then the example seems to be one in which x (the colt) is the same F (horse) as y (the adult horse), and yet x is not the same G (mass of matter) as y. So, if this is what he's saying, he accepts the second part of the Relative Identity Thesis. But a recent Locke interpreter, Vere Chappell, has argued persuasively that Locke needn't be thought to be saying this.[4] He might be saying, instead, that neither the colt nor the adult horse is identical to any mass of matter. So, although in the example an earlier mass of matter is not identical to a later one, and a colt is identical to an adult horse, it does not follow that we have identity under one kind and diversity under another; the things that are the same F (the colt and the adult horse) are not the things that fail to be the same G (the two masses of matter).[5] Further, as we will see in the next section, Locke is clear that what it is for a mass of matter to exist at a time, and thereby to exclude other masses from occupying the same place as itself, is quite different

[4] Chappell 1989. See also Chappell 1990; Uzgalis 1990.
[5] In objecting to the claim that Locke is committed to the second part of the Relative Identity Thesis, Michael Ayers (1991: II: 217) points out that the inference in E II. xxvii.1 from the Place-Time-Kind Principle to the claim that no two things of the same kind can have begun to exist at the same place and time would not follow if Locke accepted the second half of the Relative Identity Thesis. Since Locke evidently thinks the inference does follow, he must not accept that claim.

from what it is for a thing like a colt to do so. Thus, he is committed to saying that the colt and the mass of matter are distinct things. When we put this together with the fact that the colt/horse example does not require acceptance of the second part of the Relative Identity Thesis, it seems clear that Locke does not accept it.

Despite the fact that Locke does not accept the Relative Identity Thesis, he does accept the Place-Time-Kind Principle, and he does hold, consequently, that reflection on what it is for a thing of a particular kind to exist at a time is the key to determining what criteria must be met by things encountered at different times just in case they are identical. He thus turns to the question of what it is for each of the various sorts of things that we encounter in the world – atoms, masses of matter, organisms, people – to exist at a time and uses his answers to tell us what it is for each of those things to be the same over time.

2. THE IDENTITY OF ATOMS, MASSES, AND ORGANISMS

In a passage that one pair of commentators describe as a "turnip" from which nothing of value can be squeezed (Alston & Bennett 1988: 33), Locke writes,

Let us suppose an Atom, *i.e.* a continued body under one immutable Superficies, existing in a determined time and place: 'tis evident, that, considered in any instant of its Existence, it is, in that instant, the same with it self. For being, at that instant, what it is, and nothing else, it is the same, and so must continue, as long as its Existence is continued: for so long it will be the same, and no other. (E II.xxvii.3: 330)

Here Locke is trying to determine the identity conditions over time for an atom by first answering the following question: What is it for an atom to exist at a time and thereby to exclude other atoms from its location? The answer to that question is "to be a 'continued body under one immutable Superficies'," or, in other words, to occupy a continuous section of space and to be solid, to have a surface that cannot be changed, that repels other bodies. So, if at some later time we find an atom with the same "immutable Superficies," we thereby find the same atom.

To understand this theory, notice that the term "same property" is ambiguous. In one sense, two red apples have the same color – they

are both red – while in another sense, more important for our purposes, they do not: the one's color is encountered on its surface and
not on the surface of the other. Their colors, that is, can be thought of
as particulars – particular instantiations, or manifestations, of the
general property of being red. Metaphysicians sometimes refer to
such things as "tropes," to distinguish them from properties that are
shared by particular objects. Tropes aren't substances – they are not
the sorts of things in which properties inhere – nor are they shared by
distinct substances; they are particulars that inhere in other particulars. So two atoms of the same shape are nonetheless two because
each excludes all other atoms from its location in virtue of its
solidity trope. The two atoms are equally solid, but each has its own
solidity, or its own instantiation of the general property of being
solid. What makes an atom what it is at a time is its solidity trope, an
entity that adheres in it and in no other thing. And wherever that
same entity, that same solidity, is to be found, there we have the
same atom.

In a certain sense Locke's theory of atom identity is, indeed, a
turnip of a theory. The theory simply says that to answer the same-
atom question we must answer the same-immutable-surface question. And how do we do that? Locke is silent. Notice, however, that
what makes the theory a turnip is not the inadequacy of Locke's
recipe for discovering identity conditions (first, determine what
makes for the thing's synchronic existence) but our unilluminating
conception of the defining feature of the basic building blocks of
matter, namely, solidity. As Locke tells us in E II.iv, the idea of
solidity is a simple idea and that

if ... we endeavor, by Words, to make [simple ideas] clearer in the Mind, we
shall succeed no better, than if we went about to clear up the Darkness of a
blind Man's mind, by talking. (E II.iv.6: 127)

Because it is simple, we cannot say what solidity is or, equivalently,
say what it is for a particular thing's solidity to exist at a time and in
a place, and thereby to exclude other solidity tropes from that place.
And the problem is not just that *we can't say* what solidity is.
Solidity itself is not the sort of thing that can be broken down into
constituents; it is a genuinely simple quality.

Thus, Locke's approach to the same-atom question is to reduce it
to a question of the sameness of something of which we have a

simple idea, namely, in this case, solidity. In fact, this is his strategy across the board. To say what it is for a thing to exist at a time is to specify the simple ideas that are included in the complex idea of the thing; Locke takes each of those simple ideas to correspond to a simple entity, and those simple entities are combined together to make the complex thing. The identity over time of that complex thing, then, reduces to the identity over time of, first, each of those simples, and, second, their conjunction as a complex whole.

Locke takes the same approach in proposing an account of the identity of masses of matter, or collections of atoms, writing,

> [I]f two or more Atoms be joined together into the same Mass, every one of those Atoms will be the same, by the foregoing Rule: And whilst they exist united together, the Mass, consisting of the same Atoms, must be the same Mass, or the same Body, let the parts be never so differently jumbled: But if one of these Atoms be taken away, or one new one added, it is no longer the same Mass, or the same Body. (E II.xxvii.3: 330)

Taking the identity of atoms to be unproblematic, he goes on to claim, first, that what it is for a mass of matter to exist at a particular time is for it to consist of atoms jumbled together. From this he concludes that what it is for masses of matter at different times to be the same mass is for them to consist of precisely the same atoms jumbled together. Exactly *how* they are jumbled together doesn't matter: same atoms, same mass. So he's specified what a mass is by specifying, first, the simples out of which it is built, which must continue to exist if the complex is to continue to exist (atoms, each of which is solid), and, second, how those simples need to be composed in order to maintain the identity of the complex (they must be jumbled together).[6]

What follows is the same method applied to the case of organisms. However, in this case there is an important difference, for here we find that atoms are not among the simples that must remain the same if the thing is to remain the same. The dog that awaits you after your vacation had many meals while you were gone and has incorporated the food's material into her body. On your return, you don't find the same mass of matter, but you do

---

[6] For discussion of these and related issues, see McCann 1986; Bolton 1994.

find the same dog. Observations of this sort lead to Locke's next point:

We must therefore consider wherein an Oak differs from a Mass of Matter, and that seems to me to be in this; that the one is only the Cohesion of Particles of Matter any how united, the other such a disposition of them as constitutes the parts of an Oak; and such an Organization of those parts, as is fit to receive, and distribute nourishment, so as to continue, and frame the Wood, Bark, and Leaves, *etc.* of an Oak, in which consists the vegetable Life. That being then one Plant, which has such an Organization of Parts in one coherent Body, partaking of one Common Life, it continues to be the same Plant, as long as it partakes of the same Life, though that Life be communicated to new Particles of Matter vitally united to the living Plant, in a like continued Organization, conformable to that sort of Plants. (E II. xxvii.4: 330–1)

In this passage, Locke starts by asking what it is that must remain the same if the oak tree is to remain the same. We know that the atoms that compose it needn't, but then what could its identity consist in? As before, he starts by telling us what an oak tree, at a time, is; he tells us, that is, what it is for an oak tree to exist and to exclude other oak trees from its location. His view is that what it is for an oak tree to exist is for a mass of matter to have a particular complex quality: it must be organized in such a way as to maintain its own organization through changes in material stuff. An oak tree has a system for drawing moisture from the earth. But this system doesn't just draw moisture from the earth, it also uses the moisture that it draws to maintain, among other things, the structures *that allow the oak tree to draw moisture from the earth*. Oak trees have a self-supporting organization. They are homeostatic. That's what it is for an oak to exist; it is for some pile of stuff to have such a complex property: the property of making it the case that new masses of matter will have that very property. Thus, what it is for oaks existing at different times to be the same oak is for them to have the very same manifestation of this special property, or the same homeostatic organization trope. Or, as Locke puts it, they are the same so long as they "partake of the same Life."

Masses of matter are just atoms jumbled together. But what makes for their identity is not the way the atoms are put together – that is, jumbled – but the atoms themselves. Organisms are atoms organized in a special way. But what makes for their identity, by contrast, is not the atoms, but the way they are put together, the organization. Thus, where the identity of masses of matter derives from the identity of substances (same substances, same mass) the identity of an organism derives from the identity of a particular trope (same organization, same organism). This difference derives not from a difference in the mind-independent nature of masses and organisms but, instead, from a difference in our ideas; since the ideas of the two kinds of thing differ, so do the identity conditions for particulars falling under the respective ideas.

As it is in oak trees, so it is in the biological organisms that compose the human species. There is such a thing as a human animal: a creature with the peculiar human organization that is an example of a way of being organized that maintains that very form of organization. Each of your organs, and your body as a whole, is designed in such a way as to shed bits of matter and incorporate other bits and, by so doing, to maintain its organization as a thing capable of doing just that.

It's clear enough that there is no more to an oak tree than this. A full description of the particular special way in which a pile of material stuff is organized at a time captures all there is to being an oak tree at that time; and, quite plausibly, wherever we find that same manifestation of that special form of organization, we find the same oak tree. But is a full description of your peculiar physical organization, special as it is, a full description of you? Or would such a description leave something out? And, if it does leave something out, then what is it to be a person, over and above being an organism?

3. AGAINST THE SAME-ORGANISM AND SAME-SUBSTANCE THEORIES OF PERSONAL IDENTITY

What is it for a person to exist? Or, equivalently, what makes a thing such as to exclude other persons from the place that it occupies? We might think that the answer to this question is this: it is to be a human organism, a human being, what Locke calls "a man." That is, at a given moment in time, we might say, the reason that there is just one person holding this book and reading it is because there is, at a particular place, just one collection of atoms organized in the special way that human beings are organized. If this is right, then it will lead us to the following theory of personal identity: A person now and a person some time ago are the same person just in case they are the same-organism. Call this the "same-organism theory of personal identity." Locke rejects this theory, and he does so on the grounds that what it is for a person to exist at a time, and to exclude other persons from its location, is not for a human being to exist at that time and place. To prove this he shows, first, that a human being can exist at a given place and time without any person existing at that place and time; and, second, that a person can exist in a place and at a time without any human being existing at that place and time. Both claims are made in the following passage:

> [W]hoever should see a Creature of his own Shape and Make, though it had no more reason all its Life, than a *Cat* or a *Parrot*, would call him still a *Man*; or whoever should hear a *Cat* or a *Parrot* discourse, reason, and philosophize, would call or think it nothing but a *Cat* or a *Parrot*; and say, the one was a dull irrational *Man*, and the other a very intelligent rational *Parrot*. (E II.xxvii.8: 333)

What Locke here offers are the first of many thought experiments that appear in his discussion of personal identity. In each, the reader is asked to pronounce as to the nature or identity of hypothetical entities, and from our pronouncements (or, rather, what he thinks our pronouncements will be) Locke rejects or accepts various theories of personal identity. In this case, we are asked to imagine, first, the living, breathing, digesting body of a human being lacking any of the mental qualities that we think of as distinctive of persons; second, we are to imagine the mental qualities of a person housed in a nonhuman organism. Locke insists that we would say that the first is a human being (a "Man"), while the second is not. What does this pair of results show about personal identity and, particularly, about the same-organism theory? Well, nothing, by themselves; in order to know anything about that issue from consideration of the examples, we need to know whether these imaginary creatures would be considered by us to be persons. If the "dull irrational Man" is not a person, then it is possible for a human organism to exist without a person existing; and if the "intelligent rational Parrot" is a person, then it is possible for a person to exist without a human organism existing. But are these the things we are inclined to say?

Now Locke is assuming that his audience will accept the traditional Aristotelian-Scholastic definition of a person as a "rational animal." And so he is assuming that his audience will insist that the "dull irrational Man" is no person – because it's not rational – and that the "intelligent rational Parrot" is a person, since, after all, it is both rational and an animal. Of course, those of us who are not steeped in the tradition of thought that Locke is attacking might not share these intuitions; we might say that the "dull irrational Man" is a person and that the "intelligent rational Parrot" is not. But if we accept the verdict about the examples that Locke's audience would have accepted, the same-organism theory must be false: the human being and the person are separable, and so a person is not merely a human being. Thus, from reflection on *what we would say* (or, rather, what his audience would say) about his hypothetical creatures, Locke reaches a substantive metaphysical conclusion about the nature of persons: they are not identical to human beings. Parrots exclude human beings from their location; the two cannot be at the same place at the same time. In fact, they exclude any other organism from their location; as the Place-Time-Kind principle tells us, each position in space can be occupied, at a given time, by only one organism. But, as the example of the rational parrot is supposed to show, parrots do not exclude persons from their location: a person and a parrot can exist at the same place and time. What this shows is that persons are not human beings.[7]

There is an obvious alternative to the same-organism theory of personal identity – obvious, anyway, to anyone wedded either to the

---

[7] The passage just discussed can be read in a different way. It might be suggested that the passage does not concern personal identity in the least. Rather, Locke is simply attacking the Aristotelian-Scholastic equation between men and rational animals, and leaving open the possibility that persons are rational animals. This reading has its attractions. Among other things, it explains why Locke never uses the term "person" in the passage at issue. However, E II.xxvii.21 seems to indicate that Locke takes his Aristotelian-Scholastic opponent to be equivocating between an equation between men and rational animals, on the one hand, and an equation between persons and rational animals, on the other. Hence, in attacking the Aristotelian-Scholastic equation between men and rational animals, Locke understands and intends that he will be taken to be attacking the same-organism theory of personal identity, as well.

Christian conception of a soul or to the closely related Cartesian conception of the mind as an immaterial thing. According to this alternative theory, a person now and a person some time ago are the same person just in case they are (or have) the same immaterial soul. Call this the "same-soul theory of personal identity." It is no surprise that a view such as this should be allied to Christianity, with its assumption that there is an afterlife that now-embodied persons will inhabit. What could a person be but an immaterial soul, given that it survives the death and decomposition of its body?

Locke was a committed Christian and so believed in the afterlife, but he rejects the same-soul theory. He identifies two questions that must be answered in order to assess the same-soul theory: Is it possible to have different substances (souls) and yet the same person? And, is it possible to have the same substance and yet different persons? (E II.xxvii.12: 337) His answer to both questions is "yes." In support of his answer to the second question, he employs another thought experiment designed to show us that our ordinary thoughts about personal identity allow for distinction of persons without change in soul:

Let any one reflect upon himself, and conclude, that he has in himself an immaterial Spirit, which is that which thinks in him, and in the constant change of his Body keeps him the same; and is that which he calls himself: Let him also suppose it to be the same Soul, that was in *Nestor* or *Thersites*, at the Siege of *Troy*, (For Souls being, as far as we know any thing of them in their Nature, indifferent to any parcel of Matter, the Supposition has no apparent absurdity in it) which it may have been, as well as it is now, the Soul of any other Man: But he, now having no consciousness of any of the Actions either of *Nestor* or *Thersites*, does, or can he, conceive himself the same Person with either of them? Can he be concerned in either of their Actions? Attribute them to himself, or think them his own more than the Actions of any other Man, that ever existed? (E II.xxvii.14: 339)

Locke's point is that the fact that you happen to have Nestor's soul does not entail that you have the special attitude of concernment toward Nestor and his actions, and yet precisely what Locke is trying to understand is what lies at the basis of the feeling of concernment. He wants to know, that is, what facts must be in place in order to make it appropriate to feel pride or remorse, to anticipate a future with apprehension, or to look back on the past with the peculiar sense of what *you* might have done or might have been. If the same-soul theory were right, then, given that you have Nestor's soul, you ought to feel pride for having led the Pylians against Troy, for instance. But why should you care? Unless you can look back at the event and see yourself in it, what grounds do you have for feeling pride now? If the soul doesn't necessarily carry concernment, it doesn't necessarily carry identity.

Notice that Locke's description of the Nestor example is not correct if, in fact, where the soul goes, so goes concernment. Locke is just assuming that it is possible for you to have Nestor's soul without being concerned with what Nestor did. A similar assumption guides his argument for the claim that a single person could, at different times, have different souls. In fact, with respect to this issue, he is explicit that he is making such an assumption:

[I]f the same consciousness ... can be transferr'd from one thinking Substance to another, it will be possible, that two thinking Substances may make but one Person. (E II.xxvii.13: 338)

The conclusion here is conditional. He is not saying, flat out, that "two thinking Substances may make but one Person." Rather, he is saying that this would be so *if* it were possible for one soul to have the attitude of concernment toward the actions of another. (He talks here of "consciousness" rather than concernment; more about that in the next section.) Earlier he had considered the question of whether or not there is anything that *we know of* the soul that excludes the possibility of two souls being concerned with each other's actions and concluded that there is not; the claim that this is impossible can be made only "by those, who know what kind of Substances they are, that do think" (E II.xxvii.13: 337). Locke's point is that given our state of complete ignorance about the nature of our minds (he discusses this issue at length in E II.xxiii.15–36: 305–16) we cannot be sure that there is anything about them that excludes the possibility of a single person switching souls at some point in the course of its life.

It is important to see just what Locke is saying, and is not saying, in his attack on the same-soul theory. At issue is the truth or falsity of the following claim: (1) It is possible for one person to have, at different times, two different souls. In assessing this claim, Locke takes it to be given that, as much as people might claim to know the nature of their minds, they do not. This puts him in a position to assert the following claim, which is importantly different from the first: (2) *For all we know*, it is possible for one person to have, at different times, two different souls. Someone wishing to defend the same-soul theory, however, might grant that he doesn't know what his soul is, but point out that neither does Locke know. Hence, the following claim also seems true: (3) For all we know, it is *im*possible for one person to have, at different times, two different souls. If (2) and (3) are both true, that would seem to suggest that we really can't say, one way or the other, if (1) is true, and so we really can't say if the same-soul theory of personal identity is correct. This is, in fact, just Locke's point. He is not claiming to know the same-soul theory to be false; he is pointing out, rather, that no one can claim to be in a position to know that it's true, and so it can't be what informs our everyday judgments about personal identity. The same-soul theory, thus, is an idle hypothesis. We are, in fact, concerned about various past actions and future states of being and not about others; sad as I might be to know that someone is not going to live through the day, I will be much more concerned to discover that that person *is me*. And yet we don't seem to be in a position to know anything about which souls continue to exist and which souls occupy the locations of which bodies. The concept of a soul, then, seems to be invented to be the thing that carries concernment, but we don't know enough about it to know how, or why, it should be thought to do so. Further, and worse, *we can't possibly ever know anything illuminating about it*. The obstacle to knowledge here is not like, for instance, the obstacle to knowledge about what is going on, right now, a thousand miles from here; at least in that case we can imagine technological tools, or a special form of vision, that would provide us with the needed knowledge. But there is no hope at all, even in principle, of understanding the soul well enough to employ the notion when making identity judgments. To insist on the same-soul theory in the face of this is to give up hope of providing an illuminating theory of personal identity, then, rather than to offer one.[8] We might say that the mistake of the same-soul theory is to

---

[8] There is, thus, an important commonality between Locke's attack on the same-soul theory and his view of the idea of substance in general as discussed, particularly, in E II.xxiii.1–5.

leap to an account of the conditions of identity over time without first having in hand an adequate conception of what it is for a soul to exist at a time, and thereby to exclude other souls from the place it occupies.

This way of construing Locke's attack on the same-soul theory of personal identity suggests that Locke is not going to be happy with any theory of personal identity that entirely divorces what makes for our identity from the tools that we use to discover identity. This is not to say that, for him, the question is how we know if this is the same person as that, rather than what makes it the case that this is the same person as that. He is interested, first and foremost, in the question of what identity is and only secondarily in how we know that there is identity. However, he isn't going to be content with a theory of personal identity under which it is either impossible for us to know, or magical that we do know, that there is or is not identity; it's something that we know all the time, and so our account of the facts must paint them as knowable. One great advantage of the same-organism theory over the same soul theory is that we seem to be in position to know when we encounter the same human being again, and when we encounter a new one. There are very good sensory clues – such as appearance – that ordinarily, and for ordinary reasons, track identity of organism. So, we might suggest, in defense of the same-soul theory, that what makes for personal identity is the soul, but what helps us *to know* identity is the organism. There would be hope for such a view if there were reasons for thinking that where you encounter the same organism, you also encounter the same soul. Locke anticipates this theory, too, and rejects it through employing what is, perhaps, the most famous of his various thought experiments about identity:

[T]he Soul alone in the change of Bodies, would scarce to any one ... be enough to make the same *Man*. For should the Soul of a Prince, carrying with it the consciousness of the Prince's past Life, enter and inform the Body of a Cobler as soon as deserted by his own Soul, every one sees, he would be the same Person with the Prince, accountable only for the Prince's Actions: But who would say it was the same Man? The Body too goes to the making the Man, and would, I guess, to every Body determine the Man in this case, wherein the Soul, with all its Princely Thoughts about it, would not make another Man: But he would be the same Cobler to every one besides himself. (E II.xxvii.15: 340)

Locke's point here is primarily about the relationship between souls and human beings, organisms, and only secondarily about the relationship between souls and persons. His primary point is that those who met the cobbler after his soul had left and been replaced by the prince's would take themselves to be encountering the person of the cobbler again. They would, to be sure, think him crazy: he would have entirely forgotten which customers had brought him which shoes and would be raving about his right to the crown. But, and this is the important point, their inference from the recognition of the same organism to belief in the presence of the same soul would be faulty. There is no necessary connection between sameness of organism and sameness of soul, and so there is something ad hoc about a theory, such as that on offer, that has one thing (the soul) do the metaphysical work of constituting identity, and another (the human being) do the epistemological work of guiding judgments of identity.

The example of the prince and the cobbler captured the imagination of many later thinkers about personal identity, and it has at various times been taken to illustrate much more than Locke himself used it to illustrate. For instance, the example can be taken to serve as an objection to the same-organism theory: if, as Locke claims, the cobbler-bodied person, after the switch, is the same person as the pre-switch prince-bodied person, then we could have the same person without the same organism: so much for the same organism theory. Similarly, the example can be taken as an argument against the same-soul theory, for it seems to be a mere accident of the example, as Locke states it, that the soul of the prince travels to the body of the cobbler. We could imagine, just as well, that the cobbler-bodied person simply woke up one morning having forgotten everything about his life as a cobbler and with vivid memories of the life of a prince; he might then look in the mirror and be shocked at his own appearance, wondering, among other things, how it came to pass that his velvet pajamas were replaced by a leather apron. To imagine the example in this way does not require a swapping of souls, and yet to some it seems that personal identity would not follow the soul but, instead, the point of view, or perspective, that seems to have moved from the body and soul of the prince to that of the cobbler.

However, it is important to see that the lesson we take from the example depends crucially on how we tell the story and where, in the telling of it, we imply the prince and cobbler to be after the change. As Bernard Williams has emphasized,[9] while it is natural to tell the story as one of body swapping (during the night the prince and the cobbler switch bodies), it could be told differently. Say, for instance, that you, a humble cobbler, are told that you are to have your memory erased and new memories implanted that happen to match the memories of some other poor person whose memory will also be erased. This would seem a terrible thing to befall *you*, and it would seem to be scant consolation to discover that the other victim of this affair is to be given your old memories. It does not appear, when the story is told in this way, that you survive the event in another body. When the story is told in this way, that is, it seems that the poor cobbler awakes in his bed above the shoe store but having lost his mind and, worse, without even knowing it: he has lost his memory and can only prance around insisting that he went to bed in a castle and was waited on hand and foot.

The sensitivity of the moral of the story to the way in which it is told shows that thought experiments such as the example of the prince and the cobbler need to be treated with tremendous care. They are not transparent; they do not wear their meaning on their face. However, Locke almost always used them with the care that they deserve, and this is particularly clear in this particular case, for the lesson that Locke draws from the story of the prince and the cobbler is, it seems, entirely fair: it is a mistake to think that we know enough about the soul to expect it to be found without exception wherever we find the same human being. This result, like Locke's attack on the same-organism and same-soul theories more generally, is entirely negative. It does not tell us what personal identity actually is, but only what it's not. Locke's positive position, however, is the topic of the next section.

4. CONSCIOUSNESS AND MEMORY

Locke's own account of personal identity, in line with his general approach to the discovery of the identity conditions for any thing,

---

[9] Williams 1970.

begins with an analysis of what it is for a person to exist at a time and thereby exclude other persons from its location:

[W]e must consider what *Person* stands for; which, I think, is a thinking intelligent Being, that has reason and reflection, and can consider it self as it self, the same thinking thing in different times and places; which it does only by that consciousness, which is inseparable from thinking, and as it seems to me essential to it: It being impossible for any one to perceive, without perceiving, that he does perceive. When we see, hear, smell, taste, feel, meditate, or will any thing, we know that we do so. Thus it is always as to our present Sensations and Perceptions: And by this every one is to himself, that which he calls *self*. (E II.xxvii.9: 335)

The crucial quality of an entity that makes it a person is the capacity to "consider it self as it self the same thinking thing in different times and places." Or, in other words, the distinctive feature of a person is the capacity to recognize which parts of the world, parts of diverse kinds and occupying diverse places – one's pinkie finger or right ear, or one's desire for a milk shake – are parts of oneself, and the capacity to recognize which past and future parts of the world are parts of oneself. Thus the pinkie finger is part of you precisely because you recognize it to be part of you. In this case, then, there is a collapse between the fact to be known – your pinkie finger is *yours, you* occupy its position – and the knowing of it: it is yours because you know it to be, or consider it as such. Locke labels the mental act of recognizing or "considering" a part of the world to be part of yourself "consciousness." Of course, this bit of terminology is no accident, for as Locke says in the passage just quoted, consciousness is the special form of awareness that we take to accompany all of our thoughts at any given time, all of our "present Sensations and Perceptions." His claim, then, is that what makes a person what it is is also what makes its thoughts to be its own, namely, the consciousness of them, the awareness through which we both recognize our thoughts to be our own and make it the case that they are.

Locke extends his theory of what it is for a person to exist at a time into an account of what it is for persons at different times to be the same person; he extends his account of synchronic personal identity into an account of diachronic personal identity:

[S]ince consciousness always accompanies thinking, and 'tis that, that makes every one to be, what he calls *self*; and thereby distinguishes himself from all other thinking things, in this alone consists *personal Identity, i.e.* the sameness of a rational Being: And as far as this consciousness can be extended backwards to any past Action or Thought, so far reaches the Identity of that *Person;* it is the same *self* now it was then; and 'tis by the same self with this present one that now reflects on it, that that Action was done. (E II.xxvii.9: 335)

In a certain sense, this theory of personal identity is very simple: same consciousness, same person. But in another and much more important sense, it is far from clear what the theory really says. After all, what makes it the case that the consciousness possessed by the baby in the picture is the same consciousness as yours? To be sure, the baby was conscious: there were physical states and states of mind of which it was aware in that special way in which each of us is aware of his own pinkie finger. And you now are, also, conscious. But what makes for the identity, if there is one, between the baby's act of conscious awareness and yours? We might think that this question is no more puzzling than the comparable question to be asked about Locke's theory of atom identity, namely, "What makes this atom's solidity, the trope inhering in this very atom, and that past atom's solidity the same?" If we can't hope to answer this question on the grounds that solidity is simple, then perhaps, similarly, we can't hope to identify the conditions under which two acts of consciousness are the same. To say this on Locke's behalf is to see him as hiding, throughout his discussion of identity, behind the mysterianist view that it simply isn't possible to give an illuminating account of the identity over time of simples.

However, Locke resists subsuming the case of personal identity to the case of atom identity, for he insists that the earlier and later acts of conscious awareness of a single person are not, in fact, the same act of awareness. He makes a point of arguing, against the Cartesian view that the mind is always thinking, that in dreamless sleep we have no thoughts at all: "[E]very drowsy Nod shakes their Doctrine, who teach, That the Soul is always thinking" (E II.i.13: 111). And he explicitly connects this point to personal identity: "*If a sleeping Man thinks without knowing it, the sleeping and waking Man are two Persons*" (E II.i.12 (section title): 110). Further, and more explicitly, in the course of arguing against the same-substance theory of personal identity, he claims that the theory would be much more plausible were later and earlier acts of consciousness the same act; unfortunately, "that which we call the *same consciousness*, not being the same individual Act" (E II.xxvii.13: 338), this reason for the same-substance theory is not available to support it. Thus, we are left with a question: If "same person" is to be analyzed as "same consciousness," but in the relevant sense of "same consciousness" two acts of consciousness at two different times could be, in fact, two distinct acts and not one, what makes an earlier and later act of consciousness "the same" in the sense relevant to personal identity?

Trading on Locke's remark that "as far as . . . consciousness can be extended backwards to any past Action or Thought, so far reaches the Identity of that *Person*" (E II.xxvii.9: 335), commentators have frequently attributed to Locke the view that a later person is the same as an earlier just in case the later can remember the earlier's experiences.[10] After all, what is it for your "consciousness to extend backwards" except for you to remember something that took place at an earlier time? Call this the "simple memory theory of personal identity." According to the simple memory theory, distinct and separate acts of conscious awareness can be related to one another in such a way as to make it the case that their subjects are one person; for this to be the case, the later must be a remembrance of the earlier.[11] On this theory, just as your pinkie finger is part of you by virtue of your being aware of it, a past act is one done by you by virtue of your being aware of it, or remembering it. Whatever might be thought wrong with the simple memory theory, it has the virtue of simplicity.

There is, however, a great deal wrong with this theory, whether or not Locke held it. The first and most obvious objection is one that Locke anticipated: does forgetting amount to death? After all, if the future does not include a person who remembers your now reading

---

[10] Cf. Flew 1968; Brody 1972.

[11] Notice that Locke is reasonably taken to allow that a later person could be identical to an earlier one even if the later doesn't, in fact, remember the earlier's experience, so long as the later *could* remember it. He says, after all, that "as far as . . . consciousness *can* be extended backwards . . ." (E II.xxvii.9: 335, my emphasis). It is far from clear how we are to determine whether or not a person *could* remember something that he doesn't remember. Does he have this ability if it would require many hours of therapy for him to remember it?

this book, then the future does not include you; and if the future does not include you, then it is a future in which you are dead. In response to this worry, Locke seems to swallow the pill, although he also gives his reader something to wash it down with:

> But yet possibly it will still be objected, suppose I wholly lose the memory of some parts of my Life, beyond a possibility of retrieving them, so that perhaps I shall never be conscious of them again; yet am I not the same Person, that did those Actions, had those Thoughts, that I was once conscious of, though I have now forgot them? To which I answer, that we must here take notice what the Word *I* is applied to, which in this case is the Man only. And the same Man being presumed to be the same Person, *I* is easily here supposed to stand also for the same Person. But if it be possible for the same Man to have distinct incommunicable consciousness at different times, it is past doubt the same Man would at different times make different Persons. (E II.xxvii.20: 342)

So Locke is accepting that to have forgotten an experience "beyond a possibility of retrieving" it is to be a different person than the one who had it. While this follows from the simple memory theory, many would take it to show the theory to be flawed. However, Locke adds that if you think that you can continue to exist while having entirely forgotten something, it is because you are failing to distinguish between persons and human beings: the human being who did the past action continues to exist, even though the person does not. Notice that this response can be motivated by noting the ambiguity of attitude that we have toward parts of our bodies of which we are not conscious. Most of us think of our fingers and toes as bearing a much more intimate relationship to ourselves than our hair or fingernails. Locke has a tool for explaining this difference in attitude: our fingers and toes are things of which we are conscious, and so they are included within the boundaries of both the human being and the person at a time, while hair and fingernails are included only within the boundaries of the human being and not within the boundaries of the person. If this move is appealing as a way of distinguishing between fingers and fingernails, why not as a way of distinguishing between remembered and forgotten acts?[12]

---

[12] Locke's anticipation of this objection might be taken to be evidence that he accepted the simple memory theory; after all, why respond to an objection if it isn't an objection to the theory you hold? Notice, however, that what Locke is

Another objection to the simple memory theory was raised a hundred years after the publication of the *Essay* by the Scottish philosopher Thomas Reid.[13] Criticizing the simple memory theory, Reid writes,

Suppose a brave officer to have been flogged when a boy at school, for robbing an orchard, to have taken a standard from the enemy in his first campaign, and to have been made a general in advanced life: Suppose also, which must be admitted to be possible, that when he took the standard, he was conscious of his having been flogged at school, and that when made a general he was conscious of his taking the standard, but had absolutely lost the consciousness of his flogging.

These things being supposed, it follows, from Mr. Locke's doctrine, that he who was flogged at school is the same person who took the standard, and that he who took the standard is the same person who was made a general. Whence it follows, if there be any truth in logic, that the general is the same person with him who was flogged at school. But the general's consciousness does not reach so far back as his flogging, therefore, according to Mr. Locke's doctrine, he is not the same person who was flogged. Therefore the general is, and at the same time is not the same person with him who was flogged at school. (Reid 2002: 276)

Reid here exploits the fact that any theory of identity, whether of persons or anything else, must allow that we are able to infer the identity of A and C from the fact that each is identical to B. From this it follows that the general and the boy are the same person. But since, in the example, the general can't remember the boy's experiences, the simple memory theory implies that they are not identical. There is, therefore, something wrong with the simple memory theory. Reid is, therefore, exploiting the very method that Locke uses to refute the same-organism and same-substance theories: a thought experiment intended to invoke intuitions about who is identical to

---

concerned to affirm is the claim that where there is no possibility of memory, the act was not done by you. Roughly, in short: no memory, no identity. But this doesn't commit him to the claim that remembering, all by itself, is sufficient for identity. As we'll see, alternative interpretations ascribe to Locke views about what is sufficient for identity that are different from that proposed by the simple memory theory, although all efforts to cash out Locke's notion of "consciousness extending back" are committed to the claim that when it cannot be extended back, there is no identity.

[13] In fact, the objection was first offered much earlier by Berkeley in *Alciphron* (see Berkeley 1948–57: 3: 299), but it is usually attributed to Reid.

whom. However, Reid's example does not allow an easy way out for the advocate of the simple memory theory, for it simply won't do either to assert or to deny that the general and the boy are the same person; either answer creates a problem for the theory.

Another famous, and perhaps more telling, objection to the simple memory theory was raised by Joseph Butler. Butler writes,

> One should really think it self-evident that consciousness of personal identity presupposes, and therefore cannot constitute, personal identity, any more than knowledge, in any other case, can constitute truth, which it presupposes. (Butler 1754: 361)

Normally, memory is understood as a tool for discovering what happened in the past. It's a way of finding out about past facts. But under the simple memory theory, it is at once the way of finding out about the facts – you find out what you did in the past by remembering it – and also what makes the facts what they are: you are the one who did the past act because you remember it. So far this is just an observation about the simple memory theory, but it can be spun into an objection, like so: Normally we recognize a distinction between real and false memories. Real memories are representations of past events *that really happened to the rememberer;* false ones are representations of past events that didn't happen to the rememberer. Obviously, we don't want to say that a later person is identical to an earlier one if the later has a false memory of the earlier's experience; only real memory could be thought to constitute identity. But the simple memory theory seems to lack the tools for distinguishing between real and false memory: if remembering is a way of making it the case that you did what you remember, then your memory can't ever be false. Or, in other words, what makes the memory that you did something a real one is that you really did the act that you remember. But then your identity with the past actor must be a fact that precedes your remembering and not something that is produced by the act of remembering. The distinction between real and false memory is needed to make the simple memory theory plausible, but the distinction cannot be drawn without first, and independently, determining whether or not the represented past action was performed by the very person who is remembering it. The theory, then, is necessarily circular.

Given these problems, there is a strong temptation to look for a different way of interpreting Locke's same-consciousness theory of personal identity. Further, there is strong evidence to suggest that Locke never intended to be offering the simple memory theory. First, attributing the simple memory theory to Locke requires interpreting the phrase "your consciousness extends backwards to some past action" to mean "you remember doing it." If this is what Locke intended to say, why didn't he just say that? Talk of "consciousness extending backwards" is, at best, an awkward way to refer to memory. Second, to see Locke as holding the simple memory theory is to make it very difficult to make good sense of Locke's claim that

Person ... is a Forensick term appropriating Actions and their Merit; and so belongs only to intelligent Agents capable of a Law, and Happiness and Misery. (E II.xxvii.26: 346)

Locke seems to think this claim to have been earned by his theory of personal identity, to follow from that theory. But he is quite clear that animals, who are not "Agents capable of a Law" – who are not, that is, to be rewarded and punished in the afterlife for their actions – remember past experiences and past actions; he puts the point bluntly: *"Brutes have memory"* (E II.x.10 (section title): 154).[14] Much recent scholarship on Locke's theory of personal identity, then, has tried to explain how Locke's theory differs from the simple memory theory.[15]

---

[14] There may be some room to attribute the simple memory theory to Locke even in the face of his assertion that animals that are not to be held accountable for their behavior are nonetheless capable of memory. Locke holds that actions of the sort that are to be morally assessed all spring from volition, and he holds that the mental state of volition is not available to animals, but only to persons. (For discussion, see Yaffe 2000: esp. Chapter 3.) Thus, it appears that an animal could never remember a past *act*, strictly speaking, since it can't have volitions, and so can't ever really *act*, in the sense that's relevant to responsibility. However, in objection to this line, it seems at the least peculiar to assert that animals are incapable of volition while capable of "consciousness" of the sort that is constitutive of personal identity when the distinctive feature of volition that makes it available only to persons is the fact that it always involves consciousness. It would seem, that is, that the capacity for volition and the capacity for the kind of consciousness that matters for personal identity come as a package; it would seem odd, then, to allow animals the second of these capacities and not the first.

[15] Cf. Atherton 1983.

According to a particularly important interpretation, associated with Kenneth Winkler,[16] "consciousness" is to be understood as "appropriation" or "subjective constitution." According to such a view, what Locke is really saying is that the boundaries of the person, both at a time and over time, are delineated by a web of mental states of which memory is just one sort. What you have and have not appropriated is intended to be read off of neither, first, the list of actions that, at a particular moment in time, you are or could be consciously aware of performing or of having performed, nor, second, the list of actions that you recognize to have been performed by the human being with which, at a particular moment in time, you identify yourself. The first list is too short to capture all that was performed by you, as Reid's brave officer example shows: the general is not consciously aware of the acts of the boy, but between his memories and those of the soldier there are grounds for taking them to have been performed by him, grounds that the general is sadly not in a position to appreciate. The second list is too long to capture only those acts performed by the person that is you, as a number of Locke's examples show, including the example of the prince and the cobbler: after the switch, the cobbler-bodied person does not appropriate the acts performed by the cobbler before the switch, despite the fact that they were performed by the human being with whom he now associates himself; there is no route to those acts either from his psychological states when he awakes or from any of the psychological states of any of the past persons with whom he associates himself. For an act to be one that you appropriate, you must do so either directly or indirectly, where those notions are defined like so: to *directly appropriate* an act, you must be aware of having performed it; to *indirectly appropriate* an act, you must directly appropriate an act of some person who appropriates the act.[17] Thus, the general has appropriated the acts of the boy, for he appropriated the acts of the soldier who appropriated the acts of the boy by being aware that he performed them. And, similarly, the cobbler-bodied person after the switch appropriates the acts of the past prince-bodied person, but that person did not

---

[16] Winkler 1991.

[17] Thus, consciousness, for Winkler, is not the relation of awareness but, instead, the ancestral of the relation of awareness.

appropriate the acts of the cobbler, either directly or indirectly; thus, the cobbler-bodied person after the switch is not the person who, just the day before, was nailing soles on shoes.

The appropriation interpretation captures something that Locke, in certain passages, seems, undoubtedly, to be trying to say. In fact, in one place he even uses the term "appropriate" to describe what happens when we are conscious of a past action:

[P]ersonality extends it *self* beyond present Existence to what is past, only by consciousness, whereby it becomes concerned and accountable, owns and imputes to it *self* past Actions, just upon the same ground, and for the same reason, that it does the present. ... And therefore whatever past Actions it cannot reconcile or appropriate to that present *self* by consciousness, it can be no more concerned in, than if they had never been done. (E II.xxvii.26: 346)

Another advantage of the appropriation interpretation over the view according to which Locke holds the simple memory theory is the way in which the appropriation interpretation is able to explain Locke's claim that "person" is a "forensick" term. Arguably, to be morally accountable for a past action a person has to believe himself to be morally accountable for it, or else to be under rational pressure to so believe. Someone who appropriates a past action directly isn't just aware of the action; he is aware of the fact that *he* performed it. This is the difference, we might say, between, for instance, singing a song now to match one that you heard sung an hour ago, and singing a song now to match one that you recognize *you yourself* to have sung an hour ago. A bird can remember a song it heard earlier in the first sense, but it cannot remember it in the second, and it is the second that is involved in direct appropriation. Further, it is the second kind of awareness of past action that is required for moral accountability; it is not enough just to remember; to be accountable, your memory must be mediated by a thought about the identity of your present self and the person who performed the past action. In addition, in cases in which you can't remember a past action that you are nonetheless accountable for – the general may still owe an apple to the owner of the orchard that he robbed as a boy – your accountability derives from the rational pressures placed on you to appropriate the past action. Were the general, who appropriates the acts of the soldier, informed that the soldier appropriates the acts of the boy, the general would not be rational to fail to appropriate the acts of the boy, despite the fact that he can't remember them; the logic of identity requires it of him. The general himself would have to admit it just to punish him for the boy's acts once he sees that they are appropriated by the soldier; at least, he would have to admit that if he's to be rational. Thus, the very conditions for personal identity are intertwined with the conditions of accountability, under the appropriation interpretation, and this provides motivation for Locke's "forensick term" remark.

However, the appropriation interpretation does not attribute to Locke a view that can avoid the most powerful objection to be levied against Locke's theory, namely, the concern about circularity.[18] The problem is that we can have conflicts between what the logic of identity requires, on the one hand, and what we directly appropriate, on the other. Say, for instance, that twin sisters both look at a picture of a baby and both appropriate the baby's actions: each attributes to herself the action of sucking her thumb. To make the story plausible, imagine that one twin sucked her thumb and posed for the picture while the other witnessed the event; now, years later, both twins recall the event from the point of view of the picture's subject, and neither remembers being the witness. Each appropriates the very same act of thumb sucking. The logic of identity precludes the possibility that both twins are identical to the baby, since, after all, they aren't identical to each other. But appropriation is sufficient for identity on the theory, and so it seems that we can adjudicate the dispute between the sisters only by determining which is *right* to appropriate the baby's action. But it seems that there is no room to draw a distinction between right appropriation and wrong appropriation from within the theory: what a person directly appropriates is, with necessity, done by her. Hence the appropriation theory requires a prior way of drawing lines between those who are and those who are not identical to past people. Circularity looms once again, and this give us motivation to look for an alternative interpretation.

The key to understanding both what Locke means by "consciousness" and what he really means by saying that "person" is a "forensick" term lies in the connection that Locke makes between

---

[18] Winkler thinks it can. See Winkler 1991: 154.

consciousness and susceptibility to pleasure and pain. To see this, first recall that Locke is particularly interested in understanding the basis of our special feelings of *concern* for the actions and states of future and past persons whom we take to be identical to ourselves. On this understanding of the term "concern," the pride that you might feel when your child performs well in the school play is not *concern* except in a derivative sense: you might be proud *of yourself* for having raised such a talented child and see the child's performance as evidence of the fact that you performed your duties well. But you aren't proud of *the child's* actions as such, but only of your own. In the relevant sense of "concern," that is, concernment always involves belief that those acts with which you are concerned were performed by *you*. As we'll see, Locke takes concern of the relevant sort to be intertwined with susceptibility to pleasure and pain.

Now "Of Identity and Diversity" contains various remarks linking consciousness with the capacity to feel pleasure and pain. Here are two characteristic passages:

Self is that conscious thinking thing ... which is sensible, or conscious of Pleasure and Pain, capable of Happiness or Misery, and so is concern'd for it *self*, as far as that consciousness extends. (E II.xxvii.17: 341)

[P]ersonality extends it *self* beyond present Existence to what is past, only by consciousness, whereby it becomes concerned and accountable, owns and imputes to it *self* past Actions, just upon the same ground, and for the same reason, that it does the present. All which is founded in a concern for Happiness the unavoidable concomitant of consciousness, that which is conscious of Pleasure and Pain, desiring, that that *self*, that is conscious, should be happy. (E II.xxvii.26: 346)

What both of these passages indicate is that a creature that is conscious is necessarily susceptible to pleasure or pain, and, conversely, a creature that feels pleasure or pain is necessarily conscious. Consciousness is the awareness that attends pleasure and pain and that does so with necessity. (Elsewhere, Locke puts the point in no uncertain terms: "[T]o be happy or miserable without being conscious of it, seems to me utterly inconsistent and impossible" [E II.i.11: 110].) Further, Locke seems to hold that the special kind of concern that we have with past actions that we take ourselves to have performed – we feel pride or remorse, for instance, only for actions that we judge ourselves to have performed – derives from the fact that those actions are potential sources of pleasure or pain for ourselves now. As he says in the first of the two passages just quoted, you are "concern'd" about a particular chunk of the world only insofar as it is something that is capable of making you happy or miserable, of giving you pleasure or pain. Since pleasure or pain always goes along with conscious awareness, you are thus concerned with a chunk of the world only if you are conscious of its states (as you are of the states of your pinkie finger) or else its states will determine what pleasures and pains you are to feel. With this in mind, we can propose what I will call the "susceptibility-to-pain theory of personal identity." The best way to think of this theory is as an analysis of Locke's notion of consciousness. We start with the claim that a later person is the same person as an earlier one just in case they have the same consciousness. We then ask, under what conditions do they have the same consciousness? The answer, according to the susceptibility-to-pain theory, is this: the later person and the earlier one have the same consciousness just in case the earlier's actions are a potential source of pleasure or pain for the later.

The susceptibility-to-pain theory raises many questions. Notice that there are many past actions that we recognize will cause us pleasure or pain now, which are not, on those grounds, performed by ourselves. As the arrow flies toward me, I may recognize that the archer's release of it will be the cause of my future pain, but I do not think, nor is it the case, that I am the archer. Compare this to the case in which just as I begin running a marathon, I think back to the eating an hour before of a huge greasy meal. I might recognize that the act of eating the meal is going to cause me pain as I run, but in this case, in contrast to the archer case, I also recognize that the pain that I will suffer is my own fault, for I am the one who ate the meal. Or, to consider yet another kind of case, imagine that I commit a crime or a sin – a murder, say, or an act of adultery – and am never caught; later, as I suffer divine punishment in the afterlife, I may recognize that the pain that I then suffer had its source in my earlier conduct. The question is whether the susceptibility-to-pain theory is forced to say that in all three of these cases, and not just in the second and third, the prior actor and the later sufferer are the same person.

The theory need not have this implication. Or, rather, it need not if we alter it slightly. Instead of saying merely that the earlier person's action must be a potential source of *pleasure or pain* for the later person if and only if they have the same consciousness, we should say instead that the earlier's action must be a potential source of *reward or punishment* for the later person. For the sake of clarity, call this the "susceptibility-to-punishment theory of personal identity." On this view, the reason that I am not the archer, despite the fact that his action will cause me pain, is that the pain that I will suffer is not a punishment for the archer's act. By contrast, the reason that the marathon runner is the overeater is that the stomach ache is a punishment, of sorts, for the act of overeating. And, similarly, the sufferer in hell is the one who committed the earlier sin precisely because the suffering is a punishment for the sin. This line of thought begs a question or, to put the point in a more challenging tone of voice, gives rise immediately to a powerful objection, which is a version of the circularity concern: what's the difference between being punished for a prior act and merely suffering a pain for that prior act? It seems that the best answer is this: your pain is a punishment only if you are the one who performed the prior act. Thus, it seems, the pain/punishment distinction depends upon, and cannot constitute, personal identity.

However, there is a response to be made to this version of the circularity concern on behalf of the susceptibility-to-pain theory, and the response reveals what Locke means in claiming "person" to be a "forensick" term. The difference between punishment caused by a past act and mere pain caused by it is not that in the first case there is identity between actor and sufferer and in the second there is not; the difference is that in the first case the laws of nature – God's laws linking crimes with punishments and good acts with rewards – specify that the actor is to suffer, and in the second they do not.[19] Who is identical to whom depends on who is rightly rewarded or punished rather than the reverse. This is the sense in

---

[19] Unlike Locke, we tend to use the term "forensic" to refer to practices that are intertwined not with divine law, but with the laws of states, particularly criminal laws. Locke recognizes, as anyone would, that there is often a discrepancy between who is punished under divine law and who under civil law. He quite clearly indicates that the tight connection is between identity and divine law, rather than civil, at E II.xxvii.22.

which "person" is a "forensick" term, a term of law: whether or not a later and earlier act of consciousness are the same depends on the content of natural law.

The susceptibility-to-punishment theory bears a close relationship to the view that associates consciousness, in Locke's sense, with appropriation. To see this, consider the following remark:

[S]upposing a Man punish'd now, for what he had done in another Life, whereof he could be made to have no consciousness at all, what difference is there between that Punishment, and being created miserable? (E II. xxvii.26: 347)

Locke claims here that a characteristic difference between mere pain, on the one hand, and punishment, on the other, is that when a person is punished he can be made aware of having performed the prior act that the laws of nature say he is to be punished for. The kind of awareness that Locke has in mind must be the special kind of self-attributive awareness of direct appropriation. After all, as I'm being struck with the arrow I may be aware of the archer's act of releasing it, but that kind of awareness doesn't transform my pain into punishment for the releasing of the arrow. By contrast, as I double over in pain while running the marathon, there is some kind of justice to my suffering – it's my own fault – and this is justice that I am in position to perceive by being aware of having performed the prior act.

But the ability to appropriate a past act, while necessary for identity with the actor, is not sufficient for it under the susceptibility-to-punishment theory, for there is no bar to appropriating a past act for which you are not justly punished or rewarded. Locke envisions such a possibility in the following passage:

[W]hy one intellectual Substance may not have represented to it, as done by it self, what it never did, and was perhaps done by some other Agent, why I say such a representation may not possibly be without reality of Matter of Fact, as well as several representations in Dreams are, which yet, whilst dreaming, we take for true, will be difficult to conclude from the Nature of things. And that it never is so, will by us, till we have clearer views of the Nature of thinking Substances, be best resolv'd into the Goodness of God, who as far as the Happiness or Misery of any of his sensible Creatures is concerned in it, will not by a fatal Error of theirs transfer from one to another, that consciousness, which draws Reward or Punishment with it. (E II.xxvii.13: 338)

Ordinarily, commentators take Locke to be making an error here. After all, they say, if being aware of a past action is sufficient for identity with the past actor, then there could be no mistake in which a present person is aware of a past act that he didn't do; if he's aware of it, then he did it. Hence there's nothing to fear would happen if it weren't for "the Goodness of God." But Locke is not making a mistake under the susceptibility-to-punishment theory. There is no necessary, or conceptual, connection between the capacity to appropriate a past act and the appropriateness of punishment for it. It is true that wherever, and without exception, we find the one we find the other, but it is perfectly possible, on conceptual grounds, to be appropriately punished for something that you are incapable of appropriating. The reason that we never find this, however, is that as a matter of brute natural law the two never come apart. Locke's appeal to the goodness of God is his way of saying that we really don't understand *why* the ability to appropriate a past action is found just in case the act is one for which you are rightly punished, but, still, we know that it is so.[20]

The susceptibility-to-punishment theory is, in a sense, a dodge. One of the things we want to understand when we start thinking about personal identity is what fact it is that we depend upon in praising and blaming. We enter into the inquiry about personal identity in part because it seems clear that those practices would be ill-founded if there were nothing that made a past actor identical to the person whom we punish for the past act. Thus, we go looking for an account of personal identity that is given in nonmoral terms but which, nonetheless, links with our moral concepts and fixes one of the necessary conditions for their applicability. But if Locke holds the susceptibility-to-punishment theory of personal identity, as I'm suggesting he does, then he is reversing the assumed order of priority of the metaphysical and the moral: the metaphysical

---

[20] Thus, there is a close link between the point that Locke is making here in appealing to the "Goodness of God" and the appeal that he makes at E IV.iii.29: 560 to the "arbitrary Will and good Pleasure of the Wise Architect." In both, the appeal points to a conjunction between two things that we know to be without exception despite the fact that nothing in our ideas indicates that they are linked with necessity.

facts – the facts about who is the same person as whom – just are moral facts; they are facts about who is appropriately punished or rewarded for whose past acts. Still, Locke is not likely to have considered the theory to be a dodge, since, for him, the laws of nature are as much part of the universe's fabric as are the minds that are governed by them.

CONCLUSION

Locke's chapter on identity and diversity intersects with a remarkable number of philosophical issues with which Locke grapples in the *Essay*. His discussion of the principle of individuation is part of his response to, and reworking of, the Aristotelian-Scholastic approach to metaphysics. In offering his account of the principle of individuation, he is soberly participating in a debate the terms of which were set by his predecessors and, at the same time, making fun of their assumption that it is possible to find a unified and illuminating theory of the identity of a thing, no matter what kind of thing it is. His offering of the Place-Time-Kind Principle is not divorced from, but is instead part of, his nominalism about kinds of things and his closely related view to the effect that there is no kind-independent meaning to the idea of an essential quality. His discussion of the identity of atoms and, in turn, masses of matter is intertwined with his conception of matter as solid, extended stuff, a conception that is, itself, at the heart of his admiration for the corpuscularian hypothesis and his related distinction between primary and secondary qualities. His rejection of the same-organism and same-substance theories is closely connected to both his skepticism about the possibility of an illuminating conception of substratum, and his deep agnosticism as to whether or not the mind is a material thing. It is part, also, of Locke's abhorrence for excessive intellectual self-confidence, for those who think they know the answer to such grand questions as what the soul is, and what is and is not required for it to persist through time. His account of personal identity as sameness of consciousness, especially when viewed in light of the connection between consciousness and pleasure and pain, happiness and misery, is intertwined with his moral theory and his theory of value, his view to the effect that at bottom what is good or bad is linked to, respectively, pleasure or pain. And, finally, his claim that "person" is a "forensick" term – a claim that he takes to follow from his account of personal identity, rather than treating it as an add-on to the theory – is part of his attitude toward brute natural laws and the need to appeal to them, in the end, in order to make sense of the boundaries of many of our ordinary ideas. Our ideas of identity and diversity, then, sit, for Locke, at the center of a web and stretch into almost every central topic of the *Essay*.

8 Locke on Ideas and Representation

Locke's *Essay* is part of the so-called epistemological turn given philosophy by Descartes that assigned fundamental importance to the theory of knowledge. So much is clear from the introduction to Book I: "my *Purpose* [is] to enquire into the Original, Certainty, and Extent of humane Knowledge; together, with the Grounds and Degrees of Belief, Opinion, and Assent" (E I.i.2: 43). The general aim in the period was to reconcile the startling discrepancy, in all its ramifications, between the so-called manifest image, as it has come to be called, which views the world in the commonsense terms of colors, odors, and tastes, and the emerging scientific image, which sees it in the atomistic (or "corpuscularian") terms of sizes, shapes, and motion.

Locke's version of the epistemological turn took what his ecclesiastical critic Stillingfleet called the *new way of ideas*: we perceive things not as they are in themselves, but in terms of our ideas of them. By an *idea* Locke means the mind's immediate *object* whenever it thinks, which for him is something *in the mind* (E I.i.8; II.viii.8). The mind knows the mediate object outside the mind insofar as the idea represents it. The distinction between an idea and its object is Locke's way of dealing with the discrepancy between the manifest and scientific images. So far, all interpretations of Locke are in basic agreement.

There is no consensus, however, on exactly what Locke meant by 'representation', or, therefore, by an idea. According to the majority view of Locke, an idea is an item that is *really distinct* from the object it represents; they are two, numerically distinct things. And the idea represents its object by taking its place in the mind. On this *surrogate thesis*, as it might be called, an idea represents its object in the way a lawyer represents a client, by serving as a surrogate. With this sharp distinction from its object, an idea is *in the mind* in some strong sense – in the way that a quality such as roundness, for example, is in a substance such as an apple.

A weakness in this interpretation is that Locke explicitly denies that ideas are in the mind in this way, and it is not obvious how else, according to it, they could be in the mind. A further and more important difficulty it raises is that Locke is thereby committed to an unintended skepticism: if all we are ever immediately aware of are ideas in the mind, how do we know even that there are any things outside the mind? much less that they are represented by those ideas? On the surrogate thesis, ideas stand between us and what they represent, posing a *veil of perception* that hides the world from all our efforts to know it.[1]

There is a minority view, associated primarily with John W. Yolton, that offers promise of saving Locke from this unwelcome skepticism: an idea is the thing that it represents as it appears to the mind. And it represents that thing by presenting it to the mind. On this *presentation thesis*, as it might be called, an idea represents its object in the way a lawyer represents a case in court, by presenting it there. With a weakened distinction from its object, an idea can be in the mind in the way we ordinarily say that something is in the mind, namely, that it is thought of.[2] The veil of perception is thereby lifted.

Both the presentation thesis and the surrogate thesis are attempts to capture Locke's distinction between the manifest and scientific images, between appearance and reality. On the presentation thesis, to say that an idea of x represents x is to say that x appears as the idea would have it, whether it is really so or not. Again, the idea of x just is x as it appears, whether it is really the way it appears or not. On this account, the nonidentity of discernibles fails – one of the peculiarities of the logic of ideas. On the surrogate thesis, the nonidentity of discernibles holds. What we see is, or can be, qualitatively different from what there is, and therefore the idea of x is numerically different from what there is. Again, the idea of x and x

[1] Among many others, see Aaron 1955: 99–107.
[2] Yolton 1975. For a fuller bibliography of his relevant works, see Chappell 1994: 314–15. For others, see Tipton 1992: 97.

are really distinct things, which is why a veil descends between us and the world.

The tendency in the recent literature has been to soften the distinction between these two interpretations with various nuances and qualifications,[3] or to point out that it might be difficult to draw the distinction at all,[4] so that other interpretations become possible. The contest between them nonetheless remains fundamental to the interpretation of Locke, and in any case it is a useful framework for investigating Locke's views on ideas and representation. Here, the companion to his *Essay* will focus on three topics: (1) Locke's actual usage of the term 'represent', (2) how the connection between an idea and its object might be understood, and (3) what it is that makes an idea represent one object rather than another.

I

It is of interest to consider Locke's own use of the term 'represent'. Such linguistic considerations by themselves, of course, offer no definitive argument as to how Locke understood representation. For example, even if Locke had never used the term at all, he might well have raised for us exactly the same questions about representation. The fact is, however, that the term, along with its cognates, occurs with fair frequency in the *Essay*, and Locke deploys it specifically regarding the connection between an idea and its object.

In Locke's time, as it does today, the term 'represent' meant both to *take the place of* and to *make present*. So on linguistic grounds there is nothing to adjudicate between the surrogate and presentation theses. With one unique possible exception, however, there is not a single text in which Locke clearly and unambiguously uses the term in the first sense to indicate a surrogate, proxy, or stand-in. The possible exception will be considered after an investigation of the three categories into which Locke's use of the term falls.

Most of Locke's uses of the term fall into a category that might be described as ambiguous at best with respect to the surrogate thesis. None of them is inconsistent with the presentation thesis.

---

[3] Dlugos 1996; Bolton 2004; Newman 2004.   [4] Tipton 1992.

For example, he argues that no simple idea can be false in respect of external things.

> For the Truth of these Appearances, or Perceptions in our Minds, consisting ... only in their being answerable to the Powers in external Objects, to produce by our Senses such Appearances in us: and each of them being in the Mind such as it is, suitable to the Power that produced it, and which alone it represents, it cannot upon that Account, or as referr'd to such a Pattern, be *False*. (E II.xxxii.16: 390)

It might be that a simple idea represents the power producing it by taking its place in the mind. But it might also represent that power to the mind insofar as the idea is just the way in which the power, which consists in a certain corpuscular arrangement, appears to the mind – that is, the idea is the arrangement itself as it appears to the mind. In these cases of ideas of secondary qualities such as color, which is Locke's preferred example of a simple idea, the way that it appears is a matter of what he calls "superaddition." The appearance is determined by the goodness of the Creator with an eye to our material survival. But this superaddition is consistent with the fact that it is the arrangement that appears.

Some texts are at face value ambiguous in the sense that at least syntactically they can be read, as above, consistently with either the surrogate or presentation thesis, but are such that unless they are disambiguated in favor of the latter, Locke is in hot water. A good example is the idea of God. If the idea represents God as a surrogate for Him (E II.iv.13), then when Locke claims to think about God, as when he tries to worship Him, for example, it would appear, as it did in fact to Stillingfleet, that Locke worships his own ideas. In short, Locke's "new way of ideas," according to Stillingfleet, who clearly understood Locke's position in terms of the surrogate thesis, leads to religious skepticism. In reply, however, Locke insisted that he was proposing nothing new, controversial, or different from the position of Stillingfleet himself or of anyone who perceives anything at all (W IV: 134–5, 430). Again, the presentation view would seem more plausible: ideas are needed only in the sense, trivial to an empiricist, that to perceive an object we must be appeared to by it. That we perceive via ideas that are surrogates is not trivial at all, however, even on empiricist grounds (as Berkeley was soon to argue).

Moreover, Locke seems explicitly to distinguish his use of 'represent' from the notion of standing for. At least, there is a distinction between Locke's language about ideas and his language about words. (The failure to distinguish between words and ideas is a great source of mischief, according to Locke.) Both ideas and words are signs for Locke; but words are said to *stand for* what they signify, viz. ideas, whereas ideas *represent* what they signify. *"Words in their primary or immediate Signification, stand for nothing but the* Ideas *in the Mind of him that uses them,* how imperfectly soever, or carelessly those *Ideas* are collected from the Things, which they are supposed to represent" (E III.ii.2: 405).

Treating of definition, Locke appears to equate representing x with standing for or taking the place of x. But the appearance is dispelled by a close reading. Discussing the imperfections of language, he says,

but though Definitions will serve to explain the Names of Substances, as they stand for our *Ideas;* yet they leave them not without great imperfection, as they stand for Things. For our Names of Substances being not put barely for our *ideas,* but being made use of ultimately to represent Things, and so are put in their place, their signification must agree with the Truth of Things, as well as with Men's *Ideas.* (E III.xi.24: 520)

The string, "but being made use of ... to represent Things, and so ... put in their place," seems to make the equation explicit. But in the place of what? If Locke were equating 'represent' with 'put in their place', the antecedent would be 'Things'. However, the antecedent can only be '*Ideas*'. The thought is that words do not merely replace ideas, but are also used to represent things as ideas do, and in this sense words are put in the place of ideas. And, not incidentally, when this happens, great problems in communication loom.

There is no need, however, to tease out any further the presentation reading from more or less ambiguous texts. For there is a second category of texts that unequivocally show that Locke cannot mean, at least not in them, that ideas represent objects by taking their place. There are two sorts of such texts. One sort concerns what it is that is doing the representing. Locke variously says that the *mind* represents something, or that *we* represent something, either to ourselves or to others. Consider how it is that we know

God. "It is Infinity, which joined to our *Ideas* of Existence, Power, Knowledge, etc. makes that complex *Idea* whereby we represent to ourselves the best we can, the supreme Being" (E II.xxiii.35: 315). It would make no sense to say that we represent God to ourselves by taking the place of God in the mind, whereas it does make sense, on the presentation thesis, to say that we represent God to ourselves by bringing it about that He is presented to us.

The surrogate reading might be stretched by arguing that when Locke speaks in this way, in the above and other texts (e.g., II.xxii.9), he is using a circumlocution to say that we deploy or rely on ideas that represent their objects by taking their place. For representation is by means of such ideas. But consider the following text. In speaking of how memories fade and die as we grow older and in fact face our own death, Locke uses figurative language: "our Minds represent to us those Tombs, to which we are approaching" (E II.x.5: 151). It would be utter nonsense to say that our minds serve as proxies for the tombs we now contemplate and one day will inhabit. Instead, our minds make them present to us just by thinking about them. The best that a defender of the surrogate thesis might do is to say that Locke tacitly argues that the only way the mind can represent anything is by relying on an idea that stands for what is represented. But this is to give up the argument for the surrogate thesis based on Locke's use of the term 'represent'.

The surrogate thesis seems definitively snapped by texts of the second sort in this category. Here, Locke says that something represents itself. Consider: "*All our complex* Ideas, *except those of Substance,* ... cannot want *any conformity necessary to real Knowledge.* For that which is not designed to represent anything but it self, can never be capable of a wrong representation" (E IV.iv.5: 564; also II.xxxi.3 and II.xxxii.17). In particular, ideas of modes and relations represent themselves. What represents, according to Locke, in some instances represents itself, in others not. Representation is unlike both reflexive relations such as *similar to*, which everything stands in to itself, and irreflexive relations such as *larger than*, which nothing does. Instead, representation is like nonreflexive relations such as *cause of* (at least as Descartes understands it), which some things bear to themselves, others not. But on the surrogate interpretation, representation should be an irreflexive relation, for nothing stands for, or takes the place of, or serves as a proxy for itself. The surrogate interpretation must to this extent be mistaken. Meanwhile, on the presentation thesis, representation is, as it should be, nonreflexive: in some cases items always represent themselves (modes), in others not (substances).

The presentation thesis is not yet established, however. Despite the above, there is a category of texts that suggest the surrogate thesis. These texts are of three sorts. First, Locke repeatedly refers to ideas as signs, images, or pictures. Such language suggests that ideas are things really distinct from what they represent. Because Caesar is no longer present, a picture that takes his place is necessary for him to be represented to us. Moreover, in at least two texts Locke makes the equation between such terms and representation explicit: "since the Things the Mind contemplates, are none of them, besides it self, present to the Understanding, 'tis necessary that something else, as a Sign or Representation of the Thing it considers, should be present to it: And these are *Ideas*" (E IV.xxi.4: 721). Also: "it sufficing, to the unity of any *Idea*, that it be considered one Representation, or Picture" (E II.xxiv.1: 317–18). That these texts do not establish the surrogate reading would require the explanation of what it means to be a picture. The explanation is long, beyond the bounds of the discussion here (Lennon 2001: 164–6), but the short of it is that a sign or picture represents, as does an idea for Locke, by making present, not by standing for what it represents. When one *looks at* a portrait of Caesar, what one *sees* is Caesar, describing him as wearing a toga. To be sure, I could, by a shift of set, *see* the painting, describing it as rectangular and rough-textured. But then it would have ceased to be a portrait and would no longer represent anything. In his thinking about representation, Locke might have been influenced by Arnauld, who argued against the surrogate account of representation that he, along with nearly everyone else, finds in Malebranche (Yolton 1975). When I look in a mirror, what do I see? he asks. His answer is that I see myself, not some image of myself. This line of argument may or may not establish the presentation reading; at a minimum, it neutralizes the value to the surrogate thesis of texts of this sort.

Another sort of text suggesting the surrogate thesis concerns the problem of existential error (the representation of what does not exist, e.g., something that is hallucinated) in conjunction with a requirement of intentionality (all thought must have some object) (Chappell 1994c: 30). To take a familiar example not actually used by Locke, what Macbeth sees is not a real dagger, but an object in his mind, that is, an idea. Now, the dagger he hallucinates is phenomenologically indistinguishable from the real dagger he might previously have seen (if they were phenomenologically distinguishable, Macbeth would not have been fooled as he was). The argument might then be that what Macbeth sees even in the case of veridical perception of the real dagger is not a dagger but a surrogate idea of one. Yet in the texts in which this issue arises, Locke rather clearly indicates that, for him, what does not exist can in fact be represented. Discussing personal identity and the possibility of transfer of the same consciousness from one substance to another, he says,

I grant, were the same consciousness the same individual Action, it could not: But it being but a present representation of a past Action, why it may not be possible, that that may be represented to the Mind to have been, which really never was, will remain to be shewn. ... Why one intellectual Substance may not have represented to it, as done by itself, what it never did, why ... such a representation may not possibly be without reality of Matter of Fact, as well as several representations in Dreams are, ... will be difficult to conclude from the Nature of things. (E II.xxvii.13: 337–8; also II. xxxii.20)

But if what does not exist, indeed, if what has never existed, can plausibly be represented in the sense of being *stood for* by something else, then it is no more implausible for it to be *presented directly* to the mind. In either case, what is now called a nondescriptive relation or pseudo-relation must be invoked, that is, a connective like *or*, which can obtain even if one of its relata does not (it is raining *or* it is not raining), and unlike a descriptive relation such as *to the left of*, which cannot obtain unless both relata obtain (there must be two things, one to the left of the other). Such a unique relation is just what is to be expected if the unique features of mind, such as error, are to be accounted for. According to the one thesis, it would be invoked between an idea and its object; according to the other, between the object and the mind. In any case, once again the presentation reading might not yet be established; at a minimum, however, the prima facie advantage of the surrogate reading is neutralized.

A third sort of text suggesting the surrogate reading comes from Locke's discussion of the reality, adequacy, and truth of ideas. These are considerations of ideas "in reference to things from whence they are taken, or which they may be supposed to represent" (E II.xxx.1: 372). *Taking ideas from what they are supposed to represent* suggests that ideas are, or become, things distinct from what they represent. This interpretation becomes all but irresistible when Locke turns to the adequacy of ideas. "Those I call *Adequate* [those], which perfectly represent those Archetypes, which the Mind supposes them taken from; which it intends them to stand for, and to which it refers them" (E II.xxxi.1: 375). A not implausible way of reading the *taking of ideas*, however, is the *receiving of appearances*. We might be said to get appearances of a thing only in the sense that the thing appears to us, such that what we get, or take, is that thing insofar as it appears to us.

So far, then, these texts might not be any more, or less, problematic than those considered earlier. But Locke also says here that the mind intends ideas to *stand for* their archetypes. Now the expression 'stand for' is found all over the *Essay*, appearing literally hundreds of times. In every case but the one just cited, Locke uses it to refer to the relation between a word and the idea it expresses. (More precisely, it refers to the relation between a linguistic item, which can be either a word or idea forming a proposition, and what it expresses. For Locke, in at least two texts, ideas can be joined or separated according to the things they stand for [E II.xxxii.19; also E IV.v.6]. Even so, the representation by an idea of its object, and the expression of a state of affairs by ideas in judgment, are, as they should be, different.) This means that the expression 'standing for' is likely a technical one, and one that a defender of the surrogate thesis might use to disambiguate all the cases above in which it does not occur, that is, in favor of the surrogate reading. On the other hand, Locke's failure to use it except in this one case cuts the other way as well: if it means *to take the place* of something before the mind, why doesn't Locke say everywhere, or at least more often, that ideas stand for their objects? On behalf of the presentation reading, then, there are two possibilities, neither entirely satisfying. Either the single use is simply aberrant – Locke nods here by saying in effect that the thing as it appears stands for itself as it is in itself ("knowledge of it as it appears goes bail for our lack of knowledge of it in itself" might be a nonaberrant way of understanding this possibility). Or Locke here uses *standing for* in a nontechnical sense that does not necessarily involve a proxy, such as *supporting* (as in "standing for God and King Charles") or *being considered as* (as in "standing for nothing").

On balance, the evidence seems overwhelmingly weighted toward the presentation thesis. Before giving up the game, however, the defender of the surrogate thesis has a final trump card to play: the representation of many individuals by one abstract idea – for example, man – to which they all conform (E III.iii.6: 411; also III.iii.11 and IV. xvii.8). These individuals cannot all be present to the mind – that, after all, is the point of framing the abstract idea in the first place – and therefore the idea must be a surrogate. But if they are not present, how can even a surrogate idea represent them? Locke insists that reasoning and knowledge can only be about ideas, which are "truly, every one of them, particular Existences," and which may correspond to and represent many things. How might this be, on the presentation reading? The answer is that many things have the same appearance, and how this might be will be seen at the end of this chapter.

II

The preposition in the expression 'y of x' can be understood in many different ways (Lennon 2001: 157–60). In understanding Locke's use of the expression 'idea of x', three ways are of particular importance. One is to take it as indicating what the idea is *about*, viz. the object x that is represented to the mind. This is the sense in which we might speak of a statue *of* Caesar. The object represented by the statue is Caesar. This is an obvious sense of the term, and, in any case, the one assumed by most commentators. A technical term for this sense is the *objective genitive*. (In Latin, 'of x' is the genitive case, which above would modify *statue*.) It is a natural way to read Locke when he speaks of, for example, the idea of God (E II.xxiii.33–35: 314–15). One person's idea of God might in this sense be the same as another's. In fact, that people should have the same idea of such important items as God (and the dire consequences when they do not) is one of the concerns of the *Essay*.

Taking 'idea of x' to express an objective genitive establishes a real distinction between the idea and its object (as there seems to be between Caesar and a statue or picture of him), and this distinction is the linchpin of the surrogate thesis and the veil of perception that follows from it. Although it might be inviting to read Locke's expression in this way, it is not how Locke understands the expression 'idea of x', either for simple or for complex ideas. (So that if ideas are pictures for Locke, then the picturing relation itself must be understood as something other than an objective genitive.)

In the case of simple ideas, his empiricism requires a different reading. To see this, consider that with the objective genitive the action is directed toward what is expressed by the genitive. Thus, in the 'picture of Caesar', or 'the love of God', Caesar is pictured, and God is loved. But with a simple idea such as the idea of blue, it is the mind that is acted upon, not blue. (In this case, 'the love of God' would be understood with God offering the love, not receiving it.) A technical term for this case is the *subjective genitive*: the subject of the action is in the genitive. Locke must opt for the subjective genitive because we are utterly passive in our perception of simple ideas. "It is not in the Power of the most exalted Wit, or enlarged Understanding, by any quickness or variety of Thought, to *invent or frame one new simple* Idea" (E II.ii.2: 119–20). Despite being expressed by an active verb, our perception is better expressed as the "reception" of ideas (E II.xxi.73: 286).

Still, the surrogate theorist might argue, there could be a real distinction between the subjective genitive and what it modifies (as there is in 'the words of Plato', another example of this genitive). The reply is that the real distinction is between the object of the idea and the mind to which it appears. The idea itself is numerically identical to that same object (even if it is qualitatively different from that object). That is, the idea is the object as it appears to us (and the object need not appear as it really is).

Nor can complex ideas, which result from the mind's activity on simple ideas, be understood in terms of the objective genitive. A third sense of the preposition is had when we speak of a statue *of* marble. In this case, the statue does not represent marble, at least not normally. Marble is not the object. Instead, the preposition indicates the *kind of* statue it is, in the sense of what it is composed of. A technical term for this sense is the *material genitive*. Two statues of Caesar, one of which is bronze and the other marble, would thus be two different (kinds of) statues. Similarly, the preposition might indicate a kind of idea. When Locke distinguishes ideas of sensation and ideas of reflection as comprising the whole of our experience, the source of all "reason and knowledge" (E II.i.2–4), he is distinguishing kinds of ideas. An impression is not the object of these ideas. Rather, the object in the one case is something outside the mind (e.g., the idea of hard) and in the other some perception, as when we think about our thinking (e.g., the idea of doubting): "our Observation employ'd either about *external, sensible Objects; or about the internal Operations of our Minds, perceived and reflected on by our selves*" (E II.i.2: 104; also II.i.24). To put it simply, the impression or reflection is not represented by the idea; it *is* the idea.

When Locke introduces the notion of complex ideas, he says that, according to the relevant three different kinds of mental activity, they "may all be reduced under these three Heads": modes, substances, and relations (E II.xii.3: 164). That is, each of these *is* a (kind of) complex idea, not the object of such an idea. So much is syntactically clear as he continues: "First, *Modes* I call such *Ideas, ...*" Still, such an important issue cannot rest entirely on a turn of phrase, and in any case Locke does often speak of ideas of modes, which, as has just been seen, is at least ambiguous usage. Moreover, there are some commentators who, in light of Locke's self-confessed inaccuracy in speaking about ideas as if they were in things, would be inclined to disambiguate Locke's usage in favor of the objective genitive, that is, by taking mode as an object of the complex idea (Mackie: 1976: 73, note 3).

In one of the most important texts of the *Essay*, Locke distinguishes between an idea as the direct object of awareness in the mind and a quality as the power to produce the idea, which for ideas of sensation is something outside the mind. Breathtakingly, however, he concludes by saying, "which *Ideas*, if I speak of sometimes as in the things themselves, I would be understood to mean those Qualities in the Objects which produce them in us" (E II.viii.8: 134). On the attempt at disambiguation above, when Locke speaks of a mode as an idea he really means an idea of a mode such that they are really distinct. Such a reading gains plausibility from the continuation of Locke's claim about modes: "which however compounded, contain not in themselves the supposition of subsisting by themselves, but are considered as Dependencies on, or Affections of

Substances" (E II.xii.4: 165). The substances on which modes are considered to depend are, typically, other than the mind, so it would seem that ideas of modes are ideas of them as objects.

This attempt at sorting out Locke fails, however, and does so in all three cases of complex ideas, for different but serious philosophical reasons. Relations, alas, did not much interest Locke, and need not detain us, either. For there is an additional feature of relations that leaves no room for doubt but that they are kinds of ideas. It is a feature had by mixed modes as well, viz. that there is no difference between them and what they might be taken to represent. In Locke's terminology, there is a coincidence between archetype and ectype. Or, as Locke ultimately puts it, the real and nominal essences expressed by the idea are identical. Like all abstract ideas, they are the "Workmanship of the Mind, and are not referred to the real Existence of Things" (E III.v.14: 436–7). Thus, whatever properties depend on the essence and flow from the idea are the only properties of the thing represented. The real essence contains only what we put into it, so there can be no discrepancy between it and the nominal essence we create. Thus, to use Locke's (slightly emended) example, the idea of a triangle as a "plane, closed, rectilinear Figure, with three sides meeting at three angles" is complete in the sense that nothing could be discovered that was not already in it or did not follow from it. This sort of idea is, as we shall see, unlike what we conceive of as gold, for instance, in which there might well be properties that are even in principle undiscoverable. This is why such ideas are always adequate (as well as real and true). That is, they "perfectly represent those Archetypes, which the Mind supposes them taken from; which it intends them to stand for, and to which it refers them" (E II.xxxi.1: 375).

Now, it may be that this result is trivial (Chappell 1994c: 50). That is, ideas as ectypes perfectly represent their archetypes only in the apparently uninteresting sense that they represent themselves. "*Mixed Modes* and *Relations*, being Archetypes without Patterns [i.e., "standing Patterns existing anywhere" outside the mind], and so having nothing to represent but themselves, cannot but be adequate, every thing being so to it self" (E II.xxxi.3: 377). But perhaps there is something more to Locke's position. Whatever their ontological status as either creations by the mind or real things independent of it, essences have always been taken to express possibilities, kinds of things that might exist. This is precisely the notion that Locke captures with the *reality* of these ideas. "There is nothing more required ... to make them *real*, but that they be so framed, that there be a possibility of existing conformable to them. These *Ideas*, being themselves Archetypes, cannot differ from their Archetypes, and so *cannot be chimerical*, unless any one will jumble together in them inconsistent ideas" (E II.xxx.4: 373).

To say that triangularity is an essence is to say that there might be triangles. At a minimum, then, to have the idea of a mode is to establish a possibility, just by consistently thinking it. What Locke has to say about modes under this rubric is relatively intuitive, but perhaps less so when it is applied to relations. He says only that it is "with very little difference applicable also to Relations"; but he begs off the application himself, since "every Man himself may observe" it (E III.v.16: 437). Perhaps, in their way, relations express possibilities. Thus, *older than* is a thinkable idea and expresses a possible relation between x and y in the sense that x can be thought to be older than y. But *more pregnant than*, in this sense, does not.

More important than the possibilities expressed by such ideas is that they represent themselves. That is, these ideas represent their objects to the mind in the way lawyers represent cases to the court, viz. by presenting them, as opposed to the way they represent their clients, viz. by serving in their stead as surrogates. In the latter case, there is a real distinction between the representation and what is represented. In the former case, there is none. For the analogy to be perfectly precise, the lawyer would be said to bring it about that the case presents itself.

The case of the third sort of complex idea, substance, is very different. "For there desiring to copy Things, as they really do exist; and to represent to our selves that Constitution, on which all their Properties do depend, we perceive that our *Ideas* attain not that Perfection we intend." They all lack something we would like to be in them, and thus they are all inadequate (E II.xxxi.3: 377). Ideas of modes are created without metaphysical constraint – "*very arbitrarily*," as Locke puts it (E III.v.3: 429) – there being no real kinds to which they must conform. But they are not made "*at random*" (E III.v.7: 431). The constraints are the logical one that they be consistent, which we have already seen, and the pragmatic one that that they serve "the convenience of Communication." Only if we want to communicate about modes do we collect ideas into them. With respect to ideas of substance there is an additional constraint, since such ideas are intended to be of things other than themselves. "Though Men may make what complex *Ideas* they please, and give what Names they will; yet if they will be understood, when they speak of Things really existing, they must, in some degree, conform their *Ideas* to the Things they would speak of." Without this conformity, says Locke, their language "will be like that of *Babel*" (E III.vi.28: 456). It is not clear from this text what degree of conformity is required, how it might be measured, in what it consists, or even how it might be achieved. Perhaps all that Locke means is that we must intend to conform them as best we can. In any case, absent this condition of "some way answering the common appearances and agreement of Substances, as they really exist" (ibid.), we are condemned to the isolation of our own private language.

It would seem, then, that ideas of substances are *of* their objects in the way that the statue of Caesar is of its object, and that they represent their objects by taking their place as things different from them. Yet even in this case there is an ambiguity, and it occurs in the famous first paragraph of the chapter in which he elaborates the idea substance. "The Mind being ... furnished with a great number of simple *Ideas*, conveyed in by the *Senses*, ... or by *Reflection* ... takes notice also, that a certain number of these simple *Ideas* go constantly together." Taking theses ideas as belonging to one thing, says Locke, we for purposes of communication give them a single name and then inadvertently regard them as a simple idea. This happens, he continues, because "not imagining how these simple *Ideas* can subsist by themselves, we accustom our selves, to suppose some *Substratum*, wherein they do subsist, and from which they do result, which we therefore call *Substance*" (E II.xxiii.1: 295).

The ambiguity is signaled right at the outset when Locke says that ideas are "conveyed in" by the senses, for ideas are supposed to exist *only* in the mind. Nor does the issue hang on a turn of phrase. For at the end, Locke says that we suppose ideas to subsist in the substrate we call substance. Now, some have tried to disambiguate this text by appealing, in the way noted earlier, to Locke's avowal of sometimes speaking inaccurately of ideas as if they were in things (Mackie 1976: 73, note 3). This effort gains plausibility when in the next paragraph Locke switches to the idea of "pure Substance in general" as the supposed support of *qualities* capable of producing simple ideas in us.

By the same token, it seems implausible that Locke should have let an inaccuracy in such an important paragraph stand uncorrected through five editions. More likely, Locke is not inaccurate at all here, precisely because it is so important a text. As he explains elsewhere, when he speaks of "secondary *Qualities*, as being in Things; or of the *Ideas*, as being in Objects, that elicit them in us," he should be understood to mean nothing but the powers to cause those ideas. "Such ways of speaking, though accommodated to the vulgar Notions, without which, one cannot be well understood; yet truly signify nothing, but those Powers" (E II.xxxi.2: 376). For practical purposes of communication, it is often better to speak as if we knew things themselves rather than things only as they appear to us. The operator "it seems to me that" normally need be applied only in the philosophical contexts that require it. If vulgar notions are not to be accommodated here, then Locke must mean what he says.

But what does he mean? If ideas are in substances, then the substance of which he speaks must itself be an idea: a complex idea composed of a collection of simple ideas plus the supposition of a support, viz. the thing of which they are the appearances. What is the support? Locke's famous answer is that he does not know. It is a thing he knows not what. The idea of substance in general is a "confused and relative" idea; we know not what it is, but only what it does, which is to provide us with appearances of itself. As modes are mode-ideas, and relations relation-ideas, so substances are thing-ideas.

This thing-idea is *itself* a member of the collection of ideas that all together represents a thing. "The *Ideas* of *Substances* are such combinations of simple *Ideas*, as are taken to represent distinct particular things by themselves; in which the supposed, or confused *Idea* of Substance [in general], such as it is, is always the first and chief" (E II.xii.6: 165). The referent of 'which' is the combination of ideas making up ideas of particular substances such as lead. "Thus if to Substance be joined the simple *Idea* of a certain dull whitish colour, with certain degrees of Weight, Hardness, Ductility, and Fusibility, we have the *Idea* of *Lead*" (ibid.). No less than ideas of relations and modes, ideas of substances express the material genitive.

III

Whether one takes representation to mean substitution or presentation, the separate question of what grounds the representation must still be asked. What is it in virtue of which an idea is a surrogate for, or a presentation of, one thing rather than another? Or, more generally, why is the appearance I am now having an appearance of one thing rather than another? To say that the appearance of x is of x rather than of y, insofar as it is x rather than y that appears, does not answer the question. Even if the idea and object are numerically identical, we still need an account of the appearance/reality connection, as is clear from the possibility that they might be qualitatively different. Things sometimes appear different from what they are. There are four accounts of this connection to be investigated here.

1. Resemblance

Especially if one's imagination is captured by the language that Locke variously uses to describe ideas, a natural account is that ideas are like what they represent. How else is a picture, or an image, or the depiction in a camera obscura, or a diapositive projection related to its object? (E III.iii.7; II.i.15; II.xi.17; II.xiv.9). Moreover, this account seems to support the standard surrogate interpretation (Newman 2004: 276, esp. note 11). The initial obstacle to this account is that Locke explicitly denies that ideas of secondary qualities, which for him do represent, have any resemblance at all to bodies (E II.viii.15: 137). His denial is fundamental, as one of three respects in which primary and secondary qualities differ. Nor could he fail to make it without creating serious problems for his corpuscularian hypothesis.

That ideas of secondary qualities nonetheless represent is abundantly clear. All simple ideas are adequate, which is to say that they perfectly represent their archetypes; and Locke's preferred example of a simple idea, especially in this regard, is the idea of a secondary quality (E II.xxxi.1–2: 375). But in discussing the reality of ideas, which all simple ideas have – that is, they all agree with the reality of things – Locke qualifies his position: "not that all of them are the Images, or Representations of what does exist, the contrary whereof, in all but the primary Qualities of Bodies, hath already been shown [presumably in II.viii]" (E II.xxx.2: 372). In saying that an idea of a secondary quality is *not* a representation, Locke can mean only that while an idea of whiteness perfectly represents the microscopic structure causing it as opposed to that causing the idea of green or cold, and is thus real and adequate, it does not represent that structure as it is in itself, which on the corpuscularian hypothesis consists only of shape, size, and motion. The ambiguity is precisely the ambiguity of the question, do we perceive the miscroscopic structure at all? In one sense, we do not, because it is below our threshold of perception (we lack the necessary "microscopical eyes," as Locke puts it); and in another, we do perceive it, but not as it really is.

Now, Richard A. Watson, the most prominent defender of the resemblance account, is perfectly aware both that Locke takes ideas of secondary qualities to represent and that he denies that they do so in virtue of resemblance. Yet he ascribes the resemblance account to Locke, because for him all representation, "from Plato to Patricia Churchland," depends on resemblance (Watson 1995). How so, at least in the case of Locke? The answer effectively exploits the ambiguity just uncovered.

Representation depends on fixity, on a stable relation between the representer and the represented. In an utterly chaotic, Heraclitean world in which the relation constantly changed, so that the same idea could never represent the same thing twice, no idea would ever represent at all. Representation is not a one-time phenomenon; or, more precisely, an idea marks an object only in the second instance of their conjunction. Of this, more below.

Watson, meanwhile, relies on this fixity to apply his thesis even to Locke's ideas of secondary qualities. He begins by noticing that the production of ideas of primary qualities can be explained in a way that the production of ideas of secondary qualities cannot: they are like the image left by a seal in wax. But ideas of secondary qualities are "mysterious"; as Locke says, they are "superadded" according to the benevolent will of God. "They are *unlike* anything in the powers that cause them" (Watson 1995: 68, emphasis added).

But these ideas nonetheless vary concomitantly with those powers, which means, for Watson, that there must be "some isomorphism of structure or internal relations among parts between the two." The upshot is that ideas "represent their objects by resembling them exactly [primary qualities] or differentially [secondary qualities]" (Watson 1995: 68, terminology standardized). So, ideas can both resemble and be unlike what they represent.

There are three problems with this ingenious account. (i) Ideas of secondary qualities are in this context simple, hence without structure or parts with internal relations. (ii) Ideas of primary qualities involve concomitant variation, not "exact resemblance." Rotate a penny through round (face on), elliptical (at an angle), and rectangular (on edge) shapes: which idea exactly resembles it? (iii) The main problem derives from what is the central concern of the *Essay*, the "Original, Certainty, and Extent of humane Knowledge." Our knowledge in the final analysis does not extend beyond appearances to some reality beneath. In the terms deployed here, there is always a qualitative difference between representation (appearance) and represented (reality).

2. *Causation*

If one focuses on an idea as appearance, especially insofar as there must be a fixed connection between it and the reality it represents, an alternative account would be in causal terms. Different objects cause different appearances. Such an account has independent philosophical plausibility (Searle 1983: 47–9), and it seems to be supported by Locke's texts. Indeed, according to Michael Ayers, the "[causal] relation *constitutes* the basic representative relation" (Ayers 1991: I: 40).

If Locke has only a causal account of representation, however, he would seem to be in trouble, for causation, at least in any straight-forward way, seems neither necessary nor sufficient for representation. Scrooge takes the cause of his idea to be a fragment of overdone potato, although it represents Jacob Marley, who cannot be its cause, since, as Dickens makes clear, he is dead. One might try to save the causal account by viewing the representation of an idea as secured by what in normal circumstances would be its cause. But specifying "normal circumstances" requires just the representing relation the account is suppose to explain. Jacob Marley physically present before Scrooge is the normal circumstance only because the idea is of him. But why is the idea of Jacob Marley?

Nor is causation sufficient for representation. While heat causes water to boil, the boiling water does not represent the heat. This difficulty might be repaired by appeal to a special notion of cause. The Cartesian Pierre-Sylvain Regis, for example, following a lead from the third of Descartes's *Meditations*, took ideas to be exemplary or archetypal causes (Regis 1970: 76–7; Descartes 1984: II: 29). But, in addition to mobilizing a Platonist ontology inimical to Locke, Regis's account reverses the idea-object relation. For Locke, ideas are the ectypes, not the archetypes. Moreover, in the case of mixed modes, the object (a real essence) cannot cause the idea (a nominal essence), since the two are identical, whereas an archetypal cause must be distinct from what it causes. Although there are obvious difficulties in the causal account, it contains elements that are a part of any adequate account.

3. Reference

Some commentators have supplemented the causal condition with an appeal to reference. There is ample textual evidence for this addition. Representationality of idea, however, is not simply referentiality of idea, even supplemented by causation, because Locke says that the *mind* does the referring. Typically, the mind refers ideas to archetypes from which it "supposes" them to be taken, and with which it intends them to *conform* (E II.xxxi.1: 375). The case of modes and relations is atypical in that usually there is no intention that the idea conform to anything beyond the idea itself. Modes are made at will and contain only what we put into them; and as for relations, while they involve reference by the mind, that reference is of one relatum (idea) to another, not of an idea to what it represents (E II.xxxi.5: 378; also III.v.6 and II.xxv.5). Ideas of modes and relations are therefore taken to be all of them adequate. The most precise way to put Locke's position, then, is to say that an idea is adequate if is not inadequate, and that it is inadequate if the intended conformity fails.

Intended conformity never fails in the case of simple ideas, which are therefore always adequate, and it always fails in the case of ideas of substance, which are therefore never adequate (E II. xxxi.2: 375; also II.xxxi.6–13). When Locke turns to the truth or falsity of ideas, however, an additional classification emerges. This is because what is being evaluated is less the ideas, or even their conformity, than the judgment that the mind makes of their conformity, for which the more proper terminology is right or wrong, rather than true or false (E II.xxxii.26: 393–4). In any case, there are three sorts of conformity – between the idea in one's mind and (1) the idea in another's mind, (2) some real existence, and (3) some real essence. Again, it would seem that the criterion for the truth of an idea is a negative one: an idea is true if it is not false. Simple ideas cannot fail to conform and therefore are always judged rightly in this regard and are true. Ideas of substances may be true if the intended conformity is with a real existent. If the intended conformity is with a real essence, however, then the idea is never judged rightly and is always false. With respect to the first sort of conformity, with ideas in others' minds, simple ideas are least liable to be mistakenly judged (and this would seem to be so even in the face of the inverted spectrum problem, of which more below). Ideas of modes are most likely to be mistaken, since they are composed at will – to our chagrin, and Locke's examples show why: justice, cruelty, liberality, prodigality. These are just the sort of terms for which people have different ideas and thus come to blows over.

The above are just examples of how the categorization gets worked out. For the complete picture, a great deal more would need to be said. In the end, the likely value of the examples would be the illustration they provide of central Lockean doctrines from elsewhere in the *Essay*, as in the example of modes that are essentially confected at will. The philosophical issue that emerges is the basis for the mind's reference. Why is an idea referred to one thing rather than to another? – which is one of the two questions posed at the very outset of this section.

An answer to this question might take either of two forms: either the idea is encoded with information about a given object (an idea might be thought of as labeled with respect to its referent), or there is an additional perception that the accompanying idea is to be referred to a given object (as memory, for Locke, consists of an additional perception that the accompanying perception was had on a previous occasion) (Chappell 1994c: 52–5). On either account, ideas might be taken as natural signs of their objects. An apparent problem with both accounts, however, is that the additional information is precisely what the idea itself is supposed to provide – that is, in order to interpret the label or the additional perception, the mind would need another label or perception providing the very information that is being sought. (This is the homunculus problem that led to modern functionalism; see Hausman and Hausman 1997: 5–10.) As will be seen at the end of this chapter, there is an answer to this problem, but only on condition that the natural signification of ideas be relinquished. There is already a reason for abandoning it that mirrors the problem just raised. In order for smoke to be read as a natural sign of fire, both relata must be perceived at least once. But *ex hypothesi* in the case of ideas, we never perceive the signatum for which the idea is a sign, at least not in a way that would enable us to take the one as a sign for the other.

4. Convention

On any account, simple ideas must be the basis of Locke's view of representation. A final account can be had from what Locke says about the language used for them.

"The *Names of simple* Ideas *and Modes*, signify always the real, as well as nominal *Essence of their Species*" (E III.iv.3: 421). These names differ from those of substances, which "*signify* rarely, if ever, anything but *barely the nominal Essence* of those Species." On the other hand, names of simple ideas are like those used for substances in that they "intimate *some real Existence*," and they are unlike those used for modes, which "*terminate in the* Idea that is in the Mind, and lead not the Thoughts any farther" (E III.iv.2–3: 421).

These pairs of similarities and differences result from a status that simple ideas can derive only from convention. That is, both the essence (real and nominal) signified by names of simple ideas, and their intimation of real existence, that is, the reference given the idea, must be the "workmanship of the understanding." This interpretation is contrary to the currently prevailing view that ideas for Locke are natural signs (Ayers 1991: I: 40). Moreover, essence and reference are connected in that, absent the essence, there can be no reference.

It is hard to see how the name of a simple idea could get at a real essence except in the way that the name of a mode does, and that is that it stands for an idea that is the workmanship of the under-standing. In addition, simple ideas must have their reference established in the same fashion, by convention. This apparently strange view is at least suggested by Locke when he says that the reference of the term 'white' is fixed when we take it to name the color we observe in snow or milk (E III.iv.15: 427). Now, according to Locke, the reference of 'snow' or 'milk' is even harder to fix, so the problem of reference seems hereby only to be exacer-bated. But, in order to fix the reference of 'white' as the color of milk or snow, one need not know anything at all about milk or snow. It refers to whatever (color) idea one gets when viewing milk or snow. Similarly, the idea stood for by the term 'white' can be referred to whatever it is that is causing that idea. "Whilst I write this, I have, by the Paper affecting my Eyes, that *Idea* produced in my Mind, which whatever *Object* causes, I call *White*" (E IV. xi.2: 631).

For Locke, the notions of essence, kind (or sort, as he calls it), and abstract idea are intimately connected. Essences "relate to" sorts, and sorts just are abstract ideas, which, being general, are the "Workmanship of the Understanding" (E III.iii.12: 414–15). How do essences relate to sorts/abstract ideas? One way to put it is that the sort/abstract idea determines what is essential to the things falling under it. "Take but away the abstract *Ideas*, by which we sort Individuals, and rank them under common names, and then the thought of any thing *essential* to any of them, instantly vanishes: we have no notion of the one, without the other: which plainly shews their relation" (E III.vi.4: 440). In the world apart from our abstract ideas, there exist only unrelated particulars, unsorted and undifferentiated into kinds. One upshot of this view is that the distinction drawn by many philosophers between accidental and essential qualities evaporates. "All such Patterns and Standards, being quite laid aside, particular Beings, considered barely in themselves, will be found to have all their Qualities equally *essential*; and every thing, in each Individual, will be essential to it, or, which is more true, nothing at all" (E III.vi.5: 441–2). Logically speaking, anything can be classified in any way at all, so that any-thing essential on a given classification can be stripped from it by using a different classification. Or, to put it another way, nothing is essential, absent our abstract ideas.

But how can a *simple* idea be an essence? And what would be essential to it? It is one thing to say that gold is an essence and that malleability is essential to it. But how is white or blue an essence? Part of the answer is that a simple idea need not be, and often is not, a (concrete) particular idea. Instead, it can be an (abstract) general idea, arrived at by abstraction, which is to say, for Locke, by partial attention. I look at a sugar cube and attend only to its color. The sugar resembles other things in this respect, but such resemblances do not form natural kinds. It is the mind that notices such resemblances and forms them into a kind. It does so by forming a complex idea that is abstract and general, which *is* the kind by which things are sorted. Apart from the mind, all that exists are the particulars resembling each other in certain respects. Now, what is true of the complex idea is true of the simple ideas composing them. They, too, depend on the workmanship of the mind, which makes them into kinds, and without which they would not mark anything. This marking function of ideas is fundamental.

Ideas are "marks by which we distinguish things" – for example, this apple from the banana next to it, and apples, fire engines, and certain suspenders from bananas, lemons, and kernels of corn – that is, differences between individuals and kinds of individuals. Without this function, an idea would be only a neutral sensation, a "blank effect" representing nothing at all (Ayers 1991: I: 62). This very important point has been emphasized by Martha Bolton:

[A] person has the idea of blue, say, only if 'blue' sensations serve as distinguishing marks of external objects for her. Merely having phenomenally-blue sensations, and being able to think of them as such, does not suffice to possess the idea of blue. Locke says as much in a letter to Stillingfleet: 'all simple ideas, as sensible qualities, carry with them a supposition ... of a substance in which they inhere.' (Bolton 2004; W IV: 7)

The point might be expressed by saying that there are two sorts of items expressed as "ideas of blue," which are phenomenologically indistinguishable, but only one of which consists of markers.

On the one hand is the blank effect, in whose description the preposition 'of' expresses something like the material genitive: it is a kind of idea, a blue-idea, although this is not to say that the idea is blue. In this sense, one's idea of blue is particular to oneself, unshared with anyone else. On the other hand is the idea in the sense of the objective genitive. As in the case of the idea of Caesar, this is the sense in which one's idea might be the same as another's idea. What distinguishes different ideas is the object, which in this case is the same, even if we do not, and cannot, know what that object is. A blank effect becomes an idea in this sense when it is given a reference, which comes about through supposition.

Locke's claim that all simple ideas are supposed to inhere in some substance might be read in at least two ways. First, he might be drawing attention to the common mistake, and the irrelevance here of that mistake, of regarding things to be as they appear. He says that for our ideas to be marks "whereby we are to know and distinguish Things, which we have to do with; our *Ideas* do as well serve us to that purpose, and are as real distinguishing Characters, whether they be only constant Effects, or else exact Resemblances of something in the things themselves" (E II.xxx.2: 373). Whether we mistake ideas as representing things as they are, or correctly take them to be appearances caused by some microscopic structure, our ideas serve equally well in our practical dealings with the world so long as there is a certain covariance between them and the world. "To discern one Thing from another; and so chuse any of them for our uses, ... it alters not the Nature of our simple *Idea*, whether we think, that the *Idea* of Blue, be in the *Violet* it self, or in our Mind only; ... And it is equally from that Appearance, to be denominated *Blue*, whether it be that real Colour, or only a peculiar Texture in it, that causes in us that *Idea*" (E II.xxxii.14: 389). So two people one of whom has a color spectrum the inverse of the other can refer to the same object so long as their spectrums are stable.

A second reading would take Locke to have something more in mind with his notion of supposition. He might be drawing attention to what is also true for him, that we never have anything more than appearances of things (which is true whether appearances are sur-rogates or just the thing itself insofar as it appears). The point is that for appearances to be appearances, they must be given a reference to that of which they are the appearances. They must be given this reference so that they might perform their marking function. Such a reference can occur only if an otherwise blank effect is given a degree of generality. Obviously, all other things being equal, I have the gustatory idea of a pineapple that I am now biting into only if I can connect it with the gustatory idea I have when biting into another one tomorrow. This generality is required even in the case of a single enduring sensation. From moment to moment, I need to take the blank effect to be the effect of the same (sort of) object. An idea in this sense cannot be momentary. The marking function depends on generality, which depends on repeatability.

Although Locke nowhere clearly articulates how a simple idea such as blue might be made general, his only obvious way of accounting for it would be the sort of convention at the basis of all other general ideas. This convention is not unlike the baptism at the basis of the recent causal or historical theory of reference. Kripke and others hold that the reference of a term can be fixed in the absence of any defining features of the thing or kind to which it is applied, and can then be conveyed along a causal-historical chain of those using the term. A great irony is that this theory was designed to replace the so-called traditional theory of reference, according to which *each* reference requires the defining features of the referent, a theory the prime proponent of which was supposed to be Locke. To be sure, there are many texts of Locke that suggest the traditional theory; but texts have also been noted in which Locke anticipates Kripke (Mackie 1974: 77–80). Thus, Locke allows that we generally intend that our term 'gold' refer not to a nominal essence, but to a real essence. (This is why we do not think that the discovery of an additional property of so-called gold, such as solubility in aqua regia, produces a new species.) We point to the substance in the experiment before us and tacitly intend to refer to its real essence in calling it 'gold'. But this intended reference causes difficulties, since the reference fails when the body is no longer present to be pointed to. "For by this tacit reference to the real Essence of that Species of Bodies, the Word *Gold* (which by standing for a more or less perfect Collection of simple *Ideas*, serves to design that sort of Body well enough in civil Discourse) comes to have no signification at all, being put for somewhat, where of we have no *Idea* at all, when the Body it self is away" (E III.x.19: 501). The situation is very different for simple ideas. For while they (like ideas of substances) refer, they (like ideas of modes) do not purport to refer to real essences.

Insofar as appeal is made only to the causal account of a white-idea, the idea is like 'gold', restricted to the presence of the object. As reference fails when the object is removed in the case of so-called gold, so the marking function fails in the case of the white-idea. The idea needs to be made general to get beyond the present object. It must be made into an essence, which is to say, a kind created by the mind, but constrained by the causal connection. The baptism would go as follows: this blue-idea and every other blue-idea, whatever it might be, shall represent whatever it is that produces the blue-idea in me. Like a mode, the general idea of blue is produced by the mind. As in the production of a mode, there are causal constraints, but of different kinds. Modes are produced according to pure pragmatics; there are no a priori constraints on how ideas are compounded to produce them, and in this sense they are "perfectly arbitrary." Simple ideas are governed by the causal relation they have with that of which they are taken to be the appearance. In this sense they are *"not arbitrary at all"* (E III.iv.17: 428). In addition, the nominal essence represented by a mode is identical to a real essence; beyond that, there is nothing in the world represented by modes. In the case of simple ideas, while terms for them signify a real essence identical to the nominal essence we create, the ideas themselves represent something in the world, but something that is unknown. Thus, while for reference to occur there has to be an essence in the mind (which, as it happens, is both nominal and real), that essence is not the essence of what is referred to. Thus the Kripkean position of rejecting defining features as necessary for reference is preserved.

It might be asked, finally, why this same account cannot be extended to our idea of gold. The answer is simple and cuts to a main theme of the *Essay*, viz. we have no such idea. We can point to objects and intend to refer to their real essence, but that is all we can do. Our ideas are the appearances of things, not the things themselves.

9 Locke on Essences and Classification

Locke introduces his famous distinction between real and nominal essences with little fanfare halfway through the third chapter of Book III of the *Essay Concerning Human Understanding*. This distinction is his own invention. Terminologically, it is clearly intended to reflect the Scholastic distinction between real and nominal definitions, but, as Leibniz complains, it is an innovation of Locke's to use these terms to refer to essences. "It seems to me," Leibniz writes, "that your way of putting things constitutes a very novel mode of expression. People have certainly spoken of nominal *definitions*, and 'causal' or 'real' ones, but so far as I know they have not until now spoken of *essences* other than real ones" (Leibniz [1765] 1981: 293). Locke's novelty is a matter of altering terminology belonging in a theory of language to a metaphysical use, rather surprisingly, in the middle of the portion of his *Essay* entitled "On Words." This innovation of Locke's, despite its rather modest entry into his argument, has been treated by most commentators as both important and central to his theory. Genevieve Brykman, indeed, describes it as a "cornerstone" of his thinking (2001: 81). But the nature of this cornerstone and its role in Locke's metaphysics and in his theory of language have proved controversial.

Locke first presents his distinction between nominal and real essences in a very important section:

First, Essence may be taken for the very being of any thing, whereby it is, what it is. And thus the real internal, but generally in Substances, unknown Constitution of Things, whereon their discoverable Qualities depend, may be called their *Essence*. This is the proper original signification of the Word, as is evident from the formation of it; *Essentia*, in its primary notation signifying properly *Being*. And in this sense it is still used, when we speak of the *Essence* of particular things, without giving them any Name.

Secondly, The Learning and Disputes of the Schools, having been much busied about *Genus* and *Species*, the Word *Essence* has almost lost its primary signification; and instead of the real Constitution of things, has been almost wholly applied to the artificial Constitution of *Genus* and *Species*. 'Tis true, there is ordinarily supposed a real Constitution of the sorts of Things; and 'tis past doubt, there must be some real Constitution, on which any Collection of simple *Ideas* co-existing, must depend. But it being evident, that Things are ranked under Names into sorts or *Species*, only as they agree to certain abstract *Ideas*, to which we have annexed those Names, the *Essence* of each *Genus*, or Sort, comes to be nothing but that abstract *Idea*, which the General, or *Sortal*...Name stands for. And this we shall find to be that, which the word *Essence* imports, in its most familiar use. These two sorts of *Essences*, I suppose, may not unfitly be termed, the one the *Real*,the other the *Nominal Essence*. (E III.iii.15: 417)

It is important to notice that in this passage in which Locke introduces the distinction between real and nominal essences, he employs an historical frame.[1] The word 'essence', he tells us, has changed its meaning over the course of centuries from an original and Aristotelian sense of the term to its present one. The sort of essence that Locke, in the final sentence of this section, calls the real essence is the original, Aristotelian sense of essence, while what he calls the nominal essence and says is the one "in common use" is the sense of essence as it has become perverted by Scholastic philosophy. A real essence, in this original sense, is "the very being of any thing, whereby it is, what it is. And thus the real internal, but generally in Substances, unknown Constitution of Things, whereon their discoverable Qualities depend, may be called their *Essence*" (E III.iii.15: 417). In this sense, an essence is the nature, to use another Aristotelian term, the internal principle of any particular thing. This internal principle or being of a thing is what accounts for anything belonging to it. But Locke thinks the term 'essence' has become altered by the "Learning and Disputes of the Schools" and is now used as part of the project of sorting things into genera and species. Those properties essential to a thing are those that belong to it by virtue of its membership in a given genus and species, those

---

[1] This historical dimension has been noticed by Jean-Michel Vienne (1993).

that it must have because of the kind of thing it is. These essential properties can be distinguished from mere accidents, which may or may not hold of members of that species. "But it being evident," Locke writes, "that Things are ranked under Names into sorts or *Species*, only as they agree to certain abstract *Ideas*, to which we have annexed those Names, the *Essence* of each *Genus*, or Sort, comes to be nothing but that abstract *Idea*, which the General, or *Sortal* ... Name stands for" (E III.iii.15: 417). Locke proposes to call the sorting device by means of which we delineate the boundaries of sorts or species the nominal essence. This sorting device, he suggests in the passage just quoted, consists of abstract ideas.

Having told us how the term 'essence' once was used and how it is now – that is, Scholastically – being used, Locke, in E III.iii.17: 418, makes a further distinction. He says there are two different views about the real essences of corporeal substances.

The one is of those, who using the Word *Essence*, for they know not what, suppose a certain number of those Essences, according to which, all natural things are made, and wherein they do exactly every one of them partake, and so become of this or that *Species*. The other, and more rational Opinion, is of those, who look on all natural Things to have a real, but unknown Constitution of their insensible Parts, from which flow those sensible Qualities, which serve us to distinguish them one from another, according as we have Occasion to rank them into sorts, under common Denominations.

It is less rational, we now learn, to suppose there is a determinate set of kinds of things in nature, and hence improper to use the phrase "real essence" to describe such kinds. It is more rational to suppose natural things have "a real but unknown constitution" and hence, presumably, appropriate to use "real essence" to apply to such constitutions. It has seemed straightforward enough to identify the less rational opinion that there is a fixed number of "Forms or Molds" with the just-mentioned Scholastic view that things are to be distinguished into genera and species, since the Scholastics did indeed hold, as will be discussed shortly, that the categories into which we sort things have a real basis in nature. Others have pointed out, however, that the view there is a fixed number of essential kinds of things in the world is more widespread and could be held by seventeenth-century proponents of the New Science as well.[2] There is universal agreement that the more rational opinion is Locke's own, although there is less agreement, as we will see, about what this opinion commits him to.

Nevertheless, in general outline, it has proved relatively easy for commentators to give a sense of the kind of position put forward in these two paragraphs. Relying on the historical hints provided by Locke himself, the distinction between nominal and real essences is understood as a response to accounts of classification to be found among the Scholastics.[3] The best way to understand the thrust of Scholastic theory in this instance is in terms of the theoretical entity, the substantial form. The substantial form has several roles to play. As it constitutes the natures of various kinds of things, it explains why the world is, as it seems, divided into natural kinds or species. Each kind of thing is as it is because it possesses a common nature with other members of that species. The substantial form also has a role to play in accounting for our knowledge of the classifications of the natural world. As it informs our intellect, we are able to grasp the abstract nature of the kinds of things in the world and to classify them into their appropriate genera and species, according to their essential properties. Because these substantial forms play two roles, we can be satisfied that our ideas about the world map onto the way the world is. Our various intuitions – as, for example, that my mother is not and cannot be a fish – are supported by the metaphysical facts: my mother's nature is other than that of a fish.

This satisfactory state of affairs had, however, begun to unravel under pressure from the developments of the New Science. The explanatory virtues of substantial forms or natures had been replaced by the far more powerful notion of qualitatively undifferentiated, quantitatively distinguishable matter in motion. Under this pressure, the substantial form had come apart. Things are still classified into kinds according to our abstract ideas, but the explanation for the existence of that whereby they are as they are is to be sought in terms of the far different theoretical framework of matter in motion. Thus, Locke's move of dividing the essence into real and

[2] Jonathan Bennett (2001) makes this point, and credits Christopher Conn for helping him to see it.
[3] See especially M. R. Ayers 1981 and also E. J. Lowe 1995.

nominal essences can be seen as one of a number of similar moves in which explanatory jobs are located in the area that seventeenth-century science sought to describe in terms of substance, matter, corpuscles, and the like, while descriptive and classificatory functions are located within the realm of human ideas. According to this way of thinking, Locke's real essences are the explanatory entities of the natural world, while his nominal essences are the very different ideas we ordinary folk have of that world.

It is also characteristic of Locke's approach to emphasize that the division into inner constitutions in the world and abstract ideas in us contributes to the way in which our knowledge of the world is limited. Because the real essence is unknown, we have no grounds for speaking of sorted or bounded real essences: all our sorting is done by our abstract ideas. Unlike the classificatory system of the Scholastics, which is in some sense the product of the way the world is, in Locke's eyes, our abstract ideas are the "workmanship of the understanding" and are not derived from unknown real essences, but are instead based on our own ideas and their history. We frame an abstract idea of a kind of thing by noticing which of our ideas go together and then abstracting. We leave out of the composite of recurring ideas those that are peculiar to particular circumstances, to produce an abstract idea of a sort (E III.iii.6: 410–11). We cannot count on ideas framed in such a manner to map neatly onto a world of kinds with strict boundaries. Thus the consequence of noticing that the explanatory job of the essence is performed by one kind of thing, the real essence, while the descriptive or classificatory job is performed by another, the nominal essence or abstract idea, is that our knowledge, as expressed by our ideas, is limited with respect to the explanatory nature of things.

Despite the clarity provided by this general picture, however, it has seemed to numerous commentators that the two paragraphs under discussion, E III.iii.15 and E III.iii.17, still contain ambiguities, and it has not been obvious how to slot the various terms used there into the general picture just outlined. To start with one pressing problem: the original sense of 'real essence' introduced in E III.iii.15 is identified as one having to do with particulars, what any thing is, while problems about sorting are later Scholastic accretions. And particulars do not have essential properties in their own natures, but only as related to a sort. Locke writes in an often-quoted passage,

'Tis necessary for me to be as I am; GOD and Nature has made me so: But there is nothing I have, is essential to me. An Accident, or Disease, may very much alter my Reason or Memory, or both; and an Apoplexy leave neither Sense, nor Understanding, no nor Life. Other Creatures of my shape, may be made with more, and better, or fewer, and worse Faculties than I have: and others may have Reason, and Sense, in a shape and body very different from mine. None of these are essential to the one, or the other, or to any individual whatsoever, till the Mind refers it to some Sort or *Species* of things; and then presently, according to the abstract *Idea* of that sort, something is found *essential*. (E III.vi.4: 440)

If the lump in front of me is to be counted as a magnet, then it is essential that it attract iron, but if it does not do so, it is clearly ridiculous to say, of the existing lump, that it lacks something essential to *its* being.[4] So the original, Aristotelian use of 'real essence', that whereby a thing is what it is, applies to particulars – in which case, all qualities are essential qualities – and does not describe something belonging to sorts. But when in E III.iii.17, Locke discusses the two opinions about real essences, both are opinions about sorting. Has Locke abandoned the original sense of 'real essence' for a new one, reflecting the issue raised by the Scholastics of sorting by essences into what is essential about a kind of thing and what is not essential?

On at least one popular reading, the answer to this question is yes. While it is less rational to suppose that nature itself comes already sorted, it is held to be more rational, according to Locke, to suppose that nature can be sorted into real essences, sometimes called "Lockean real essences," by means of the nominal essence. It is more rational, that is, to suppose that a subset or aspect of the real essence of particulars can be identified as containing just those qualities responsible for the ideas of the nominal essence. This Lockean real essence would thus constitute a bit of the mind-independent world, but one identifiable only through mind-dependent ideas. On an alternative reading, the answer is no. Locke is not held, in E III.iii.17, to be embracing the Scholastic view that essences sort. Rather, Locke would be saying some people, less

---

[4] This is an example of Locke's. See also E III.vi.6 and E III.vi.4.

rationally, think nature comes sorted into kinds, whereas the more rational opinion is that nature is merely the origin of those qualities on which the ideas by means of which we sort depend. On this reading, ideas sort, but they merely depend upon and do not sort real essences. There are no alleged "Lockean real essences" but only the original Aristotelian real essences of particulars.[5]

A related puzzle concerns the way in which Locke is assumed to understand the notion of an inner constitution. Picking up on the context of the New Science, which has proved so helpful in getting a general picture of what Locke is up to, many have assumed that, since the inner constitution is that from which sensible qualities flow (E III.iii.17), it must, in fact, be identical with the causal basis for sensible qualities, as identified by the New Science. Thus, David Owen, for example, identifies internal constitutions with "internal corpuscularian structures" (1991: 105), and this is in fact a very common move. It is very common, that is, to assume that the explanation provided by an inner constitution is a causal explanation, and further to assume that Locke was prepared to endorse corpuscularian microstructures as the model for causal explanations. An alternative view, however, suggests that Locke intended something much stronger as an explanation, namely, that from which discoverable or sensible qualities *necessarily* flow, reflecting the original definition of a real essence as the "the very being of a thing, whereby it is, what it is" (E III.iii.15: 417). On such a view, the inner constitution might well account for the form that causal, corpuscularian explanations take, but would not be identical with such explanations.[6]

---

[5] These issues have been raised by Jean-Michel Vienne (1993) and by David Owen (1991). Other discussions may be found in Pauline Phemister (1990), Susanna Goodin (1997), and Pauline Phemister (1997). The view that Locke allows for the possibility of real essences as aspects of particulars sorted by nominal essences is most closely associated with Michael Ayers, and put forward in Ayers 1991.

[6] This latter position has recently been argued by P. Kyle Stanford (1990). Proponents of the first view, in addition to Owen, are too numerous to mention. A classic statement has been provided by Michael Ayers, who says, "What explains the properties of a species so defined [by the nominal essence] ... is corpuscularian structure (or at least something like it, if Boyle's theory is less than the whole truth). Those aspects of the structure of the individual members of a species which they have in common and in virtue of which they all possess the defining properties of the species, comprise what Locke called the 'real essence' of the species" (1991: II: 67–8).

Questions have also been raised about Locke's conception of the nominal essence, particularly nominal essences of substances. Locke tells us, as I said, that all abstract ideas are the workmanship of the understanding, but he also thinks the understanding does different things when it frames the ideas of what he calls mixed modes, like jealousy and adultery, than it does when it puts together ideas of substances like gold and water. Locke illustrates this difference through his story of Adam, who, of course, first gave names to things. In the case of mixed modes, Locke says Adam "put *Ideas* together, only by his own Imagination, not taken from the Existence of any thing; and to them he gave Names to denominate all Things, that should happen to agree to those his abstract *Ideas*, without considering whether any such thing did exist, or no: the Standard there was of his own making" (E III.vi.46: 468). Adam's idea tells us what adultery or jealousy is, whether or not there are any instances of either in the world. When Adam frames an idea of a new substance like gold, however, he proceeds differently.

> But in the forming his *Idea* of this new Substance he takes the quite contrary Course; here he has a Standard made by Nature; and therefore being to represent that to himself, by the *Idea* he has of it, even when it is absent, he puts in no simple *Idea* into his complex one, but what he has the Perception of from the thing it self. He takes Care that his *Idea* be conformable to this *Archetype*, and intends the Name should stand for an *Idea* so conformable. (E III.vi.46: 468)

In the case of ideas of substances, Adam cannot include any idea he wants to, but must guide the framing of his idea by a natural archetype.

Questions arise when we attempt to pin down the nature of this archetype. An important difference between the ideas of mixed modes, where Adam is free to include whatever he wants, and the ideas of substances, where his ideas conform to an archetype, is the introduction of a normative dimension. In the case of mixed modes, for example, all our ideas are adequate, because, containing just what we say they contain, these ideas cannot lack anything. But ideas of substances are imperfect and inadequate, that is, they can be judged to lack something that ought to be included. But with respect to what do we make this judgment?[7] Or similarly, Locke

---

[7] This issue has been raised by Ruth Mattern (1986). See also Martha Bolton 1988.

introduces normative concerns when he urges that we should perfect our ideas of substances by making them more complete (E IV. xii.14). Again, it seems relevant to ask, more complete with respect to what?[8] The most obvious answer to questions of this sort seems to be to say that our ideas of substances would be more perfect if they contained ideas of those qualities belonging to the real essence. Our ideas of substances would then be lacking when they leave out qualities of the real essence. That is, it would seem reasonable to identify the archetype to which substance terms conform with the real essence of that kind of substance. But Locke specifically rules out such an identification. He writes:

> For though the Word *Man* or *Gold*, signify nothing truly but a complex *Idea* of Properties, united together in one sort of Substances: Yet there is scarce any Body in the use of these Words, but often supposes each of those names to stand for a thing having the real Essence, on which those Properties depend. Which is so far from diminishing the Imperfection of our Words, that by a plain Abuse, it adds to it, when we would make them stand for something, which not being in our complex *Idea*, the name we use, can no ways be the sign of. (E III.x.18: 500)

We are quite wrong, however tempted we are to do so, to identify the archetype of substance terms with real essences. But if the archetype made by nature is not the real essence, then what is it, and how does it function to make our ideas of substances more or less perfect?

One final area of disagreement has recently emerged that is perhaps more important, or, at least, more central than any of the others. This concerns the motivation for Locke's distinction between nominal and real essence. In particular, why is it that Locke maintains as he does that our words do not pick out mind-independent kinds but instead only mind-dependent abstract ideas? What purpose can he have in urging that my clear intuitions about the boundaries of natural kinds, that this is gold and that is water, are not grounded in any metaphysical differences, but merely on the different ways in which we choose to categorize? There are two kinds of answers to this question now current in the literature. One, perhaps the standard position, sees Locke as rejecting a Scholastic

---

[8] This matter has been raised and discussed by Lionel Shapiro (1999).

theory of natural kinds because of the respect he felt for the New Science, particularly in its corpuscularian version, as developed by Boyle.[9] The second view, which has more recently emerged, holds that, whatever might be the case with respect to the ontological commitments of corpuscularianism, Locke's claims are in fact mandated by his new theory of ideas. Proponents of this view hold that it is due to the nature of ideas, as Locke sees it, that words cannot apply to unknown real essences.[10]

When Locke's reasons for holding that our ideas do not reflect mind-independent kinds are taken to depend upon his defense of corpuscularianism, the argument goes something like this. While it is true that it may seem crystal clear to me that my mother cannot possibly be a fish, this intuition cannot be based on a grasp of the inner constitutions of mothers and fish. This is because the observable qualities of a woman like my mother depend upon an ever-shifting structure of corpuscles that could perfectly conceivably alter into that structure of corpuscles on which the observable qualities of a mackerel or a walleye depend. If, therefore, I find there to be something wrong with the claim that my mother is a fish, this has to do with the ideas that I attach to the words 'mother' and 'fish', which are indeed strongly antithetical, and not with the inner constitution of my mother or a walleye. Locke's commitment to corpuscularianism leads him to endorse the notion of a great chain of being, in which there are no abrupt gaps between species. Rather, the inner constitution of a woman like my mother shades by imperceptible degrees into the inner constitution of a walleye. Hence, the possibility of entities not readily classifiable into natural species, such as monsters (physically impaired humans), changelings (reason-impaired humans), and the offspring of cats mated to mice.

In sum, what makes our general words not apply immediately to general things or sorts are the simple facts of the matter. Well-bounded sorts do not exist in nature. Our general terms are mediated by the ideas of sorts we construct in order to understand a world in which, helpfully, nature has made many things alike. On

[9] Proponents of this approach include R. S. Woolhouse (1971), Peter Alexander (1985), M. R. Ayers (1981), and Nicholas Jolley (1984, 1999).
[10] Various versions of this approach have been developed by Martha Bolton (1992), Paul Guyer (1994), and Genevieve Brykman (2001).

the basis of these observable similarities, we devise classifications that pick out those aspects of nature responsible for the observable similarities of ideas. On this account, Locke would be wrong if it turned out that there were in fact ways of picking out well-defined sorts in nature, independent of our ideas of those sorts. Many commentators hold that progress in science has revealed that this is in fact the case. By reference to things like atomic numbers and molecular structures, they argue we are now in a position to identify what is really gold or really water, whether or not the sample in question conforms to our abstract idea of gold or water. For it has seemed to many that a clear difficulty with an account like Locke's is that it provides no room for the possibility of "apparent gold" or "apparent water." So long as a given sample conforms to our abstract idea, it is gold or water.

On the alternative interpretation, however, Locke's position is not one that is so easily refutable by progress in the natural sciences. On this account, Locke's views on the way in which words pick out things start from his seminal claim that ideas are the immediate objects of thought. This being the case, words will not stand immediately for things, but only through the mediation of ideas. Our capacity to think about things is constrained by the nature of our ideas and by the processes by means of which ideas are generated. Several features in particular have been mentioned by proponents of this approach. First, the content of our ideas is determined by what is immediately perceivable and contained in the idea. It is nonsensical to suppose that ideas can outrun their content or stand for something not immediately present in them. So there can be nothing more to a species than what is contained in our abstract idea of it. Second, the nature of our ideas is constrained by the nature of our cognitive faculties. In the case of abstract ideas of sorts, our ideas are limited to whatever sensible qualities our sense organs have provided and then are constructed according to our various capacities to combine, relate, and abstract. It is not nature that determines which ideas will be put together in complex ideas; rather, these combinations are the product of the understanding. The result of these combining processes is always a loose federation of qualities, containing whatever ideas we happen to have observed co-occurring. Such a loose federation does not provide the kind of structure that would allow us to distinguish essential from accidental qualities or to determine which ideas depend upon which qualities. Whatever ideas we have the capacity to acquire can never reflect some way things have to be, but instead are the result of our present histories and present choices. Since scientific progress, like progress in all other areas of knowledge, depends upon the nature of our cognitive faculties, while we certainly can, through new discoveries, add new features, such as atomic number and molecular structure, to our idea of gold or water, we do not in any serious way change the kind of idea we are producing.

Each of these interpretations results from stressing the importance and the uniqueness of one of Locke's two novel entities. We get one kind of reading if we take what is important to Locke to be his discoveries about the nature of the abstract ideas for which our words must stand, and we get another kind of reading if Locke is held to be working out the implications of identifying real essences with quasi-mechanical structures thrown up out of ever-changing arrays of corpuscles. The first depends on a theory of what language is like, while the second depends upon a theory of what the world is like. It is worth pointing out that while each theory has been claimed to have suggestive connections with contemporary positions in philosophy – the first with Quinean approaches to language and the second to versions of scientific realism – both approaches to Locke's account of essences are thoroughly grounded in important seventeenth-century issues: the nature of ideas, on the one hand, and mechanistic corpuscularianism on the other. Nothing can be gained by accusing proponents of either view of historiographical failings.

While there is ample textual evidence that Locke admired mechanical corpuscularianism and was willing on occasion to adopt its modes of explanation, evidence specifically linking this admiration with his views on real essences is on thinner ground.[11] Nevertheless, Michael Ayers, in defense of a corpuscularian-based approach, has challenged Paul Guyer to defend his language-based approach by explaining the presence of certain passages in which Locke appears to give empirical support to Ayers's position

---

[11] It should be noted that Locke frequently accompanies his endorsements of corpuscularian explanations with disclaimers, suggesting that other, better explanations might come along.

(Ayers 1997). Perhaps the most telling of these is a passage in which Locke apparently denies that there is any such thing as species and boundaries between them in nature. In the passage in question, Locke writes:

> ... in all the visible corporeal World, we see no Chasms, or Gaps. All quite down from us, the descent is by easy steps, and a continued series of Things, that in each remove, differ very little one from the other. ... There are some Brutes, that seem to have as much Knowledge and Reason, as some that are call'd Men: and the Animal and Vegetable Kingdoms, are so nearly join'd, that if you will take the lowest of one, and the highest of the other, there will scarce be perceived any great difference between them; and so on till we come to the lowest and most inorganical parts of Matter, we shall find everywhere, that the several *Species* are linked together, and differ but in almost insensible degrees. (E III.vi.12: 447)

This passage provides support, especially in its final invocation of a great chain of being, for the view that there are no species in nature, that each species shades imperceptibly into the next. It seems reasonable to suppose, then, that Locke is arguing that our ideas of species must be the product of our understanding, since there are no species in nature for them to copy. "Surely," Ayers argues, "much like Boyle, Locke at least wants to impress on us that the continuing and unpredictable changes in the world are incompatible with the doctrine of fixed specific forms and objective boundaries between sorts, but can be accounted for by a hypothesis with the shape of corpuscularianism" (1997: 172). Since there can't be any real essences in a world of corpuscularian flux, we can't possibly know them, or base our ideas of species on them.

This crucial passage, however, if we take a closer look at it, is not quite so cut-and-dried as it at first appears. In particular, it does not occur as part of a direct argument about the nature of real essences, but is, instead, a subpart of a larger argument that begins one section earlier, in E III.vi.11. That paragraph is about the possibility of different species of spirits, and the reason for calling our attention to such a possibility is to spell out or illustrate a way in which our ideas are limited. Our ideas of spirits, Locke argues, like all our ideas, are restricted to those simple ideas available to us. In this case, because we have ideas of spirits only by reflection, we are limited to those simple ideas derived from our own case, which can consist only of operations found within us. "And though we are told," Locke argues,

that there are different *Species of Angels*; yet we know not how to frame distinct specific *Ideas* of them; not out of any Conceit, that the Existence of more *Species* than one of *Spirits*, is impossible; But because having no more simple *Ideas* (nor being able to frame more) applicable to such Beings, but only those few, taken from our selves, and from the Actions of our own Minds in thinking, and being delighted, and moving several parts of our Bodies; we can no otherwise distinguish in our Conceptions the several *Species of Spirits*, one from another, but by attributing those Operations and Powers, we find in our selves, to them in a higher or lower degree. (E III. vi.11: 445–6)

The problem Locke is calling to our attention is this: Our idea of spirit is limited to those simple ideas of reflection available to us. But we know there are many more species of spirits than the human species, with more and different mental powers. Our inability to conceptualize this vast variety of different kinds of spirits is an indication that our ideas of spirits are nominal essences, abstracted from the ideas we receive from ourselves, and are not based on real essences. We know these real essences of other spirits exist, but we lack the resources to think about them; they are unknown. The subsequent passage on varieties of species in nature is intended as an analogical argument. Just as there are many different species in nature other than ourselves, differing imperceptibly one from another, so we can extrapolate to the existence of many different species of spirits, even though we can't have ideas of them. This claim is in fact the conclusion of E III.vi.12: 447:

And when we consider the infinite Power and Wisdom of the Maker, we have reason to think, that it is suitable to the magnificent Harmony of the Universe, and the great Design and infinite Goodness of the Architect, that the *Species* of Creatures should also, by gentle degrees, ascend upward from us toward his infinite Perfection, as we see they gradually descend from us downwards: Which if it be probable, we have reason then to be perswaded, that there are far more *Species* of Creatures above us, than there are beneath; we being in degrees of Perfection much more remote from the infinite Being of GOD, than we are from the lowest state of Being, and that which approaches nearest to nothing. And yet of all those distinct *Species*, for the reasons above-said, we have no clear distinct *Ideas*.

While the original passage claiming the existence of a great chain of being does seem to support a corpuscularian reading of Locke's project, the passage when taken in its entirety instead provides support for those, like Guyer, who wish to emphasize the importance to Locke of his theory of language and of his stress on the limitations in the way ideas are possible.

Locke's use of borderline cases, like monsters and changelings, is also frequently cited as evidence of the corpuscular basis for Locke's account of essences.[12] Locke did indeed set much store by such cases; they form an important element of his initial dismissal of the "less rational opinion" that all natural things are cast by their essences into "Forms or Molds." "The frequent Productions of Monsters," Locke argues,

> in all the Species of Animals, and of Changelings, and other strange Issues of humane Birth, carry with them difficulties, not possible to consist with this *Hypothesis*: Since it is as impossible, that two Things, partaking exactly of the same real *Essence*, should have different Properties, as that two figures partaking in the same real *Essence* of a Circle, should have different Properties. (E III.iii.17: 418)

Locke is arguing here that, if you are committed to the view that species membership is determined by the possession of a real essence, then you are going to be discomforted by the existence of individual offspring lacking the essential properties of their parents. What is probably significant about this argument is that, while it may be true that corpuscularian theory can provide a better account of deviant offspring, this is no part of Locke's argument at this point.[13] Locke never explicitly links borderline cases to corpuscularianism. Instead, they seem to serve two purposes. As in the passage just quoted, he thinks the existence of such entities causes problems for Scholastic essentialism. He is not, as some have imagined, arguing that the existence of monsters indicates that natural species don't have fixed boundaries. It is therefore not a refutation of Locke's claim to point out, as does Jolley, that the

---

[12] See, for example, M. R. Ayers 1997 and Nicholas Jolley 1999.

[13] Jolley appears to imagine that Locke's argument goes through only if forms and molds are understood in terms of geometric corpuscularianism. But I think this misses Locke's target, which is not explanations in terms of molds, but rather essentialism.

problem can be overcome by labeling monsters (e.g., physically deformed humans) and changelings (reason-impaired humans) members of new species. Locke ultimately regards the existence of these so-called borderline cases as a reason to recognize that our ideas of species are not made by nature, and cannot be based on real essences. The most extensive use of such cases, occurring in E III. vi.22–24, makes this point and follows it up by arguing that borderline cases are for many of us hard cases. We don't know what to say about them, and we each of us end up saying different things. Therefore, Locke concludes, we are each of us operating with our own speaker-relative abstract idea of what constitutes, for example, a human, and not with a set of necessary conditions for humanity. Again, when we pay attention to the way in which Locke deploys these examples, they are in service of his theory of language rather than his ontology.[14]

Perhaps, however, even though Locke does not, it appears, cite corpuscularian evidence in support of his real/nominal essence distinction, it is nevertheless the picture provided by corpuscularianism that underlies the development of the distinction. It still could be that it was Locke's understanding of corpuscularianism that allowed him to draw the conclusion that the abstract ideas by means of which we sort do not map onto real essences on which qualities depend. For it is undoubtedly the case that Locke frequently makes reference to corpuscularian conclusions and seems happy to suppose that substances have internal, microscopic constitutions of textured, moving parts.[15] So surely it is Locke's understanding of this inaccessible nature of things that led him to distinguish a thing's real essence from its nominal essence. Surely,

[14] Michael Ayers also challenges Paul Guyer with respect to a passage at E III.vi.39, where Locke argues that to most people watches, despite internal dissimilarities, all constitute a single species. Ayers urges that this passage shows Locke arguing that, with respect to watches, there are no lowest species, rather than, as Guyer claims, demonstrating that what counts as a watch relies on human choices. It seems to me, however, that despite Locke's references to "minuter Divisions from Differences" the overall thrust of the passage is to argue that it is observable and superficial differences, and not their internal structure, that lead people to categorize objects as watches. The lesson Locke is seeking to draw from this passage therefore seems to be that differences in internal structure, surely the analog of corpuscularian structure, don't affect the choices made when people classify things as watches.

[15] Most notably in E II.xxiii.11–13.

therefore, we ought to use this background assumption when we attempt to elucidate Locke's motives for drawing the distinction.

For this approach to be helpful, however, it must be that an appeal to corpuscularianism can help us to understand (or, at the very least, not hinder us from understanding) what the distinction can do, not just in the case of substances, but in the case of ideas of mixed modes and simple ideas as well. For an important element in Locke's deployment of the concepts of real and nominal essences is the clarification that he believes they give to a proper understanding of ideas of mixed modes and simple ideas, as well as ideas of substances. Our understanding of the notion of real essence and its relation to nominal essence should apply equally perspicuously to what Locke says about the nominal and real essences of mixed modes and kinds of simple ideas, as well as of substances. But it is not clear that reading Locke's concept of real essence through the lens of corpuscularianism is entirely helpful in dealing with these other cases.

For Locke, important differences are revealed among simple ideas, ideas of mixed modes, and ideas of substances by the relations between their respective real and nominal essences. The various kinds of mixed modes and kinds of simple ideas, like kinds of substances, have both nominal and real essences. Mixed modes and simple ideas both differ from the case of substances, however, because kinds of mixed modes and kinds of simple ideas have real essences that are the same as their nominal essences, while, in the case of substances, the real essence is different from the nominal essence. At first glance, the claim with respect to mixed modes looks to be fairly straightforward. Ideas of mixed modes are ideas that are framed, at least initially, quite arbitrarily, and without any reference to any real existence. In Locke's extended example (E III. vi.44–51), the ideas of jealousy and adultery contain just those ideas Adam puts into them, because, in framing them, Adam was not attempting to capture an archetype made by nature, but instead trying to convey his thoughts to his listener. The case is otherwise when Adam puts together his idea of gold, because here he is trying to convey something about the stuff brought to him by his children by matching his idea to an archetype found in nature. It would be reasonable to take this set of actions by Adam to describe a situation where, in the case of gold, the qualities conjoined have a corpuscularian structure causally responsible for them, while in the case of jealousy and adultery, they do not. So, in the case of gold, our idea has a real but unknown essence, whereas in the case of jealousy and adultery, there is none. At first glance, it looks as though an underlying corpuscularianism accounts for this difference.

What is left unexamined, however, on this approach, is that Locke says that ideas of mixed modes *have* real essences, even though these real essences are identical to their nominal essences. The same essence, in *this* case, plays two roles. It is, first of all, of course, the abstract idea that is the workmanship of the understanding, and that provides the boundaries of a given species, but as a real essence, it is also "the very being of any thing, whereby it is, what it is" (E III.iii.15: 417). Locke makes this clear in his initial discussion of the identification a few paragraphs later: "Thus a Figure including a Space between three Lines, is the real, as well as nominal *Essence* of a Triangle; it being not only the abstract *Idea* to which the general Name is annexed, but the very *Essentia*, or Being, of the thing it self, that Foundation from which all its Properties flow, and to which they are all inseparably annexed" (E III.iii.18: 418). When you have grasped the nominal essence of a mixed mode, you not only have at your disposal the means for recognizing entities that fall into its category, but you also have within your grasp the capacity to recognize all other properties necessarily depending upon and following from that essence. In order to do proper justice to Locke's claim that the nominal and real essences of mixed modes are identical, we are pushed to adopt an interpretation of the concept of real essence that identifies it as the necessary basis for all properties of a thing or sort of thing. This is, of course, Locke's original sense of the term 'essence'. Used in this sense, the corpuscularian structure of a substance could be identical with its real essence only if it is clear Locke thought that you could, through the knowledge of an entity's corpuscularian structure, grasp all of the properties of that entity that could be said to follow from it. Locke's repeated strictures, however, about the limitations on our knowledge, even assuming corpuscularianism, make it unlikely that he would endorse such a view.[16] If we assume that Locke intended to

---

[16] Consider, for example, the well-known passages in E II.xxiii, where Locke says we have no understanding of how particles cohere so that bodies are extended (E II. xxiii.23–6), or of how bodies move other bodies (E II.xxiii.28).

use the term 'real essence' in the same way when talking about the real essence of substances and of mixed modes, then it seems that we are driven to an understanding of real essence that undercuts an identification with corpuscularian structures.

The situation is even more complicated when we turn to the case of simple ideas. For simple ideas, unlike ideas of mixed modes, are not arbitrary. It is, in fact, completely impossible for us to make them up, and the only way for anyone to have a simple idea is to receive it passively. Simple ideas, moreover, like ideas of substances, and unlike ideas of mixed modes, do, in Locke's words, *"intimate* also *some real Existence,* from which was derived their original pattern" (E III.iv.2: 421). But Locke says, just as in the case of mixed modes, that the real essence of kinds of simple ideas is identical to the nominal essence. The nominal essence in this case is based on nothing more than the having of some simple idea; since simple ideas cannot be defined, they can be acquired only as passive impressions on the mind. It is therefore the having of a simple idea of red that is the basis of our understanding of what kind of thing red is. But we have that idea of red because of the presence of something real in the world that the idea signifies. It would seem reasonable to suppose that the something really existing is a corpuscularian structure of some sort, and to suppose that our idea of red signifies that unknown structure. It would seem reasonable, that is, to suppose that the case of simple ideas replicates that of substances, since they share the characteristic of being derived from some really existing pattern. But Locke, somewhat surprisingly, denies this, and instead classifies kinds of simple ideas with the thoroughly arbitrary mixed modes.

The explanation for this state of affairs derives from Locke's conviction that simple ideas are undefinable and contain nothing more within them than their perspicuous content. His reasoning is laid bare in his discussion of the indefinability of the simple idea of light, where Locke interestingly moves from what had been a critique of the unintelligibility of Scholastic attempts to define simple ideas to consider a more modern example. "Those who tell us," Locke writes,

that *Light* is a great number of little Globules, striking briskly on the bottom of the eye, speak more intelligibly than the Schools: but yet these

Words never so well understood, would make the *Idea*, the Word *Light* stands for, no more known to a Man that understands it not before, than if one should tell him, that *Light* was nothing but a Company of little Tennis-balls, which Fairies all day long struck with Rackets against some Men's Fore-heads, whilst they passed by others. For granting this explication of the thing to be true; yet the *Idea* of the cause of *Light*, if we had it never so exact, would no more give us the *Idea* of *Light* it self, as it is such a particular perception in us, than the *Idea* of Figure and Motion of a sharp piece of Steel, would give us the *Idea* of that Pain, which it is able to cause in us. For the cause of any Sensation, and the Sensation it self, in all the simple *Ideas* of one Sense, are two *Ideas*; and two *Ideas* so different and so distant one from another, that no two can be more so. (E III.iv.10: 423–4)[17]

The cause of any simple idea, Locke is saying here, no matter how well understood, is no more than a contingent fact about that thing, and tells us nothing about what kind of thing that simple idea really is. Light really is as we experience it, and light really is not the globules hypothesized as causing that experience. What light or red really is is what is manifested in the simple idea itself. Anything that matches my simple idea of red just is red and belongs to the kind of thing that is red. Unlike the case of mixed modes, I have a simple idea of red because of something in the external world acting upon me that is its cause, and my simple idea signifies this. But the mere presence of the simple idea in me is enough to guarantee the presence of *something* that is its cause. There is no further guarantee that all the "somethings" that give rise to ideas of red form a natural or resembling kind. Red is a kind based only on matching ideas of red. Thus, the simple idea not only constitutes the boundary of the species red, but is also what constitutes the very being of the species itself. Again, the way in which Locke talks about simple ideas reflects the kind of idea-theoretic considerations Bolton stresses, to do with the nature of the content of our ideas, and leaves no room for an account of essences in terms of a commitment to corpuscularian structure, however useful appeals to corpuscularian structure might be in other contexts.

---

[17] Locke continues this passage by claiming the authority of Descartes on his side: Descartes, he tells us, also distinguished the idea of light from the cause of that idea.

If corpuscularian assumptions have no role to play in the account of nominal and real essences of simple ideas and mixed modes, it is worth wondering also whether they have a significant role to play in the case of ideas of substances. Crucially, what distinguishes ideas of substances is that nominal essences of substances are not the same as real essences. This divergence, however, cannot be due to facts about a corpuscularian structure associated with real essences. It cannot, for example, be due simply to our ignorance or our present ignorance of the corpuscularian structures causing sensible qualities, or the real essences of kinds of simple ideas would also be different from their nominal essences. Nor can it have to do simply with the undoubted flux and diversity found among the different corpuscularian structures of different particulars falling under the same nominal essence. For what emerges in the case of ideas of mixed modes is that the nominal essence tells us something that the nominal essence of substances does not. It does not just tell us what ideas of qualities go together; it also shows us the basis on which all properties of that kind follow. This is what in the case of substances we remain ignorant of, and constitutes the real essence of the substance. The problem is not a metaphysical one, that there are no real essences of substances, but is a problem rooted in our ignorance of such substances. This is not, moreover, an ignorance that a greater knowledge of corpuscularian structures can cure, for, while corpuscularian structures might well be causes, they are not essences. There are therefore compelling reasons not to read Locke's account of real and nominal essences as a piece of corpuscularian metaphysics dropped into the middle of a discussion of language. To the contrary, with this reading dispelled, the discussion of essences fits neatly into the project about language to which Locke devotes the third book of the *Essay*.

The subject matter of Book III is words, but Locke's primary care in his discussion of words is to spell out the implications of his theory of ideas with respect to words. The cornerstone of this approach is the conviction that *"Words in their primary or immediate Signification, stand for nothing, but the* Ideas *in the Mind of him that uses them"* (E III.ii.2: 405). This is a dictum that has caused a certain amount of discomfort, as it seems to imply that our words can only reverberate within our own heads. But of course the important terms here are "primary" and "immediate." Words can indeed secondarily or mediately stand for things other than our own ideas, but this practice is mediated by ideas. Locke indeed goes straight on, after having maintained that words stand for ideas, to describe two what he calls "secret references" people give to their words: "*First, they suppose their Words to be Marks of the* Ideas *in the Minds also of other Men, with whom they communicate*: For else they should talk in vain, and could not be understood, if the Sounds they applied to one *Idea*, were such, as by the Hearer, were applied to another, which is to speak two Languages" (E III.ii.4: 406–7). I have plainly failed to communicate my thoughts to another if that person takes my words to refer to entirely different ideas than mine. "*Secondly*," Locke adds, "Because *Men* would not be thought to talk *barely* of their own Imaginations, but of Things as really they are; therefore they *often suppose their Words to stand also for the reality of Things*" (E III.ii.5: 407). I do not communicate with others just about the products of my fancy; I intend my words to stand for real things out there in the world. Much of the motivation of Book III is to explore the ramifications of these communicative desiderata, the ways in which they can be accomplished, and the various roadblocks that stand in the way of communicative success.

In this chapter, Locke puts these points positively: we need to be able to share our ideas with others, and we need to be able to talk about things, not ideas. In later chapters, however, Locke's more negative assessments of these various ways in which we use our language have proved puzzling. Jonathan Bennett has called attention to a later passage where Locke first says that, in using general names of substances, "we do most commonly tacitly suppose, or intend, they should stand for the real Essence of a certain sort of Substance." But Locke goes on:

Yet there is scarce any Body in the use of these Words, but often supposes each of those names to stand for a thing having the real Essence, on which those Properties depend. Which is so far from diminishing the Imperfection of our Words, that by a plain Abuse it adds to it, when we would make them stand for something, which not being in our complex *Idea*, the name we use, can no ways be the sign of. (E III.x.18: 500)

"Which is it?" Bennett asks, given that in the same passage Locke "writes that by a 'secret supposition' we make the word stand for a real essence; that 'we would' – that is, we try to – make the word stand for a real essence; and that in 'no ways' can the word stand for a real essence" (2001: 105). It is less often noticed, but it is no less troubling, that Locke also seems to contradict himself about the other "secret supposition," that our words stand for the same ideas in our minds and in the minds of others. Consider this passage:

> There remains yet another more general, though, perhaps, less observed *Abuse of Words*; and that is, that Men having by a long and familiar use annexed to them certain *Ideas*, they are apt *to imagine so near and necessary a connexion between the names and the signification* they use them in, that they forwardly suppose one cannot but understand what their meaning is, and therefore one ought to acquiesce in the Words delivered, as if it were past doubt, that in the use of those common received sounds, the Speaker and Hearer had necessarily the same precise *Ideas*. (E III.x.22: 503)

Again, one asks, which is it? Communication demands that speakers assume that their hearers attach the same ideas to their words that they do, but it is an abuse of language so to assume.

The key to unraveling these contradictions is to notice that both secret suppositions that Locke introduces as necessary to communication and then condemns as abuses of language can be understood in terms of his discussion of essences. The supposition about the ideas in the speakers' and hearers' minds concerns the nominal essences or abstract ideas they attach to their words, and the supposition about general names of substances concerns real essences. A plausible assumption is that Locke supposes that communication is facilitated by a correct understanding of the notions of real and nominal essences and is hindered by incorrect understandings of these concepts. The role, therefore, of the discussion of real and nominal essences in Book III is to show how a faulty grasp on the concept of essences leads to breakdowns in communication, while a just understanding makes communication possible.

The false assumption about the nature of ideas in the minds of others is one that is embedded in the Scholastic account of essences, the account Locke seeks to replace. If we did indeed sort based on the Scholastic forms that inform our intellect, then the ideas by means of which we sort would be made by the world. They would express the necessary and sufficient conditions for the boundaries of a species. Under *these* circumstances, it would be perfectly appropriate to assume that the idea that informs my intellect is exactly the same as that which informs the intellect of others. But Locke repeatedly stresses that the ideas by means of which we sort are made by us, not by the world. More importantly, he holds that when we pay attention to the process by means of which we construct abstract ideas, we will find that it is a process that allows for considerable variation from one speaker to another. "Nor will any one wonder," Locke writes,

that I say these *Essences*, or abstract *Ideas*, (which are the measures of Names, and the boundaries of Species) are the *Workmanship of the Understanding*, who considers, that at least the complex ones are often, in several Men, different Collections of simple *Ideas*: and therefore that is *Covetousness* to one Man, which is not so to another. Nay, even in Substances, where their abstract *Ideas* seem to be taken from the Things themselves, they are not constantly the same; so not in that Species, which is most familiar to us, and with which we have the most intimate acquaintance: It having been more than once doubted, whether the *Foetus* born of a Woman were a *Man*, even so far, as that it hath been debated, whether it were, or were not to be nourished and baptized: which could not be, if the abstract *Idea* or Essence, to which the Name Man belonged, were of Nature's making; and were not the uncertain and various Collection of simple *Ideas*, which the Understanding puts together, and then abstracting it, affixed a name to it. (E III.iii.14: 416)

The various puzzles and disagreements with which we are faced show that the process by which ideas are attached to words is not simple or automatic, or the same for everyone. The work my understanding undertakes when I frame abstract ideas is to collect different simple ideas into a single bundle. There is no structure to the list of ideas I collect beyond the fact that they have recurred in my past history or appear salient to me. Each abstract idea is therefore speaker-relative, reflecting each speaker's history and choices.

The usefulness for communication of ideas collected in such a manner will depend upon the stability of the collection and on the likelihood that others will attach the same collection to the same word. Neither of these desiderata can be guaranteed. Locke points out that

when a word stands for a very complex *Idea*, that is compounded and decompounded, it is not easy for Men to form and retain that *Idea* so exactly, as to make the Name in common use, stand for the same precise

Idea, without any the least variation. Hence it comes to pass, that Men's Names, of very compound *Ideas*, such as for the most part are moral Words, have seldom, in two different Men, the same precise signification, since one Man's complex *Idea* seldom agrees with anothers, and often differs from his own, from that which he had yesterday, or will have tomorrow. (E III. ix.6: 478)

So long as each speaker is both idiosyncratic and careless in the construction of our ideas, the result, taken together, is that each of our ideas cannot be assumed to agree with those of others. Failure to pay attention to the very real possibility that each speaker has constructed a different set of ideas to attach to a word results, Locke warns, in a great deal of unnecessary argument, in which combatants, who think they are arguing about things, are actually using words with different meanings (E III.xi.6). It is by recognizing the nature of the process by which speakers attach ideas to words that we can take steps to ensure that the ideas of each speaker are sufficiently precise and sufficiently in line with common practice to make communication possible.

When Locke terms the speaker-relative abstract ideas "nominal *essences*," therefore, he is employing what Brykman calls a "conceptual trompe l'oeil." The nominal essence behaves like an essence inasmuch as it delineates a species, but we can be fooled if we don't recognize that *"every distinct abstract* Idea, *is a distinct Essence*: and the names that stand for such distinct *Ideas*, are the names of Things essentially different"* (E III.iii.14: 416). Once we recognize that our words stand for speaker-relative abstract ideas and not for fixed essences in nature, then we can also recognize that the sharing of ideas that underlies successful communication is a project and not a given. The truth that communication is facilitated when speaker and hearer attach the same ideas to the same words is obscured by the falsehood that nature will guarantee this result for us, leading us to suppose that we do not have to work to achieve it.

If we return to Bennett's original "Which is it?" question about Locke's attitude toward real essences, we should be able to make a similar sorting into truth and falsehood. The truth that communication about substance terms is "regulated" by real existences in nature (E III.ix.11: 481) is obscured by the falsehood that they are controlled by real essences. Locke maintains that if we suppose the standard governing the correct use of terms to be a real essence, then, since the real essence is always unknown, we are never in a position to know whether a present use of a term is correct, whether, as Locke says, a present instance is a real horse or real gold or not. In fact, Locke not only thinks we are unable to make use of the supposition of a common internal constitution as a standard for the application of terms, but also thinks this supposition is most probably false (E III.x.20). This is presumably because two individuals called by the same name differ from one another as much as, or more than, they resemble each other and hence must have different internal constitutions to account for these differences. But if the false supposition of an internal constitution obscures the real standard governing the application of our terms, what is the real standard? How do things themselves or real existence function to determine the content of ideas of substances?

The rule by which Locke thinks we frame ideas of substances is well known: we put together ideas that in our experience have been found to recur, to "go constantly together," and we give them one name. It is worth noticing, however, that a "going together" rule is not quite the same as a "resemblance" rule based on the notion that nature makes many things alike. A going-together rule, in fact, has different and more useful implications. So far, what we have noticed about Locke's discussion of this process is his emphasis on its arbitrary and speaker-relative nature. Where in this process do we find the standards set by nature? We need here to take into account that Locke holds that a collection of recurring ideas is not enough to constitute an idea of a substance or substances. In E III. vi.21: 450, for example, he reminds us of what ideas of general words do contain, since they do not contain real essences: "The *Essence* of any thing, in respect of us, is the whole complex *Idea*, comprehended and marked by that Name; and in Substances, besides the several distinct simple *Ideas* that make them up, the confused one of Substance, or of an unknown Support and Cause of their Union, is always a part." Whenever we construct an idea, a nominal essence, of a substance, we include as a part of that idea the confused, obscure, and relative idea of substance. That idea points to the supposition that all of the ideas found to be recurring and hence put together by us, recur because of a real union in nature.[18] This confused, obscure, relative idea of substance as a part of our ideas of substances is a place holder for things themselves. As such, it does indeed function normatively. It tells us that we ought to include within our idea of any substance whatever ideas are found to co-occur with those ideas that have already been found to go together, and that we ought to exclude ideas that do not recur. We have, that is, a way to identify a real horse or real gold. The particular thing in front of me is a real horse or real gold if it presents me with those ideas that have been found to go together. We also have a standard we can use in altering our existing ideas. An idea of a substance will be more perfect if it includes more of those reliably recurring ideas. The idea of substance does not provide an extramental standard by means of which we assess our idea construction, but rather it provides reasons for including or excluding simple ideas from a complex. As a confused and obscure idea, of course, it will never provide us with hard and fixed boundaries for our ideas of kinds of substances. Instead, as Locke repeatedly emphasizes, it provides a standard that is open-ended, resulting in ideas that are always inadequate. Again, it is appropriate and conversationally necessary to take substance terms to refer to things, and it is this reference that the presence of the idea of substance within any abstract idea supplies. Alternatively, however, if we suppose that reference to things obtains only when our substance terms apply to real essences, we will fail.

Genevieve Brykman calls attention to a remark Berkeley made in his *Philosophical Commentaries* about Book III of the *Essay*: "Locke's great oversight seems to be that he did not Begin wth his Third Book at least that he had not some thought of it at first. Certainly the 2 1st books don't agree wth wt he says in ye 3d" (Berkeley 1948–57: I: 87). I leave to another time the merits of Berkeley's allegations of inconsistency.[19] What is clear from Berkeley's own practice, since he took his advice to Locke, is that he read Book III as centrally about the issue I have been foregrounding, nominal essences or abstract ideas. And these essences, in a lesson Berkeley fully exploited, are essences in name only,

---

[18] I am influenced in my discussion of this point by Lex Newman 2000.

[19] It is probably worth thinking about the fact, however, that most of the passages where Locke seems to be committing himself to a corpuscularian inner constitution occur in Book II.

since, in our ignorance of essential nature, we construct the ideas by means of which we classify. The explanation for the novelty Leibniz mentions is that, for Locke, the only essences we know are linguistic essences, since we lack the knowledge of metaphysical essences. Locke himself raises the question why he had not treated these matters as a failure of our knowledge rather than of our language. He explains:

> I must confess then, that when I first began this Discourse of the Under-standing, and a good while after, I had not the least Thought, that any Consideration of Words was at all necessary to it. But when having passed over the Original and Composition of our *Ideas*, I began to examine the Extent and Certainty of our Knowledge, I found it had so near a connexion with Words, that unless their force and manner of Signification were first well observed, there could be very little said clearly and pertinently con-cerning Knowledge: which being conversant about Truth, had constantly to do with Propositions. And though it terminated in Things, yet it was for the most part so much by the intervention of Words, that they seem'd scarce separable from our general Knowledge. At least they interpose themselves so much between our Understandings and the Truth, which it would contemplate and apprehend, that like the *Medium* through which visible Objects pass, their Obscurity and Disorder does not seldom cast a mist before our Eyes, and impose upon our Understandings. (E III.ix.21: 488)

The role Book III plays in Locke's overall argument, then, is the one he lays out in this passage: to teach us, through an explanation of how words function, to guard against the various ways in which we may be misled through confusions in the way words are used, and to show us how to improve communication through a careful and conscious understanding of how words gain, through our own handiwork, meaning.

10 Language, Meaning, and Mind in Locke's *Essay*

I

Locke's *Essay concerning Human Understanding* is a philosophical landmark devoted to understanding the nature and limits of human knowledge in terms of the concept of an idea. The term 'idea' plays such an important role in the *Essay* that contemporary critics derided it for following a "new way of ideas" that would "promote scepticism and infidelity" (W IV: 129–30). Locke himself was apologetic for his frequent use of the term 'idea', but he believed that he "could not avoid frequently using it" (E I.i.8: 47). Locke writes, "[m]y *new way by ideas* ... may ... comprehend my whole Essay," but he adds that this "new way of *ideas*, and the old way of speaking intelligibly, was always, and ever will be the same" (W IV: 134, 430). Locke uses the concept of an idea to develop accounts of sensation, reflection, perception, memory, and knowledge, which became the central themes that exercised his successors and critics such as Berkeley, Hume, and Reid.

But there is another distinctive feature of Locke's *Essay*. It also includes a turn to language that has a significant place in the history of philosophy. Locke not only relies on the concept of an idea to explain perception and knowledge, but also uses it to develop a theory of language. After a critique of the doctrine of innate ideas in Book I and an extensive discussion of the origins and the classification of ideas in Book II, Locke turns to language in Book III, which begins with a chapter "Of Words or Language in General." It is only in the fourth and last book of the *Essay* that Locke turns to human knowledge.

Several things are clear about Locke's linguistic turn in the *Essay*.[1] It is clear that, in Locke's words, this third book is devoted to "the Nature, Use, and Signification of Language" (E II.xxxiii.19: 401). It is also clear why he turns to language. After having discussed the origins and types of ideas we have, Locke initially wanted to turn to the role ideas play in human cognition and what human beings can expect to know given the nature of our ideas. However, he postponed this discussion of human knowledge and turned to language instead because he concluded that language plays a central role in human cognition. He writes:

> [B]ut upon nearer approach, I find, that there is so close a connexion between *Ideas* and Words; and our abstract *Ideas*, and general words, have so constant a relation one to another, that it is impossible to speak clearly and distinctly of our Knowledge, which all consists in Propositions, without considering, first, the Nature, Use, and Signification of Language; which therefore must be the business of the next Book. (E II.xxxiii.19: 401; also see III.ix.21)

These closing remarks of Book II accurately reflect Locke's intellectual development. The earliest known draft of Locke's *Essay*, written in 1671, has very little discussion of human language. Even the third known draft of the *Essay*, known as Draft C and written in 1685, does not contain a book on language. However, by then Locke had already made his linguistic turn. The closing remarks of Book II of the *Essay* are anticipated in the last paragraph of Draft C, where Locke "confesses" that when he began examining "what use the understanding made of these Ideas & what knowledge it attaind by them," he "found words by constant use soe neare a Connection with them & were by inadvertency soe often put for our Ideas that it was impossible to speake clearly & destinctly of our knowledge ... without considering first the nature use and signification of language which therefor must be the businese of my next booke."[2]

It is also clear that, in his discussion of language, Locke continues on the "way of ideas," but adds a new term: the "Signification of Language." Locke introduces this term in the second

---

[1] The term "linguistic turn" is from Rorty 1967. For an account of the role of Locke's linguistic turn in modern philosophy, see Losonsky 2006.

[2] I am very indebted to John Rogers for information about Draft C.

chapter of Book III, called "*Of the Signification of Words*," where he writes:

Words in their primary or immediate Signification, stand for nothing, but the Ideas *in the Mind of him that uses them,* how imperfectly soever, or carelesly those *Ideas* are collected from the Things, which they are supposed to represent. (E III.ii.2: 405)

There is no doubt that for Locke the relation of signification between words and ideas is a human artifact and a product of voluntary activity. "*Words,*" Locke argues, "come to be made use of by Men, as *the Signs of* their *Ideas* ... not by any natural connexion, that there is between particular articulate sounds and certain *Ideas*, ... but by a voluntary Imposition, whereby such a Word is made arbitrarily the Mark of such an *Idea*" (E III.ii.1: 405). In fact, "[s]ounds have no natural connexion with our *Ideas,*" Locke writes, and it is only "the arbitrary imposition of Men" that connects words and ideas (E III.ix.4: 477). Thus words are "voluntary Signs in every one," including Adam (E III.vi.47: 468). Accordingly, Locke rejects the then-current view that there is a nonconventional language of nature, usually associated with Adam's language as described in Genesis 1:27.[3]

Finally, it is clear that Locke assigns a very high degree of importance to the study of language. The very last chapter of the *Essay* is devoted to the "*Division of the Sciences,*" of which there are three, the third being "σημειωτική [*sēmeintikē*], or *the Doctrine of Signs*, the most usual whereof being Words, it is aptly enough termed also λογική [*logikē*], Logick" (E IV.xxi.4: 720). The task of the doctrine of signs is to "consider the Nature of Signs, the Mind makes use of for the understanding of Things, or conveying its Knowledge to others." The class of signs studied by this science includes not only words, but also ideas that are signs of extramental objects. The "Things, the Mind contemplates," Locke writes, "are none of them, besides it self, present to the Understanding," and therefore "'tis necessary that something else, as a Sign or Representation of the thing it considers, should be present to it: And these are *Ideas*" (E IV. xxi.4: 720–1). With words that signify ideas and ideas that represent objects, human beings pursue and communicate their knowledge.

---

[3] On language of nature doctrines, see Aarsleff 1982 and Losonsky 2001: 105–15.

This much is relatively clear in Locke's discussion about language, but what appears to be unclear about Locke's philosophy of language, at least as far as recent scholarship is concerned, is what Locke's discussion of language is exactly about. Clearly, the focal point of his philosophy of language is the relation of signification between words and ideas, but today there appears to be a lack of a consensus about what Locke had in mind when writing about the signification of language. I turn to the traditional view and its critics in the following section; in the subsequent sections, I respond to the critics and defend the traditional reading of Locke's theory of signification.

II

The traditional view is that Locke's theory of signification is a theory of linguistic meaning. Mill in his *System of Logic* takes Locke to be discussing linguistic meaning (1974 VII: I.2.1), and W. P. Alston in his widely used introduction to the philosophy of language probably expressed the consensus forty-five years ago when he characterized Locke's theory of signification as a theory of meaning, specifically an "ideational theory" of meaning (1964: 22–3).[4] A more detailed and fine-tuned treatment of Locke's theory of signification as a theory of linguistic meaning is the late Norman Kretzmann's essay "The Main Thesis of Locke's Semantic Theory" (1967). Kretzmann called Book III of Locke's *Essay* "the first modern treatise devoted specifically to philosophy of language" and Locke's discussion of signification a "semantic theory" (1967: 379–80; also 1968: 175–6). The importance of Locke's semantic theory, Kretzmann argues, "lay in the fact that Locke had expressly connected semantic inquiry with theory of knowledge" (*ibid.*). Locke turns to the signification of words, primarily categorematic words such as common names, in order to further his work in epistemology, and Locke's concept of signification, according to Kretzmann, is primarily the concept of a semantic relation between names used by a speaker and the ideas that speaker has in mind.

---

[4] Also, Bennett 1971; Martin 1987; Ayers: 1991: I: 269–76; Losonsky 1990, 1994; Guyer 1994; and Jolley 1999: 162–8.

Kretzmann argues that there is also a secondary semantic relation implicit in Locke's theory. While "[w]ords *in their primary or immediate Signification, stand for nothing, but the* Ideas *in the Mind of him that uses them,*" Locke also believes that an idea is "a Sign or Representation" of things (E IV.xxi.4: 721) and that some names, for example, names of substances such as "gold," are used "ultimately to represent Things," and so "their signification must agree with the Truth of Things, as well as with Men's *Ideas*" (E III. xi.24: 520). Kretzmann infers from these and similar passages that although names *primarily* and *immediately* signify ideas in the minds of the speaker who uses them, in Locke's view they can *secondarily* and *mediately* signify the things ideas represent (1967: 380; 1968: 187–8). Kretzmann's use of the term 'refer' when discussing Locke's secondary or mediate signification suggests that Locke's distinction parallels Frege's distinction between sense and reference (1968: 188; Frege 1892). While the sense of a name is the ideas the speaker using the name has in mind, it refers to the objects, if any, that these ideas represent.

This reading of Locke has been challenged on several grounds. An early challenge came from the medievalist E. J. Ashworth, who argued that Locke uses 'signify' in the same way late sixteenth- and early seventeenth-century scholastics used '*significare*', and that '*significare*' and its cognate '*significatio*' are not about linguistic meaning strictly speaking (1981: 309–11; 1998: 183–91). Ashworth argued that by "the early sixteenth century the standard definition of '*significare*' was 'to represent some thing or some things or in some way to the cognitive power'" (1998: 187). Thus a term can signify its "total denotation" – for example, 'man' can signify Plato, Socrates, Cicero, and so forth – because by using a term a speaker can intend to make known the term's total denotation (1998: 188). But a term also signifies what a speaker has in mind, that is, concepts, because "it is by means of concepts that things are signified, and the means of signifying must itself be signified" (Ashworth 1981: 324). Thus '*significare*' and its cognates cover both the sense and the reference of a term, but it is also about "psychological states as opposed to abstract entities such as meanings" (Ashworth 1981: 310; also 1998: 187–8; 1977: 57–79; and Spade 1982: 188).

While Kretzmann and Ashworth disagree about Locke's concept of signification, they agree that signification is a species of representation and that on Locke's view, words can represent objects, not just our ideas. Walter Ott (2004) rejects this assumption. He denies that Locke's theory of signification includes, implicitly or explicitly, a semantic relation between words and extramental objects. Ott argues that understanding Locke's concept of signification in terms that include the senses/reference distinction runs counter to Locke's own text. Instead, for Locke signification is indication, that is, a sign signifies when it is "an evidence, a grounds for inference" (2004: 24, also 32). On this interpretation, Locke's claim that words signify ideas in the mind of the speaker who is using them means "that words serve as indicators or signals of those ideas" (Ott 2004: 24.) Ott maintains that this meaning of 'signification' accords with a "semiotic tradition" that includes Aristotle, Hobbes, and Arnauld and Nicole of the *Port-Royal Logic* and that is "deeply at odds with that of the late Scholastics" (Ott 2004: 14).

To support his thesis that Locke's signification is wholly distinct from "sense, reference, or any mixture of both," Ott cites Hobbes's famous discussion in *De Corpore* of the nature of signs and signification (2004: 13–14). Hobbes there writes that signs "are the *antecedents of their consequents, and the consequents of their antecedents, as often as we observe them to go before or follow after in the same manner*" (1839: I: I.2.2). When this regularity is a fact of nature, we have natural signs – for instance, when "a thick cloud is a sign of rain to follow." In the case of arbitrary signs, the regularity is established by "choice ... at our own pleasure, as a bush, hung up, signifies that wine is to be sold there ... and words so and so connected, signify the cogitations and motions of our mind" (1839: I: I.2.2).

Ian Hacking is another writer who cites Hobbes's text to reject the view that Locke's theory of signification is a theory of linguistic meaning. Hacking maintains that for Hobbes A signifies B when A and B regularly follow or precede each other, and that given this account of sign and signification "it becomes very difficult to foist any theory of meaning on to Hobbes," and by extension onto Locke (1975: 20, 47). Hacking also argues that theories of linguistic meaning "have to do with the essentially public features of language," and since Locke "did not have a theory of public discourse," he "did not have a theory of meaning" (1975: 52–3). Hacking highlights the fact that for Locke, the ideas that words signify are private: they "are all within [man's] own Breast, invisible, and hidden from others, nor can of themselves be made appear" (E III. ii.1: 405). Consequently, "unless a man's words excite the same ideas in the hearer which he makes them stand for in speaking, he does not speak intelligibly" (E III.ii.8: 408). Given that ideas on Locke's account are private, Hacking argues that either Locke was "unusually unreflective" or he was not concerned with giving an account of meaning and public discourse (1975: 44). Had Locke been reflective and serious about meaning and public discourse, Hacking argues, he would have been concerned with the sameness of ideas between speakers. But Locke was not concerned with the sameness of ideas between speakers, so Hacking concludes that Locke was not concerned with linguistic meaning.

III

I maintain that Locke's theory of signification is indeed a theory of linguistic meaning. His theory of signification aims to explain what distinguishes language from mere articulate sounds. He argues that the ability *"to frame articulate Sounds"* is "not enough to produce Language; for Parrots, and several other Birds, will be taught to make articulate Sounds distinct enough, which yet, by no means, are capable of Language" (E III.i.1: 402). Locke maintain that "[b]esides articulate Sounds" something else is necessary for language, and this additional ingredient is that a human being is *"able to use these Sounds, as Signs of internal Conceptions,"* that is, "to make them stand as marks for the *Ideas* within his own Mind" (E III.i.2: 402). Locke is interested in what it is for human beings to "use the *Words* they speak (with any meaning)" (E III.ii.3: 406), that is, what it is to "speak intelligibly" (E III.ii.8: 408). As he puts it very clearly in *"Of the Conduct of the Understanding,"* if a word does not stand for an idea, it is "a mere empty sound without a meaning" (CU §29: 64). It certainly appears on a first reading that Locke intended that signification is what distinguishes mere articulate sounds from meaningful language.

That Locke was concerned with linguistic meaning is confirmed by the fact that Locke indeed has a theory of communication and an account of the sameness of ideas. Locke begins his discussion of language in Book III by tying language to communication. Language, Locke writes, is "the great Instrument, and common Tye of Society," and one of the uses of language is that "the Thoughts of Men's Minds be conveyed from one to another" (E III.i.1–2: 402). Signification is what makes communication possible. Locke writes:

The Comfort, and Advantage of Society, not being to be had without Communication of Thoughts, it was necessary, that Man should find out some external sensible Signs, whereby those invisible *Ideas*, which his thoughts are made up of, might be made known to others. (E III.ii.1: 405)

Because words are "well adapted to that purpose," they came to be used by human beings

as *the Signs of* their *Ideas.* ... The use then of Words, is to be sensible Marks of *Ideas*; and the *Ideas* they stand for, are their proper and immediate Signification. (ibid.)

But signification is not the only element of Locke's theory of communication. An integral part of Locke's theory of communication is his theory of rectification.[5]

According to Locke, human beings intend that their ideas have a *"double conformity."*[6] We take our ideas to conform to external objects as well as to the ideas that other people have, and successful communication depends on the latter conformity (E II.xxxii.8: 386). Rectification is the process of determining when our ideas conform to the ideas of others. Although judgments about the sameness of ideas are always fallible (E II.xxxii.9), there can be good reasons for believing that ideas conform to the ideas of others if they are rectified.

The basic strategy of rectification is to fix the signification of a term by a standard in nature. For Locke a standard in nature is what is given passively to the understanding without the contribution of voluntary activity, because when the mind is passive with respect to its ideas, their content is determined by their causes.[7] Simple

---

[5] See Losonsky 1994. Ashworth (1998: 64–5) notices several crucial passages that belong to Locke's theory of rectification, but she sees them only as "practical hints" inessential to Locke's theory of language.

[6] Aarsleff's reading of Locke also emphasizes the 'double conformity' of language (1982: 24–5). For a critique, see Hacking 1988: 135–53.

[7] On the role Locke assigns to causality in determining content, see Ayers 1991: I: 38; I: 62–6; and Ayers 1994.

ideas are paradigm cases of such standards in nature.[8] Two people have the same kind of simple idea if their perceptions are brought about by the same causal powers, both the powers of the object and the powers of our sensory organs (E II.xxxii.14; also II.vii.4). Since simple ideas are classified by their causes, Locke is not worried about the possibility that because people have different sense organs, simple ideas might actually appear differently to different people. If two people have sense organs that are similar enough regularly to produce distinct simple ideas in response to distinct causes, their simple ideas are the same because they are produced by the same powers, and thus they can rely on these simple ideas to distinguish the same things no matter how these ideas appear to them (E II.xxxii.15).

Consequently, in the case of simple ideas of sensation I am justified in believing that my simple ideas conform to another person's simple ideas if I have reason to believe that our ideas causally covary with the same object. Hence the best way to "mak[e] known the signification of the name of any simple *Idea, is by presenting to his Senses that Subject, which may produce it in his Mind,* and make him actually have the *Idea,* that Word stands for" (E III.xi.14: 515; also II.xxxii.9).

Complex ideas are more difficult to rectify because they are in part products of our voluntary activity (E II.xxx.3; II.xxxii.12; III. ix.7). Voluntary activity is not subject to reliable nomological regularities, and so we cannot rely on causality to classify complex ideas.[9] However, complex ideas of substances do have natural features that can be used for rectification. Complex ideas of substances are constructed on the basis of passively given, co-occurring simple ideas. These ideas are given in groups – for instance, the "simple ideas of Bright, Hot, Roundish, having a constant regular motion, at a certain distance from us, and, perhaps, some other" occur together in experience (E II.xxiii.6: 298–9). A group of simple ideas can then be unified and formed by the human understanding into a complex idea of substance annexed to a name (E III.vi.28; also see Losonsky 1989). These patterns of co-occurring simple ideas are the

---

[8] For a possible exception to the passive nature of simple ideas, see Bolton 1994.

[9] Compare Fodor (1987: 99–100), who argues that the language of thought is subject to laws because it is involuntary, but that public speech acts are voluntary and hence not subject to reliable nomological regularities.

"archetypes" by which the "Significations [of natural kind terms] may best be rectified" (E III.ix.13: 482).

Locke recognizes that rectification is not a source of certain knowledge. First, rectification suffers from the uncertainty that belongs to any empirical inquiry. Knowledge of what people have in mind when using words is arrived at by making and testing hypotheses about what people have in mind based upon their responses to objects and our beliefs about the structure of their perceptual apparatus.[10] This means that human communication is a source of probable opinion, not of knowledge in the sense Locke uses the term 'knowledge' (E IV.ii.1: 531; IV.ii.14: 536–7). Just as there is no certain knowledge of physical bodies, there is no certain knowledge of what others have in mind (E IV.iii.29).

Second, rectification is made uncertain by the instability of our ideas. For instance, we cannot agree on the *"precise number of simple Ideas, or Qualities, belonging to any sort of Things, signified by its name"* (E III.vi.30: 457). There are too many simple ideas that are given to us in groups for us to have exactly conforming ideas of substances, and consequently "the complex *Ideas* of Substances ... will be very various; and so the signification of [their] names, very uncertain" (E III.ix.13: 483). Moreover, our ideas are constantly changing as a result of new experiences, and consequently linguistic meaning is also in constant flux, entailing that *"Languages constantly change"* (E II.xxii.7: 291).[11]

Consequently, Locke's assessment of our capacity to communicate is pessimistic. For Locke, language by its very nature is imperfect, because the "very nature of Words, makes it almost unavoidable, for many of them to be doubtful and uncertain in their significations" (E III.ix.1: 476; also III.x.1). In short, the source of *"the Imperfection of Words is the doubtfulness of their Signification"* (E III.ix.4: 476). It cannot be overemphasized that for Locke

---

[10] See Locke's account of his own interpretive efforts in his preface to the *Paraphrase*. Locke's philosophy of communication anticipates Davidson (1986), who argues that we communicate using a "passing theory" that we develop and revise as we communicate.

[11] Harris (1981: 88) is wrong when he claims that Locke imposes an "invariance condition" on language, namely, that "[w]hatever may vary as between speaker and hearer, or between the conveyance of a given message on one occasion and conveyance of the same message on another occasion, cannot count as part of the language."

the problems of language are not only due to *"wilful Faults and Neglects,* which Men are guilty of," but also due to "the Imperfection that is naturally in Language" (E III.x.1: 490). This is not an idle observation on Locke's part. If we were more aware of the

imperfections of Language, ... a great many of the Controversies that make such a noise in the World, would of themselves cease; and the way to Knowledge, and, perhaps, Peace too, lie a great deal opener than it does. (E III.ix.21: 489)

So it is true that Locke's account limits the certainty and scope of human communication, but this was an intended consequence of his theory of signification. Locke had a theory of signification that captured his skepticism about communication, and if we do not share his skepticism about the human capacity to communicate, then we should attack his doubts, not his theory of signification (Losonsky 1990).[12]

IV

Placing Locke in the context of Hobbes's philosophy is an important aid to better understanding Locke's philosophy (Rogers 1988; Ott 2004: 13–14), but this context does not undermine the semantic interpretation of Locke's theory of signification. Hobbes's discussion of signification as natural or artificial regularities undermines neither that Hobbes nor that Locke was discussing linguistic meaning. There are contemporary theories of meaning that attempt to fashion semantic content out of causal regularities or covariance, and so the mere fact that Hobbes is discussing meaning in terms of regularity does not count against reading him as making a contribution to the theory of meaning. In fact, Hobbes, for whom signification clearly is a causal relationship, has been cited as the father of contemporary attempts to naturalize mind and meaning (Haugeland 1981: 1).

Still, given the paucity of Hobbes's discussion of signification, it is difficult to pin down his concept of signification. It is possible that all Hobbes meant by signification is the relation of indicating or signaling, where what does the signifying serves as

[12] Also see Ayers 1991: I: 275; Guyer 1994: 121; and Jolley 1999: 165.

evidence or grounds for inference, as smoke serves as evidence for fire. But Locke's discussion of signification is rich and detailed enough to show that Locke's concept of signification is not to be identified with indication. Of course, signification, understood as linguistic meaning, is compatible with indication. After all, that a speaker uses a meaningful phrase is evidence for what the speaker has in mind. But it is the fact that a speaker uses a phrase that already has a certain meaning that makes it possible for that phrase to be evidence for what the speaker has in mind. Consequently, linguistic meaning has to be more than indication, and the same holds for Locke's signification. Locke makes this clear when he writes that words "being immediately the Signs of Mens *Ideas*; and, by that means, the Instruments whereby Men communicate their Conceptions, and express to one another those Thoughts and Imaginations, they have within their own Breasts" (E III.ii.6: 407). Here Locke explicitly states that it is *by means of* signification, that is, by means of words "being immediately the Signs of Mens *Ideas*," that we indicate our thoughts to others. Hence, Locke's concept of signification cannot be defined in terms of indication.

Moreover, if signification were conventional indication, Locke would have to limit signification to cases where words are used as *instruments* for giving evidence that allows people to infer what they have in mind. This covers two cases that Locke mentions: "either to record their own Thoughts for the Assistance of their own Memory; or ... to bring out their *Ideas*, and lay them before the view of others" (E III.ii.2: 405). Words are used to indicate to others, or to remind oneself later, what one was thinking (Ott 2004: 25). But for Locke language, and hence signification, has another important function.

As early as the second draft of the *Essay*, Locke writes that human beings use language not only to communicate and record, but "also even to think upon things" (D I: 166). Locke develops this view in the *Essay*, where he writes in the first chapter of Book III: "It is not enough for the perfection of Language that Sounds can be made signs of *Ideas*, unless those *signs* can be so made use of, as *to comprehend several particular Things*" (E III.i.3: 402). Words are needed to think about "a multitude of particular existences," that is, to think about classes and kinds.

Locke rejects the view that how human beings classify objects rests solely on a natural and objective classification that is independent of the mind's activity. For Locke, human language plays a central role in our thinking about classes or kinds. If "we will warily attend to the Motions of the Mind," Locke writes already in Book II, "we shall ... find, that the Mind having got any *Idea*, which it thinks it may have use of, either in Contemplation or Discourse, the first Thing it does, is to abstract it, and then get a Name to it; and so lay it up in its ... Memory, as containing the Essence of a sort of Things, of which the Name is always to the Mark" (E II.xxxii.7: 386). Later in Book III he concludes the chapter on general terms as follows:

To conclude, ... all the great Business of *Genera* and *Species* ... amounts to no more but this, That Men making abstract *Ideas*, and settling them in their Minds with names annexed to them, do thereby enable themselves to consider Things, and discourse of them, as it were in bundles, for the easier and readier improvement, and communication of their Knowledge. (E III.iii.20: 420)

But if names annexed to ideas enable us not just to discourse about things and communicate our knowledge to others (or to ourselves at a later time), but also to think about classes of things and improve our knowledge, signification cannot be indication in the sense of serving as a ground or evidence for inferences. When a person thinks about a class of objects with the help of a general term, the term is not used as a piece of evidence from which she infers what she has in mind!

Consequently, for Locke words are sometimes formal signs. An instrumental sign is (i) an object of thought, particularly sensation, that indicates another object and (ii) that is not itself a means of thinking. A formal sign is primarily something "*by which* thought is accomplished" (Ott 2004: 19; Ashworth 1990: 39). On Locke's account, names sometimes are formal signs because they are used to think, and it requires reflection to recognize this. Locke turns to language after Book II because upon reflection Locke found "that there is so close a connexion between *Ideas* and Words" and that "our abstract *Ideas*, and general Words, have so constant a relation to one another" (E II.xxxiii.19: 401).

The "close connexion" or "constant relation" Locke has in mind is names annexed to ideas. The annexation of names is a topic throughout Book III.[13] The "whole *mystery* of *Genera* and *Species*," Locke writes, "is nothing else but abstract *Ideas*, more or less comprehensive, with names annexed to them" (E III.iii.9: 412; also III.iii.20). He repeats this in his discussion of essences in the chapter *"Of the Names of Substances"*:

The measure and boundary of each Sort, or *Species*, whereby it is constituted that particular Sort, and distinguished from others, is what we call its *Essence*, which *is* nothing but that *abstract* Idea *to which the Name is annexed*. (E III.vi.2: 439)

The annexation of names is especially important for the ideas of what Locke calls "mixed modes." Mixed modes are general ideas that combine simple ideas that do not appear to occur together in nature, but are "scattered and Independent" (E II.xxii.1: 288). These are ideas that *"are* not only *made* by the Mind, but made *very arbitrarily*, made without Patterns, or reference to any real Existence" (E III.v.3: 429). Locke believes that moral ideas are ideas of mixed modes, claiming that there is no more special connection between killing and a human being than between killing and a sheep, but we have a special idea and word for the former – 'murder' – but not for the latter. Similarly, the idea of incest combines scattered and independent ideas that are connected only in the mind, not in nature (E III.v.7).

Since ideas of mixed modes are made "without Patterns," the mind needs something that keeps the disparate ideas together, and Locke maintains that names perform this function:

The near relation that there is *between Species, Essences, and* their *general Names*, at least in *mixed Modes*, will farther appear, when we consider, that it is the Name that seems to preserve those *Essences*, and give them their lasting duration. For the connexion between the loose parts of those complex *Ideas*, being made by the Mind, this union, which has not particular foundation in Nature, would cease again, were there not something that did, as it were, hold it together, and keep the parts from scattering, Though therefore it be the Mind that makes the Collection, 'tis the Name which is, as it were the Knot, that ties them fast together. What a vast variety of different *Ideas*, does the word *Triumphus* hold together, and

---

[13] The term "annexed" is used fifty-four times in Book III and always in order to discuss the annexation of names.

deliver to us as one *Species*! ... I think, that which holds those different parts together, in the unity of one complex *Idea*, is that very word annexed to it. (E III.v.10: 434)

Locke's observation that words are like knots that tie ideas together marks the beginning of an historical trend that gives language a constitutive role to play in the construction of thought (Aarsleff 1982; Losonsky 1999: xxvi–xxvii).

Names have a smaller role to play in the construction of general ideas of substances, because those ideas, as we saw earlier, are based on archetypes or patterns of simple ideas co-occurring in experience; for instance, the idea of gold is based on the fact that malleability, fusibility, and the color yellow (among other qualities) are found together in the experience. Consequently, ideas of substances have "a lasting Union" compared to ideas of mixed modes (E III. vi.42: 465). Nevertheless, names still have a role to play here as well. Locke writes in the chapter *"Of the Names of Substances"* that *"the making of* Species *and* Genera *is in order to general names,* and ... general Names are necessary, if not the Being, yet at least to the completing of a *Species,* and making it pass for such" (E III.vi.39: 463).

The reason complex ideas of substances need names is that nature does not make "precise and *unmovable Boundaries"* (E III. vi.27: 454). There is still *"confusion and uncertainty"* (E III.vi.40: 464) in the given patterns of ideas in human experience, and human beings need more order than is found in experience (E III.vi.36). The simple ideas that coexist in the patterns of our experience are "very numerous" (even "almost infinite"), and all of them have an "equal right to go into the complex, specifick *Idea"* that human beings construct on the basis of this pattern (E III.ix.13: 482). Locke refers to the great variety of properties a metal can have when heated and "in the Hands of a Chymist, by the application of other Bodies," and so the properties that coexist are "not easy to be collected, and to be completely known." Accordingly, different people, depending on their skill, attention, and circumstances, will construct different general ideas of gold, and this holds for all substances. Locke concludes "that the complex *Ideas* of Substances, in Men using the same Name for them, will be very various; and so the significations of those names, very uncertain" (ibid.).

Nevertheless, names introduce some stability into our ideas of substances, and for this reason Locke always defines substantial kinds in terms of an *"abstract* Idea *to which the Name is annexed"* (E III.vi.2: 439). By combining several ideas and annexing a name to it, our ideas of substances are supposed to remain steadily the same, whatever mutations the particular substances are liable to (E III. iii.19: 419). Locke anticipates this role for names in Book II when he writes: *"Names,* as supposedly steady signs of Things, and by their difference to stand for, and keep Things distinct, that in themselves are different, are the *occasion of denominating* Ideas ... by a secret and unobserved reference, the Mind makes of its *Ideas* to such Names." He adds: "This perhaps, will be fuller understood, after what I say of Words, in the Third Book, has been read and considered" (E II.xxix.10: 366–7).

In sum, for Locke there is a close tie between classification and language because the ideas humans use for classification are so unstable – either because, in the case of mixed modes, classification does not rest on any natural pattern whatsoever, or because the given patterns are too complex and fluid for our classificatory needs – that human beings must rely on the stability of outward signs, particularly words, to keep the ideas combined in general ideas together. This is why Locke concludes in Book II that "there is so close a connexion between *Ideas* and Words" that he cannot properly discuss human knowledge without focusing on language.

V

Since words are needed "even to think upon things" (D I: 166), specifically to *"comprehend several particular Things"* (E III.i.3: 402), Locke worries that in our thinking words come to replace our ideas. Most human beings, if not all, Locke writes, "in their Thinking and Reasonings within themselves, make use of Words instead of *Ideas"* (E IV.v.4: 574). Since our ideas are unstable, Locke maintains that

when we would consider, or make Propositions about the more complex *Ideas,* as of a *Man, Vitriol, Fortitude, Glory,* we usually put the Name for the *Idea*: Because the *Ideas* these Names stand for, being for the most part imperfect, confused and undetermined, we reflect on the *Names* themselves because they are more clear, certain, and distinct, and readier occur to our Thoughts, than the pure *Ideas*: and so we make use of these Words instead of the *Ideas* themselves, even when we would meditate and reason within ourselves, and make tacit mental Propositions. (E IV.v.4: 575)

For example, instead of using the word 'man' annexed to our complex idea of man in order to add stability to the complex idea, we replace the complex idea with the name 'man'.

In this way words are a *"Medium* through which visible objects pass,"* and they "impose upon our Understandings" (E III.ix.21: 488). In fact, words "interpose themselves so much between our Understandings, and the Truth ... that ... their Obscurity and Disorder does not seldom cast a mist before our Eyes" (ibid.). This role words appear to have in Locke's philosophy conflicts with his central view that *"the Mind*, in all its Thoughts and Reasonings, hath no other immediate Object but its own *Ideas"* and consequently that "our Knowledge is only conversant about them" (E IV.i.1: 525). Locke concludes that it is "evident, the Mind knows not Things immediately, but only by the intervention of the *Ideas* it has of them" (E IV.iv.3: 563). If words "interpose themselves ... between our Understandings, and the Truth," then ideas are not the only immediate objects of our understanding.

This conflict also infects Locke's discussion of propositions. Locke writes at the end of Book II of the *Essay* that the reason language is relevant to the human understanding is that all human knowledge "consists in Propositions" (E II.xxxiii.19: 401; also III.ix.21). Locke identifies "two sorts of Signs commonly made use of" in propositions, namely, ideas and words; accordingly, there are mental and verbal propositions (E IV.v.2: 574). Mental propositions consist of ideas, and verbal propositions, as he writes, *"are Words ... put together or separated in affirmative or negative Sentences"* (E IV.v.5: 575–6). Sometimes, according to Locke, knowledge consists of sentences (E III.ix.21: 488). But knowledge has ideas only as immediate objects, and consequently knowledge cannot *consist* in sentences, that is, words cannot be proper parts of human knowledge.

One way of resolving this conflict is to suppose that Locke was careless and that for Locke, strictly speaking, when we rely on language in our thinking, the *immediate* objects of such thoughts are *ideas* of words, not words themselves. For example, strictly speaking, when the word 'gold' comes to replace the idea of gold, the idea of the word 'gold' replaces the idea of gold in thinking and reasoning about gold.

Unfortunately, Locke is not clear about this issue, and the historical context offers few clues. Both Hobbes and Leibniz assign an important role to language in human reasoning, particularly abstract reasoning. In the *Leviathan*, Hobbes defines reason as "nothing but *Reckoning* (that is, Adding and Subtracting) of the Consequences of generall names" (Hobbes 1996: 1.v: 32), and Leibniz allows for "blind" or "symbolic" thinking, where human beings "use ... words ... in place of the ideas" they have of objects (1960: VI: 423; 1970: 292). Unfortunately, there is too much room for interpretation about whether they mean literally that words themselves are constituent parts of these thoughts or hold the weaker view that *ideas* of words are constituents of these thoughts, and that words function only as causes of these ideas.[14]

Condillac is clearly committed to the stronger thesis in his *Essai sur l'Origine des Connaissances Humains* (Essay Concerning the Origins of Human Knowledge), first published in 1746 and translated into English in 1756 with the subtitle *Being a Supplement to Mr. Locke's Essay on the Human Understanding*.[15] Condillac maintains that the human understanding is so dependent on language that Locke should have incorporated Book III of the *Essay* into Book II, which is devoted to the origins of ideas (1947: I: 5). For Condillac, external symbols are constitutive of human reasoning: chains of human reasoning actually include words (Ricken 1994: 80). What makes the voluntary control over the mind's operations possible is the ability to voluntarily produce *signs*, and not simply the ability to produce *ideas of signs* (Condillac 1947: I: 21–4). However, Condillac sees his own position as correcting shortcomings of Locke's philosophy (1947: 5), suggesting that Condillac himself thought Locke was not clear enough about the role language plays in human reasoning.

Kretzmann (1968: 196) offers some textual evidence that suggests that Locke holds the weaker thesis. Locke defines words as articulate sounds (E II.xviii.3; III.i.1), and Kretzmann maintains

---

[14] See Dascal 1987; Losonsky 2001: 160–3, 171–3; and Pécharman 1992.
[15] On Locke's reception in France, see Bonno 1990; Yolton 1991; and Aarsleff 1994.

that, for Locke, every sound is an idea and hence words are ideas (1968: 190). Additional evidence, I believe, is the passage from Book IV quoted at the start of this section. This is the passage where Locke argues that we use names instead of complex ideas, such as the idea of *man* or *vitriol*, "because they are more clear, certain, and distinct, and readier occur to our Thoughts, than the pure *Ideas*: and so we make use of these Words instead of the *Ideas* themselves, even when we would meditate and reason within ourselves, and make tacit mental Propositions" (E IV.v.4: 575). His use of the phrase 'pure *Ideas*' suggests that Locke believes that when we use words to think, we rely on *impure* ideas, that is, ideas of words rather than ideas of the qualities of objects.

Still more evidence is Locke's claim that "when we make any Propositions within our own Thoughts, about *White* or *Black*, *Sweet* or *Bitter*, a *Triangle* or a *Circle*, we can and often do frame in our Minds the *Ideas* themselves, without reflecting on the Names" (ibid). This again suggests a contrast between "*Ideas* themselves," for example, ideas of black or sweet, on the one hand, and ideas of names that we have when "reflecting on the Names," for example, ideas of the words 'black' or 'sweet'. Finally, when Locke writes that words play a role even in unspoken ("tacit") mental propositions, he describes this use of words in tacit mental propositions as reasoning "within ourselves," which strongly suggests that Locke again has *ideas* of words in mind, because mental propositions "within ourselves" can consist only of ideas.

Nevertheless, these passages are not decisive, and there are passages where Locke clearly distinguishes between words and ideas. In the concluding chapter of the *Essay*, Locke describes "*Ideas* and *Words*, as the great Instruments of Knowledge" (E IV.xxi.4: 721). Locke also writes that "Words, by their immediate operations on us, cause no other *Ideas*, but their natural Sounds" (E II.xviii.3: 224), that they are "external sensible Signs" that allow us to communicate "invisible *Ideas*" (E III.ii.1: 405), and that "Words ... do really exist without me" (E IV.xi.7: 634). These passages not only distinguish between words and ideas, but also strongly suggest that words are qualities or powers in objects that produce ideas in us, and not ideas in the human understanding (E II.viii.8: 134). After all, if words were ideas, which for Locke are private, invisible, and inaudible to others, they could not be used to communicate our ideas to other people. Therefore, I think the judicious conclusion is that Locke simply had not worked through this issue carefully.

VI

If Locke's concept of signification is a concept of linguistic meaning, then Locke's *Essay* should exhibit close ties among the terms 'signification', 'meaning', and 'definition', and this is indeed the case. Locke writes that "Definitions [are] ... only the explaining of one Word, by several others, so that the meaning, or *Idea* it stands for, may be certainly known" (E III.iii.10: 413). To define a word is to give its meaning:

I think, its is agreed, that *a Definition is* nothing else, but *the shewing the meaning of one word by several other not synonymous Terms.* The meaning of Words, being only the *Ideas* they are made to stand for by him that uses them; the meaning of any Term is then shewed, or the word is defined when by other words, the *Idea* it is made the Sign of, and annexed to in the Mind of the Speaker, is as it were represented, or set before the view of another; and thus its Signification ascertained. (E III.iv.6: 422)

Although 'signification' is Locke's preferred term, Locke's use of 'meaning' is not infrequent or casual.[16] Locke uses 'meaning' twice in the crucial second chapter of Book III, where he introduces signification. The first occurrence is in section 3 of Chapter ii, where Locke writes:

This is so necessary in the use of Language, that in this respect, the Knowing, and the Ignorant; the Learned, and Unlearned, use the *Words* they speak (with any meaning) all alike. They, *in every Man's Mouth, stand for the* Ideas *he has,* and which he would express by them. (E III.ii.3: 406)

The second occurrence is in the last sentence of this chapter:

But whatever be the consequence of any Man's using of Words differently, either from their general Meaning, or the particular Sense of the Person to whom he addresses them, this is certain, their signification, in his use of them, is limited to his *Ideas,* and they can be Signs of nothing else. (E III.ii.8: 408)[17]

---

[16] *Pace* Ashworth 1998: 183. For results of a search of the electronic text, see Losonsky 1994.

[17] The terms 'Meaning' and 'Sense' in this passage were added in the fourth edition (1700) of the *Essay.* Ashworth (1998: 183), who misses the first occurrence but

Locke uses 'meaning' and 'signification' synonymously in other important passages. In his discussion *"Of the Abuses of Words,"* Locke writes that one way in which people abuse words is when they *"imagine so near and necessary a connexion between the names and the signification* they use them in, that they forwardly suppose one cannot but understand what their meaning is." A consequence of this, Locke continues, is that they "never trouble themselves to explain their own, or understand clearly others meaning," and are surprised if you ask them for "the meaning of their Terms" (E III.x.22: 503). When discussing "remedies" for the abuse of language, Locke writes that if a speaker deviates from common use, "it is sometimes necessary for the ascertaining the signification of Words, to *declare their Meaning"* (E III.xi.12: 515).

Although Locke's account of signification is an account of linguistic meaning, it must be admitted that he does not sharply distinguish between sense and reference. When Locke introduces the concept of signification, it seems that he has primarily sense in mind. He is aiming to explain what the understanding and intelligibility of speech consists of, and he explains this in terms of the signification of ideas (E III.ii.2). This is corroborated by the fact that Locke frequently uses 'express' when discussing what ideas signify – for example, when he writes that a name is used to "express and signify" ideas (E II.xxxi.4: 377).[18] A particularly telling passage occurs in the second chapter of Book III, where Locke brings together meaning, expression, and signification: "the Knowing, and the Ignorant; the Learned, and Unlearned, use the *Words* they speak (with any meaning) all alike," namely, "[t]hey, *in every Man's Mouth, stand for the* Ideas *he has,* and which he would express by them" (E III.ii.3: 406).

While in these passages Locke has something like sense in mind, Locke's discussion of signification often appears to aim at

---

notices this second one, maintains that here Locke is *contrasting* meaning and sense, on the one hand, and signification, on the other. This is a strained reading of this passage. Locke is simply distinguishing among the ideas that people usually have when using a word, the idea that a hearer may have upon hearing a word, and the idea that a speaker has when using it. Locke's point is that a speaker is always limited to signifying her own ideas.

[18] Also see E III.ii.6; III.v.14; III.vi.44; III.vii.5; III.ix.9; and III.x.10, among many other places where Locke uses 'express' to discuss signification.

reference – for instance, when he writes that human beings "would not be thought to talk *barely* of their own Imaginations, but Things as really they are; therefore they *often suppose their Words to stand for the reality of Things*" (E III.ii.5: 407). What people often suppose, Locke seems to be saying, is that their words refer to the reality of extramental objects, and this is especially true of the substance terms. Locke writes that "*common Names of Substances ... stand for Sorts*" (E III.vi.1: 438; also III.vi.4), which for Locke is "*nothing but the ranking them under distinct Names, according to complex* Ideas *in us*" (E III.vi.8: 443).

That Locke's concept of signification mixes sense and reference is not surprising. Frege himself begins with a concept of content that combines sense and reference, and his "splitting of content" into sense and reference is an achievement of Frege's essay "On Sense and Reference" (Beaney 1996: 151–2). What Locke's concept of signification captures is a pre-theoretical concept of linguistic meaning that does not sharply distinguish between sense and reference. The fact that it is still far from settled whether an adequate account of linguistic meaning must involve senses, what speakers have in mind, referential relations, referents, or all of the above underscores the ambiguity that still prevails in the concept of meaning. The ambiguities of Locke's concept of signification track the ambiguities of our own concept of *meaning*.

Locke's position in the *Essay* about the legitimacy of the supposed reference of names to extramental objects appears to vacillate. He calls it "a perverting the use of Words" (E III.ii.5: 407) and says that it is an "*Imperfection of Words*" (E III.ix, Chapter Title) when words "are made to stand for, and so their signification is supposed to agree to, *The real Constitution of Things*" (E III.ix.12: 482). At the same time, he writes that the correct use of the names of substances requires something more than "*determined Ideas*: In these *the Names must also be conformable to Things, as they exist*" (E III.xi.10: 513). A little later, Locke writes: "For our Names of Substances being not put barely for our *Ideas*, but being made use of ultimately to represent Things, and so are put in their place, their signification must agree with the Truth of Things, as well as with Men's *Ideas*" (E III.xi.24: 520). A person who has "*Ideas* of Substances, disagreeing with the real Existence of Things, so far wants the Materials of true Knowledge in his Understanding, and hath, instead thereof, *Chimæras*" (E III.x.31: 506).

This vacillation, however, is only apparent. What is an abuse of language, according to Locke, is to suppose or assume that words refer to things *without the appropriate evidence.* In "common Controversies, and the ordinary Affairs of Life" it cannot be expected that substance terms are *"conformable to Things,* as they exist," that is, that they "represent Things" (E III.xi.10: 514). The reason is that the ideas human beings ordinarily collect into general ideas are simpler than the patterns found in nature. Human beings limit themselves to "a few sensible obvious Qualities" (E III.vi.29: 456; also III.vi.25), while nature, even as we experience it, is much more complex.[19] While these ordinary complex ideas are good enough to get by in "the Market, and the Wake" (E III.xi.10: 514), conformity to things "is absolutely necessary in Enquiries after philosophical Knowledge and in Controversies about Truth" (E III. xi.10: 513–14). When we are after truth, we aim to use terms "ultimately to represent Things," and thus we "must go a little farther" than "the ordinary complex *Idea,* commonly received as the signification" of a name of a substance (E III.xi.24: 520). We must "enquire into the Nature and Properties of the Things themselves, and thereby perfect, as much as we can, our *Ideas* of their distinct Species" (ibid.). "Therefore," Locke concludes, *"to define their Names right, natural History is to be enquired into"* (E III.xi.24: 521).[20]

In short, we cannot take for granted that our names of substances refer to something, but must ground our beliefs about the reference of our names of substances in empirical research. Although we will not attain certain knowledge about this, and there will always be some uncertainty about the reference of our natural kind terms, this is the same uncertainty that attaches to our *"Science* of natural bodies" (E IV.iii.29: 560).

It has been argued that since Locke maintains that ideas are the "proper and immediate Signification" of names (E III.ii.1: 405), any

---

[19] Locke's attack on using the obvious appearances of objects to classify them is central to his attack on Aristotelian classification of species and genera in terms of their salient perceptual qualities. See Guyer 1994: 116.

[20] Natural history is required not only because we intend that the names of substances signify "such Collection of simple *Ideas,* as do really exist in Things themselves," but also because we want these names to stand "for the complex *Ideas* in other Men's Minds" (E III.xi.24: 521).

other signification, such as signifying extramental objects, is *im*proper or incorrect (Ott 2004: 27). Consequently, Locke's concept of signification cannot include reference. This argument assumes that 'proper' is used in the sense of "correct" or "genuine" and does not admit of degrees, but 'proper' can also mean "belonging to something distinctively (more than any other)" (*Oxford English Dictionary* 1971), and in this sense propriety can come in degrees. Locke's own use of "proper" when discussing signification does admit of degrees, for example, when he writes that he thought the term 'solidity' was "more proper" than 'impenetrability', although both are acceptable (E II.iv.1: 123), or that "*active Power* ... is the more proper signification of the word *Power*" (E II.xxi.4: 235; also see II.xxxii.12). Moreover, only four lines after Locke uses the phrase "proper and immediate Signification" he writes that ideas are the "*primary and immediate Signification*" of words (E III.ii.2: 405). He is clearly restating his position and using 'proper' and 'primary' synonymously.

VII

If Locke's concept of signification is a concept of meaning that combines sense and reference, as I have argued, then it follows that for Locke, albeit confusedly, ideas are also the referents of all names. This view seems absurd enough to many readers to cast doubt on the assumption that for Locke signification is linguistic meaning (Ashworth 1998: 183), or causes them to look for qualifications and refinements in Locke's own statement of the theory. This latter approach drives Kretzmann's (1968) interpretation that Locke distinguishes between immediate and mediate signification, suggesting that the former is sense, while the latter is reference. Accordingly, when speakers use the term 'sun', they are referring not to the idea of the sun, but to the sun itself. The idea of the sun is the sense of that term, but the sun itself is its referent.

Kretzmann's refinement leaves Locke still committed to the view that ideas are the senses of words, but Locke's position is sufficiently qualified to avoid the easiest objections to this view. Most importantly, Locke does not assume that the sense of *every* word is an idea. While there is some initial plausibility to the view that the sense of a name or a categorematic word is an idea, the suggestion that the copula 'is' or the conjunction 'but' signifies an idea certainly seems implausible. But Locke explicitly excepts particles and syncategorematic words such as 'is', 'not', and 'but' from his theory that names signify ideas. Particles do not signify ideas, but instead exhibit "the several Postures of the Mind" and are *"marks of some Action, or Intimation of the Mind"* (E III.vii.4: 472). In order to properly understand the particles of language, Locke writes, we need to study "the several views, postures, stands, turns, limitations, and exceptions, and several other Thoughts of the Mind" (ibid.)[21]

Although Kretzmann's strategy is available for developing Locke's theory, Locke himself simply does not distinguish between sense and reference, and consequently Locke cannot be absolved fully of the charge of semantic idealism. After all, Locke does state quite simply that "Words ... are names of *Ideas*" or "referr" to ideas (E III.vii.1: 471 and III.iv.17: 428; also II.xxvii.7; II.xxxi.6; III. iv.1; and III.vi.51). But Locke can be cleared of the charge that all names refer *only* to ideas. While names of mixed modes indeed refer to complex ideas and nothing else, "in *Substances* it is not so" (E III. x.19: 501) because when human beings seek to "speak of Things really existing, they must, in some degree conform their *Ideas* to the Things they would speak of" (E III.vi.28: 456). In these situations, we can claim also to name extramental objects in addition to ideas as long as we have appropriate evidence that the ideas our names of substances signify conform to objects.

Was Locke's belief that our names refer to ideas so absurd? Mill, in his critique of Locke, thought so and aimed to refute Locke quickly with the observation that "When I say, 'The sun is the cause of day,' I do not mean that my idea of the sun causes or excites in me the idea of day" (1974: VII: I.ii.1). Of course, Mill's paraphrase is sloppy, and therein lies its force. First, it does not analyze "cause" correctly. According to Locke, the appropriate idea of cause in cases where we are dealing with complex ideas of natural substances is an idea of "constant change of ... *Ideas*," that is, a regularity of our ideas (E II.xxi.1: 233). Although when reflecting on our own mental operations we have a clear idea of an active power that excites or brings about changes, we do not have a clear idea of

---

[21] For example, see Locke's analysis of the various senses of 'but' (E III.vii.5).

such a power when it comes to natural bodies like the sun (E II. xxi.4: 235). All that is clear in the case of the sun are the regularities and changes of ideas associated with the idea of the sun. So the proper Lockean paraphrase is that what I mean, in part, when I say "The sun causes the day" is that my idea of sun is regularly connected with the idea of day, which is more plausible than Mill's incomplete paraphrase.

But on Locke's account this would be only part of the meaning. In the case of substances, we also aim to refer to things themselves, and thus we also have a secondary reference in mind. When I say, "The sun is the cause of day," I also mean that the thing that conforms or agrees with my idea of the sun has an active power to bring about what conforms to my idea of day. Consequently, the statement "The sun is the cause of day" has, if true, "a double *reference*" (E III.ix.12: 482). It immediately refers to the ideas of the person making the statement, but it also has a secondary reference, namely, to the things that conform to or agree with those ideas. I can refer to things themselves, on Locke's philosophy, but only indirectly as the objects that conform to my ideas. Direct reference, as far as human beings are concerned, is possible only to the ideas of the human understanding.

Appropriately qualified, Locke's account might still be false, of course, but it is far from absurd. It is Locke's fundamental view that our access to nature apart from us is indirect, mediated by our ideas – that indeed there is a veil of perception that hangs between the mind and "Things themselves" (E IV.iv.3: 563).[22] If we take this view seriously, then what our mind encounters primarily and immediately are phenomena. I do not perceive the sun itself, but the sun-as-I-experience-it, or the sense data I have when perceiving the sun (Bennett 1971: 27). So when I use language to refer to what I experience, I refer to phenomena, and the perceived sun is no less phenomenal than a flower's scent or Macbeth's "dagger of the mind" (*Macbeth* II.i).

None of this precludes that in addition to phenomena we can also aim to refer to objects themselves. Just as Macbeth wonders if the

---

[22] Locke frequently uses the locution 'things themselves' (for instance, E II.xxx.2; II. xxxii.18; III.xi.24; and IV.iii.23) and even uses the Kantian phrase 'Things in themselves' (E II.xxxii.8: 386).

dagger of his mind is "a false creation, Proceeding from the heat-oppressed brain," I can wonder if there is something that conforms or agrees with the 'sun of my mind' and gather evidence that indeed there is. I can also aim to refer to it, and when something indeed agrees with my idea of the sun, I succeed. On the other hand, "he that hath *Ideas* of Substances, disagreeing with the real Existence of Things, so far wants the Materials of true Knowledge in his Understanding, and hath, instead thereof, *Chimæras*" (E III.x.31: 506). In such cases, he still refers to the ideas he has, but fails to refer to things themselves.

In sum and in Locke's terms, names *"in their primary and immediate Signification, stand for nothing, but the* Ideas *in the Mind of him that uses them,"* but they *"stand also for the reality of Things"* when persons who use them "conform their *Ideas* to the Things" (E III.ii.2: 405; also III.ii.5; III.vi.28). When the signified ideas do not conform, the speaker is still signifying something – ideas – but not the things themselves. Not only is this view not absurd, but it might even be true. When I refer to an object before me as I am looking at it, I believe with some justification that what I am directly perceiving is a product of visual processing and a property of my nervous system, just as the pain in my foot is in my brain and not in my foot. Still, I also believe with some justification that what I am perceiving is a product of causal interaction with external objects in my environment that, in an important and relevant sense, agree with my experience.[23] So when I refer to phenomena before me, I also wish to refer to those external objects, even if they may be quite different from the color and solidity that I am directly perceiving. Locke's theory of "double reference" serves this point of view and is worthy of proper development.

---

[23] I am assuming that there are phenomenal objects of experience, or qualia, that have the qualities that are experiences – for example, when I perceive something red, there is a red experience. This assumption conflicts with the contemporary naturalist suggestion that there are no phenomenal objects and that, strictly speaking, mental states do not have objects but only intensional or representational properties (Harman 1990; Jackson 2003). Although my Lockean assumption may be false, it certainly is not absurd and has a firm place in the history of philosophy.

11 Locke on Knowledge

The primary aim of this essay is to explain the central elements of Locke's theory of knowledge. A secondary aim arises from the official definition of knowledge introduced in the opening lines of Book IV. Though Locke's repeated statements of the definition are consistent with the initial formulation, the consensus view among commentators is that the official definition is in tension with other Book IV doctrines. My broader interpretation involves an effort to render the various doctrines consistent with the official definition.

The order of discussion: section 1 explicates the definition of knowledge. Section 2 explains two main divisions of knowledge – namely, its three degrees, and the four sorts of knowable truths. In section 3, I consider whether Locke understands knowable truths on a model of analyticity. Section 4 addresses potential problems about the objectivity of knowledge, given Locke's account. Section 5 focuses on knowledge of the external world – Locke calls this "sensitive knowledge," and it poses special difficulties for the official definition of knowledge.

1. DEFINITION OF KNOWLEDGE

Book IV opens with a statement of the definition of knowledge, along with its rationale:

§1. SINCE *the Mind*, in all its Thoughts and Reasonings, hath no other immediate Object but its own *Ideas*, which it alone does or can

---

[1] I would like to thank Sam Rickless, Shaun Nichols, David Owen, Paul Hoffman, Tom Lennon, Nick Jolley, Alan Nelson, Vere Chappell, and several audiences (including the 1999 New England Colloquium in Early Modern Philosophy, the 2001 meeting of the Pacific Division of the American Philosophical Association, a 2002 meeting of the Cartesian Circle in Irvine, and the 2005 meeting of the Pacific APA) for helpful feedback on various ideas in this essay.

contemplate, it is evident, that our knowledge is only conversant about them.

§2. *Knowledge* then seems to me to be nothing but *the perception of the connexion and agreement, or disagreement and repugnancy of any of our Ideas.* Where this Perception is, there is Knowledge, and where it is not, there, though we may fancy, guess, or believe, yet we always come short of Knowledge. . . . (E IV.i.1–2: 525)

(For brevity, I typically refer simply to an "agreement" of ideas, not to an "agreement or disagreement.") These opening two articles together entail that in referring to agreements *of* ideas Locke means agreements *between* ideas. The express rationale (§1) for the definition makes no sense except on a between-ideas understanding of the definition.[2] Locke chooses as the heading for §2, "Knowledge is the Perception of the Agreement or Disagreement *of two Ideas*" (ibid., my italics); and later, in summarizing the entire range of cases of knowledge, he states the definition in terms of an agreement "of any two *Ideas*" (E IV.ii.15: 538). Commentators generally worry that the between-ideas formulation is in tension with Locke's commitment to existential knowledge – an apparent tension to which I return in sections 2, 3, and 5. My interpretation assumes the between-ideas understanding of the definition. Note too that the definition entails that the objects of knowledge are true propositions, because Locke takes the latter to be constituted by agreements between ideas.[3]

My aim in the present section is an explication of the definition just given. I first explain (a) the requirement, of knowledge, that the idea agreement is to be *perceived*; then (b) the restriction of

---

[2] Elsewhere (2004) I elaborate the case for the between-ideas understanding of the definition.

[3] Knowledge is of false propositions in the case of perceiving not agreements but disagreements. Explaining his conceptions of both truth and propositions, Locke writes: "*Truth* then seems to me, in the proper import of the Word, to signify nothing but *the joining or separating of Signs, as the Things signified by them, do agree or disagree one with another.* The *joining* or *separating* of signs here meant is what by another name, we call Proposition" (E IV.v.2: 574). Joining makes propositions affirmative, and separating makes them negative. Acknowledging "two sorts of Signs . . . *viz. Ideas* and Words" (E IV.v.2: 574), Locke allows for two kinds of propositions: "purely *mental Propositions*" consist of the ideas "stripp'd of Names," while *verbal* propositions include also the names (E IV.v.3: 574), as when words are "*put together or separated in affirmative or negative Sentences*" (E IV.v.5: 576).

knowledge to *ideas*; and finally (c) the relationship between Locke's account and justified true belief accounts.

First, a terminological clarification. Locke generally relegates the language of *judgment* and *belief* to cognition that falls short of strict knowledge. When the mind knows a proposition, it of course *affirms* it, and Locke sometimes uses the language of *assent* to refer to such affirmation.[4] Throughout this essay I follow Locke in my use of judgment- and belief-talk, and I use the language of assent to refer neutrally to the mind's affirmation – neutral as between knowledge and judgment.

1.a. Knowledge Requires a Perception of Agreement

The requirement that agreements of ideas be *perceived* marks a contrast between knowledge and judgment. In both, the mind perceives a relation of ideas – a proposition.[5] Only in knowledge does the mind perceive the proposition to be true – perceiving the relation to be an agreement, as opposed merely to presuming it:

[T]he Mind has two Faculties, conversant about Truth and Falsehood.

First, Knowledge, whereby it certainly perceives, and is undoubtedly satisfied of the Agreement or Disagreement of any *Ideas.*

Secondly, Judgment, which is the putting *Ideas* together, or separating them from one another in the Mind, when their certain Agreement or Disagreement is not perceived, but *presumed* to be so; which is, as the Word imports, taken to be so before it certainly appears. (E IV.xiv.4: 653; cf. IV.xvii.17)

Knowledge is grounded in perception. Judgment is grounded in presumption. Locke sometimes portrays knowledge-making perception

---

[4] Locke uses *assent*-talk for both intuitive knowledge (cf. E IV.ii.4; IV.vii.2–10) and demonstrative knowledge (cf. E IV.ii.4; IV.vii.19). In these contexts I take him to be employing assent-talk in a neutral way: he's referring to generic affirmation that happens to be directed at propositions that are known, rather than judged; he's not referring to a species of affirmation unique to knowledge. More frequently, Locke uses assent-talk not in this neutral sense, but in a narrow sense aligned specifically with *belief* (cf. E IV.xv–xvi, passim).

[5] As Locke explains to Stillingfleet, knowledge and judgment always involve a relation between ideas: "Every thing which we either know or believe, is some proposition: now no proposition can be framed as the object of our knowledge or assent, wherein two ideas are not joined to, or separated from one another" (W IV: 357f.).

in terms of *seeing* an agreement (cf. E IV.ii.2; IV.xvii.2) and judg-
ment-making presumption in terms of *taking* there to be one (cf. E
IV.xiv.3; IV.xvii.17).

Requiring that the agreement be perceived enforces a high epistemic standard. Locke is in a tradition that reserves knowledge-talk
for what we're *certain* of, as opposed to what we think *probable*. He
holds that certainty "is requisite to Knowledge" (E IV.vi.13: 588); that
"to know, and be certain, is the same thing" (W IV: 145); and
importantly, that "the highest Probability, amounts not to Certainty" (E IV.iii.14: 546). The difference between knowledge and
judgment is well illustrated in his treatment of expert testimony.
Suppose "a Mathematician, a Man of credit," demonstrates a
proposition of geometry; whereas, "another Man, who never took the
pains to observe the Demonstration," has as the "foundation of his
Assent" the testimony of the mathematician. Only the mathematician has knowledge; only his assent is grounded in "an evidence,[6]
which clearly shews the Agreement" (E IV.xv.1: 654). Like Descartes,
Locke is committed to an "epistemological individualism"[7] that
prevents knowledge from transferring from one person to another.

The notion of certainty Locke invokes is not that of sheer subjective
conviction. Though he acknowledges such convictions, the epistemic
notion of interest is connected with the success of one's perception in
revealing an agreement. He call this *certainty of knowledge*. To have
such certainty is "to perceive the agreement or disagreement of *Ideas*,
as expressed in any Proposition" (E IV.vi.3: 579f; cf. IV.iv.7).[8]

1.b. Knowledge Is Restricted to Ideas

We've seen that in introducing the definition of knowledge (E IV.
i.1–2), Locke bases it in part on the following thesis about ideas:
that because the mind "hath no other immediate Object but its own
Ideas, which it alone does or can contemplate, it is evident, that our
knowledge is only conversant about them." Elsewhere Locke
makes related statements. He characterizes an *idea* as "whatsoever
the Mind perceives in it self, or is the immediate object of

---

[6] Locke uses the language of *evidence* broadly to refer to *grounds*, whether what is
grounded is certain knowledge or probable judgment.
[7] In this terminology I follow Jolley (1999: 171).
[8] See Wolterstorff (1996: 44ff.) for a helpful discussion of Locke on certainty.

Perception" (E II.viii.8: 134; cf. W IV: 362). He explains that these immediate perceptual objects mediate the mind's awareness of external things: a man has "no notion of any Thing without him, but by the *Idea* he has of it in his Mind" (E II.xxxii.25: 393; cf. IV.iv.3). I take such statements to suggest some version of a representational theory of perception.[9] Other commentators deemphasize these texts, having Locke regard ideas not as perceptual *objects* but as mental acts or operations (cf. Ayers 1986: 17ff.; Yolton 1970: 128ff.). I propose that we take seriously Locke's references to ideas as the immediate objects of perceptual awareness. In making this thesis about ideas the basis of his definition of knowledge, I take Locke to be making two related points. The one point concerns our *apprehension* of the truths we know: in having "no other immediate Object but its own *Ideas*," it is only its ideas that the mind "does or can contemplate" in achieving knowledge. The other point concerns the nature of the *truths* thus apprehended: because we can contemplate none other than our ideas, it is "evident, that our knowledge is only conversant about them [ideas]" – the truths we apprehend express mere relations between ideas. He makes a similar twofold point elsewhere in stating that "Knowledge is founded on, and employ'd about our *Ideas* only" (E IV.ii.15: 538).

Grounding an agreement/truth by the mere contemplation of the related ideas is a form of what has come to be called a priori apprehension. The contrasting case involves apprehending a truth from experience. Though Locke's idea empiricism entails that the genesis of the related *ideas* is always experiential, apprehending their *agreement* is another matter. He views the two basic experiential sources – external sense and internal sense (reflection) – as the "Fountains of Knowledge" only in the sense that these are the sources "from whence all the *Ideas* we have, or can naturally have, do spring" (E II.i.2: 104). In perceiving agreements between ideas, the mind's apprehension arises

---

[9] Though I won't argue it here, I take it that the kind of representationist account that Locke holds entails (i) that ideas are *mental entities*, (ii) that ideas are the *immediate objects* of perceptual awareness, and (iii) that in veridical sense perception ideas *conform to* the real things producing them (though the conformity need not be one of resemblance) (cf. my 2004). On some competing interpretations involving a direct-perception account, Locke instead holds that in veridical sense perception the immediate objects of awareness are extramental things themselves. See the essay by Thomas Lennon in the present volume for a powerful defense of a nonrepresentationist interpretation.

from a contemplation of the ideas alone, not from an experienced connection. Hume helped to clarify a related distinction, writing that the objects of enquiry "may naturally be divided into two kinds, to wit, *Relations of Ideas*, and *Matters of Fact*." Propositions of the first sort "are discoverable by the mere operation of thought, without dependence on what is any where existent"; while propositions of the second sort are discoverable "entirely from experience, when we find, that any particular objects are constantly conjoined with each other" (Hume 1748: §4: 108–09). Hume's distinction overlaps Locke's distinction between knowledge and judgment. In judgment, the mind's apprehension is grounded not in the mere contemplation of the related ideas, but in experience: the mind presumes an agreement, writes Locke, that "it does not perceive, but hath observed to be frequent and usual" (E IV.xvii.17: 685). Describing exemplary cases of judgment, Locke notes that the mind is "left only to Observation and Experiment"; the ideas "have a constant and regular connexion, in the ordinary course of Things" (E IV.iii.28: 558–9).

Does Locke hold that knowledge, insofar as it is a priori, is of necessary truths? The texts suggest that he does. At issue is the nature of the agreement – the connection. Recall that the official definition of knowledge is in terms of perceiving the "connexion and agreement," or, in the case of knowledge of falsehoods, perceiving the "disagreement and repugnancy" of the two ideas (E IV.i.2: 525). That knowledge of falsehoods would entail a perception of *repugnancy* – what Locke at one point equates with an *incompatibility* (E IV.iii.15: 546) – suggests that knowledge of truths entails a perception of *necessity*. This suggestion finds expression in passages discussing general knowledge, contexts in which Locke regularly refers to the agreement as a *"necessary Connexion"* (cf. E IV. iii.16: 548, passim). Perhaps surprising is that his understanding of knowable agreements in terms of necessary connections is not limited to cases of general knowledge. Locke indeed frames the E IV.xi discussion of external-world knowledge in terms of the conditions needed for the account to enable the apprehension of a *necessary connection*.[10] In section 3, I address whether Locke understands necessary connections on a model of analyticity.

---

[10] He opens that discussion by clarifying the need to employ ideas of *sensation*, not memory, "there being no necessary connexion of *real Existence*, with any *Ideas* a

Our interpretation portrays Locke as a moderate skeptic. Unlike thoroughgoing skeptics, he allows for genuine achievements of knowledge. Unlike commonsense realists, he denies that ordinary knowledge claims about the world are typically among such achievements. The Introduction to the *Essay* casts this cognitive situation in an optimistic light. There Locke explains that many situations are ill-suited to knowledge, though they allow for practical assurances: an appreciation of the limits of knowledge makes us less likely to "perplex our selves and others with Disputes about Things, to which our Understandings are not suited" (E I.i.4: 45); an appreciation of the achievements possible in mere judgment makes us less likely to "peremptorily, or intemperately require Demonstration, and demand Certainty, where Probability only is to be had" (E I.i.5: 46). The clarification helps us to avoid skepticism, because in "extending their Enquiries beyond their Capacities," inquirers are apt to "increase their Doubts, and to confirm them at last in perfect Scepticism" (E I.i.7: 47). In short, "when we know our own *Strength*, we shall the better know what to undertake with hopes of Success" (E I.i.6: 46).

1.c. Locke's Account in Relation to Justified True Belief Accounts

In stating his definition, Locke is clear that knowledge is "nothing but" the perception of an agreement of ideas, that "in this alone it consists" (E IV.i.2: 525). These statements appear to establish that he understands the *perception of agreement* as wholly constitutive of knowledge – not merely as a central element of it. Thus understood, Locke's account falls outside of the tradition rendering knowledge as *justified true belief*, a tradition widely thought to trace to Plato. I suggest that this distinction between Locke and the

---

Man hath in his Memory" (E IV.xi.1: 630); the account thus focuses on "the actual receiving of *Ideas* from without" (E IV.xi.2: 630). At the close of the discussion, Locke clarifies that the reason such knowledge only "*extends as far as the present Testimony of our Senses*, employ'd about particular Objects, that do then affect them, *and no farther*" is precisely that, otherwise, "there is no necessary connexion" at play (E IV.xi.9: 635). The dual-cognized-relations account of sensitive knowledge that I attribute to Locke (to be discussed) helps to resolve the tension inherent in holding that knowledge of nongeneral truths involves apprehension of a necessary connection.

tradition is, in one regard, merely verbal; in another regard it is more substantive, albeit a distinction without any epistemic difference.

The merely verbal regard concerns terminology. As we've seen, Locke restricts *belief*-talk to cases of probable judgment. This merely verbal difference is easily resolved, however, for one can recast the traditional account in terms of *justified true assent*.

A substantive difference remains. For Locke, the mind's assent to an agreement is distinct from its perception of the agreement. He maintains, like Descartes, that having the right sort of perception is what "makes the Mind assent":

For that which makes the Mind assent to such Propositions, being nothing else but the perception it has of the agreement, or disagreement of its *Ideas*...(E IV.vii.9: 595)

The perception is the *ground* of assent (cf. E IV.xviii.9); the *reason* of the assent (cf. E IV.vii.2). It follows that the assent is not a constitutive element of knowledge. For in being "nothing but" the perception of agreement, knowledge is effectively reduced to the *justified truth* part of the traditional rendering: agreements constitute *truths*; perception of them constitutes having a knowledgeworthy ground – having epistemic *justification*.[11] Knowledge consists entirely in having the right sort of apprehension; being in the right sort of doxastic state is in no way constitutive of knowledge.[12]

There is, therefore, more than a merely verbal difference between Locke's account and justified true assent accounts. But the difference is of no practical epistemic significance, precisely because Locke holds that the mind *always* assents to what it

[11] The express jargon of *justification* is, of course, optional to the point being made. Whether one insists, with Locke, that the truth be perceived with certainty – or instead be indubitable, or apprehended reliably, or whatnot – these amount to variations on the theme of grounding a proposition.
[12] Note that on interpretations that render the mind's perception of an agreement *identical* with its assent (cf. note 14), Locke's account *does* fall within the justified true assent tradition. My contention that, to the contrary, his account falls outside that tradition depends not on any particular view as to the nature of assent, but only on his denying that the perception and the assent are identical. As to its nature, I am aware of no texts that directly settle whether Locke conceives of assent as more properly a mode of the will or of the understanding (in accord with his E II.xxi.5 distinction). Indirect textual arguments can be made on behalf of either reading.

knows.[13] His broader commitments thus imply that there is knowledge if, and only if, there is justified true assent.[14]

---

[13] Even for some cases of judgment, Locke thinks assent is typically unavoidable. He holds that in cases involving sufficiently "cogent and clear" support for an agreement, the inquirer "cannot refuse his Assent"; and of cases involving undisputable testimony, Locke writes: "In all such Cases, I say, I think it is not in any rational Man's Power to refuse his Assent; but that it necessarily follows, and closes with such Probabilities" (E IV.xx.15: 716f). In these regards, Locke contends that assent in judgment "is no more in our Power than Knowledge" (E IV.xx.16: 717). In other kinds of cases, Locke allows that "Assent, Suspense, or Dissent, are often voluntary Actions" (E IV.xx.15: 716).

[14] The foregoing analysis assumes that Locke distinguishes the following cognitive elements: (i) the justifying apprehension (i.e., the *perception* of the agreement); (ii) the *proposition* that's true (i.e., the agreement); and (iii) the mind's *assent* (i.e., the affirmation). Such assumptions have recently been challenged in the literature. One sort of competing interpretation conflates (i) and (ii) – e.g., Owen writes that, for Locke, "there is no distinction between perceiving the agreement or disagreement of ideas, forming the proposition, and knowing it to be true" (1999b: 47). Another sort of competing interpretation conflates (i) and (iii) – e.g., Ayers writes that, for Locke, "it is the perception which itself constitutes the mental act of affirmation" (1991: I: 86). Contra Owen and Ayers, I take Locke to allow for three distinct kinds of steps in acquiring knowledge. First, there may be inquiry – neutral consideration of a proposition already formed, but not yet apprehended. Second, the inquiry may lead to apprehension – the perception of agreement. Third, the perception of agreement makes the mind assent. The distinctness of these steps is perhaps clearest for inquiry leading to demonstrative knowledge. Typical of such inquiry (unlike the case of self-evident propositions) is that the mind initially considers the proposition prior to perceiving whether it counts as an agreement. As Locke writes: "though in *Demonstration*, the Mind does at last perceive the Agreement or Disagreement of the *Ideas* it considers; yet 'tis not without pains and attention" (E IV.ii.4: 532). Locke therefore does not conflate (i) and (ii). Were the very *being* of the agreement itself identical to the perception of it, Locke would be mistaken in telling us that the expert mathematician perceives the same agreement that another person merely presumes (E IV.xv.1). Locke does write that in perceiving an agreement of ideas the mind "does tacitly within it self put them into a kind of Proposition affirmative or negative" (E IV.v.6: 576). But this remark immediately follows his clarification that there is, distinct from mental affirmation, a purely grammatical sort of affirmation constituted by words being "put together or separated in *affirmative or negative Sentences*" (E IV.v.5: 575f.). (For a carefully argued defense of the kind of view I mean to oppose, see the essay by David Owen in the present volume.) Neither does Locke conflate (i) and (iii). As we've seen, he holds that the perception "makes the Mind assent," rather than being identical with it. And he even allows that the assent may occur in the absence of the perception: in cases of habitual knowledge, where the mind merely remembers having perceived an agreement, rather than occurrently perceiving it, Locke maintains that the mind nonetheless "assents" (E IV.i.8: 528).

2. TWO MAIN DIVISIONS OF KNOWLEDGE

Book IV introduces several distinctions in the course of elaborating Locke's theory of knowledge. The present section focuses on divisions in terms of (a) three degrees of knowledge and (b) four sorts of knowable agreements.

2.a. Three Degrees of Knowledge

All knowledge is marked by perceptual certainty. Not all certainty is achieved via the same route. Locke's three *degrees* of knowledge arise from three different routes, or "ways of Evidence" (E IV.ii.14: 538). The resulting degrees Locke calls "intuitive" knowledge, "demonstrative" knowledge, and "sensitive" knowledge (E IV.ii).

The most certain degree is *intuitive* knowledge, wherein the perception of agreement arises via a self-evident grasp of the proposition. Among Locke's examples: "that *White* is not *Black*, That a *Circle* is not a *Triangle*, That *Three* are more than *Two*, and equal to *One* and *Two*." In such cases, there is no need for inference – "the Mind is at no pains of proving" the proposition, instead perceiving its truth simply "by being directed toward it." According to Locke, "'tis on this *Intuition*, that depends all the Certainty and Evidence of all our Knowledge," implying that intuition plays a role in the other two degrees of knowledge (E IV.ii.1: 531).

The second degree is *demonstrative* knowledge, wherein the perception of agreement arises via proof. Locke's notion of demonstration involves a literal chain of ideas. Suppose you have intuitive knowledge of two identities, A = B and B = C. By arranging the ideas A, B, and C into a chain with B in the middle, B plays the epistemic role of helping the mind to perceive that A = C. In this demonstration, B functions as the proof: "those intervening *Ideas*, which serve to shew the Agreement of any two others, are called *Proofs*" (E IV.ii.3: 532). One of Locke's examples concerns the agreement between the idea of the *sum of the interior angles of a triangle* and the idea of the *sum of two right angles*. To demonstrate this, the mind finds ideas of "other Angles, to which the three Angles of a Triangle have an Equality," while noticing that these other angles are "equal to two right ones," whereby it "comes to know their Equality to two right ones" (E IV.ii.2: 532).

Locke sometimes characterizes the distinction between intuition and demonstration in terms of epistemic directness or immediacy. Accordingly, intuition is epistemically *immediate*, in that the mind *directly* apprehends the agreement by considering the two ideas "by themselves, without the intervention of any other" – that is, not via proof but "by their immediate Comparison" (E IV.ii.1–2: 531f.). In demonstration, the perception of agreement is *mediated*, in that the mind *indirectly* apprehends the agreement between ideas – that is, "not immediately," but instead with the help of "intermediate *Ideas*" (E IV.ii.2–3: 531f.).

Importantly, this notion of *epistemic* directness or immediacy is distinct from the notion of *perceptual* directness or immediacy, though both notions involve perceptual awareness. Locke acknowledges distinct sorts of perceptual awareness: one is "the Perception of the Connexion or Repugnancy, *Agreement or Disagreement*, that there is between any of our Ideas"; another is "the Perception of *Ideas* in our Minds" (E II.xxi.5: 236, my italics). Related to the former is the notion of *epistemic* immediacy: the mind's perception of the truth value of a proposition is either direct or indirect. Related to the latter sort of perceptual awareness is the notion of *perceptual* immediacy: the mind's awareness of an (nonpropositional) object is either direct or indirect; for example, its awareness of its own ideas is direct, whereas its awareness of external things is mediated by an awareness of its ideas. A frequent mistake is to conflate these two notions of directness/immediacy.[15] Their distinctness is illustrated well in Locke's third degree of knowledge: while demonstratively apprehending a proposition, the mind's awareness of the agreeing *ideas* is perceptually immediate, though its perception of their *agreement* is epistemically mediated.

Locke's third, and least certain, degree is *sensitive* knowledge, the only degree of knowledge essentially involving veridical sensation. Unlike intuition and demonstration, sensitive knowledge purports, via sensation, both to make cognitive contact with external things and to *be* knowledge – thus encompassing an

---

[15] Many hold that if our awareness of tables and chairs is *perceptually* indirect – i.e., if we're aware of tables via an awareness of ideas of them – then our cognition *that* there are such objects, or *that* they have such-and-such properties, would have to be *epistemically* indirect. I am sympathetic to this view, though even in this example the two notions are distinct.

agreement between ideas. As I understand Locke, the key to this twofold cognitive status stems from the twofold role of *sensation*: as *veridical*, sensations stand in causal relations with external things, thus establishing a cognitive link (though not strictly a *known* link) with external reality; as *ideas*, sensations can stand in relations of agreement with other ideas, thus making possible that reflective awareness of sensation would satisfy the definition of knowledge. These dual cognized relations are both essential to achieving the third degree of knowledge. Only a relation between two ideas can strictly be known. That one of the ideas is a veridical sensation is what qualifies the known relation as *sensitive* knowledge.

How, according to Locke, do intuition, demonstration, and sensation result in *differing degrees* of certainty – "different degrees and ways of Evidence and Certainty" (E IV.ii.14: 538)? One kind of approach that would yield variations in degree is on the conception of certainty as a psychological feeling – there being felt variations of conviction. As noted earlier (section 1.a), however, this is not the epistemic conception of certainty that Locke takes to be integral to knowledge. He needs a different approach. Yet because he construes the relevant certainty in terms of a perception of agreement, a potential problem arises in that each of the three degrees results in such perception. How, then, could there *be* variations in degree?

Locke appears to ascribe the variations to the relative likelihood of error. On this reading, intuition is the most certain because of its resistance to error. Locke holds of "intuitive Evidence" that it "infallibly determines the Understanding" (E IV.xv.5: 656); he thinks "there is no room for any the least mistake or doubt" (E IV. xvii.15: 684).

Demonstration is less certain, because, unlike intuition, it is susceptible to errors of memory. In long proofs, the mind inevitably relies on memory as it surveys the links of the chain. The longer the proof, the greater the reliance, and thus an increased chance of errors of memory: "for there must be a Remembrance of the Intuition of the Agreement of the *Medium*, or intermediate *Idea*, with that we compared it with before, when we compare it with the other: and where there be many *Mediums*, there the danger of the Mistake is the greater" (E IV.xvii.15: 684). Memory does therefore explain why demonstration is "more imperfect" than intuition (E IV.i.9: 530).

One strategy to eliminate such error would restrict demonstrative knowledge to just those chains of ideas that the mind apprehends all at once. Locke invokes this strategy in early editions of the *Essay*, but he later amends his position, arriving at the view that reliance on memory is not, in itself, a disqualification: "upon a due examination I find that it comes not short of perfect certainty, and is in effect true Knowledge," so that what a man "once knew to be true he will always know to be true, as long as he can remember that he once knew it" (E IV.i.9: 528f.). This role for memory underwrites Locke's distinction between actual and habitual knowledge. *Actual* knowledge arises from "the present view" the mind has of the agreement; *habitual* knowledge arises from the memory of a "foregoing" perception of the agreement (E IV.i.8: 527f.).

Less obvious is how relative likelihoods of error account for sensitive knowledge being a yet lower "degree" of certainty. Though "not reaching perfectly to either of the foregoing degrees of certainty," writes Locke, sensitive knowledge "passes under the name of Knowledge" (E IV.ii.14: 537). But how could a degree of knowledge introduce *more* room for error than long chains of demonstration, while managing to *be* knowledge? Our interpretation of sensitive knowledge as involving dual cognized relations provides an answer. As earlier noted, sensitive knowledge has a twofold cognitive status (unlike intuition or demonstration), in that an idea of sensation stands in dual cognitive relations: it stands both in a perceived agreement with another idea, *and* in a causal relation with an external cause. Though cognition of the former relation explains why sensitive knowledge "passes under the name of Knowledge," cognition of the latter relation is integral and yet could pass for nothing stronger than probable judgment. Sensitive knowledge, therefore, incorporates the vulnerabilities of probable judgment, rendering it *more* susceptible to error than demonstration.

That the three degrees are degrees *of knowledge* underscores an important difference between Locke's account of demonstration and the contemporary notion of deduction. Locke's notion of demonstration is fundamentally *epistemic*, not logical. Demonstration is achieved only if knowledge is; proofs that fail to terminate in knowledge are ipso facto probabilistic, not demonstrative. By contrast, the notion of deduction in contemporary logic is not epistemic; the criteria by which an argument counts as deductive are independent of what anyone knows about it.[16] Nor is Locke's notion of demonstration comparable to a *sound* deduction, for neither is soundness an epistemic notion.[17]

On a related note, Locke's notion of demonstration is also distinct from Aristotelian syllogism. It is because his fundamental concerns in the *Essay* are epistemological (cf. E I.i.2) that he finds little use for syllogism. Aristotle's "Forms of Syllogism," writes Locke, "are not the only, nor the best way of reasoning ... *for the attainment of Knowledge*" (E IV.xvii.4: 671f.). Like our notion of deduction, syllogism is not knowledge-entailing. Locke thinks that the "hardest Task" in the effort to increase knowledge "is *the finding out of Proofs*" (E IV.xvii.6: 679) in *his* sense of proof – that is, the task of *"finding out* those *Intermediate Ideas"* by which we come demonstrably to know new truths (E IV.xii.14: 648). Yet it is precisely here that syllogism fails us:

The Rules of *Syllogism* serve not to furnish the Mind with those intermediate *Ideas*, that may shew the connexion of remote ones. This way of reasoning discovers no new Proofs, but is the Art of marshalling, and ranging the old ones we have already. ... A Man knows first, and then he is able to prove syllogistically. So that *Syllogism* comes after Knowledge, and then a Man has little or no need of it. (E IV.xvii.6: 679)

Locke dissociates his account of demonstration from yet another theoretical notion linked to Aristotle, namely what has come to be called *foundationism*. The foundationist doctrine to which he principally objects has it that systematic knowledge is built up from

---

[16] Locke's account does not allow for the possibility of a demonstration that has, say, good reasoning but false premises (cf. Owen 1999b: 38ff.). Arguably, Locke could recognize such distinctions, as between validity and soundness, in connection with *reason* per se. In E IV.xvii.2 he defines reason as an inferential faculty concerned with the finding and ordering of the "intermediate *Ideas*, as to discover what connexion there is in each link of the Chain"; it is "the Faculty which finds out the Means, and rightly applies them." And Locke does say, in the same chapter, that "all right reasoning may be reduced to [Aristotle's] Forms of Syllogism" (E IV.xvii.4: 671). (He does not say that demonstration itself thus reduces.) Syllogism admits of distinctions comparable to validity and soundness. Since Locke's aims in the *Essay* are epistemic, his broader treatment of reason focuses not on its logic, but on its application in realizing either knowledge or probable judgment.

[17] Note that Locke's own use of *deduction*-talk is neutral as between demonstrative proof and probable proof (cf. E IV.xvi.2; IV.xvii.18; IV.xvii.23; IV.xviii.2).

some few, self-evident, general principles: "The beaten Road of the Schools has been, to lay down in the beginning one or more general Propositions, as Foundations whereon to build the Knowledge that was to be had of that Subject" (E IV.xii.1: 639). Locke maintains, to the contrary, that *particular* truths are far more epistemically accessible than are general truths – an inversion of foundationist doctrine. And of these self-evident particular propositions, he maintains that they are not few in number, but "infinite, at least innumerable" (E IV.vii.10: 597). Locke conjectures that the genesis of the foundationist doctrine is a misguided assumption that mathematics proceeds in such a manner. Questioning the assumption in regards to the generality of our most basic knowledge, Locke asks

whether it be clearer, that taking an Inch from a black Line of two Inches, and an Inch from a red Line of two Inches, the remaining parts of the two lines will be equal, or that *if you take equals from equals, the remainder will be equals*: Which, I say, of these two, is the clearer and first known, I leave to any one to determine.... (E IV.xii.4: 641)

Locke thinks that "that which has carried them [mathematicians] so far, and produced such wonderful and unexpected discoveries" is not foundationist doctrine, but the "admirable Methods they have invented for the singling out, and laying in order those intermediate *Ideas*, that demonstratively shew the equality or inequality" (E IV.xii.7: 643). He therefore holds that his own account of demonstrative knowledge is better modeled after successful inquiry in mathematics than is foundationist doctrine.

2.b. Four Sorts of Knowable Agreements

Another of Locke's central taxonomic schemes divides knowledge according to the sorts of knowable agreements/truths. Locke explains four main sorts (E IV.i.3ff.).

The first sort – "*Identity*, or *Diversity*" – includes, as its heading suggests, identity claims. To the extent that knowledge admits of foundations, Locke thinks these claims play the foundational role (cf. E IV.vii.4). Of this first sort, Locke writes: "there can be no *Idea* in the Mind, which it does not presently, by an intuitive Knowledge, perceive to be what it is, and to be different from any other"

(E IV.iii.8: 544); "a Man infallibly knows ... that the *Ideas* he calls *White* and *Round*, are the very *Ideas* they are, and that they are not other *Ideas* which he calls *Red* or *Square*"; any doubts here will "always be found to be about the Names, and not the *Ideas* themselves" (E IV.i.4: 526).[18]

The second sort – "*Relation*" – is "the largest Field of our Knowledge" (E IV.iii.18: 548f.). Locke appears to regard this as a catchall category.[19] This hardly diminishes its importance, however, as this sort includes truths of mathematics and of morality (E IV.iii.18ff.).

The third sort – "*Co-existence*, or *necessary connexion*" – "belongs particularly to Substances" (E IV.i.6: 527). In discussing this sort, Locke reminds readers of the position articulated in Book II (cf. E II.xxiii.3ff.) whereby our ideas of varying sorts of substances are "nothing but certain Collections of simple *Ideas* united in one Subject, and so co-existing together" (E IV.iii.9: 544). The third sort of agreement particularly concerns such coexistences:

Thus when we pronounce concerning *Gold*, that it is fixed, our Knowledge of this Truth amounts to no more but this, that fixedness, or a power to

---

[18] Included in this first sort are truths about the present contents of consciousness. Locke writes that a man "can never be in doubt when any *Idea* is in his Mind, that it is there," explaining this by appeal to "it being impossible but that he should perceive what he perceives" (E IV.vii.4: 592). But this leaves unclear how such truths count as agreements between ideas. An explanation is suggested in connection with his Book II discussion of perception: "*What Perception is*, everyone will know better by reflecting on what he does himself, when he sees, hears, feels, *etc.*" – that is, "reflects on what passes in his own Mind" (E II.ix.2: 143). This implies that the general idea of perception subsumes all manner of occurring ideas, thereby suggesting how to formulate the relevant agreement. Suppose a sensation of red is occurring in my mind. To know that that idea is presently occurring – that it is *in* the present contents of my consciousness – is to perceive an agreement between that idea and my general idea of perception. (To know, in addition, that the occurring sensation is of *red* is to perceive, in addition, an agreement between that idea of sensation and my general idea of red.)

[19] Since each of the four sorts is a sort of relation, the catchall reading finds some support in the very heading "Relation" – suggesting a generic category for further relations of agreement of various odds and ends. Locke indeed says that this sort includes agreements "of what kind soever" (E IV.i.5: 526), elsewhere qualifying it to include "any *other* Relation" (E IV.iii.18: 548, italics added) – presumably, any "other" than whatever falls under the other three sorts. And of the other three sorts, he says they "deserve well to be considered as distinct Heads, and not under Relation in general" (E IV.i.7: 527). For a contrary interpretation, see Ayers (1991: I: 99f.), who argues that it is not a catchall.

remain in the Fire unconsumed, is an *Idea*, that always accompanies, and is join'd with that particular sort of Yellowness, Weight, Fusibility, Malleableness, and Solubility in *Aqua Regia*, which make our complex *Idea*, signified by the word *Gold*. (E IV.i.6: 527)

Agreements of this third sort figure importantly in the theoretical claims of natural philosophy. They figure also in practical contexts, in our ordinary object identifications.

On the theoretical front, natural philosophers wish to discover the qualities coexisting in corporeal things. This would help to explain how bodies impact one another – their power to "change the sensible Qualities of other Bodies." The account "thought to go farthest in an intelligible Explication" is the corpuscularian hypothesis: Locke thinks it affords a "fuller and clearer discovery of the necessary Connexion, and *Co-existence*, of the Powers, which are to be observed" (E IV.iii.16: 547). But how is knowledge of coexisting *ideas* supposed to yield an account of coexisting *qualities*? The answer lies in doctrines expounded in Book II: the "power to produce" simple ideas Locke calls a *quality* of the thing producing it (E II.viii.8: 134); such simple ideas, "being in us the Effects of Powers in Things without us," are the "Marks" by which we "distinguish the Qualities, that are really in things themselves" (E II.xxx.2: 372). This relationship suggests a way to discover connections among qualities, even though our perception strictly extends only to our ideas: namely, by finding necessary connections among our simple ideas.[20] Just as we can demonstrate "the Properties of a Square, or a Triangle" not by experiment but by contemplation of the ideas themselves, similar contemplation of our simple ideas would allow us to demonstrate how bodies impact one another – "we should know without Trial several of their Operations one upon another" (E IV.iii.25: 556). In theory, this all comes together as a promising demonstrative science of natural bodies, but Locke thinks there is a series of obstacles. For one thing, the ideas we actually have do not reveal the hoped-for

[20] Locke thus writes: "Could any one discover a necessary connexion between *Malleableness*, and the *Colour* or *Weight* of *Gold*, or any other part of the complex *Idea* signified by that Name, he might make a *certain* universal Proposition concerning *Gold* in this respect; and the real Truth of this Proposition, That *all Gold is Malleable*, would be as *certain* as of this, *The three Angles of all right-lined Triangles, are equal to two right ones*" (E IV.vi.10: 585).

connections.[21] But the "more incurable part of Ignorance" arises from our inability to conceive how there even *could* be a relevant connection between primary qualities and our secondary-quality ideas (E IV.iii.12: 545).[22] Though we observe "a constant and regular connexion, in the ordinary course of Things," the connections are "not discoverable in the *Ideas* themselves" (E IV.iii.28: 559). Locke concludes:

> In vain therefore shall we endeavour to discover by our *Ideas*, (the only true way of certain and universal Knowledge,) what other *Ideas* are to be found constantly joined with that of our complex *Idea* of any Substance. ... So that let our complex *Idea* of any Species of Substances, be what it will, we can hardly, from the simple *Ideas* contained in it, certainly determine the *necessary co-existence* of any other Quality whatsoever. (E IV.iii.14: 545f.)

Of the goal of a demonstrative "*Science* of natural Bodies," he adds: "we are, I think, so far from being capable of any such thing, that I conclude it lost labour to seek after it" (E IV.iii.29: 560).

On the practical front, the exigencies of life involve us in identifying the ordinary objects of experience. For example, I may identify an object – as being an item of food, or a dangerous animal, and so on – by comparing the coexisting simples in my complex idea of it to my existing library of ideas of various sorts of substances. In perceiving an agreement between the complex idea and an idea in the library, I not only identify it, I may *know* its sort – say, that it is a hunk of *gold*. Locke adds a caveat. Such claims are not knowable where one refers them to a supposed real essence in nature, but only insofar as they are referred to a nominal essence: it is "in this proper use of the word *Gold*" that we can "know what is, or is not *Gold*" – namely, insofar as there is "a discoverable connexion, or inconsistency with that nominal Essence"

---

[21] Locke observes that "the simple *Ideas* whereof our complex *Ideas* of Substances are made up, are, for the most part such, as carry with them, in their own Nature, no visible necessary connexion, or inconsistency with any other simple *Ideas*, whose *co-existence* with them we would inform our selves about" (E IV.iii.10: 544).

[22] Locke notes that "we can by no means conceive how any *size, figure, or motion* of any Particles, can possibly produce in us the *Idea* of any *Colour, Taste,* or *Sound* whatsoever; there is no conceivable *connexion* betwixt the one and the other" (E IV.iii.13: 545).

(E IV.vi.8: 583).[23] Properly understood, the certainty derives entirely from the composition of one's complex ideas: the proposition that *Gold is malleable* "is a very certain Proposition, if *Malleableness* be a part of the complex *Idea* the word *Gold* stands for." In terms of existential import, therefore, the resulting knowledge is of a piece with the knowledge whereby we identify chimerical objects: for there "is nothing affirmed of *Gold*, but that that Sound stands for an *Idea* in which *Malleableness* is contained: And such a sort of Truth and Certainty as this, it is to say *a Centaur is four-footed*" (E IV. vi.9: 583). Knowledge claims with existential import belong to the fourth sort of knowable agreement – to which I now turn.

The fourth sort – "*Real Existence*" – involves "*actual real Existence* agreeing to any *Idea*" (E IV.i.7: 527). This sort includes existential propositions. Locke explains three kinds of cases, one for each of the three degrees of certainty: we can achieve "intuitive Knowledge of our own *Existence*"; "demonstrative Knowledge of the *Existence* of a God"; and sensitive knowledge "of the *Existence* of any thing else" (E IV.iii.21: 552f.; cf. IV.ix.2).

This fourth sort of agreement is notorious in the secondary literature. It is virtually axiomatic among commentators that sensitive knowledge of real existence is in tension with the official definition of knowledge, where the definition is understood to require an agreement between two ideas.[24] The assumption underwriting this widespread opinion is that Locke intends the fourth sort to involve an agreement not between two ideas, but between an idea and an *actual real existence*. I reject this assumption. The relevant texts suggest, to the contrary, that Locke understands knowledge of this fourth sort to involve the perception of an agreement involving the *idea of* actual existence, not actual existence itself. Ironically, that this is Locke's meaning is most clear in the case commentators regard as most contentious, namely, sensitive knowledge. In reply to Stillingfleet, who raises precisely

---

[23] On Locke's theory of language, the "proper and immediate Signification" of the word *gold* is an *idea of* gold: "*Words in their primary or immediate Signification, stand for nothing, but the Ideas in the Mind of him that uses them*" (E III.ii.1–2: 405).

[24] Cf. Aaron 1971: 240; Ayers 1991: I: 159; Gibson 1968: 166; Green 1874–75: I: 20; Jolley 1999: 187; Loeb 1981: 58; Woolhouse 1994: 154; Woozley 1964: 48; and Yolton 1970: 109f.

the worry under consideration – objecting that existential knowledge is in tension with the official definition of knowledge – Locke explains that there is no tension because the *idea of* existence is in play:

Now the *two ideas*, that in this case are *perceived to agree*, and do thereby produce knowledge, are the *idea of* actual sensation ... and the *idea of* actual existence of something without me that causes that sensation. (W IV: 360, my italics)

Though Locke does us the favor of explicitly specifying the two ideas only for existential knowledge of the third degree, I read him to be similarly invoking the idea of existence in the other cases of existential knowledge.[25]

This understanding of the fourth sort of agreement comports with Locke's handling of the other sorts. Whether the agreement concerns an identity, a geometric figure, or a substance, knowledge is in each case achieved by perceiving agreements that involve ideas *about* the items in question – *ideas of* white and red, *ideas of* triangles, *ideas of* gold, and so on. Likewise, agreements of the fourth sort involve *ideas of* existence. That Locke intends the fourth sort to be thus similar to the other three sorts – in involving an agreement "of two ideas" – is surely the most natural reading of the opening articles of E IV.i leading up to article three, wherein the four sorts of agreements are introduced. Consider the summaries/headings of these three articles:

§ 1. Our Knowledge conversant about our Ideas.
§ 2. Knowledge is the Perception of the Agreement or Disagreement of two Ideas.
§ 3. This Agreement fourfold.

In context, "*This Agreement fourfold*" certainly refers to four sorts of agreement "*of two* ideas."

I suggest that we therefore take seriously Locke's official definition of knowledge in terms of agreements "of two ideas," taking it

---

[25] In the case of existential knowledge of God, Locke writes in reply to Stillingfleet: "I dare venture to say to your lordship, that I have proved there is a God, and see no inconsistency at all between these two propositions, that certainty consists in the perception of the agreement or disagreement of ideas, and that it is certain there is a God" (W IV: 289).

to apply even to particular existential knowledge.[26] With this understanding of existential knowledge, the apt worry properly shifts to a different potential problem – more happily, a problem Locke recognizes and addresses. Since knowledge, per se, is utterly restricted to the mind's own ideas, the *seeming* implication is that knowledge can have no relevance whatever to real things. And yet, to the contrary, Locke clearly allows for what he calls *real* knowledge – knowledge that *is* relevant to real things. Locke devotes E IV. iv to the topic, and I address it later in section 4.

Of the three kinds of cases of existential knowledge, two of them yield external-world knowledge (in the epistemologist's sense of *external*): knowledge "of the Existence of GOD by Demonstration," and knowledge "of other Things" via sensitive knowledge (E IV. ix.2: 618). Knowledge of God carries with it information about both the nature and existence of something external. Sensitive knowledge carries information only about the existence of something external – whatever its nature – that functions as the cause of sensation.[27]

3. KNOWLEDGE AND ANALYTICITY

Section 1.b argued, among other things, that Locke's notion of *perceiving* agreements is best understood in connection with *apriority*. The present section argues that his notion of perceivable *agreements* is best understood in connection with an extended form of *analyticity*. Though this interpretation is consistent with Kant's

---

[26] Rebutting Stillingfleet's insistence that a different formulation is needed for existential knowledge, Locke writes: "Your lordship is pleased here to call this proposition, 'that knowledge or certainty consists in the perception of the agreement or disagreement of ideas', my general grounds of certainty; as if I had some more particular grounds of certainty. Whereas I have no other ground or notion of certainty, but this one alone..." (W IV: 287).

[27] Distinguish perceiving the idea of sensation to agree with (as Locke tells Stillingfleet) the idea of an *external* cause, versus its agreeing with the idea of an external *corporeal* cause. What sensitive knowledge establishes is only the former – a point implied in all of the central passages treating sensitive knowledge (cf. E IV.ii.14; IV.iv.4; IV.xi). I argue this at length in Newman 2004. Locke thinks our best hypothesis gives us probability, but not knowledge, that such external causes have a corporeal nature (cf. E IV.xii.10). Some commentators read Locke as instead holding that sensitive knowledge provides knowledge of external *corporeal* existence. Cf. Mandelbaum 1964: 1–4 and Yolton 1970: 110–11, 119.

understanding of such figures as Locke – whereby a priori apprehension is always of analytic truths – it puts me at odds with the
consensus view in Locke scholarship. That view has Locke allowing
for knowable agreements that are synthetic. This standard reading
of Locke is based on an understanding of his trifling/instructive
distinction that assumes that his trifling propositions are analytic
and his instructive propositions are synthetic.[28] That assumption
entails that Locke allows for synthetic knowledge, for it is beyond
dispute that he allows for knowledge of instructive propositions. In
what follows, I first argue (a) that that assumption underwriting the
standard reading is false – that Locke's category of trifling propositions should not be equated with analytic propositions, but instead
with a special case of them; then (b) that Locke is best understood as
holding that all knowable agreements are analytic in the extended
sense of being idea-containment truths.

3.a. Trifling Propositions Are a Subset of
Analytic Propositions

Prima facie, the assumption that Locke's E IV.viii distinction
between *trifling* and *instructive* propositions anticipates Kant's
analytic/synthetic distinction enjoys textual support. Locke introduces two sorts of trifling propositions. The first sort (E IV.viii.2–3:
609–12) includes "*All purely identical Propositions.*" Locke offers
numerous examples: "*a Soul is a Soul*," "*a Law is a Law*," and so
on. The second sort of trifling proposition (E IV.viii.4–7: 612–14)
includes definitional truths: namely, "*when a part of the complex*
Idea *is predicated of the Name of the whole*; a part of the Definition
of the Word defined." If, for example, "the name *Gold* stands for
this complex *Idea* of *Body, Yellow, Heavy, Fusible, Malleable,*
'twill not much instruct me to put it solemnly afterwards in a
Proposition, and gravely say, *All Gold is fusible.*" Locke summarizes both sorts of trifling propositions as being "not instructive" –
a result owed to a *containment*; whereas *instructive* propositions
"affirm something of another" that is "not contained in it" (E IV.
viii.8: 614). It might thus seem that the trifling/instructive distinction

---

[28] Cf. Ayers 1991: I: 101; Fraser 1959 [1894]: 247, 292; Gibson 1960: 135ff.; Jolley
1999: 180f.; Owen 1999b: 42ff.; Woolhouse 1994: 163.

does indeed anticipate the analytic/synthetic distinction, and, as a consequence, that Locke allows for knowledge of synthetic propositions.

Notwithstanding the seeming support for this reading, I contend that it is mistaken. The reading presupposes that the notion of *containment* Locke invokes is of a piece with the containment of analyticity, thus making trifling propositions and analytic propositions uninformative in the same sense. Let me argue to the contrary.

Though there is no single, uncontroversial way to understand analyticity, I take as fundamental the characterization in terms of concept containment. But I will instead invoke *idea* containment, thereby expanding analyticity to include both general and particular propositions. Accordingly, analytic truths are uninformative in that the predicate idea is contained in the subject idea – nothing new is predicated. By contrast, synthetic truths are informative in that the predicate idea is not contained in the subject idea – something new is predicated. The relevant ideational containment is straightforwardly illustrated for propositions in which the predicate idea helps to compose the subject idea. For example, assume that A and B are simple ideas that combine to form the complex idea AB, and consider the proposition *AB is A*. The idea AB literally *contains* the idea A. Apply this to the proposition *Cherries are red* and assume that the complex idea of a cherry – its nominal essence – includes the simple ideas of a particular *red* color and a *roundish* shape. In this case the proposition is, like the case of *AB is A*, an idea-containment truth. Consider instead the proposition *Cherries are bitter tasting*. I take it that this is true of some cherries. Unless the nominal essence of cherry includes the idea of bitter taste, however, this is not an idea-containment agreement but is instead synthetic. Consider yet another case, the proposition *Cherries are not red*. Given the nominal essence of cherry just stated, this proposition would be an idea-containment falsehood: the subject idea includes the idea of red, thus excluding the predicate, *not red*. All idea-containment agreements involve the same broad notion of containment, though the containments may not be as straightforward as those in the cherry examples.[29] It is this

---

[29] Where the subject idea is abstract, the resulting containments may depend on idiosyncratic conceptions. For example, given one person's conception, the idea of

notion of analyticity – on the model of idea containment – that I'll argue (in section 3.b) is at play in all of Locke's knowable agreements.

My thesis concerning trifling propositions is that they are a special case of analytic propositions – a special case characterized by an additional notion of containment. Characteristic of analytic propositions is an *ideational* containment: they predicate *no new idea* not already contained in the subject idea. Characteristic of trifling propositions is that they involve, in addition, an *epistemic* containment: they predicate no new idea *not already noticed* as being contained in the subject idea. These are distinct notions of containment. Of knowable agreements, Locke writes: "it does not always happen, that the Mind sees that Agreement or Disagreement, which there is between them [the ideas]" (E IV.ii.2: 531). Using an example from contemporary logic, DeMorgan's theorems *are* analytic truths in first-order logic, whether or not the beginning logic student notices the containment. For such students the theorems are instructive, not trifling. We do not always notice everything contained in our ideas. In having the sensation of a spherical object – say, a cherry – we might fail to notice that our idea contains variations of color shading, variations helping to suggest the spherical shape. Addressing such a case in connection with the Molyneux problem, Locke notes that we suppose the object to have "uniform Colour," failing to notice that "the *Idea* we receive from thence, is only a Plain variously colour'd, as is evident in Painting" (E II.ix.8: 145). Locke does therefore allow that ideas may contain

---

bachelor contains the idea of being *not presently married*; on another's conception, it contains the idea of having *never been married*. Where instead the subject ideas are of individual substances, the details of the containment might vary from experience to experience. On one occasion, the complex idea of one's morning coffee might contain the idea of being too strong, while the next morning containing the idea of being too weak. Where the sentences involves negative predication, this introduces the possibility of indefinitely many idea-containments – there being indefinitely many possible negative conceptions. One negative conception of a triangle might explicitly contain the idea of being *not four-sided*, while another contains the idea of having *no curves*. One negative conception of the idea of white might contain the idea of being *not black*, while another contains the idea that it is *not red*. In general, how one regards what is named by the subject term is determinative of the predications that result in idea-containment agreements (cf. E IV.vii.15–18).

elements that are unnoticed.[30] But not only is the mind's notice essential to a proposition counting as trifling, Locke holds that the mind must *already* have noticed the containment – the mind must have perceived the predicated agreement *before*. It is in this sense that trifling propositions involve epistemic containment: because the mind has already perceived the agreement, Locke counts trifling propositions as epistemically uninformative – they "bring no increase to our Knowledge" (E IV.viii.1: 609).

Let's reconsider Locke's two sorts of trifling propositions in light of this understanding of them. I begin with the second sort of trifling proposition, whereby *"a part of the complex Idea is predicated of the Name of the whole; a part of the Definition of the Word defined"* (E IV.viii.4: 612). Elsewhere, Locke explains his understanding of definitions: "I think, it is agreed, that a Definition is nothing else, but the shewing the meaning of one Word by several other not synonymous Terms. The meaning of Words, being only *the Ideas they are made to stand for by him that uses them...*" (E III.iv.6: 422, italics added). Since Locke allows for variation in the ideas that different people make words stand for, definitions do likewise vary. A proposition counts as trifling, for a person, when it predicates something that that person has already noticed as being a part of the subject idea – when the predicate idea is "nothing but what he before comprehended, and signified by the name" of the subject idea. If I already know "the name *Gold* stands for this complex *Idea* of *Body, Yellow, Heavy, Fusible, Malleable,*" then, writes Locke, "'twill not much instruct me to put it solemnly afterwards in a Proposition, and gravely say, *All Gold is fusible*" (E IV.viii.5: 613). Since the containment has *already* been noticed, the proposition is trifling. Or suppose the name *triangle* is already known to stand for the idea of a three-sided figure. In this case, the proposition *Triangles are three-sided* is trifling – it conveys no information not *already* noticed: "And therefore he trifles with

---

[30] Of course, Locke needs to avoid the implication that the mind can straightforwardly have an idea without noticing it – an issue he discusses earlier in the same chapter (cf. E II.ix.3ff.; I.ii.5). But he does not require that the mind be fully cognizant of every aspect of the ideas it has – as if simply in order to have the idea of a right triangle, the mind must be cognizant of its Pythagorean properties. Locke can invoke notions of *attention* and *confusion* to explain how our ideas might actually have elements that we fail to notice (cf. E II.xxix; IV.vii.4, 10–11).

Words, who makes such a Proposition, which when it is made, contains no more than one of the Terms does, and which a Man was supposed to know before: *v.g. a Triangle hath three sides*" (E IV. viii.7: 614). Beginning geometers, however, may not notice that such ideas contain the idea of being three-angled. In that context, the proposition *Triangles are three-angled* is instructive.

The texts similarly support this epistemic interpretation for Locke's first sort of trifling proposition – namely, cases such as that "*a Soul is a Soul*", and "*a Law is a Law*" (E IV.viii.3: 610). Locke does not count all self-evident idea-containments as trifling, only those expressed by *verbal* identities wherein the same *term* is affirmed of itself. In the hope of preempting misunderstandings on this point, Locke writes that "by *Identical Propositions*, I mean only such, wherein the same *Term* importing the same Idea, is affirmed of it self" (E IV.viii.3: 611, italics added).[31] Locke is concerned specifically with cases involving verbal identity, because these are the cases guaranteed to involve epistemic containment: "For when we affirm the same Term of it self," writes Locke, "it shews us nothing, but what we must certainly know before"; "the same Word may with great certainty be affirmed of it self, without any doubt of the Truth of any such Proposition" (E IV.viii.2: 609). What is essential to self-evident propositions more generally is not this notion of epistemic uninformativeness, but merely that the mind perceive the agreement "at the first sight of the *Ideas* together" (E IV.ii.1: 531) – a characterization consistent with their being instructive, not trifling. Trifling propositions are truths "we must certainly know before," not simply "at the first sight of the *Ideas* together." Self-evident truths are *easily* known, but, unlike trifling propositions, they need not be *already* known. This way of demarcating the class of trifling truths allows for the possibility of intuitive knowledge that's instructive.

It is therefore a mistake to see Locke's trifling/instructive distinction as an anticipation of the analytic/synthetic distinction. A proposition may be analytic in the sense of an idea-containment truth without being trifling in Locke's sense.

---

[31] Ayers nonetheless concludes (cf. 1991: I: 101) that Locke, in referring to identical propositions, is referring to the entire category of identities that fall under the first sort of knowable agreement (cf. section 2.b here, and E IV.i.3–4).

3.b. The Case for an Analyticity Interpretation

I contend that, on the best reading of Locke, to perceive an agreement between ideas just is to perceive an idea-containment. Truths are knowable only if they are analytic in the sense of idea-containments. Synthetic truths are at best judgeable.[32] The case for this reading rests primarily on the nature of the claims Locke makes both in distinguishing between knowable and unknowable agreements, and in distinguishing how the mind apprehends the agreements it knows versus those it judges. These two kinds of claims dovetail with two kinds of features of analytic truths. First, in analytic truths the agreement is *intrinsic* to the ideas. Second, and as a consequence of the first, in analytic truths the agreement may be apprehended by consideration of the ideas alone. Neither of these features holds of synthetic truths, yet Locke portrays knowable agreements as having both:

> In some of our Ideas there are certain Relations, Habitudes, and Connexions, so *visibly included in the Nature of the Ideas themselves*, that we cannot conceive them separable from them, by any Power whatsoever. And *in these only*, we are *capable* of certain and universal Knowledge.[33] (E IV. iii.29: 559, italics added)

In this passage, the context concerns general truths. Similar remarks elsewhere concern *all* sorts of knowable agreements: the key to "*finding* their Agreement," writes Locke, lies in "*barely considering those Ideas*, and by comparing them one with another" (E IV.xii.6: 642, italics added).[34] Note that we can only find, or apprehend, agreements by solely considering the ideas if those agreements are intrinsic to the ideas – if, as Locke writes in the earlier text, the agreement is "visibly included in the Nature of the *Ideas* themselves" (cf. E IV.iii.14; xii.9; xv.1). That Locke holds that knowable agreements are apprehended by consideration of the ideas

---

[32] Some idea-containment truths are know*able* but not known, as in Locke's example of the demonstrable proposition of geometry that the nonmathematician merely judges (E IV.xv.1).

[33] In the continuation of this passage, Locke illustrates his remarks with a demonstrable proposition of geometry.

[34] Of course, since demonstrations depend on proofs, they rely on *further* ideas, rather than on "*barely considering those Ideas*, and by comparing them one with another." But the role of these further ideas is not to provide a bridge that is extrinsic to the original two ideas (as occurs in the case of probable proofs), but instead to help reveal the agreement that is intrinsic to them.

alone marks a contrast with his view of probable judgment. In judgment and belief, the mind's apprehension is grounded in something extrinsic to the ideas in the proposition believed:

That which makes me believe, is *something extraneous to the thing I believe*; something not evidently joined on both sides to, and so not manifestly shewing the Agreement, or Disagreement of those *Ideas*, that are under consideration. (E IV.xv.3: 655, my italics)

This way of contrasting knowledge and judgment does not square with the standard interpretation whereby knowledge extends to synthetic truths. Since synthetic truths do not consist in agreements that are "in the Nature of the Ideas themselves," it is *not* the case that "finding their Agreement" lies in "barely considering those Ideas." Kant makes a related point – that the apprehension of synthetic truths depends on something extrinsic to the ideas. With the analytic, he writes, "I keep to the given concept, in order to establish something about it"; with the synthetic, "I am to go outside the given concept, in order to consider, in relation with this concept, something quite different from what was thought in it":

If it is granted, then, that one must go outside a given concept in order to compare it synthetically with another concept, then something third is needed wherein alone the synthesis of two concepts can arise. (Kant 1996: 225)

Kant thus appeals to an elaborate system of cognitive structure in order to explain the possibility of a priori apprehension of synthetic truths. Such an appeal is unavailable to Locke. Experience is his only cognitive resource for apprehending synthetic relations among ideas, yet experiential apprehension yields at best probable judgment, not knowledge. It is therefore no surprise to find Locke explaining cases of unknowable truths in terms of the needed agreement being "remote from the nature of our *Ideas*," the "connexion being not discoverable in the *Ideas* themselves"; concluding of such cases that we're "left only to Observation and Experiment" (E IV.iii.28: 558f.). The theoretical pressures push in the direction of limiting knowable agreements to relations of idea-containment, and the texts suggest that Locke is cognizant of this.

Those who interpret Locke as allowing for synthetic knowledge have a powerful resort. They can cite apparent counterexamples – alleged cases that Locke counts as *both* knowable and synthetic.

Space doesn't permit a comprehensive examination of such cases, but I want to consider a sample. Doing so will help to clarify the kind of account I attribute to Locke. In selecting a representative sample, I follow the division into four sorts of agreements (E IV.i.3).

The first sort of agreement – "*Identity, or Diversity*" – includes such self-evident propositions as *White is not black*. But while *White is white* obviously is an idea-containment, cases of negative predication are not so obvious. Fundamental to such knowledge is noticing what Locke calls a *disagreement* between the ideas. Such a disagreement is not a mere difference, but, as he sometimes says, a "*repugnancy*" (cf. E IV.i.2: 525). I take him to mean an exclusion. The ideas of a triangle and of white do not exclude one another – I can image a *white triangle*. The ideas of white and black do exclude one another. Locke thinks that by juxtaposing the ideas in the mind we apprehend the disagreement. Though not every idea of white explicitly contains an idea of not-black, when considering them in relation to one another the mind apprehends in the idea of white that it is not black (cf. note 29). I take Locke to thus hold that such cases are analytic, whether or not trifling.

The second sort – "*Relation*" – is the catchall. Among what might seem hard cases for my interpretation, Locke thinks we know "by an intuitive Certainty, that bare *nothing can no more produce any real Being, than it can be equal to two right Angles*" (E IV.x.3: 620). Prima facie, the underlying assumption – that "*Bare nothing cannot produce something*" – looks synthetic. But attention to Locke's rendering of the component ideas shows it to be an idea-containment truth. He takes our ideas of productive power to derive from such experiences as of volitions followed by limb movements, or of motion in one body followed by motion in another (cf. E II.xxi.4). That is, the experiential concept of causal production is abstracted from experiences always involving *something* as the supposed cause or producer. As such, the concept contains the idea of something as the cause. Causal production being thus conceived, the two ideas – that of *bare nothing*, and that of a *cause/producer* – are perceived to *disagree*. They exclude one another.

The third sort – "*Co-existence, or necessary connexion*" – concerns our ideas of coexisting qualities. The few such cases that Locke thinks we actually know include that "Figure necessarily supposes Extension" (E IV.iii.14: 546) – that is, that there's a knowable agreement between the *idea of figure* and the *idea of extension*. Prima facie, this might appear synthetic.[35] Again, attention to Locke's rendering of the component ideas reveals an idea-containment truth. He holds that the idea of *figure*, or shape, is – whether by sight or touch – a modification of the idea of space, or extension (E II.xiii.5). In picturing or imaging a shape,[36] the mind thereby images extension – the figure is represented as spread out. On Locke's view, therefore, the idea of figure straightforwardly contains an idea of extension.

The fourth sort – *"Real Existence"* – might seem notably problematic for the thesis that knowable agreements are always idea-containments. Recall that Locke details the two ideas that he takes to agree: the *idea of actual sensation*, and the *idea of an external cause of ideas*. Prima facie, these ideas seem not to stand in a relation of idea-containment. But consider further details of Locke's account. He thinks a distinctive feature of ideas of external sensation is their involuntary production in the mind – they "obtrude" on the mind (E II.i.25: 118; cf. II.ii.2; II.xii.1). Where sensation is thus conceived, to regard an idea *as* an actual sensation is to regard it as an idea produced by an external cause, rather than by the will (cf. E II.xxi).[37] This rendering helps to explain why Locke would hold that the *idea of actual sensation* and the *idea of an external cause of ideas* do agree, by idea-containment.

4. KNOWLEDGE AND OBJECTIVITY

That the objects of knowledge are agreements between ideas raises potential problems about its objectivity. In the present section, I develop two strands of concern. I first consider (a) whether Locke's account of concept formation commits him to a relativism about general truths, and therefore about general knowledge; then (b)

---

[35] It has been reported to me that this example was raised in the discussion period of an APA session, with the participants concluding it to be exemplary of a synthetic proposition in Locke.

[36] Locke likens ideas to *pictures* (cf. E II.xi.17; II.xxix.8; III.iii.7, passim) as well as to *images* (cf. E II.i.15; II.i.25; II.x.5, passim).

[37] Locke is clear that this aspect of sensation plays a central role in its contribution to sensitive knowledge (cf. E IV.ii.14; IV.iv.4; IV.xi.1–2, 5).

the objection that knowledge construed as the perception of agreements of *ideas* is – as Locke's hypothetical critic puts it – "only building a Castle in the Air," and therefore worthless, because it is "the Knowledge of *things* that is only to be prized" (E IV.iv.1–2: 563, italics added).

4.a. Does Locke's Concept Relativism Imply Truth and Knowledge Relativism?

In our complex ideas of various sorts of substances, the list of ingredient simple ideas is apt to be perceiver-relative. For in the process of concept formation, the list is determined not by the external world alone, but with significant help from the mind.[38] The resulting list of simples "*depends upon the various Care, Industry, or Fancy*" of the one making the complex idea (E III.vi.29: 456). Variations arise, in part, because "in making their general *Ideas*" people concern themselves more with "the convenience of Language" than with "the true and precise Nature of Things, as they exist" (E III.vi.32: 459f.). Locke illustrates this for gold:

> But however, these *Species* of Substances pass well enough in ordinary Conversation, it is plain that this complex *Idea*, wherein they observe several Individuals to agree, is, by different Men, made very differently.... The yellow shining Colour, makes *Gold* to Children; others add Weight, Malleableness, and Fusibility; and others yet other Qualities.... And therefore *different Men* leaving out, or putting in several simple *Ideas*, which others do not, according to their various Examination, Skill or Observation of that subject, *have different Essences of Gold*; which must therefore be of their own, and not of Nature's making. (E III.vi.31: 458f.)

The world's contribution is just this: "Nature in the Production of Things, makes several of them alike." And things with like qualities produce like collections of simple ideas ready for sorting. But "the *sorting* of them under Names, *is the Workmanship of the Understanding, taking occasion from the similitude* it observes amongst them, to make abstract general *Ideas*" (E III.iii.13: 415).

This conceptual relativism might seem to underwrite a truth relativism. Since the truth of general propositions is a function

---

[38] In referring to *concepts*, I mean simply to refer to what Locke calls abstract or general ideas – ideas with general content.

solely of relations between concepts, divergent conceptions give rise to divergent truths – a worry seemingly confirmed in Locke's discussion of divergent seventeenth-century conceptions of *body*. On Descartes's conception, the whole essence of body is *extension*, that is, space. Relative to this conception, there could be no empty space in the sense of a region devoid of bodies. On the competing conception, an atomist account, extension is only one part of the essence of body, the other essential part being *solidity*. Relative to this conception, there can be regions of empty space, that is, vacua. Note that these divergent conceptions seem to give rise to divergent idea-containment truths. As Locke points out, the claim that *"Space is Body"* is a true predication, on the Cartesian conception; the claim that *"Space is not Body"* is a true predication, on the atomist conception. Propositional truth, per se, is neutral as to the correctness of the conception, depending only on the relation between the component ideas. Both propositions about space may therefore be true, though seeming to express contradictory content. And since knowledge, per se, is simply the perception of such agreements, these seemingly contradictory propositions might both be *known*. As Locke writes, a Cartesian "may easily demonstrate, that there is no *Vacuum*; i.e. no Space void of Body" – "his Knowledge, that Space cannot be without Body, is certain." Whereas, if solidity is included in one's conception, we can "as easily demonstrate, that there may be a *Vacuum*, or Space without a Body, as *Des-Cartes* demonstrated the contrary." Both cases "may be equally demonstrated, *viz*. That there may be a *Vacuum*, and that there cannot be a *Vacuum*" (E IV.vii.12–14: 604f.).

Is Locke therefore committed to a radical relativism? Specifically, is he committed to holding that numerically the same *proposition* (qua relation of *ideas*) might be true for one person, while false for another person? No. What Locke is committed to is a weaker thesis, namely, that numerically the same *sentence* (the *words*) might express a truth relative to one person's conceptions, while expressing a falsehood relative to another's.[39] Compare the two sentences *S is P* and *It is not the case that S is P*. These

---

[39] Locke himself draws the distinction in terms of contrasting sorts of propositions, rather than a contrast between propositions and sentences (cf. note 3). The underlying distinction is the same.

sentences express a *propositional* contradiction only if the terms *S* and *P* are used with the same signification in each sentence. If instead the terms signify different ideas, then we have not a propositional contradiction but an equivocation in the use of terminology. By the same diagnosis, the sentences *There can be a vacuum* and *There cannot be a vacuum* express a propositional contradiction only if the terms have the same signification in each sentence. If they do not – if in one case the term *vacuum* signifies *a region devoid of solid objects*, while in the other, *a region devoid of extension* – it is possible that the two sentences express fully consistent propositions. Locke thinks it a common mistake to suppose that there's a contradiction in such cases – the mistake of "thinking that where the same Terms are preserved," the resulting sentences "are about the same things, though the *Ideas* they stand for are in truth different." The seeming contradiction turns out to be merely "in sound and appearance," not in the ideas (E IV.vii.15: 606).

Locke is not, therefore, committed to a radical relativism about truth or knowledge. Indeed, at the level of ideas, Locke maintains that his general truths are appropriately designated as *eternal truths* – not because they're innate, but because the ideas would agree in any mind that contemplated them. Referring to general truths (and supposing the terms to signify the same ideas), Locke writes:

Such Propositions are therefore called *Eternal Truths*, not because they are Eternal Propositions actually formed, and antecedent to the Understanding, that at any time makes them; nor because they are imprinted on the Mind from any patterns, that are any where of them out of the Mind, and existed before: But because being once made, about abstract *Ideas*, so as to be true, they will, whenever they can be supposed to be made again at any time past or to come, by a Mind having those *Ideas*, always actually be true. (E IV. xi.14: 638f)

What Locke writes about the divergent conceptions of body may nonetheless seem deeply unsatisfying. One wants to say – contra what he seems to allow – that the contrary accounts of body cannot both be true, much less both known; that in such cases, at most one of the accounts could be *really* true and thus *really* known. Locke is not blind to these concerns, and he addresses them. In doing so, he indeed introduces the notions of "real" truth and "real" knowledge. Interestingly, however, he does not give up his fundamental rendering of truth and knowledge in terms of *ideas*, thus allowing that both the Cartesian and atomist accounts might actually be true and known. As will emerge, by *really* true/known Locke does not mean *actually* true/known, but something more like actually true/known *plus* something more.

4.b. Knowledge Per Se versus Real Knowledge

The definition of knowledge, per se, allows both the Cartesian and the atomist conceptions of body to give rise to genuine knowledge. Yet even Locke is convinced that the Cartesian conception gets the world wrong. It might therefore seem either that Locke's definition of knowledge is incomplete (and likewise for his rendering of truth), or that on his conception knowledge is so hopelessly bound up with subjective ideas as to be useless in inquiries concerning real objective things. Locke addresses this apparent problem in E IV.iv, titled *"Of the Reality of our Knowledge."*

IV.iv opens with a potential objection arising from the official definition of knowledge:

I Doubt not but my Reader, by this time, may be apt to think, that I have been all this while only building a Castle in the Air; and be ready to say to me, To what purpose all this stir? Knowledge, say you, is only the *perception of the agreement or disagreement of our own Ideas*: but who knows what those Ideas may be? ... If it be true, that *all Knowledge lies only in the perception of the agreement or disagreement of our own Ideas*, the Visions of an Enthusiast, and the Reasonings of a sober Man, will be equally certain. 'Tis no matter how Things are: so a Man *observe but the agreement of his own Imaginations*, and talk conformably, it is all Truth, all Certainty. ... But of what use is all this fine Knowledge of Men's own Imaginations, to a Man that enquires after the reality of Things?[40] (E IV.iv.1: 562f., italics added)

---

[40] A parallel objection arises for Locke's account of *truth*, a point he develops in the very next chapter: "here again will be apt to occur the same doubt about Truth, that did about Knowledge." The chimerical thoughts of *"Harpies and Centaurs"* count as *"Ideas* in our Heads, and have their agreement and disagreement there, as well as the *Ideas* of real Beings, and so have as true Propositions made about them" (E IV.v.7: 577).

Shifting to his own voice, Locke writes:

To which I answer, That if our Knowledge of our Ideas terminate in them, and reach no farther, *where there is something farther intended*, our most serious Thoughts will be of little more use, than the Reveries of a crazy Brain.... But, I hope, before I have done, to make it evident, that this way of certainty, by the Knowledge of our Ideas, goes *a little farther* than bare Imagination.... (E IV.iv.2: 563, italics added)

But how *could* knowledge go even "a little farther"? For given Locke's official definition of knowledge, "the Visions of an Enthusiast, and the Reasonings of a sober Man, will be equally certain" – their perceptions of agreement should count "equally" *as* knowledge.

As a first step in understanding Locke's reply to the objection, note that he takes the problem to be limited in scope. As the remarks just quoted indicate, that knowledge would "reach no farther" than our ideas makes for a problem specifically in situations "where there is something farther intended." But Locke doesn't think this situation is typical:

Nor let it be wondred, that I place the Certainty of our Knowledge in the Consideration of our *Ideas*, with so little Care and Regard (as it may seem) to the real Existence of Things: Since most of those Discourses, which take up the Thoughts and engage the Disputes of those who pretend to make it their Business to enquire after Truth and Certainty, will, I presume, upon Examination be found to be *general Propositions*, and Notions in which Existence is not at all concerned. (E IV.iv.8: 565f.)

Though Locke views the problematic cases as limited, his broader treatment of the issues is perfectly general. His solution does not involve altering his fundamental conception of knowledge – what I'll refer to as knowledge *per se*. He instead formulates a special case of knowledge that imposes a further requirement – what he calls *real* knowledge. Knowledge per se requires only the perception of an agreement between ideas. *Real* knowledge requires – in addition – that the ideas conform to the reality of which they purport to be ideas: "*Our knowledge* therefore is *real*, only so far as there is a [further] conformity between our *Ideas* and the reality of Things" (E IV.iv.3: 563); "to make our Knowledge *real*, it is requisite, that the *Ideas* answer their *Archetypes*"

(E IV.iv.8: 565).[41] The "visions of an enthusiast" can in principle satisfy the requirements of knowledge per se, but they cannot – insofar as they are delusional – satisfy the requirements of real knowledge. Consider again the divergent seventeenth-century conceptions of body. What Locke concedes to both Cartesians and atomists is an ability to achieve knowledge per se. Real knowledge is achievable only if one's ideas are real ideas (in the E II.xxx sense):

Whatever Ideas we have, the Agreement we find they have with others, *will still be knowledge*. ... But to *make it real* concerning Substances, the Ideas must be taken from the real existence of things. (E IV.iv.12: 568f., italics added)

Locke's recapitulation of the chapter clarifies the two sets of requirements:

Where-ever we perceive the Agreement or Disagreement of any of our Ideas *there is certain Knowledge*: and where-ever we are sure those Ideas agree with the reality of Things, there is certain *real* Knowledge. (E IV.iv.18: 573, italics added)

Locke adopts an analogous solution to the analogous problem that arises for truth, distinguishing between truth per se and real truth.[42]

In knowledge per se, the mind apprehends an agreement by *perceiving* it. In real knowledge, how does it apprehend the further relation between an idea and its archetype? The question is pressing, because only relations between ideas can be perceived and thus known. It is no mistake, then, that in characterizing the *real*-making requirement, Locke employs weaker epistemic language. As he writes in his recapitulation: though knowledge per se requires that "we perceive" the agreement, the further real-making requirement is merely that "we are sure" those same ideas agree

---

[41] The appeal to archetypes allows the solution to apply whether the relevant "reality of Things" is mental or extramental. Moreover, it renders the account continuous with Locke's Book II treatment of *real* ideas. Real ideas are a special case of ideas that successfully link with their intended archetypes: "By *real Ideas*, I mean such as have a Foundation in Nature; such as have a Conformity with the real Being, and Existence of Things, or with their Archetypes" (E II.xxx.1: 372).

[42] Propositional truth, per se, is defined in terms of agreements between ideas. *Real* truth is defined as a special case of truth involving also "an agreement with the reality of Things": insofar as the constituent ideas "agree to their Archetypes, so far only is the *Truth real*" (E IV.v.8–9: 577f.).

with reality. Importantly, being *sure* – having *assurances* – does not entail having perceptual certainty, though it allows it. Locke regularly uses assurance-talk in contexts of mere probability.

Under what circumstances can we achieve real knowledge? Locke explains two kinds of cases arising from "two sorts of *Ideas*, that, we may be assured agree with Things" (E IV.iv.3: 563). The first case arises from simple ideas. Since in Locke's theory simple ideas constitute veridical sensations, he maintains that they have the requisite conformity to their archetypes in virtue of being produced by them: "this conformity between our simple *Ideas*, and the existence of Things, is sufficient for real Knowledge" (E IV.iv.4: 564). This first case of real knowledge results in sensitive knowledge. This is the one sort of real knowledge guaranteeing cognitive contact with *external* real things, because it's the one case involving external archetypes.

The second case arises from "*All our complex* Ideas, *except those of Substances.*" These complex ideas give rise to real knowledge because of the status of their archetypes: "being *Archetypes* of the Mind's own making, not intended to be the Copies of any thing, nor referred to the existence of any thing, as to their Originals," they "*cannot want any conformity necessary to real Knowledge.*" As a consequence, "all the Knowledge we attain concerning these *Ideas* is real, and reaches Things themselves" (E IV.iv.5: 564). Locke thus counts mathematical ideas as real (E II.xxxi.3), such that "the *Knowledge* we have of *Mathematical Truths*, is not only certain, but *real Knowledge*" (E IV.iv.6: 565). And he extends the account to "*moral Knowledge*": like our mathematical ideas, "our *moral Ideas*" count as "*Archetypes* themselves"; and therefore "all the Agreement, or Disagreement, which we shall find in them, will produce real Knowledge, as well as in mathematical Figures" (E IV. iv.7: 565).

5. SENSITIVE KNOWLEDGE OF THE EXTERNAL WORLD

Sensitive knowledge has struck many commentators as being in tension with the official definition of knowledge. For by definition, knowledge is limited to agreements between ideas, yet sensitive knowledge purports to extend *beyond* ideas to the external causes of veridical sensation. It has therefore seemed that sensitive knowledge could not count *both* as knowledge (thus defined) *and* as external-world cognition.[43] Commentators have tended to conclude either that Locke doesn't really mean to define all knowledge in terms of an agreement "of two ideas," or else that he errs in extending knowledge to external existence.

Over the course of this essay I have put forward various elements of an interpretation that resolves this apparent tension, all the while adhering to Locke's definition of knowledge in terms of perceiving an agreement of two ideas. I have argued that sensitive knowledge essentially involves dual cognized relations arising from the twofold nature of ideas of sensation (see section 2.a). Ideas of sensation function as veridical links to the external world. They also function as *ideas* that can stand in perceivable agreement with other ideas. We've seen that Locke identifies for Stillingfleet the two ideas that can be perceived to agree (see section 2.b): the *idea of actual sensation* and the *idea of an external cause of ideas*. The appearance of tension bothering commentators does therefore rest on a false assumption: namely, that sensitive knowledge does not encompass *both* the perception of an agreement between ideas *and* a further cognized relation between one of these ideas and its external cause. By encompassing both relations, sensitive knowledge qualifies as *real* knowledge (see section 4.b).

This dual-cognized-relations interpretation explains why Locke characterizes sensitive knowledge both in the terminology of knowledge *and* in terms apropos of judgment. With regard to its known aspect, we've seen that Locke discusses sensitive knowledge in terms of necessary connections (see section 1.b), suggesting that he thinks it in line with the general picture of knowable agreements as apprehended a priori. And of the two ideas he identifies for Stillingfleet, I have argued that they comport with the understanding of knowable agreements as idea-containments, where such containments include truths about particulars (see section 3.b).

Insofar as sensitive knowledge extends beyond the mind's ideas, we should expect that Locke would support cognition of this further relation by appeal to probable judgment. It is no surprise, then, that he puts forward, in E IV.xi, a series of *probabilistic* proofs in support of sensitive knowledge. The point of the proofs is to help *assure* us

---

[43] Cf. note 24.

that the ideas we take as veridical sensations *are* veridical – that they are not mere fictions of the imagination, but do indeed give notice *"of the existing of Things without us"* (E IV.xi.3: 631). By these proofs, writes Locke, we are "confirmed in this assurance" (E IV.xi.3: 632). The assurance arises from reflecting on the manner in which the putative sensation is induced in the mind: "the having the *Idea* of any thing in our Mind, no more proves the Existence of that Thing, than the picture of a Man evidences his being in the World. ... 'Tis therefore the actual receiving of *Ideas* from without, that gives us notice of the *Existence* of other Things" (E IV.xi.1–2: 630). Our assurance is grounded in "that perception and Consciousness we have of the actual entrance of *Ideas*" from external things (E IV. ii.14: 538). The four proofs of E IV.xi amount to four ways of being sure that an idea has an external cause, rather than being fictions of the imagination.

The texts do therefore lend support to the thesis that Locke takes sensitive knowledge to involve dual cognized relations – one known, the other judged. I take his view to be that reflection on an occurring sensation does at once establish both a judged result vis-à-vis a presumed external cause, and a known result vis-à-vis the *idea of* such a cause. Locke does not offer details of how this twofold cognitive act unfolds, and further explanation is needed beyond that provided here. My principal aim has been to sketch the basis for a dual-agreements understanding of sensitive knowledge while clarifying it as consistent with Locke's official definition of knowledge.

12   Locke's Ontology

I. INTRODUCTION

One of the deepest tensions in Locke's *Essay*, a work full of profound and productive conflicts, is one between Locke's metaphysical tendencies – his inclination to presuppose or even to argue for substantive metaphysical positions – and his devout epistemic modesty, which seems to urge agnosticism about major metaphysical issues. Both tendencies are deeply rooted in the *Essay*. Locke is a theorist of substance, essence, and quality. Yet his favorite conclusions are epistemically pessimistic, even skeptical; when it comes to questions about how the world is constituted, our understandings cannot penetrate very far. Locke seems torn between metaphysics and modesty, between dogmatism and skepticism. This chapter will consider two specific examples of this sort of tension. The first involves the ontology of body, and the second the ontology of mind.

The conflict concerning bodily natures looks like this: As is well known, Locke typically describes bodies in the terms of the corpuscularian science of his day, as exemplified especially by the natural philosopher Robert Boyle. Locke's characterizations of the real essences of bodies are mechanist. He envisions them as corpuscularian textures – spatial arrangements of particles possessing size, shape, solidity, and motion.[1] Thus, Locke seems inclined to

---

[1] For present purposes, I will use "mechanist" and "corpuscularian" interchangeably. The meaning of "corpuscularian" is, I take it, fixed by Boyle, who coined that term (Boyle 1991: 4; Boyle 1999–2000: V: 289). The meaning of "mechanist" is more fluid, but it is uncontroversial that Boyle's corpuscularianism, as expressed in the *Origin of Forms and Qualities*, is a mechanist theory. I also use the phrase "strict mechanism" specifically to denote the view that all macroscopic bodily phenomena should be explained in terms of the motions and impacts of

presuppose a corpuscularian account of the nature of bodies. Furthermore, in making his famous distinction between primary and secondary qualities, Locke sometimes seems (as in E II.viii.9) to be putting forward *arguments* in favor of a corpuscularian ontology, that is, in favor of the view that bodies can be completely described in terms of size, shape, solidity, motion, and spatial arrangement. This is Locke's dogmatic side: it seems that he thinks that we can determine that the nature of bodies is captured by mechanist theory. On the skeptical side, however, Locke modestly proclaims that corpuscularianism is merely an hypothesis, and an hypothesis whose truth value lies outside the scope of the *Essay*'s concerns. Any resolution of this tension will have implications for Locke's distinction between primary and secondary qualities, his understanding of real essences, and his philosophy of science.

The second tension to be examined, concerning the nature of mind, looks even more dramatic, for here Locke seems saddled with an outright contradiction. Here, Locke's dogmatic side can be precisely located: its site is his proof of God's existence. More specifically, in the course of his argument (in E IV.x) for the traditional, substantive metaphysical claims that (1) an eternal, most powerful, thinking thing exists and that (2) that thing (i.e., God,) is not material, Locke seems to argue that no materialist account of thought and volition is possible. Yet just a few chapters earlier, in E IV.iii, Locke in his agnostic mode defends (at great risk to his reputation) the theologically dangerous proposition that for all we know, matter might think; that is, our thinking might be carried out by matter, rather than by some sort of immaterial, spiritual substance. For Locke's contemporaries, especially his critics, this was one of the most striking features of the *Essay* – Locke was seen as threatening our immortal souls and encouraging the worst sort of free thinking by allowing for the (epistemic) possibility of thinking matter. Locke argues that, although we cannot understand how matter could think, because we *also* cannot understand how a material and a spiritual substance could causally interact,[2] we ought to modestly rest in agnosticism:

---

submicroscopic particles, or corpuscles, each of which can be fully characterized in terms of a strictly limited range of (primary) properties: size, shape, motion (or mobility), and solidity or impenetrability.

[2] Nor even how a spiritual substance might think (E II.xxiii.25).

For since we must allow he [our Maker] has annexed Effects to Motion, which we can no way conceive Motion able to produce, what reason have we to conclude, that he could not order them as well to be produced in a Subject we cannot conceive capable of them, as well as in a Subject we cannot conceive the motion of Matter can any way operate upon? (E IV. iii.6: 541)

This is to say that we cannot know whether dualism or materialism is true of finite thinkers. This agnosticism about thinking matter, so controversial in Locke's day, looks appealing and insightful in our own. Unfortunately, it seems to land Locke in contradiction: he appears to support both the dogmatic, dualist claim that materialism (about any thinkers) cannot be true, and the agnostic/skeptical claim that we do not know whether or not materialism (about finite thinkers such as ourselves) is true.

We will see that both of these tensions can be resolved. The first will be dealt with quickly, in section 2. The second will occupy us for the rest of the chapter. What we gain by resolving these tensions, in addition to clearing Locke of charges of inconsistency, is an accurate understanding of Locke's ontology of body and mind. Locke does not in fact waver unsteadily between dogmatism and skepticism; a consistent thread can be woven among his positions. Moreover, reflection on the implications of these positions will provide us with a better understanding of the level of his metaphysical commitments and their basis.

2. ONTOLOGY OF BODY: THE STATUS OF MECHANISM

In this section, the interpretation I offer will be argued for in a somewhat peremptory fashion. There are three reasons for this. (1) I have argued for this interpretation of Locke elsewhere (Downing 1998). (2) The questions at issue here overlap significantly with those treated in other chapters of this volume. (3) The interpretation offered will be reinforced by its fit with the conclusions drawn in later sections of this chapter, from issues concerning Locke's ontology of mind.

As noted in the introduction, the puzzle concerning Locke's ontology of body stems from the fact that Locke typically characterizes bodies, physical substances, from the perspective of the new mechanist science – as configurations of particles analyzable entirely in terms of size, shape, solidity, and motion/rest. Is he presupposing the truth of Boylean corpuscularianism – just founding the *Essay* on the best scientific theory going?[3] Does he think he can give philosophical arguments for this account of the nature of body (as he might seem to be doing with the thought experiment about the grain of wheat in E II.viii.9)?[4] Or should we take him at his word when he declares corpuscularianism to be an hypothesis, and an hypothesis whose truth goes beyond the concerns of the *Essay*? For surely that is what he straightforwardly states as his position:[5]

I have here instanced in the corpuscularian Hypothesis, as that which is thought to go farthest in an intelligible Explication of the Qualities of Bodies; and I fear the Weakness of humane Understanding is scarce able to substitute another, which will afford us a fuller and clearer discovery of the necessary Connexion, and Co-*existence*, of the Powers, which are to be observed united in several sorts of them. This at least is certain, that which ever Hypothesis be clearest and truest, (for of that it is not my business to determine,) our Knowledge concerning corporeal Substances, will be very little advanced by any of them, till we are made see, what Qualities and Powers of Bodies have a *necessary Connexion or Repugnancy* one with another; which in the present State of Philosophy, I think, we know but to a very small degree: And, I doubt, whether with those Faculties we have, we shall ever be able to carry our general Knowledge (I say not particular Experience) in this part much farther. (E IV.iii.16: 547–8)

I suggest that we take Locke quite literally here. Corpuscularianism functions in the *Essay* as an *instance* or *example*. But an instance of what, exactly? An answer to that question is indicated in E III.iii.15–17:

First, Essence may be taken for the very being of any thing, whereby it is, what it is. And thus the real internal, but generally in Substances, unknown Constitution of Things, whereon their discoverable Qualities depend, may be called their *Essence*. This is the proper original signification of the Word, as is evident from the formation of it; *Essentia*, in its primary notation signifying properly *Being*. And in this sense it is still used, when we speak

---

[3] Many scholars have suggested this in one way or another, most notably Peter Alexander (1985: 6–7). See also Mandelbaum 1964: 1–3 and Yolton 1970: 11.
[4] See, e.g., Norbert and Hornstein 1984.   [5] See also E IV.iii.11.

of the *Essence* of particular things, without giving them any Name. (E III. iii.15: 417)

Concerning the real Essences of corporeal Substances, (to mention those only,) there are, if I mistake not, two Opinions. The one is of those, who using the Word *Essence*, for they know not what, suppose a certain number of those Essences, according to which, all natural things are made, and wherein they do exactly every one of them partake, and so become of this or that *Species*. The other, and more rational Opinion, is of those, who look on all natural Things to have a real, but unknown Constitution of their insensible Parts, from which flow those sensible Qualities, which serve us to distinguish them one from another, according as we have Occasion to rank them into sorts, under common Denominations. (E III. iii.17: 417–8)

As Locke explains it here, the real essence or real constitution of something is what makes the thing what it is.[6] Locke understands this as meaning that it is what causes something to have the discoverable qualities that it has. He mentions two opinions about what these real essences might be like, in the case of corporeal (bodily) substances: (1) the purportedly unintelligible scholastic opinion and (2) a broadly corpuscularian opinion according to which discoverable qualities flow from an internal constitution of submicroscopic parts. The corpuscularian hypothesis thus provides an *instance* or *example* of what the real essences of bodies might be like.[7]

In providing an example of what the real constitutions of bodies might be like, corpuscularianism also provides an example of what the primary qualities of bodies might be. On this interpretation, Locke's core notion of primary quality emerges as that of an intrinsic and irreducible quality.[8] It is a metaphysical notion at the

[6] This notion of real essence is the one that, following Guyer 1994: 133–4, I label "real constitution" in section 6. See notes 30–32.

[7] Locke's discussion at E III.iii.15–17 is in fact complex in ways that cannot be fully addressed here. Part of Locke's negative characterization of the scholastic opinion derives from its failure to distinguish between real and nominal essences, whereas the more rational modern opinion realizes that *types* of substances must be set by our ideas.

[8] I take it that this is what Locke means by contrasting qualities that *"are really in them* [objects], whether any ones Senses perceive them or no" (E II.viii.17) and are therefore primary, versus those that are *"imputed"* (E II.viii.22) and "nothing in the Objects themselves, but Powers" (E II.viii.10) and are therefore secondary.

same level as, and logically linked to, the metaphysical notion of real essence. Locke acknowledges this logical connection at E IV. vi.7, where he writes of secondary qualities as depending upon real constitutions. More typically, Locke describes secondary qualities as depending on primary qualities, but the two formulations are both appropriate, since a real constitution is a particular combination of intrinsic and irreducible (primary) qualities, a combination that is responsible for some relevant set of observable qualities, including secondary ones. Corpuscularianism provides an example of what might fill these metaphysical roles and, in doing so, illustrates what it would be for observable qualities to flow from a real constitution, and for secondary qualities to be produced by primary ones.

It would be misleading to say that it is *merely* an illustration, however, since Locke clearly sees corpuscularianism as in some way unique among natural philosophies (scientific theories). Locke views the theory as uniquely natural to us, for it asserts that bodies are as we conceive them to be via some simple reflection on sensory experience. This, I suggest,[9] is what Locke is getting at in E II.viii.9: 134–5, where he argues[10] that the corpuscularian list of primary qualities – solidity, extension, figure, and mobility – reflects what "Sense constantly finds in every particle of Matter" *and* "Mind finds inseparable from every particle of Matter." Locke is pointing out the theory's special status as our natural physics, but this does not reflect an official commitment to the truth of the theory.[11] Because of corpuscularianism's naturalness, its clarity (based as it is on simple ideas of sensation), and its reductive character (promising to explain many qualities in terms of a few), it provides a uniquely good *illustration* of the abstract notions of real essence and primary quality. Further, the corpuscularian example allows us to grasp the ideal of *scientia* – the sort of knowledge we would ideally have if we

[9] See also McCann 1994: 59–62.
[10] The argument is less than fully convincing, though the basic point about the psychological naturalness of a mechanist notion of body is surely plausible.
[11] Contra Jacovides 2002: 178, this is not to say that Locke did not believe corpuscularianism to be true. What I am specifically denying is that the central doctrines of the *Essay* presuppose or depend on the truth of corpuscularianism. As will emerge later, however, I also think that by sometime in the 1690s, Locke had concluded that strict mechanism could not be true because of its inability to explain Newton's results.

knew the real essences of things, wherein we could deduce the observable qualities and powers of bodies from their internal constitutions.[12] Corpuscularianism's apparent ability to model the flow of physical behavior from essences is highlighted by the lock and key analogy. Locke suggests that if we knew the corpuscularian real essences of opium and human being, we would understand why opium has its famous dormitive power in the same way that we understand why a certain key has the power to turn a certain lock. Moreover, we would be able to assert "without Trial" that opium can put humans to sleep (E IV.iii.25: 556).[13]

Scientia is what we aspire to by way of knowledge of substances, Locke holds, but it eludes us for a trio of increasingly grave reasons. First, *if* corpuscularianism is the correct theory, then the real essences of physical things are not available to us, because of their minuteness.[14] Second, *if* corpuscularianism is the correct theory, we will be left unable to explain cohesion, the communication of motion, and body-mind interactions. That is, as Margaret Wilson (1979) has emphasized, Locke goes out of his way to point out in the

[12] For this ideal of deducibility, see E II.xxxi.6 (and also E IV.vi.11, quoted in section 5).

[13] For a nice illustration of how corpuscularianism might promise deductive explanations, see Alexander 1985: 161. Rozemond and Yaffe (2004) have argued that Locke does not see mechanism as promising deductive explanation from real essences, but instead sees it as offering and actually providing a different sort of explanation – mechanistic explanation. This interesting proposal, as they acknowledge, faces some difficulty in characterizing this different sort of explanation (a difficulty that they plausibly connect to the recurring difficulty of analyzing the supposed special intelligibility of mechanism). There is also a textual issue here. In *Some Thoughts Concerning Education* (TE: 244–8), Locke characterizes corpuscularianism as one of the systems of natural philosophy that pretends "to give us a body of *Natural Philosophy* from the first Principles of Bodies in general." That is, it aims at *scientia*, demonstration from real essences, but fails to achieve it. The only actual virtue of corpuscularianism, compared to other schools, is its clear, intelligible language. Locke does not mention here any special explanatory success had by corpuscularianism, and he seems to go out of his way not to recommend the system as actually useful. This fits with my own view that Locke sees corpuscularianism as a uniquely good illustration of what *scientia*, deductive knowledge from real constitutions, *would be* like, although (at least by the 1690s) he does not think corpuscularianism will actually provide it. It should be noted that Locke's attachment to corpuscularianism does shift over time, with Draft C of 1685 representing the strongest apparent degree of attachment. For more on the chronology of Locke's views here, see Downing forthcoming.

[14] Locke views this as a practical problem that we are unlikely to overcome, not as an in principle barrier (Downing 1994).

Essay that corpuscularianism, though it promises *scientia*, cannot deliver on that promise because of explanatory gaps in the theory. Third, corpuscularianism might not be the right theory, in which case a deductive understanding of the qualities of bodies is "yet more remote from our Comprehension" (E IV.iii.11: 544). For Locke in the *Essay*, the second point reinforces the third point. That is, the explanatory failures of corpuscularianism reinforce the otherwise merely abstract possibility that it might not in fact provide the correct account of what the primary qualities of bodies are and what the real essences of bodies are like. Thus, we have reason to back away from our natural physics.

I have argued that when it comes to Locke's ontology of body, the conflict between skepticism and dogmatism, modesty and metaphysics, can be adjudicated in favor of skepticism/modesty. Locke, though he views corpuscularianism as our natural physics, does not commit himself to the truth of the theory. Its official role in the *Essay* is to illustrate the more basic notions of real essence and primary quality. This resolution raises a further question, however, about the nature and basis of Locke's commitment to these more abstract, metaphysical notions. This question, however, we should defer until we can approach it again through considering Locke's ontology of mind.

3. ONTOLOGY OF MIND: THE CONTRADICTION

As we observed in section 1, Locke's ontology of mind seems deeply conflicted. He typically writes as a dualist, but his official position (judging from E IV.iii as well as the correspondence with Stillingfleet) is that materialism about finite minds cannot be ruled out. Thus far there is no contradiction, of course. The gravest challenge to attributing a consistent position to Locke comes from his proof of God's existence, which seems to entail that thought cannot be carried out by mere matter. It appears, then, that Locke commits himself to contradictory claims: that we know that matter cannot think, and that we do not know whether some matter does think. I will argue that this contradiction is resolvable, though the resolution comes at a price – it requires us to carefully reconsider our views about (1) what gets proved in proving God's immateriality and (2) what the hypothesis of thinking matter amounts to.

The discussion will proceed as follows. First, we will consider a number of apparently straightforward and attractive ways of dissolving or resolving the contradiction. These options turn out, I will argue, to be unsatisfactory. Having refocused the inquiry on Locke's notion of superaddition, we will examine one prominent account of this notion that would also permit a resolution of the contradiction. On this interpretation, God might superadd thought to matter as an extrinsic power. Leibniz thought this an unattractive view to attribute to Locke, but it is not obvious what alternative is available. In section 6, I will carve out an alternative understanding of the superaddition of thought to matter, compatible with the essentialism that Michael Ayers has attributed to Locke. I will argue that the bulk of the available evidence favors attributing this understanding of superaddition to Locke. We will then examine the consequences of this new reading of superaddition for both the hypothesis of thinking matter and the proof of God's immateriality. We will conclude by briefly reflecting on what this resolution reveals about the extent of Locke's metaphysics and the nature of his commitment to that metaphysics.

The first step in resolving the contradiction, however, is to characterize it more precisely through an examination of Locke's proof of God's existence. Locke begins by proving (purportedly) that an eternal thinking thing, most knowing and most powerful, exists. He then turns to the question of whether this eternal thinking thing might be material. Locke argues against the possibility of such a Hobbesian material God as follows. Either (1) every particle of matter thinks, or (2) only one atom does, or (3) thought arises from some system of matter. The first option is dismissed as absurd, and the second as arbitrary and absurd, but the third requires further consideration:

... it only remains, that it is *some certain System of Matter* duly put together, that is this *thinking eternal Being*. This is that, which, I imagine, is that Notion, which Men are aptest to have of GOD, who would have him a material Being, as most readily suggested to them, by the ordinary conceit they have of themselves, and other Men, which they take to be material thinking Beings. But this Imagination, however more natural, is no less absurd than the other: For to suppose the eternal thinking Being, to be nothing else but a composition of Particles of Matter, each whereof is incogitative, is to ascribe all the Wisdom and Knowledge of that eternal

Being, only to the *juxta*-position of parts; than which, nothing can be more absurd. For unthinking Particles of Matter, however put together, can have nothing thereby added to them, but a new relation of Position, which 'tis impossible should give thought and knowledge to them.

But farther, this *corporeal System* either has all its parts at rest, or it is a certain motion of the parts wherein its Thinking consists. If it be perfectly at rest, it is but one lump, and so can have no privileges above one Atom.

If it be the motion of its parts, on which its Thinking depends, all the Thoughts there must be unavoidably accidental, and limited; since all the Particles that by Motion cause Thought, being each of them in it self without any Thought, cannot regulate its own Motions, much less be regulated by the Thought of the whole; since that Thought is not the cause of Motion (for then it must be antecedent to it, and so without it) but the consequence of it, whereby Freedom, Power, Choice, and all rational and wise thinking or acting will be quite taken away.... (E IV.x.16–17: 627)

Surely this looks like an argument that, *if* it rules out a material God, *also* rules out material thinkers of *any* kind, and thus motivates dualism.[15]

---

[15] This point merits elaboration: Of course, the conclusion that Locke wants here is specifically that God – the eternal, most powerful, most knowing thing – cannot be material. But his argument has broader implications. How could matter then be made to think at all? Arranging the particles in some special way won't do, since "'tis impossible" this "should give thought and knowledge to them." Will setting them in motion help? Since the particles themselves are unthinking (it being absurd that all matter thinks or that some particular atom does), their motions will be unregulated and thus cannot constitute rational thought, etc. Here it might be objected that once an immaterial God is established, he can do the regulating, so that ordinary finite thinkers could just be ordinary mechanist matter. But what form will the regulation take? Configuring the system in some particular arrangement won't work. Configuring the system and then setting it in motion won't work. Could God somehow set up the merely material system so that its motions are self-regulating? The suggestion would have to be that if the preceding motion of the system is of the right (thought-constituting) kind, it could somehow guide the next motion appropriately. Locke cannot mean to allow this, since then the possibility that God is such an eternally self-regulating, merely material system could not be eliminated. (To eliminate this possibility is, after all, the point of the argument. Locke's argument here is *not* that it is enormously unlikely that God is a merely material being. As noted in section 4, Locke claims in E IV.iii.6 that he has shown in E IV.x that it is a *contradiction* for God to be material.) That Locke views this suggestion as a nonstarter is, moreover, clearly implied by the first paragraph (section 16): spatial arrangement is a relation of position, and motion is a relation of position that changes over time; these are all that can be added to particles of matter, and neither can give thought to them. (That is to say, section 16 is supposed to be a self-standing argument that a system of mere matter, in whatever state, cannot

4. EASY RESOLUTIONS SKETCHED AND REJECTED

A tempting interpretive strategy at this point is to try to minimize the force or scope of Locke's conclusion in order to preserve agnosticism about thinking matter. Michael Ayers (1981: 240) attempts to narrow the proof's scope by arguing that Locke's main point is that because thought can be only a contingent, not an essential, property of matter, its presence in matter requires explanation; thus, to attribute thought to a material *first* cause is unacceptable. Though this is certainly one argumentative strand that can be seen in E IV.x,[16] it offers little help in saving the possibility of thinking matter. For the problem for thinking matter is created by the fact that the only obvious way for thought to be *contingently* added to matter, by configuring some system of matter and setting it in motion, cannot succeed, according to Locke's argument in E IV.x.

An obvious rationale for minimizing the *force* of the proof is that the context is charged with religious concerns. One might suggest that in order to distinguish himself from Hobbes's heterodoxy, Locke is tempted to present overzealously what are in fact intelligibility considerations. Locke holds that although intelligibility considerations do weigh against thinking matter, they are countered by intelligibility problems with dualism. On this interpretation, Locke's true position in the "proof" of God's immateriality would be just that this same balance does not obtain in the case of God, where Locke is content to presuppose that some version of the traditional Christian conception of God is intelligible or at least does not present the sort of challenge to the understanding posed by

---

produce divine thought, because it cannot produce thought. Section 17 then reconsiders the *same* question via a dilemma – is the system in motion or at rest?) The third paragraph seems not to foreclose the possibility that God might configure a system, move it, and *perpetually* regulate that motion so that it could constitute wise thought. But this proposal has three strikes against it: (1) This sort of occasionalist materialism is not what the hypothesis of thinking matter was supposed to amount to. (2) The first paragraph again rules it out as impossible: no matter how nicely God shifts the positions of particles of matter, this can't bestow thought. (3) The passage itself suggests the thought that an other-regulated system of this kind could not constitute a rational and free thinker.

[16] Ayers's point is especially useful in understanding Locke's remarks in the correspondence with Stillingfleet at W IV: 469. If this were the only consideration raised in E IV.x against God's materiality, however, the chapter would presumably have been quite a bit shorter.

a Hobbesian God. Thus, intelligibility problems with a material God, which are essentially the *same* intelligibility problems that confront thinking matter,[17] in this case properly motivate us to reject the problematic hypothesis, because an intelligible *alternative* is available.[18]

Unfortunately, this attractive suggestion runs up against Locke's own clearly expressed attitude toward his proof:

> For I see no contradiction in it, that the first eternal thinking Being should, if he pleased, give to certain Systems of created sensless matter, put together as he thinks fit, some degrees of sense, perception, and thought: Though, as I think, I have proved, *Lib.* 4. *c.* 10th. it is no less than a contradiction to suppose matter (which is evidently in its own nature void of sense and thought) should be that Eternal first thinking Being. (E IV.iii.6: 541)

It's clear that Locke views the conceptual difficulties with finite material thinkers and with a material God as entirely different in kind. Most significantly, if the claim that God is material is to be a contradiction, then the proof must be demonstrative, and it must amount to a contradiction to suppose that mere matter can think via some arrangement or motion of its parts. I submit that a constraint on any acceptable interpretation of *Locke* on thinking matter is that it should acknowledge the force that Locke accords to his conclusion here.

It is not at all clear, of course, that Locke *should* have accorded his proof such force. If he were to admit that he had only raised a challenge, based on intelligibility considerations, to a material God, the contradiction could be eliminated as suggested earlier: Locke simply holds that intelligibility considerations militate against a material God, but weigh equally against materialist and dualist accounts of finite thinkers, so that we do not have reason to choose between them. This would provide a sort of epistemological resolution of the contradiction. This is evidently not Locke's view of the situation, however, assuming that he writes with consistent sincerity. Our goal here should be to locate a resolution that Locke could have, and perhaps actually did, endorse. By adhering to Locke's own views, we open up the possibility of learning how he thought not just about thinking matter, but also about some more basic issues.

---

[17] Or, at least, they include the same intelligibility problems.

[18] See Jacovides 2002: 183–4 on the moderate epistemic weight that Locke accords to conceivability/intelligibility considerations.

How, then, can we understand the hypothesis of thinking matter? Locke's own, all-too-brief attempt to reconcile these doctrines
in the *Essay* takes place in the quotation just given and the lines
leading up to it:

> We have the *Ideas* of *Matter* and *Thinking*, but possibly shall never be able to
> know, whether any mere material Being thinks, or no; it being impossible for
> us, by the contemplation of our own *Ideas*, without revelation, to discover,
> whether Omnipotency has not given to some Systems of Matter fitly dis-
> posed, a power to perceive and think, or else joined and fixed to Matter so
> disposed, a thinking immaterial Substance: It being, in respect of our Notions,
> not much more remote from our Comprehension to conceive, that GOD can,
> if he pleases, superadd to Matter a Faculty of Thinking, than that he should
> superadd to it another Substance with a Faculty of Thinking; since we know
> not wherein Thinking consists, nor to what sort of Substances the Almighty
> has been pleased to give that Power, which cannot be in any created Being,
> but merely by the good pleasure and Bounty of the Creator. (E IV.iii.6: 540–1)

Locke's claim that God may superadd to matter a faculty of
thinking allows us to usefully relabel our problem: What we want
to understand is the superaddition of thought to matter. How is it
possible, and what sort of process, if any, is it?

In one passage from the correspondence with Stillingfleet (the
site of Locke's most extended discussion of the issue), Locke seems
to suggest an easy answer to this question:

> The idea of matter is an extended solid substance; wherever there is such a
> substance, there is matter, and the essence of matter, whatever other
> qualities, not contained in that essence, it shall please God to superadd to
> it. For example, God creates an extended solid substance, without the
> superadding any thing else to it, and so we may consider it at rest: to some
> parts of it he superadds motion, but it has still the essence of matter: other
> parts of it he frames into plants, with all the excellencies of vegetation, life,
> and beauty, which are to be found in a rose or a peach-tree, &c. above the
> essence of matter in general, but it is still but matter: to other parts he adds
> sense and spontaneous motion, and those other properties that are to be
> found in an elephant. (W IV: 460)

One might think from *this* passage that superadding thought to
matter could be as easy as setting matter into motion,[19] that is, that

---

[19] As Ayers (1981: II: 229, 238) strongly suggests by emphasizing this passage and the
analogy between superadding motion to matter and thought to matter.

it might be done by appropriately arranging and moving some set of merely material parts. Unfortunately, this is precisely what is ruled out by Locke's proof of God's immateriality, according to the constraint argued for earlier.

Another apparently easy response is suggested by Locke's tendency to invoke the poverty of our ideas in the course of describing the superaddition of thought to matter. Indeed, superaddition often occurs in Locke's thought as an hypothesis to which we are forced by our limited viewpoint. One might thus argue that Locke has no answer to the question – What is superaddition? – because to appeal to God's superaddition of X to Y is just to say that God has bestowed X upon Y in some way that surpasses our understanding. This gives us what Matthew Stuart (1998) has called the epistemic reading of superaddition. On this reading, we can modestly acknowledge our ignorance and God's omnipotence in order to avoid explaining how thought might be added to matter.

The epistemic reading is surely correct in holding that Locke offers no *general* account of what superaddition amounts to, and that the only thing that unites all his references to superaddition is our ignorance. However, invoking an epistemic reading does nothing to dissolve the tension between the God proof and thinking matter. For, of course, Locke does not claim in E IV.x merely that we cannot understand how God could be material, but rather that we can understand that it is impossible for God to be material, for volition and thought cannot arise from mere matter in motion.[20] Thus, we *do* know that the superaddition of thought to matter cannot simply involve the configuration and motion of purely material parts.

5. THE EXTRINSIC-POWERS READING OF SUPERADDITION

Furthermore, some of Locke's references to superaddition seem to be describing a metaphysical proposal about how an all-powerful God can bestow qualities upon things:

Here are now two distinct substances, the one material, the other immaterial, both in a state of perfect inactivity. Now I ask what power God can give to one of these substances (supposing them to retain the same distinct

---

[20] As Stuart (1998: 366) in effect points out.

natures, that they had as substances in their state of inactivity) which he cannot give to the other? (W IV: 464)

... if you mean that certain parcels of matter, ordered by the divine Power, as seems fit to him, may be made capable of receiving from his omnipotency the faculty of thinking; that indeed I say.... (W IV: 468)

Famously, Leibniz saw a metaphysical proposal here, one that he took to be profoundly confused. To put it bluntly, Leibniz thought that Locke's God was arbitrarily attaching powers to bodies not naturally capable of them, that is, that he was taking refuge in Scholastic real qualities. His response was to give Locke a rather patronizing little lecture on the proper way to understand modifications:

... it must be borne in mind above all that the modifications which can occur to a single subject naturally and without miracles must arise from limitations and variations of a real genus, i.e. of a constant and absolute inherent nature. For that is how philosophers distinguish the modes of an absolute being from that being itself; just as we know that size, shape and motion are obviously limitations and variations of corporeal nature (for it is plain how a limited extension yields shapes, and that changes occurring in it are nothing but motion). Whenever we find some quality in a subject, we ought to believe that if we understood the nature of both the subject and the quality we would conceive how the quality could arise from it. So within the order of nature (miracles apart) it is not at God's arbitrary discretion to attach this or that quality haphazardly to substances. He will never give them any which are not natural to them, that is, which cannot arise from their nature as explicable modifications. So we may take it that matter will not naturally possess the attractive power referred to above, and that it will not of itself move in a curved path, because it is impossible to conceive how this could happen – that is, to explain it mechanically – whereas what is natural must be such as could become distinctly conceivable by anyone admitted into the secrets of things. (Leibniz 1981: 65–6; Leibniz 1923–: VI. vi: 65–6)

Matthew Stuart has more recently defended Leibniz's interpretation of Locke. He does not share Leibniz's obvious horror at the position he attributes to Locke, an attitude he justifies by couching the interpretation in terms of extrinsic powers anchored in divinely established, voluntaristic laws of nature, rather than in terms of bare powers arbitrarily glued onto substances (Stuart 1998: 369–70). A similar interpretation is put forward by Edwin McCann, who explains superaddition in terms of arbitrary laws set by God (McCann 1994: 74–5).[21] I will refer to this interpretation as the "extrinsic powers" reading of superaddition. A minor weakness in this interpretation is Locke's virtual silence on the question of laws of nature and their status.[22] By contrast, he is famously vocal about the potential explanatory power of real essences. Indeed, Locke's descriptions in the *Essay* of what it would be to know the real essences of things, that we would then understand how all of their properties followed from those essences, just as we can deduce the properties of a triangle from its essence, suggest a fundamental sympathy with Leibniz's own picture, in particular, sympathy with the claim that "if we understood the nature of both the subject and the quality we would conceive how the quality could arise from it."[23] A representative example is E IV.vi.11: 585 (see also E II. xxxi.6):[24]

Had we such *Ideas* of Substances, as to know what real Constitutions produce those sensible Qualities we find in them, and how those Qualities flowed from thence, we could, by the specifick *Ideas* of their real Essences in our own Minds, more certainly find out their Properties, and discover what Qualities they had, or had not, than we can now by our Senses: And to know the Properties of *Gold*, it would be no more necessary, that *Gold* should exist, and that we should make Experiments upon it, than it is necessary for the knowing the Properties of a Triangle, that a Triangle

---

[21] Langton (2000) also belongs in this camp.

[22] As Stuart (1996: 460) acknowledges. McCann (1994: 75) cites E IV.iii.29 as establishing that Locke's God ordains laws as (brute) necessary connections. But what Locke writes here is more naturally read as subordinating laws to causes:

> The Things that, as far as our Observation reaches, we constantly find to proceed regularly, we may conclude, do act by a Law set them; but yet by a Law, that we know not: whereby, though Causes work steadily, and Effects constantly flow from them, yet their *Connexions* and *Dependancies* being not discoverable in our *Ideas*, we can have but an experimental Knowledge of them.

That is, where we see a regularity, we infer a law sustained by causes (not a brute law imposed by God). The causes and effects *have* connections and dependencies, though we are ignorant of them.

[23] See Wilson 1999: 197.

[24] For a different interpretation of these passages, see Stuart 1996. Stuart suggests reading such passages as expressing merely deductivism about explanation.

should exist in any Matter, the *Idea* in our Minds would serve for the one, as well as the other. But we are so far from being admitted into the Secrets of Nature, that we scarce so much as ever approach the first entrance towards them.

Michael Ayers has made this side of Locke a centerpiece of his interpretation of the *Essay*, attributing to Locke a "pure mechanism" according to which "the understanding which is in principle possible of mechanical processes is the same in kind as the understanding which can be achieved in geometry" (1991: II: 135).[25] Apart from finding this a somewhat idiosyncratic use of "mechanism,"[26] I am in considerable agreement with Ayers's position here, contra Leibniz, Stuart, and McCann. I will argue, specifically, that there is no good reason to suppose that Locke actually disagrees with anything but the last sentence of Leibniz's little lecture, and thus, no good reason to suppose that he is committed to superaddition amounting to the arbitrary attaching of powers to bodies. So, in keeping with passages like E IV.vi.11, I will provisionally attribute to Locke what I will call "essentialism": the view that the qualities and behavior of a body follow from its real constitution (some particular configuration of its intrinsic and irreducible qualities), together with the real constitutions of other bodies and the spatial relations among bodies.[27] Essentialism thus rules out an extrinsic-powers reading of superaddition.

But what alternative understanding of superaddition is available?[28] We should observe that the extrinsic-powers interpretation put forward by Leibniz, Stuart, and McCann has an important virtue: it explains the compatibility of thinking matter with the proof of God's immateriality. For matter can think, on this interpretation, only through the imposition of nonnatural powers via the forging of (arbitrary) laws of nature. Presumably only God (if anyone) could

---

[25] See also Ayers 1991 II: 153, 190, and Ayers 1981: 210.

[26] The term, applied in a seventeenth-century context, typically denotes a far more specific theory, more physical than metaphysical, committed to the principle that all bodily action is by impact at contact, as well as to a particular short list of primary qualities. See note 1.

[27] Arguably, this ought to be called "constitutionalism." But that term is surely uglier and potentially at least as misleading as "essentialism."

[28] Here I think Ayers fails us, though he makes a crucial point which will help lead us in the right direction. See note 29.

bring this off; thus, God himself could not be (or always have been) a material being functioning in this way. The extrinsic-powers interpretation, then, resolves the contradiction as follows: We know that matter could not think simply by means of size, shape, solidity, and motion/rest. We do not know whether some matter thinks in virtue of God's having attached further powers to it, not derived from its real constitution. But, if the superaddition of thought to matter is not this sort of arbitrary imposition of powers, what is it, and can it render thinking matter compatible with the proof of God's immateriality?

6. ESSENTIALIST SUPERADDITION

The first step in answering this question is to see where Leibniz went wrong in his Locke interpretation. Leibniz's mistake lay in failing to keep in mind Locke's distinction between real and nominal essences. Here we need to examine the Locke's "peach tree passage" (cited earlier) at greater length.

The idea of matter is an extended solid substance; wherever there is such a substance, there is matter, and the essence of matter, whatever other qualities, not contained in that essence, it shall please God to superadd to it. For example, God creates an extended solid substance, without the superadding any thing else to it, and so we may consider it at rest: to some parts of it he superadds motion, but it has still the essence of matter: other parts of it he frames into plants, with all the excellencies of vegetation, life, and beauty, which are to be found in a rose or a peach-tree, &c. above the essence of matter in general, but it is still but matter: to other parts he adds sense and spontaneous motion, and those other properties that are to be found in an elephant. Hitherto it is not doubted but the power of God may go, and that the properties of a rose, a peach, or an elephant, superadded to matter, change not the properties of matter; but matter is in these things matter still. But if one venture to go on one step further, and say, God may give to matter thought, reason, and volition, as well as sense and spontaneous motion, there are men ready presently to limit the power of the omnipotent Creator, and tell us he cannot do it; because it destroys the essence, "changes the essential properties of matter." To make good which assertion, they have no more to say, but that thought and reason are not included in the essence of matter. I grant it; but whatever excellency, not contained in its essence, be superadded to matter, it does not destroy the essence of matter, if it leaves it an extended solid substance; wherever that is, there is the essence of matter: and if every thing of greater perfection, superadded to such a substance, destroys the essence of matter, what will become of the essence of matter in a plant, or an animal, whose properties far exceed those of a mere extended solid substance? (W IV: 460–1)

Locke clearly states at the beginning of this passage that we are talking about our *idea* of matter. That is, we are talking about a nominal essence: a complex, abstract idea according to which we sort things into kinds, including the kind – matter.[29] Anything that causes in us ideas of extension and solidity satisfies the nominal essence of matter and thus *is* matter, whatever the real essence, that is, the real, physical constitution that allows it to causally produce those ideas in us. The passage misleads because the series of examples Locke gives next may be taken to suggest that he supposes the real essence of matter to be exhausted by solidity and extension, and that superaddition can then be done simply by reconfiguring that solid, extended stuff. With Leibniz, then, we may be shocked at Locke's continuing on to sense, reason, and volition, when (as we know from the God proof) Locke agrees with Leibniz that thought cannot arise from any arrangement of merely material parts. Note, however, that Locke ends with the same point with which he began: wherever we have solid, extended stuff, we have the essence of matter; no essences have been violated. In fact, this is true in two senses: Of course, the nominal essence remains the same, defined as it is by our abstract idea, and the stuff continues to satisfy it as long as it is solid and extended. We can also be sure that whatever is extended and solid has the real essence of body, since real essences of kinds are officially defined in relation to nominal ones, as whatever sort of real constitution produces the observable qualities cataloged by the nominal essence as definitive of that kind (E III.vi.6: 442).[30] This makes "real essence" a rather technical term; we should thus regiment Locke's (more haphazard) usage along lines suggested by Paul Guyer, using "real constitution" for the configuration of intrinsic and irreducible qualities responsible for

---

[29] Ayers (1981: 229 [see also 222]) notes that "for Locke 'extended solid substance' gives a sort of nominal essence of matter rather than its real essence." See also Atherton 1984b: 418.

[30] See Guyer 1994: 133–4 and Owen 1991: 105–18. Though that real essence might be a disjunctive one, as we will see.

all of a thing's qualities/powers,[31] while reserving "real essence" for constitutions relative to nominal essences, that is, for whatever constitution is responsible for a set of observable properties enshrined by us as a kind.[32]

The superaddition Locke writes of here, then, is with respect to the nominal essence. He asks: Why should it be controversial to affirm that God can bestow a quality upon something that goes beyond the qualities that we take to be definitive of that kind of thing? Why suppose that "God can give no power to any parts of matter, but *what men can account for* from the essence of matter in general?" (W IV: 461, my emphasis). That superaddition is with respect to the nominal essence is further supported by Locke's treatment of the thinking-matter issue in his first letter to Stillingfleet, where he tells us that the question comes down to this: whether there exists any substance that has both the (observable) quality of solidity and the power of thought (W IV: 33).[33] Leibniz, like some later commentators, supposes that Locke has been misled by his obscure idea of substance-in-general into thinking that powers can be arbitrarily glued onto a bare and uncharacterizable substratum (Leibniz 1981: 63–4; Leibniz 1923–: VI.vi: 63–4). But there is no such confusion. Nothing Locke says here goes against the (more or less Leibnizian) view that when thought is superadded to a particular substance, that thought, like the rest of its behavior, follows from its particular real constitution. These powers look extrinsic from our perspective; they don't follow

---

[31] I disagree, however, with Guyer's claim that Locke "suggests that the concept of a thing's real constitution is nonrelational, that constitution in no way depending upon our own mental activity" (1994: 133). Though Locke would hold, I think, that the constitution of the entire world as a whole is nonrelational and depends in no way on mental activity, he is aware that individuation, the carving of one thing out from its neighborhood, must be done by us. We might, e.g., do so by implicitly referring to 'that brown, rectangular thing that tends to move around together', thus demarcating an individual with a real constitution, a configuration of intrinsic and irreduceable qualities grounding all of its other qualities.

[32] Owen (1991: 108) similarly distinguishes between real essence of an unsorted particular and real essence of a sorted particular. He rightly notes that the former is not properly an *essence* for Locke, since no distinction between essential and accidental properties is possible without reference to a kind.

[33] See also a letter to Collins, W X: 285, as well as E IV.iii.6, where the question of thinking matter is described as the question of whether God can give perception and thought "to a Substance, which has the Modification of Solidity."

from the nominal essence. But that is not to say that they are extrinsic with respect to the natures/real constitutions of bodies. But if Locke does not reject this sort of essentialism here, how exactly might superaddition be understood, so as to be compatible with it?

The first point we need to keep in mind is that given Locke's proof of God's immateriality, thought cannot follow from the real constitution of a substance unless that constitution is more than merely mechanical, that is, unless it is not characterizable simply in terms of extension and solidity (and their modifications). So, if Locke accepts essentialism, the real constitutions of thinking things must be nonmechanical. The second is that Locke assumes that it is obvious from experience that not all material stuff (that is, stuff that satisfies the nominal essence of matter by manifesting the observable qualities of extension and solidity) thinks. This leaves us with the following two options for superaddition. God's super-adding thought to matter involves either

(1)   Disjunctive real constitutions: God gives some stuff a nonmechanical real constitution that allows it to manifest thought as well as extension and solidity, while he gives nonthinking material stuff a different type of real constitution, which might well be purely mechanical.

or

(2)   Uniform nonmechanical[34] real constitutions, differently configured: the real constitutions of all material things (things that satisfy the nominal essence of matter) are nonmechanical; God configures some of them so as to allow them to think.

First, let us examine these two options a little further by considering their intelligibility and how they fit with the texts. These characterizations may seem disagreeably abstract, but this poses no serious problem. One thing we need in order to make sense of them is an abstract notion of the real constitution that produces a thing's observable qualities; Locke supplies us with that at E III.iii.15. Another is the analogy with mechanism, which, as argued in section 1, is presented by Locke as a uniquely intelligible *example* of

[34] In both (1) and (2), "nonmechanical" just means "not merely or strictly mechanical," that is, not exhausted by size, shape, solidity, and motion/rest.

what the real constitutions of bodies might be like. Relying on that analogy, we can make sense of the idea of "configuring" the real constitutions of some things, by analogy to arranging and moving mechanical parts, so as to make them think.[35] Note that "configuration" need not be taken too literally. All that proposal (2) requires is that some particular co-instantiations of primary qualities will work to produce thought and others will not; God sets some up so as to allow for thought. Of course, we can't understand how that would work, given that we have no idea of these non-mechanical constitutions, but that's just as we would expect. The disjunctiveness of the first option may seem peculiar, but remember that Locke's views about classification clearly allow that the real essences of types might be highly disjunctive; it might, for example, be that two very different sorts of constitutions produce that set of observable qualities (yellow, malleable, etc.) that are necessary and sufficient for something to count as gold. Likewise for matter.[36]

7. SUPPORT FOR ESSENTIALIST SUPERADDITION

So, if Locke is a consistent essentialist, he ought to understand superaddition along the lines we have just indicated. Is there any more direct textual evidence favoring (1) or (2) over the "extrinsic powers" reading? In fact, there is. Many of the very passages that

[35] An interesting challenge might be raised to essentialist superaddition à la (2), however: Locke argues in E IV.x that configuring purely mechanical qualities (putting extended solid bodies into particular spatial arrangements and setting them in motion) can't produce thought. Why would he think that some analog of configuration might work, given different primary qualities/real constitutions? (This is related to a question posed to me by Jonathan Schaffer.) Once we realize that "configuration" need not be taken literally, as including just repositioning and setting into motion, I think the objection loses most of its force. To whatever objection remains, I think the appropriate reply is just: Why suppose that it can be ruled out? What argument would establish that?

[36] For Locke's acknowledgement of the possible, even probable disjunctiveness of real essences, see E III.x.20. Interestingly, Ayers's interpretation of Locke's "pure mechanism" rules out (1) by specifying that all matter must have one uniform nature (1981: 210; 1991: II: 153). Although I think Locke is inclined to assume that matter is catholic (as Boyle put it, 1991: 18; Boyle 1999–2000: V: 305), I cannot see any basis for building this into the very foundations of Locke's system, especially given Ayers's own point that "solid, extended substance" gives the nominal essence of matter.

most seem to suggest an extrinsic-powers reading turn out, on closer inspection, to better support an essentialist reading. Note that W IV: 468, which has divine omnipotency bestowing the faculty of thinking on certain parcels of matter, also states that these parcels must first be "made capable of receiving" them. On the Leibnizian reading, it is unclear why the powers could not simply be bestowed at will.[37] The passage from W IV: 464, also quoted earlier, is followed by this illuminating little internal dialog:

If it be asked, why they limit the omnipotence of God, in reference to the one rather than the other of these substances; all that can be said to it is, that they cannot conceive how the solid substance should ever be able to move itself. And as little, say I, are they able to conceive how a created unsolid substance should move itself; but there may be something in an immaterial substance, that you do not know. I grant it; and in a material one too: for example, gravitation of matter towards matter, and in the several proportions observable, inevitably shows, that there is something in matter that we do not understand, unless we can conceive self-motion in matter; or an inexplicable and inconceivable attraction in matter, at immense and almost incomprehensible distances: it must therefore be confessed, that there is something in solid, as well as unsolid substances, that we do not understand. (W IV: 464)

The hypothesis of thinking matter leads us not to the view that an omnipotent God could bestow thought even on mere solid, extended stuff, but rather to the view that there may be something in material substances, that is, in things that manifest solidity and extension, that we do not know. This strongly suggests that there must be something internal to the thinking thing that would, in principle, explain its ability to think.

The connection that Locke makes here to attraction is one that we should follow. Recall that thinking matter is just an hypothesis, something that Locke claims is, for all we know, possible, and thus not to be ruled out. He takes it, however, that Newton has shown that universal gravitation is actual and that it cannot be accounted for mechanically, in terms of the impacts of bodies possessing size,

---

[37] McCann and Stuart could perhaps accommodate such passages by, say, suggesting that God may need to configure bodies so that they fall under the relevant divinely established general laws. The point remains that these passages offer no positive support for an extrinsic-powers reading over an essentialist one.

shape, solidity, and motion/rest. If Locke is an essentialist, this implies that mechanism is a false or incomplete account of the nature of bodies.[38] But this is exactly what Locke acknowledges in stating that Newton has shown that there *is* something in solid substances that we do not understand.

Most tellingly, if Locke were content to allow that laws of nature are arbitrary divine additions to the natures of things, he should have no problem at all with gravity; it would pose no challenge to his understanding of how the world works.[39] One thing that is clear is that this is not Locke's response to Newton. He is deeply troubled by Newton's results, as he famously reports to Stillingfleet:

> It is true, I say [in the *Essay*], "that bodies operate by impulse, and nothing else." And so I thought when I writ it, and can yet conceive no other way of their operation. But I am since convinced by the judicious Mr. Newton's incomparable book, that it is too bold a presumption to limit God's power, in this point, by my narrow conceptions. The gravitation of matter towards matter, by ways inconceivable to me, is not only a demonstration that God can, if he pleases, put into bodies powers and ways of operation above what can be derived from our idea of body, or can be explained by what we know of matter, but also an unquestionable and every where visible instance, that he has done so. And therefore in the next edition of my book I shall take care to have that passage rectified. (W IV: 467–8)

Note that Locke does not say that the powers God put into bodies cannot be derived from *any* idea of body, or that they cannot be explained *full stop*, but that they cannot be derived from *our* idea of body and cannot be explained by what *we* know of matter. Further, to add those powers to bodies is to do something *to bodies*, not simply to establish a law that bodies fall under. The result is something whose nature we do not, at least fully, comprehend. Locke writes in his *Elements of Natural Philosophy* that the force of attraction "is inexplicable by us, though made evident to us by experience, and so to be taken as a principle in natural philosophy" (W III: 305). But if the extrinsic-powers interpretation were correct,

---

[38] Here Locke self-consciously takes a step beyond his position in the *Essay*, which, as argued in section 1, is that corpuscularianism is the most intelligible theory available, but that it has severe explanatory gaps and may be false.

[39] Compare Berkeley's position: Berkeley holds that all laws of nature are mere regularities in our ideas, established by God. As a result, he finds gravitational "attraction" no more problematic than impact.

there would be no explanatory problem: God bestows a power, establishes a law, and there is nothing further that needs explanation, nothing that eludes us.[40]

8. CONSEQUENCES FOR THINKING MATTER AND DIVINE IMMATERIALITY

We have seen that there is good reason to read Locke's talk of the (possible) superaddition of thought to matter, as well as the actual superaddition of gravity to matter, as compatible with essentialism and, thus, along the lines of (1) or (2). We must, however, consider the consequences of this reading, some of which may seem less than attractive. First, the sort of materialism that Locke contemplates under the rubric of thinking matter is not what we might have thought at first glance. The hypothesis that cannot be ruled out is not that *matter* – understood as something whose *nature* is exhausted by extension and solidity – might think, but that something

---

[40] In *Some Thoughts Concerning Education*, there is a discussion of gravity that might seem to lend strong support to an extrinsic-powers or occasionalist reading of superaddition:

> ... it is evident, that by mere Matter and Motion, none of the great Phænomena of Nature can be resolved, to instance but in that common one of Gravity, which I think impossible to be explained by any natural Operation of Matter, or any other Law of Motion, but the positive Will of a Superiour Being, so ordering it. (TE: 246)

Stuart (1998: 355–6) lays considerable stress on this passage in arguing for his extrinsic-powers view. Note how the passage continues, however:

> And therefore since the Deluge cannot be well explained without admitting something out of the ordinary course of Nature, I propose it to be considered whether God's altering the Center of gravity in the Earth for a time (a thing as intelligible as gravity it self, which, perhaps a little variation of Causes unknown to us would produce) will not more easily account for *Noah's* Flood, than any *Hypothesis* yet made use of to solve it. (TE: 246)

The first part of the passage is admittedly somewhat awkward for my interpretation; I read it as stating that we cannot explain gravity via our idea of matter, and must therefore have recourse in some fashion to God. This does not entail, however, that what God did was to attach extrinsic powers to purely mechanical matter; it may be that what he did was to create material stuff whose nature transcends our ideas. The second half of the passage reinforces my interpretation and undercuts Stuart's (or an occasionalist interpretation), since it implies that gravity has some underlying cause, which might be altered in some fashion so as to shift the Earth's center of gravity.

material – something that *exhibits* extension and solidity – might think. Thus, Hobbes's materialism is not a live option for Locke. Of course, this is no more than we should expect at this point, since, as argued in section 2, if we take Locke's God proof seriously, we must see it as implying that strictly mechanist matter cannot think. Thus, the hypothesis of thinking matter is the hypothesis that something whose nature is not fully captured by our idea of matter, but that falls under our idea of matter by exhibiting solidity and extension, might think.[41] In short: not that *mere* matter might think but that something *material* might think.

We must then return to the question of what exactly the proof of God's immateriality establishes and what it leaves open. What it establishes is that God could not be mere matter: God's nature could not be exhausted by extension and solidity. But of course this is also true of me: I could not be mere matter. Indeed, I have argued that Locke saw Newton as having established that *matter* is not mere matter, that its nature is not captured by our idea of matter, that is, by mechanism. So showing that God could not be mere matter may not seem like much of an achievement. And my analysis invites the question: If I could be *material*, could God be material? That is, could God manifest the properties of extension and solidity? The answer here must be yes, but that much should be untroubling. After all, the extrinsic-powers interpretation too must allow that God could bestow upon himself the relevant powers to manifest solidity and extension and thus count as material by falling under our idea of matter. It's also true that for all the proof tells us, God and finite thinkers might share the same type of real constitution, that is, our constitutions might be characterizable in terms of the same primary qualities. But, of course, dualism too allows for this.

What might seem genuinely troubling is the possibility, allowed by option (2), that I, God, and a rock might share the same type of real constitution, the same sorts of primary qualities. Now, (1) and (2) were explicitly formulated by me, not by Locke, and one might respond to this concern by suggesting that Locke favors or should favor (1) over (2). It seems to me, however, that both possibilities are

---

[41] Recall that this fits quite precisely with the way Locke describes the question of thinking matter at W IV: 33 and W X: 285: the question is whether one substance can have the affections of solidity, extension, and thought.

available to him, but that his descriptions of superaddition and the lack of any direct acknowledgement of the possibility that matter itself might be highly disjunctive in its nature suggest (2) somewhat more than (1).[42] My response is to observe that Locke's central concern in E IV.x is to eliminate Hobbes's God, and his purportedly demonstrative proof, on my interpretation, is simply aimed at that. In leaving open (2)'s version of thinking matter – that God might configure some material stuff so that it can also manifest thought – the proof thereby leaves open that possibility that God might *be* that sort of configured material stuff. Note, however, that as observed in section 2, Ayers has plausibly identified in Locke a further argument that would apply against this sort of material God – a God whose essence is not mechanist, but whose essence differs only in complexity and configuration from a rock's. That argument is that if thought is a matter of configuration, it is merely a contingent property of its bearer, and thus its presence requires explanation and cannot be attributed to a *first* cause.

9. CONCLUSION: LOCKE'S METAPHYSICAL COMMITMENTS

We are now in a position to appreciate the convergence between Locke's philosophy of body and his philosophy of mind. In considering Locke's view of body, I argued that Locke is not committed to the corpuscularian theory he so often helps himself to; what he is committed to is a much more abstract metaphysics of real constitution and primary quality. His ontology of mind reveals these same commitments, together with the same official agnosticism about what the real constitutions of bodies and minds are actually like. It is this agnosticism that allows him to entertain the possibility of a sort of thinking matter, a substance that is extended, solid, and thinking, compatible with essentialism, despite the fact that he maintains that something whose real constitution is

---

[42] His descriptions of the superaddition of thought to matter do often suggest that God is organizing or adjusting a system, which, lacking such specific organization, would be unable to think (as in E IV.iii.6). That Locke has not specifically contemplated (1) is also suggested by W IV: 469, where Locke concludes from the fact that not all matter thinks that thought is not essential to any matter. If (1) is an option, and if we are interested in real rather than nominal essences, this inference looks problematic.

exhausted by extension, solidity, and their modifications cannot think.

I have suggested elsewhere that Locke's metaphysical commitments are fairly modest, that they amount to a refinement of the view that appearance and reality may diverge and that appearance is causally dependent on reality (Downing 1998: 395). This position might fairly be described as the metaphysical backdrop to mechanism. Of course, one might well find the view and/or the "refinement" controversial. We ought to ask, therefore, about the basis for Locke's commitments, especially about his attachment to the essentialist view that all of a thing's qualities follow from its own real constitution, together with the real constitutions of other substances and the spatial relations among those substances. This seems the most controversial aspect of Locke's ontology, and it may well sound like the sort of metaphysical commitment that a proponent of epistemic modesty ought to eschew, though we would not be disconcerted to find it held by a rationalist such as Leibniz.

In fact, there are (at least) two questions here that Locke should answer, as a student of the human understanding. First, how do we come up with such a view, and second, why should we take it to be true? The answer to the first question must be that this is the view that we naturally derive from reflection on our experience, including the sort of reflection conducted in the *Essay*.[43] And I think this is exactly Locke's position, though his account of it is, of course, less than satisfying if one holds him to his expressed strictly empiricist standards. As for the second, I think Locke's only answer is: this is what it would be for the world to be intelligible in principle. Locke has already given up on the world's being fully intelligible *to us*, as we are presently constituted, with the faculties that we have. As we saw in section 1, Locke holds that we cannot achieve a *scientia* of body, that our best attempt, via our natural physics, the mechanical hypothesis, falls short. Here he disagrees with Leibniz, who insists that the world must be intelligible *to us* and clings, on that basis, to mechanism. That the world is *in*

---

[43] Locke's notions of real constitution and primary quality must, like any other, be derived from reflection on experience. In E II.viii, one thing that Locke shows us is how reflection on sensory experience allows us to distinguish between appearance and reality and arrive at the very notion of a primary quality – a quality that bodies have intrinsically, that grounds other powers.

principle intelligible, intelligible to other spirits and perhaps to us, given other ideas, is a view that Locke shows no signs of abandoning. He ought to regard it as a defeasible assumption – his epistemic modesty demands this much – but he does not regard it as defeated.[44]

[44] Many thanks to Lex Newman and Abraham Roth for helpful comments on this paper. Thanks also to audiences at the University of Massachusetts (Amherst), the University of Illinois at Urbana/Champaign, The Ohio State University, and the Oxford Seminar in Early Modern Philosophy for profitable discussions of this material.

13 The Moral Epistemology of Locke's *Essay*

Locke's general moral theory presents formidable difficulties for the commentator. Depending on where in the *Essay* one looks, the content of morality appears to depend on the Bible, or on the requisites of our fellows, or on our personal needs and interests. Our knowledge of moral principles seems in turn to depend on a priori reflection, social learning, religious instruction, and the analysis of terms and sentences.[1] Locke's generous attempt to accommodate every moral intuition makes it difficult to characterize his doctrines in standard terms. Is Locke a conventionalist who anticipates Hume, or a realist who believes firmly in moral truth? Is he a divine command theorist who looks to the Word of God, or a naturalist who looks to the Law of Nature for moral orientation? Why does he insist that moral reasoning is comparable to mathematical reasoning while at the same time presenting the history of ethics in an unmathematical way as a history of insoluble squabbles between moral sects?

Yet this Easter basket of thoughts and doctrines is not the chaos it seems. To bring some order into it, it is useful to remember that Locke was the first philosopher to give sustained attention to moral epistemology, to treat moral practices as reflecting the acquired concepts and beliefs of practitioners. Although Descartes describes morality as presenting a problem of theory choice, pointing to the difference between a provisional morality to be used whilst undertaking one's inquiries and a perfected, scientific morality that will cap them off,[2] no philosopher before Locke compares and contrasts our ability to discover facts about the natural world with our ability

[1] For an overview, see Schneewind 1994: 199–225.   [2] Descartes 1984: I: 14–5.

to discover the truths of morality, considering both from an epistemological standpoint. As he explained to his critic James Lowde, Locke was not interested in "laying down moral Rules" in the *Essay* but rather in "shewing the original and nature of moral *Ideas*, and enumerating the Rules Men make use of in moral Relations, whether those Rules were true or false..." (E II. xxviii.11: 354 note).[3]

Locke wrote in an era in which there was astonishing progress in the physical sciences, in mathematics, optics, and experimental philosophy, and his interest in the accomplishments of Boyle, Sydenham, and Newton in chemistry, medicine, and physics is well documented. Though the expansion of natural history and anthropology occurred after his death in 1704, Locke's awareness of the plenitudes of nature and culture comes through vividly in the *Essay*. His claim that the mind at birth is tabula rasa, "white Paper, void of all Characters" (E II.i.2: 104), to be written on by experience and education, inspired reformers; the declaration that the mind is pure and good though naïve at birth was a condition of the eighteenth-century faith in progress and perfectibility. Abraham Tucker praised him (somewhat inaccurately, since Locke allowed moral "things" real essences) for "clearing away that incumbrance of innate ideas, real essences, and such like rubbish."[4] Yet Locke is far from an optimist philosopher. He frequently emphasizes that humans exist in what he calls a "twilight of Probability" or a "State of Mediocrity" (E IV.xiv.2: 652; cf. E IV.xii.10; C 1: 559).

Experience inscribes ideas on our tablets, not facts or knowledge of the internal working of things. Our minds, on Locke's view, have no special affinity for truth. His caution contrasts not only with that of other English philosophers like Bacon, Boyle, and Hooke, who hoped for quick and useful results from experimental philosophy, but also with the confidence of Cartesians and Platonists, who considered the human mind happily equipped for insight into the true and immutable natures of things. At times, Locke's harping on the mediocrity of our senses and our intellects and on the complexity and obscurity of the universe seems a dreary parroting

---

[3] Locke is usually considered the first of the British Moralists. Ralph Cudworth, Samuel Clarke, Anthony Ashley Cooper, and Francis Hutcheson all published their major works after the *Essay*.

[4] Tucker 1768, quoted in Sell 1997: 120.

of the old complaints and reproaches of the theologians. His faith in the power of education overlay a belief in intrinsic human depravity, a pessimistic estimation of the power of inclinations and appetites and of the effects of the human search for gratification, indulgence, and pleasure.[5] Locke's attack on innate ideas did not presuppose the view that human beings are entirely blank slates at birth. On the contrary, Locke thought of the infant as possessing native instincts and drives that education and culture needed to subdue.

Locke's refusal to ascribe an innate tropism toward the good to humans and his focus on the social acquisition of ideas seemed cynical to many of his contemporaries. James Lowde saw Locke as a destroyer of morality (Lowde 1694), and Locke's young friend the third earl of Shaftesbury deplored his retributivist emphasis on the punishing authority of God and complained that the attack on innate ideas in the *Essay* "struck at Fundamentals, threw all *Order* and *Virtue* out of the World..." (Cooper 1716: 39). Newton was forced to apologize to Locke for giving out that "you struck at ye roots of morality in a principle you laid down in your book of Ideas."[6]

Locke writes within two thought complexes. In one, he adopts a descriptive perspective on the study of moral ideas in keeping with his general programme. This "idealist" or, more properly, "ideaist" commitment leads him in the direction of relativism and conventionalism, and to an interest in the genealogy and maintenance of normative beliefs, and in the role played by reputation and disgrace in the formation of the moral person. At the same time, Locke had strong realist intuitions. He considered certain traits – sobriety, gentleness with children, responsible parenthood and custodianship of property, respect for womanhood – to be undeniable virtues and to be grounded in the natural law and perhaps in the will of God: things outside the human mind and transcending social convention. His realist intuitions push him toward a conception of absolute right and wrong independent of ideas and cultural practice.[7]

---

[5] See Spellman 1988: 104ff.

[6] Newton was likely referring to Locke's enunciation of the Hobbesian principle that good and evil are understood in reference to pleasure and pain (E II.xx.2). Trumbull and Scott 1959: II: 280, cited in Rogers 1979: 191–205.

[7] Michael Ayers describes the relation between secular conceptions and divine command conceptions of morality as "a standing theme of moral philosophy in the

Within each complex, Locke is both optimistic and pessimistic. As an "idealist optimist," he envisions an orderly and decent society in which human beings pursue their selected ends without mischief, disorder, and confusion because they have acquired and retained sound moral ideas. As an "idealist pessimist," however, he sees the human mind as infested with false beliefs and our perceptions as distorted by prejudice. Human beings are disposed to rigid dogmatism of judgment.

There is scarce any one so floating and superficial in his Understanding, who hath not some reverenced Propositions, which are to him the Principles on which he bottoms his Reasonings; and by which he judgeth of Truth and Falsehood, Right and Wrong: which some, wanting skill and leisure, and others the inclination, and some being taught, that they ought not, to examine; there are few to be found who are not exposed by their Ignorance, Laziness, Education, or Precipitancy, to *take them upon trust*. (E I.iii.24: 82)

Men who are "either perplexed in the necessary affairs of Life, or hot in the pursuit of Pleasures," do not trouble to examine their principles. For one thing, it is time-consuming; for another, it is dangerous to do so:

Who is there almost, that dare shake the foundations of all his past Thoughts and Actions, and endure to bring upon himself the shame of having been a long time wholly in mistake and error? Who is there, hardy enough to contend with the reproach, which is everywhere prepared for those who dare venture to dissent from the received Opinions of their Country or Party?[8]

As a "realist optimist," Locke believes that most human beings agree on what constitutes virtue and vice. Further, their common understandings "in a great measure every-where correspond with

---

seventeenth century" and points to Pierre Nicole's complex handling of the conflict in his *Essais de Morale* (Paris, 1672–85), which Locke endeavoured to translate, as an important influence on his thinking. See Ayers 1991: II: 184ff.

[8] "And where is the Man to be found, that can patiently prepare himself to bear the name of Whimsical, Sceptical, or Atheist, which he is sure to meet with, who does in the least scruple any of the common Opinions? And he will be much more afraid to *question those Principles*, when he shall think them, as most Men do, the standards set up by God in his Mind, to be the Rule and Touchstone of all other Opinions. And what can hinder him from thinking them sacred, when he finds them the earliest of all his own Thoughts, and the most reverenced by others?" (E I. iii.25: 83)

the unchangeable Rule of Right and Wrong, which the Law of God hath established. . . . [W]hereby, even in the corruption of manners, the true boundaries of the Law of Nature, which ought to be the rule of Vertue and Vice, were pretty well preserved" (E II.xxviii.11: 356). Different systems of morals merely reflect different, though equally reasonable, understandings of happiness (E I.iii.6). In his "realist pessimist" moods, however, Locke sees human beings all over the world flagrantly contravening the law of nature. Book I of the *Essay* lays out a discouraging picture of the behaviour human beings engage in to assuage their lusts, their hungers, and their reluctance to be burdened with the care of dependents. According to Locke's sources, they abandon their sick relatives to the elements, bury their unwanted children alive, use female captives to breed children to eat, and eat the mothers when they are past breeding.[9]

Moral laws are "a curb and restraint to . . . exorbitant Desires," Locke maintains (E I.iii.13: 75), but the exorbitant desires that different societies wish to curb are different, and they do not do a consistently good job of curbing them. "View but an Army at the sacking of a Town," he says, ". . . *Robberies, Murders, Rapes,* are the Sports of Men set at Liberty from Punishment and Censure" (E I.iii.9: 70). In war and in distant countries, men often behave as though the rules they would observe at home and with their neighbours are suspended. The hot pursuit of pleasure is evident in the self-indulgence of the upper classes, represented by the drunkard whose decaying health and wasting estates are described in the chapter on "Power" (E II.xxi.35: 253). Though morality is in our long-term interest and conducive to happiness (E II.xx.2: 229), the *"weak and narrow Constitution of our Minds"* limits our ability to perceive our long-term interests and especially our very long-term interests (E II.xxi.64: 276–7). Our epistemic weakness accordingly

---

[9] "In a part of *Asia*, the Sick, when their Case comes to be thought desperate, are carried out and laid on the Earth, before they are dead, and left there, exposed to Wind and Weather, to perish without Assistance or Pity. It is familiar amongst the *Mengrelians*, a People professing Christianity, to bury their Children alive without scruple. There are places where they eat their own Children. The *Caribes* were wont to geld their Children, on purpose to fat and eat them. And *Garcilasso de la Vega* tells us of a People in *Peru*, which were won't to fat and eat the Children they got on their female Captives, whom they kept as Concubines for that purpose; and when they were past Breeding, the Mothers themselves were kill'd too and eaten" (E I.iii.9: 71).

places limits on our moral performance, as he says in a letter to Denis Grenville, and "we are not capeable of living altogeather exactly by a strict rule, nor altogeather without one" (C 1: 559). In trying, as Voltaire described it, to write the history of the soul and not its romance, Locke's concern to describe morally relevant phenomena exactly as he had observed them came into persistent conflict with his desire to encourage his readers to understand morality as rational and universal.

I. MORAL IDEAS AND THEIR FOUNDATIONS

The task of philosophy, according to the Introduction to Locke's *Essay*, is to determine what is useful to life; his friend James Tyrell reported that the idea for the *Essay* had occurred to Locke after a discussion of morals and revealed religion with five or six friends.[10] Though the *Essay* is interpreted more commonly as a theoretical treatise on epistemology than as a prescriptive ethical text, Locke has views about worthwhile, destructive, and useless activities that come through strongly at many places in the work, and his summary of the human condition informs the overall shape and structure of the *Essay*.

Our Business here is not to know all things, but those which concern our Conduct. If we can find out those Measures, whereby a rational Creature put in that State, which Man is in, in this World, may, and ought to govern his Opinions, and Actions depending thereon, we need not be troubled, that some other things escape our Knowledge. (E I.i.6: 46)

The "other things that escape our Knowledge" are, famously, the inner constitutions of substances, the relation between their corpuscular constitutions and the properties flowing from them, the genesis of our perceptual experiences, the existence of immaterial substances (including the human soul), the resurrection of the dead, the future state of the Earth, the existence of angels, and extraterrestrial life (E IV.iii.22–28: 554–60). The barriers to our acquiring such knowledge lie in the limitations of our perceptual faculties; we cannot see atoms, souls, the future, faraway objects and places, or the process of quality generation. However, our ignorance in all

---

[10] See Rogers 1998: 1–22.

these matters does not impact upon the "Condition of our eternal Estate." Moral inquiry, by contrast, is "suited to our natural Capacities, and carries in it our greatest interest" (E IV.xii.11: 646). It is the *"proper Science, and Business of Mankind in general"* (ibid.).

Locke takes it for granted that human beings do acquire some forms of knowledge, including moral knowledge. His chief concern is not with combating skepticism, or showing that the beliefs acquired are not delusory, but with detailing the process by which this normally happens and identifying the impediments to knowledge acquisition. Locke thus allows religious instruction and religious insight a central role in the formation of moral belief, leaving it unclear, however, whether he means to exhibit the grounds of morality or to exhibit what men take to be the grounds of morality. Often his language suggests that the task is genuinely meta-ethical: "[T]he true ground of Morality ... can only be the Will and Law of a God, who sees Men in the dark, has in his Hand Rewards and Punishments, and Power enough to call to account the Proudest Offender" (E I.iii.6: 69).

That God has given a Rule whereby Men should govern themselves, I think there is no body so brutish as to deny. He has a Right to do it, we are his Creatures: He has Goodness and Wisdom to direct our Actions to that which is best: and he has Power to enforce it by Rewards and Punishments of infinite weight and duration, in another Life. ... This is the only true touchstone of *moral Rectitude*. ... (E II.xxviii.8: 352)

Nevertheless, Locke seems in other places to suggest that the notion of a divine command is better construed as one of the regulative ideas – to anticipate Kant's language – that men employ to guide their conduct. His view is that when a child arrives at the ideas of (a) a morally commanding God who (b) has made his requirements clear in Scripture and who (c) requires obedience from that child and everyone else, and at the idea of (d) a future life in which his and everyone else's obedience or disobedience will be rewarded or punished, and sees that (e) she must fear God's wrath, then that child has grasped, for the first time, the *idea of* a real moral obligation.

To forestall the objection that since ideas (a)–(e) are not possessed universally, and since they are inserted by force into young human minds, chiefly in places like England, they are mere superstitions and cannot be the foundations of morality, Locke must ascend from the anthropological standpoint of Book I of the *Essay* to show why the ideas inculcated in England are good ones to have. He does so by shifting his focus from man-as-member-of-a-social-species in Book I to man-as-philosopher in Book II, and then, in Book IV, from man-as-philosopher to man-as-critical-epistemologist, considering the difference between rational persuasion, on the one hand, and justified and unjustified varieties of nonrational faith, on the other. The ideas of God and a future state, though the former is said to be "self-evident" on reflection, are not innate. Whole nations, not just ignorant savages, have "no Notion of a God, no Religion." The Chinese are a highly civilized people, and many atheists close to home are, he suspects, deterred from free expression only by "fear of the Magistrate's Sword, or their Neighbour's Censure" (E I.iv.8: 88). Book II nevertheless shows how we [can] each "frame the best *Idea* of him our Minds are capable of ... by enlarging those simple *Ideas*, we have taken from the Operations of our own Minds, by Reflection; or by our Senses, from exterior things, to that vastness, to which Infinity can extend them" (E II.xxiii.34: 315). Book IV completes this intellectual journey. The "framing" procedure described in Book II does not construct the idea of a law giver with unlimited powers of punishment. Ascending from pagan ignorance to a knowledge of the Christian God by experience and reflection, the subject rounds out his knowledge by accepting on faith, though not by reason, the doctrines in Scripture regarding the commandments of God and the life to come (E IV.xviii.7: 694).

This ascent is problematic. If Locke remains concerned, as a student of the human mind, with the formation of our theological-moral ideas as an individual psychological process, or as an historical process undergone by different cultures at different times, he has not accounted for the normative force of any set of moral prohibitions or commands. If, however, Locke means to show that there are objective obligations, as expressed in the Old and New Testaments, and not merely that some portion of humanity has ideas of them, he must show that (a)–(e) are all true and that we come to know them, not merely to believe them. For if we merely believed (a)–(e), it would follow not that there were objective obligations, but only that we believed them to exist. And demonstrating the truth of ideas (a)–(e) was a task for which Locke was radically unequipped.

Indeed, the existence of a future state and future rewards and punishments are not assured by demonstration but are merely probable, according to Locke's epistemology. As Thomas Burnet pointed out in his critique of the *Essay*, Locke is at best entitled to infer that there are *probably* genuine moral obligations and that they are *probably* those laid down in Scripture (Burnet 1697: 20). Rational theology really assures us only of the existence of an eternal cogitative being, according to E IV.x.11: 625. Faith, Locke tells us, is an epistemic state that is "beyond doubt" and that "perfectly excludes all wavering as our Knowledge itself." But Locke denominates this state chiefly in order to warn his reader that it is possible to have "Faith and Assurance in what is not a divine Revelation." And he frequently emphasizes that truths discovered through "Knowledge and Contemplation of our own *Ideas*, will always be certainer to us, than those which are conveyed to us by *Traditional Revelation*" (E IV.xviii.4: 690–1). The existence of an objective moral law thus seems to depend on conditions that we cannot know for certain to obtain.

II. INNATE IDEAS, RELATIVISM, AND CONVENTION

One might wonder why Locke did not compare the physical laws of nature – the laws of collision mechanics, Newton's law of gravitation, Boyle's law of gases – with the prohibitory laws of justice and morality, of whose force he appears to be certain, and which, like moral rules, are not innate and are not known to certain ignorant and uncultivated persons. Originally a concept in Roman jurisprudence, the law of nature referred to tendencies that were both normal and normative, tendencies shared with the (better-behaved) animals, whose violation constituted what later legal theorists of the Christian era considered a particularly horrific category of *crimen contra natura*; incest, parricide, parental neglect, homosexuality, and bestiality were principal examples of such *crimen*.[11]

---

[11] Occasionally, philanthropy, obedience to the sovereign, and the right of self-defense, as well as the common ownership of resources, fell under the law of nature. A useful discussion can be found in Greene 1997.

Yet the analogy between a universal physical and a universal moral law – later so impressive to Kant – did not occur to Locke, for reasons quite independent of his weaker grip on the mathematical portions of physical science. The idealistic-descriptive strain in Locke is bound up with his thesis that moral terms, unlike substance terms, refer to mind-dependent entities. At the same time, he is convinced that some aspects of morality are not mere fashion or accepted practice. This leads him to compare moral to mathematical rather than to physical knowledge and to suggest that both can be acquired by effort and application.

In politics, Locke was just as mistrustful of introspection by the downtrodden and the upheavals it could effect as he was of the appeal to authority and its repressive sequelae. The radical Protestants of the Revolution searched their own minds for principles of social justice and found there, with the help of their knowledge of primitive Christianity, the anti-authoritarian, anti-property sentiments that disturbed the civil peace and put the country in an uproar. Their views, the results of "immediate Revelation; of Illumination without search; and of certainty without Proof, and without Examination..." (E IV.xix.8: 700), are criticized by Locke as "groundless opinions." Yet it is difficult to see Locke as worried in 1690 about outbreaks of enthusiasm and political radicalism. His polemic is directed against the claim that all the morality a human being needs to know is contained in a few simple maxims engraved into the heart of man by God, and that, provided this knowledge is not corrupted by education and custom, humans will be drawn spontaneously to the good. The theory of innate ideas, already ridiculed by Samuel Parker as implying that God has hung "little pictures of Himself and all his Creatures in every man's Understanding" (Parker 1666),[12] was too sanguine for Locke. He feared, moreover, that its naiveté led to moral and religious cynicism. For if some recently encountered humans lacked any native imprint of the Christian God (and this could easily be shown in Locke's time), this could be taken to mean that the idea of the Christian God was in fact imprinted by books and teachers and was a fiction.

In the *Essay*, Locke associates innate ideas with the Deist Herbert of Cherbury. Cherbury was an exponent of what he called

---

[12] Cited in Rogers 1979: 194.

"layman's religion," a kind of universal system with minimal doctrinal content. Herbert posits a Platonic *instinctus naturalis*, guiding human beings toward goodness and happiness.[13] His book on truth presents five ethico-religious maxims as *"Veritates nostrae Catholicae."* Examples of these maxims are that there is a supreme God, that He ought to be worshipped, that "Vice and crime must be expiated by repentance," and that "There is reward or punishment in the afterlife." Locke may also have had in mind, as proponents of innate ideas, John Smith, Isaac Barrow, Henry More, Benjamin Whichcote,[14] and Ralph Cudworth, whose *True and Immutable Morality* is thought to have circulated in manuscript, and to which Locke's long and intense relationship with Cudworth's daughter Damaris Masham might have given him access. The notion that God implants moral notions in our souls was, however, as Yolton has pointed out, ubiquitous in early seventeenth-century English texts.[15] It fit in well with the Cartesian doctrine that the idea of God is innate (Descartes 1984: II: 31; I: 309).

The rather different point that moral qualities are not apprehended by the rational intellect but are registered by another, more emotional faculty, which nevertheless corresponds to a basic human endowment, is one that is taken up by moral sense theorists from Shaftesbury and Cudworth to Hume. Cudworth's main point, as a Platonist and as an opponent of Hobbes's materialism, is that sensory experience cannot impress the rightness or wrongness, beauty or ugliness, of external objects and events on us. These evaluations presuppose an intrinsic quality in the thing perceived and "an inward and active energy of the mind itself" (Cudworth 1996: 73) in evaluating them, as well as a native disposition toward the good. If the soul were tabula rasa, "there could not be any such thing as moral good and evil, just and unjust, forasmuch as these

---

[13] Herbert of Cherbury's *De veritate* (1624) has been republished in an English translation by Meyrick Carre (London, 1992); *De religione laici* (1645) was translated by Harold Hutcheson (New Haven, CT: Yale University Press, 1944); for an overview, see Nuovo 2000.

[14] Rogers 1979.

[15] See also the discussion in Yolton 1956: 25–48. "Some variant of the theory [of innate ideas]," Yolton comments, "can be found in almost any pamphlet of the early part of the [seventeenth] century dealing with morality, conscience, the existence of God or natural law" (31).

differences do not arise merely from the outward objects or from the impresses which they make upon the senses."[16] Locke is, however, far from granting such a faculty. Above and beyond his reluctance to expose religion and morals to critique on the grounds of the total absence of certain ideas in untutored persons, Locke's view of human depravity and his anti-metaphysical bias rendered Platonism unacceptable. His keen awareness of the extreme forms of cruelty of man to man and the casual dissipation of his contemporaries prevented his taking seriously the philosopher's claim that the human soul is drawn to it by a Platonic form of the good, and that there is a preexisting harmony between objectively good and beautiful forms and our minds. The human soul, in Locke's dim view of it, responds chiefly to hedonistic incentives. As the soul is tabula rasa with respect to its evaluations, and egoism is the primitive, default state, the human child needs education and correction through social approval and disapproval to arrive at an understanding of proper conduct. The child and the savage are not specially corrupted; their cruel and self-centered behaviour is not degeneration from a pure and innocent state, but simply lack of socialization and knowledge.

It is this broader claim that underlies Locke's attack on innate ideas. If any moral rule were innate, he says, "Parents preserve and cherish your children" would be such a one, yet even the Greeks and Romans, not to mention the savages, did not observe it: they were known to have deliberately exposed their inconvenient children, leaving them to their deaths or to the mercy of strangers. "There is scarce that Principle of Morality to be named, or *Rule* of *Vertue* to be thought on (those only excepted, that are absolutely necessary to hold Society together, which commonly are neglected betwixt distinct Societies) which is not, somewhere or other, *slighted* and condemned by the general Fashion of *whole Societies* of Men, governed by practical Opinions, and Rules of living quite opposite to others" (E I.iii.10: 72).

To the implicit objection that there are principles that might well command universal assent, at least among adults, such as Herbert's principles, Locke's answer is that they contain terms such as "virtue" and "sin" that are differently understood by different

[16] Ibid., 145.

persons. To suggest that God has imprinted these maxims on our hearts is to suggest that what is there is ambiguous and without determinate content, hence useless. Locke does not dispute that we can recognize Herbert's propositions as self-evidently true, that is, that we can attach meanings to them "at first hearing" that make them recognizable as obviously true, but he doubts that there are only five such basic moral truths and that they are *in foro interiori descriptae*. For, if all self-evident principles were innate, we should have to conclude that the mind is stocked with a plethora of useless trivialities, such as that red is not blue, a square is not circle, and so on (E I.ii.19–20: 58). Conscience, then, does not reveal moral principles, but only assesses the conformity of a person's behaviour to preexisting moral principles. Interesting, substantive moral truths are hard won:

[I]t will be hard to instance any one moral Rule, which can pretend to so general and ready an assent as, *What is, is,* or to be so manifest a Truth as this, *That it is impossible for the same thing to be, and not to be.* Whereby, it is evident, That they are farther removed from a title to be innate; and the doubt of their being native Impressions on the Mind, is stronger against these moral Principles than the other. (E I.iii.1: 65)

Locke appears finally to think that the theory of innate ideas promotes nihilism. The Platonists overplay their hand, for, failing to find innate moral ideas in themselves, or impressed by their apparent absence in others, disgusted readers react by rejecting Platonism and all its idealistic apparatus and conclude that they are mere machines that cannot help what they do: "[T]hey take away not only innate, but all Moral Rules whatsoever, and leave not a possibility to believe any such" in the name of mechanism (E I.iii.14: 76). Now, Locke is a kind of mechanist. He believes that visible effects depend on subvisible corpuscular causes, that we do not know whether the mind is a thinking, active, immaterial, and imperishable substance, and that matter may be endowed with a power of thought (E IV.iii.6: 542). Yet he is not a libertine, and he has a strong sense of agency and moral responsibility. He will try the difficult task: "to *put Morality and Mechanism together*" (ibid., 77), and this project is one to which he applies himself seriously in his discussion of weakness of the will and in his advancing of a compatibilist view of agency.

III. DEMONSTRATION

Locke's claim that morality is demonstrable might seem at odds with his notion that faith-based theological ideas support our notion of morality. However, in insisting that practical knowledge (he blurs the lines between moral and political philosophy) is analogous to mathematical knowledge, he expresses the hopeful view that a certain system of morality can be articulated in regions in which revelation is silent and Scripture provides inadequate guidance. "The *Idea* of a supreme Being, infinite in Power, Goodness, and Wisdom, whose Workmanship we are, and on whom we depend; and the *Idea* of our selves, as understanding rational Beings, being such as are clear in us, would, I suppose, if duly considered and pursued, afford such Foundations of our Duty and Rules of Action, as might place *Morality amongst the Sciences capable of Demonstration* ... " (E IV.iii.18: 549). At the same time, the hope of demonstrability reflects the superiority of proved knowledge over faith, for propositions "whose Certainty is built upon the clear Perception of the Agreement, or Disagreement of our *Ideas*" are preferable to those obtained by revelation (E IV.xviii.5: 691–2).

I doubt not, but from self-evident Propositions, by necessary Consequences, as incontestable as those in Mathematicks, the measures of right and wrong might be made out, to any one that will apply himself with the same Indifferency and Attention to the one, as he does to the other of these Sciences. (E IV.iii.18: 549)

Locke devotes considerable ingenuity to establishing a parallel between a mathematical concept and a moral concept. The key lines of parallelism are these:

1   Moral ideas are "mixed modes" made by the mind (E III.v.3–6). (Most) mathematical ideas are "complex" modes made by the mind (E II.xxxi.3).

2   Mathematical objects (triangle, square, circle), morally relevant actions (parricide), and virtues (sincerity) have a conceptual reality as *ideas*. Even if there were no circles in the world, if no one had ever committed parricide, and if no one was ever perfectly sincere, there are truths about, and there can be knowledge of, these "beings" (E III.v.5; E IV.iv.8).

3   The real essences of mathematical concepts and of "the Things moral Words stand for" may be "perfectly known" (E III.xi.16: 516), though our knowledge of them is often "wrong, imperfect or inadequate" (E II.xxxi.5: 378).

On these points (and on an obscure theory of "Archetypes or Patterns" to which the mind intends its inventions to correspond [ibid.]) are founded Locke's hope of a science of ethics. "...I am bold to think, that *Morality is capable of Demonstration*, as well as Mathematics: Since the precise real Essence of the things moral Words stand for, may be perfectly known; and so the Congruity, or Incongruity of the Things themselves, be certainly discovered, in which consists perfect Knowledge" (E III.xi.16: 516). Locke thinks that reflection on terms like "justice" brings genuine insight and that clarification of concepts confers moral knowledge without costly and troublesome experimental intervention into reality.

> It is far easier for Men to frame in their Minds an *Idea*, which shall be the Standard to which they will give the name *Justice*, with which Pattern so made, all Actions that agree shall pass under that denomination, than, having seen *Aristides*, to frame an *Idea*, that shall in all things be exactly like him, who is as he is, let Men make what *Idea*, they please of him. For the one, they need but know the combination of *Ideas*, that are put together in their own Minds; for the other, they must enquire into the whole Nature, and abstruse hidden Constitution, and various Qualities of a Thing existing without them. (E III.xi.17: 517)

Locke tries to show that a natural kind like "gold" or "water" is very different from what might be called a "moral kind" such as "murder" in ways that, on his view, are advantageous for the theoretical study of morality. Moral terms are framed, he says, according to human interest. A man's killing a sheep does not fall under the concept of "murder," as a man's killing a man under particular circumstances does. Human needs, dispositions, and beliefs, one might say, render the disjunctive concepts "killing a man or a sheep" or even "killing a man or another animal" so unimportant that we have no special word for them. Locke's discussion further brings out the way in which notions of intention and relation enter into the idea of a moral kind. Actions that superficially appear highly dissimilar are made by the mind into instances of the same thing. The shooting of an uncle might look to an observer more like the shooting of a sheep than it does the slow poisoning of a spouse, to borrow an example of John Colman's, yet there is a deep connection between the two superficially dissimilar actions.[17] Locke concludes that although murder, the thing meant by the word 'murder', has a real essence, the complex idea is nevertheless made by the mind, which, "by its free choice, gives a connexion to a certain number of *Ideas*" (E III.v.6: 431).

Some of our ideas, then, contain "certain Relations, Habitudes, and Connexions [e.g., murder is connected to man] ... that we cannot conceive them separable from them, by any Power whatsoever. And in these only, we are capable of certain and universal Knowledge" (E IV.iii.29: 559). Locke does not suggest that the idea of "wrongness" can be seen to stand in an intrinsic relation to or connection with the ideas of theft, murder, and adultery, or that the idea of "rightness" is disconnected from them. It is, moreover, unclear how men can come to know that their self-made moral ideas are not, after all, weak, imperfect, and inadequate. If there are no "archetypes" for moral concepts, it is hard to see how moral knowledge can fail; if there are archetypes, it is hard to see how it can succeed, since we have no independent access to them. Locke offers several examples of how he thinks relations and connections between ideas furnish us with knowledge.

First, we may follow out a chain of inferences such as the following: From the idea that God punishes, we may infer that God punishes justly, and thence that God punishes the guilty. From this it follows that we are sometimes guilty, which implies that we have the power to do otherwise. Self-determination, in case we doubted that we had it and thought we were mere machines, can thus be inferred from the notion of God as judge (E IV.xvii.4: 673). Elsewhere (E IV.iii.18: 549–50), Locke offers two examples of demonstrable propositions of political philosophy: "Where there is no property, there is no injustice" and "No government allows absolute liberty." The argument for the truth of the first proposition runs as follows: The idea of property is the idea of a right to a thing, and the idea of injustice is the idea of a violation of the right to a thing. Hence the concept of injustice presupposes that of the right to a thing. There is an "agreement of ideas" between justice and

[17] Colman 1983: 128.

property, such that a condition of the world without property would be a condition of the world without injustice. The idea of a government is the idea of a force that establishes society on certain rules or laws, while absolute liberty is the right of anyone to do as he pleases. The idea of government thus disagrees with or excludes the idea of absolute liberty. A condition of the world with absolute liberty would be a condition of the world without government.

How convincing is Locke's claim that we can demonstrate important moral principles? Berkeley joked that "[t]o demonstrate Morality it seems one need only make a Dictionary of Words & see which included which."[18] In fact, as Colman observes, Locke had just such a dictionary of mixed modes in mind (cf. E II.xxii.12). Yet there are several difficulties with Locke's position. First, moral concepts like "murder" and "property" are "essentially contested," to borrow W. B. Gallie's term.[19] Some believe that abortion and killing by soldiers in war are both murder; others deny that one or both is murder. Some speakers of English will insist that the claim "Robin was justified in murdering Jean" is semantically aberrant on the grounds that murder cannot be justified and that there is accordingly nothing it would be like for the claim to be true. Others will think the sentence could be true or false. Disagreement over precisely what murder entails or excludes cannot be resolved by mathematical methods, since mathematics begins with precise, stipulative definitions. Second, even if we came to perfect agreement on what acts were to count as murder, there would remain many things about murder that we could discover only empirically, by observation and experiment, if at all. The causes of murder, the statistical incidence of murders of various types, the motives that lead murderers to murder are not demonstrable from consideration of the concept of murder. Changes in our factual beliefs about the phenomenon, murder, can produce changes in our normative views about how it is morally right to treat murderers.

Locke's allegedly demonstrable statement "Where there is no property, there is no injustice" implies that one can behave cruelly toward a propertyless person, such as a homeless beggar or a

[18] George Berkeley, *Philosophical Commentaries*, 690. In his *Works*, ed. A.A. Luce (London: Thomas Nelson, 1948), vol. 1, p. 84.
[19] Gallie 1964.

nomadic savage, but not unjustly. Accepting the claim and its entailments, however, carries no implication whatsoever about what we may do to beggars or nomads or are forbidden to do to them, and we cannot claim to have demonstrated a normative statement. One might insist that the statement can be interpreted as a genuine normative claim, that is, as "The institution of private property cannot be basically unjust," or even as "Everyone has a right to his or her property and cannot be justly required to give it up." Both claims would be contested by a radical who asserts that "All property is theft" or that "All property as it is currently obtained and held is obtained and held unjustly." Such a person may mean by "property" and "just" the same thing as his opponent. In short, we cannot demonstrate substantive moral-political propositions such as:

1   Slavery is not unjust, since it deprives no one of his property.
2   Governments may repress free speech.

Locke indeed seemed to lose confidence in his view that morality is demonstrable. In a letter to Molyneux of 1692, he retracted his earlier confident statement. "Though by the view I had of moral ideas, whilst I was considering that subject, I thought I saw that morality might be demonstratively made out, yet whether I am able so to make it out, is another question" (C 4: 524). In the *Reasonableness of Christianity* of 1695, he concedes that human reason "never from unquestioned principles, by clear deductions, made out an entire body of the law of nature."[20] In another letter to Molyneux written the following year, he decides that the Gospels "contain so perfect a body of Ethicks, that reason may be excused from that enquiry, since she may find man's duty clearer and easier in revelation than in herself" (C 5: 595). To Carey Mordaunt, he recommends a programme of reading, consisting of the New Testament, Cicero, Aristotle, and Pufendorf, avoiding, however, Scholastic ethics and all works dealing with "how to difine, distinguish, and dispute about the names of virtues and vices."[21]

Locke is surely right to emphasize that when we are interested in questions like "What are the appropriate limits to the exercise of

[20] W VII: 140.   [21] Letter to Carey Mordaunt, September/October 1697, C (2320).

government power with regard to the control of seditious literature or movement across national borders?" we must reflect on the function of government – the actions, intentions, and relations involved in the concept of government. Beyond that, however, we must call up our experience of repressive and permissive regimes and predict as well as we can the effects of various policies. Fortunately, this experience is available to us historically and narratively; it is not hopelessly distant or hopelessly small. To be sure, this is not "demonstration" in the sense of mathematical proof, nor is it the pure "showing" of Royal Society demonstrations. Yet Locke's suggestion that this knowledge is available to us so long as we employ cognitive effort, and that this effort is not merely introspective, seems correct. If the propositions of morality are discovered, not intuited, they can become known only through inquiry into matters of fact regarding nature and society, or into relations of ideas, or by some combination of the two.

Locke's claim that morality – and we should understand by this political philosophy as well – is demonstrable is important in another respect. It communicated his expectation that law and government power could be constructed on a reasonable and non-authoritarian, nonsectarian basis. He thinks of "indifferency and attention" as capable of raising the study of morality from doxology to science, in much the way that the seventeenth century raised the study of nature from doxology to science. For, traditionally, formulating a moral philosophy had been a matter of choosing which sect to follow. The Epicureans defended atomism and pleasure; the Stoics attacked Epicurean hedonism and defended Providence and a world-spirit; the Platonists held to the Forms, including the Form of the Good; the Aristotelians, to form and matter and *eudaimonia*, and so on.

Seventeenth-century philosophers insisted that they were discarding the old model for selecting ontologies. They looked admiringly on the consensus of mathematics and on the beginnings of consensus in experimental science. The quest for "certitude" meant the quest for undisputed knowledge, which, by definition, could not be sectarian. Certain results, therefore, could best be arrived at by a mind that was not an adherent of any system of nature or of morals. The ideal of impartial inquiry was articulated by Thomas Sprat in his *History of the Royal Society* of 1667, in which he proposed to examine all matters without prejudice or deference to the ancients. Yet the Royal Society avoided discussing politics and religion, which were seen as unfit for objective inquiry. Academicians like John Wilkins doubted that morality could be demonstrated. The notion of an impartial investigation of moral duties was very much a conceptual novelty.[22]

Locke refers to the doubtfulness of sectarian principles and the propensity of sectaries to be "confirmed in Mistake and Errour" (E IV.xii.5: 642; cf. IV.xii.4–6). Locke's critics, accustomed to thinking of morality as articulated by one ancient school and defended against another, perhaps found his combination of rationalist ambition and historical rootlessness disconcerting. Yet Locke's commitment to "indifferency" and the avoidance of sectarianism is exemplary. Actually to seek moral knowledge is not the same thing as seeing how far utilitarianism, for example, or virtue theory, or another particular doctrine can be defended against objections by a partisan committed to it in advance. Above all, Locke's view that moral knowledge is hard won and often involves the reversal of long-established custom is appealing: "[M]oral principles require Reasoning and Discourse, and some Exercise of the Mind, to discover the certainty of their Truth. They lie not open as natural Characters ingraven on the Mind ... and by their own light ... certain and known to every Body" (E I.iii.1: 66). Effort is necessary, even if it is not always sufficient.

This effort does not, however, condemn us to unceasing moral inquiry or overscrupulousness. Though some aspects of our conduct are fixed by Scripture, or by the law of nature, or are demonstrable, and others are constrained by local custom and convention, a good deal is up to the individual. That we have considerable moral liberty and need not "clog every action of our lives, even the minutest of them ... with infinite Consideration before we began it and unavoidable perplexity and doubt when it is donne" was the substance of the letter Locke wrote to Denis Grenville in 1678 (C 1: 558). The actions forbidden or mandated as a matter of real obligation are therefore few. Other performances are elicited and constrained by the regard or scorn of men, and it is presumably prudent to take

---

[22] Conroy (1961) summarizes contemporary and post-Lockean views on moral demonstration. See also Smith 1962.

note of this, but we still enjoy considerable freedom in deciding how to live. Though this rather existentialist-sounding message is muted in the *Essay*, it comes through in Locke's rejection of perfectionism. Our inability to demonstrate the existence and uniqueness of a *summum bonum* by philosophical argument allows us a certain latitude in pursuing what appears and feels good to us:

Hence it was, I think, that the Philosophers of old did in vain enquire, whether the *Summum bonum* consisted in Riches, or bodily Delights, or Virtue or Contemplation: And they might have as reasonably disputed, whether the best Relish were to be found in Apples, Plumbs, or Nuts; and have divided themselves into Sects upon it. ... So the greatest Happiness consists, in the having those things, which produce the greatest Pleasure; and in the absence of those, which cause any disturbance, any pain. Now these, to different Men, are very different things. (E II.xxi.55: 269)

Our pursuits are constrained only by what God (= the Law of Nature) explicitly prohibits. Locke's commitment to pleasure is even more evident in his early journal entries. "The business of man ... [is] to be happy in this world by enjoyment of the things of nature subservient to life health ease and pleasure and the com-fortable hopes of an other life when this is ended."[23] Since we have a powerful drive toward happiness, moral steering often requires only the correction of false beliefs concerning what will make us happy.

In the meantime, Locke's conventionalism is evident: "[W]hatever is pretended," he says, "these Names, *Vertue* and *Vice*, in the particular instances of their application, through the several Nations and Societies of Men in the World, are constantly attrib-uted only to such actions, as in each Country and Society are in reputation or discredit" (E II.xxviii.10: 353). He refers to the "secret and tacit consent" established in "Societies, Tribes, and Clubs of Men in the World: whereby several actions come to find Credit or Disgrace amongst them according to the Judgment, Maxims, or Fashions of that place" (ibid.). He anticipates Hume's notion that we do an effective job of policing one another and guiding one another's conduct into tolerable channels by allocating affection and esteem. Our desire for honour and a good reputation helps us to

---

[23] Locke, journal entry of February 8, 1677, in Aaron and Gibb 1936: 88.

perform appropriately in our own small societies, though aggression and recklessness pose constant threats to the social order.

The distortions of reasoning power induced by pleasure and desire are treated with great seriousness by Locke. We make wrong judgments of our long-term interests, since "[o]bjects, near our view, are apt to be thought greater, than those of a larger size, that are more remote" (E II.xxi.63: 275). We estimate present pains as needing immediate removal even if suffering them is conducive to greater happiness. The pain of deprivation of a desired object "forces us, as it were, blindfold into its embraces" (E II.xxi.64: 277). Further, we minimize the evil consequences of our actions, or suppose them avoidable (E II.xxi.66). Moreover, our emotions make us impervious to moral reasoning and blind to our own true interests. We are liable to "extreme disturbance [that] possess our whole Mind, as when the pain of the Rack, an impetuous *uneasiness*, as of Love, Anger, or any other violent Passion, running away with us, allows us not to liberty of thought, and we are not Masters enough of our own Minds to consider thoroughly, and examine fairly" (E II.xxi.53: 267–8). Yet, so long as we forbear from "too hasty compliance with our desires" and aim for "the moderation and restraint of our Passions" and sober reflection on our true happiness, God, "who knows our frailty, pities our weakness, and requires of us no more of us than we are able to do, and sees what was, and was not in our power, will judge as a kind and merciful Father" (ibid.). When we honestly do not know what to do and must somehow take action anyway, we can only hope that such reasonings as we do bring to bear on the matter are indifferent and attentive, and that if we were to be regarded by a judge who sees into the heart, that judge would not conclude that we were, after all, self-serving, ignorant, and lazy.

Locke's stress on the "arbitrariness" of moral notions – our framing of moral concepts according to what we value and disparage – implies that we could well have cared about different things than we do, in which case quite different actions would have been right and wrong. We could have regarded the killing of a sheep as "murder," or defined theft so that food items could not be "stolen." His view that we construct or "frame" the moral notions that we believe we need is not unrelated to modern notions of concept formation and their relation to human interests, to Searle's "collective intentionality." This might be taken to imply full-blown relativism: since there is no "we" who share a universal common understanding of moral right and wrong, all local understandings must be on the same footing. Locke rejects this inference, though he does not reconcile his commitment to natural law and revealed morality with his idealist emphasis on the variety of moral understandings that exist.

Locke was misled by the too-sharp distinction he draws between moral concepts conceived as "mixed modes," which he regards as the "Workmanship of the understanding" (E III.v.6: 431) and as "arbitrarily" constructed (ibid.), and substances, which he regards as given in nature, even if the names of species also reflect the workmanship of the understanding. In fact, we can discover, by empirical investigation, a great deal about mixed modes that is morally relevant, for example, the best ways to prevent theft, the motives behind rape, the frequency of adultery in a particular society, the conditions that provoke civil wars and revolutions. The moral-political terms "theft" and "revolution," though they do not name substances like "water" and "gold," nevertheless name phenomena that are as real and robust as snowstorms and volcanoes, and we might be said to know approximately as much about them. The better we understand them, the better our moral beliefs ought to be, and the kind of effort required to understand them is not only analytical but also observational and experimental.

IV. MORAL BELIEFS AND MORAL PROGRESS

What evidence is there that moral theory has flourished to the extent that it has abandoned sectarian commitments, such as Stoicism, hedonism, and Aristotelianism, or, alternatively, the ethics of revealed religion? What of Locke's hope that ethics and politics would yield to the same methods – assiduous, impartial inquiry – that had brought progress in other disciplines? To be sure, modern philosophy of science is not convinced that impartiality rather than commitment, sometimes irrational commitment, to a paradigm brings theoretical progress, and theoretical progress in the sciences does not necessarily improve human life. Yet Locke is surely right to insist that "indifferency and attention," rather than blind defensiveness applied to well-worked-out positions, is a precondition of theoretical progress and that such theoretical progress is progress in terms of what persons actually value.

In trying to decide whether moral progress is a kind of intellectual progress, as Locke often, though not always, insists that it is, we are perhaps handicapped by our limited comprehension of the everyday lives of past people and of the local understandings of various strata of their societies. The vices mentioned in the *Essay* include drunkenness, financial irresponsibility, adultery, murder, rape, robbery, and destruction of property. Though we are familiar with all these phenomena, the reader of Locke's text is naturally curious. Did middle-class persons forge wills and cheat their business partners? How common was blackmail? Did most servants, or only a few, steal from their masters? Did Locke's contemporaries smother their illegitimate or malformed infants, confine their schizophrenic adolescents in attics, starve their demented parents? And were such practices regarded with horror or as tragically necessary? Where were Locke's friends inclined to draw the line between a *Kavaliersdelict* and a seriously wrong action? The *Essay* itself provides few clues. Yet readers who assume that the moral understandings of Locke's time have changed little over the past three centuries might reflect on the discomfort that a modern audience would experience if a typical Restoration plot of chicanery and getting around people were set by Steven Sondheim as a musical comedy with modern scenes, language, and characters.

Though he is hardly the first philosopher to comment on the diversity of human customs and opinions, Locke is the first philosopher to treat morality as a set of anthropological and psychological phenomena. Though this was a novel and fruitful way to initiate an investigation, the relationship between ideas and practices is perhaps not as straightforward as Locke seems to assume. The Caribs may no more have believed that it is right to eat children (assuming they did so) than we believe it is right to impose suffering on animals or to exploit workers. Like us, they might have deplored these practices as reflecting a sad necessity and lack of appealing alternatives. A message taken from Locke's "Book of Ideas" was that through the examination and refinement of our ideas, the world itself can be changed. But his discussion makes amply clear that, to influence what happens in the world, it is insufficient to change beliefs about moral right and wrong, or rather, that beliefs about what is right and wrong cannot be changed unless there are also changes in expectations, hopes, desires, and beliefs about what is the case in the world.

14 Locke on Judgment

I. INTRODUCTION

Locke usually uses the term "judgment" in a rather narrow but not unusual sense, as referring to the faculty that produces probable opinion or assent.[2] His account is explicitly developed by analogy with his account of knowledge, and like that account, it is developed in terms of the relation various ideas bear to one another. Whereas knowledge is the *perception* of the agreement or disagreement of any of our ideas, judgment is the *presumption* of their agreement or disagreement. Intuitive knowledge is the immediate perception of the agreement or disagreement of two ideas, for example, white is not black. If we perceive the idea of white, and the idea of black, nothing more is needed to perceive that white and black disagree with respect to identity. We just see or intuit it. Demonstrative knowledge is more complicated. Suppose we have or perceive the idea of the internal angles of a triangle, and also the idea of two right angles. Unless one is a prodigy, one can't just "see" that these two ideas agree with respect to equality; a demonstration is needed. For Locke, such a demonstration requires that we find another idea, such as 180 degrees, so that we can intuit that this

---

[1] Some of the themes in this paper were first explored in Owen 1999a, 1999b, and 2003. I am very grateful to Lex Newman, Michael Jacovides, Walter Ott, Dario Perinetti, and Don Garrett for critical comments and advice.

[2] See entry 7a under "judgement or judgment" in the OED: "The formation of an opinion or notion concerning something by exercising the mind upon it; an opinion, estimate." Characteristically, Locke uses the term "judgment" to refer, not just to the faculty that produces beliefs or opinions, but also to the characteristic activity of the faculty, and to the belief or opinion produced by the faculty. "Knowledge" is used in a similarly broad way.

idea stands in the relation of equality both to the internal angles of a triangle, and to two right angles. Thus a demonstration, for Locke, is a chain of ideas, such that each idea in the chain is intuitively seen to agree or disagree with its neighbours. A demonstration is a series of intuitions.

But now suppose that instead of constructing a demonstration to show that the internal angles of a triangle are equal to two right angles, we simply take the word of our math teacher. She tells us that the internal angles of a triangle are equal to two right angles, and we believe her. In this case we do not have demonstrative knowledge, but only probable belief or opinion. We presume an agreement between two ideas, an agreement that we could have perceived if we had constructed the demonstration. And note that this presumption must always have grounds or a cause.[3] The testimony and veracity of our teacher causes us to believe that the internal angles of a triangle are equal to two right angles. According to Locke, this grounding of our belief just is probable reasoning. There is no immediate belief, as there is immediate knowledge. All belief is the result of probable reasoning; that is to say, all belief is inferential.

Locke developed his account of judgment, probability, and belief to supplement his account of knowledge. Knowledge, it turns out, is very limited, and in many matters, including the empirical investigation of nature, we must use our judgment and be guided by probability. As knowledge is the perception of the agreement or disagreement of ideas, so judgment is the presumption of such agreement or disagreement. Belief is seen as an approximation to knowledge; belief is like knowledge but less so. Judgment shares an important characteristic with knowledge: it is more or less involuntary. Although we can choose whether or not to open our eyes, and in which direction to look, we can't control which ideas appear to us, or whether they agree or disagree. Similarly, although we can decide whether or not to continue our enquiries, we cannot decide what to believe, given the evidence we have.

The ascription of several of these theses to Locke is controversial, and I will defend them in some detail in section 3 of this paper. But

---

[3] The two grounds of probability are the uniformity of nature and the veracity of testimony. Unlike Hume, Locke does not seem very interested in the question of how these grounds themselves are to be accounted for.

one thing is no longer controversial.[4] Even in this narrow sense, judgment is clearly an important topic for Locke. At the very beginning of the *Essay*, Locke announces that the purpose of his essay is to enquire into, not just knowledge, but also opinion or belief. Locke's account of it, combined with his account of sensitive knowledge, can be seen as the beginning of the modern conception of empirical knowledge.

There is a broader sense of 'judgment' that Locke is concerned with, though he never addressed it using that term.[5] Descartes distinguished between the intellect and the will. The intellect perceives various ideas or propositions, but it is the will that asserts or denies such a proposition to be true. Judgment in the broad sense is judging something to be true or false. According to Descartes, making a judgment requires not only the intellect but also the will. In some respects, this is similar to the modern, post-Fregean view. The grasping or understanding of the content of a proposition is one matter; our asserting or denying it is another. When I assert the truth-functional conditional "If the president dies when in office, the vice president becomes president," I assert neither that the president died in office nor that the vice president became president. But I must understand the content of those unasserted propositions if I am to understand the content of the conditional.

The modern view about the distinction between understanding a proposition and asserting or denying it is very familiar to contemporary philosophers, and it is similar enough to Descartes's view that it is very easy to think that Descartes's view was pretty standard in early modern philosophy. It is thus tempting to read that view into Locke. In section 2 of this chapter, I will argue that

---

[4] I say "no longer" because until recently, belief, judgment, and probability were topics in Locke that were largely ignored. There was, for instance, no chapter devoted to it in *The Cambridge Companion to Locke* (Chappell 1994), though Wolterstorff's essay (1994) in that volume presents an interpretation. But more recently, even introductory books on Locke contain discussions of it. See Jolley 1999 and Lowe 1995. Jolley says, "A major theme of Book 4 is thus the very limited nature of our knowledge in the strict sense; in many of the areas of enquiry, including what we now call science, we must be content with probability" (Jolley 1999: 188).

[5] See entry 9b under "judgment or judgment" in the OED: "The action of mentally apprehending the relation between two objects of thought; predication, as an act of mind. With *pl*. A mental assertion or statement; a proposition, as formed in the mind."

Descartes's view was nonstandard in early modern philosophy, and that Locke, like many others, held the view that forming a proposition and understanding its content is the very same thing as affirming or denying the proposition. The act of judgment, broadly conceived, is an act of the understanding, and not divisible into separate acts of the intellect and the will, as Descartes thought. Furthermore, Locke thought it to be a *single* act of the understanding. One might still reject the Cartesian view and claim that that judgment involves only the understanding, while maintaining that judgment has two components: grasping or understanding a proposition, on the one hand, and asserting or denying the proposition, on the other. But Locke thought that there aren't two acts of the understanding here, but only one. Predication just is affirming or denying.

2. JUDGMENT AND PROPOSITIONS

In "Of Power," Locke says:

The power of Perception is that which we call the Understanding. Perception, which we make the act of the Understanding, is of three sorts: 1. The Perception of *Ideas* in our Minds. 2. The Perception of the signification of Signs. 3. The Perception of the Connexion or Repugnancy, Agreement or Disagreement, that there is between any of our *Ideas*. All these are attributed to the *Understanding*, or perceptive Power, though it be the two latter only that use allows us to say we understand. (E II.xxi.5: 236)

The perception of ideas is the most fundamental psychological relation for Locke. Perceiving an idea is the way we are aware of our ideas. Ideas are here functioning like terms in traditional logic. Just as in logic terms can be combined in special ways to produce propositions, so for Locke, ideas can be combined to produce propositions. This involves the third sort of perception, the perception of the agreement or disagreement between any of our ideas. It is very difficult to read what Locke says here without thinking of his famous account of knowledge:

Knowledge then seems to me to be nothing but *the perception of the connexion and agreement, or disagreement and repugnancy of any of our Ideas*. In this alone it consists. Where this perception is, there is

Knowledge, and where it is not, there, though we may fancy, guess, or believe, yet we always come short of Knowledge. (E IV.i.2: 525)

When "the Mind perceives the Agreement or Disagreement of two *Ideas* immediately by themselves, without the intervention of any other" (E IV.ii.1: 530–1), we have intuitive knowledge. "[W]hen the Mind cannot so bring it *Ideas* together, as by their immediate Comparison...to perceive their Agreement or Disagreement, it is fain, by the Intervention of other *Ideas* (one or more, as it happens) to discover the Agreement or Disagreement, which it searches" (E IV.ii.2: 532). This process is called demonstrative reasoning or demonstration, and the result is demonstrative knowledge. The third degree of knowledge is sensitive knowledge, or the knowledge "of the existence of particular external Objects, by that perception and Consciousness we have of the actual entrance of *Ideas* from them" (E IV.ii.14: 537–8). Sensitive knowledge is problematic, as it does not seem to be a matter of perceiving the agreement or disagreement of two ideas. But note, it is still a form of perception, the perception "we have of the actual entrance of *Ideas* from" external objects. It is arguable that this is the second of the three sorts of perception that Locke distinguishes in "Of Power," quoted earlier; sensitive knowledge is the perception of the signification of signs. We perceive not only ideas (the first sort of perception) but also their signification (the third sort of perception).[6]

Knowledge is the perception of the agreement or disagreement of ideas. How can we map this account onto talk of propositions as representing the content of knowledge? And once we do that, how should we answer the question about judgment in the broad sense? Is it one thing to understand a proposition, and another thing to assent to it or judge it to be true? According to Locke, is there a single act of judgment, or is the process divided into two stages, understanding and assent? The answer is clear with respect to Descartes. Consider *Principles* I: 32:

We possess only two modes of thinking: the perception of the intellect and the operation of the will.

---

[6] See also "Of the Division of the Sciences" (E IV.xxi.1–5). This is the merest suggestion of how one might think of sensitive knowledge. The problem is deep and troublesome and has concerned Locke scholars for decades, if not centuries. Lex Newman presents an elegant and novel account in his contribution to this volume.

All the modes of thinking that we experience within ourselves can be brought under two general headings: perception, or the operation of the intellect, and volition, or the operation of the will. Sensory perception, imagination and pure understanding are simply various modes of perception; desire, aversion, assertion, denial and doubt are various modes of willing.

The understanding presents us with a proposition, and the will asserts or denies it. As far as I can tell, Descartes is not very interested in the structure of such propositions. Sometimes they are merely ideas, such as the idea of God. But when presented with a proposition, it is up to the will to assert or deny it. And it is this assertion or denial that constitutes making a judgment. Consider *Principles* I: 34:

Making a judgement requires not only the intellect but also the will.

In order to make a judgement, the intellect is of course required since, in the case of something which we do not in any way perceive, there is no judgement we can make. But the will is also required so that, once something is perceived in some manner, our assent may then be given.

I don't think there is much doubt about Descartes's motivation. Putting judgment in the hands of the will helps to solve the problem of error. "Now when we perceive something, so long as we do not make any assertion or denial about it, we clearly avoid error." Furthermore, the division of labour between the understanding and the will fits into Descartes's theory of clear and distinct perception. "And we equally avoid error when we confine our assertions or denials to what we clearly and distinctly perceive should be asserted or denied" (*Principles* I: 33). Note that the proposition must be understood in order for it to be asserted or denied; understanding is logically prior to assent.[7] So Descartes divides judgment, in the broad sense, into two parts: understanding a proposition is a process of perception, and belongs to the understanding; affirming or denying a proposition is a matter of assertion, and belongs to the will.[8]

---

[7] The details of Descartes's account are complicated by his doctrine of clear and distinct perception. In ordinary cases, we understand the proposition, and then give our assent. But when we clearly and distinctly perceive something, the will is determined to assent; the act is no longer voluntary.

[8] Again, for our purposes, it is not important that Descartes divides judgment between the understanding and the will. For the contrast with Locke, what is

Although their motivation is entirely different, post-Fregean philosophers have a broadly similar account. Geach is perhaps the clearest:

A thought may have just the same content whether you assent to its truth or not; a proposition may occur in discourse now asserted, now unasserted, and yet be recognizably the same proposition. This may appear so obviously true as to be hardly worth saying; but we shall see it *is* worth saying. (Geach 1972: 254–5)

Geach calls this *"the Frege point,* after the logician who was the first (so far as I know) to make the point clearly and emphatically." Several of Geach's arguments claim that the Frege point is needed to understand truth-functional connectives. When we assert *P or Q*, we assert neither *P* nor *Q*. "[S]o if we say that the truth value of the whole proposition is determined by the truth values of the disjuncts, we are committed to recognizing that the disjuncts have truth values independently of being actually asserted" (Geach 1972: 258).

Another argument, more relevant to our purposes, concerns predication and assertion. According to Geach, many logicians confuse predicating *P* of *S* with affirming that *S is P*:

A further difficulty arises over the expression "assertion about something". Round this and similar expressions there is piled a secular accumulation of logical error; we have here a suggestion that *"P"* is predicated of *S* only if it is actually asserted, affirmed, that *S* is *P*. A moment's consideration ought to have shown that this will not do: *"P"* may be predicated of *S* in an *if* or a *then* clause, or in a clause of a disjunction, without the speaker's being in the least committed to affirming that *S* is *P*. Yet it took the genius of the young Frege to dissolve the monstrous and unholy union that previous logicians had made between the import of a predicate and the assertoric force of a sentence. Even when a sentence has assertoric force, this attaches to the sentence as a whole; not specially to the subject, or to the predicate, or to any part of the sentence. (Geach 1960: 24)

Who were the logicians who perpetrated this monstrous and unholy conflation of predication and affirmation? Geach had in mind Frege's immediate predecessors, as well as mid-twentieth-century philosophers such as Ryle and Strawson.[9] It looks as if

---

important is that Descartes requires two acts for judgment: one of grasping the content of a proposition, the other of assenting to it.

[9] For further discussion by Geach, see Geach 1963: 131–4.

Descartes and his followers are exempt, but if Geach and I are right, then most other philosophers in the early modern period are guilty. Predicating *S* of *P* just was affirming that *S* is *P*. In the remainder of this section I'll argue that this is certainly true of Locke.[10]

For Locke, knowledge is the perception of the agreement or dis-agreement of ideas. Propositions represent the content of what we know. The question is, does Locke think that it is one thing to form a proposition, and another to assent to it in a separate act of mind? Does Locke have a propositional-attitude psychology? Or does he think, as Geach alleges that so many pre-Fregeans thought, that the act of assertion or affirmation just is an act of predication or proposition formation? There are some texts that give support to the propositional-attitude interpretation. In "Of Universal Propo-sitions, their Truth and Certainty," he distinguishes certainty of truth from certainty of knowledge:

Certainty of Truth is, when Words are so put together in Propositions, as exactly to express the agreement or disagreement of the *Ideas* they stand for, as really it is. *Certainty of Knowledge* is, to perceive the agreement or disagreement of *Ideas*, as expressed in any Proposition. This we usually call knowing, or being certain of the Truth of any Proposition. (E IV.vi.3: 579–80)

This could be interpreted as saying that it is the agreement of ideas that constitutes a proposition, while it is perception of that agree-ment that constitutes knowledge. If Locke could also account for what it is to consider or entertain a proposition, independently of

---

[10] Of course, this is very controversial. The best discussion I know is in Ott 2002 and Ott 2004 (Chapter 2), though Ott and I come to diametrically opposed conclusions. Ott argues that the philosophers of the early modern period did not conflate assertion and predication. Instead, he suggests, their concerns with predication were much like Russell's concerns about the unity of the proposition. For discussion of Russell and the unity of the proposition, see Hylton 1984, and for more detail, Hylton 1990. Buroker (1993) argues that Arnauld and Nicole, in the *Port Royal Logic*, present a single-act account of judgment, where predication just is affirmation or denial. Wolterstorff (1994, 1996) and Nuchelmans (1983: 139–47) present a view of Locke that separates understanding a proposition from affirming or denying it. Bennett (1994) suggests that Locke might be sympathetic to the view of belief where we first entertain a proposition in some neutral way, and then take some attitude toward it. Michael Ayers criticizes both Bennett 1994 and Wolterstorff 1994 in Ayers 1997. See also Ayers 1991, especially volume I, *Epistemology*, Chapters 3 and 13. Ayers's views on Locke, in these chapters as elsewhere, have been very influential on me.

affirming or denying it, then it looks as if he could escape Geach's charge.[11]

Locke's main treatment of propositions is found in the first six sections of Chapter v of Book IV, "Of Truth in General."[12] He there says that truth is

the joining or separating of Signs, as the Things signified by them, do agree or disagree one with another. The joining or separating of signs here meant is what by another name, we call Proposition. (E IV.v.2: 574)

So a proposition is constructed by the joining or separating of signs. There are two sorts of signs, ideas and words, so there are two sorts of propositions, mental and verbal. Locke has this to say about these propositions:

First, Mental, wherein the *Ideas*, in our Understandings *are* without the use of Words *put together, or separated* by the Mind, perceiving, or judging of their Agreement, or Disagreement.

Secondly, Verbal Propositions, which *are Words* the signs of our *Ideas put together or separated in affirmative or negative Sentences.* By which affirming or denying, these Signs, made by Sounds, are as it were put together or separated one from another. (E IV.v.5: 575–6)

Mental propositions are constructed by putting together or separating ideas. Ideas are put together or separated by perceiving, or judging, of their agreement or disagreement.[13] But perceiving, or judging, of two ideas' agreement or disagreement just is knowing or believing something. So constructing a proposition is the very same mental act as knowing or believing. Verbal propositions are constructed in an analogous fashion, by affirmation or denial. Constructing a verbal proposition is the very same thing as affirming or denying it.

Consider again what Locke says about mental propositions. Mental propositions are ideas *"put together, or separated* by the

---

[11] Other problems would remain. As Don Garrett has pointed out to me, if Locke thought that it was the agreement or disagreement of ideas that constituted a proposition, then it is utterly unclear what a false proposition could be.

[12] See also E II.xxxii.1, 19: 384, 391; and E III.vii.1: 471, where Locke says *"Is,* and *Is not,* are the general marks of the Mind, affirming, or denying."

[13] "Judging" is here used in Locke's technical sense. To judge, presume, or suppose, rather than perceive, two ideas to agree or disagree is to believe, rather than know, some proposition.

Mind, perceiving, or judging of their Agreement, or Disagreement."
I have suggested that the most natural way of reading this is to
interpret Locke as claiming that there is but one act here. We put
together, or separate, ideas *by* perceiving, or judging, their agreement or disagreement. But another reading is possible, one that
renders this passage consistent with a two-act reading.[14] First of all,
there is the joining or separating of ideas. This is the act of proposition formation. Then there is a second act of perceiving, or judging, the ideas already put together, to agree or disagree. This results
in affirming the proposition to be true. Some support for this
interpretation comes from E IV.v.6: 576, where Locke talks about a
person who "perceives, believes, or supposes" the agreement or
disagreement of ideas. According to this line of thought,[15] it is one
thing to suppose or consider a proposition, by joining or separating
ideas, but quite another thing to affirm the proposition by perceiving or judging the proposition to be true.

I do not think this interpretation can be sustained. Locke reaf-
firms this single-act theory of judgment, in the broad sense, in the
very next section:

Every one's Experience will satisfie him, that the Mind, either by perceiving
or supposing the Agreement or Disagreement of any of its *Ideas*, does
tacitly within it self put them into a kind of Proposition affirmative or
negative, which I have endeavoured to express by the terms *Putting together*
and *Separating*.[16]

This passage is unambiguous. Constructing a proposition is putting
together or separating ideas. But the mind puts together or separates
ideas simply by perceiving or presuming agreement or disagreement. One constructs a proposition by affirming or denying.
Predicating *P* of *S* just is affirming that *S is P*. It looks as if Locke
had the resources to put forward a two-act theory. He could have

---

[14] This possibility was pointed out to me by Don Garrett and Lex Newman, in
correspondence.
[15] Suggested to me by Walter Ott, in correspondence.
[16] Note that "[p]erceiving or supposing" here is just like "perceiving or judging" in
the previous quotation. Perceiving leads to knowledge, while supposing leads to
belief. This helps us properly understand the "perceives, believes, or supposes"
passage. There are not three things here, but only two. One the one hand, we can
perceive agreement; on the other hand, we can believe or suppose such an
agreement.

held that it is one thing to join or separate ideas, thus forming a proposition that is understood, and quite a different thing to assert a proposition, by perceiving or presuming the agreement or disagreement of the ideas previously joined or separated. But I think the textual evidence clearly points to the view that Locke held a one-act theory. Proposition formation, predication, assertion, and affirmation all come down to a single act of perceiving or presuming agreement of ideas. Geach's charge stands.

If this indeed is Locke's theory, then he is going to have trouble with conditionals.[17] This is hardly surprising; everybody had trouble with conditionals before Frege. What is more troublesome is that the single-act account of judgment seems to rule out what every philosopher needs to allow. We need to be able to consider, suppose, or entertain propositions prior to committing ourselves to their truth or falsity. Locke is well aware of this need. For instance, when discussing the limitations of what we know, he says:

We have the *Ideas* of a *Square*, a *Circle*, and *Equality*; and yet, perhaps, shall never be able to find a Circle equal to a Square, and certainly know that it is so. (E IV.iii.6: 540)[18]

But if proposition formation just is affirmation or denial, how is this possible? The question is not settled by reflection on the relatively involuntary nature of knowledge and belief in Locke. Consider a geometric demonstration. Suppose we want to demonstrate that the internal angles of a triangle are equal to two right angles. We need to construct a chain of ideas, such that each idea is intuitively seen to agree with its adjacent neighbours in the chain. If the chain is successfully constructed, we then indirectly see the agreement in size between the two angles. We can't follow the chain of reasoning and refuse to accept the fact that the ideas agree. It is not up to us. But before we construct the chain, can't we wonder or consider whether the two angles are equal? We must be able to; otherwise we wouldn't know what the demonstration was supposed to show. It is arguable that the same is true of intuition. It doesn't take much

---

[17] See, for instance, the discussion in *Logic or the Art of Thinking*, Arnauld and Nicole 1996: 99–101.
[18] Thanks to Michael Jacovides for reminding me of this passage, and of its importance to the matter at hand.

thought to intuit that three is greater than two. But can't we raise the question before perceiving their agreement?

The way Locke sets up the issue in the demonstration case is this: "Thus the Mind being willing to know the Agreement or Disagreement in bigness, between the three Angles of a Triangle, and two right ones, cannot by an immediate view and comparing them, do it" (E IV.ii.2: 532). Being ignorant of and wanting to know whether two ideas agree or disagree may be enough. We want to know whether to affirm or deny the equality of the one angle with another. That is to say, we want to know which proposition to construct.

This does not solve the problem; it only restates it. To wonder which proposition to construct, and whether two ideas agree or disagree, is to consider whether a proposition is true or not. But this cannot be done without having the proposition in mind. Locke does have a solution to the problem, and it involves his account of belief and assent (judgment in the narrow sense), the topic of the next section of this chapter. This much can be said now. Belief is the presumption of agreement or disagreement between two ideas, and it ranges from near-certainty of agreement to near-certainty of disagreement. Locke calls the relation the mind has to these states "entertainment."[19] One such list of entertainments seems to go from full belief to full disbelief: "*Belief, Conjecture, Doubt, Wavering, Distrust, Disbelief*" (E IV.xvi.9: 663). So when we make a conjecture, we are actually presuming that the two ideas agree or disagree. There is a continuum, ranging from full belief to full disbelief. And it has a midpoint. So when we are wondering whether a proposition is true or false, we are actually judging (in Locke's technical sense) that it is true, with a certain degree of probability, (e.g., 50 percent). Elsewhere, Locke talks about "Assent, Suspense, or Dissent" (E IV.xx.15: 716). Suspense seems to be midway between full assent and full dissent. Locke thus has a way out of the problem. Even with a single-act account of judgment in the broad sense, Locke has an adequate way to allow us to consider propositions prior to constructing a demonstration or investigating the

[19] See E IV.xv.3: 655 and E IV.xvi.9: 663. It is important to realize that "entertainment" in these places doesn't mean "hypothetical consideration." It means "the belief or disbelief" we have in some claim or other.

grounds of probability: we can form a belief state midway between full assent and full dissent.

3. JUDGMENT, PROBABLE REASONING, AND BELIEF

Locke thought that knowledge is the perception of the agreement or disagreement of ideas. But knowledge, Locke thought, is "very short and scanty" (E IV.xiv.1: 652). Fortunately, the "Mind has two Faculties, conversant about Truth and Falshood." The mind not only has the faculty of knowledge, "whereby it certainly perceives, and is undoubtedly satisfied of the Agreement or Disagreement of any *Ideas*." It also has judgment, "which is the putting *Ideas* together, or separating them from one another in the mind, when their certain Agreement or Disagreement is not perceived, but *presumed* to be so" (E IV.xiv.4: 653). This is Locke's technical sense of "judgment," to the examination of which we shall now turn. Knowledge is the perception of agreement or disagreement of ideas, while belief, judgment, or assent is the presumption or supposition that the ideas agree or disagree. Belief seems to be an approximation to knowledge; where we cannot or do not perceive agreement, we make do with supposing it.

From the very beginning of the *Essay*, Locke emphasizes the importance of belief or opinion as something needed to supplement knowledge. The three main tasks of the *Essay* are an enquiry into the origin of ideas, an enquiry into the nature of knowledge, and, Locke says,

Thirdly, I shall make some Enquiry into the Nature and Grounds of *Faith*, or *Opinion*: whereby I mean that Assent, which we give to any Proposition as true, of whose Truth yet we have no certain Knowledge: And here we shall have Occasion to examine the Reasons and Degrees of *Assent*. (E I.i.3: 44)

A little later, he points out the importance of not demanding demonstration and certainty where only opinion and probability is available to us:

And we shall then use our Understandings right, when we entertain all Objects in that Way and Proportion, that they are suited to our Faculties; and upon those Grounds, they are capable of being propos'd to us; and not peremptorily, or intemperately require Demonstration, and demand

Certainty, where Probability only is to be had, and which is sufficient to govern all our Concernments. If we will disbelieve every thing, because we cannot certainly know all things; we shall do much-what as wisely as he, who would not use his Legs, but sit still and perish, because he had no Wings to fly. (E I.i.5: 46)

The bulk of Locke's discussion of judgment comes in Chapters xiv to xxi of Book IV. Although some of the important themes of these chapters are matters of faith and religion, Locke's discussion of judgment is not limited to these. Our knowledge of the natural world is severely limited. Intuitive and demonstrative knowledge is hampered by our lack of the perception of any necessary connection between many of our ideas:

This, how weighty and considerable a part soever of Humane Science, is yet very narrow, and scarce any at all. The reason whereof is, that the simple *Ideas* whereof our complex *Ideas* of Substances are made up, are, for the most part such, as carry with them, in their own Nature, no visible necessary connexion, or inconsistency with any other simple *Ideas*, whose *co-existence* with them we would inform our selves about. (E IV.iii.10: 544)

Locke says that whatever comes short of intuition and demonstration, "with what assurance soever embraced, is but Faith, or Opinion, but not knowledge, *at least in all general Truths*" (E IV. ii.14: 537; emphasis mine). Sensitive knowledge does pick up some of the slack, but it has to do only with *"the particular existence of finite Beings* without us." General truths about substances, such as "All gold is fixed," cannot be known, either through intuitive, demonstrative, or sensitive knowledge: "it is impossible that we certainly know the Truth of this Proposition, That *all gold is fixed"* (E IV.vi.8: 583).[20]

Sensitive knowledge is not just limited to the particular; it is also limited to the present testimony of the senses. Sensitive *"Knowledge extends as far as the present Testimony of our senses,* employ'd about particular Objects, that do affect them, *and no farther"* (E IV.xi.9: 635). To use Locke's example, if I see a man in

---

[20] A qualification needs to be made to this negative claim. Certain trivial general truths about substances can be known, when the idea of the predicate is contained in the idea of the subject. *"All gold is malleable ...* is a very certain Proposition, if *Malleableness* be part of the complex *Idea* that the word *Gold* stands for" (E IV. vi.9: 583).

my room, I have sensitive knowledge of his existence. If he leaves my presence, I have a memory that he did exist while he was in my room, but I no longer have knowledge of his current existence: "by a thousand ways he may cease to be, since I had the Testimony of my Senses for his Existence." Probability steps in to fill the void left by our limited knowledge:

And therefore though it be highly probable, that Millions of Men do now exist, yet whilst I am alone writing this, I have not that Certainty of it, which we strictly call Knowledge; though the great likelihood of it puts me past doubt, and it be reasonable for me to do several things upon the confidence, that there are Men . . . now in the World: but this is but probability, not Knowledge. (E IV.xi.9: 635–6)[21]

Those who would enquire into the nature of the physical world must make do with experience, and the general beliefs thereby provided. "Our Knowledge in all these Enquiries, reaches very little farther than our Experience" (E IV.iii.14: 546). But we need not, and should not, confine ourselves to knowledge, either in ordinary life or in physical enquiries:

He that will not eat, till he has Demonstration that it will nourish him; he that will not stir, till he infallibly knows the Business he goes about will succeed, will have little else to do, but sit still and perish. (E IV.xiv.1: 652)[22]

As mentioned in the introduction to this chapter, Locke thinks that, although we are forced to rely on judgment or probability where knowledge is unavailable, we sometimes rely on probable belief even where knowledge is possible. For instance, we might believe that the internal angles of a triangle are equal to two right angles, or we might know it on the basis of demonstration. In general,

The Mind sometimes exercises this *Judgment* out of necessity, where demonstrative Proofs, and certain knowledge are not to be had; and sometimes out of Laziness, Unskilfulness, or Haste, even where demonstrative and certain Proofs are to be had. (E IV.xiv.3: 653)

---

[21] Note that Locke is here setting up the problem that so exercised Hume: how do we come to have beliefs in the unobserved, which go beyond the present evidence of the senses and memory?

[22] See also E IV.xi.10: 636: "He that in the ordinary Affairs of Life, would admit of nothing but direct plain Demonstration, would be sure of nothing, in this World, but of perishing quickly."

Judgment is introduced as analogous to knowledge, and the product of judgment is like the product of knowledge, only weaker. In knowledge, we perceive the agreement or disagreement of ideas; in judgment, we only presume such an agreement or disagreement:

Thus the Mind has two Faculties, conversant about Truth and Falshood.

First, Knowledge, whereby it certainly perceives, and is undoubtedly satisfied of the Agreement or Disagreement of any *Ideas*.

Secondly, Judgment, which is the putting *Ideas* together, or separating them from one another in the Mind, when their certain Agreement or Disagreement is not perceived, but *presumed* to be so . . . (E IV.xiv.4: 653)

Just as Locke introduced judgment by analogy with knowledge, so Locke introduces probability by analogy with demonstration:

As Demonstration is the shewing the Agreement, or Disagreement of two *Ideas*, by the intervention of one or more Proofs, which have a constant, immutable, and visible connexion one with another: so *Probability* is nothing but the appearance of such an Agreement, or Disagreement, by the intervention of Proofs, whose connexion is not constant and immutable, or at least is not perceived to be so, but is, or appears for the most part to be so, and is enough to induce the Mind to *judge* the Proposition to be true, or false, rather than the contrary. (E IV.xv.1: 654)

Probability is the appearance of agreement or disagreement of ideas, and it causes our assent. That is, it causes us to presume the ideas to agree or disagree, where we do not perceive that agreement.

For Locke, a demonstration is a series of intuitions. A demonstration is a chain of ideas; each idea is intuitively connected to its adjacent ideas in the chain. We immediately see the intuitive relation between any two ideas in the chain. Locke calls these intermediate ideas "proofs." We indirectly or inferentially see the agreement or disagreement of the ideas at each end of the chain, via the immediate perception of the agreement or disagreement of the intermediate ideas or proofs.[23] For example, when we know that the internal angles of a triangle are equal to two right angles, we have the idea of the internal angles of a triangle, and the idea of the two right angles. We cannot immediately see the agreement between them. But it is easy enough to construct another angle, and

---

[23] See E IV.ii.2–8: 531–4. For an extended discussion, see Owen 1999b, Chapter 3.

to see immediately that that angle is equal both to the internal angles of a triangle and to two right angles. Since Locke makes so much of the analogy between demonstrative and probable reasoning, one might think that the structure of probable reasoning is as follows. Just as demonstrative knowledge is the indirect perception of the agreement of two ideas, via a chain of intermediate ideas or proofs, so probable judgment is the indirect presumption of the agreement of two ideas, via a chain of intermediate ideas or proofs. In a demonstration, we immediately perceive the agreement of any two adjacent ideas in the chain; in probable reasoning, we immediately judge or presume the agreement of any two ideas in the chain.

This picture will not do. There is nothing in probable reasoning corresponding to intuition. In intuition, "each immediate *Idea*, each step has its visible and certain connexion; in belief not so" (E IV.xv.3: 655). The connection between ideas perceived by intuition is intrinsic to the nature of the ideas themselves. But that "which makes me believe, is something extraneous to the thing I believe." Locke's account of judgment and probable reasoning is supposed to *explain* how we judge things to be true; on the picture just sketched, it would presuppose that we can immediately judge or presume two ideas to agree. But such judgments are caused by something extraneous to the ideas, and probable reasoning is supposed to explain that.

Perhaps the clearest way to see that the picture of Locke's account of judgment just sketched is inaccurate is to realize that Locke does not think there is any such thing as immediate belief. All beliefs are the result of probable reasoning. We have already quoted extensively from E IV.xv.1: 654, where Locke describes probability as "nothing but the appearance of such an Agreement, or Disagreement, by the intervention of Proofs"; and the title of this section is *"Probability is the appearance of agreement upon fallible proofs."* And again, later in Book IV, he compares *"Demonstration by reasoning"* to *"Judgment upon probable reasoning"* (E IV. xvii.15, 16 (titles of paragraphs): 683, 685), and describes the operation of judgment as follows:

There are other *Ideas*, whose agreement, or Disagreement, can no otherwise be judged of, but by the intervention of others, which have not a certain Agreement with the Extremes, but an usual or likely one: And in these it is, that the *Judgment* is properly exercised. (E IV.xvii.16: 685)[24]

Probable reasoning is always compared to demonstrative reasoning, and judgment always operates with intermediate ideas. All beliefs or opinions are produced in this way; there are no immediate beliefs. But if there is no immediate judgment, and no probable equivalent of intuition, just what is the relation between ideas that makes up the chain of ideas that constitutes a piece of probable reasoning? This turns out to be an extremely difficult question to answer. The brief answer is that the intermediate ideas are ideas of testimony or past experience that cause us to presume the agreement of the two ideas at each end of the chain. But before explaining this more fully, we first need to say more about judgment, belief, and assent.

Locke sometimes speaks of this judgment as assent: "The entertainment the Mind gives this sort of Propositions, is called *Belief, Assent,* or *Opinion,* which is the admitting or receiving any Proposition for true, without certain Knowledge that it is so" (E IV. xv.3: 655). And just as there are degrees of knowledge, viz., intuitive, demonstrative, and sensitive, so too there are degrees of assent "from full *Assurance* and Confidence, quite down to *Conjecture, Doubt,* and *Distrust*" (E IV.xv.2: 655). Indeed, Locke devotes a whole chapter of Book IV to the degrees of assent. So for Locke, assent is not an attitude we take toward various propositions, whereby sometimes we assent to something that we know, while at other times we assent to what we believe. Like "judgment," "assent" is a technical term for Locke. It is just another term for belief or opinion. According to Locke, believing or assenting to a proposition is a sort of pale imitation of knowing it, a presuming rather than a perceiving. Both knowledge and belief involve proposition formation; predication is a form of affirmation or denial.

---

[24] See also E IV.xvii.17: 685:

> *Intuitive Knowledge,* is the perception of the certain Agreement, or Disagreement of two *Ideas* immediately compared together. *Rational Knowledge,* is the perception of the certain Agreement, or Disagreement of any two *Ideas,* by the intervention of one or more other *Ideas.*
>
> *Judgment,* is the thinking or taking two *Ideas* to agree, or disagree, by the intervention of one or more *Ideas,* whose certain Agreement, or Disagreement with them it does not perceive, but hath observed to be frequent and usual.

Assent is not an attitude one takes toward a proposition already formed. So when Locke speaks of a self-evident proposition as something that one "assents to at first sight" (E IV.vii.2: 591), he is not saying that we believe or assent to something known; he is just saying that we come to know it.[25]

An important aspect of Locke's denial of immediate judgment is the claim that all judgments are based on evidence or have grounds. But what is such evidence, and how does it function in the probable reasoning that produces beliefs? To understand Locke's position here, first consider the analogous question concerning knowledge. When we perceive the agreement of two ideas, we have knowledge, which is certain. What determines us to have this certainty Locke calls "evidence," as in "perceiving a demonstrative Evidence in the

---

[25] For Locke, knowledge does not evoke assent, where assent is belief. Knowledge is the perception of the agreement or disagreement of ideas, while belief or assent is the presumption of such agreement. Assent, for Locke, is not some further act or attitude one takes toward a perceived or presumed agreement or disagreement of ideas. Just as belief, the presumption or supposition of the agreement or disagreement of ideas, involves "taking to be true," so too does knowledge, which is the perception of such agreement. There is no need to posit a further act of assent. On Locke's account, belief or assent approximates to knowledge. Part of the trouble in understanding Locke is that in places he *does* speak as if assent were a separate act or attitude one takes toward a piece of knowledge. But this is hardly decisive. The vast majority of the occurrences of "assent" and its cognates in Book IV concern belief only, not an attitude one might take toward knowledge. Of the remaining occurrences, all but three occur in Chapter vii, "*Of maxims*," and in a moment I shall argue that there is a special reason why that should be so. Of the remaining three, one concerns maxims (E IV.xvii.14: 683) and one occurs at E IV. i.8: 528. That leaves only one occurrence, at E IV.xvii.19: 686, of the use of "assent" or its cognates as pertaining to knowledge as well as belief that comes after Locke's "official" account of "assent" in E IV.xiv–xv. And even there, the discussion makes it clear that the topic is as much about belief as about knowledge. Of the other occurrences in Book IV, all but two concern maxims, and only one of those does not occur in E IV.vii, "*Of maxims*." Why is this significant? That chapter is Locke's account of the self-evidence of certain maxims and axioms, which "because they are *self-evident*, have been supposed innate" (E IV.vii.1: 591). Locke has owed his readers an account of self-evidentness ever since his discussion of innateness in Book I. Part of that debt was cleared when Locke talked about intuition in the early chapters of Book IV. But Locke returns to the issue here, with explicit reference to the innateness controversy. As much of that debate concerned "universal assent" (E I.ii.4: 49) and "immediate assent" (E I.ii.17: 56), it is not surprising that when Locke returns to that debate, he retains some of the original terminology. Almost everywhere else in Book IV, "assent" concerns only belief or judgment, not an attitude we take toward known propositions.

Proofs" (E IV.xiv.3: 653) and "intuitive Evidence, which infallibly determines the Understanding" (E IV.xv.5: 656). The evidence that determines us to perceive the agreement or disagreement of ideas is not some proposition, already known, from which we infer some other proposition. That would make nonsense of the notion of "intuitive evidence." Intuitive evidence is the intrinsic nature of the ideas in the chain that makes possible our perception of their agreement. Demonstrative evidence is the intrinsic nature of the ideas in the chain that allows us to perceive immediately the agreement of any two adjacent ideas, and to perceive indirectly the agreement between the two ideas at the end of the chain.

The case is similar with respect to probability and belief. The grounds of probability are what induces, causes, or makes[26] us presume two ideas to agree. The presumption of agreement is not due to the intrinsic nature of the ideas. Instead,

That which makes me believe, is something extraneous to the thing I believe; something not evidently joined on both sides to, and so not manifestly shewing the Agreement, or Disagreement of those *Ideas*, that are under consideration. (E IV.xv.3: 655)

The person who demonstratively knows that the internal angles of a right angle are equal to two right angles indirectly perceives that the two ideas agree, via the relevant intermediate ideas. What of the person who believes that equality because of the testimony of a reliable mathematician?

That which causes his Assent to this proposition, that the three Angles of a Triangle are equal to two right ones, that which makes him take these *Ideas* to agree, without knowing them to do so, is the wonted Veracity of the Speaker in other cases, or his supposed Veracity in this. (E IV.xv.1: 654)

Grounds of probability are what cause us to believe, and an instance of decisive grounds "carries so much evidence with it, that it naturally determines the Judgment, and leaves us as little liberty to believe, or disbelieve, as a Demonstration does, whether we will know, or be ignorant" (E IV.xvi.9: 663). The talk here is mainly

---

[26] "[T]hat which causes his Assent" (E IV.xv.1: 654); "[t]hat which makes me believe" (E IV.xv.3: 655); "some inducements to receive them for true" (E IV.xv.4: 655–6).

causal, but the ideas of "grounds" and "evidence" are also normative. And Locke intends them to be so, as is shown throughout Book
IV. Consider the following passage:

*[T]he Mind if it will proceed rationally, ought to examine all the grounds
of Probability*, and see how they make more or less, *for or against* any
probable Proposition, before it assents to or dissents from it, and upon a due
ballancing the whole, reject, or receive it, with a more or less firm assent,
proportionably to the preponderancy of the greater grounds of Probability
on one side or the other. (E IV.xv.5: 656)

The grounds of probability are the circumstances that cause us to
presume agreement. But they have normative force as well: the
degree of assent ought to be proportional to the preponderancy of
the greater grounds. Has Locke simply confused the normative with
the psychological here? The situation is not as simple as that. In spite
of the normative nature of his concerns, Locke is not much interested in the logical nature, considered in isolation from the faculty of
judgment, of the evidential relationships between what we would
now call the "evidence" for an empirical proposition, on the one
hand; and the degree of "justification" a belief based on that evidence
might have, on the other. Instead, he is concerned to explain what it
is for our "understanding faculties" to function properly. Although
we "ought to examine all the grounds of probability," doing so is no
guarantee that we will get things right. Right judgment, for Locke, is
not a matter of judging according to some established rules, so that
the belief produced by the judgment is justified even though it may
be false. Right judgment is a matter of getting things right: if judgment "so unites, or separates them [ideas], as in Reality Things are, it
is *right Judgment*" (E IV.xiv.4: 653). For Locke, the causal and evidential nature of the grounds of belief are inextricably linked.[27]

---

[27] The situation is more complicated than these brief remarks might indicate. See
Hatfield 1997, especially pp. 31–6. I suspect that a full understanding of Locke's
views on probability and belief cannot be achieved in isolation from an
understanding of his views on sensitive knowledge. In each, there is the intimate
connection between the relevant faculty, the characteristic activity of that faculty,
and the result of that activity. In each, there is a lack of concern with modern
questions about justification. And in each, testimony seems to play a crucial role.
Locke is as happy to talk of the testimony of the senses as he is to speak of the
testimony of other persons. Just as another's testimony may cause us to presume
that two ideas agree, so an item in the world may cause us to have an idea such
that we perceive it as a sign of that item.

The grounds of probability, Locke asserts, are two: testimony, as we saw in the mathematics case, and "conformity of any thing with our own Knowledge, Observation, and Experience" (E IV.xv.4: 656). Locke thought conformity with "Knowledge, Observation, and Experience" could provide grounds for belief or opinion in unobserved matters of fact and was careful to point out that this did not result in knowledge. Our past experience of objects grounds our beliefs about such unobserved objects. Suppose I perceive a body of water, with some fine colours and a bubble upon that water. A little later,

[B]eing now quite out of the sight both of the Water and Bubbles too, it is no more certainly known to me, that the Water doth now exist, than that the Bubbles or Colours therein do so; it being no more necessary that Water should exist to day, because it existed yesterday, than that the Colours or Bubbles exist to day because they existed yesterday, though it be exceedingly much more probable, because water hath been observed to continue long in Existence, but Bubbles, and the Colours on them quickly cease to be. (E IV.xi.11: 636–7)

Our beliefs about what is unobserved should conform to our past experience: it is more probable that the water exists now than that the bubbles still exist because water has been observed in the past to continue in existence longer than bubbles. The man who believes in the equality of the three angles of a triangle to two right angles on the basis of testimony reasons from the idea of the three angles to the idea of two right ones, and he reasons via the "fallible proof" (E IV.xv.1 (section title): 654) or "probable medium" (E IV.xvii.16: 685) of testimony. The person who believes that the water he saw a minute ago still exists reasons from the idea of water once existing to the idea of the same water still existing via the probable medium of conformity to past experience.

We have already argued against the view that considers Locke as holding that judgment binds together ideas in a chain of probable reasoning the way intuition binds together ideas in a demonstrative chain of ideas. Locke does not think there is any such thing as "immediate judgment"; such a judgment would result in a belief formed on no grounds whatsoever, a possibility Locke does not countenance. Judgment is our ability to presume that two ideas agree or disagree, but such a judgment, and the resulting belief, always has grounds (testimony or our own experience). And of course, the account we are rejecting cannot be saved by suggesting that we can judge that any two adjacent ideas in the chain agree, on grounds of testimony or conformity to our own experience. For then between any two ideas in the chain, we would have to interpose a third, and our chain of ideas would become infinite.

If a chain of probable reasoning results in a belief, we judge, rather than perceive, that the first idea suitably agrees with the last. We make this judgment because we take each idea in the chain to be suitably related to its adjacent idea. This agreement is not perceived, for then the chain would constitute a piece of demonstrative reasoning. But our awareness or "presumption" of the first idea being related to the last still must depend on our awareness of each idea in the chain being related to its neighbour, and we need some account of this latter awareness. On the present account, we cannot call it judgment, because that is limited to a more complex operation that requires intermediate ideas, and we are here looking to explain immediate awareness. Worse, this immediate awareness cannot be grounded in testimony or experience, as that grounding is explained via the intervention of intermediate ideas. We seem to need the probable equivalent of intuition to explain why each idea in the chain is held to agree with its neighbour, and on the present account it is not clear that such an equivalent is even possible, at least if it is to involve testimony or experience.

We need to remember the extrinsic nature of probability judgments, in contrast to the intrinsic nature of knowledge claims:

And herein lies the *difference between Probability* and *Certainty, Faith* and *Knowledge*, that in all parts of Knowledge, there is intuition; each immediate *Idea*, each step has its visible and certain connexion; in belief not so. That which makes me believe, is something extraneous to the thing I believe; something not evidently joined on both sides to, and so not manifestly shewing the Agreement, or Disagreement of those *Ideas*, that are under consideration. (E IV.xv.3: 655)

Locke, as we have seen, speaks in causal language of the external source of the link between ideas in judgment:

So that which causes his Assent to this Proposition, that the three Angles of a Triangle are equal to two right ones, that which make him take these

Ideas to agree, without knowing them to do so, is the wonted Veracity of the Speaker in other cases, or his supposed Veracity in this. (E IV.xv.1: 654)

The grounds of probability are extraneous to the ideas presumed to be related. I might judge the proposition "The three angles of a triangle are equal to two right ones" to be true (i.e., presume the two ideas to be suitably related) *because* someone told me so. Here the idea of the speaker's veracity is functioning as a proof or intermediate idea, but in a manner rather different from the way intermediate ideas function in demonstrative reasoning. In demonstrative reasoning, each idea is intuitively perceived to agree with its neighbour. In probable reasoning, intermediate ideas cause the mind to presume agreement of the two ideas between which the intermediate idea stands. In demonstrative reasoning, there is an intrinsic connection between any two ideas in the chain; in probable reasoning, there is an extrinsic connection between the two ideas at the extremes, caused by the intermediate ideas. So I might judge that there are currently people existing, and the grounds for this judgment might be past experience. The idea of the relevant past experience acts as a sort of causal glue that enables us to presume the ideas to agree. This possibility accords well with Locke's claim that we judge not just out of necessity, when no demonstration is to be had, but "sometimes out of Laziness, Unskilfulness, or Haste." (E IV.xiv.3: 653) When we are inclined to presume ideas to agree, we may not bother to look for the demonstrative intermediate ideas that would enable us to perceive their intrinsic agreement.

On this interpretation, proofs are that which binds two ideas together. In demonstrative reasoning, such proofs are intermediate ideas such that each idea can be intuitively perceived as agreeing or disagreeing with its neighbour. In probable reasoning, such proofs are ideas of actual experience we have had or testimony we have received that cause us to presume a connection between the two ideas at the ends of the chain.[28]

---

[28] Probable reasoning, like demonstrative reasoning, may consist of several ideas or proofs causing us to presume an agreement between the ideas at the extremes. A particularly clear example occurs at E IV.xvii.4: 672:

Tell a Country Gentlewoman, that the Wind is South-West, and the Weather louring, and like to rain, and she will easily understand, 'tis not safe for her to go

Grounds of probability can cause us to presume relations between ideas without perceiving their intrinsic connection, if any. Furthermore, we are supposed to consider all sorts of conflicting evidence and come up with a balanced judgment. By what mechanism does this occur? In the end, I do not think Locke has the resources to answer this question. Let us reconsider a passage of Locke's already cited:

> [T]he Mind if it will proceed rationally, ought to examine all the grounds of Probability, and see how they make more or less, *for or against*, any probable Proposition, before it assents to or dissents from it, and upon a due ballancing the whole, reject, or receive it, with a more or less firm assent, proportionably to the preponderancy of the greater grounds of Probability on one side or the other. (E IV.xv.5: 656)

The idea seems to be that, although some propositions may have all the evidence in their favour, for most propositions not known, there will be experience and testimony for and against. The crucial ingredient seems to be the "degree of conformity with what is usually observed to happen." So if a man in England tells me he saw someone walk upon ice, "this has so great conformity with what is usually observed to happen, that I am disposed by the nature of the thing it self to assent to it." Since, in this case, there appear to be few grounds for denying the proposition, we judge it to be true. But if the same man says the same thing to the "King of *Siam*," there is little conformity with what the king has observed, and he may well not believe the proposition, but judge the man to be a liar.

It is difficult to assess just how we are to evaluate the probability of propositions on conflicting evidence. Any question of weighing evidence appears to be a matter of allowing one bit of evidence to function as grounds for or against taking two ideas to be related, another bit of evidence to function as grounds for another judgment,

---

abroad thin clad, in such a day, after a fever: she clearly sees the probable Connexion of all those, *viz.* South-West-Wind, and Clouds, Rain, wetting, taking cold, Relapse, and danger of death, without tying them together in those artificial and cumbersome Fetters of several Syllogisms, that clog and hinder the Mind. . . .

The point is that this piece of probable reasoning is better understood by the reasoner if it is laid out as a chain of ideas, and not forced into syllogistic mold. A similar example with respect to demonstrative reasoning is given at E IV.xvii.4: 672–3.

and so on. When all the grounds are exhausted, the winner is somehow supposed to emerge. One bit of evidence inclines us to presume one way; another bit of evidence inclines us to presume another way. Locke thinks that when the evidence is overwhelmingly one way, "it naturally determines the Judgment, and leaves us as little liberty to believe, or disbelieve, as a Demonstration does, whether we will know, or be ignorant" (E IV.xvi.9: 663). The difficulty comes when the evidence is mixed. But even here, if the evidence is functioning causally, will we not presume whichever way the evidence is stronger? The answer to this is yes, but it does not follow that the beliefs we have are entirely arbitrary. We do not know, based on some calculation, just what degree of assent is due a proposition for which there is contradictory evidence; but if we pay attention to all the evidence, and let it weigh with us, the belief we eventually form will reflect the variety of evidence and its force. Probability is the appearance or presumption of the agreement of ideas; it is not knowledge that there is some specific likelihood that a belief we have may be true.[29]

---

[29] See, for instance, E IV.xvi.9: 663:

> These [testimony and past experience] are liable to so great variety of contrary Observations, Circumstances, Reports, different Qualifications, Tempers, Designs, Over-sights, *etc.* of the Reporters, that 'tis impossible to reduce to precise Rules, the various degrees wherein Men give their Assent. This only may be said in general, That as the Arguments and Proofs, *pro* and *con*, upon due Examination, nicely weighing every particular Circumstance, shall to any one appear, upon the whole matter, in greater or less degree, to preponderate on either side, so they are fitted to produce in the Mind such different Entertainment, as we call *Belief, Conjecture, Guess, Wavering, Distrust, Disbelief*, etc.

There is no knowledge of the appropriate degree of assent; it just emerges as the evidence is duly considered. I thus find myself in disagreement, in some respects, with Wolterstorff over the interpretation of Locke on probability. For instance, he says of Locke: "My believing the proposition, upon 'perceiving' the fact, *that P is highly probable on this evidence*, is certain; my believing the proposition P itself is merely probable" (Wolterstorff 1996: 89). Wolterstorff thinks that Locke's theory holds that we *know* how probable P is, given the evidence, though we do not know P. I do not think this is true of Locke. Suppose that P is the proposition "A is B." Then to judge that P is true is to presume that A stands in some relation to B, a relation such that if it were perceived would result in knowledge that A is B. If we *know* that some evidence gives high probability to P, then we would have to perceive the agreement between the idea of the evidence and the idea of P's being true. But what is this agreement, and how do we perceive it? On my view, the evidence or grounds of our judgment that P is whatever it is that causes us to

Some evidence that this is the correct interpretation comes in Locke's discussion of "Wrong Assent, or Error" in E IV.xx. Error seems to result mainly from a lack of proofs, or the lack of the ability or will to use them. Not having such proofs, or failing to consider the evidence they provide (i.e., failing to allow the idea of such evidence to incline one to presume agreement or disagreement) will result in a judgment not based on all the evidence available. On this conception, beliefs finally arrived at are in some sense both voluntary and involuntary, and yet this is a consistent view.[30] They are in a way involuntary because, once the various proofs have been taken into account, that is to say, once all the available evidence has been considered, the final judgment emerges independently of one's will:

But that a Man should afford his Assent to that side, on which the less Probability appears to him, seems to me utterly impracticable, and as impossible, as it is to believe the same thing probable and improbable at the same time. (E IV.xx.15: 716)

But they are, in a way, voluntary, as well. A person can refuse to consider evidence for whatever reason: lack of interest or inclination, or even laziness (see E IV.xx.6: 710). Or it may require effort to get at the proofs, effort that the greater part of mankind may not be able to afford:

And in this State are the greatest part of Mankind, who are given up to Labour, and enslaved to the Necessity of their mean Condition; whose Lives are worn out, only in the Provisions for Living. These Men's Opportunity of Knowledge and Enquiry, are commonly as narrow as their Fortunes; and their Understandings are but little instructed, when all their whole Time and Pains is laid out, to still the Croaking of their own Bellies, or the Cries of their Children. 'Tis not to be expected, that a Man, who drudges on, all his Life, in a laborious Trade, should be more knowing in the variety of things done in the World, than a Pack-horse, who is driven constantly forwards and backwards, in a narrow Lane, and dirty Road, only to Market, should be skilled in the Geography of the Country. (E IV.xx.2: 707)

---

presume that the relevant relation between A and B holds, where the relation is such that if we did perceive it, we would know that P, i.e., know that A is B.

[30] Here I side with Ayers 1991 over Passmore 1986 on the issue of Locke and the voluntariness of belief.

Locke clearly has a lot of sympathy with the plight of such people, much more than with he who would refuse to consider certain evidence simply because it goes against his own interest or preconceived opinion.[31] Nonetheless, Locke is convinced that:

GOD has furnished Men with Faculties sufficient to direct them in the Way they should take, if they will but seriously employ them that Way, when their ordinary Vocations allow them the Leisure. (E IV.xx.3: 708)

4. CONCLUSION

Locke had extraordinary and important views on judgment, both in the broad sense and in his narrower technical sense. In the broad sense, he had a carefully worked out view about the nature of propositions, and how the mind forms them out of ideas. Although his identification of proposition formation with the perception or presumption of the agreement or disagreement of ideas seems antiquated to us, and leaves Locke with serious problems, it is important for an overall understanding of Locke. In particular, it is important for understanding his views on knowledge and judgment, in the narrow sense.

Locke thought that our knowledge is very limited. Intuitive and demonstrative knowledge cannot be extended to our knowledge of the physical world. Sensitive knowledge is limited to current sense

---

[31] There is also the matter of lacking the skill or ability to use the proofs one has. Locke says:

> Those who *want skill to use those Evidences they have* of Probabilities; who cannot carry a train of Consequences in their Heads, nor weigh exactly the preponderancy of contrary Proofs and Testimonies, making every Circumstance its due allowance, may be easily misled to assent to Positions that are not probable. (E IV.xx.5: 709)

This seems to be a case of the faculty of reason not functioning correctly. The proofs, which would ordinarily incline one toward the appropriate presumption of the agreement of ideas, do not have their ordinary causal upshot. Locke does not seem very interested in how or why this might happen. He says:

> Which great difference in Men's Intellectuals, whether it rises from any defect in the Organs of the Body, particularly adapted to Thinking; or in the dulness or untractableness of those Faculties, for want of use; or, as some think, in the natural differences of Men's Souls themselves; or some, or all of these together, it matters not here to examine. (E IV.xx.5: 709)

experience. Furthermore, it is limited to particulars. Through memory, such knowledge can be extended into the past. But when we consider our cognitive awareness of general truths about the world, or of matters of fact that we have never observed or have yet to occur, we need to rely on judgment and belief formation, not knowledge. Judgment extends sensitive knowledge, in much the same way that demonstration extends intuition. The analogy is not exact. Demonstration is a series of intuitions, and results in knowledge; Judgment is not a series of sense perceptions, and results in belief, not knowledge. Although both intuitive and sensitive knowledge are immediate and noninferential, there is no immediate belief. All belief or opinion is the product of probable reasoning.

Although there are these disanalogies between knowledge and belief, we need to understand Locke on knowledge if we are to understand what he says about judgment and belief. Knowledge is the perception of the agreement or disagreement of ideas, and such a perception contributes both to the act of knowing and to the proposition known. Belief is the presumption of the agreement or disagreement of ideas, and such a presumption contributes both to the act of assent and to the proposition believed. Assenting to a proposition just is believing it. Assent or belief is not some further act directed toward a proposition known or believed. Knowing a proposition is one thing, assenting to or believing a proposition is another. Believing or assenting is sort of a watered-down version of knowing. We can even believe a proposition – that is, presume agreement between ideas – when it would be perfectly possible, with a little effort, to perceive the agreement and hence to achieve knowledge.

Locke thinks that the production of belief is causal. Evidence, whether based on past experience or on testimony, causes the presumption of the agreement or disagreement of ideas. Belief is formed by the preponderance of the evidence. Belief formation is normative as well as causal, though Locke is very sketchy on the details. Although it is rational, according to Locke, to take as much evidence into account as possible, his notion of "right judgment" is judgment that gets things right. Judgments formed on the basis of all the relevant evidence may still be wrong judgments.

Locke's account of judgment, in both the wide and narrow senses, may seem naïve by modern standards. Nonetheless, it is of the greatest importance. Locke was one of the first philosophers of the early modern period to realize the importance of supplementing knowledge with belief. Furthermore, he held that belief could meet standards of rationality, and was produced by probable reasoning. In fact, in his account of sensitive knowledge, probable reasoning, and belief, we can see the emergence of the modern account of empirical knowledge. This is a remarkable achievement.

15 Locke on Faith and Reason

In the "Epistle to the Reader," Locke famously recalls how the idea for the *Essay Concerning Human Understanding* originated in a conversation among five or six friends (E: 7). According to James Tyrrell, one of the friends who were present on that occasion, the topic of the conversation was the principles of morality and revealed religion.[1] As a guide to the focus of the *Essay*, Tyrrell's remark, even if accurate, may seem of dubious value, for Locke himself goes on to describe the subject of the conversation as "very remote" from that of the finished work that he is setting before the reader (E: 7). Nonetheless, there is a sense in which the topic of revealed religion, no less than that of morality, remains close to the heart of Locke's concerns in the published *Essay*. In a couple of brilliant chapters, Locke shows himself to be deeply interested in issues about the rationality of assent to propositions that are supposed to be divinely revealed. If the subject of the original conversation was remote from that of the *Essay*, this may have been true only in a limited sense; Locke's interest in the issues was transformed by his discovery of the need for a critique of the human understanding.

The structure of the present chapter is as follows. In the first section, I seek to explain the place of Locke's philosophy of religion in the project of the *Essay* as a whole; we shall see, in particular, that Locke's contribution needs to be understood in the wider context of his demarcation of the spheres of knowledge and belief in general. In the second section of the essay, I examine the central arguments of Locke's chapter "Of Faith and Reason"; here it is

---

[1] See Cranston 1957: 140–1.

shown that Locke is expanding the role of reason with regard to revelation. The third section is devoted to an analysis of Locke's polemic against the religious enthusiasts of his day who lay claim to private revelation; it is argued that this chapter not only supplements the discussion in "Of Faith and Reason" but also makes a significant contribution to the overall epistemology of the *Essay*. The final section of the chapter is devoted to an internal critique of Locke's philosophy of religion; in particular, I seek to defend Locke against charges of inconsistency and circularity.

I. PHILOSOPHY OF RELIGION AND THE PROJECT OF THE *ESSAY*

Locke's discussion of faith and reason has become a classic contribution to the philosophy of religion, but his interest in problems about the rationality of religious belief is not a merely academic one. At the beginning of IV.xviii, Locke remarks that confusion about the boundaries between faith and reason "may possibly have been the cause, if not of great Disorders, yet at least of great Disputes, and perhaps Mistakes in the World" (E IV.xviii.1: 688). One of Locke's goals in what we may call his philosophy of religion is clearly to undermine the threats to civil order posed by enemies such as the "enthusiasts" who mistakenly denigrate the role of reason in religion. In its concern to defuse the heat and violence of seventeenth-century debates, Locke's philosophy of religion is of a piece with the whole project of the *Essay*. In the Introduction to the work, Locke explains that he seeks to demarcate the spheres of knowledge and belief or opinion, and in subsequent chapters it becomes clear that he hopes for a practical payoff from the successful execution of his project; it will contribute to a more tolerant intellectual atmosphere (see E I.i.4–5: 44–5). Once people are convinced by argument how narrow is the sphere of knowledge, they will realize that in many cases they are opposing belief in the name, not of knowledge, but of other beliefs that are more or less rationally justified. In the same way, Locke expects that a proper demarcation of the spheres of reason and faith will defuse the violence of debates about religion among his contemporaries. But it is not enough to notice how the discussion of faith and reason is infused with the same practical objectives as the *Essay* as a whole; we need a deeper and more precise understanding of the place of Locke's philosophy of religion in the project of the work.

No reader of the *Essay* can fail to see, at least in broad terms, how in the last book Locke executes his project of demarcating the spheres of knowledge and belief or opinion in general. There are indeed two dimensions to Locke's project. In the first place, Locke seeks to offer a philosophical analysis of the nature of knowledge and belief, and how they differ from one another. From the standpoint of contemporary theory of knowledge, Locke's analysis is rather surprising. In contrast to standard contemporary accounts, knowledge, for Locke, is not justified true belief; indeed, it is not a species of belief at all. On the contrary, for Locke knowledge is a mental act or state that logically excludes believing. Something of Locke's view emerges in his response to Stillingfleet in a passage where the immediate issue is religious belief or faith:

> That which your Lordship is afraid it [i.e., Locke's definition of knowledge] may be dangerous to, is an article of faith: that which your Lordship labours, and is concerned for, is the certainty of faith. Now, my Lord, I humbly conceive the certainty of faith … has nothing to do with the certainty of knowledge. And to talk of the certainty of faith, seems all one to me, as to talk of the knowledge of believing, a way of speaking not easy for me to understand. …
>
> Faith stands by itself, and upon grounds of its own; nor can be removed from them, and placed on those of knowledge. Their grounds are so far from being the same, or having anything common, that when it is brought to certainty, faith is destroyed; it is knowledge then, and faith no longer. (W IV: 146)

It is tempting to suppose that Locke is making a point here simply about the nature of religious faith, but that, I think, would be a mistake; he is saying something about the nature of belief in general. Locke's official definition of religious faith will be discussed in the next section, but here we may note that, for Locke, such faith is a species of belief in general; as such, it can lay no claim to certainty or knowledge, which for Locke are equivalent (W IV: 143). Locke is not to be numbered among those thinkers who regard religious faith as sui generis.

The other main dimension of Locke's project of demarcation is his attempt to show where the standards of knowledge can be satisfied, and where we must rest content with something less than knowledge, namely, belief. In recent years, interest in Locke's project of demarcation has tended to center on his thesis that in natural science, as we would call it today, knowledge in the strict sense, or *scientia*, is not available; as Locke puts it, "how far so ever humane Industry may advance useful and *experimental* Philosophy in *physical Things, scientifical* will still be out of our reach" (E IV. iii.26: 556). But as the late chapters of Book IV of the *Essay* show, Locke is scarcely less concerned with advancing the same thesis with regard to religion: religion is an area of great concern to us where the prospects for knowledge in the strict sense are poor. The shrinking of the sphere of knowledge and the corresponding expansion of the sphere of belief are thus major themes of the last book of the *Essay*.

To say that Locke seeks to shrink the sphere of knowledge in religion is not to say that he allows no room for knowledge, even in the strict sense. According to Locke, the second degree of knowledge in the strict sense is demonstration; and Locke, like Descartes and Aquinas before him, is insistent that it is possible not only in principle to achieve demonstrative knowledge of the existence of God; he claims actually to be in possession of such a demonstrative proof. Locke indeed advances a version of the cosmological argument for God's existence that has struck almost all its readers as clearly defective; ever since Leibniz, philosophers have noticed that it seems to involve at least one instance of the fallacy of equivocation.[2] Thus, the premise, "from Eternity there has been something" (E IV.x.3: 620), is ambiguous between "There has never been a time when nothing existed" and "Some one thing has always existed." It is the second, stronger thesis that Locke requires if his argument is to go through, but he is entitled at most to the weaker thesis. Whatever the glaring defects of Locke's argument, however, it is at least billed as a demonstration of the existence of God that is as certain as any proof in Euclid.

Locke, then, follows tradition in holding that knowledge of the existence of God is possible. In general, however, by the standards of his age Locke is conspicuous for his willingness to assign to the province of faith doctrines that were often assigned to the province

---

[2] See Leibniz, *New Essays on Human Understanding*, IV.x; Leibniz 1996: 435–6.

of knowledge. One striking illustration of this point is the doctrine of personal immortality, which was of course of great moment to Locke and his contemporaries. Other philosophers, especially those (like Leibniz) who were raised in the Platonic tradition, argue that the truth of this doctrine could be known a priori; the immortality of the soul follows from the fact of its simplicity, which is itself knowable independently of experience. Of course, such philosophers are prepared to concede that what we can know by reason needs to be supplemented by the voice of revelation; that there will be a general resurrection of the dead in which souls will be reunited with their bodies is an article of faith for which our authority is the Bible and the teaching of the church. In a sense, then, the full Christian doctrine of immortality straddles the divide between knowledge and faith. Locke, by contrast, is not impressed by allegedly demonstrative proofs that seek to derive immortality from the immateriality or simplicity of the soul, since he believes that such immateriality itself, however probable, falls short of knowledge or certainty. Moreover, Locke holds that even if such a proof of the soul's immateriality were available, it would not serve to establish personal immortality. According to Locke, simply by virtue of being a substance, an immaterial soul would, if it existed, be indestructible; but such indestructibility is not sufficient, and perhaps not even necessary, for personal immortality.[3] Thus, for Locke, for whom all philosophical arguments for personal immortality fail, the doctrine is exclusively an article of faith, not of knowledge; epistemologically, it belongs in the same class as the tenet that Jesus is the messiah (which was almost universally assigned to the sphere of faith). Although he would not have been willing to acknowledge the point of kinship, Locke agrees with Hobbes's terse remark that "there is no naturall knowledge of mans estate after death."[4] As Locke says in controversy with Stillingfleet, it is Jesus Christ who has brought life and immortality to light through the Gospel (W IV: 480).

Before we conclude this section, we should take note of one further distinctive feature of Locke's epistemology of religion. We have seen that, according to Locke, the existence of God is almost

---

[3] Journal entry dated February 20, 1682; Aaron and Gibb 1936: 121–3.
[4] Hobbes, *Leviathan* I.15; Hobbes 1968: 206.

the only proposition regarding religion with respect to which knowledge in the strict sense is possible. Now, to say this does not of itself entail that, for Locke, there is a corresponding shrinkage of the area of natural theology – that is, that part of theology that appeals exclusively to reason. Consider, for instance, the case of the Argument from Design for the existence of God. As it is traditionally presented – for instance, in Hume's *Dialogues Concerning Natural Religion* – this is not a demonstrative argument, and does not claim to be, for it is an inductive argument from analogy.[5] Nonetheless, it clearly falls within the sphere of natural or rational theology. Locke, however, appears to regard the areas of demonstrative religious knowledge and natural theology as coextensive; he seems to allow no case where there are strong probabilistic arguments for religious doctrines such as the existence of God.

2. FAITH AND REASON: THE MAIN THESES

Locke's brilliant discussion of faith and reason may perhaps best be introduced by way of a striking observation: Locke seeks both to expand and to shrink the area of faith. The contradiction here is only apparent. Locke seeks to expand the area of faith – that is, belief in general – in relation to that of knowledge; as we have seen, a major theme of Book IV is that in most areas of intellectual enquiry the prospects for *scientia*, or knowledge in the strict sense, are poor, and that we must rest content with something less, namely, faith or belief. But Locke also seeks to shrink the area of faith in relation to reason: in two chapters (E IV.xviii and IV.xix) Locke opposes those, ranging from Roman Catholics to the Puritans, who claim that there is little or no role for reason to play where matters of religious faith are concerned: as Locke says, his opponents cry out "'Tis matter of faith, and above reason." His project of demarcating the provinces of faith and reason is a subtle and carefully wrought attempt to defend the competence of reason in this area in a way that, in Michael Ayers's suggestive phrase, effectively clips the wings of revelation.[6]

---

[5] For this reading of the argument from design, as it is presented by Cleanthes in Hume's *Dialogues*, see Gaskin 1978: 9–40, esp. 22–3.

[6] Ayers 1991: I: 121.

At first sight it is not obvious that this is Locke's purpose. Just as Locke had earlier argued that knowledge and faith are contradistinguished, so he now begins by conceding that there is a sense in which reason and faith are contradistinguished:

Reason therefore here, as contradistinguished to *Faith*, I take to be the discovery of the Certainty or Probability of such Propositions or Truths, which the Mind arrives at by Deductions made from such *Ideas*, which it has got by the use of its natural Faculties, *viz.* By Sensation or Reflection.

Faith, on the other side, is the Assent to any Proposition, not thus made out by the Deductions of Reason; but upon the Credit of the Proposer, as coming from GOD, in some extraordinary way of Communication. This way of discovering Truths to Men we call *Revelation*. (E IV.xviii.2: 689)

Locke may seem to be staking out the boundaries of reason and faith in such a way as to defend the autonomy of faith. But carefully read, the ensuing discussion shows that his purpose is to make two related points that have the effect of enhancing the role of reason.

In the first place, Locke's implicit purpose is to identify two senses of the term 'reason'. Contrary to what we might suppose, the definition that Locke offers at E IV.xviii.2 is not intended as a definition of 'reason' in general; as Locke says, it is a definition of 'reason' only insofar as it is contradistinguished from faith. Locke's intention is to isolate a narrow sense of the term 'reason' in which it may be contrasted to faith (we may call this the "discovery" sense of the term 'reason').[7] Reason in this sense is not confined to the faculty of finding demonstrative arguments; as Locke indicates, even in this narrow sense reason is the faculty involved in finding out the probability as well as the certainty of propositions; it is thus at home in inductive arguments. But Locke is clear that there is in addition a broader sense of the term 'reason' in which it is equivalent to our "natural faculties" in general (E IV.xviii.3: 690). Such a definition of reason may seem a broader one than Locke needs, but for our purpose the important point is the existence of the distinction rather than the precise terms in which it is drawn; moreover, the breadth of Locke's definition seems to do no harm to his case.

The use that Locke seeks to make of this distinction may be illustrated by means of an example close to his heart. Consider, for

[7] Locke offers a similar definition of 'reason' at E IV.xvii.2.

instance, the article of faith expressed in the proposition "The dead shall rise and live again." As we have seen, Locke holds that, unlike the existence of God, this is not a proposition that can be demonstrated. And he further holds – implicitly, at least – that there are no nondemonstrative, inductive arguments for the truth of the proposition. As Locke says, reason cannot discover or "make out" the truth of the proposition; that is, reason in the narrow sense has nothing to do with this proposition. But, according to Locke, it does not follow that there is no role for reason to play here, when reason is understood in the broad sense. Where a purportedly revealed proposition is concerned, reason in this sense has a role to play in examining the grounds for belief; that is, reason is competent to decide whether p is, in fact, divinely revealed. It is the function of reason in this sense to examine not only the credibility of witnesses to an alleged revelation but also the meaning of the texts in which it is reported. For example, if the Bible seems to say that a virgin shall conceive, it is the function of reason in the broad sense to determine what is meant by the word in the original Greek or Hebrew that is translated into English as 'virgin'. As we shall see in the next section, such a distinction between two senses of 'reason' is implicitly acknowledged in the later chapter "Of Enthusiasm" (E IV.xix.14: 704).

The second point that Locke makes in order to enhance the role of reason in this area and to clip the wings of revelation concerns the object of faith. Again, Locke seeks to make a distinction that his opponents have ignored at their peril, but in this case it involves not two senses of a term, but rather two propositions that are easily conflated. In Locke's view, it is important to distinguish between the alleged divinely revealed proposition p and the further proposition "It is divinely revealed that p." According to Locke, it is only the former that is an object of faith and off limits to reason even in the broad sense (unless "It is divinely revealed that p" is part of the content of the alleged revelation). If p is indeed divinely revealed, then reason has no role in discovering its truth value: Locke accepts that it is a necessary truth that if God reveals that p, then p; for, as Locke puts it, God cannot lie (E IV.xviii.5: 692). But it does not follow from this that reason has no role to play when what is at issue is the proposition "It is divinely revealed that p" (and assuming this does not fall within the scope of the alleged

revelation). Here again, Locke wants to insist that there is a legitimate, and indeed indispensable, role for reason to play in discovering whether the second proposition is in fact true. As Ayers
appropriately says, the sting of Locke's argument is in the tail.[8] By
conceding to his opponents that the proper object of divine faith is
indeed off limits to reason, Locke is giving very little away: all the
emphasis in the account falls on the issue of whether there are good
grounds for supposing that p is in fact divinely revealed.

The central purpose of the main arguments in "Of Faith and
Reason," then, may well be aptly described in terms of clipping the
wings of revelation. Locke seeks to buttress the central argument of
"Of Faith and Reason" by making two further points that in their
different ways draw on the basic, or at least central, principles of his
epistemology; these points may seem innocuous enough, but they
both serve the same central purpose. In the first place, Locke
appeals to the foundational principles of his theory of knowledge to
put limits on the content of traditional revelation. According to
Locke, whatever experiences St. Paul may have had when he was
"rapp'd up into the Third Heaven," he cannot communicate any
new simple ideas to us (E IV.xviii.3: 690); for in conveying a revelation, the prophets, however divinely inspired they may have been,
are forced to make use of language, and language is limited to signs
expressing the simple ideas we receive from sensation or reflection,
and the various complex ideas that arise from them. Locke is careful
to observe that his point applies only to the case of traditional
revelation – that is, revelation that is communicated to us by others
(for example, in the Bible); he does not deny that St. Paul and other
holy men may indeed have had the ineffable experiences they claim
to have had; God may have supernaturally inspired them with
experiences that transcended the normal channels of sensation and
reflection. But, as we shall see, in the chapter on enthusiasm Locke
is generally skeptical about claims to original revelation.

Locke also invokes other central theses of his theory of knowledge to set limits to the epistemic weight of alleged revelations.
Once again, Locke begins with a seemingly innocuous concession:
God could reveal to us a proposition, such as a theorem in Euclid,
that we can discover by the use of our natural faculties (i.e., that we

---

[8] Ayers 1991: I: 122.

can know in the strict sense). Such a supposition, for Locke, involves no absurdity. But here too the sting of Locke's argument is in the tail. For it is clear that Locke is less interested in expanding the scope of revealed religion than in emphasizing the lower epistemic status of claims to revelation. Suppose that someone claims that God has directly revealed to him or her the truth of the Pythagorean theorem. On Locke's theory of knowledge, our assurance that the Pythagorean theorem has in fact been divinely revealed to the person can never be as epistemically weighty as the certainty of the truth of the proposition, which derives from the perception of the agreement and disagreement of ideas. Of course, as we have seen, if God has indeed revealed a proposition in mathematics, then the proposition is true, but for Locke there is always room for doubt about whether the proposition has been divinely revealed.

This last argument invokes the principles of Locke's general epistemology to set limits to revelation, but it has no obvious polemical intention. Locke now invokes the principles of his epistemology to mount an attack on the Catholic dogma of transubstantiation (E IV.xviii.5: 692). The Catholic dogma entails that one and the same body can be in two places at the same time; indeed, it claims that this happens when the Mass is celebrated simultaneously in different churches. But according to Locke, such a dogma conflicts with the principles of our clear intuitive knowledge in this area, and must therefore be rejected. As we have seen, it is a central tenet of Locke's epistemology that knowledge trumps faith in the sense that there is always room to doubt whether an article of faith is in fact divinely revealed: where the supposedly revealed proposition contradicts the principles of our intuitive knowledge, we have grounds for believing that the proposition is not in fact divinely revealed. The principles of our knowledge are thus criteria for divine revelation. As Locke puts it, "*Faith* can never convince us of any Thing, that contradicts our Knowledge" (E IV.xviii.5: 692).

Locke's general thesis is clearly an important application of his overall epistemology, but it is somewhat misleadingly expressed. His phrasing of the sentence might suggest that he is making a descriptive point about human psychology; the Catholics cannot in fact be convinced of the truth of the dogma that they claim to believe. But it is clear in context that Locke is not questioning that the Catholics really believe their dogma. The point that he is making is a normative one, not a descriptive one: given the principles of his epistemology, the Catholics have *no right* to be convinced of the dogma, for it contradicts the principles of our intuitive knowledge. Of course, since the dogma in question is supposed to involve a contradiction, the non-normative thesis involves philosophically interesting issues. It might plausibly be argued that it is incoherent to talk of believing what is logically impossible; similar claims to incoherence are often made about the notion of deciding to believe or believing at will. But interesting as they may be, such issues are not raised by Locke's normative thesis.

Locke's discussion of revelation in the case of what we can know by the use of our natural faculties is an important part of the project of clipping the wings of revelation, but it seems to suffer from an oversight. Consider the case where what is allegedly revealed is not a mathematical theorem whose truth we already know but a conjecture (Goldbach's, for example) for which we as yet have no proof. Of course, Locke would insist that we could come to have greater assurance of the truth of this proposition by the use of our natural faculties; the alleged revelation could in principle be made redundant by the proper use of these faculties. But in the absence of a proof, the alleged revelation, if well authenticated, would be a useful addition to our stock of well-supported beliefs, though not, of course, to our body of knowledge in the strict sense. Locke arguably makes life too easy for himself by overlooking this kind of case.

3. THE CRITIQUE OF ENTHUSIASM

Locke's critique of religious enthusiasm is one of the most famous and influential contributions to the philosophy of religion. Despite its fame, the critique was something of an afterthought on Locke's part; the chapter in question was not added until the fourth edition of the *Essay*. Indeed, Locke went ahead and added the chapter against the initial advice of his friend William Molyneux to the effect that such a discussion was unnecessary (March 26, 1695; C 5: 317). It is natural to ask, then, why Locke felt the need to supplement his philosophy of religion in the *Essay* in this way. We shall have gone a long way toward answering this question if we can show not only that the discussion fills a gap in the argument left by

"Of Faith and Reason," but also that it plays an integral role in the philosophy of the *Essay* as a whole. These desiderata can, I believe, be satisfied.

Locke's critique of enthusiasm complements the earlier discussion of faith and reason in at least two ways. In the first place, as Michael Ayers notices, the discussion in "Of Faith and Reason" was in one way incomplete.[9] Locke had reminded the reader of the standard distinction between original and traditional revelation, but he had concentrated almost all his attention on the claims of the latter; that is, he had been interested in claims to the effect that the Bible or the Catholic Church is a repository of truths divinely revealed to others. By contrast, Locke had largely ignored the claims of those who say that they have been in direct communication with God or the Holy Spirit. In Locke's time such claims were made by the Quakers and Puritan zealots or extremists.[10] Second, the target of Locke's polemic in "Of Enthusiasm" embodies a distinctive attitude toward reason in religious matters. Near the beginning of "Of Faith and Reason," Locke says that every sect "as far as Reason will help them, make use of it gladly: and where it fails them, they cry out, *'Tis matter of Faith, and above Reason"* (E IV.xviii.2: 689). By contrast, Locke's opponents in "Of Enthusiasm" adopt a more extreme attitude, "which laying by Reason would set up Revelation without it" (E IV.xix.3: 698). It is true that Locke later ironically characterizes the enthusiasts as holding that reason is a "dim Candle" that can be eclipsed by the "Sun" of private revelation (E IV.xix.8: 700), and that seems to suggest that they recognize that reason has some epistemic authority (perhaps in other, more prosaic areas of life). But in general it is clear that Locke's target in "Of Enthusiasm" adopts a more openly hostile attitude toward reason than is at issue in the chapter "Of Faith and Reason."

The critique of enthusiasm not only complements the discussion in "Of Faith and Reason"; less obviously and more controversially,

---

[9] Ayers 1991: I: 111.

[10] The target of Locke's polemic in the chapter "Of Enthusiasm" is controversial. Thomas Lennon has recently argued that the target is less religious than philosophical: the polemic is principally directed against Cartesian philosophers such as Nicolas Malebranche and his English disciple John Norris (Lennon 1993: 173). I have criticized Lennon's position in Jolley 2003: 179–91, esp. 180–3. See also Ayers 1991: I: 122.

it also embodies and develops a principal theme of the *Essay* as a whole. In one of its chief aspects, the *Essay* is a sustained attack on what we might call the "divine direct assistance" model of knowledge.[11] Earlier in the work Locke had criticized the most philosophically respectable version of this doctrine, namely, the doctrine of innate knowledge associated with Descartes and the Cambridge Platonists. According to such a doctrine, God has directly inscribed truths on our minds, either at birth or before it, and our task as responsible epistemic agents, as it were, is to uncover the truths that are present, though often latent, in our souls. At the time of writing the chapter "Of Enthusiasm," Locke was engaged in attacking a more recent version of the theory, namely, Malebranche's doctrine of "seeing all things in God";[12] according to this theory, God directly assists us in our search for knowledge not by inscribing truths in the depths of our souls but rather by granting us access to ideas and truths in his own mind. Against such theories Locke argues that God confines his role to endowing us with natural faculties, and then leaves us to cultivate these faculties in such a way that they yield either knowledge in the strict sense or at least justified true belief.

The doctrines of innate knowledge and of divine illumination (or vision in God) differ from one another in important respects, but to see why Locke's extended polemic against such theories still leaves a gap in his argument, it is helpful to notice what they have in common. As we should expect from the philosophers who advance them, such theories are at once universalistic and rationalistic. To say that they are universalistic is to say that they claim that God provides direct cognitive assistance to all human minds; the truths that for Descartes and others are directly inscribed by God on our souls may be obscured in some minds, but they are nonetheless present and can in principle be uncovered if only people will direct their attention aright. To say that these theories are rationalistic is to say that reason is either the instrument for the discovery of such truths or perhaps, in some sense, the object of discovery; in Malebranche's philosophy, for instance, God is actually identified

---

[11] Cf. Jolley 2003: 186–7.
[12] Locke's essay "An Examination of P. Malebranche's Opinion of Seeing All Things in God" (W IX: 211–55) was posthumously published in 1706.

with Universal Reason. Locke's famous polemics against these doctrines thus leave untouched versions of the "divine direct assistance" model that are particularistic or antirationalist. The polemic against enthusiasm goes a long way toward filling this gap in the argument. The enthusiasts are particularistic in the sense that they claim that God has provided direct assistance only to his chosen or "peculiar" people. And they are antirationalist in the sense that they claim that God provides such assistance not through reason but through supernatural revelation. Sticklers for completeness will observe that Locke's polemic against enthusiasm still leaves two versions of the model in the field – the particularistic/rationalist and the universalistic/antirationalist. But on Locke's behalf it could be said that neither of these positions was a serious, as opposed to a merely academic, option in the controversies of the period. Moreover, Locke arguably operates with a simpler classificatory scheme that divides the proponents of the "divine direct assistance" model into rationalists and antirationalists, and in terms of this classification his attack on the "divine direct assistance" model is complete.

Locke is not the only seventeenth-century philosopher to mount a sustained critique of religious enthusiasm; he had been anticipated in this area by the Cambridge Platonist Henry More.[13] But it is important to notice that there is a major difference in the character of their critiques. More largely confines himself to seeking to offer a diagnosis of religious enthusiasm; it is a form of mental pathology caused by an overheated imagination. This sort of critique is not wholly absent from Locke's discussion; he writes, for instance, of the enthusiasts as "Men, in whom Melancholy has mixed with Devotion, or whose conceit of themselves has raised them into an Opinion of a greater familiarity with GOD and a nearer admittance to his Favour than is afforded to Others" (E IV. xix.5: 699). But what is distinctive about Locke's discussion is that it takes the form of a genuine critical engagement with the claims of the enthusiasts. Locke's critique may be unsympathetic or myopic, but its philosophical character is not in doubt.

In opposition to the enthusiasts Locke returns to his favorite strategy, first seen in the polemic against innate knowledge, of

---

[13] Henry More, *Enthusiasmus Triumphatus* (1662).

arguing through a dilemma.[14] He challenges his opponents to tell us just what is the proposition that they claim to see with a light from heaven; he thinks it must be either the religious proposition p (e.g., that the millennium is at hand) or the proposition that p has been divinely revealed. Suppose that they say the former. In that case they can be confronted with a further dilemma: either they know that p in Locke's strict sense, in which case revelation is unnecessary, or they merely believe that p without strictly knowing it. If they believe that p without knowing it, they can be challenged about the grounds for their belief. If they respond by saying that they believe that p because it has been revealed by God, they are caught in a circle, for their only ground for believing that p is divinely revealed is their assurance that p. And the enthusiasts can be convicted of just the same circular reasoning if they embrace the second horn of the initial dilemma – that is, if they choose to claim that what they see with a light from heaven is that the proposition has been divinely revealed. Thus, as Locke says, their position comes down to the bald assertion that they are sure because they are sure.

Locke, then, augments his polemic against the "divine direct assistance" model of knowledge through a critique of the enthusiasts that employs the same argumentative strategy – the argument through a dilemma – as his earlier attack on the doctrine of innate knowledge. Yet it is important to note that Locke is not in a position to mount an unqualified attack on the particularistic and antirationalist version of this model; in this respect, his polemic against this version differs from his polemic against the universalistic and rationalist version embodied in the doctrine of innate knowledge. As Locke himself notes, he does not go so far as to deny that God can, or even does, communicate directly with individual human beings. Nonetheless, Locke argues that the exceptions to the rule that God does not do so are principled ones:

Thus we see the holy Men of old, who had *Revelations* from GOD, had something else besides that internal Light of assurance in their own Minds, to testify to them, that it was from GOD. They were not left to their own Perswasions alone, that those Perswasions were from GOD; But had

---

[14] For this interpretation of Locke's strategy of argument against the doctrine of innate principles, see Jolley 1999: 32–7.

outward Signs to convince them of the Author of those Revelations.
(E IV.xix.15: 705)

Such outward signs – that is, miracles, such as the burning bush that
Moses saw – function as epistemic criteria by which we (and the holy
men themselves) can distinguish genuine revelations from the
spurious, or at least dubious, revelations of the enthusiasts. But of
course, as Wolterstorff notes, the invocation of miracles simply raises
a new set of problems that Locke does not address in the *Essay*.[15]

4. THE ROLE OF REASON: PROBLEMS

Locke's philosophy of revealed religion is no doubt open to criticism
on external grounds. His polemic against the enthusiasts has been
described as "highly tendentious," and he has been taken to task for
never exploring the possibility that religious experience, of one sort
or another, can provide evidence for religious belief.[16] Indeed, to
many readers Locke's conception of the nature of both religious
belief and experience will seem an impoverished one; it may seem
to exhibit the same limitations that are often ascribed to his contemporaries' view of poetry and of the imagination in general.
However fascinating it might be, pursuing such a line of criticism
would involve us in murky and highly controversial issues and
would run the risk of leading us far away from Locke and his concerns. In this section, I shall focus instead on the more modest but
also more profitable goal of mounting an internal critique of Locke's
philosophy of religion. I shall focus, in particular, on problems of
consistency and circularity arising from Locke's various claims
about the role of reason.

In the course of criticizing the enthusiasts Locke makes an unusually eloquent and surprisingly unqualified claim: "*Reason* must be
our last Judge and Guide in every Thing" (E IV.xix.14: 704). It is
natural to ask whether Locke does not pay a price for the seemingly
extravagant and unqualified nature of his claim; it may seem that

---

[15] Wolterstorff 1994: 196. Wolterstorff cites two problems: "how much of what a
person claims to be divinely revealed is confirmed as divinely revealed by his
performance of a miracle?" and "under what circumstances, if any, are we
permitted to accept testimony to the effect that a miracle has occurred?"
Wolterstorff observes that this last problem was addressed by Hume.
[16] Wolterstorff 1994: 195.

Locke commits himself here to a position about the role of reason that is inconsistent with the more measured claims of the previous chapter, "Of Faith and Reason"; there, after all, he was prepared to concede that there is a sense in which faith and reason may be contradistinguished and have distinct provinces. But in fact such an objection seems mistaken. For even in IV.xix, Locke does qualify, or at least clarify, the claim about the role of reason in a way that brings it into line with the dominant position of "Of Faith and Reason." Consider the passage that immediately follows the eloquent claim that reason must be our last judge and guide in everything:

I do not mean, that we must consult Reason, and examine whether a Proposition revealed from God can be made out by natural Principles, and if it cannot, that then we may reject it: But consult it we must, and by it examine, whether it be a *Revelation* from God or no: And if *Reason* finds it to be revealed from GOD, *Reason* then declares for it, as much as for any other Truth, and makes it one of her Dictates. (E IV.xix.14: 704)

Locke may not operate here with a distinction between two senses of the term 'reason'; rather, he seems to be thinking in terms of two roles for reason. Nonetheless, what he says could easily be expressed in terms of the distinction between two senses drawn in the previous chapter. It is not reason in the narrow, discovery sense that must be our last judge and guide in everything; rather, it is reason in the broad sense that covers critical enquiry. Locke is saying that any alleged divine revelation must be subject to such tests as the critical examination of witnesses and the interpretation of texts: there is no appeal beyond reason in the broad sense. Even in "Of Enthusiasm" Locke allows logical space for justified assent to propositions of the form "It is divinely revealed that p," where p is above reason in the sense that its truth cannot be discovered by demonstrative or probabilistic arguments.

Locke's striking claim that reason must be our last judge and guide in everything gives rise to another sort of objection of consistency. Locke makes his resounding claim in the course of opposing the enthusiasts, who have a very low view of our faculty of reason. Locke characterizes their position with pleasing irony:

When the Spirit brings Light into our Minds, it dispels Darkness. We see it, as we do that of the Sun at Noon, and need not the twilight of Reason to shew it us. This Light from Heaven is strong, clear, and pure, carries its own

Demonstration with it, and we may as rationally take a Glow-worme to assist us to Discover the Sun, as to examine the Celestial Ray by our dim Candle, Reason. (E IV.xix.8: 700)

For the enthusiasts, then, our faculty of reason is a dim candle that is eclipsed by the sunshine of private divine revelation. But if we cast our mind back over the *Essay*, we might wonder whether Locke does not himself really agree with the enthusiasts that reason is a dim candle; certainly, in the Introduction to the *Essay* and elsewhere he makes many statements about the narrowness of our minds, and he even characterizes this fact by invoking the traditional image of the candle.[17] It is natural to ask, then, whether Locke can consistently hold both that reason is a dim candle and that it must be our last judge and guide in everything.

It may be tempting to suppose that the key to resolving the problem lies in the distinction between two senses of the term 'reason'. We might say that, for Locke, it is reason in the narrow sense that is a dim candle; in other words, there are few propositions whose certainty or even probability we can discover by deductive or inductive arguments. But as we have seen, it is reason in the broad sense that must be our last judge and guide in everything. And from the fact that reason in the narrow sense is a dim candle, it does not follow that reason in the broad sense is a dim candle; in this latter sense, reason might be a rather bright light. Thus no problem of consistency is involved.

But in fact such a strategy for resolving the problem is both misguided and unnecessary. The strategy is misguided, for it seems that it is reason in the broad sense that is a dim candle; that is, it is reason in the sense in which it is equivalent to our natural faculties in general that Locke is inclined to characterize as modest and limited in scope. And the strategy is unnecessary because the consistency of Locke's overall position can be defended without invoking a distinction between different senses of the term 'reason'. It is true that Locke's claims about reason are in some tension with one another, but they are not in contradiction: reason is indeed a dim candle, but dim as it is, it is the best light available to us, and

---

[17] The image of reason as a candle derives from Proverbs 20:27. The image was prominent among the Cambridge Platonists, especially Nathanael Culverwel. Locke exploits the image to emphasize the weakness of reason or our natural faculties.

NICHOLAS JOLLEY

this is why it must be our last judge and guide in everything. Moreover, it is perfectly coherent for Locke to claim that it is reason itself that enables us to see that it is the best light available to us; it is reason, for instance, that exposes the spurious, or at least doubtful, claims of the enthusiasts. We can see that this is a coherent position by taking the metaphor literally. Daylight and electric light are both brighter than candlelight, but by candlelight I might discover that it is dark outside and that there is no electric light in the room; I might, for instance, use the candle to read, perhaps rather laboriously, a newspaper that informs me that power outages have been scheduled for that very day.

Locke's position on the role of reason is a consistent one, but it may seem that he is in trouble from a different quarter. We have seen that Locke can answer the question why reason must be our last judge and guide by saying that it is the best light available to us, and that it is reason itself that enables us to discover this fact. Nonetheless, one might still seek to press the question of how we know that reason is a reliable faculty; how do we know that it does not systematically distort reality, like the curved mirrors in an amusement park? It seems that Locke's answer to this question is that reason – that is, our natural faculties in general – has been given us by a benevolent God who would not deceive us in this way; such a God would not endow us with faculties that are systematically unreliable. But then, as Michael Ayers suggests, it may seem that a Lockean circle looms: "The question arises whether Locke is not in the end guilty of something like the famous Cartesian circle, employing reason to justify reason: by mean of my faculties, I can prove the existence of God; since God is not a deceiver I can trust my faculties."[18]

It is possible to reply to this objection that it mistakes the nature of Locke's project. Whether Descartes is trying to justify the reliability of reason by reason itself is of course a controversial issue, on which we do not need to take a stand here. But whatever the truth on that score, it seems fair to say that the situation in Locke's case is clear. In the *Essay Concerning Human Understanding*, Locke is not trying to show that reason is reliable. What is at issue for Locke is not the reliability of reason or of our natural faculties in general, but rather their scope; Locke wants to chart the limits of our human

[18] Ayers 1991: I: 123.

understanding in such a way that we come to know where we may reasonably hope to achieve knowledge. Whether such a project is coherent is of course a subject for legitimate question, but it is a different project from that of justifying the reliability of reason or our natural faculties in general. Since Locke does not seek to argue for the reliability of reason at all, a fortiori he is not guilty of a circular argument.

CONCLUSION

No one can read carefully Locke's discussion of faith and reason without noticing that its treatment of revealed religion is almost uniformly negative. Whenever Locke seems to make concessions to the claims of revelation, he proceeds to qualify these concessions in such a way that they amount to very little; in effect, what he gives with one hand he takes away with the other. It is true that Locke creates logical space for rational assent to the proposition that some further proposition has been revealed by God. But nowhere does Locke show that the conditions for rational assent are in fact satisfied; nowhere does he show that there are grounds for believing that the Bible is a repository of divine revelation. Indeed, in the case of the Bible it seems highly unlikely that the conditions for rational assent to the claims of revelation are in fact satisfied. No doubt the negative emphasis of Locke's treatment of revelation is a function of his particular polemical concerns; as Ayers says, Locke's target is not atheists or deists, but rather those – whether Catholics or Protestants – who promote uncritically some arbitrary interpretation of Scripture or lay claim to private revelation.[19] The tone and emphasis of Locke's discussion are understandable in context, but even so, the situation is most ironic. We know that Locke was a theist and a Christian (if a rather unorthodox one) who seems to have believed that the Bible contains divinely revealed truths. But his most sustained discussion of the philosophy of religion is highly corrosive; whatever he intended, it gives aid and comfort to the enemies of revealed religion. Here, perhaps more clearly than anywhere else in the *Essay*, we see why Locke was a hero and an inspiration to philosophers of the Enlightenment such as Voltaire.

[19] Ayers 1991: I: 122.

Bibliography

WORKS OF LOCKE CITED IN THIS VOLUME

The Correspondence of John Locke, ed. E. S. de Beer. 9 vols. Oxford: Clarendon Press, 1976–.

Drafts for the Essay concerning Human Understanding, *and Other Philosophical Writings*, ed. Peter H. Nidditch and G. A. J. Rogers. 3 vols. Oxford: Clarendon Press, 1990–.

An Essay concerning Human Understanding, ed. Peter H. Nidditch. Oxford: Clarendon Press, 1975.

Essays on the Law of Nature, ed. W. von Leyden. Oxford: Oxford University Press, 1954.

"A Letter to the Right Reverend Edward, Lord Bishop of Worcester, Concerning some Passages relating to Mr. Locke's Essay of humane Understanding: In a late Discourse of his Lordship's, in Vindication of the Trinity." London, 1697.

"Mr. Locke's Reply to the Right Reverend the Lord Bishop of Worcester's Answer to his Second Letter." London, 1699.

Of the Conduct of the Understanding, fifth edition, ed. Thomas Fowler. Oxford: Oxford University Press, 1901.

Some Thoughts concerning Education, ed. John W. Yolton and Jean S. Yolton. Oxford: Clarendon Press, 1989.

The Works of John Locke, new edition, corrected. 10 vols. London 1823; repr. 1963.

OTHER WORKS CITED

Aaron, Richard I. *John Locke*. Oxford: Oxford University Press, 1937; 3rd ed. 1971.

Aaron, Richard I., and Jocelyn Gibb, eds. *An Early Draft of Locke's Essay Together with Excerpts from His Journals*. Oxford: Oxford University Press, 1936.

Aarsleff, H. *From Locke to Saussure: Essay on the Study of Language and Intellectual History*. Minneapolis: University of Minnesota Press, 1982.

Aarsleff, H. Locke's Influence. In *The Cambridge Companion to Locke*, ed. Vere Chappell. Cambridge: Cambridge University Press, 1994, pp. 252–89.

Acworth, Richard. Locke's First Reply to John Norris. *The Locke Newsletter* 2 (1971): 7–11.

Alexander, Peter. *Ideas, Qualities and Corpuscles: Locke and Boyle on the External World*. Cambridge: Cambridge University Press, 1985.

Alston, W. P. *Philosophy of Language*. Englewood Cliffs, NJ: Prentice-Hall, 1964.

Alston, William, and Jonathan Bennett. Locke on People and Substances. *Philosophical Review* 47 (1988): 25–46.

Anscombe, G. E. M., and P. Geach. *Three Philosophers*. Ithaca, NY: Cornell University Press, 1961.

Anstey, Peter. Boyle on Occasionalism: An Unexamined Source. *Journal of the History of Ideas* 60 (1999): 57–81.

Anstey, Peter R. *The Philosophy of Robert Boyle*. London: Routledge, 2000.

Aquinas, Thomas. *Summa Theologiae*. Blackfriars edition, ed. and tr. Thomas Gilby et al. 60 vols. London: Eyre and Spottiswoode, 1964ff.

Arnauld, Antoine, and Pierre Nicole. *Logic or the Art of Thinking* (1683), trans. Jill Vance Buroker. Cambridge: Cambridge University Press, 1996.

Ashworth, E. J. *Language and Logic in the Post-Medieval Period*. Dordrecht: D. Reidel, 1974.

Ashworth, E. J. Chimeras and Imaginary Objects: A Study of the Post-Medieval Theory of Signification. *Vivarium* 14 (1977): 57–79.

Ashworth, E. J. 'Do Words Signify Ideas or Things?' The Scholastic Sources of Locke's Theory of Language. *Journal of the History of Philosophy* 19 (1981): 299–326.

Ashworth, E. J. Mental Language and the Unity of Propositions: A Semantic Problem Discussed by Early Sixteenth Century Logicians. *Franciscan Studies* 41 (1981): 61–69.

Ashworth, E. J. Locke on Language. In *Locke*, ed. Vere Chappell. Oxford: Oxford University Press, pp. 175–98. First published in *Canadian Journal of Philosophy* 14 (1984): 45–73.

Ashworth, E. J. Domingo de Soto (1494–1560) and the Doctrine of Signs. In *De Ortu Grammaticae: Studies in Medieval Grammar and Linguistics Theory in Memory of Jan Pinborg*, ed. G. L. Brusill-Hall, S. Ebbesen, and K. Koerner. Philadelphia: John Benjamins, 1990, pp. 35–48.

Atherton, Margaret. Locke's Theory of Personal Identity. In *Midwest Studies in Philosophy VIII: Contemporary Perspectives on the History of Philosophy*, ed. Vere Chappell. Minneapolis: University of Minnesota Press, 1983, pp. 273–93.

Atherton, Margaret. The Inessentiality of Lockean Essences. *Canadian Journal of Philosophy* **14** (1984): 277–93.

Atherton, Margaret. Knowledge of Substance and Knowledge of Science in Locke's *Essay. History of Philosophy Quarterly* **1** (1984): 413–27.

Atherton, Margaret. 'Ideas in the Mind, Qualities in Bodies': Some Distinctive Features of Locke's Account of Primary and Secondary Qualities. In *Minds, Ideas, and Concepts: Essays on the Theory of Representation in Modern Philosophy*, ed. Phillip D. Cummins and Guenter Zoeller. Atascadero, CA: Ridgeview, 1992.

Axtell, James L. Locke's Review of the *Principia. Notes and Records of the Royal Society of London* **20** (1965): 152–61.

Ayers, Michael R. Ideas of Power and Substance in Locke's Philosophy. In *Locke on Human Understanding*, ed. I. Tipton. Oxford: Oxford University Press, 1977, pp. 77–104.

Ayers, Michael R. Review of P. H. Nidditch, *John Locke: An Essay Concerning Human Understanding. Philosophy* **52** (1977): 227–30.

Ayers, Michael R. Locke versus Aristotle on Natural Kinds. *Journal of Philosophy* **78** (1981): 247–71.

Ayers, Michael R. Mechanism, Superaddition, and the Proof of God's Existence in Locke's *Essay. Philosophical Review* **90** (1981): 210–51.

Ayers, Michael R. Are Locke's 'Ideas' Images, Intentional Objects or Natural Signs? *Locke Newsletter* **17** (1986): 3–36.

Ayers, Michael R. *Locke: Epistemology and Ontology.* 2 vols. London: Routledge, 1991.

Ayers, Michael R. The Foundations of Knowledge and the Logic of Substance: The Structure of Locke's General Philosophy. In *Locke's Philosophy: Content and Context*, ed. G. A. J. Rogers. Oxford: Oxford University Press, 1996.

Ayers, Michael R. Review Article: *The Cambridge Companion to Locke*, ed. Chappell. *The Locke Newsletter* **28** (1997): 157–88.

Bacon, Francis. *The New Organon* (1620), ed. Lisa Jardine and Michael Silverthorne. Cambridge: Cambridge University Press, 2000.

Baeumker, Clemens. Primäre und Sekundäre Qualitäten: Ein Nachtrag. *Archiv für Geschichte der Philosophie* **22** (1909): 380.

Barnes, Johathan. *Early Greek Philosophy.* London: Penguin, 1987.

Beaney, M. *Frege: Making Sense.* London: Duckworth, 1996.

Bennett, Jonathan. Substance, Reality, and Primary Qualities. In *Locke and Berkeley: A Collection of Critical Essays*, ed. C. B. Martin and D. M. Armstrong. Garden City, NY: Anchor Books, 1968.

Bennett, Jonathan. *Locke, Berkeley, Hume: Central Themes.* Oxford: Oxford University Press, 1971.

Bennett, Jonathan. A Note on Interpretation. *Canadian Journal of Philosophy* **12** (1982): 753–5.

Bennett, Jonathan. Substratum. *History of Philosophy Quarterly* **4** (1987): 197–215.

Bennett, Jonathan. Locke's Philosophy of Mind. In *The Cambridge Companion to Locke*, ed. Vere Chappell. Cambridge: Cambridge University Press, 1994, pp. 89–114.

Bennett, Jonathan. *Learning from Six Philosophers: Descartes, Spinoza, Leibniz, Locke, Berkeley, Hume.* 2 vols. Oxford: Clarendon Press, 2001.

Berkeley, George. *The Works of George Berkeley*, ed. T. E. Jessop and A. A. Luce. 9 vols. London: Thomas Nelson and Sons, 1948–57.

Bill, E. G. W. *Education at Christ Church Oxford 1660–1800*. Oxford: Clarendon Press, 1988.

Bolton, Martha Brandt. The Origins of Locke's Doctrine of Primary and Secondary Qualities. *Philosophical Quarterly* **26** (1976): 305–16.

Bolton, Martha Brandt. Substances, Substrata, and Names of Substances in Locke's *Essay. Philosophical Review* **85** (1976): 488–513.

Bolton, Martha Brandt. Locke and Pyrrhonism: The Doctrine of Primary and Secondary Qualities. In *The Skeptical Tradition*, ed. Myles Burnyeat. Berkeley: University of California Press, 1983.

Bolton, Martha. Locke on Substance Ideas and the Determination of Kinds: A Reply to Mattern. *The Locke Newsletter* **19** (1988): 17–45.

Bolton, Martha. The Idea-Theoretic Basis of Locke's Anti-Essentialist Doctrine of Nominal Essences. In *Minds, Ideas, and Objects: Essays on the Theory of Representation in Modern Philosophy*, ed. Phillip D. Cummins and Guenter Zoller. Atascadero, CA: Ridgeview, 1992.

Bolton, Martha Brandt. The Real Molyneux Question and the Basis of Locke's Answer. In *Locke's Philosophy: Context and Content*, ed. G. A. J. Rogers. Oxford: Clarendon Press, 1994, pp. 75–100.

Bolton, Martha Brandt. Locke on Identity: The Scheme of Simple and Compounded Things. In *Individuation and Identity in Early Modern Philosophy*, ed. K. F. Barber and J. J. E. Garcia. Albany: State University of New York Press, 1994, pp. 103–31.

Bolton, Martha Brandt. The Relevance of Locke's Theory of Ideas to His Doctrine of Nominal Essence and Anti-Essentialist Semantic Theory. In *Locke*, ed. Vere Chappell. Oxford: Oxford University Press, 1998, pp. 214–25.

Bolton, Martha Brandt. Locke. In *The Blackwell Guide to the Modern Philosophers: From Descartes to Nietzsche*, ed. Steven M. Emmanuel. Malden, MA: Blackwell, 2001.

Bolton, Martha Brandt. Locke's Theory of Sensible Representation. In *Perception and Reality: From Descartes to the Present*, ed. Ralph Schumacher. Paderborn, Germany: Mentis-Verlag, 2003, pp. 146–67.

Bolton, Martha Brandt. Locke on the Semantic and Epistemic Role of Simple Ideas of Sensation. *Pacific Philosophical Quarterly* **85** (2004): 301–21.

Bonno, G. The Diffusion and Influence of Locke's *Essay Concerning Human Understanding* in France before Voltaire's *Lettres Philosophiques*. In *A Locke Miscellany: Locke Biography and Criticism for All*, ed. J. S. Yolton. Bristol: Thoemmes, 1990, pp. 75–85.

Boyle, Robert. *Selected Philosophical Papers of Robert Boyle*, ed. M. A. Stewart. Manchester: Manchester University Press, 1979.

Boyle, Robert. *A Free Enquiry into the Vulgarly Received Notion of Nature*, ed. E. B. Davis and M. Hunter. Cambridge: Cambridge University Press, 1996.

Boyle, Robert. *The Works of Robert Boyle*, ed. Michael Hunter and Edward B. Davis. 14 vols. London: Pickering & Chatto, 1999–2000.

Brody, Baruch. Locke on the Identity of Persons. *American Philosophical Quarterly* **9** (1972): 327–34.

Brykman, Genevieve. *Locke: Idees, language et connaissance.* Paris: Ellipses, 2001.

Buchdahl, G. *Metaphysics and the Philosophy of Science.* Cambridge, MA: MIT Press, 1969.

Burgersdijk, Franco. *Institutionum logicorum libri duo.* Cambridge, 1637.

Burnet, Thomas. *Second Remarks upon an Essay Concerning Humane Understanding, In a Letter address'd to the Author* (1697). New York: Garland, 1984.

Buroker, Jill. The Port-Royal Semantics of Terms. *Synthese* **96** (1993): 455–76.

Butler, Joseph. *The Analogy of Religion*, fifth edition. Glasgow, 1754.

Campbell, John. Locke on Qualities. *Canadian Journal of Philosophy* **10** (1980): 567–85.

Carter, W. B. The Classification of Ideas in Locke's *Essay. Dialogue* **2** (1963): 25–41.

Chappell, Vere. Locke and Relative Identity. *History of Philosophy Quarterly* **6** (1989): 69–83.

Chappell, Vere. Locke on the Ontology of Matter, Living Things and Persons. *Philosophical Studies* **60** (1990): 19–32.

Chappell, Vere. Locke on the Freedom of the Will. In *Locke's Philosophy: Content and Context*, ed. G. A. J. Rogers. Oxford: Oxford University Press, 1994.

Chappell, Vere. Locke on the Intellectual Basis of Sin. *Journal of the History of Philosophy* **32** (1994): 197–207.

Chappell, Vere. Locke's Theory of Ideas. In *The Cambridge Companion to Locke*, ed. Vere Chappell. Cambridge: Cambridge University Press, 1994, pp. 26–55.

Chappell, Vere. Locke on the Suspension of Desire. *Locke Newsletter* **29** (1998): 23–38.

Chappell, Vere. Review of *Liberty Worth the Name*, by Gideon Yaffe. *Mind* **113** (2004): 420–4.

Cohen, Sheldon. St. Thomas Aquinas on the Immaterial Reception of Sensible Forms. *Philosophical Review* **91** (1982): 193–209.

Colman, John. *John Locke's Moral Philosophy*. Edinburgh: Edinburgh University Press, 1983.

Combach, Johannes. *Metaphysicorum libri duo*, third edition. Oxford, 1633.

Condillac, E. B. de. *Oeuvres philosophiques*, ed. Georges Le Roy. Paris: Presses Universitaires, 1947.

Condillac. E. B. de. *An Essay on the Origin of Human Knowledge*, trans. T. Nugent. Gainesville, FL: Scholars' Facsimiles & Reprints, 1971.

Conroy, Graham P. George Berkeley on Moral Demonstration. *Journal of the History of Ideas* **22** (1961): 205–14.

Cooper, Anthony Ashley, third earl of Shaftesbury. *Several Letters Written by a Noble Lord to a Young Man at University*. London, 1716.

Coudert, A. Some Theories of Natural Language from the Renaissance to the Seventeenth Century. *Studia Leibnitiana Sonderheft* **7** (1978): 106–14.

Cranston, Maurice. *John Locke: A Biography*. London: Longman, 1957.

Cudworth, Ralph. *A Treatise Concerning Eternal and Immutable Morality (1731)*. In *A Treatise Concerning Eternal and Immutable Morality, With A Treatise of Freewill*, ed. Sarah Hutton. Cambridge: Cambridge University Press, 1996.

Cummins, Robert. Two Troublesome Claims about Qualities in Locke's Essay. *Philosophical Review* **84** (1975): 401–18.

Curley, Edwin. Locke, Boyle, and the Distinction between Primary and Secondary Qualities. *Philosophical Review* **81** (1972): 438–64.

Dascal, M. *Leibniz: Language, Signs and Thought*. Philadelphia: John Benjamins, 1987.

Davidson, Arnold L., and Norbert Hornstein. The Primary/Secondary Quality Distinction: Berkeley, Locke, and the Foundations of Corpuscularian Science. *Dialogue* **23** (1984): 281–303.

Davidson, D. A Nice Derangement of Epitaphs. In *Truth and Interpretation*, ed. E. LePore. London: Blackwell, 1986.

Descartes, René. *Oeuvres de Descartes*, ed. Charles Adam and Paul Tannery. Paris: J. Vrin, 1904.

Descartes, René. *The Philosophical Writings of Descartes*, ed. and trans. John Cottingham, Robert Stoothoff, and Dugald Murdoch. 3 vols. Cambridge: Cambridge University Press, 1984–.

Descartes, René. *Discourse on Method, Optics, Geometry, and Meteorology*, revised edition, trans. Paul J. Olscamp. Indianapolis: Hackett, 2001.

Dlugos, Peter. Yolton and Rorty on the Veil of Ideas in Locke. *History of Philosophy Quarterly* **13** (1996): 317–29.

Downing, Lisa. Are Corpuscles Unobservable in Principle for Locke? *Journal of the History of Philosophy* **30** (1992): 33–51.

Downing, Lisa. The Status of Mechanism in Locke's *Essay*. *Philosophical Review* **107** (1998): 381–414.

Downing, Lisa. The "Sensible Object" and the "Uncertain Philosophical Cause." In *Kant and the Early Moderns*, ed. D. Garber and B. Longuenesse. Princeton, NJ: Princeton University Press, forthcoming.

Feingold, Mordechai. The Humanities. In *The History of the University of Oxford*, ed. Nicholas Tyacke, vol. 4, *Seventeenth-Century Oxford*. Oxford: Clarendon Press, 1997, pp. 211–358.

Feingold, Mordechai. The Mathematical Sciences and the New Philosophies. In *The History of the University of Oxford*, ed. Nicholas Tyacke, vol. 4, *Seventeenth-Century Oxford*. Oxford: Clarendon Press, 1997, pp. 359–448.

Flew, Anthony. Locke on Personal Identity. In *Locke and Berkeley*, ed. C. B. Martin and D. M. Armstrong. New York: Anchor Books, 1968.

Flower, Desmond, ed. *Voltaire's England*. London: The Folio Society, 1950.

Fodor, J. *Psychosemantics*. Cambridge, MA: MIT Press, 1987.

Frank, Robert G., Jr. *Harvey and the Oxford Physiologists*. Berkeley and Los Angeles: University of California Press, 1980.

Fraser, Alexander Campbell. Annotations on Locke's *An Essay Concerning Human Understanding*. 2 vols. New York: Dover, 1959.

Frege, G. *Translations from the Philosophical Writings of Gottlob Frege*, first edition, ed. and trans. P. Geach and M. Black. Oxford: Blackwell, 1952.

Frege, G. Über Sinn und Bedeutung. *Zeitschrift für Philosophie und Philosophische Kritik* **100** (1892): 25–50. Translated in Frege 1952.

Galileo. The Assayer. In *Discoveries and Opinions of Galileo (1623)*, trans. and ed. Stillman Drake. Garden City, NY: Anchor Books, 1957.

Gallie, W. B. Essentially Contested Concepts. In his *Philosophy and the Historical Understanding*. London: Chalto and Windus, 1964, pp. 157–91.

Gaskin, J. C. A. *Hume's Philosophy of Religion*. New York: Macmillan, 1978.

Gassendi, Pierre. *Institutio Logica* (1658), trans. Howard Jones. Assen, The Netherlands: Van Gorcum, 1981.

Geach, P. T. *Reference and Generality*. Ithaca, NY: Cornell University Press, 1960.

Geach, P. T. Frege. In Geach and Anscombe 1963, pp. 131–62.

Geach, P. T. Identity. *Review of Metaphysics* **21** (1967): 3–12.

Geach, P. T. *Logic Matters*. Oxford: Basil Blackwell, 1972.

Geach, P. T. *God and the Soul*. Bristol: Thoemmes Press, 1994.

Geach, P. T., and G. E. M. Anscombe, eds. *Three Philosophers*. Oxford: Basil Blackwell, 1963.

Gibson, James. *Locke's Theory of Knowledge and Its Historical Relations (1917)*. Cambridge: Cambridge University Press, 1931.

Goldstick, D. Secondary Qualities. *Philosophy and Phenomenological Research* **48** (1987): 145–6.

Goodin, Susanna. A Refutation of the Possibility of Real Species in Locke. *The Locke Newsletter* **28** (1997): 67–75.

Green, T. H. Introduction to Hume's *Treatise of Human Nature*. In *The Philosophical Works of David Hume*, ed. T. H. Green and T. H. Grose. London: Longmans, 1874–75, vol. I, pp. 1–299.

Greene, Robert A. Natural Law, Synderesis and the Moral Sense. *Journal of the History of Ideas* **58** (1997): 173–98.

Griffin, Nicholas. *Relative Identity*. Oxford: Clarendon Press, 1977.

Guerlac, Henry. Can There Be Colors in the Dark? Physical Theory before Newton. *Journal of the History of Ideas* **47** (1986): 3–20.

Guyer, Paul. Locke's Philosophy of Language. In *The Cambridge Companion to Locke*, ed. Vere Chappell. Cambridge: Cambridge University Press, 1994, pp. 115–45.

Hacking, I. *Why Does Language Matter to Philosophy?* Cambridge: Cambridge University Press, 1975.

Hacking, I. Locke, Leibniz, Language and Hans Aarsleff. *Synthese* **75** (1988): 135–53.

Hankinson, R. J. Stoic Epistemology. In *The Cambridge Companion to the Stoics*, ed. Brad Inwood. Cambridge: Cambridge University Press, 2003, pp. 59–84.

Harman, G. The Intrinsic Qualities of Experience. *Philosophical Perspectives* **4** (1990): 31–52.

Harris, R. *The Language Myth*. New York: St. Martin's Press, 1981.

Harrison, John, and Peter Laslett. *The Library of John Locke*. Oxford: Oxford University Press, 1965; 2nd ed. 1971.

Hatfield, Gary. The Workings of the Intellect: Mind and Psychology. In *Logic and the Workings of the Mind: The Logic of Ideas and Faculty Psychology in Early Modern Philosophy*, ed. Patricia Easton, vol. 5. Atascadero, CA: Ridgeview, 1997.

Haugeland, J. Semantic Engines: An Introduction to Mind Designs. In *Mind Design*, ed. J. Haugeland. Cambridge, MA: MIT Press, 1981.

Hausman, David B., and Alan Hausman. *Descartes's Legacy: Minds and Meaning in Early Modern Philosophy*. Toronto: University of Toronto Press, 1997.

Herbert of Cherbury, Edward. *De Veritate: Prout Distinguitur a Revelatione, a Verisimili, a Possibili, et a Falso* (1624), trans. Meyrick H. Carré. Bristol: J. W. Arrowsmith, 1937.

Heyd, Thomas. Locke's Arguments for the Resemblance Thesis Revisited. *The Locke Newsletter* **25** (1994): 13–28.

Hill, Benjamin. 'Resemblance' and Locke's Primary-Secondary Quality Distinction. *Locke Studies* **4** (2004): 89–122.

Hobbes, Thomas. *Leviathan*, ed. C. B. Macpherson. Harmondsworth: Penguin, 1968.

Hobbes, Thomas. *Leviathan*, ed. R. Tuck. Cambridge: Cambridge University Press, 1996.

Hobbes, Thomas. *Leviathan* (London, 1651). Indianapolis: Hackett, 1994.

Hobbes, Thomas. *The English Works of Thomas Hobbes*, ed. W. Molesworth. 11 vols. London: John Bohn, 1839.

Hobbes, Thomas. Part I of *De Corpore*, trans. Aloysius Martinich. New York: Abaris Books, 1981.

Hobbes, Thomas. *Hobbes and Bramhall on Liberty and Necessity*, ed. Vere Chappell. Cambridge: Cambridge University Press, 1999.

Humboldt, W. v. *On Language: On the Diversity of Human Language Construction and Its Influence on the Mental Development of the Human Species*, ed. M. Losonsky, trans. P. Heath. Cambridge: Cambridge University Press, 1999.

Hume, David. *An Enquiry Concerning Human Understanding* (1748), ed. Tom L. Beauchamp. Oxford: Oxford University Press, 1999.

Hume, David. *A Treatise of Human Nature*, ed. David Norton and Mary Norton. Oxford: Oxford University Press, 2000.

Hylton, Peter. The Nature of the Proposition and the Revolt against Idealism. In Rorty et al. (1984).

Hylton, Peter. *Russell, Idealism and the Emergence of Analytic Philosophy*. Oxford: Clarendon Press, 1990.

Jackson, F. Mind and Illusion. In *Minds and Persons*, ed. Anthony O'Hear. Cambridge: Cambridge University Press, 2003, pp. 251–71.

Jackson, Reginald. Locke's Distinction between Primary and Secondary Qualities. *Mind* **38** (1929): 56–76.

Jacovides, Michael. Locke's Resemblance Theses. *Philosophical Review* **108** (1999): 461–96.

Jacovides, Michael. Cambridge Changes of Color. *Pacific Philosophical Quarterly* **81** (2000): 142–63.

Jacovides, Michael. The Epistemology under Locke's Corpuscularianism. *Archiv fur Geschichte der Philosophie* **84** (2002): 161–89.

Jacovides, Michael. Locke's Construction of the Idea of Power. *Studies in History and Philosophy of Science* **34** (2003): 329–50.

Jolley, Nicholas. *Leibniz and Locke*. Oxford: Clarendon Press, 1984.

Jolley, Nicholas. *Locke: His Philosophical Thought*. Oxford: Oxford University Press, 1999.

Jolley, Nicholas. Reason's Dim Candle: Locke's Critique of Enthusiasm. In *The Philosophy of Locke: New Perspectives*, ed. P. Anstey. London: Routledge, 2003, pp. 179–91.

Kant, Immanuel. *Critique of Pure Reason*, trans. Werner S. Pluhar. Indianapolis: Hackett, 1996.

Kenny, Anthony, ed. *Rationalism, Empiricism, and Idealism*. Oxford: Clarendon Press, 1986.

Kim, Halla. Locke on Innatism. *Locke Studies* **3** (2003): 15–39.

Kretzmann, N. History of Semantics. In *The Encyclopedia of Philosophy*, ed. Paul Edwards, vol. 7. New York: Collier Macmillan, 1967, pp. 358–406.

Kretzmann, N. The Main Thesis of Locke's Semantic Theory. *Philosophical Review* **77** (1968): 175–96.

Kulstad, Mark. Locke on Consciousness and Reflection. *Studia Leibnitiana* **16** (1984): 143–67.

Langton, Rae. Locke's Relations and God's Good Pleasure. *Proceedings of the Aristotelian Society* **100** (2000): 75–91.

Langtry, Bruce. Locke and the Relativisation of Identity. *Philosophical Studies* **27** (1975): 401–9.

Laudan, Larry. The Clock Metaphor and Probabilism: The Impact of Descartes on British Methodological Thought, 1650–65. *Annals of Science* **22** (1966): 73–104.

Leibniz, G. W. *Die Philosophischen Schriften von Gottfried Wilhelm Leibniz*, ed. C. J. Gerhardt. 7 vols. Hildesheim: Olms, 1960.

Leibniz, G. W. *G. W. Leibniz: Sämtliche Schriften und Briefe*. Berlin: Akademie Verlag, 1923–.

Leibniz, G. W. *Philosophical Papers and Letters*, second edition, ed. and trans. L. Loemker. Dordrecht: Reidel, 1970.

Leibniz, G. W. *New Essays on Human Understanding* (1765), trans. Peter Remnant and Jonathan Bennett. Cambridge: Cambridge University Press, 1981.

Lennon, T. *The Battle of the Gods and Giants*. Princeton, NJ: Princeton University Press, 1993.

Lennon, Thomas M. Locke and the Logic of Ideas. *History of Philosophy Quarterly* **18** (2001): 155–76.

Lievers, Menno. The Molyneux Problem. *Journal of the History of Philosophy* **30** (1992): 399–416.

Loeb, Louis E. *From Descartes to Hume.* Ithaca, NY: Cornell University Press, 1981.

Losonsky, M. Locke on the Making of Complex Ideas. *Locke Newsletter* **20** (1989): 35–46.

Losonsky, Michael. Locke on the Making of Complex Ideas. *Locke Newsletter* **20** (1989): 35–46.

Losonsky, M. Locke on Meaning and Signification. In *Locke's Philosophy: Content and Context,* ed. J. Rogers. Oxford: Clarendon Press, 1994.

Losonsky, M. Introduction. In Humboldt 1999, pp. vii–xxxiv.

Losonsky, M. *Enlightenment and Action from Descartes to Kant: Passionate Thought.* Cambridge: Cambridge University Press, 2001.

Losonsky, M. *Linguistic Turns in Modern Philosophy.* Cambridge: Cambridge University Press, 2006.

Lowde, James. *A Discourse Concerning the Nature of Man.* London, 1694.

Lowe, E. J. Necessity and the Will in Locke's Theory of Action. *History of Philosophy Quarterly* **3** (1986): 149–63.

Lowe, E. J. *Locke on Human Understanding.* London: Routledge, 1995.

Mackie, J. L. Locke's Anticipation of Kripke. *Analysis* **34** (1974): 177–80.

Mackie, J. L. *Problems from Locke.* Oxford: Clarendon Press, 1976.

Magri, Tito. Locke, Suspension of Desire, and the Remote Good. *British Journal for the History of Philosophy* **8** (2000): 55–70.

Maier, Anneliese. Die Mechanisierung des Weltbilds im 17. Jahrhundert. In *Zwei Untersuchungen zur Nachscholastischen Philosophie,* second edition. Rome: Edizioni di Storia e Letteratura, 1968.

Mandelbaum, Maurice. Locke's Realism. In *Philosophy, Science, and Sense Perception: Historical and Critical Studies.* Baltimore: Johns Hopkins University Press, 1964.

Martin, R. M. *The Meaning of Language.* Cambridge, MA: MIT Press, 1987.

Mattern, Ruth. Locke on Natural Kinds and the Workmanship of the Understanding. *The Locke Newsletter* **17** (1986): 45–92.

McCann, Edwin. Cartesian Selves and Lockean Substances. *Monist* **69** (1986): 458–82.

McCann, Edwin. Locke on Identity: Matter, Life, and Consciousness. *Archiv für Geschichte der Philosophie* **69** (1987): 54–77.

McCann, Edwin. Locke's Philosophy of Body. In *The Cambridge Companion to Locke,* ed. Vere Chappell. Cambridge: Cambridge University Press, 1994, pp. 56–88.

McCann, Edwin. Locke's Theory of Substance under Attack! *Philosophical Studies* **106** (2001): 87–105.

Menn, Stephen. The Greatest Stumbling Block: Descartes' Denial of Real Qualities. In *Descartes and His Contemporaries: Mediations, Objections, and Replies*, ed. Roger Ariew and Marjorie Grene. Chicago: University of Chicago Press, 1995, pp. 182–207.

Mill, J. S. *Collected Works of John Stuart Mill*, ed. J. M. Robson. Toronto: University of Toronto Press, 1974.

Milton, J. R. The Scholastic Background to Locke's Thought. *The Locke Newsletter* **15** (1984): 25–34.

Milton, J. R. Locke and Gassendi: A Reappraisal. In *English Philosophy in the Age of Locke*, ed. M. A. Stewart. Oxford: Clarendon Press, 2000.

More, Henry. *An Antidote Against Atheisme, or, An Appeal to the Natural Faculties of the Minde of Man, Whether There be not a God*. London, 1653.

More, Henry. *Collection of Several Philosophical Writings* (1662). New York: Garland, 1978.

Newman, Lex. Locke on the Idea of Substratum. *Pacific Philosophical Quarterly* **81** (2000): 291–324.

Newman, Lex. Locke on Sensitive Knowledge and the Veil of Perception – Four Misconceptions. *Pacific Philosophical Quarterly* **85** (2004): 273–300.

Noonan, Harold. Locke on Personal Identity. *Philosophy* **53** (1978): 343–51.

North, Roger. *Autobiography*. Uni. Libr. Camb., MS. Baker 37, fols. 163–163v. Quoted in M. H. Curtis, *Oxford and Cambridge in Transition 1558–1642*. Oxford: Clarendon Press, 1959.

Nuchelmans, Gabriel. *Judgment and Proposition from Descartes to Kant*. Amsterdam: North-Holland, 1983.

Nuovo, Victor. Edward, 1st Lord Herbert of Cherbury. In *Dictionary of Seventeenth Century Philosophers*. Bristol: Thoemmes, 2000, vol. 1, pp. 409–16.

Odegard, Douglas. Identity through Time. *American Philosophical Quarterly* **9** (1972): 29–38.

Ott, Walter. Propositional Attitudes in Modern Philosophy. *Dialogue* **41** (2002): 551–68.

Ott, Walter. *Locke's Philosophy of Language*. Cambridge: Cambridge University Press, 2004.

Owen, David. Locke on Real Essence. *History of Philosophy Quarterly* **8**, 2 (April 1991): 105–18.

Owen, David. Locke on Reason, Probable Reasoning, and Opinion. *Locke Newsletter* **24** (1993): 35–69.

Owen, David. Critical Notice of Wolterstorff (1996). *The Locke Newsletter* 30 (1999): 102–27.

Owen, David. *Hume's Reason*. Oxford: Oxford University Press, 1999.

Owen, David. Locke and Hume on Belief, Judgment and Assent. *Topoi* 22 (2003): 15–28.

Palmer, David. Locke and the 'Ancient Hypothesis'. *Canadian Journal of Philosophy* 1 (supp.) (1974): 41–8.

Parker, Samuel. *A Free and Impartial Censure of the Platonick Philosophie: Being a Letter Written to his much Honoured Friend Mr. N. B.* (1666). New York: AMS Press, 1985.

Passmore, John. Locke and the Ethics of Belief. In *Kenny* 1986, pp. 23–46.

Pécharman, M. Le Discourse Mental Selon Hobbes. *Archives de philosophie* 55 (1992): 553–73.

Phemister, Pauline. The Possibility of Real Species in Locke: A Reply to Goodin's Response. *The Locke Newsletter* 28 (1997): 77–86.

Phemister, Pauline. Real Essences in Particular. *The Locke Newsletter* 21 (1990): 27–55.

Pringle-Pattison, A. S., ed. *An Essay Concerning Human Understanding by John Locke*. Oxford: Clarendon Press, 1924.

Puffendorf, Samuel. *On the Laws of Nature and Nations* (1688), trans. C. H. Oldfather and W. A. Oldfather. Oxford: Clarendon Press, 1931.

Putnam, Hilary. *Reason, Truth, and History*. Cambridge: Cambridge University Press, 1981.

Quine, W. V. On What There Is. In his *From a Logical Point of View*, second edition. Cambridge, MA: Harvard University Press, 1980, pp. 1–19.

Rabb, J. Douglas. Are Locke's Ideas of Relation Complex? *Locke Newsletter* 5 (1974): 41–55.

Regis, Pierre-Sylvain. *Cours entier de philosophie* (1691). New York: Johnson, 1970.

Reid, Thomas. *The Works of Thomas Reid*, 7th ed., edited with preface and notes by William Hamilton. 2 vols. Edinburgh: MacLachlan and Stewart, 1877.

Reid, Thomas. *Essays on the Intellectual Powers of Man*, ed. Derek Brookes. University Park: Pennsylvania State University Press, 2002.

Rickless, Samuel C. Locke on Primary and Secondary Qualities. *Pacific Philosophical Quarterly* 78 (1997): 297–319.

Rickless, Samuel C. Locke on the Freedom to Will. *Locke Newsletter* 31 (2000): 43–67.

Rickless, Samuel C. The Cartesian Fallacy Fallacy. *Noûs* 39 (2005): 309–36.

Rogers, G. A. J. Locke's *Essay* and Newton's *Principia*. *Journal of the History of Ideas* 39 (1978): 217–32.

Rogers, G. A. J. Locke, Newton, and the Cambridge Platonists on Innate Ideas. *Journal of the History of Ideas* 40 (1979): 191–205.

Rogers, G. A. J. Hobbes's Hidden Influence. In *Perspectives on Thomas Hobbes*, ed. G. A. J. Rogers and A. Ryan. Oxford: Oxford University Press, 1988, pp. 189–205.

Rogers, G. A. J. *Locke's Enlightenment: Aspects of the Origin, Nature, and Impact of his Philosophy*. Hildesheim: Olms, 1998.

Rogers, G. A. J. "Locke and the Platonists." Unpublished manuscript.

Rorty, R. M., ed. *The Linguistic Turn: Essay in Philosophical Method*. Chicago: University of Chicago Press, 1967.

Rorty, R. M., ed. *The Linguistic Turn: Essays in Philosophical Methods with Two Retrospective Essays*. Chicago: University of Chicago Press, 1992.

Rorty, R., J. B. Schneewind, and Q. Skinner, eds. *Philosophy in History*. New York: Cambridge University Press, 1984.

Rozemond, Marleen, and Gideon Yaffe. Peach Trees, Gravity, and God: Mechanism in Locke. *British Journal for the History of Philosophy* 12 (2004): 387–412.

Ryle, Gilbert. *The Concept of Mind*. London: Hutchinson, 1949.

Ryle, Gilbert. Negative 'Actions' (1973). In his *On Thinking*, ed. Konstantin Kolenda. Oxford: Blackwell, 1979, pp. 105–19.

Sanderson, Robert. *Logicae artis compendium*, fourth edition. Oxford, 1640.

Sargent, Rose-Mary. *The Diffident Naturalist: Robert Boyle and the Philosophy of Experiment*. Chicago: University of Chicago Press, 1995.

Schneewind, J. B. Locke's Moral Philosophy. In *The Cambridge Companion to Locke*, ed. Vere Chappell. Cambridge: Cambridge University Press, 1994, pp. 199–225.

Schouls, Peter. *Reasoned Freedom*. Ithaca, NY: Cornell University Press, 1992.

Schumacher, Ralph. What Are the Direct Objects of Sight? Locke on the Molyneux Problem. *Locke Studies* 30 (2003): 41–61.

Searle, John R. *Intentionality: An Essay in the Philosophy of Mind*. Cambridge: Cambridge University Press, 1983.

Sell, Alan P. F. *John Locke and the Eighteenth-Century Divines*. Cardiff: University of Wales, 1997.

Shapiro, Lionel. Toward 'Perfect Collections of Properties': Locke on the Constitution of Substantial Sorts. *Canadian Journal of Philosophy* 29 (December 1999): 551–92.

Smith, Constance. Locke and John Austin on the Idea of Morality. *Journal of the History of Ideas* 23 (1962): 141–2.

Spade, P. V. The Semantics of Terms. In *The Cambridge History of Later Medieval Philosophy*, ed. Norman Kretzmann, Anthony Kenny, and Jan Pinborg. Cambridge: Cambridge University Press, 1982, pp. 188–96.

Spellman, W. M. *John Locke and the Problem of Depravity*. Oxford: Clarendon Press, 1988.

Sprat, Thomas. *History of the Royal Society*, ed. Jackson I. Cope and Harold Whitmore Jones. St. Louis: Washington University Press, 1959.

Stanford, P. Kyle. Reference and Natural Kind Terms: The Real Essence of Locke's View. *Pacific Philosophical Quarterly* **79** (1990): 78–97.

Stewart, M. A. Locke's Mental Atomism and the Classification of Ideas: I and II. *Locke Newsletter* **10** (1979): 53–82 and **11** (1980): 25–62.

Stillingfleet, Edward. *Origines Sacrae: Or, A Rational Account of the Grounds of Christian Faith, as to the Truth and Divine Authority of the Scriptures, And the Matters Therein Contained*. London, 1662.

Stillingfleet, Edward. *The Bishop of Worcester's Answer to Mr. Locke's Letter Concerning Some Passages relating to his Essay of humane Understanding, Mentioned in the late Discourse in Vindication of the Trinity*. London, 1697.

Stillingfleet, Edward. *A Discourse in Vindication of the Doctrine of the Trinity: with an Answer to the Late Socinian Observations against it from Scripture, Antiquity and Reason and A Preface concerning the different Explications of the Trinity, and the Tendency of the present Socinian Controversie*. London, 1697.

Stillingfleet, Edward. *The Bishop of Worcester's Answer to Mr. Locke's Second Letter, Wherein his Notion of Ideas is prov'd to be Inconsistent with it self, and with the Articles of the Christian Faith*. London, 1698.

Stone, Lawrence. *Uncertain Unions: Marriage in England 1660–1753*. Oxford: Oxford University Press, 1992.

Stuart, Matthew. "Locke's Metaphysics." Unpublished manuscript.

Stuart, Matthew. Locke's Geometrical Analogy. *History of Philosophy Quarterly* **13** (1996): 451–67.

Stuart, Matthew. Locke on Superaddition and Mechanism. *British Journal for the History of Philosophy* **6** (1998): 351–79.

Stuart, Matthew. Locke's Colors. *Philosophical Review* **112** (2003): 57–96.

Thackray, Arnold. Matter in a Nut-Shell: Newton's *Opticks* and Eighteenth-Century Chemistry. *Ambix* **15** (1968): 29–53.

Tipton, Ian. 'Ideas' and 'Objects': Locke on Perceiving Things. In *Minds, Ideas, and Objects: Essays on the Theory of Perception in Early Modern Philosophy*, ed. P. D. Cummins and G. Zoeller. Atascadero, CA: Ridgewood, 1992, pp. 97–110.

Trumbull, H. W., and J. F. Scott, eds. *Correspondence of Isaac Newton*. Cambridge: Cambridge University Press, 1959–.

Uzgalis, William. Relative Identity and Locke's Principle of Individuation. *History of Philosophy Quarterly* **7** (1990): 283–97.

Vienne, Jean-Michel. Locke on Real Essences and Internal Constitution. *Proceedings of the Aristotelian Society* NS: **93** (1993): 139–53.

Walmsley, Jonathan. Locke's Natural Philosophy in Draft A of the *Essay*. *Journal of the History of Ideas* **65** (2004): 15–37.

Watson, Richard A. *Representational Ideas: From Plato to Patricia Churchland*. Dordrecht: Kluwer, 1995.

Whichcote, Benjamin. The Glorious Evidence and Power of Divine Truth (1698). In *The Cambridge Platonists*, ed. E. T. Campagnac. Oxford: Clarendon Press, 1901, pp. 1–28.

Williams, Bernard. The Self and the Future. In *Personal Identity*, ed. John Perry. Berkeley: University of California Press, 1970, pp. 179–98.

Willis, Thomas. *Thomas Willis's Oxford Lectures*, ed. Kenneth Dewhurst, collated from notes by John Locke and Richard Lower. Oxford: Sandford Publications, 1980.

Wilson, Catherine. *The Invisible World: Early Modern Philosophy and the Invention of the Microscope*. Princeton, NJ: Princeton University Press, 1995.

Wilson, Margaret. Leibniz and Locke on First Truths. *Journal of the History of Ideas* **28** (1967): 347–66.

Wilson, Margaret. Superadded Properties: The Limits of Mechanism in Locke. *American Philosophical Quarterly* **16** (1979): 143–50.

Wilson, Margaret. Descartes on Sense and "Resemblance." In *Reason, Will, and Sensation: Studies in Cartesian Metaphysics*, ed. John Cottingham. Oxford: Clarendon Press, 1994, pp. 209–228.

Wilson, Robert A. Locke's Primary Qualities. *Journal of the History of Philosophy* **40** (2002): 201–28.

Winkler, Kenneth. Locke on Personal Identity. In *Locke*, ed. Vere Chappell. Oxford: Oxford University Press, 1991, pp. 149–74.

Winkler, Kenneth. Ideas, Sentiments, and Qualities. In *Minds, Ideas, and Concepts: Essays on the Theory of Representation in Modern Philosophy*, ed. Phillip D. Cummins and Guenter Zoeller. Atascadero, CA: Ridgeview, 1992, pp. 151–65.

Wolterstorff, Nicholas. Locke's Philosophy of Religion. In *The Cambridge Companion to Locke*, ed. Vere Chappell. Cambridge: Cambridge University Press, 1994, pp. 172–98.

Wolterstorff, Nicholas. *John Locke and the Ethics of Belief*. Cambridge: Cambridge University Press, 1996.

Wood, Anthony. *Athenae Oxoniensis*, vol. 4. Oxford, 1813.

Woolhouse, R. S. *Locke's Philosophy of Science and Knowledge*. London: Barnes and Noble, 1971.

Woolhouse, R. S. *Locke's Philosophy of Science and Knowledge*. Oxford: Basil Blackwell, 1969.

Woolhouse, R. S. *Locke*. Minneapolis: University of Minnesota Press, 1983.

Woolhouse, Roger. Locke's Theory of Knowledge. In *The Cambridge Companion to Locke*, ed. Vere Chappell. Cambridge University Press, 1994, pp. 146–71.

Woozley, A. D. Introduction. In *An Essay Concerning Human Understanding*, by John Locke, ed. A. D. Woozley. London: Collins, 1964, pp. 9–51.

Woozley, A. D. Some Remarks on Locke's Account of Knowledge (1972). In *Locke on Human Understanding*, ed. I. C. Tipton. Oxford: Oxford University Press, 1977, pp. 141–8.

Yaffe, Gideon. *Liberty Worth the Name: Locke on Free Agency*. Princeton, NJ: Princeton University Press, 2000.

Yaffe, Gideon. Locke on Refraining, Suspending and the Freedom of the Will. *History of Philosophy Quarterly* **18** (2001): 373–91.

Yolton, John W. *John Locke and the Way of Ideas*. Oxford: Clarendon Press, 1956.

Yolton, John W. *Locke and the Compass of Human Understanding*. Cambridge: Cambridge University Press, 1970.

Yolton, John W. Ideas and Knowledge in Seventeenth-Century Philosophy. *Journal of the History of Philosophy* **13** (1975): 373–88.

Yolton, John W. *Locke and French Materialism*. Oxford: Oxford University Press, 1991.

Index of Names and Subjects

Index of Passages Cited